GARRISONING THE BORDERLANDS OF MEDIEVAL SIENA

Through a close study of local demographies and topographies, this study considers patterns of piety, charity and patronage, and by extension, the development of art and architecture in Siena's southern contado during the thirteenth and fourteenth centuries.

Garrisoning the Borderlands of Medieval Siena describes Sant'Angelo in Colle as a designated 'castello di frontiera' under the Sienese Government of the Nine (1287–1355), against the background of Siena's military and economic buoyancy during the early fourteenth century. At the same time, mining thoroughly the Tax Record of 1320 and the Boundary Registration of 1318 and presenting a large number of individual records that have not been published before – including wills, tenancy agreements, land exchange and sharecropping contracts – the author constructs a portrait of the people, buildings and surrounding countryside of Sant'Angelo in Colle. Finally, adopting the methodological approach of first considering patterns of ownership of land and property in the context of identifying potential patrons of art, the study considers patterns of piety and charity established in the early fourteenth-century village and the extent to which these affected the development of the urban fabric and the embellishment of key buildings in medieval Sant'Angelo in Colle.

After a career in University teaching in the UK, most recently in the department of Art History at Birkbeck College, University of London, Anabel Thomas has for the last ten years lived in Tuscany. She is the author of The Painter's Practice in Renaissance Tuscany *(Cambridge University Press, 1995) and* Art and Piety in the Female Religious Communities of Renaissance Italy *(Cambridge University Press, 2003) as well as of articles in learned periodicals in the UK, USA, and Italy.*

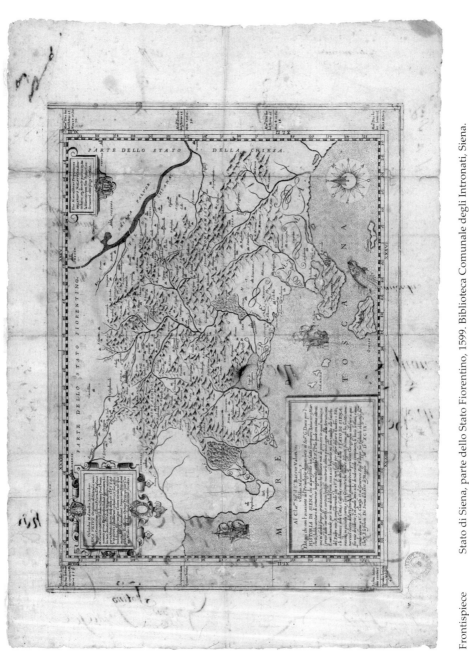

Frontispiece   Stato di Siena, parte dello Stato Fiorentino, 1599. Biblioteca Comunale degli Intronati, Siena.

Garrisoning the Borderlands of Medieval Siena

Sant'Angelo in Colle: Frontier Castle under the Government of the Nine (1287–1355)

Anabel Thomas

ASHGATE

Published by
Ashgate Publishing Limited
Wey Court East
Union Road
Farnham
Surrey, GU9 7PT
England

Ashgate Publishing Company
Suite 420
101 Cherry Street
Burlington, VT 05401-4405
USA

Ashgate website: http://www.ashgate.com

British Library Cataloguing in Publication Data
Thomas, Anabel.
Garrisoning the Borderlands of Medieval Siena : Sant'Angelo
in Colle : Frontier Castle under the Government of the Nine
(1287-1355).
1. Siena (Italy)--History--Rule of the Nine, 1287-1355.
2. Sant'Angelo in Colle (Italy)--History. 3. Sant'Angelo
in Colle (Italy)--Social conditions. 4. Sant'Angelo in
Colle (Italy)--Population--History--To 1500.
5. Sant'Angelo in Colle (Italy)--Buildings, structures,
etc.--History--To 1500. 6. Geography, Medieval--Italy--
Sant'Angelo in Colle.
I. Title
945.5'804-dc22

Library of Congress Cataloging-in-Publication Data
Thomas, Anabel.
Garrisoning the Borderlands of Medieval Siena : Sant'Angelo in Colle, Frontier Castle
under the Government of the Nine, 1287-1355 / Anabel Thomas.
    p. cm.
Includes bibliographical references and index.
ISBN 978-1-4094-2603-5 (hardcover : alk. paper) 1. Siena (Italy)--History--Rule of the
Nine, 1287-1355. 2. Castles--Italy--Siena--History. 3. City walls--Italy--Siena--History.
4. Gates--Italy--Siena--History. 5. Architecture, Medieval--Italy--Siena--History.
6. Social history--Medieval, 500-1500. I. Title.
DG975.S5T47 2011
945'.58104--dc22

2011005540

ISBN 9781409426035 (hbk)

Printed and bound in Great Britain by the MPG Books Group, UK.

For my Mother

Contents

PART I   TOPOGRAPHY AND DEMOGRAPHY

The Territory

The Urban Fabric

PART II   SOCIETY AND SOCIETAL VALUES

The People

Civic Awareness

Illustrations

Front cover

(colour/portrait) *Palazzaccio*, Sant'Angelo in Colle
Photograph by Andrea Rabissi

Frontispiece

(black and white/landscape) Stato di Siena, parte dello Stato Fiorentino, 1599
Biblioteca Comunale degli Intronati, Siena, Ex Museo Civico III.0001
Su autorizzazione della Biblioteca Comunale degli Intronati di Siena

Colour plates

Black and white illustrations

Diagrams

Cluster diagrams

Tables

Preface

The farmer cleaves the earth with his curved plough.
This is his yearlong work, thus he sustains
His homeland, thus his little grandchildren,
His herds and trusty bullocks. Never a pause!
The seasons teem with fruits, the young of flocks,
Or sheaves of Ceres' corn; they load the furrows
And burst the barns with produce. Then, come winter,
The olive-press is busy; sleek with acorns
The pigs come home; the arbutes in the woods
Give berries; autumn sheds its varied windfalls;
And high on sunny terraces of rock
The mellow vintage ripens.

> Virgil, *The Georgics*, Book Two, Penguin Classics, translated into English verse with introduction and notes by L.P. Wilkinson, Penguin Group, 1982, Courtesy Penguin Group (UK)

This is the story of Sant'Angelo in Colle, a medieval Tuscan frontier castle guarding Siena's southern borders, under the Government of the Nine. The period of the Government of the Nine – a group of nine governing priors, who managed the affairs of Siena between 1287 and 1355 – was when Sant'Angelo in Colle achieved its greatest military and political significance. It was also the period during which most of the local inhabitants, as in Virgil's *Georgics*, were daily involved in the working of the land, the rearing of livestock and the production of oil, cheese and wine.

Sant'Angelo in Colle sits like a crown upon the top of its own individual hill, eight kilometres south of Montalcino, and overlooking the broad plains of the Orcia and Ombrone Rivers (see Colour Plate 1). To the east, south and west, Sant'Angelo in Colle looks out over cascading slopes covered with vines, olive trees, holm oaks, scrubland and densely variegated woods. Beyond the valleys, it confronts a majestic sweep of mountains that culminates in Monte Amiata, the highest peak in southern Tuscany (see Colour Plate 2). To the north, Sant'Angelo in Colle is overlooked by thickly wooded slopes that rise up steeply towards Montalcino, and beyond that, Siena. It is flanked on its north-western side by a sweep of cypresses that follows the modern access road up to the site of the old *cassero*, or fortified military outpost (see Colour Plate 3) which was imposed on Sant'Angelo in Colle by the Republic of Siena in the last years of the thirteenth century. Larger than a hamlet, but much smaller than a town or city, medieval Sant'Angelo in Colle might best be described as a village, although the existence there of a *Palazzo Comunale*[1] by the end of the thirteenth century establishes it as one of the early Tuscan communes.

Eight centuries later, what was once a buzzing hive of activity seems unnaturally quiet. Within the original perimeters of Sant'Angelo in Colle there is now a sense of shutters closing. More and more buildings fall empty. The memories are increasingly those of loss. The last resident priest, Don Antonio Brandi, retired in 2006 and – to the great sadness of his many friends, colleagues and parishioners – died shortly thereafter. The bells continue to punctuate the daily round, but more often than not, they seem to mark another departure. With each passing, the accompanying funeral cortege that winds its way down from the main square and parish church of San Michele Arcangelo appears more aged, but not less purposeful in the common desire to render an appropriate farewell.

In the twenty-first century there is a significant decline in the population inside the old historic centre, partly because of a move to new accommodation on the surrounding slopes. Yet, despite the passing of time and changing circumstances, this wider community remains close-knit. While the young and not so young may lament the increasingly silent alleys and squares and the echoes of those voices of loved ones long since departed from the old historic centre, older 'angels' (both on and below the hill) continue to record with animation and pride the experiences of their youth. Those memories in large part nourish the present study, which looks back to the people and life of Sant'Angelo in Colle of the early medieval period. Even then, this community was confronting change with all of its attendant challenges. In the thirteenth and fourteenth centuries this included dealing with the impositions of new masters in the form of officials and military sent by the Republic of Siena; surviving famine and drought and avoiding contagious disease; and confronting the vagaries of weather when cultivating the land and nurturing their livestock.

The nature of the local agriculture has changed radically even within the last 50 years. Older members of the community still recall diverse arable crops and a varied husbandry with sheep, cows, poultry and goats. While some traces of this remain, most of the territory is now worked only for the olive and the vine. Where once there was a flourishing business based on the rearing of pigs in the densely forested slopes surrounding Sant'Angelo in Colle, priority is now given to the production of Brunello wine aged over several years in wooden casks made from imported French oak. There is in fact no end, only a series of beginnings. Different sounds now resound within the folds and upon the inclines of Sant'Angelo in Colle and its surrounding terrain. New and different buildings emerge in the shade of the old historic centre. There are new births on the slopes below. Gradually, new 'Angiolesi' establish other kinds of existence in a place where once, and until quite recently, each day was marked by the sound of church bells, the specific demands of each seasonal change, and the constantly changing but ever present tasks associated with working the land.

As a more recent resident of Sant'Angelo in Colle, I have witnessed the slow but inexorable passing of old traditions as well as the passing away of many companions. I have also seen – as perhaps only an 'outsider' can – how this *fiumana*,[2] although constantly changing in its individual components, and perhaps cutting a different course as it confronts the changes of the twenty-first century, nevertheless continues to flow.

As a producer of Brunello wine, Sant'Angelo in Colle, like the quality of that wine continues to grow. In this context, advice offered by Padre Emanuele of Sant'Antimo and temporary officiating priest to Sant'Angelo in Colle at the funeral in the parish church of San Michele Arcangelo on 20 February 2007 of Oreno Andreini, aged 80 – beloved and respected by young and old – seems most apt:

We must try to become, over time, like good wine …
For we, like wine, can become better with age.

I dedicate this study to all today's 'angels' in the hope that it will serve three specific functions. First, I hope that the description of the density and variety of buildings existing in Sant'Angelo in Colle during the medieval period will breathe new life into the present historic centre, increasingly emptied of people, but nevertheless pulsating with memories of the past. Second, I hope that the description of people who lived in Sant'Angelo in Colle so many years ago will stimulate the sensibilities of those who confront it in its modern state. Third, I hope that modern 'angels', in acquainting themselves with something of their past history, will see how the passing of time, the changing of established traditions, as well as the passing away of people we love, does not diminish in essence this place where we have lived, and where many of us, if fortune smiles upon us, will end our days well aged – like the good local wine.

Anabel Thomas, December, 2010

Notes

1   Town hall.

2   River of humanity.

Acknowledgements

First and foremost, I would like to offer thanks to the many residents of Sant'Angelo in Colle, who have shown interest in this project and who have offered insights concerning the village's old traditions. Amongst these, and for their advice on particular issues: Luciana Andreini, Stefania Fatorella Bindocci, Lorenza Granai Favilli, Gastone Ferretti, Enza Granai, Giuliana Guerrini, Giuliano Guerrini, the late Maria Gentile Lisini Baldi, Gina Martini, Wanda De Merli, Carmen Nutolo, Chiara and Pietro Ricci, Alessandra and Ivalda Severini. In particular, I offer gratitude to the late Don Antonio Brandi.

Special thanks, also, to the following friends, helpmates and colleagues: Mario Ascheri, Bruno Bonucci, Stefano Cinelli Colombini, Alessandra Dami, Raffaele Giannetti, Helen Humphreys, Philippa Jackson, Helen Langdon, Nicola McGregor, Rachel Moriarty, Annibale Parisi, Mirco Sanchini, Jemima Thomas, Nat Thomas, Quentin Thomas and Giulia Zoi, who have followed this project during various stages of its development, offering advice and encouragement. To my daughter Abigail I offer particular thanks for her constructive comments on an early draft, and in particular the scope and purpose of Chapter 1.

I would also like to thank all the staff of the State archives and library in Siena, for their patience, courtesy and unflagging assistance in providing and analysing archival material, and in particular Maria Assunta Ceppari Ridolfi, Luciana Franchino, Maria Ilari, Carla Sanelli, Fulvia Sussi and Patrizia Turrini. I am especially grateful to Cristina Paccagnini in the Communal Archives in Montalcino for her professional support throughout the project.

In procuring photographs I am grateful for the help of Rosanna de Benedictis and Annalisa Pezzo at the Biblioteca degli Intronati in Siena; Alessandro Bagnoli, Maria Mangiavacchi and Anna Maria Emanuele in the Soprintendenza per i beni storici artistici ed etnoantropologici per le province di Siena e Grosseto. Above all, my thanks go to Andrea Rabissi in Montalcino for his generosity and skill in providing photographic material of Sant'Angelo in Colle and its environs, as well as of images of archival records in the Communal Archive in Montalcino.

Introduction

Sant'Angelo in Colle, *Castello di Frontiera* in the southern Sienese *contado*

Sant'Angelo in Colle, some 50 or so kilometres to the south of Siena, was often described in documents drawn up by Sienese officials during the medieval period as a *castello* (castle), and, more specifically, from 1265 (some 20 or so years before the creation of the Government of the Nine), as a *castello di frontiera* (frontier castle).[1] Now, little remains of the fortified *cassero*, or military barracks, established by the Sienese at Sant'Angelo in Colle, and nothing apparently remains of the village's early statutes. However, many surviving records chronicle the affairs of Sant'Angelo in Colle under the Sienese yoke.

The relationship between Sant'Angelo in Colle and Siena dates back to the early thirteenth century, when that increasingly powerful city set about expanding its territory, and defending itself in the face of provocation from Florence to the north, the feudal counts of Monte Amiata to the south, and other centres of power to the south-east. Sant'Angelo in Colle was one of the first communities in the southern territories of what is now Tuscany to be successfully subdued by Siena. Tributes were exacted from the people there as early as 1208, and in July 1212, the commune's consul, Ildibrandino di Bando, and other members of the community gathered together in the old church of San Michele, to offer a formal oath of loyalty to the Sienese government.[2] Significantly, Ildibrandino di Bando had obtained the consent of the parish priest of Sant'Angelo in Colle, 'domini Bonaventurae', before confirming the oath.

Thirteen years later, in 1225, and in a much more detailed transaction, two consuls, with the authority of the majority of the men of Sant'Angelo in Colle who had reached maturity, placed themselves under the supreme authority of Siena.[3] One hundred and eighty-nine named individuals are listed in the main body of the document recording this event as accepting the terms of the new oath of loyalty drawn up by the notary Appuliese. A further 63 men – in groups ranging from 3 to 19, and gathered together in front of a number of different witnesses – appear to have sworn to observe the same oath. In the case of two of these groups the priest of Sant'Angelo in Colle, 'domino

Ranerio' is named as a witness. In one of the two cases, that involving the largest number of men, Don Ranerio was also supported by Martino, *cherico*, or cleric. There was no apparent reason why these 63 men should have offered their oath of allegiance separately, or indeed why they were gathered together in front of different witnesses. However, if all of the individuals named in the oath of allegiance of 1225 were associated with Sant'Angelo in Colle, there must have been 200 or so men in the village who had reached the age of maturity by that date. Odile Redon suggests that if a community consisted of about 150 men, it could be considered as of medium importance.[4] Where there were 200 or so men, the commune in question must be considered large. On that basis, it seems that Sant'Angelo in Colle had already achieved a status of some significance by the second quarter of the thirteenth century.

No reference was made during the oath of allegiance of 1225 to any prior permission being sought or given by the parish priest, although Don Ranerio and at least one member of his clergy clearly played a part in the ceremony as witnesses. Nor was the precise location in which the oath-swearing ceremony took place recorded. However, while the phrase 'Actum in castro Sancti Angeli in Colle' included in the 1225 document may have merely reflected the fact that the oath took place inside the village, it is also possible that the ceremony took place within the space of a fortified structure already embedded within the urban fabric of Sant'Angelo in Colle.[5] As we shall see, particular locations and spaces were often politically charged in the medieval period. This was especially the case when one power attempted to exert its authority over another. The transfer from a religious space under the authority of the local priest to a lay space governed by a different authority in the confirmed oath of allegiance of 1225 could thus have been highly significant.

In effect, and apart from a number of individually stipulated dues, each of the individuals appearing in the first list of named men recorded in the 1225 oath promised Guidone, the mayor of Siena (acting on behalf of the Commune of Siena), that they would in no way obstruct the allegiance as notarised; that they would protect, look after and defend all Sienese citizens (and any property belonging to them) against attack from any other people or places or communes (with the exception of the Imperial dominion and the abbey of Sant'Antimo); that they would fight any war and resolve any conflict required of them by any mayor or consul of Siena; that they would in no way extract tax for any purpose from any Sienese citizen coming into their territory; and last, but not least, that they committed themselves and all their goods to the authority of Siena.

Siena fought hard and long to establish and then maintain her southern territories, not only because they offered access to the sea, and the promise of trade to equal that of rival powers such as Florence and Genoa to the north, but also because the lush pastures of the Maremma and the rich cornfields of the Orcia valley guaranteed the well-being of Sienese citizens through the rearing of livestock and the production of grain. In this way the Sienese were assured not only of meat and flour, but also of milk and cheese, essential ingredients for the support of everyday existence. As an armed frontier post, Sant'Angelo in Colle assumed an important role, not only during Siena's territorial expansions towards the Maremma and the military outpost of Talamone (the southern gateway to the Mediterranean), but also in subduing the nearby town of Montalcino to the north. Indeed, by 1337 Sant'Angelo in Colle had clearly assumed a central position in Siena's military affairs, since in that year it was recorded as heading one of the nine vicariates in the Sienese state.[6]

Although theoretically protected by Siena after its subjugation in 1208 Sant'Angelo in Colle was, nevertheless, continually terrorised by rebels to the Sienese cause. It also seems that not everyone in the village was happy with the *status quo*. Less than a decade after the ratification of allegiance to Siena in 1225, the records of the Sienese *Biccherna* refer to discord amongst the 'angels' on the hill.[7] In November 1229 Bonincontro Leonesi was paid 30 *soldi* to go to Sant'Angelo in Colle and make peace between the inhabitants there.[8] Further reference was made to the village's internal factions in July 1231.[9] Several months later, in October 1231, Ugolino Paoletti was paid 100 *soldi* for the five days he spent on another peacemaking mission together with Ildibrandino Trombetti and Arnolfo di Ciabatti – 'pro facto discordie inter illos de S. Angeli in Colle' (on account of the unrest amongst the inhabitants of Sant'Angelo in Colle).[10] It seems that unrest amongst the inhabitants of the village continued, since a further reference was made to the unsettled state of affairs at Sant'Angelo in Colle in 1232.[11] Nor was this the last occasion that the unruly nature of this southern frontier castle was brought to the attention of officials in Siena, or that attempts were made by central government to bring it to heel. Another reference to unrest inside the village was recorded as late as 1280. On that occasion, two individuals – Messer Fortebraccio and Messer Iacopo Marescotti – were deputed to resolve local issues in the unsettled southern border post.[12]

Records dating to the second half of the thirteenth century show that the Sienese realised at an early stage the need to fortify the key strategic points in their southern territory, and to protect them from attack by nearby communities. In particular, reference was made to the dangers posed to the castle and people of Sant'Angelo in Colle by the neighbouring town of Montalcino, not yet firmly under the Sienese yoke. For three years between 1252 and 1255 Sant'Angelo in Colle became the seat of control for Sienese military engaged in laying siege to Montalcino.[13] It seems that the villagers may have suffered reprisals from Montalcino as a result of this, for in June 1260 the *Consiglio Generale*, or General Council, in Siena noted the need to protect their frontier castle from attack and probable devastation by Montalcino.[14]

Siena and Florence had been in conflict over ownership of Montalcino since the end of the twelfth century. In the Battle of 1174–76, Montalcino had sided with Siena against Florence, only to see the enemy victorious. Thus, at that time, Montalcino fell to the Florentines. This battle seems to have marked the beginning of the contest between Florence and Siena for ownership of Montalcino. Following the Sienese victory at the Battle of Montaperti in 1260, Montalcino not only fell to the Sienese but was also virtually razed to the ground for having previously sided with Florence.[15] Before the Battle of Montaperti, Montalcino had frequently been treated as a tradable pawn in treaties hatched by the two super powers. But Montalcino itself had resisted takeover attempts by Siena throughout the first half of the thirteenth century.[16] They were to suffer dearly for this. The destruction of Montalcino following the Battle of Montaperti was certainly not the result of a decision taken in the heat of or in the aftermath of battle. As early as 1251, members of the *Consiglio Generale* in Siena were giving voice to the manner in which Montalcino might be destroyed, and who should be selected to carry out that task.[17] When it came to it, few details were missing. In June 1260, it was suggested in a meeting of the General Council that foot soldiers and horsemen should be positioned around Montalcino to stop anyone coming in or going out, which might otherwise possibly impede the destruction of the town.[18] Even after their ignominious defeat, many of the local inhabitants of Montalcino resisted the Sienese yoke, and must thus have been regarded as potential troublemakers. Uncertainties of this kind no doubt contributed to Siena's procrastination in offering the people of Montalcino the right to call themselves Sienese citizens. That right was only established in October 1361, over 100 years after the victory at Montaperti, and several years after the fall of the Government of the Nine.[19] Under the establishment of the Twelve, Montalcino was finally allowed a certain amount of autonomy, although it was forced at the same time to swear obedience to the new government in Siena.

In terms of political stability, the medieval frontier post of Sant'Angelo in Colle was more fortunate than its nearby neighbour Montalcino. Yet between the thirteenth and fourteenth centuries, the villagers witnessed dramatic changes in their economic fortunes, in local demography, and even in the urban structure itself. On occasion Sant'Angelo in Colle was hard put to meet the demands imposed on it by its new masters. A surviving record of January 1262/3 describes how the commune and castle had been forced to elect a *sindaco*, or chief official, to sell a large number of local possessions in order to pay Sant'Angelo in Colle's dues.[20] Although clearly compromised by subjugation to Siena, and the visible manifestation of this in the garrisoning of troops in the village, the imposition of foreign officials to carry out local business, and the constant need to raise money for taxes for its new masters, Sant'Angelo in Colle nevertheless clearly benefited from the influx of Sienese 'outsiders'.[21] As this study will show, a number of Sienese citizens played an important part in injecting new life and investment into the existing community, not least by establishing a system of *mezzadria*, or sharecropping, and hiring local residents of Sant'Angelo in Colle to work the land they acquired in the vicinity of the village.[22] At the same time, these newcomers brought with them the cultural experience and expectations of the city.

Unlike Montalcino, Sant'Angelo in Colle was offered a degree of autonomy in dealing with local affairs at a comparatively early date. As early as 1256 the Sienese government agreed, for example, that the commune and men of the village should be free to elect their own rector, so long as that individual was a committed resident Sienese citizen ('cives senenses assidue habitatores').[23] In January 1266 the General Council also agreed that Sant'Angelo in Colle should have its own resident 'podestà', or mayor.[24] It may have been at this date, therefore, if not before, that the village acquired an official town hall.[25] Ugo Ricci maintained that Sant'Angelo in Colle at first adopted a policy similar to numerous other small rural communes where village officials, instead of meeting in communal offices, gathered together on the *sagrato*, or square, in front of the parish church.[26] In such situations, the parish priest was in effect the *maestro*, or head of the community, acting as chancellor and peacekeeper. This may explain why in 1212, the consent of the village priest was sought prior to the oath of allegiance to Siena, but why in 1225 the two consuls of Sant'Angelo in Colle appear to have been acting independently of the religious authorities. In effect, the pre-existing authority in the village was challenged through the procedural framework of the second oath. In bypassing the authority of the village priest, whilst at the same time co-opting his services in the oath-taking ceremony as a witness, the Sienese sent out a clear message confirming the superiority of power of central government over the newly subject commune. The fact that the oath of 1225 seems not to have taken place inside the church of San Michele may well have formed part of the same strategy.

That said decentralisation, in the form of handing over to individual communes the responsibility for managing their own internal affairs, seems on occasion to have suited the central government. Self-interest, and in particular the reinforcement at minimum cost of hard-won territory in the southern *contado*, underlay many apparently generous gestures made by the Sienese to their subject towns and villages. Sienese citizens finding themselves in the position of guarding newly established frontiers received particular support. Castelfranco di Paganico, to the south of Sant'Angelo in Colle and on the other side of the Orcia River provides a useful case study. In March 1295, officials of the General Council in Siena recorded that compensation was due to those individuals who had decided to relocate to the 'Castello e Terra di Castelfranco di Paganico' following the construction of what was in effect a new town there.[27] Many of these people had built homes in the town, and were now demanding the farmhouses that had been promised them, so that they could work the surrounding land and establish new livelihoods there. By the spring of 1295, some of the Sienese colonists were even threatening to leave. Noting that the entire project of the new town had been undertaken 'p(er) conservazione e utilita delle Terre di Maremma, e p(er) sicurezza de viaggiatori e mercanti dalle ruberie dei ladri e assassini di strada' (for the conservation and use of the lands of the Maremma, and for the security and protection of travellers and merchants from robbers and assassins along the road), the Sienese officials of the General Council were forced to consider how to carve up the existing territory in order to allocate plots of land and individual farm buildings to their own pioneering citizens.

In the case of a new settlement like Castelfranco di Paganico it was particularly important that the central government should keep their frontier men happy. No town built as a safe haven for those travelling backwards and forwards from the southern territories could have flourished without the presence of local inhabitants along the way who were friendly to the Sienese state. Equally, the Sienese frontier men would not stay in the new settlement if they had no means of providing for themselves and their families. But, establishing a Sienese presence must on occasion have involved acquisition of land previously held by others, inevitably causing some degree of tension.

For the Sienese government there was clearly an ulterior motive to such initiatives as the 'land-grab' at Castelfranco di Paganico. It was obviously in the interests of the Sienese that they should establish a visible presence in any newly acquired territory. Moreover, each time a Sienese citizen laid claim to land or property, the *contado* was expanded and new frontiers were established. Towards the end of the thirteenth century, and during the early years of the fourteenth century the records of the General Council contain numerous references to the purchase of land and houses in the southern *contado*, and to inducements offered to those who were prepared to invest their money there. Thus, in August 1299 concessions of *casalini* (little houses normally in the country) and *poderi* (farms) were offered to anyone who would go and live in Rocca Albegna.[28] And on 2 June 1301 reference was made to one specific individual, Musciatto di Guido di Francesco, in the context of his buying land, castles and houses 'in the Sienese state'.[29] On more than one occasion it seems that such acquisitions were in effect appropriated from owners who were no longer regarded as *bonafide* supporters of the Sienese government. Elsewhere it seems that a forced sale was imposed even on those who, on the surface, professed to be on the side of Siena. Thus, in February 1285/6 Count Ranieri d'Elci and his sons are said to have 'sworn friendship to the Commune of Siena' and to have 'put at their disposition' their castles at Elci, Giuncarico and Sticciano.[30] As we shall see, similar patterns of appropriation of land by Sienese 'outsiders' were established in the vicinity of Sant'Angelo in Colle.

By the early fourteenth century, several 'outsiders' including a considerable number of Sienese citizens and Sienese religious and charitable institutions had acquired property in and around the southern garrison of Sant'Angelo in Colle. These included the Augustinian community of Sant'Agostino and the hospitals of Santa Maria della Scala and Monna Agnese and, from Montalcino, a group of religious women known as the *fratesse*, or female friars, as well as the local Augustinian friars of the convent of Sant'Agostino. Such influx must have dramatically influenced the closely knit community of Sant'Angelo in Colle, not least through the establishment of a new social hierarchy with a variety of cultural experiences and expectations. Events described here will show how the Sienese presence in particular stimulated change, through the construction of new buildings inside the garrison's walls. There is some evidence also to show that local affluence deriving from the increased political significance of Sant'Angelo in Colle within the Sienese sphere resulted in a number of endowments to the village's two churches by the village's own residents. There seems little doubt that such local patronage was coloured by artistic know-how newly introduced to the frontier castle by outsiders arriving from the city. It is probably no coincidence, for example, that painted panels and fresco work associated with Sant'Angelo in Colle reflect the artistic style of fourteenth-century Sienese artists. Medieval craftsmen frequently followed the movements and fortunes of their city patrons, as the latter moved from the centre to the periphery, or looked to their business concerns outside their own city walls. As models of cultural activity at the centre, Sienese artists no doubt also assumed a particular cultural cachet in the provinces where individuals newly subject to Siena were more often than not, and for a variety of reasons, eager to assume or be associated with contemporary fashions.[31] As this study will attempt to show, early fourteenth-century residents of Sant'Angelo in Colle were probably also anxious to reflect patterns of piety and charity established inside Siena itself. Indeed, surviving documents show that endowments were frequently made to Sienese institutions as well as to the village's own local organisations.

Such practice was no doubt a natural by-product of Sant'Angelo in Colle's subject status. Surviving records indicate that the internal affairs of subject communes were subjected to constant scrutiny by a central government that was not only concerned to control local unrest and prevent rebellion, but also engaged in a process of acculturation. That this included physical rearrangement of the various urban fabrics under the authority of Siena is confirmed by the frequent references to the construction of fortified military barracks in newly subdued communes, most noticeably in the wake of confrontations with the central government.[32] On occasion, it seems that there was in addition a practical and even aesthetic element to interventions in the internal layout of individual towns. It was clearly preferable not only that subject communes should be defended against possible attack, but also that they should offer adequate accommodation for visiting dignitaries. By the same count, it was no doubt deemed appropriate to establish good access to and transport through such urban fabrics. Such preoccupations may well have influenced the election on 12 July 1279 of several Sienese deputies who were authorised to go to Colle Sabbatini to 'design and finish the streets, gates and squares' there, as well as to construct ditches and moats as fortifications.[33]

That subject communes like Sant'Angelo in Colle were on occasion expected to host Sienese citizens and their allies and even their livery is clear from such commands as that emanating from the *Concistoro* in August 1381, that the villagers should extend a warm welcome to 36 horses belonging to Francesco Orsini.[34] Merely finding the space to house, water and feed so many horses must have presented a problem, quite apart from any hospitality that might have been extended to, or expected by Francesco Orsini and his retinue.

Having the Sienese military encamped within the urban fabric did not only mean the physical presence of soldiers. On occasion, Sienese barracks also functioned as armament centres. When in March 1285 Sozzino di Deo Tolomei relinquished his position as one of the commanders of the Sienese state and betrayed Siena by independently occupying Montegiove on the other side of the River Orcia from Sant'Angelo in Colle, an army was immediately despatched against him.[35] This assault was to include the use of *battifolle*, or battering rams. At the same time, it was decided that the stones for the *trabocchi*, or catapults, should be made at Sant'Angelo in Colle. The harshness of such punitive measures as well as the manufacturing of armaments on their own doorstep would surely not have escaped the notice of the villagers. Some of them may even have been co-opted to the enterprise. Thus, while on the one hand responding to disobedience within its own ranks through immediate and aggressive military manoeuvres, the Sienese government may also have been intent on delivering a passive message of warning as to the dire consequences of disobedience to its subjects in the southern frontier castle at Sant'Angelo in Colle.

The minutes of the Sienese General Council show that great attention was paid to the various ways in which a rebellious town or village might be punished, as well as the extent to which the meting out of such punishment might have a lasting visual impact, as a way of discouraging other disobedient acts. In some cases it was decided that the whole urban fabric should be razed to the ground; in others that only certain buildings should be targeted. Elsewhere, attention focused on the dismantling of perimeter walls, gates and ditches. Clearly, the aim was to effect sufficient physical damage so that potential dissidents elsewhere would be dissuaded from similar acts of rebellion. At the same time, the Sienese clearly appreciated the advantages of drawing subject communes into the net by a process of protectionism and munificence. For perhaps obvious reasons, although the records of the General Council contain numerous references to destruction following misdemeanours of subject towns and villages, there are just as many, if not more, descriptions of compensation to injured parties and restoration work in the wake of such punishment. It was often the case that swift reparation was made for damage done to the urban fabric. Thus, on 13 February 1259/60 payment was made to the nuns of Grosseto and the city's hospital 'in ricompensa dei danni e destruzione fatta dall'esercito senese ai medesimi' (in recompense for the damage and destruction wrought on the same by the Sienese army).[36] At the same time, Siena was clearly anxious to protect itself from future threats. A few weeks after reparation to the city's nuns and hospital, the decision was taken in May of the same year to send 30 builders with one superintendent in order to construct a new castle at Grosseto.[37] Some 70 or so years later, after another local insurrection in Grosseto, the General Council decided that the surrounding walls should be razed to the ground and all the 'fossi' (protective ditches) should be filled in.[38] Shortly thereafter, however (in 1345), we find references to the completion of both the *cassaro* (military barracks) and the *muri* (walls) of Grosseto, indicating that what had been destroyed was quickly rebuilt.[39] In some cases the threat of destruction of city walls and buildings was lifted altogether. In November 1317, for example, the *Consiglio della Campana*, after considering whether or not to destroy Castello di Civitella, proposed instead to maintain it and in fact to fortify it.[40]

Often, officials in Siena appear to have been anxious to present a sympathetic face in the event of local troubles, whilst at the same time making sure that their own interests were protected. When a local tyrant set fire to Castello di Camigliano in 1339, apparently leaving the settlement vulnerable to the 'vento marino' (sea breeze) – which caused the illness and death of many of the residents – the Sienese General Council decreed that the locals should be exempt from tax for the period of four years.[41] There was, nevertheless, a significant condition. All monies saved were to be spent on the reconstruction of the town's walls. The Sienese were no doubt conscious that if Camigliano remained defenceless, and its residents in ill health, the entire community would be vulnerable. Clearly, no *castello di frontiera* would have served any useful purpose if it were left without adequate fortifications over anything more than a very short period. The temptation for other powers to attempt a take over and thus whittle away the Sienese state would have been too great. The latter is spelt out clearly in a decision by the *Consiglio della Campana* of 2 August 1322, that reparations should be made to the walls of Rocca Albegna.[42] In that case it had been noted that the walls on one side of Rocca Albegna were 'smurata', or fallen down, and that the 'enemies of Rocca Albegna' could thus easily penetrate the urban fabric. It was thus decided that the 'men and people' of Rocca Albegna should be allowed to cut down a number of trees in a nearby wood in order to raise sufficient funds to reconstruct the walls. Significantly, the number of trees felled was not to exceed that necessary to cover the cost of the building work. In other words, there was no question that any of the local population should benefit individually from the cutting of the trees and their subsequent sale. The Government of the Nine was nevertheless anxious not to overstretch the loyalty of their subject citizens in Rocca Albegna. There seems little doubt that the inhabitants of Rocca Albegna were miserably poor in the early fourteenth century. Only a few weeks after the stipulation concerning the rebuilding of the walls, reference was made to the *povertà* (poverty) and *miseria* (misery) of the people of Rocca Albegna, and the extreme difficulties they were facing 'because of the war'.[43] The decision was thus taken to relieve Rocca Albegna of all dues and taxes for the period of five years, with the sole exception that they should continue to present wax to Siena for the annual celebration of the feast of the Assumption of the Virgin.

Nonetheless, the Sienese clearly also knew how to wring the most humiliating punishment from those who rebelled against them. When, in 1261 the people of Montelaterone forged a peace plan with the monks of Abbadia San Salvatore without Siena's permission, the General Council decided that the whole community should reap the consequences.[44] It was subsequently agreed that the most appropriate punishment would be to force the townsmen of Montelaterone to complete at their own expense the military barracks already partially constructed by the Sienese.[45]

Despite theoretical protection from Siena, the inhabitants of Sant'Angelo in Colle frequently suffered attack from those wishing to destabilise Siena, or merely intent on sowing havoc and distress. Much strife arose as a result of tension between Guelfs and Ghibellines.[46] During the second half of the thirteenth century, any opponent of the Sienese government tended to side with the Ghibellines. According to Giovanni Antonio Pecci, when in 1281 Sant'Angelo in Colle was occupied by Amadeo da Montenero and Guglielmo d'Orso – supporters of the Ghibelline faction – the whole village was deemed to be in open rebellion to Siena.[47] On that occasion the *podestà*, or local mayor, had apparently been expelled from the village by the rebels, along with the company of Sienese soldiers billeted there.[48] The order was subsequently sent out from Siena that all those who had been involved in the rebellion should be rounded up and punished. In particular, it was stressed that the leader of the Ghibelline rebels, Neri da Sticciano, should be captured and killed and that a new company of soldiers should be formed and sent to Sant'Angelo in Colle.[49] Once the village was retaken by Sienese troops, Siena plotted revenge on Sant'Angelo in Colle, threatening in a meeting of the General Council in between June and July 1281 to tear down the walls of the village, as 'punishment for harbouring their enemies'.[50]

Tradition has it that all of the village's fortifications were pulled down following the insurrection of 1281. An entry in the *Biccherna* records dated 14 February 1280/1281 does in fact refer to payment made to the 50 individuals who are said to have razed the walls of Sant'Angelo in Colle to the ground.[51] The total destruction of the walls is, however, probably an exaggeration. The eighteenth-century chronicler, Giovanni Antonio Pecci, cites an anonymous source that describes Sant'Angelo in Colle as completely surrounded by fortified walls in 1282.[52] It seems more likely, therefore, that the Sienese, having threatened to humiliate Sant'Angelo in Colle by rendering them vulnerable to the outside world, in fact imposed a lighter punishment. It is possible, as Ugo Ricci suggests, that only the main gate of the village was destroyed following the Ghibelline rebellion.[53] This, combined with the partial dismantling of adjacent walls, would clearly have driven home a hard message. Damage of this kind would, moreover, have been comparatively easy to repair. There is some physical support for such a course of events in the surviving urban fabric. Parts of the one remaining gateway are clearly of ancient construction, although variations in the stonework indicate different working processes.[54]

It is, of course, also possible that it was an earlier circuit of walls that suffered the main brunt of the Sienese assault in 1281, and that later building work (including the construction of new gateways and additional stretches of wall) and subsequent infillings have rendered the path of these pre-existing fortifications invisible. The fact that one stretch of walls to the south of the village reveals a different kind of construction from other surviving sections does indeed support such a hypothesis.

Figure I.1   North portal Sant'Angelo in Colle (internal view, detail of stonework)

Figure I.2
Southern external
wall, Sant'Angelo
in Colle

In any event, surviving records dating to 1281 indicate that although the General Council was anxious to canvas a number of punitive measures following the insurrection at Sant'Angelo in Colle, no firm conclusions were reached.[55]

Nevertheless, there seems little doubt that the Sienese effected a number of changes in their southern frontier castle in the face of continued unrest there. Even before the Ghibelline-inspired rebellion at Sant'Angelo in Colle, a member of the Salimbeni clan – one of the leading families in Siena at that time, and staunch supporters of the government – was elected to assume control over affairs at Sant'Angelo in Colle.[56] Surviving records also speak of intense building work, not only on the walls of Sant'Angelo in Colle, but in addition in the construction of a new military headquarters in the village during the early 1280s. On 11 April 1282, payment was made to three individuals, Pietro di Scotto, Ranieri di Turchio and Mino di Piero for the five days they spent visiting Sant'Angelo in Colle in order to decide where to site the barracks.[57] Building work was finished in 1286, a year before the election of the Government of the Nine.[58] The scene was apparently set for a new period of order.

According to contemporary accounts the 70 or so years of the Government of the Nine was the period of greatest peace and prosperity for Siena. In his *Cronaca Senese*, the fourteenth-century chronicler Agnolo di Tura del Grasso wrote 'ognuno attendeva ai suoi guadagni e cosi il contado, e tutti s'amavano come fratelli' (everyone looked after their own affairs, both in the city and in the countryside, and they all treated each other like brothers, with love).[59] This was not only a period of relatively stable government. It was also a time during which there was a particular flourishing of the combined arts of painting, architecture and town planning. Under the Government of the Nine, many impressive architectural projects were undertaken inside the walls of Siena, such as the laying out of the *Piazza del Campo*, the construction of the *Palazzo Pubblico* and the adjacent *Torre del Mangia*, as well as the grandiose enlargement of the cathedral – all, still, potent symbols of the city's well-being during the early medieval period.[60] These were the years, also, that witnessed the art of such great painters as Duccio di Buoninsegna and Ambrogio and Pietro Lorenzetti.[61] In 1311, Duccio's painting of the *Maestà* (the Virgin in Majesty) was placed – after much celebration and procession throughout the city – on the high altar of the city's Cathedral, thus celebrating and reinforcing the myth established in the wake of the victorious Battle of Montaperti in 1260, that Siena was particularly favoured by the Virgin Mary.[62] Three decades after the completion of the *Maesta*, Ambrogio Lorenzetti was commissioned to decorate the *Sala dei Nove* in the *Palazzo Pubblico* with on two walls scenes expostulating the virtues of good government, and on another, the disasters of war and the social unrest that arose under bad government, where evil reigned and where bad counsel was the order of the day.[63]

Such scenes must have had a particular significance for frontier garrisons such as Sant'Angelo in Colle. Despite her protected status as a subject Sienese commune, she continued to confront age-old rivals to the south. Surviving records speak of the damage done to the village when a *cavalcata*, or group of armed horsemen, from Campagnatico stormed Sant'Angelo in Colle in 1295.[64] Four years later, the counts of Civitella were condemned for a similar assault.[65] During this period, many small groups of armed men from the slopes of Monte Amiata roamed the plains of the Orcia and Ombrone rivers and infiltrated the surrounding hillsides. Their trademarks were violent confrontations, arson, theft, and physical assault. The Sienese *Caleffo Vecchio* includes almost daily chronicles of such events in the ever-expanding, but frequently under-protected Sienese *contado*. In many cases, mercenaries ran amok, bringing death or injury to local residents. Marauding miscreants also frequently created mayhem in the countryside, setting pastures alight, stealing cattle and provoking armed combat. Victims of such lawlessness were forced to watch as their homes were invaded, their loved ones wounded, and their cattle stolen, often in the conspicuous absence of the forces of law and order. On some occasions, events in and around Sant'Angelo in Colle must have reflected only too clearly those scenes representing the effects of bad government painted on the walls of the *Palazzo dei Nove* in Siena.

Surviving records indicate that Ambrogio Lorenzetti's depiction of the effects of misrule was by no means exaggerated.[66] This was not so much political propaganda as an objective depiction of events as they occurred on the ground, even under the watchful eyes of the Government of the Nine. Unrest in the *contado*, whether in the form of local miscreants or rebellion by subject communes, clearly threatened the fortunes of the city itself, through disruption of trade and commerce. Not only were Siena's food supplies threatened. Tax revenues were also endangered, particularly in those cases where individuals hostile to Siena assumed even temporary positions of power.[67] On occasion, attacks on the southern frontier post of Sant'Angelo in Colle must have resulted in acute damage to both the local economy and the revenues of central government. When the commune and men of Campagnatico, described as 'ribelli e nemici del comune di Siena' (rebels and enemies of the commune of Siena) stormed Sant'Angelo in Colle in March 1294 and made off with 700 sheep, they must not only have deprived the local inhabitants of produce in the form of cheese and wool, but also have dented the expectations in kind of the city of Siena itself.[68]

One group of troublemakers associated with the sons of Guidone di Bonifazio, count of Civitella di Ardinghesco, is constantly cited in the context of Sant'Angelo in Colle. Described as enemies and rebels, and subjected to numerous bans and fines by the Government of the Nine, Fazio, Longaruccio, Ghinozzo, Bino and Niccoluccio di Guidone terrorised the southern Sienese *contado* over a number of decades. In the tense summer days of June 1288, only a year after the formation of the Government of the Nine, Guidone di Bonifazio and his sons were accused of attacking the church of Santi Fabiano e Sebastiano in Civitella, of expelling the rector from his home and of setting fire to the church itself.[69] On another occasion, in July 1291, 'hostiliter et armati' (armed and with hostile intent), the same group of miscreants rode up to Sant'Angelo in Colle and, coming upon two men in the area known as Quarata on the outskirts of the village, hurled insults at them, before hacking them to death with their lances.[70] The Sienese government promptly banned Guidone and his followers from the territory. Each one of them was in addition fined 3,000 'libris denariorum Senesium'.

But not all such incidents were fuelled by a desire to defy the central government. There is some evidence to suggest that there had been a long-running vendetta between the supporters of the Ardinghesca clan and the residents of Sant'Angelo in Colle. Although the slaughter of Piero di Ruggero and Giovanni di Bencivenne in the fields of Quarata might seem at first sight to have been a gratuitous act of violence by rebels to the Sienese cause, it appears that this particular incident was fired by personal quarrels, rather than by open defiance to the Republic of Siena. Only a few months before the killing at Quarata, another group – including Mone, brother of Migliacci, and son of Francesco, the notary of Sant'Angelo – had wounded and killed Gratiolo di Caffarelli, a member of the Ardingheschi.[71] For this killing, which took place in the district of Sasso Marittima, the 'angels' had, in their turn, been fined and reprimanded by the Government of the Nine. The incident at Sasso Marittima may, nevertheless, have prompted a revenge excursion on the part of the Ardingheschi. In any event, there were not only two incidents of this kind. This particular vendetta seems to have been running for some time.

A couple of years before the incident at Sasso Marittima, Longaruccio, Fazio, Ghinozzo and Bino of the Civitella clan had, in an incident in June 1289, insulted Duccio di Leonardo of Sant'Angelo in Colle, and his companion Nuccio di Falcona, before wounding Duccio with a sword thrust to his arm, and stoning Nuccio.[72] During the same month, Longaruccio's gang was denounced by Nerio, or Neri di Giucciardo (who was related to Nuccio di Falcona) for having insulted and wounded his brother Ticcio.[73] It seems as if the two groups were locked in a perpetual cycle of attack and counter attack, which had little to do with the politics of the super powers.

The unruly Count of Civitella and his sons were, nevertheless, finally brought to heel. Imposing massive fines on all members of the family, and listing in full numerous crimes committed by them over a number of years, the Government of the Nine confiscated all of Count Guidone's possessions in March 1299/1300, and assumed power over one eighth of the *corte*, or territory, of Civitella itself.[74] Sant'Angelo in Colle, for its part, had once more been placed firmly under the authority of Siena, and there she remained throughout the fourteenth century and beyond.[75] Surviving records confirm that money was made available by the Sienese government for the fortification and protection of Sant'Angelo in Colle at regular intervals. These continued right up to the period prior to Siena's defeat by the combined military forces backing Florence, during the siege of Montalcino between 1555 and 1559.[76]

The economic conditions of Sant'Angelo in Colle improved rapidly under the Government of the Nine, and, more particularly, in the 100 years between 1280 and 1380. For one thing, the population was expanding. Like many other settlements in the early modern period, Sant'Angelo in Colle witnessed a particularly rapid expansion during the thirteenth century. At the beginning of the thirteenth century, there were probably some 350 'angels' on the hill, since 87 *fuochi*, or households, were listed there in 1212.[77] A decade later, in 1225, some 250 men over the age of maturity are documented as signing the oath of loyalty to Siena.[78] Many of these must have had dependents, including women, children and old folk. It is probable, therefore, that during this short period of time, the population of Sant'Angelo in Colle had increased by at least 50 percent. Fifty years later, in 1278, 175 *fuochi* were declared, indicating that the early thirteenth-century population had more than doubled in size.[79] In 1320, 128 named individuals and the heirs of 66 others (some 100 of which were recorded as possessing property inside the walls) were included in the *Estimo*, or *Tavola delle possessioni* for Sant'Angelo in Colle.[80] It is possible, therefore, that there were as many as 1,000 souls established inside the walls of the village by the early fourteenth century.[81] In terms of potential work force, alone, such expansion in the population of this southern frontier castle must have increased the production of food crops and facilitated the rearing of livestock. But it must also have placed an increasing burden on what was a comparatively small urban fabric, where only so many buildings could be accommodated within the existing circle of walls.

By the end of the fourteenth century, Sant'Angelo in Colle was in fact established as a significant centre for the rearing and sheltering of cattle and pigs, the curing of ham, the production of *pecorino*, or sheep's milk cheese, the tending of vines and olives, and the nurturing of chickens.[82] Many of these activities were drawn into the ambit of the Sienese Ospedale di Santa Maria della Scala, which had established a presence in and around the village by the beginning of the fourteenth century. Indeed, it is possible that this institution had already established a *grancia*, or grange, at Sant'Angelo in Colle several decades earlier.[83]

Much has been written about the hospital institution that was first recorded in Siena in 1090 as the 'xenodochium et hospitalis de canonica Sancte Marie'. More recently, a fundamental work was published by Stephan Epstein in 1986, a year that witnessed a number of other seminal studies on Santa Maria della Scala.[84] Epstein deals with all aspects of Santa Maria della Scala's history, from its ecclesiastical foundation through to the expansion of its patrimony in the southern Sienese *contado*, and the central role the hospital assumed in the affairs of the Sienese Government of the Nine. In effect, and following in the footsteps of earlier historians concerned with the history of Santa Maria della Scala, Epstein prepared the way for a whole raft of studies considering individual hospital granges; the general development of medical assistance and social welfare in the early medieval period; the relationship between art, piety and charity as reflected in the imposing series of frescoed images in the hospital's old *pellegrinaggio*, or public ward; and everyday life within the walls of the great Sienese hospital itself.[85]

There seems little doubt that Santa Maria della Scala was initially dependent on the Canons of the Cathedral of Siena, because the hospital complex itself was built on land belonging to that entity. A close association was also formed at an early date between the hospital and the Augustinian order, through the creation at the end of the twelfth century of the so-called 'Oblati di Santa Maria'.[86] The independent autonomy of this 'ordine ospedaliere degli Oblati' was recognised in a papal bull dating to 1195.[87] However, few now question the early importance of the hospital in terms of what Anne Katherine Isaacs calls a 'civic system of devotion' and Siena's 'territorial projection'.[88] Isaacs argues that the hospital of Santa Maria della Scala was the central nucleus of a widespread system of assistance and political influence, which depended in part on Siena's position on the Via Francigena. She suggests that the diverse functions that the hospital established by the early fourteenth century, ranging from curing the sick and the distribution of bread to the poor, to the acceptance of abandoned infants and their wet-nursing (both inside the city and in the surrounding countryside), underpinned the development of Santa Maria della Scala's own independent territory and resources in the southern Sienese *contado*. According to Isaacs, such development was at first confined to the more accessible areas close to the main road, and was restricted in the main to principal conurbations in the Val d'Orcia. A high point in the acquisition of territory occurred during the third decade of the fourteenth century,[89] the hospital's statute of 1322 listing those areas that were never to be alienated (amongst them, property at Sant'Angelo in Colle).[90] Isaacs suggests that such patterns of acquisition reflected Siena's steady expansion to the south, as well as the city's confrontation with the Aldobrandeschi counts of Monte Amiata on the other side of the River Orcia. Thus, a complex form of symbiosis was established between the hospital and central government by the early fourteenth century. But long before this, there is evidence that the Commune was offering financial assistance for the development of the hospital complex, and that the internal affairs of Santa Maria della Scala were being scrutinised by government officials.[91]

Meanwhile, Santa Maria della Scala was intent on building up an impressive portfolio of possessions both inside and beyond the city. As early as 1280, the hospital's patrimony included some 500 properties.[92] Epstein traces the origin of this in numerous contracts of sale and donation of land that became ever more frequent during the second decade of the thirteenth century.[93] Noting that various rural hospitals along the Via Francigena also began at that time to place themselves under the authority of Santa Maria della Scala, Epstein demonstrates how the hospital consolidated a number of possessions in the vicinity of individual urban fabrics such as the small village of Cuna, and subsequently established individual headquarters there, known as *grancie*, or granges. Elsewhere, the donation of houses and individual pieces of land led to the development of hospitals, such as that at San Quirico d'Orcia, which not only served as hospices, but also as refuges for abandoned babies and children. While serving in the main as depots for local produce, which was subsequently transferred to Siena, such granges also functioned as outposts for local surveillance. In effect, and as we shall see, individual *grancia* officials and associates in the form of members of the Augustinian order (sent either from the city or established in local communities in the vicinity of individual subject communes) not only reinforced the central power of Santa Maria della Scala, but also played a significant part in monitoring everyday happenings in the southern Sienese *contado*. As Epstein points out, such power and widespread local activity must have been of mounting interest to the Government of the Nine, which was intent on consolidating its own presence in the same areas to the south of Siena. Indeed, Epstein suggests that a direct correlation may be drawn between the hospital's expanding patrimony and the government's attempt in 1305 to draw Santa Maria della Scala and other charitable institutions in the city under its direct control.[94]

There seems little doubt that one such *grancia* or office had been established in Sant'Angelo in Colle by 1356, since in that year reference was made to Friar Niccolo Tori, 'granciere' of Sant'Angelo in Colle.[95] This initial granary seems to have been expanded (both in size, business and significance) during the second half of the fourteenth century. According to a register drawn up between May 1385 and April 1386, during that period the hospital's *grancia* at Sant'Angelo in Colle sent to Siena 18 *staia* (a unit of measurement equivalent to a bushel) of grain, 190 *staia* of wine, 16 *staia* of olive oil, 200 *libre* (pounds) of linen, 2773 forms of cheese, 13 fowl, 600 eggs, 10 sheep and 8 pigs.[96]

It seems clear that Sant'Angelo in Colle had already become an important centre of wine production, although by contrast the export of oil was low. It also appears that there was a significant local cloth industry. However, the number of cheeses produced – roughly a third of the overall number produced at the same date by the 12 or so *grancie* in the southern Sienese *contado* – indicates that this was the most significant local product in the early fourteenth-century village. Records concerning the production of cheese in other areas cite much lower figures.[97] The fact that eight live pigs had been sent to Siena from Sant'Angelo in Colle between 1385 and 1386 is also significant. Pigs were particularly important in the medieval period for both diet and trade. They not only provided fresh meat for the local peasants' daily needs, but were also used for the production of long-lasting salted hams for consumption at home and abroad. Preserved meat formed an essential part of the medieval diet.[98] Like the pig ambling up to the walls of Siena in Ambrogio Lorenzetti's fresco of a landscape under the protection of a good government in the *Sala dei Nove*, livestock from Sant'Angelo in Colle was clearly transported alive along the dusty road from the foothills of Montalcino, to staging posts in various parts of the southern Sienese territory, before finally reaching Siena.[99]

Quite apart from contributing to the financial well-being of the Ospedale di Santa Maria della Scala, such bullishness in the market of essential goods must have stimulated the local economy of Sant'Angelo in Colle, and in turn have affected the construction of new buildings as well as the embellishment of the urban fabric. Yet famine also stalked the closing years of the fourteenth century, and the southern frontier castle was not immune to the consequences of this. But even then, it seems that Sienese 'outsiders' played a part in ameliorating the suffering of the local inhabitants. The hospital of Santa Maria della Scala, for example, lent money to the commune of Sant'Angelo in Colle during the particularly lean year of 1390, so that it might cover its expenses and protect the interests of the people there.[100]

Much earlier in the century, the Republic of Siena itself was facing increasing financial burdens. In 1304 the Government of the Nine was virtually bankrupt. In a money-saving operation, the decision was taken to withdraw the *corpo di guardia*, or resident military corps, from a number of communes.[101] Despite this, and no doubt mainly because of its strategic position, guarding Siena's southern flank, Sant'Angelo in Colle continued to serve as a fortified outpost. Hardly a decade seems to have passed between the second half of the fourteenth century and the end of the fifteenth century, without some reference being made either to the rebuilding, or restoration of existing walls, or expenses deemed necessary for the construction of completely new sections in the southern frontier castle.[102] Nevertheless, the institutions that had protected Sant'Angelo in Colle and contributed to its wealth during the fourteenth century began gradually to disappear. In 1355, the Government of the Nine fell, giving way to the Government of the Twelve.[103] By 1380, the Sienese military had completely abandoned its southern post, handing over its barracks in 1376 to the hospital of Santa Maria della Scala, which at that time was clearly intent on expanding its affairs in Sant'Angelo in Colle.[104] However, after a comparatively brief period of successful business, the hospital transferred its headquarters first to Argiano, and then to Piana, virtually abandoning the 'angels' on the hill.[105] At the same time Santa Maria della Scala arranged the removal and redistribution in *grancie* elsewhere of the sheep they had kept in the territory of Sant'Angelo in Colle. For the villagers of that date, it must have seemed as if they were witnessing not only the end of a golden age but also the demise of a significant part of their livelihood. In 1403, after a disastrous series of drought and famine years, the officials of Santa Maria della Scala let out the Sant'Angelo in Colle grange to a private Sienese citizen – Goro di Goro Sansedoni.[106] This signalled the end of a mutually beneficial relationship established between Siena at the centre and Sant'Angelo in Colle on the periphery that had lasted for nearly 200 years. Thereafter Sant'Angelo in Colle, whilst ostensibly still under the protection of Siena, confronted increasingly lean times.

The crisis of the countryside in the late-fourteenth century closed a significant chapter in the life of Sant'Angelo in Colle.[107] Depleted by famine and outbreaks of the plague, and increasingly weighed down by poverty, declining numbers, and the continuing burden of taxes that they could no longer accommodate, the inhabitants of Sant'Angelo in Colle presented a miserable picture to the outside world by the mid-fifteenth century. In August 1435, the villagers made an impassioned plea for exemption from tax by the Sienese government.[108] Referring to the village's continual decline, the people of Sant'Angelo in Colle drew attention to the fact that whereas once they had numbered 300, they were at that date reduced to 70 souls, in just 11 households. They had nothing from which they could squeeze even a *quattrino* (or small coin) except for the *terra*, or ground. How could so few manage the vines, the olives, the fields and the woods, when, before, so many more households – each, presumably, with their own extended family members – had contributed to and supported the daily endeavours of working the land and raising livestock? Meantime, large urban centres, albeit in their turn disadvantaged by disease, demographic change and years of financial insecurity, were benefiting from recession on the land, and the translocation of a large number of individuals from the countryside to the city. Cities such as Florence were not only busily establishing themselves as bustling centres of successful entrepreneurial activities in what came to be known as the Age of the Renaissance, but were also increasing in size, authority and power.

Despite this, the Sienese continued to fortify the old *castello di frontiera* of Sant'Angelo in Colle, as if in denial of the village's waning prosperity. Clearly, Sant'Angelo in Colle's strategic position outstripped its actual viability as a living community, as Florence and Siena locked jaws in continual hostility. In 1494, the huge sum of 500 florins was recorded for work on the walls of Sant'Angelo in Colle, indicating, perhaps, a complete rebuild and encircling of the village. At the same time, whether through poverty or disaffection, the residents of Sant'Angelo in Colle resolutely turned their backs on impending disaster. In the sixteenth century, when Siena made its last stand against Florence, there was frenetic speculation about the old frontier post. But the population of Sant'Angelo in Colle was in open rebellion. It may even have decided upon a form of auto-vandalism. Surviving records refer to the enforced evacuation of Sant'Angelo in Colle in December 1552, just before the arrival of the Florentines and their allies, and the siege of Montalcino between 1553 and 1555.[109] The 'angels' had apparently broken a promise to fortify the village, and, as a result, all the inhabitants were ordered to leave Sant'Angelo in Colle and seek shelter, either in Montalcino, or in Siena.[110] At the same time the order was sent out that the villagers should take away with them all the grain, wine, oil and other produce and likewise lodge it either in Montalcino or Siena.[111] Subsequently, it was decided that it would be impossible to lodge Sienese troops in Sant'Angelo in Colle itself, because the urban fabric was void of any kind of practical support in the form of local manpower or the provision of bed and board. To all intents and purposes Sant'Angelo in Colle was an empty shell.

After the fall of Montalcino and the subjugation of Siena to Florence in 1559, the southern frontier post of Sant'Angelo in Colle must have presented a piteous aspect. When Francesco Piccolomini visited the hospital of Sant'Angelo in Colle in 1573, he suggested that the building was suitable for animals, rather than humans.[112] The rest of the urban fabric may have been reduced to a similar state. Presumably, much of the circuit of walls must have been in a state of semi-collapse. Although the war between Siena and Florence no doubt played its part in such deterioration, degradation of the urban fabric was inevitable given that the village was, if not entirely derelict, in effect, semi-abandoned. Siena was, moreover, no longer in a position to oversee or finance repair work there. Despite this, original inhabitants and new residents seem gradually to have returned. At this point, some of the stones from the old walls were no doubt carried away for the construction of new dwellings, or for repair work on older structures and public buildings that had long lain empty and were themselves threatening collapse.

Some walls must, nevertheless, have been left standing, or considerable reparation work carried out on them during the 100 years following the fall of Siena, since Bartolomeo Gherardini, when visiting the village in 1676 in his guise as Sienese auditor general for Grand Duke Cosimo III of Tuscany, recorded that Sant'Angelo in Colle was circled by walls and that the external *carbonaie*, or ditches forming a moat, were partially left fallow and partially worked.[113]

In fact, a number of private individuals had assumed authority for the welfare of the village as early as the beginning of the sixteenth century. In 1520, Pope Leo X conceded the parish church of San Michele Arcangelo to the Brogioni.[114] Several decades later, the same family also assumed responsibility for the adjacent hospital of Sant'Antonio.[115] Other wealthy individuals such as the Ciaia assumed responsibility for a number of structures that had most probably functioned previously as communal offices.[116] These individuals brought new life to the village's religious and charitable institutions, as well as making considerable changes to the urban fabric. The church of San Michele and hospital of Sant'Antonio remained in the possession of the Brogioni family for over 200 years. Following the death of the last member of the family, Urania Brogioni, and the death of her husband (in 1742), the administration of the hospital was passed to the Knights of Saint Stephen. The hospital's patrimony was at the same time passed to Santa Maria della Scala.[117] By then, as the studies of recent historians have shown, the village and its territory was once again a mere shadow of its former self.[118]

There seems little doubt that Sant'Angelo in Colle's importance and prosperity at the time of the Government of the Nine reflected its strategic value to Siena, and was to a large extent the result of that city's external support. With hindsight, it seems obvious that once Siena's relations with Montalcino were settled in 1361 and the impressive structural additions made to the fortress there by the Sienese, Sant'Angelo in Colle's significance as a military outpost of the Sienese state should inevitably diminish. It is, moreover, clear that after 1361 Montalcino achieved a privileged position of semi-autonomy within the Republic of Siena. It was thus well placed to expand its own territory at the expense of Sant'Angelo in Colle.

Accounts of Montalcinco's affairs during the early modern period pay little attention to the strategic significance of the neighbouring commune of Sant'Angelo in Colle on the southern fringes of the Sienese *contado*. This study attempts to redress the balance between the two centres through an account of the history of Sant'Angelo in Colle, at a period when, rather than being a subordinate part of the commune of Montalcino (as was the case from 1777), it was able to challenge its neighbour as a rival centre of military and economic significance.

Notes

1 Vincenzo Passeri, *Documenti per la Storia delle Località della Provincia di Siena*
   (hereafter Passeri), (Siena, 2002), p. 308. For an overview of surviving documents
   concerning Sant'Angelo in Colle see Passeri pp. 307–9. See also Ugo Ricci, *S.
   Angelo in Colle nella storia e nella vita del contesto Senese e Toscano* (typescript,
   1985), (hereafter Ricci, 1985), *Sant'Angelo in Colle nella Storia* (typescript, 1989),
   (hereafter Ricci, 1989) and *Sant'Angelo in Colle: Appendice* (typescript, 1989),
   (hereafter Ricci, *Appendice*); Don Antonio Brandi, *Parrocchia di S. Michele
   Arcangelo in S. Angelo in Colle* (typescripts, 1972, 1991, and 2004); and Paolo
   Cammarosano, Riccardo Francovich, Vincenzo Passeri, Carlo Perogalli, Gabriella
   Piccinni and Giulio Vismara (eds), *I Castelli del Senese, Strutture fortificate dell'area
   Senese-grossetana* (Siena, 1985), pp. 327–28; and Emanuele Repetti, *Dizionario
   geografico, fisico, storico della Toscana*, (ristampa anastatica, 6 vols, Reggello, 2005),
   1, p. 86. Most recently, see also Silvana Biasutti (ed.), *Don Antonio Brandi, Il
   senso della memoria: ricerche sulla storia di Sant'Angelo in Colle* (Vicenza, 2010) – a
   compilation of Don Brandi's work published on the occasion of the most recent
   25 year celebrations in honour of the 'Madonna della Misericordia'.

2 Passeri, p. 307.

3 Ibid. See also Ricci, 1985, p. 29.

4 Odile Redon, *Uomini e comunità del contado senese nel Duecento* (Siena, 1982), pp. 99
   and 102.

5 The village of Camigliano, which also offered fealty to Siena in 1212, is likewise
   described as a 'castle', see Giovanni Cecchini (ed.), *Il Caleffo Vecchio del Comune
   di Siena* (hereafter *Caleffo Vecchio*) (Siena, 1931), vol. 1, no. 102, pp. 155–56. As
   at Sant'Angelo in Colle, the consul of Camigliano, Ildibrandino di Ardimanno,
   reported that he had obtained the consent of the local priest, Domino Gregorio,
   prior to agreeing to the oath. A slightly different turn of phrase was used when
   Montepinzuto offered its allegiance to Siena in 1213, see Cecchini, *Caleffo Vecchio*,
   1, no. 107, pp. 159–60. The oath of allegiance from that community begins
   by referring to 'the men (or people) of Montepinzuto'. Halfway through the
   document, there is a further reference to the 'men' of the village and a separate
   reference to the 'rectors of the castle'. The oath itself is said to have been sworn
   'in Montepinzuto', no reference being made to any specific structure such as the
   parish church, or fortified structure in the form of a castle.

6 In 1337 some 40 or so other settlements were associated with the military outpost
   of Sant'Angelo in Colle, including nearby Argiano. (See Donatella Ciampoli,
   *Il Capitano del popolo a Siena nel primo Trecento. Con il rubricario dello statuto del
   comune di Siena del 1337* (Siena, 1984), p. 102.) According to Giovacchino Faluschi
   and Ettore Romagnoli (*Manoscritti*, Siena, Biblioteca degli Intronati, C.II 5–6,
   vol. I, fol. 27r), Sant'Angelo in Colle was already positioned at the centre of a
   'gran vicario' in 1310. For vicariates, see Mario Ascheri, *Lo spazio storico di Siena*,
   Fondazione Monte dei Paschi di Siena (Milan, 2001), pp. 136–61 (144). See also
   Lucia Nardi, 'La distrettualizzazione dello stato: i Vicariati della Repubblica
   di Siena 1337–1339', in Mario Ascheri and Donatella Ciampoli (eds), *Siena e il
   suo territorio nel Rinascimento* (Siena, 1986), vol. 1, pp. 55–67. In 1310 the statutes
   of the *Capitani del Popolo* recorded that the Sienese territory was divided into
   nine vicariates, each comprising a number of rural communities. A *capitano*,
   or captain, holding military and judicial powers, headed each vicariate. Such
   powers had originally been in the hands of the *rettori*, or rectors, of individual
   communities. However, the title of 'rettore', or 'signore naturale', was abolished

in 1291. Under the Government of the Nine it was agreed that each captain in each vicariate should serve for six months and that in each of those months he should spend at least six days in the vicariate's relevant central commune. For a discussion of the role assumed by rectors during the thirteenth century, see Andrea Barlucchi, *Il contado senese nell'epoca dei Nove. Asciano e il suo territorio tra Due e Trecento* (Florence, 1997), pp. 133–34. According to Barlucchi, the vice rector was frequently the *notarius offitialis*, or official notary. In this guise, he was responsible for calling together the communal council, for deciding the agenda and introducing questions, as well as acting as arbiter in local affairs. The official notary also took the minutes of council meetings and kept a note of public expenditure decided by the commune. These individuals thus assumed an important role in linking the *contado* (or surrounding territory owned) with the city. The role of treasurer seems likewise to have included a number of responsibilities. In this respect, it is interesting to note that in January 1307/8 Bindo di Accorso in Sant'Angelo in Colle was referred to as 'camerarius, rectore offitiale ipsius castri' (the treasurer and official rector of this castle), see Archivio di Stato di Siena (hereafter ASS), *Diplomatico di Montalcino*, Busta 32, no. 133.

7   The principal function of the *Biccherna*, which took its name from the place of the treasury in Constantinople, was to administer communal expenses. It was also responsible for overseeing the security of the city and the *contado*, see Ricci, 1985, p. 37. For a more detailed consideration of the activities and functions of the *Biccherna* and the later *Gabella Generale e dei Contratti* and the *Ufficio di Gabella Generale* which was created to deal with the increasing number of dues levied, see ASS, *Archivio della Biccherna del Comune di Siena, Inventario* (Rome, Siena, 1953), pp. IX–XXI; Cosimo Cecinato, *L'amministrazione finanziaria del Comune di Siena nel sec. 13* (Milan, 1966), pp. 164–235. See also Luigi Borgia, Enzo Carli, Maria Assunta Ceppari, Ubaldo Morandi, Patrizia Sinibaldi, Carla Zarrili (eds), *Le Biccherne. Tavole Dipinte delle Magistrature Senesi (secoli 13–18)* (Rome, 1984), pp. 1–11.

8   Brandi, 1972, p. 6 and 2004, p. 6. According to the original document, Bonincontro spent four days altogether on this mission. At least two of the days were probably spent in the village, listening to local reports and acting as intermediary.

9   Passeri, p. 307.

10   Ibid. See also ASS, *Biccherna* 4, fol. 150, for a slightly earlier peace-making mission to Sant'Angelo in Colle in June 1231. On that occasion Bonsignori Balitore was paid the slightly lower sum of 3 *lire*, 10 *soldi* and 8 *denari* for travelling to Sant'Angelo in Colle 'pro facto discordie que errant in dicto castro' (on account of the disorders existing in that castle).

11   Redon, *Uomini e comunità*, p. 198, footnote 132.

12   Brandi, *Parrocchia di S. Michele Arcangelo*, 1972, p. 6.

13   In this context, see Redon, *Uomini e comunità*, p. 215, footnote 238. In 1252 a member of the Piccolomini family, 'messer Ranieri di messer Chiaromontese', was recorded as billeted at Sant'Angelo in Colle, together with his *compagnia*, or company, see Giovanni Antonio Pecci, *Notizie storiche della città di Montalcino*, with preface by Giuliano Catoni (Montalcino, 1989), p. 35. For the series of wars in which Montalcino was involved during the medieval period, see Antonio Pecci, *Memorie storico-critiche della città di Siena*, facsimile reproduction, Mario Pavolini and Ennio Innocenti (eds), (Siena, 1988), pp. 25–53. See also Lucia Carle, *Storia e storie di una città, Montalcino* (Siena, 1998), pp. 59–63; and Passeri, pp. 167–69.

14   Passeri, p. 307.

15   Ibid. For a recent overview of the Battle of Montaperti, see Duccio Balestracci (ed.), *Alla ricerca di Montaperti: mito, fonti documentarie e storiografie*, Convegno, Accademia dei Rozzi, Siena, 30 novembre 2007 (Siena, 2009). See also, Sergio Raveggi, 'La vittoria di Montaperti', with associated bibliography, in Roberto Barsanti, Giuliano Catoni and Mario De Gregorio (eds), *Storia di Siena, I, Dalle origini alla fine della Repubblica* (Siena, 1995), pp. 79–94. For Siena's fortunes following the victory at Montaperti, see Giuseppe Martini, 'Siena da Montaperti alla caduta dei Nove (1260–1355)', *Bullettino senese di storia e patria* (hereafter *BSSP*), 68 (1961), pp. 3–56 and 75–128.

16   For a recent synopsis of relationships between Montalcino, Florence and Siena during the thirteenth century, see Mario Ascheri, 'Montalcino nella storia: alle sorgenti del Brunello', in Mario Ascheri and Vinicio Serino (eds), *Prima del Brunello, Montalcino Capitale Mancata* (San Quirico d'Orcia, 2007), pp. 13–42.

17   See, for example, ASS, *Consiglio Generale*, 3, fols. 47r, 47v, and 65r.

18   Passeri, p. 168.

19   Ibid., p. 169. For a brief overview of Montalcino's political status between the thirteenth and fourteenth centuries, and for the town's relationship with Siena during the thirteenth century, including its final subjugation in 1361, see Alfio Cortonesi, 'Demografia e popolamento nel contado di Siena: Il territorio montalcinese nei secoli 13–15', in Rinaldo Comba, Gabriella Piccinni, Giuliano Pinto (eds), *Strutture familiari epidemie migrazioni nell'Italia medievale* (Naples, 1984), pp. 153–81 (153–57). For a survey of documents concerning Montalcino during the same period, see also Passeri, pp. 167–9. Ricci (1985, p. 35) maintains that the construction of the Sienese 'Rocca' at Montalcino, which in effect constituted an addition to a pre-existing fortress, marked the end of Sant'Angelo in Colle's privileged role as a military outpost of the Sienese *contado*.

20   Passeri, p. 307. See also Redon, *Uomini e comunità*, p. 199, footnote 137.

21   For an analysis of the influence of Sienese 'outsiders' in other parts of the Sienese *contado*, and in particular in the region of nearby Camigliano and Argiano, see Roberto Farinelli and Andrea Giorgi, *Camigliano, Argiano e Poggio alle Mura (secoli 12–14)*, presentazione di Alfio Cortonesi, Associazione Culturale e ricreativa Camigliano, Siena 1995 (hereafter Farinelli and Giorgi, 1995), pp. 31–39. See also, Roberto Farinelli and Andrea Giorgi, 'Contributo allo Studio dei rapporti tra Siena ed il suo territorio', *Rivista di storia dell'agricoltura*, 32 no. 2 (1992), pp. 3–72; Andrea Giorgi, *I 'casati' Senesi e la terra. Definizione di un gruppo di famiglie magnatizie ed evoluzione dei loro patrimoni immobiliari (fine sec 11 – inizio sec. 14)*, Tesi di dottorato di ricerca in Storia Medievale, Università degli Studi di Firenze, V ciclo, Anno Accademico 1989–90/1992–93; David L. Hicks, 'Sources of Wealth in Renaissance Siena: Business men and Landowners', *BSSP*, 93 (1986), pp. 9–42 and Irene Polverini Fosi, 'Proprietà cittadina e privilegi signorili nel contado senese', *BSSP*, 87 (1980), pp. 158–66.

22   For a seminal and recent study of sharecropping in medieval Tuscany and an extensive bibliography, see Gabriella Piccinni (ed.), *Il contratto mezzadrile nella Toscana medievale*, vol. 3, *Contado di Siena 1349–1518 (Appendice: la normativa, 1256–1510)* (Florence, 1992).

23   ASS, *Manoscritti*, D 79, Galgano Bichi, *Notizie relative ai Capitanati di Siena* (hereafter, *Bichi*), fol. 24. Ugo Ricci (Ricci, 1985, p. 30) notes that this concession was included in the Sienese statutes of 1262.

24   ASS, *Consiglio Generale*, 12, fol. 4.

25   For an early fourteenth-century reference to what was probably the structure that functioned as the *Palazzo Comunale* in Sant'Angelo in Colle following the erection of the military barracks on the site of the original communal offices there during the 1280s, see ASS, *Diplomatico di Montalcino*, Busta 32, no. 134. According to this record, which is dated 27 January 1307/8, a number of individuals, including Giannetto di Griffo of Montalcino and Bindo di Accorso in his capacity of treasurer of Sant'Angelo in Colle, assembled together in the *domo*, or house, 'dci castri' (of this castle) to consider a 'presentation' or case submitted by Giannetto.

26   Ricci, 1985, p. 24.

27   ASS, *Consiglio Generale*, 47, fol. 74r (new pencil pagination). For the development of the new town of Castelfranco di Paganico, see Patrizia Angelucci, 'Genesi di un borgo franco nel Senese: Paganico', in I. Deug Su and Ernesto Menestò (eds), *Università e tutela dei beni culturali: il contributo degli studi medievali e umanistici*, Atti del Convegno promosso dalla Facoltà di magistero in Arezzo dell'Università di Siena, Arezzo and Siena, 21–23 January1977 (Florence, 1981), pp. 95–140.

28   ASS, *Consiglio Generale*, 56, fols 69r–69v.

29   Ibid., 59, fols 96r–97v.

30   *Il Caleffo Vecchio del Comune di Siena*, vol. 4, (eds), Mario Ascheri, Alessandra Forzini, Chiara Santini (Siena, 1984), no. 1059, pp. 1654–58.

31   In this respect, see Diana Norman, *Siena and the Virgin. Art and Politics in a Late Medieval City* (New Haven – London, 1999).

32   In this respect, see William M. Bowsky, 'City and Contado: Military Relationships and Communal Bonds in Fourteenth-century Siena', in Anthony Molho and John A. Tedeschi (eds), *Renaissance studies in Honor of Hans Baron* (Florence, 1970), pp. 75–98.

33   ASS, *Consiglio Generale*, 23, fol. 7r (new pencil pagination).

34   Passeri, p. 308. For an explanation of 'Concistoro', the term adopted after the fourteenth century in reference to the 'Signoria', see Borgia, Carli, Ceppari, Morandi, Sinibaldi, and Zarrili, *Le Biccherne. Tavole Dipinte*, pp. 11–12.

35   ASS, *Consiglio Generale*, 29, fols 48r–48v (new pencil pagination).

36   Ibid., 10, fol. 58v.

37   Ibid., fol. 102r. (Not March 16, as recorded in ASS, *Manoscritti*, C1, fol. 47r.)

38   Ibid., 119, fols 33r–34r (new pagination).

39   Ibid., 136, fols 28r–28v (new pencil pagination).

40   Ibid., 89, fols 191v–192v (new pencil pagination).

41   Ibid., 124, fols 39v–40v (new pencil pagination).

42   Ibid., 97, fols 57r–60r (new pencil pagination).

43   Ibid., fol. 90v (new pencil pagination).

44   Ibid., 11, fol. 48r (old pagination fol. 47r).

45   This may well explain the evidence of diverse construction methods noted in recent analysis of the surviving structure at Montelaterone, see Michele Nucciotti, 'Il cassero senese di Montelaterone. L'Indagine Archeologica', *Amiata Storia e Territorio*, anno 13, 38/39 (March 2002), pp. 19–23.

46   For the Government of the Nine, see William M. Bowsky, *Le finanze del Comune di Siena 1287–1355* (Florence, 1976), originally published as *The Finance of the Commune of Siena* (Oxford, 1970) and *Un comune italiano nel Medioevo, Siena sotto il regime dei Nove, 1287–1355* (Bologna, 1986), originally published as *A Medieval Italian Commune: Siena under the Nine, 1287–1355* (Berkeley, Los Angeles and London, 1981). See also William M. Bowsky, 'The Buon Governo of Siena (1287–1355): A Medieval Italian Oligarchy', *Speculum*, 37 (1962), pp. 368–81 and Mario Ascheri, 'La Siena del 'Buon Governo' (1287–1355)', in Simonetta Adorni Braccesi and Mario Ascheri (eds), *Politica e cultura nelle repubbliche italiane dal medioevo all'età moderna*, Atti del convegno, Siena, 1997 (Rome, Istituto storico italiano per l'Età moderna e contemporanea 43–44, 2001), pp. 81–107. For the essentially Guelf nature of the Government of the Nine, see Giustino Francini, 'Appunti sulla costituzione guelfa del comune di Siena secondo il costituto del 1274', *BSSP*, n.s. 10 (1939), pp. 11–28. See also Mario Ascheri, *Siena e la Città-stato del Medioevo Italiano* (Siena, 2003), pp. 67–90; and Gabriella Piccinni (ed.), *Fedeltà ghibellina, affari guelfi: saggi e riletture intorno alla storia di Siena fra Due e Trecento* (Pisa, 2008).

47   ASS, *Manoscritti*, D 67, *Memorie storiche politiche, civili, e naturali delle città, terre, e castella, che sono, e sono state suddite della città di Siena. Raccolte dal Cavaliere Gio(vanni) Antonio Pecci, Patrizio Sanese* (hereafter *Pecci*), fol. 89. There is some confusion about the identity and names of these two rebels. Some sources (for example, Brandi, 2004, p. 7), record the second rebel's name as Gualchino. The eighteenth-century historian, Galgano Bichi (*Bichi*, fol. 25) for his part maintained that this individual was called Gualcherino del Cotone. In the original document (ASS, *Consiglio Generale*, 25, fol. 2.), the first rebel is said to have come from Arezzo, and the second is definitely named as Gualchino.

48   *Bichi*, fol. 25.

49   *Pecci*, fol. 89.

50   Passeri, p. 308.

51   See *Bichi*, fol. 24 and *Biccherna*, libro B, 66, fol. 102 (14 February 1280/81) for a payment to Maffeo or Matteo 'fabbro al Casato' for 45 *picconi* or pickaxes and other tools to 'devastare le mura' (destroy the walls) of Sant'Angelo in Colle. See also, Brandi, 2004, p. 7.

52   *Pecci*, fol. 85–90 (89). The same fact is recorded by Galgano Bichi (*Bichi*, fol. 22). Indeed, Bichi suggested that Sienese action at Sant'Angelo in Colle in the early 1280s was a calculated exercise to frighten other communities away from accommodating rebels. Bichi noted that during the same period Monte a Follonica and Monticiano received similar treatment.

53   Ricci, 1985, p. 32.

54   I am grateful to Giuliano Guerrini for pointing out the probable different stages of construction and reparation of this surviving gateway as revealed not only by variations in the stonework, but also by the size of the stones, themselves.

55   ASS, *Consiglio Generale* 25, fols 2r–3v.

56 According to Ricci (1985, pp. 30–2), this individual took office on November 29, 1274. Citing Repetti, Ricci further maintains that Sant'Angelo in Colle was given over 'in feudo', or feudal ownership, to the Salimbeni following the Ghibelline rebellion of 1280. Antonio Sigillo, for his part (*Montalcino. Itinerarii turistici* (Città di Castello, 1994), p. 80) maintains that the Salimbeni assumed power at Sant'Angelo in Colle around 1282. In fact, the records show that Notto Salimbeni was elected as *podestà* on 29 November 1272 for a fixed period of time, see ASS, *Manoscritti*, D75 (hereafter Ms 75), fol. 151, based on the *Libro dei'consigli della Campana del 1271*, fol. 96 [*Archivio delle Riformagioni*]. By contrast, other members of the Salimbeni clan, such as the sons of Salimbene di Giovanni Salimbene, are documented as assuming feudal ownership of a number of outposts in the Val d'Orcia (including Tintinnano) in 1274, see Vincenzo Passeri, 'La Torre di Tentennano e Castiglione', in Carlo Avetta (ed.), *'Tintinnano'. La Rocca e il territorio di Castiglione d'Orcia* (San Quirico d'Orcia, 1988), pp. 31–43 (31–32). According to Passeri, the Salimbeni received such favours in recognition of the financial support they offered to the Sienese government in the wake of the Battle of Montaperti. In this context see also, Donatella Ciampoli, 'Uno statuto signorile di fine duecento: I Salimbeni e la comunità di Rocca d'Orcia novant'anni dopo la "Carta Libertatis"', in Donatello Ciampoli and Chiara Laurenti (eds), *Gli statuti di Rocca d'Orcia – Tintinnano dai Salimbeni alla Repubblica di Siena (secoli 13–15)* (Siena, 2006), pp. 11–64.

57 *Bichi*, fol. 26.

58 Brandi, 1972, p. 7.

59 'Agnolo di Tura del Grasso, *Cronaca Senese*', in Alessandro Lisini and Fabio Iacometti (eds), *Cronache senesi, Rerum Italicarum Scriptores*, 15, part 6 (Bologna, 1931–1939), pp. 255–564 (367).

60 For architectural projects under the Government of the Nine, see Odile Redon, *Lo spazio di una città. Siena e la Toscana meridionale (secoli 13–14)* (Siena, 1999); and Mario Ascheri, *Siena e la Città-Stato*, pp. 25–44; 'La Siena del Buon Governo (1287–1355)'; and 'Siena in the Fourteenth century: State, Territory and Culture', in Thomas W. Blomquist and Maureen F. Mazzaoui (eds), *The 'other Tuscany': essays in the history of Lucca, Pisa, and Siena during the thirteenth, fourteenth and fifteenth centuries* (Kalamazoo, 1994), pp. 163–97. See also Duccio Balestracci and Gabriella Piccinni, *Siena nel Trecento. Assetto urbano e strutture edilizie* (Florence, 1977), and, in particular, Duccio Balestracci, 'From Development to Crisis: changing urban structures in Siena between the Thirteenth and Fifteenth centuries', in *'The Other Tuscany'*, pp. 199–213.

61 For the latest research on Duccio di Buoninsegna, see the catalogue of the exhibition, *Duccio Alle origini della pittura senese*, (eds) Alessandro Bagnoli, Roberto Bartalini, Luciano Bellosi, Michel Laclotte (Milan, 2003). For a recent survey of Ambrogio and Pietro Lorenzetti, see Chiara Frugoni (ed.), *Pietro e Ambrogio Lorenzetti* (Florence, 2002).

62 For Duccio's *Maestà*, see *Duccio alle origini*, pp. 208–31. For a recent survey of Siena's special relationship with the Virgin Mary, see Norman, *Siena and the Virgin*.

63 For a recent survey of literature covering the so-called frescoes of Good and Bad Government, see Ascheri, 'La Siena del "Buon governo" (1287–1355)'.

64 Passeri, p. 308.

65   Ibid. For the various condemnations pronounced on the Counts of Civitella during the last decades of the thirteenth century, see *Caleffo Vecchio*, 4, no. 1028, pp. 1541–57.

66   For the political implications of the Lorenzetti frescoes in terms of the aspirations of the Government of the Nine, see Ascheri, 'La Siena del "Buon Governo" (1287–1355)', and Maria Monica Donato, 'Il Pittore del Buon Governo: Le opere "politiche" di Ambrogio in Palazzo Pubblico', in Chiara Frugoni (ed.), *Pietro e Ambrogio Lorenzetti*, pp. 201–9. See also Chiara Frugoni, 'Il governo dei Nove a Siena e il loro credo politico nell'affresco di Ambrogio Lorenzetti', *Quaderni Medievali* 7 (1979), pp. 14–42 and *Quaderni Medievali*, 8 (1979), pp. 71–103; Quentin Skinner, 'Ambrogio Lorenzetti: The Artist as Political Philosopher', *Proceedings of the British Academy*, 72 (1986), pp. 1–56; and Diana Norman, 'Pisa, Siena and the Maremma: A Neglected Aspect of Ambrogio Lorenzetti's Paintings in the Sala dei Nove', *Renaissance Studies*, 11 (1997), pp. 310–57. For the regular outbreaks of unrest in the Sienese *contado*, see Mario Ascheri, 'Per la storia del Territorio: un itinerario dai comuni al comune', in Avetta (ed.), *'Tintinnano'*, pp. 73–85 (78–79).

67   Michael Baxandall ('Art, Society and the Bouguer Principle', *Representations*, 12 (1985), pp. 32–43), noting that Ambrogio Lorenzetti's landscape was 'articulated by a sense of territory being something that produces food', points out that in the year the frescoes in the *Palazzo dei Nove* were begun there was an acute shortage of grain in Siena's southern *contado*. Developing a theme first considered under the title 'The fresco of Good Government in Action 1338–40', Baxandall argues that Lorenzetti's depiction of the Sienese *contado* was significant for the emphasis placed on the need for easy transit within and across the territory.

68   *Bichi*, fol. 25.

69   *Caleffo Vecchio*, 4, no. 1028, pp. 1547–48.

70   Ibid., p. 1554.

71   Ibid., p. 1552.

72   Ibid., pp. 1546–47.

73   Ibid., pp. 1545–46. This may be the same Neri di Guicciardo who emerges as a powerful individual in so far as the affairs of Sant'Angelo in Colle during the early fourteenth century were concerned, through his ownership of a large amount of land in the vicinity of the village, as well as multiple properties inside the walls.

74   Ibid., no. 1031: 1566–72.

75   Elsewhere, Siena was involved over an even longer period of time in attempts to stamp its authority over other communities in the southern *contado*. Nearby Argiano, for example, did not finally cede to Siena until 1391 (despite signing a first oath of loyalty together with Sant'Angelo in Colle in 1212, see *Caleffo Vecchio*, 1, no. 101, pp. 154–55), and Montenero, which faced Sant'Angelo in Colle on the southern side of the River Orcia, only finally buckled to the Sienese will in 1400. In this respect, see Lucia Nardi, 'La distrettualizzazione dello stato: I Vicariati della Repubblica di Siena 1337–1339', in Mario Ascheri and Donatella Ciampoli (eds), *Siena e il suo territorio nel Rinascimento* (Siena, 1986), pp. 55–67.

76   Passeri, pp. 308–9.

77 Farinelli and Giorgi, 1995, p. 16. These authors estimate that, on average, each *fuoco*, or household, consisted of at least four individuals. See also, 'Cortonesi, 'Demografia e Popolamento', p. 155, footnote 7.

78 *Caleffo Vecchio*, 1, no. 222, pp. 321–24.

79 Farinelli and Giorgi, 1995, p. 16.

80 ASS, *Tavola delle possessioni del contado*, *Estimo* (hereafter throughout the text, as *Estimo* 24).

81 See Roberto Farinelli and Andrea Giorgi, 'La "Tavola delle possessioni" come fonte per lo studio del territorio: l'esempio di Castelnuovo dell'Abate', in Alfio Cortonesi (ed.), *La Val d'Orcia nel Medioevo e nei primi secoli dell'età moderna*, Atti del convegno internazionale di studi storici, Pienza 15–18 settembre, 1988 (Rome, 1990), pp. 213–56, where the authors suggest that in estimating the overall population a factor of five should be applied to male proprietors, and a factor of two to female proprietors. Where there were groups of heirs, the size of the population is almost unquantifiable, since widows as well as siblings and children of the deceased may have been included. At the very least a factor of two should be applied. In 1320, 89 male and some 20 female householders are listed, along with 13 groups of heirs. See also, Cortonesi, 'Demografia e Popolamento', p. 155, footnote 8.

82 For a seminal study of this Sienese institution, see Stephan R. Epstein, *Alle origini della fattoria toscana. L'ospedale della Scala di Siena e le sue terre (metà '200 – metà '400)* (Florence, 1986), arising from *idem*, 'Dall'espansione alla gestione della crisi: L'ospedale di Santa Maria della Scala di Siena e il suo patrimonio (1260–1450)', Tesi di laurea, Facoltà di Lettere, L'Università degli Studi di Siena, Anno Accademico, 1983–84. See also Giuseppina Coscarella and Franca Cecilia Franchi, 'Le Grance dello Spedale di Santa Maria della Scala nel contado senese', *BSSP*, 92 (1985), pp. 66–92.

83 Coscarella and Franchi ('Le Grance', p. 67) maintain that the majority of the hospital's granges were established during the last decade of the thirteenth century.

84 Epstein, *Alle origini*, p. 7. See also see the special edition of the *Bollettino d'Arte*, *La Fabbrica del Santa Maria della Scala*, (Siena, 1986), and *Il Santa Maria della Scala nella storia della città*, Atti del Convegno Internazionale di Studi, 20 novembre 1986, Comune di Siena (Siena, Monte dei Paschi di Siena, 1986) (and especially Anne Katherine Isaacs, 'Lo Spedale di Santa Maria della Scala nell'antico stato senese', pp. 14–29).

85 In this context, see Daniela Gallavotti Cavallero and Andrea Brogi (eds), *Lo spedale grande di Siena: fatti urbanistica e architettonici del Santa Maria della Scala: ricerche, riflessioni, interrogativi* (Florence, 1987); Gabriella Piccinni and Laura Vigni, 'Modelli di assistenza ospedaliera tra Medioevo ed Età Moderna. Quotidianità, amministrazione, conflitti nell'ospedale di Santa Maria della Scala', in Giuliano Pinto (ed.), *La società del bisogno: povertà e assistenza nella Toscana medievale* (Florence, 1989), pp. 131–74; Gabriella Piccinni, 'L'ospedale della Scala di Siena. Note sulle origini dell'assistenza sanitaria in Toscana (14–15 secolo) in *Città e servizi sociali nell'Italia dei Secoli 12–15*, Twelfth Convegno di Studi, Pistoia, 9–12 ottobre 1987 (Pistoia, 1990), pp. 297–324, and Gualtiero Bellucci and Piero Torriti, *Il Santa Maria della Scala in Siena: l'ospedale dei mille anni, xenodochium Sancte Marie* (Genoa, 1991). See also, amongst a large number of more recent works which include extensive bibliographic references, Duccio Balestracci, *L'Invenzione dell'ospedale: assistenza e assistiti nel Medioevo* (Milan,

2000); Alessandro Orlandini, *Gettatelli e pellegrini: gli affreschi nella sala del Pellegrinaio dell'ospedale di Santa Maria della Scala di Siena: itinerario didattico su una summa figurativa dell'assistenza ospedaliera fra Medioevo e Rinascimento* (Siena, 2002); Gabriella Piccinni and Carla Zarrilli (eds), *Arte e assistenza a Siena: le copertine dipinte dell'Ospedale di Santa Maria della Scala*, exhibition catalogue, Siena Archivio dello Stato (Pisa, 2003); Roberta Mucciarelli, *La terra contesa: I Piccolomini contro Santa Maria della Scala 1277–1280* (Florence, 2001); Maddalena Belli, *La cucina di un ospedale del Trecento: gli spazi, gli oggetti, il cibo nel Santa Maria della Scala di Siena* (Pisa, 2004); Michele Pellegrini, *La comunità ospedaliera di Santa Maria della Scala e il suo piu antico statuto: Siena 1305* (Pisa, c.2005); the exhibition catalogue, *Pulcherrima res: preziosi ornamenti del passato: Siena, complesso museale Santa Maria della Scala*, Palazzo Squarcialupi, 21 April–4 November 2007 (Siena, c.2007), and Paolo Fedeli, *Un fratello dell'antico ospedale Santa Maria della Scala. San Bernardo Tolomei: la società medioevale del suo tempo* (Siena, c.2009).

86 Gianfranco di Pietro and Paolo Donati, 'Cronologia e iconografia storica dal 11 secolo alla fine del 18 secolo', in *Siena, La Fabbrica del Santa Maria della Scala*, special edition, *Bollettino d'Arte* (1986), pp. 5–14 (5).

87 Ibid.

88 Isaacs, 'Lo Spedale', 1986, p. 19.

89 Apart from Epstein, *Alle origini*, 1986, pp. 29–57, see Gallavotti Cavallero, *Lo Spedale*, 1985, pp. 25–28 for a detailed analysis of the expansion of the hospital's patrimony.

90 Isaacs, 'Lo Spedale', 1986, pp. 22–23. See also Mucciarelli, *La terra contesa*, 2001, p. 72.

91 Gallavotti Cavallero and Brogi, *Lo spedale*, 1987, p. 42, and p. 58 for the hospital's financial affairs prior to that date.

92 Bellucci and Torriti, *Il Santa Maria della Scala*, 1991, p. 41.

93 Epstein, *Alle origini*, 1986, pp. 29–32.

94 In this context, see also Gallavotti Cavallero and Brogi, *Lo spedale*, 1987, p. 69. For a more recent and succinct analysis of the foundation of the hospital and its developing relationship with the commune of Siena, see Michele Pellegrini, 'L'Ospedale e il comune: immagini di una relazione privilegiata', in Piccinni and Zarrilli (eds), *Arte e assistenza a Siena*, pp. 29–45.

95 Biblioteca Comunale degli Intronati, Siena, *Manoscritti*, B. VI. 20, new pagination fol. 34r.

96 Epstein, *Alle origini*, p. 99, Table 2.

97 Ibid. San Quirico for example sent only 10 cheeses. Twenty-six more cheeses came from Stigliano and 350 from Serre. Even in those cases such as Cuna or Montisi, where a larger number of cheeses were recorded, the total number of forms did not exceed 2,000.

98 For preserved meat and fat as principal sources of nourishment in medieval diet, see Laura Galoppini (ed.), *Il lardo nell'alimentazione toscana dall'antichità ai nostri giorni*, Atti della Giornata di studio, Massa, 1 settembre 2001, Deputazione di storia patria per le antiche province modenesi (Massa–Modena, 2003). See also Franca Leverotti, 'Il consumo della carne a Massa all'inizio del 15 secolo. Prime considerazioni', *Archeologia medievale*, 8 (1981), pp. 227–38 and Epstein, *Alle origini*, pp. 218–19.

99   See Epstein, *Alle origini*, pp. 73–75, for a consideration of the links between the various *grancie*. See also, Coscarella and Franchi, 'Le grance'.

100 Epstein, *Alle origini*, p. 82.

101 See Ricci, 1985, p. 38. See also, Brandi, 1972, p. 7 and 2004, p. 7.

102 See Passeri, p. 308.

103 For the institution of the Government of the Twelve, see Stefano Moscadelli, *Siena sotto i dodici (1355–1368): amministrazione e finanze*, Tesi di laurea, Università di Siena, Facoltà di Lettere e Filosofia, Anno Accademico 1981–1982 (Siena, 1982).

104 In 1376, it was decreed that the hospital of Santa Maria della Scala should not only take possession of 'el casserone overo palazzo el quale fu gia cassero del Comune' (the large barracks or palace that had previously served as the military headquarters of the commune), but also be responsible for its restoration, fortification and general protection, see Brandi, 2004, p. 8.

105 Epstein, *Alle origini*, pp. 242 and 263.

106 Ibid., p. 263. Passeri (p. 308) does not refer to this event, but notes instead a transaction between Goro Sansedoni and Viva di Giovanni of Sant'Angelo in Colle on 5 May 1410 [based on ASS, *Concistoro* 1875, nos. 26 and 28].

107 For the crisis in the countryside during the late fourteenth century, see Giovanni Cherubini, 'Risorse, paesaggio ed utilizzazione agricola del territorio della Toscana sud-occidentale nei secoli 14–15', in *Civiltà ed economia agricola in Toscana nei secc. 13–15. Problemi della vita delle campagne nel tardo Medioevo*, Atti dell'ottavo Convegno Internazionale del Centro Italiano di studi di Storia e d'Arte, Pistoia, 21–4 aprile 1977 (Pistoia, 1981), pp. 91–115. See also, Gabriella Piccinni, 'I "villani incittadinati" nella Siena del 14 secolo', *BSSP*, 82–83 (1975–1976), pp. 158–219. For a consideration of the changes in demography in the southern Sienese *contado* at the end of the medieval period, and a survey of related bibliography, see Maria Ginatempo, 'Il Popolamento della Valdorcia alla fine del medioevo (15–16 secolo)', in Cortonesi, *La Val d'Orcia*, pp. 113–53, and (by the same author) *Crisi di un territorio. Il popolamento della Toscana senese alla fine del Medioevo* (Florence, 1988).

108 ASS, *Consiglio Generale*, 218, fol. 189r.

109 Passeri, p. 309.

110 Ibid.

111 ASS, *Balia*, 467, fols 207v–208r.

112 Archivio Vescovile di Montalcino (hereafter AVM), *Visite Pastorali*, 225, fol. 12v.

113 ASS, *Manoscritti*, D 84, *Visita fatta nell'Anno 1676 alle Città, Terre, Castella, dello Stato della Città di Siena dall'Ill(ustrissi)mo Sig(no)re Bartolomeo Gherardini, Auditore Generale in Siena per la A.S. di Cosimo III de' Medici Granduca VI di Toscana* (eighteenth-century copy), fols 72–80 (72). See also Don Antonio Brandi, *Notizie relative a Argiano – Poggio alle Mura – S. Angelo in Colle Tratte dalla Visita fatta nell'anno 1676 dall'Ill.mo Sig.re Bartolomeo Gheradini* (undated transcription in typescript), p. 7.

114 AVM, *Sant'Angelo in Colle, Prepositura*, 131 (second book, loose sheet with end date 1751). See also ASS, *Ospedale* 1183, Eredità Brogioni. The Brogioni may have become involved in the affairs of the parish church even earlier than 1520, since reference is made to them in the context of San Michele in a papal bull of 1508,

see ASS, *Ospedale*, 1182, fol. 24r. I am grateful to Philippa Jackson for drawing my attention to this.

115   Ricci, 1985, pp. 64–65, quoting from Pecci, dates this handover to 1574. See also ASS, *Ospedale* 1183, Eredità Brogioni.

116   For the Ciaia, see Ricci, 1985, pp. 66–67 and 86–88. See also Brandi, 2004, pp. 64–66.

117   AVM, *Sant'Angelo in Colle, Prepositura*, 131 (second book, loose sheet with end date 1751). See also Ricci, 1985, p. 65, citing ASS, *Eredità Brogioni Ugolini, Archivio Santa Maria della Scala.*

118   For the history of Sant'Angelo in Colle during the second half of the sixteenth century and from then until the modern period, see Ricci, *Appendice* (1989), pp. 12–38.

Documentary Sources and Medieval Toponyms

Two principal documents underpin this analysis of Sant'Angelo in Colle under the Government of the Nine: the first, a *Tavola delle Possessioni* drawn up for the village in 1320; the second, a boundary document for the *corte*, or territory, of Sant'Angelo in Colle drawn up in 1318.

The 1320 *Tavola delle possessioni* for Sant'Angelo in Colle

The early fourteenth-century *Tavole delle possessioni* (tables of possessions) formed a constituent part of the Sienese *Estimo*, or *Lira*.[1] Instituted in the middle of the second decade of the fourteenth century under the auspices of the Government of the Nine, the *Lira* was in effect a form of poll tax, or rateable evaluation of land and accommodation belonging to anyone who was subject to the authority of the city of Siena.[2] The *Tavola*, or comprehensive record, was compiled from a number of individual reports known as *Tavolette*. With the help of the initial *Tavolette* each entry in the *Tavole delle possessioni* contained details not only of the size and value of property owned (whether building or land), but also of its innate characteristics (house, country house, shack, building plot, field used for agricultural purposes, woodland, vineyard, olive grove, orchard). It was on the basis of these entries that the *Lira*, or precise calculation of tax due, was formed.

As might be expected, size was a ruling factor when assessing the amount of tax to be levied. The larger the house, or living unit, the greater its perceived value. But there were also variations within different categories. Thus, a *casa*, or living house inside the walls of a built up environment was normally valued at a higher rate per square *braccia*, or metre than a *capanna*, or shack-like hut in the country. Distinctions were also drawn between different types of constructions and sites inside the walls. For example, a *platea*, or building plot, even if containing some form of rudimentary or deteriorated structure carried a different value from a house that was being lived in. Entries in the *Tavole delle possessioni* were normally arranged in alphabetical order according to the first name of the proprietor (even if not in strict sequence within each letter section), and included not only each adult male or female with assets, but also individual institutions. Heirs were also listed, although they were normally treated as group entries, with few detailed references to specific members. Elderly men and women and young children were rarely allotted separate entries. This is understandable, for in many cases such individuals must have fallen into the category of dependents subsumed into larger family units, or as under- or over-age, and thus exempt from taxation.

Recent analysis of fourteenth-century tax records, and in particular the Sienese *Tavole delle possessioni* has shown how useful such documents can be when attempting to establish the size of medieval populations, the nature of individual households, and even the layout of the urban fabrics themselves.[3] The 1320 *Tavola delle possessioni* for Sant'Angelo in Colle has figured in a number of demographic studies of medieval Siena and its southern *contado*. However, in none of these has there been any detailed consideration of ownership of property in the village during the early fourteenth century, or any attempt made to match individual entries in the *Tavola delle possessioni* with the existing urban fabric of Sant'Angelo in Colle. Nor has there been any acknowledgement of the fact that the survival of this particular document may be due in large part to the historical significance of Sant'Angelo in Colle during the early medieval period. Indeed, many surveys of Siena's southern *contado* seem to prioritise early modern Montalcino over Sant'Angelo in Colle, apparently ignoring the key role assumed by the southern frontier post in ensnaring its larger neighbour within the Sienese net. An attempt is made here to redress that imbalance. At the same time, questions are raised about the comprehensiveness of individual *Tavole*.

The introduction to the 1320 *Tavola delle possessioni* for Sant'Angelo in Colle notes that the survey had been ordered by 'Ser Petram Jacobi', 'Ser Buonfigliuoli', and 'Ser Nofrum Orlandi', and that they have been 'elected in the name of the Government of the Nine of Siena'. It further claims that the *Tavola* contains references to every single possession, patrimony and goods belonging to the people of that frontier castle.[4] As such, one would expect it to offer a complete survey of the medieval village. However, although this record would at first sight appear to provide a unique opportunity to establish the precise number and position of houses in the medieval village and to relate these to the surviving urban fabric, closer examination reveals that this is not as straightforward as it might seem. Not only are there inconsistencies between individual entries, it is also clear that the existing urban fabric differs from that confronting the early fourteenth-century officials of the *Lira*.

Visitors to the village in the twenty-first century are enchanted by what appears to be the virtually intact *centro storico*, or historic centre. Many assume, indeed, that the surviving urban fabric has undergone little change, and that it is a faithful reflection of the medieval frontier castle. The 1320 *Tavola delle possessioni* offers a rather different perspective. Several parts of medieval Sant'Angelo in Colle as recorded in the 1320 *Tavola delle possessioni* are clearly no longer standing, or are only partially recognisable. The village has not only lost most of its encircling walls but also appears to have lost several of its official buildings, including the medieval *Palazzo Comunale*, its old hospital, and a number of other public facilities such as the communal olive press. The site of the fortified grange belonging to the Sienese hospital of Santa Maria della Scala is still marked in the one remaining tower now housing the village *circolo*, or social club, but little else of what was possibly quite a complex structure remains. It also seems likely that the village has lost an ancient church that was dedicated to Saint Peter.

As we shall see from the detailed consideration of the urban fabric in Chapter 1, the 1320 *Tavola delle possessioni* also prompts questions about the actual number of structures standing in the early fourteenth-century village, and the extent to which these were individually owned and occupied, as opposed to being rented or let out to third parties. Cross-referencing between individual entries throws light on a number of different patterns of ownership of property operating in the early fourteenth-century village. While a considerable proportion of those listed in the *Tavola* owned their own living accommodation, many others appear not to have owned any property inside the walls. Yet others appear to have been multiple property owners. As will become clear, multiple ownership of property, and particularly where the property was owned by 'outsiders', could affect living conditions inside the village through systems of renting and sub-letting. As discussion in Chapter 4 will show, multiple ownership of property could also affect individual livelihoods in the surrounding territory, especially when such property was situated outside the walls, and where patterns of *mezzadria*, or sharecropping, were in place.

Documents such as the Sienese *Lira* are increasingly mined for the information they can offer about the livelihoods of those living in subject Sienese communes during the medieval period. Individual entries in the 1320 *Tavola delle possessioni* for Sant'Angelo in Colle indicate that local revenue must have come almost exclusively from the land. This was put to a number of uses. By far the most common references were to terrain suitable for pasture or arable work, but some of the largest tracts declared by individual proprietors were covered by forest, or wood. Individual entries also show that particular areas in the surrounding countryside were designated for different kinds of cultivation, from orchards and kitchen gardens nestling in the shadow of the walls to olive groves and vineyards to the south and south-west of the village, and more distant pastures for sheep to the east. In between, there were numerous plots of land suitable for crops, as well as copious brushland and thick woodland that provided firewood and an appropriate environment for the rearing of pigs, and even grazing by cattle. There were also large tracts of *terra sode*, or uncultivated land, indicating that a system of rotation was being practised. All in all, it seems clear that the early fourteenth-century inhabitants of the village were for the most part engaged in the cultivation of crops, the rearing of pigs, the pasturing of cattle, the making of cheese, the shearing of sheep, the spinning of yarn and – with the help of ample supplies of fresh spring water – the dipping of animal hides and the various stages of working cloth.

Establishing a viable livelihood was, however, dependent on a number of factors. Not the least of the challenges faced by the residents of early fourteenth-century Sant'Angelo in Colle must have been the nature of the land they worked, the size and position of individual plots, varying weather conditions and the cost of grain for sowing. For the lone land worker, these alone must have presented considerable challenges. But, as we shall see, many plots of land in the vicinity of the early fourteenth-century village belonged to Sienese 'outsiders'. Any produce or profit from the working of such land was thus necessarily shared. Daily endeavours and livelihoods were in any event compromised by the fact that Sant'Angelo in Colle was a subject Sienese commune. A source of regular revenue was clearly needed to pay the various taxes levied on behalf of the Sienese government. A proportion of any profit arising from working the land was thus forfeited in direct taxation. Individual Sienese citizens must also have benefited as a result of sharecropping agreements. But even in the absence of formal arrangements of that kind, many villagers must in effect have been working much of their land for the ultimate benefit of their Sienese masters.

A number of other factors no doubt impinged on the fortunes of land workers and their dependents. Prime amongst these must have been famine, disease and attack from other communes not subjected to the Sienese yoke. As we have seen, individuals hostile to Siena and Sant'Angelo in Colle itself were regularly involved in acts of sabotage, burning crops and stealing livestock. There were also other, less obvious threats. Conflicting interests where land was jointly owned could obstruct natural rhythms of planting and harvesting. Owners of neighbouring land could contest boundaries or restrict the flow of essential resources such as water. There are hints of such issues in a number of entries in the 1320 *Tavola delle possessioni*. This record thus serves as a basis of enquiry on a number of very different levels.

In terms of the present enquiry the 1320 *Tavola delle possessioni* is, moreover, particularly useful for the light it throws on changes within the landscape. Comparison of details entered in individual entries in respect of the early fourteenth-century terrain, indicates that there have been a number of significant changes. There have, it seems, always been vines and olive trees in the area.[5] Vestiges of some of the oldest olive groves in the territory of Sant'Angelo in Colle are, for example, located in the vicinity of Saproia and Sesta to the east of the village (an area frequently mentioned in the 1320 *Tavola delle possessioni* in the context of olives). Moreover, several of the areas given over to vineyards on the western borders can also be traced back to the early fourteenth century.[6] However, over the course of time, much of the woodland covering the territory on its northern and north-western sides has been cleared to accommodate new lines of vines and new olive groves. Indeed, these new plantations are increasingly obscuring earlier topographies. How individual plots of land fitted together in the early fourteenth century is in some part explained by the toponyms and details of contiguity included in surviving records. One such record (referred to here as the '1318 boundary document') that defines the boundaries between the communes of Sant'Angelo in Colle and Montalcino in 1318 is subjected to detailed analysis here.

The 1318 boundary document[7]

The 1318 boundary document is one of a number of parchments gathered together in the *Diplomatico* of Montalcino in the State Archives in Siena. For the most part un-catalogued, this *fondo*, or section, of the State Archives contains a diverse collection of records ranging from wills to the sale of land and sharecropping agreements. Drawn up and witnessed by a number of key individuals from Montalcino and Sant'Angelo in Colle, the 1318 boundary document records in detail the boundaries of land owned by Sant'Angelo in Colle, and the particulars of its confines to the north, south, west and east. It is clear from this that medieval Sant'Angelo in Colle was important, not only in terms of the overall size of its territory, but also in terms of its geographical position immediately adjacent to the commune of Montalcino. When comparing the fourteenth-century boundaries as outlined in the 1318 boundary document, with those defined in more recent maps, it is obvious that the present-day territory of Sant'Angelo in Colle is a mere shadow of its former self (see Colour Plate 4).

By contrast, the territory of Montalcino increased exponentially. Sant'Angelo in Colle was drawn within the borders of the new Diocese of Montalcino in the middle of the fifteenth century, and by the eighteenth century, the Vicariate of Montalcino extended well south of the River Orcia.

While the 1320 *Tavola delle possessioni* offers valuable insights about the varying kinds of terrain in the vicinity of Sant'Angelo in Colle during the early fourteenth century, it is a cumbersome tool when attempting to establish the overall confines of the territory and the more specific distinctions within it. The 1318 document is not only more succinct, but also offers a general overview of the territory. It also provides answers to very diverse questions. Yet, by contrast with the 1320 *Tavola delle possessioni* for Sant'Angelo in Colle the 1318 boundary document seems to have generated very little, if any interest. This is remarkable, given that it maps out the extent of Sant'Angelo in Colle's territory at the end of the second decade of the fourteenth century. For this reason, if none other, it merits detailed consideration.

The 1318 boundary document was drawn up in the *contrada* 'at the bottom, or far end of the commune of the Montalcino wood' on behalf of Deus, son of the deceased Dietanive of Montalcino, mayor of the commune of Montalcino, and Ser Petruccius Pieri of Sant'Angelo in Colle, mayor of the commune of Sant'Angelo.[8] The legal expert called in to help with the process of establishing individual demarcations was the lawyer Angelo, son of the

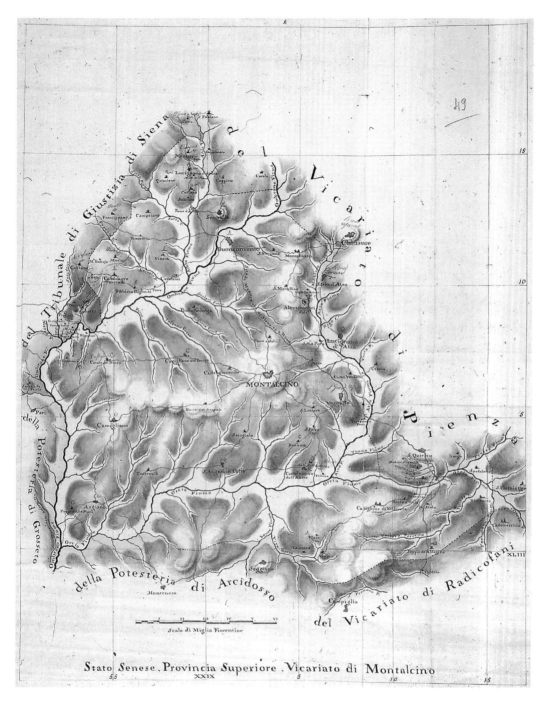

Figure Doc.sources 1   Eighteenth-century map of the Vicariate of Montalcino. Archivio di Stato, Siena, Vicariato dello Stato Senese – Montalcino n. 8 'Stato Senese, Provincia Superiore.Vicariato di Montalcino

deceased Nini Vulpis of Montepulciano. The notary responsible for drawing up the document itself is identified as the Sienese citizen, Ser Mino di Accorso. Another individual, Vivianum di Forteguerra, acted as arbitrator. There were six witnesses: three from Montalcino (Betto di Pasquale, Cione di Dote and Ser Morandi di Ser Pepi), and three from Sant'Angelo in Colle (Lunardutio di Giovanni, Michele Genovesis and Berto Ramaioli).

According to its opening statement, the 1318 boundary document had been requested by the presiding mayor of each commune in an attempt to maintain good relations between them, and to establish a common peace and concord for each and every individual living in their lands. Clearly, both communes appreciated the advantages of having well-defined borders.

It is, however, significant that at least two of the individuals called in to oversee the drawing up of the 1318 boundary document were associated with the Sienese government: Ser Mino di Accorso was described as a Sienese notary; Vivianum di Forteguerra as a 'noble Sienese knight'. Mino di Accorso was also involved in the affairs of Sant'Angelo in Colle as 'by order of the syndicate of the commune'. As we shall see, he was also probably related to one of the richest men of the early fourteenth-century village, Bindo di Accorso. Against such a background, one might expect that the interests of Sant'Angelo in Colle would be uppermost. In other words, in case of doubt, the positioning of individual boundary markings might be in their favour. That being the case, it would of course follow that the government of Siena would be assured of eliciting the maximum amount of tax from their subject commune.

There can be little doubt that Sant'Angelo in Colle was well represented locally. At least two of the individuals called to witness the 1318 boundary document on behalf of Sant'Angelo in Colle – Lonarduccio di Giovanni and Michele Genovesis – must have assumed important roles in the affairs of the village, since the 1320 *Tavole delle possessioni* reveals that they owned a considerable amount of property. As we shall see in Chapter 6, their individual patrimonies placed them amongst the five richest men in Sant'Angelo in Colle in 1320. The third witness – Berto di Ramaiolo – was also an individual of some standing, although his overall patrimony was much lower than that of either Lonarduccio di Giovanni or Michele Genovesis. But, as we shall see, Berto's joint ownership of a number of pieces of land indicates that he belonged to an extended family clan with considerable assets in and around Sant'Angelo in Colle. All in all, it seems likely that the three individuals called to witness the drawing up of the boundaries of Sant'Angelo in Colle's territory in 1318 had been selected from the village's elite.

There seems little doubt that establishing the boundaries between Montalcino and Sant'Angelo in Colle in the early fourteenth century was regarded as a matter of some local importance. It seems likely that there had been conflicts of interest in the past, and especially following Sant'Angelo in Colle's formal subjugation by Siena in the early thirteenth century. In 1318 Montalcino was still not entirely pacified by the Sienese. Sant'Angelo in Colle, by contrast, had been subject to Siena's legal system and taxation laws for over a century. In terms of taxation alone, it was clearly in the interests of the Government of the Nine that the borders of their frontier castle should be defined accurately. Whilst ensuring this, the 1318 boundary document also identified those individuals holding land on the borders of Sant'Angelo in Colle's territory that may over time have been claimed by neighbouring communes. Land owners not falling under the jurisdiction of Siena were not only likely to fight to maintain the boundaries of their own land, but could potentially become engaged in disputes with those individuals holding neighbouring plots who were answerable to Siena. Border disputes could thus present a problem to officials of the Sienese government attempting to levy tax.

Records such as the 1318 boundary document would no doubt also have been extremely useful when drawing up the contemporary *Tavole delle possessioni*. For the modern historian, such records also throw light on medieval power politics. As we shall see, not all those owning land at the outer limits of Sant'Angelo in Colle's territory were local residents. Indeed, it appears that a large number of them resided elsewhere. Some lived in Siena; some were residents of the potentially hostile commune of Montalcino; several others came from the neighbouring hamlet of Villa a Tolli, which in the early fourteenth century was controlled by Montalcino. In effect, a number of different interests were at work.

The 1318 boundary document thus offered (and offers) far more than an itemised account of demarcation points dividing the two communes of Montalcino and Sant'Angelo in Colle in the second decade of the fourteenth century. Most significantly, it provided the Government of the Nine with precious information as to possible areas of conflict, by pinpointing those parts of the terrain where neighbouring landowners had differing political affiliations. In effect, the 1318 boundary document illustrates how the conflicting interests of Siena and Florence might have been played out on a daily basis in the patchwork of woodland, pasture and arable plots that defined the peripheries of the frontier castle of Sant'Angelo in Colle in the southern Sienese *contado*.

Toponyms and topography

Increasing attention is paid to the ways in which toponyms can reveal the nature of local topography in earlier times.[9] Several of the names allotted to different areas in the vicinity of Sant'Angelo in Colle in both the 1320 *Tavola delle possessioni* and the 1318 boundary document not only indicate the lie of the land, but also help locate a number of specific features that combined to form the early fourteenth-century landscape. As might be expected, the contours of the land seem to have changed little since the medieval period, although there have clearly been considerable changes in land usage.

A number of areas are described in the early fourteenth century records as *poggio* – clearly in reference to elevated areas – whilst others described as *plano* or *piano* no doubt referred, instead, to the intervening plains and lowlands, which even now define the area. There are numerous references, also, to *fonte*, indicating the plentiful presence of water, presumably in the form of natural springs. Several locations are assigned the toponym, *fossatellus*, indicating that there was also a number of ditches or streams.[10] The 1320 *Tavola delle possessioni* also contains references to stretches of water, which (like the 'fossato castellani',[11] and the 'fossatus gorge canete')[12] appear to have taken their name from nearby structures or natural features in the landscape. At the beginning of the fourteenth century it seems that much of the territory in the vicinity of Sant'Angelo in Colle was bounded and criss-crossed by streams and other water conduits (ranging from deep channels to shallow ditches). Apart from the Tredine *fossa*, or ditch, there are references to at least two other established streams, the Campuazi and the Rigagnoli, as well as to numerous other minor waterways. Over time much of this surface water has disappeared. In nineteenth-century *catastal* maps only the Tredine stream appears to have any significance.

One area in particular, the 'contrada lame di Sant'Angelo', appears to have been covered by springs and streamlets throughout the year. Although there is now little evidence of marshland in the vicinity of Sant'Angelo in Colle, and much of the surrounding land remains dry for most of the year, modern maps reveal the extent to which the land on the south side of the Sesta road has been criss-crossed over time by conduits of water – all of which originally led into the Orcia. Evidence of this remains in the many long-dry ditches and gullies that still puncture the terrain to the east and south-east of the territory, although many other parts of the terrain have been razed and cleared for the cultivation of vines, thus smudging earlier topographies.

Individual toponyms contained in both the 1320 *Tavola delle possessioni* and the 1318 boundary document throw light on the ways in which the inhabitants of the medieval village profited from their watery environment. Thus, 'fossatello del cuio' implies that one particular ditch, or stretch of water was used for the washing, or curing of animal hides. Elsewhere, 'fossatus porcis' indicates that the stream in question was a watering place for pigs. Other toponyms reveal how the water supply in the vicinity of Sant'Angelo in Colle had already changed, perhaps forcing the villagers to search for water further afield. There is, for example, a reference to the 'vallis secche', or dry valley, presumably an area that had once contained a rushing stream, but that had since dried up.

During the fourteenth century several of the water conduits around Sant'Angelo in Colle were also described in terms of nearby woodland and even individual trees. There are references, for example, to the 'leccio', or semi-evergreen holm oak, and to the 'quercia', the deciduous variety. From these, it is clear that the early fourteenth-century landscape was densely covered by different species of oak. Traces of this still remain to the immediate south and north-east, but many other parts have been cleared. Individual toponyms in both the 1320 *Tavola delle possessioni* and the 1318 boundary document not only provide us with information about the distribution of other trees such as the olive, but at the same time help to identify those parts of the territory that have remained virtually untouched over seven centuries. There are references, for example, to the 'oliveto di Sexta' to the east of the village, confirming that land close to the hamlet of Sesta was, as now, so covered by olive trees that the whole area was referred to as 'the olive grove'.

Quite apart from the courses etched by water, the terrain surrounding early fourteenth-century Sant'Angelo in Colle was clearly also criss-crossed by a number of thoroughfares ranging from quite sizeable roads to narrow tracks. While some of these served to connect the village with the outside world, many more appear to have functioned as local links between one farmhouse and another, or for transport over the various tracts of land owned by individual proprietors. For the most part, the names of these have been lost in the mists of time, but frequent references to the 'via vicinale', or near road, in nineteenth-century *catastal* records may reflect older toponyms adopted for such connecting roads or tracks in the vicinity of the medieval village.

Many of the toponyms in both the 1320 *Tavola delle possessioni* and the 1318 boundary document also throw light on the ways in which local people moved around the territory, whilst at the same time identifying some of the local landmarks associated with such everyday activities. The 'via carraie', for example, was presumably a road used by carts and wagons, and was thus probably an important thoroughfare for the transport of harvest crops and other goods as well as the movement of livestock.[13] The, 'via fornelle', presumably like the 'via carraie' a well-trodden road rather than a narrow track, must by contrast have led to some kind of furnace works.[14] The 'stradella ma(?n) gmeta', in turn, was probably quite a narrow track established in connection with the quarrying of manganese of lime.[15] Toponyms such as these not only reveal (as might be expected) that there were a number of different kinds of roads (some amounting to little more than tracks) in the vicinity of the early fourteenth-century village, but also throw light on the diverse kinds of activities practised. There seems little doubt, for example, that as well as agricultural pursuits, the villagers of Sant'Angelo in Colle were involved in brickmaking. The remains of one brickmaking furnace still survive to the east of the village, in the area now referred to as 'frabiche', or 'fabbriche', to the north of Saproia. To the south-west, the 'Podere Fornace' still bears witness to the brickmaking that continued in the vicinity of the village even into the modern period.

While many medieval toponyms clearly fell away as old trades ceased and new modes of transport were developed, others appear to have survived for many centuries. In the case of the naming of roads, surviving toponyms are often those that depended upon general notions of direction. Thus, where a road ran between two urban centres it was the case, even until quite recently, that the thoroughfare in question was named after one or both of the built up areas. One such example is the 'via detto castelnuovo', which in nineteenth-century records was also known as the 'via da Sant'Angelo a Castelnuovo', or road from Sant'Angelo to Castelnuovo. Until recently, inhabitants of Castelnuovo dell'abate also referred to one nearby thoroughfare as the 'via di Siena', or the Sienese road.[16]

The 1318 boundary document shows that the practice of naming roads in terms of the areas they served was already well established in the medieval period. Thus, we find references to 'via qua re . a sco Anglo in colle ad villam tollis', the road that goes from Sant'Angelo in Colle to Villa i Tolli; the 'viarum quibus itur a Sco Angelo in Colle ad villa tollis et ad eta (?terra) montisalcini', the roads that go from Sant'Angelo in Colle to the Villa i Tolli and (?)towards the territory of Montalcino; and the 'viam qua itur a castro Sci Angli in colle ad t.ram montisilcini', the road that goes from the castle of Sant'Angelo towards the territory of Montalcino. Such toponyms are revealing in a number of ways. We learn, for example, that a number of thoroughfares existed to the north and north-east of Sant'Angelo in Colle in the early fourteenth century. At least three, and possibly four of these connected Sant'Angelo in Colle with Villa a Tolli and Montalcino, although their trajectories were probably not the same as those existing in the twenty-first century.

As we shall see in the following chapter, it was not only the edges of particular fields, or the courses of individual stretches of water that played a significant part in defining the boundaries of individual plots of land. Frequent reference was made, also, to tracks and thoroughfares. However, establishing the trajectories of medieval thoroughfares is often hazardous, not least because the construction of more recent roads has often destroyed the evidence of earlier tracks or resulted in overgrowth of scrub and woodland. In this respect both the 1320 *Tavola delle possessioni* and the 1318 boundary document offer unique insights into the medieval topography and ancient toponyms of Sant'Angelo in Colle, *castello di frontiera* in the Sienese southern *contado*.

Notes

1   For the creation and drawing up of the *Tavola delle Possessioni* for the *Massa* and *Contado* of Siena between 1316 and 1320, see Luciano Banchi, 'La Lira, la Tavola delle possessioni e la Preste nella Repubblica di Siena', *Archivio Storico Italiano*, ser 3, 7, part 2 (1868), pp. 53–88. See also, Ernestò Fiumi, 'L'imposta diretta nei comuni medievali della Toscana', in *Studi in onore di Armando Sapori* (Milan, 1957), pp. 329–53; Maria Luisa Pavolini, 'Aspetti della politica finanziaria e comunale nel basso Medio Evo (Siena nel Due-Trecento)', *Economia e Storia* (1977), pp. 271–92 (281–83); Ann Katherine Chiancone Isaacs, 'Fisco e politica a Siena nel Trecento.' *Rivista storica italiana*, 85 (1973), pp. 22–46; Giovanni Cherubini, 'Proprietari, contadini e càmpagne senesi all' inizio del Trecento', in Giovanni Cherubini (ed.), *Signori, contadini, borghesi. Ricerche sulla società Italiana del Basso Medioevo* (Florence, 1974), pp. 231–311 (232–36); Duccio Balestracci and Gabriella Piccinni, *Siena nel Trecento: assetto urbano e strutture edilizie* (Florence, 1977), p. 8; and William M. Bowsky, *The Finance of the Commune of Siena. 1287–1355* (Oxford, 1970), Italian translation, *Le Finanze del comune di Siena (1287–1355)* (Florence 1976), pp. 94–115, 118–31 and 309–50. See also Paolo Cammarosano's review of Bowsky in *Studi Medievali*, ser. 3a, 12 (1971), pp. 301–22 and by the same author, *Monteriggione. Storia, architettura, paesaggio* (Milan, 1983), pp. 58–67. For two more recent overviews of the levying of tax on behalf of the Sienese government, including comprehensive bibliographies, see Vincenzo Passeri and Laura Neri (eds), *Gli insediamenti della Repubblica di Siena nel catasto del 1318–1320* (Siena, 1994), pp. III–IV and Alberto Grohmann (ed.), *Le fonti censuarie e catastali tra tarda romanità e basso medioevo, Emilia Romagna, Toscana, Umbria, Marche, San Marino* (San Marino, 1996). For a meticulous analysis of the various stages involved in drawing up such records, and a detailed consideration of the contents of two individual *Tavole delle possessioni*, see Roberto Farinelli and Andrea Giorgi, 'La "Tavola delle Possessioni" come fonte per lo Studio del territorio: l'esempio di Castelnuovo dell'Abate', in Alfio Cortonesi (ed.), *La Valdorcia nel Medioevo e nei primi secoli dell'Età moderna*, Atti del convegno internazionale di studi storici, Pienza, 15–18 settembre 1988 (Rome, 1990), pp. 213–56, and (by the same authors) 'Radicondoli: società e territorio in una "curia" attraverso la "Tavola delle Possessioni" ', in Costanza Cucini (ed.) *Radicondoli. Storia e Archeologia di un comune senese* (Rome, 1990), pp. 353–91.

2   As Banchi (La Lira, la Tavola', p. 55) notes, *Estimo* was the term commonly adopted by the Florentines. The Sienese for their part adopted the term *Lira*. In this context, see also Luciano Banchi, 'Gli ordinamenti economici dei comuni toscani nel medioevo e segnatamente del Comune di Siena, I: La Lira o l'Estimo', *Atti della R. Accademia dei Fisiocritici di Siena*, ser 3a, 2 (1879), pp. 9–80.

3   See, in particular, David Herlihy and Christiane Klapisch-Zuber, *Les Toscans et leurs familles. Une étude du catasto florentin de 1427* (Paris, 1978). English translation, *Tuscans and their families: A study of the Florentine catasto of 1427* (New Haven, Conn., 1985); Italian translation: *I toscani e le loro famiglie: uno studio sul catasto fiorentino del 1427* (Bologna, *c*.1988), and more recently, the work of Giovanni Cherubini and his equipage.

4   See Appendix I for a complete index of first names and patronyms.

5   In this context, I am grateful to Lorenza Favilli Granai for allowing me to consult her thesis 'Tipografia storica del territorio di Montalcino. Insediamenti antichi nel territorio di Montalcino', Tesi di laurea, Università degli studi di Firenze, Facoltà di Magistero, relatore Giovanni Uggeri, Anno Accademico 1984–85.

6 Amongst these was the vineyard at Fonterenza.

7 Archivio di Stato, Siena (hereafter ASS), *Diplomatico di Montalcino*, Busta 33 bis, no. 134.

8 See Appendix II for a full transcription.

9 In this context, see Giovanni Uggeri, 'Questioni di metodo. La toponomastica nella ricerca topografica: il contribuito alla ricostruzione della viabilità', *Journal of Ancient Topography*, 1 (1991), pp. 21–36. See also, Carlo Alberto Mastrelli, 'Nota toponomastica', in Passeri and Neri, *Gli insediamenti*, pp. IX–XVII; Farinelli and Giorgi, 'Radicondoli', pp. 368–74; Vincenzo Passeri and Paolo Cammarosano, *Repertorio dei toponimi della provincia di Siena, desunti dalla cartografia dell'Istituto Geografico Militare* (Siena, 1983); Giovanni Battista Pellegrini, *Toponomastica italiana* (Milan, 1991); Cammarosano, *Monteriggioni*, pp. 111–12, and Silvio Pieri, *Toponomastica della Toscana Meridionale e dell'Arcipelago toscano* (Siena, 1969).

10 In this respect see Luciano Logazzi, 'I segni sulla terra. Sistemi di confinazione e di misurazione dei boschi nell'alto Medioevo', in Bruno Andreolli and Massimo Montanari (eds), *Il bosco nel medioevo* (Bologna, 1988), pp. 17–34 (19). See also Laura Cassi, 'Distribuzione geografica dei toponimi derivati dalla vegetazione in Toscana', *Rivista Geografica Italiana*, 80, fasc. 4, dicembre (1973), pp. 389–432.

11 See ASS, *Estimo* 24, fols 109v, 184r, 191r, 382r, 397v, 429r, 451r.

12 Ibid., fol. 465r.

13 For 'via carraie', see ASS, *Estimo* 24, fols 114v, 128v, 129r, 130r, 179r, 187v, 329r, 344r.

14 For 'via fornelle', see ASS, *Estimo* 24, fols 272r and 315r.

15 For 'stradella ma(?n)gmeta', see ASS, *Estimo* 24, fols 236r and 445r.

16 I am grateful to Bruno Bonucci for this information.

Appendix I

Index of *Estimo* 24[1]

31	Comune Sci Angli	LVIII
32	Casinus Bini	LXVI
33	Chola Johanis	LXVIII
34	Cecchinas (Cici)[7] Ghezzi	LXXI
35	Chele Ruggerii	LXXIII
36	Conte Venture	LXXVII
37	Chiniis (Ghinus)[8]Bonaiuti	LXXVIII
38	Cecchus Ture	LXXIX
39	Cecchus Johannis	LXXXII
40	Cecchus Bindi	LXXXIV
41	Cen(n)inus Cennis	LXXXV
42	Cecchus Nucci	LXXXVII
43	Chola (Chele)[9] Freduccii	LXXXVIII
44	Chele Ferrantis	LXXXIX
45	Cenne Bartali	XC
46	Cenne Lactarini	XCI
47	Ceccha Guidi	XCII
48	Cecchinus Cecchi	XCIII
49	Ciana Guidarelli	XCV
50	Ciellina Niccholucci	XCVI
51	Chola Michaelis	XCVII
52	Cenellus Ugolini	XCVIII
53	Cignone Benvenuti	XCIX
54	Casinus Altemanni (Altimanni)[10]	CI
55	Ceccha Bononis	CII
56	Ciattus (Ciactus)[11] Nuccii	CIII
57	Chasella di Mo(n)talcino	CIV
58	Chola Micchelucci	CV
59	Chola Marzuoli	CVI
60	Dominichellus Romauioli	CIX
61	Dominichus Buiriacci (Biriutii)[12] (Brunacci)[13] (Brunatii)[14]	CXII
62	D(omi)na Rosa Pieri pecoraio[15]	CXII[16]
63	Drudas (Drudus)[17] Cennis	CXVII
64	Dominichus Guidi	CXVIII
65	D(omi)na Nuta uxor Ciaffi	CCCLX
66	D(omi)na Rosa uxor Futii	CCCC
67	D(omi)na Tessina Peruzzi	CCCCXX
68	D(omi)na Cellina uxor d(omin)i Micchelutii	CCLIX
69	Dadus Valchericci (Valcherini)[18]	CCLX
70	Eccl(es)ia S(an)c(t)i Ang(e)li	CXXI
71	Eccl(es)ia S(an)c(t)i Petri	CXXXII
72	Fuccius Andelonis	CXXXIX
73	Figlius Lunardi	CXL

74	Finuccius Ranuccini (Finutii Ranutii)[19]	CXLI
75	Folchinus Johanis	CXLIII
76	Fatuiola Maffei (Maffuccii)[20]	CXLV
77	Gilius Ranucci	CXLVII
78	Ganus Guigliolmucci	CXLIX
79	Gerinus Gregorii	CL
80	Guarneruccius (Guarnerii)[21] Bruni	CLI
81	Ghinuccuis (Ghini)[22] Filipputii	CLII
82	Ghuccuis Petrucci	CLIII
83	Giacobus Micchelucci	CLV
84	Griffuccuis Bruni	CLVI
85	Gratia Ugolini	CLVII
86	Guiduccius Tebaldi	CLIX
87	Giannollus Credis di Villa a Tolle	CLX
88	Guido Vannis	CLXI
89	Giannos (Gani) Lamberti (Lambertini)[23]	CLXII
90	Gianinius Accorsi (Accorsi)[24]	CLXIII
91	Heredes Venture	CLXV
92	Heredes Cennis	CLXVI
93	Heredes Ser Francisci	CLXVII
94	Heredes Johanis Appare	CLXVIII
95	Heredes Naldi Jacobi	CLXIX
96	Heredes Janis Jacomini	CLXX
97	Heredes Cecchi Pieri	CLXXI
98	Heredes Petrucci (Pierucci)[25] Guillielmi	CLXXVIII
99	Heredes Banducci	CLXXX
100	Heredes Bini Tassini	CLXXXII
101	Heredes Bini Ranuccii	CLXXXIII
102	Heredes Bini	CLXXXIV
103	Heredes Brunaccii	CLXXXV
104	Heredes Franchi	CLXXXVI
105	Heredes Bini Jacomini	CXC
106	Heredes Bindi Ranuccii	CXCI
107	Heredes Maffuccii	CXCII
108	Hospitale S(an)c(t)i Ang(e)lo	CXCIII
109	Heredes Alteman(n)i (Altimanni)[26]	CXCIV
110	Heredes Muiccii (Muccii)[27]	CXCVI
111	Heredes Vitalis di Vico	CXCVII
112	Heredes Cennis Gratie	CXCIX
113	Heredes Romanuioli	CC
114	Heredes Mini Argomenti	CCII
115	Heredes D(omi)ne Becche	CCIII
116	Heredes Cecchi Franchi	CCIV
117	Heredes Nigri di Mo(n)te Alcino	CCV

118	Heredes Nerii Rubei	CCVI
119	Heredes Nerii Fabri	CCVIII
120	Heredes Nerii Sossie di Tolle (Villa a Tolle)[28]	CCIX
121	Heredes Nerii Orlandi di Villa a Tolle	CCX
122	Heredes Vive Jacobi	CCXII
123	Heredes Fatii de la Villa	CCXIV
124	Heredes Ghezzi	CCXV
125	Heredes Guidi Schifalorzo	CCXVII
126	Heredes Berto(e)[29] Martini	CCXIX
127	Heredes Cioli	CCXX
128	Heredes Gian(n)is Uguiccionis	CCXXI
129	Heredes Nuti Brunacci	CCXXII
130	Heredes Micchelutii	CCXXIII
131	Heredes Leti Sabbatini	CCXXIV
132	Heredes Cecchi cavalieri[30]	CCXXV
133	Heredes Feduccci di Villa a Tolle	CCXXVI
134	Heredes Accorsi	CCXXVII
135	Heredes Blanchi	CCXXVIII
136	Heredes Ture Bene(n)casa	CCXXIX
137	Heredes mag(ist)ri Puccii	CCXXXI
138	Heredes Binocci (Binozzi)[31]	CCXXXII
139	Heredes Johanelli	CCXXXIII
140	Heredes Berti mag(ist)ri Ma(r)tini	CCXXXIV
141	Heredes Ciantis di Villa a Tolle	CCXXXV
142	Heredes Ciani di Villa a Tolle	CCXXXVI
143	Heredes Nuta de la fante[32] di Villa a Tolle	CCXXXVII
144	Heredes Nerii Venture	CCXXXVIII
145	Heredes Nerii Tassini	CCXXXIX
146	Heredes Guadagni	CCXL
147	Heredes Becche fratesse	CCXLI
148	Heredes Nerii	CCXLII
149	Heredes Peri pecorai[33]	CCXLIII
150	Heredes Borgognonis	CCXLIV
151	Heredes Benaventis (Bencivenis)[34]	CCXLV
152	Heredes Cremonesis	CCXLVI
153	Heredes Tori	CCXLVII
154	Heredes Ranuccetti	CCXLVIII
155	Heredes Guidi di Colona (Accolone)[35]	CCLVI
156	Heredes Giannis Orlandi	CCLVII
157	Heredes Perucci Assalti	CCLVIII
158	Iohanes Vitalis	CCL
159	Johininus Raynaldi	CCLI
160	Johanes Gualterii	CCLIII
161	Johaninus Rainucci	CCLIV

162	Landutuis Berti	CCLXIII
163	Landutuis (Landuccio) Giontarelli (Juntarelli)[36]	CCLXIV
164	Landus Pepi	CCLXV
165	Lucannus (?Lucarinus)[37] ser Francisci	CCLXVIII
166	Landutuis Duccii	CCLXX
167	Lonarduccius (Lonardelli)[38]Benvegnate	CCLXXI
168	Landus Gionte (?Junte)[39]	CCLXXII
169	Lonardutuis Johanis	CCLXXV
170	Lonardutuis Terni	CCLXXVII
171	Lonardutuis Jontarelli	CCLXXVIII
172	Lonardutuis Vecci	CCLXXIX
173	Landus Guadagni	CCLXXX
174	Mon(n)a Neccha nigozzantis[40]	CCLXXXI
175	Martinus Berti	CCLXXXIII
176	Mon(n)a Scholai	CCLXXXIV
177	Michus Genovesis[41]	CCLXXXVI
178	Maffeus (Massi)[42] Januarii	CCXC
179	Minutius Sozzi (Sozza)[43]	CCXCII
180	Mon(n)a Gem(m)a Accorsi	CCXCIV
181	Minutius Bandacci (Bandutii)[44]	CCXCV
182	Mon(n)a Beccha Ser Francisci	CCXCVI
183	Menchinus Ghezzi	CCXCVII
184	Mon(n)a Mita Baldiccionis	CCXCVIII
185	Mon(n)aster(io) di fratessis di Mo(n)te Alcino	CCXCIX
186	Martinus Gian(n)is	CCC
187	Mutuis Orlandi	CCCI
188	Marchus Johanelli	CCCII
189	Mon(n)a Gioia	CCCIII
190	Marchutius (Marrutuis) Angololli (Angelelli)[45]	CCCIV
191	Martino(?e)llus Guidarelli	CCCVI
192	Menchinus Lamb(er)ti	CCCVII
193	Minus Johanis	CCCVIII
194	Mita Peri[46]	CCCIX, CCCXXX
195	Mita Tora (Torrci)[47]	CCCX
196	Mina Maffutii	CCCXI
197	Maffuccia Benciven(n)is	CCCXII
198	Mita Brunacci	CCCXIII
199	Mita Nerii	CCCXIV
200	Martinutuis In(?n)segnie (Ensegne)[48]	CCCXV
201	Mideris (Mideus)[49] Fuccii	CCCXVI
202	Marchus Johinolli (Johanelli)[50]	CCCXVII, CCCII
203	Mo(?e)ldina Guidarelli	CCCXIX
204	Minus Ser Guilli (?Guillielmi)	CCCXX

205	Mon(n)a Lucia Guidi	CCCXXII
206	Martinutius Ma(r)tini	CCCXXIII
207	Meus Pepi	CCCXXV
208	Mencinus Orlandi	CCCXXVI
209	Mina Giannis	CCCXXVII
210	Man(n)us Maffucci	CCCXXVIII
211	Mon(n)a Mita Pieri[51]	CCCXXX, CCCIX
212	Mon(n)a Duccia Cioli	CCCXXXI
213	Mon(n)a Neccha Venture	CCCXXXII
214	Maffuccinus Maffucci	CCCXXXIII[52]
215	Mon(n)a Mita Minucci[53]	CCCXXXIII[54]
216	Mon(n)a Mita Minucci	CCCXXXV
217	Mutia Gionte	CCCXXXVI
218	Mon(n)a Jacomina Sozzi	CCCXXXVII
219	Mon(n)a Becca Petrini	CCCXXXVIII
220	Netius (Nennus)[55] Ranieri	CCCXL
221	Ninus Johanis	CCCXLII
222	Novolhinus (Novellinus)[56] Venture	CCCXLVI
223	Nardellus Venture	CCCXLVII
224	Nardus Cambii	CCCXLIX
225	Naldus Jacomi	CCCLI
226	Nutus Venture	CCCLII
227	Naccinus Nutii	CCCLIII
228	Nuta Sozzi	CCCLIV
229	Naccinus Giordanelli	CCCLV[57]
230	Nucciarellus Ranerii	CCCLVII
231	Nuta Nuccii	CCCLVIII
232	Necchina Ture	CCCLIX
233	Neccha Brunacci	CCCLX[58]
234	Neri Dietavive (Diotavive)[59]	CCCLXII
235	Nerituis (Nerutuis)[60] Nolsi	CCCLXIV
236	Nenus (Nerius)[61] Ciantis de Villa a Tolle	CCCLXV
237	Nuccius Credis di d(e)c(t)a Villa	CCCLXVI
238	Novellaria (Novellina)[62] Bini	CCCLXVII
239	Nuccius Massai(?n)e	CCCLXV[63]
240	Nardutius Johanis	CCCLXXI
241	Nutius Sanne	CCCLXXII
242	Nerius Guadagni	CCCCLIV
243	Propostia S(an)c(t)i Angeli	CCCLXXIV
244	Petrutius Bonan(n)i	CCCLXXVI
245	Petrutuis Peri	CCCLXXVIII
246	Paganellus Johanis	CCCLXXX
247	Petrinus Nerii	CCCLXXXII
248	Petratinis (Petrutuis)[64] Johannis	CCCLXXXIII

249	Plebes a Sexta	CCCLXXXV
250	Petrus Bindi de Mo(n)tealcino	CCCLXXXVI
251	Petrutius Pepi	CCCLXXXVII
252	Pieriis Nerii	CCCLXXXVIII
253	Petrutius Alaman(n)i	CCCXC
254	Pagolus Nerii Rubei	CCCXCI
255	Pia Farolfi	CCCXCII
256	Petrutuis Ciani di Villa a Tolle	CCCXCIII
257	Petrucciuolus Saliti	CCCXCIV
258	Ristornectus (Ristorucciius)[65]Vitalis	CCCXCV
259	Ristoruccius Borgognonus	CCCXCVII
260	Riccuccuis (Riccutuis)[66] Guidi	CCCCIII
261	Scolarriolus (Scholai)[67] Gian(n)elli	CCCCI
262	Sozzus Melde	CCCCIV
263	Sozzus Jacomi (Jacobi)[68]	CCCCV
264	Ser Tollus Ghollii[69]	CCCCVII
265	Sozzus Mainetti	CCCCIX
266	Sozzus Ranucci	CCCCX
267	Salitus Orlandi	CCCCXI
268	Sozzinus Sozzi	CCCCXII
269	Ser Guccius Ser Francisci	CCCCXLIX
270	Ser Franciscus et Ser Nere q(uon) dam Cecchi Pieri[70]	CCLV
271	Scolauiolus Buonomi de Mo(n)te alcino	CCCCXV
272	Tura Guilli (Guillielmi)[71]	CCCCXIII
273	Tura Martini	CCCCXIV
274	Tinus de Mo(n)tenero	CCCCXVI
275	Tessina Lasie (Lascie)[72]	CCCCXVII
276	Tinus Maffucci	CCCCXVIII
277	Tura Morolli (Morelli)[73]	CCCCXIX
278	Torazzuolus Tori	CCCCXXI
279	Turellus Jan(n)ini	CCCCXXII
280	Turellus Leti	CCCCXXIII
281	Tura Manni	CCCCLIII
282	Vivianus Mendi	CCCCXXIV
283	Van(nu)tuis q(uon)da(m) Berti mag(ist)ri Martini	CCCCXXVI
284	Vese Michi	CCCCXVIII
285	Vivianus Ranucci	CCCCXXIX
286	Ulivutius (Ulivicci)[74]Johan(n)is	CCCCXXXI
287	Vannos Cholis (Vannes Chelis)[75]	CCCCXXXIII
288	Van(n)utuis Cremonosis (Cremonesis)[76]	CCCCXXXV
289	Vivatuis (Vinnuccci)[77]Ciampoli	CCCCXXXVI
290	Van(n)utuis Johannis	CCCCXXXVIII
291	Van(n)utuis Massaie	CCCCXL
292	Van(n)utuis Tori	CCCCXLII

293	Vina Morelli (Moregli)[78] (Meglioregli)[79]	CCCCXLIII
294	Vanutuis Ranieri	CCCCXLIV
295	Vannes Gherardi di Villa a Tolle	CCCCXLV
296	Villanus Brunus	CCCCXLVI
297	Van(n)utius Insegne (Ensegne)[80]	CCCCXLVII
298	Vinitiana uxor Guidarolli (Guidarelli)[81]	CCCCXVIII

Analysis

The existing index contains Latin numerals indicating folio numbers. Where relevant, the precise recto or verso reference or alternative page number is noted here in the endnotes.

Notes

1   Archivio di Stato di Siena, *Estimo del Contado*, 24. The index is transcribed in its original Latinate form. Pagination within the document itself is in Arabic form. All second names included in the index are given capital letters, although in the original document the use of lower and upper case is inconsistent. A number of individuals listed in the index have more than one entry. Such duplications are noted, together with the Arabic page references. Where a professional title such as 'magister' occurs, the lower case is adopted. When an individual's name appears in the main body of the document in a recognisably different form, the alternative spelling is included in parenthesis with an Arabic page reference indicated in an end note.

2   fol. 23r.

3   fol. 30r.

4   This is possibly a duplicate entry for Bindus Ranerii (see no. 12). However, a clear distinction is made between the spelling of Bindus and Binus both in the index and in the two entries within the document itself. It is possible, therefore, that these two individuals were siblings. However, it also seems that the patronym of Ranieri allotted to Bindus was incorrect, since he is referred to as Bindus di Nerio Casini in the context of land owned by him in the plain at Sesta (see fol. 25v.). One of the neighbours to that piece of land was said to be the church of San Michele; another, the heirs of Cecco di Piero. In the equivalent entry concerning property at Sesta owned by the church of San Michele, there is a reference to 'Bini di Nerii Tassini' as a neighbouring landowner (see fol. 123v.). In that owned by the heirs of Cecco di Piero, there is a reference to 'Bindi Nerii' (see fols 176r–176v.). It seems more likely, therefore, that the individual listed as Bindus Ranieri in the 1320 *Tavola delle Possessioni* was in fact named Bindus di Nerio Casini (or Tassini). There is further evidence of possible confusions in drawing up details for these two individuals in a reference in the entry for Bindus to one of the individuals described as owning property abutting the house belonging to Bindus inside the walls of the village as Petri, or Petrus Ranieri (see fol. 25r.). That individual is not included in the index to *Estimo* 24. Nor is there a separate entry for him within the document itself.

5   fol. 49r.

6   fol. 54r.

7   fol. 68r.

8   fol. 78r.

9   fol. 88r.

10   fol. 40r.

11   fol. 103r.

12   fol. 328v.

13   fol. 225r.

14   fol. 328v.

15   Pecoraio is possibly used here in the sense of Rosa's father being a shepherd.

16   Actually fol. 116r.

17   fols 117r and 73v.

18   fol. 260r.

19   fol. 343r.

20   fol. 440r

21   fol. 174r.

22   fol. 140r.

23   fol. 129v.

24   fol. 163r.

25   fol. 178r.

26   fol. 194r.

27   fol. 196r.

28   fol. 209r.

29   fol. 219r.

30   Cavalieri is possibly used here in the sense of Cecco having been a knight.

31   fol. 232r.

32   Fante is possibly used here in the sense of Nuta being the offspring of a servant.

33   Pecoraio is possibly used here in the sense of Piero being a shepherd.

34   fol. 245r.

35   fol. 256r.

36   fol. 74v.

37   fol. 268r.

38   fol. 221r.

39   fol. 134v.

40 Nigozzantis is possibly used here in the sense of Necca being a shopkeeper.

41 Genovesis no doubt indicates that this individual came from Genoa.

42 fol. 175v.

43 fol. 292r.

44 fol. 295r.

45 fol. 304r.

46 There are two entries for this individual in the index. In the second instance in the index she is given the title 'Mon(n)a', and references are made both to her father and to her husband.

47 fol. 310r.

48 fol. 315r.

49 fol. 315v.

50 There are two entries for this individual in the index.

51 See footnote 46 above.

52 Actually, fol. 334r.

53 This individual's name appears twice in the index. Within the document itself, there are two separate entries, the first of which refers to Mon(n)a Mita Miu(?n)ucci, and the second of which spells out the patronym as Minutii.

54 Actually fol. 334r.

55 fol. 340r.

56 fol. 346r.

57 An entry on the page following that for Naccinus Giordanelli purports to record the patrimony of Naccius, or Naccini Giordani, see fol. 355v. This individual is not listed in the index. Given the similarity between the names and the fact that there is only one recorded patrimony on fol. 355v, it seems likely that there was an error in drawing up the details, and that only one individual was involved.

58 Actually fol. 361r.

59 fol. 362r.

60 fol. 364r.

61 fol. 197r.

62 fol. 367r.

63 In fact fol. 370r.

64 fol. 383r.

65 fol. 395r.

66 fol. 403r.

67 fol. 47r.

68 fol. 114v.

69 This individual is described in other surviving documents of the period as a notary.

70 There is no individual entry for Ser Nere in *Estimo* 24, but he appears to have been the (perhaps underage) brother of Ser Francischus di Cecchi Pieri.

71 fol. 185r.

72 fol. 417r.

73 fol. 419r.

74 fol. 103r.

75 fol. 433r.

76 fol. 435r.

77 fol. 27r.

78 fol. 443r.

79 fol. 125v.

80 fol. 447r.

81 fol. 448r.

Appendix II

Transcription of the 1318 boundary document[1]

In Dei nomine amen Anno eiusdem annativitatis Millesimo CCCXVIII Indictione prima, die quinta mensis Octubris. De lite et questione litibus et questionibus que sunt seu esse possent inter commune et homines terre Montisalcini ex una parte et commune et homines Castri de Sancto Angelo in Colle ex altera ratione Seu occasione confinium seu terminorum inter districtos dicte terre montisalcino predicti et communis Castri Sci Angeli in colle quorum confinium seu terminorum discordia seu lix erat et essere poterat inter dicta duo communia de ipsis confinibus ponendis in disctrictu seu […] districtum cuislibet dicte terre adserens quelibet partium predictarum Iurisditiones ipsarum terrarum ultra protendi quam sint inconcordia partes predicte Ideo volentes homines dictorum duorum communium dictas lites et questiones sedare et de ipsis litibus et questionibus ad concordiam pervenire pro bono pacis et concordie communium predictorum et singularium personarum ipsorum Deus olim Dietanive de montalcini sindicus dicti communis montisalcini ad infrascripta spetialiter constitutus ut de infrascriptas syndicatu apparet manu mei notari infrascrpti syndicario nomine dicti communis ex parte una Et Petruccius Pieri de Sancto Angelo in Colle syndicus dicte terre Sancti Angeli in Colle ut de ipsius syndicatu apparet manu Ser Mini Accursi notario de Senis ad infrascripta spetialiter ordinatus syndicario nomine dicti communis Sci Angli in Colle ex altera parte lites et questiones que sunt seu in posterum esse possent inter dicta duo communia occasione terminorum seu confinium supra dictorum ponendorum inter districtos utriusque terre de quibus ponendis est discordia inter dicti communa supra dicta conpromiserunt vice et nomine dictorum communium et singularum personarum ipsorum communium in Nobilem militem dominum Vivianum de Forteguerris de Senis presentem et suscipientem tamquam In arbitrum Arbitratore et amicum communem. Et dantes et concedentes supradicti syndici et quilibet eorum vice et nomine communium predictorum dicto domino .Viviano Arbitro arbitratori seu amico communiter ab eis electo licentiam et liberam potestatem supradictis lites et questiones et qualibet earum cognoscendi difinendi et terminandi de iure et de facto et quomodocumque ipsi placuerit et ponendi terminos et poni faciendi inter districto dictarum terrarum in quibuscumque locis ei placuerit non servata in predictis vel aliquo predictorum aliqua iuris solepnitate et quod possit ipsas lites et questiones cognoscere et difinire et ipsos terminos seu confines ponere seu poni facere sumarie et sine strepitu et figura Iudicii presentibus partibus et absentibus citatis et non citatis die ferriata et non ferriata sedendo et sedes stando promictentes supradicti syndici syndicario nomine dictorum communium ad invicem unus alteri solepni stipulatione interveniente firmum et ratam habere et perpetuo tenere et observare quicquid ed totum per dictum dominum Vivianum arbitrum supradictum in predictis et circa predicta vel aliqua predictorum laudatum sententiatum pronunptiatum et arbitratum fuerit et non convenire de iure vel de facto inuidicio vel extra aliqua ratione vel extra (omnia) in integrum refici rationem petere ser (cancelled) in totum executione mandare et ipsos terminos ponere seu poni facere in illis locis et illis modis et conditionibus prout per dictum dominum Vivianum arbitrum supradictum sententiam et mandatum fuerit etiam declaratum sub pena Mille librarum denarom senensium minutorim ab una parte altris solepniter stipulatum promissum et etiam dana expensas et interesse ad invecem reficere promisserunt que pena totiens comictatur quotiens in predictis vel aliquo predictorum ab una partium fuerit contraventum et sub obligatione bonorum utriusque communis Que bona syndici supradicti nomine et vice dictorum communium constituerunt se unus nomine alterius precario possidere donec corporalem possessionem acceperint quam possessionem accipiendi et aprehendendi unus alteri nomine supradicto dederunt in casu quo contraventum fuerit in aliquo predictorum auctoritate propria licentiam et liberam potestatem et ipsa bona tenendi fructandi et vendendi usque ad consecutionem dicte pene dampnorum inter essere expensarum que pena soluta vel non ratis et firmis manentibus supradictis (crossed out) omnibus supradictis

Actum in districtu Montisalcini in contrata dicta in pede silve communis montisalcini presentibus Becto Pasqualis, Cione Dote, Ser Morando Ser Pepi de montalcino Lunarduccio Johannis, Micho Gienovesis et Becto Ramaioli di Sco Anglo in Colle testibus ad predicta vocatis ad hibitis et Rogatis

Ego Angelus olim Nini Vulpis de montepolitiano Imperiali auctorite Iudex ordinarius et notarius predictis omnibus et singulis interfui et ea ut supra continetur scripsi et publicavi Rogatus Et quod supra scriptum remissum interlineatum et signatum est videlicet: inter districtos dicte terre montisalcini predicti et Castri Sci Angeli in Colle quorum confinium seu terminorum propria manu scripsi remisi intellineavi et signavi:

In Dei nomine amen Nos Vivianus de Forteguerris de Senis arbiter et arbitrator etiam amicus communis electus a Deo olim Dietavive sindico communis montisalcini ex parte una et Petruccio Ser (cancelled) Pieri syndico communis Sci Angeli in Colle ex parte altera super litibus et questionibus dirimendis que sunt et esse possent in posterum inter dictam dua communa occasione seu ratione confinium seu terminorum ponendorum inter districtos predictorum duorum communium ut de compromisso in nos facto plenius patet manu Ser Angeli olim Nini Vulpis de montepulitiano pro parte dicti communis montisalcini et pro parte dicti communis Sci Angeli in Colle manu Ser Mini Acursi notari de Senis iuso dicto compromissu ac etiam iusis et diligenter examinatis Iuribus utriusque partis et auditis que dicte partes dicere et allegare voluerunt et occulata fide inspectis locis in quibus seu de quibus erat discordia seu esse poterat inter dicta duo communa de dictis confinibus ponendis et de predictis districtibus et Iurisdictionibus utriusque communis terminandi volentes homines predictorum communium et etiam ipsa communa ad pacem et concordiam perducere finem litibus et discordii inponentes ex vigore dicti compromissi in nos facti et omni iure et modo quibus melius possumus Christi nomine invocato sic inter dictas partes laudamus arbitramus sententiamus et diffinimus ac etiam declaramus videlicet quod fossatellus qui est in pede lame Sci Angeli sit primus terminus prout trahit et respicit recta linea ad campum Albicini Johannis videlicet ad aream existentem in dicto campo posita in dicta contrata lame Sci Angeli cui a capite dicti campi est Neri Ciantis et ex alio latere est Perucci Ciani et siqui sunt eidem veriores confines. Item quod in area predicta ponatur et ficcetur alius terminus et sit supradictus terminus qui terminus trahat et respiciat recta linea ad capud plani campi Bernarduccii pietri positam in contrata dicta Sotteragiolo cui a capite est Naldini Nuti et a pede est Caselli Nuccii Gratiani et ex uno latere est Gianelli Credis Et in capite plani Bernarduccii Pietri predicti ponatur et ficcetur unus alius terminus et sit tertius terminus et dictus terminus trahat et respiciat recta linea ad pedem strate veteris a capite aree bernarducci pietri existentis in quodam campo dicti Bernarduccii positam in contrata dicta el magnattaio cui a capite est supradicti Naldini et ex uno latere est supradicti Giannelli et siqui sunt eidem veriores confines. Et quod in pede dicte strate veteris in capite aree supradicti Bernarducci ponatur mictatur et ficcetur alius terminus qui sit quartus terminus et dictus terminus sic missus et positus trahat et respiciat recta linea ad campum Peruccii Ciani positum in contrata delmagnactaio cui a capite est Ciati et a pede est fossatus triedine et siqui sunt eidem veriores confines. Et quod in campo dicti Peruccii ponatur mictatur et ficcetur alius terminus et sit quintus terminus qui terminus sic missus positus et ficcatus mictat trahat et respiciat recta linea ad campum Peruccii predicti positum in dicta contrata et iuxta supradictos confines (… cancelled) videlicet ad sassum pincutum existentem in dicto campo. Et quod super dictum sassum pincutum ponatur mictatur et ficcetur unus alius terminus et sit sextus terminus, qui terminus sic missus et positus mictat et respiciat recta linea in fossatum triedine. Item quod dictus fossatus Triedine sit septimus terminus et habeatur et teneatur pro vii termino sicut dictus fossatus triedine labitur currit et respicit versus et usque ad campum dne Mite uxoris minuccii banduccii positus in contrata dictam frale macchie cui a capite est via et a pede est fossatus Triedine et siqui sunt eidem veriores confines. Et quod in dicto campo mictatur ficetur et ponatur unus alius terminus et sit octavus terminus qui terminus sic missus et positus trahat et respiciat ad campum Naldini Nuti predicti positum in dicta contrata dicta fralemacchia cui a capite est Ciati Nuccii et ex uno heredum Ciantis et siqui sunt ei veriores confines Et in dicto campo mictatur ficcetur et ponatur unus alius terminus et sit nonus terminus qui terminus sic missus et positus trahat mictat et respiciat recta linea ad alium campum Naldini dicti positum in dicta contrata fralemacchie cui a capite est via qua itur a Sco Angelo in Colle ad villam tollis Et in dicto campo ponatur mictetur et ficcetur unus alius terminus et sit decimus terminus qui terminus sic positus et missus mictat respiciat et vadet recta linea per supradictam viam usque ad crocicchuim existens in capite viarum quibus itur a Sco Angelo In Colle ad villam tollis et ad terram montisalcini quod crocicchuim dictarum viarum est in contrata dicta elpianodelemaglie. Et quod in dicto crocicchio mictatur ponatur et ficcetur unus alius terminus et sit undecimus terminus qui terminus sic missus et positu respiciat et mictat et vadat et trahat recta linea per viam qua itur a castro Sci Angeli in colle ad terram montisalcini usque ad campum heredum Ciantis predicti positum in contrata predicta del piano delemaglie cui ex uno latere est dicta via Et in dicto campo mictatur ficetur et ponatur unus alius terminus et sit duodecimos terminus qui terminus sic missus et positus trahat respiciat et vadat recta linea per supradictam viam usque ad terminum veterem missum et positum in pede silve terre montisalcini. Et in pede dicte silve ubi est dictus terminus vetus ponatur et mictatur alius terminus tertiodecimus terminus qui terminus sic missus et positus vadat trahat et respiciat recta linea usque ad terminum veterem missum et positum in contrata del cerreta cui a capite est boscus Chelis Feduccii et Perucci Azzonelli et a pede est communis Sci Angeli in colle Et in dicto loco ubi est dictus terminus vetus ponatur et mictatur alius novus terminus et sit quartodecimus terminus qui terminus sic missus et positus recta linea respiciat et vadat usque ad alium terminum veterem positum et missum in contrata campuoci inter campum communis sci Angeli in colle et campum heredum feduccii di tolle Et ubi est dictus vetus terminus ponatur mictatur et ficcietur alius terminus novus qui terminus sic missus et positus respiciat vadat et mictat recta linea per Rigagnolum qui est iuxta campum Neri Guicciardi et mictit in fossatum campuoci usque ad conbarbium dicti fossati campuoci et rigagnoli et in dicto conbarbio ponatur et mictatur alius terminus et sit quintodecimus terminus et In dicto termino ponendo in dicto conbarbio fossati prout mictit dictus fossatus Campuoci in fossatum deribolgare sit alius terminus et a dicto fossato de Ribolgare prout currit mictit et vadit dictus fossatus de ribolgare usque ad conbarbium fossati Ranucci et sit et esse debeat alius terminus. Item dicimus et mandamus ac etiam arbitramur quod omnis et singuli termini et confines prout supra declarati sunt ponantur in supradictis locis et in eis ficcentur et murentur infrascripto modo et forma videlicet quod per commune Sci Angeli in colle murentur vi supradictorum terminorum quorum .v. positi sunt ultra fossati triedine alii vero termini murentur per commune montisalcini quorum omnium terminorum mura[n]dum per dicta communa: (… cancelled) altitudo sit duorum bracchiorum a terra qui termini (.crossed out) omnes murentur lapidibus et calcina Et predicto fiant et fieri mandamus per dicta duo communia usque ad kalendas decembris proxime venturi sub pena .C. florenorum auri Item madamus arbitramur et sententiamur quod omnis et singule vie que sunt dictos confines et terminos sint communes inter dicta communia ita quod hominibus et singularibus personis singulariter et communiter supradictorum communuim sit licitus ire et comoditatem habere per dictas vias ac si proprie essent Que omnia et singula predicta mandamus a dictis partibus observari in omnibus et singulis supradicto articulis et capitilis executione mandari sub pena in dicto compromisso inserta;

Latum datum et pronunptiatum fuit dictum laudum et laudi sententiam per dominum Vivianum arbitrum et arbitratorem predictum sub annis domini annativitate millesimo CCCXVIII Indictione prima, die quinta mesis Octubris in curia Sci Angeli in Colle in contrata que dicetur elamoni in campo Viviuccii Ciampoli di Sco Angeli in Colle presentibus consentientibus et volentibus supradictis syndici[s] et quolibet eorum syndicario et nominee pro dictis communibus presentibus Becto pasqualis, Cione Dote Ser Morando Ser Pepi di montalcino, lunarduccio Johannis, Micho Gienovesis et Becto Ramaioli di Scto Angelo in Colle testibus ad omnia predicta vocatis ad litis et Rogatis;

Ego Angelus olim Nini Vulpis de montepuliciano Imperiali auctoritate Iudex ordinarius et notarius predictis ominibus inter fui et ea ut supra continetur scripsi et pubblicavi Rogatus

Note

1 Archivio di Stato, Siena, *Diplomatico di Montalcino*, Busta 33 bis, no. 134. With grateful thanks to Dottoressa Maria Assunta Ceppari for her help in transcribing this document. Any errors that remain are my sole responsibility.

Measurements

Money

1 *florin* = 4 *lire*   (according to conventional valuation, although in practice
                          the *lira* fluctuated against the *florin*)
1 *lira* = 20 *soldi*
1 *soldo* = 12 *denari*

Linear measurements

1 *braccio* = *c.*half a metre
1 *staio* of land = 100 *tavole* = roughly between 300 and 600 square metres

Weights

1 *moggio* = about 8 sacks or 24 *staia*
1 *staio* of oil = 10 flasks

PART I

TOPOGRAPHY AND DEMOGRAPHY

The Territory

Boundaries, Demarcations and the Politics of Land Ownership

The 1318 boundary document shows that some fifteen or so demarcation points were established between the two communes of Montalcino and Sant'Angelo in Colle on the north-western, northern and north-eastern fringes of the southern frontier castle. These demarcation points were in the main described in terms of individual proprietors of land, but some were defined in terms of ditches, streams and roads, and on at least one occasion there is a reference to a geological feature in the form of a large pointed rock. There are, in addition, a number of references to individual *contrade* within the territory of Sant'Angelo in Colle itself, many of which are described in terms of the existing landscape. From these we learn that the outer reaches of Sant'Angelo in Colle's territory consisted of the '*contrada in pede silve comunis montisalcino*', the '*contrada lame di Sant'Angelo*', the '*contrada Sotteragiolo*', the '*contrada elmagnattaio*', the '*contrada el piano dele maglie*', the '*contrada del cerreta*', and the '*contrada campuozi*'.

This was clearly a landscape of extremes: in one part marshy and possibly even waterlogged; in another, scrubland; and in yet another, dense wood. In between, there was rich arable land.[1] While it is clear that there have been changes both in the description of local landmarks and in the landscape itself, much is still recognisable. To the north and west, land that was once covered by dense forest has been cleared in order to establish a semi-industrialised vista of vineyards and olive groves. However, vestiges of forest in the area once known as 'at the foot of the wood of Montalcino' are still clearly visible at either side of the 'strada Traversa i Monti', the modern ridge road which now connects Montalcino to Sant'Angelo in Colle, before plunging down the hill towards the Orcia valley.[2] Traces of some of the old roads are also recognisable, although in some cases they have been truncated.

The 1318 boundary document indicates that a road connecting Sant'Angelo in Colle with Montalcino originally ran at a lower level than the present 'strada Traversa i Monti', and that it originally branched off from the Sesta road. It was from the Sesta road, also, that another thoroughfare pushed up towards Villa a Tolli, in the direction of Montalcino. Any tracks that existed amongst the dense holm oak and scrubland to the north-west of the village must have been narrow and more suitable for local husbandry and the tending of livestock, than passage from one settlement to another.

There seems little doubt, however, that a network of roads to the north of Sant'Angelo in Colle was created as early as the sixth century AD.[3] On the basis of the need for visual contact between the summit of one hill and another for the construction of roadways in the early Christian period, Luigi Donati and Letizia Ceccarelli suggest that a road was originally cut down towards Sant'Antimo and Villa a Tolli from a point on the ridge road in the vicinity of Poggio Civitella. At the same time another line of contact was established between the latter and Sant'Angelo in Colle. A third road was then carved out to the west down to Roselle and the sea. Donati and Ceccarelli are of the opinion that there was originally no direct link between Poggio Civitella and Montalcino, or between Poggio Civitella and Poggio alle Mura, because of the intervening thick forest and sloping land.

Before the nineteenth century and the construction of the 'strada Traversa i Monti', there was in fact no direct route between Montalcino and Sant'Angelo in Colle along the ridge, now known as the 'Passo del Lume Spento'. During the late eighteenth century, the road connecting the two settlements carved a much lower course, thus avoiding the steep pull up to the ridge. This road wound its way up from Montalcino past Podere Pioggiolo, and on towards Villa le Prata, joining two other thoroughfares – one running down to Tavernelle, and the other cutting across to Poggio la Pigna. The Tavernelle road offered the main route to the Maremma, running down towards Poggio alle Mura and Volta Salcio, before crossing the River Ombrone and thus reaching l'Osteria dei Cannicci. It seems likely that this road followed the course of a much older thoroughfare directed towards the Maremma and the maritime south-west. During the late eighteenth century, the internal route south from Montalcino branched off at Poggio Civitella in the direction of Villa a Tolli.

That a road from Siena to the Maremma skirted Montalcino on its northern and western side at the end of the thirteenth century is confirmed by an entry in the 1290 *Statuto dei Viari di Siena*.[4] Referring to a bridge that was to be made in the 'aqua de Sarlata' in the vicinity of Santa Cristina, the Sienese officials ruled that the new structure should be built on the road that went from Abbadia Ardenga to Sant'Angelo in Colle, and that the expense of its construction should be shared between the communes of Percenna, Sant'Angelo in Colle, Abbadia Ardenga, Castiglione Lungombrone and Bibbiano. This road thus clearly traced a low trajectory around Montalcino, presumably branching back towards Sant'Angelo in Colle in the vicinity of Tavernelle.

In the medieval period, the road which cut off from the ridge in the vicinity of Poggio Civitella seems first to have passed through Villa a Tolli, and then to have continued on to join the Sesta road at a point to the north-east of Sant'Angelo in Colle. The first part of this thoroughfare must have more or less followed the path traced by the existing road connecting Poggio Civitella with Villa a Tolli. No evidence now remains, however, of any continuation of that thoroughfare in the direction of Sant'Angelo in Colle. Indeed, the only clear track in the vicinity of Villa a Tolli leads down to Sant'Antimo and Castelnuovo dell'Abate. Yet it is logical that the two centres should at one time have been connected. As discussion here will show, several of the inhabitants of Villa a Tolli owned land on the borders of Sant'Angelo in Colle's territory. This, together with the physical proximity of the two villages, must have favoured the creation of tracks, if not roads, between the two settlements. According to Roberto Farinelli and Andrea Giorgi, there was indeed a *sentiero* or track running west from Castelnuovo dell'Abate towards Sant'Angelo in Colle during the early fourteenth century.[5] Although those authors probably had in mind what is now known as the Sesta road, it seems likely that a similar track once connected Villa a Tolli with Sant'Angelo in Colle. The intervening terrain, which is scoured by gorges, would clearly have favoured such a link, rather than a more formal thoroughfare. Records contained in the *Campione delle strade della Comunità di Montalcino compilato l'Anno 1778* do in fact reveal that as late as the end of the eighteenth century there was still a connecting road between Villa a Tolli and Sant'Angelo in Colle at a lower level than the present Passo del Lume Spento, or 'Traversa dei Monti'. Another road seems to have continued on in the direction of Santa Restituta.[6] It also seems clear that there was still a connection between Sant'Angelo in Colle and Villa a Tolli during the second quarter of the nineteenth century, although it was clearly in a state of disrepair. Indeed, a record in the *Circondario dell'Ingegnere* archive covering the period 1836–1837, described repair work necessary for safe and comfortable passage along the road connecting Sant'Angelo in Colle with the church at Villa a Tolli.[7] According to this record, the distance covered was 2036 *braccia*, equivalent to about one and three quarter miles.

During the medieval period the hill directly to the north of Sant'Angelo in Colle seems to have been virtually impenetrable. Indeed, the thick cover of trees may explain why the officials involved in drawing up the 1318 boundary document chose to initiate proceedings in the 'contrada in pede silve cois montisalcino'. Here, more than anywhere else, there must have been scope for confusion. Elsewhere, the boundaries of individual fields offered much clearer evidence of territorial limits.

The first half a dozen or so demarcations of the 1318 boundary document were established in the eastern part of Sant'Angelo in Colle's territory, in the area known as the *contrada lame Sci Angeli*, and in the area around the Tredine stream. But this was by no means the only stretch of water in the territory. Descriptions of the last few demarcation points in the 1318 boundary document include references to the 'Ranuccii', 'Rigagnolum' and 'Campuozi' ditches as well as to the 'contrada campuozi' to the west of the village, indicating that the Campuozi ditch was something more than a mere trickle of water.

In its northern reaches, the Tredine stream ran close to the area known as the 'Poggio de Arno', on the northern side of the Sesta road. In the fourteenth century the Tredine stream marked the western border of the commune of Castelnuovo dell'Abate. According to the 1320 *Tavola delle possessioni* it

was in this area that Bernarduccio da Seggiano owned a palace, a house, a
capanna, or shack, and a flour mill.[8] Bernarduccio presumably lived on his
mill complex, which was bordered on one side by the Tredine stream, on
another, by a road and on a third side by property belonging to the commune
of Sant'Angelo in Colle. Given the *campanalismo*[9] that even now exists in the
village of Sant'Angelo in Colle, it seems likely that Bernarduccio da Seggiano
would have been regarded as something of an outsider. Moreover, at least
one of his close neighbours probably fell into the same category. In the details
furnished on behalf of the commune of Sant'Angelo in Colle itself in the 1320
Tavola delle possessioni, there is a reference to a piece of arable land lying fallow
in the area known as Poggio Vannuccio (or Manuccio), which was bordered
on one side by a stream; on another, by land belonging to Tino of Montenero;
and on another by land belonging to Lonarduccio (sic) of Seggiano.[10] Tino,
like Bernaduccio, was clearly associated with territory beyond the confines of
the commune of Sant'Angelo in Colle, on the south side of the River Orcia. As
we shall see, such distinctions were on occasion significant, particularly in the
context of tax levied from pasture land and the movement of livestock from
one territory to another.

While no reference was made to 'Bernardo' of Seggiano in the entry
furnished on behalf of the commune of Sant'Angelo in Colle in the 1320
Tavola delle possessioni, it seems likely that the commune's fallow land abutted
Bernardo's property, and that the mill complex was thus positioned on the
so-called Poggio Vannuccio. The Tredine stream presumably provided the
power for the mill, whilst the slope of Poggio Vannuccio accelerated the flow
of water. Land to the north-west of Bernardo of Seggiano's property was
clearly somewhat rough. This section of Sant'Angelo in Colle's territory was
known as the *contrada fra le macchie*. Given its toponym, it seems likely that
much of the land here was covered with low bush-like vegetation unsuitable
for the location of a mill powered by water, and probably not appropriate
either for the cultivation of crops or the rearing of livestock. It seems unlikely,
also, that there could have been any abundance of vines or olives in this area.
To the south of the Sesta road, however, the terrain changed dramatically.
According to the 1318 document, this was the area known as the *contrada lame
Sci Angeli*, the marsh of Sant'Angelo. Given the reference to marshland, there
seems little doubt that at least some parts of the land traversed by the Tredine
stream were waterlogged during early spring. However, throughout the drier
summer months, this part of the territory no doubt turned into lush pasture.
Despite the increasing lines of vines, there is still some evidence of rolling
meadowland suitable for the pasturing of cattle and sheep on the eastern
side of the village. The eastern stretches of the territory may thus have been
regarded as particularly important, both for the residents of Sant'Angelo in
Colle and for the Sienese government. It is perhaps no coincidence, therefore,
that the officials responsible for drawing up the 1318 boundary document
started on the eastern side of the village. Nor is it perhaps surprising that
they took particular care to establish the identity of those individuals who

not only controlled this side of the territory, but who also owned dairy land appropriate for the production of milk, cheese, meat and wool vital for the general well-being of the medieval village. As will become clear, several landowners on the eastern borders had outside connections. It was thus perhaps not coincidental that it was the commune of Sant'Angelo in Colle itself that owned land pushing up against that belonging to Bernardo of Seggiano and Tino of Montenero.

The political affiliations of those established on the borders of any territory could clearly impact on both internal and external affairs. In some senses, landowners in the outer reaches might be regarded as pioneers. During those times when Sant'Angelo in Colle was under threat or even invaded, such individuals may have felt that they and their property were on the front line. They may even have been seen as holding the line. It is probably significant, however, that several of the individuals recorded as owning property on the borders of Sant'Angelo in Colle's territory in the early fourteenth century were not local residents. The 1318 boundary document reveals that there were a number of contiguous areas on the eastern border that could have given rise to a conflict of interests, since they were all owned by residents of Villa a Tolli. Far from feeling threatened by owning land on what might be a disputed border, such proprietors may have considered themselves to be in a privileged position, continually edging forward into disputed territory. At the very least, they must also, on occasion, have been intent on expanding their own individual holdings. As already suggested, such manoeuvres may not always have been in the interests of the Republic of Siena, particularly where the landowner might claim immunity from Sienese taxes, by dint of having residence outside Siena's jurisdiction. This was presumably the case for 'Albicini Iohannis', 'Neri Ciantis' and 'Petruccio Ciatti', all of whom were residents of nearby Villa a Tolli, and all of whom, according to the 1318 boundary document held land on the eastern borders of Sant'Angelo in Colle's territory.

The *fossatellus*, or ditch, at the lower end of the 'contrada lame di Sant'Angelo' was named as the first demarcation line in the 1318 boundary document. A straight line drawn from this ditch defined the edges of a field belonging to the first individual, 'Albicini Iohannis'. The field at the far end of this belonged to 'Neri Ciantis', and that on the other side of Albicini's property belonged to 'Petruccio Ciatti', or Ciacci. All of these proprietors may have been regarded as potentially hostile to the Sienese government, since they were answerable not to Sant'Angelo in Colle, but to the commune of Montalcino. As such, and certainly prior to Montalcino's final subjugation, they would have been under no obligation to respect Sienese legislation. In addition, many of the individuals cited as residents of Villa a Tolli were interrelated. They thus affected a strong (and 'outside') family nexus that was a potential threat to neighbouring landowners affiliated with Sant'Angelo in Colle.

The 1320 *Tavola delle possessioni* reveals that landowners from Villa a Tolli clustered together in adjacent plots, as if to compound their presence in the adjacent subject Sienese commune. It also shows that these 'outsiders' clung to the outer reaches on the eastern side of Sant'Angelo in Colle's territory. The field belonging to 'Albicini Iohannis', or Albicino di Giovanni in the 'contrada lame Sant'Angelo' was clearly situated on the farthest extremes of the frontier castle's eastern border, since a neighbouring plot is described as belonging to the adjacent commune of Castelnuovo dell'Abate.[11] Measuring some eight and a half *staia*, Albicino's land was located in the area known as 'Poggio', and was described as *terre labor* (worked, or agricultural land). It was the only piece of land owned by Albicino in the territory of Sant'Angelo in Colle. Property belonging to Albicino's neighbour, 'Nerius Ciantis', or Nerio di Cianti, or Ciacci, in the area known as 'Quercis', was likewise described as worked, or agricultural land.[12] Neighbouring plots to Nerio's land are recorded as belonging to the heirs of Nerio di Orlandini (who are also mentioned as neighbours to the land belonging to Albicino), Albicino di Giovanni, and – once again – the *curia*, or community of Castelnuovo dell'Abate. It seems clear from this that the two areas of 'Poggio' and 'Quercis' were either adjacent, or in one and the same area which was known locally by a number of different names. A close reading of the 1320 *Tavola delle possessioni* for Sant'Angelo in Colle confirms this. While Nerio di Cianti (or Ciacci), in acknowledging the heirs of Nerio di Orlandini as neighbours, referred to his own property as being in the area known as 'Quercis', the heirs of Nerio di Orlandini for their part described their land as being at 'Quercus Ubertis'. Thus 'Quercis' and 'Quercus Ubertis' were presumably interchangeable terms for land that, together with the area known as 'Poggio', was in the *contrada* 'lame di Sant'Angelo'.

There seems little doubt that the heirs of Nerio di Orlandino, like Albicino and Nerio di Cianti (or Ciacci), were all residents of Villa a Tolli, rather than Sant'Angelo in Colle.[13] However, unlike Albicino and Nerio, the former group of individuals seems to have established a foothold in a number of places. Of the three clans, the heirs of Nerio di Orlandini must have presented the strongest outside presence. There are references to two pieces of worked land at 'Plebis a Sexte' (the Pieve at Sesta); three pieces of worked land in the area known as 'Quercus Ubertis'; two pieces of worked land in the area known as 'Poggio Vannucci'; and yet another in an area known as 't(?l)anis' (possibly 'lamis', or marsh). One of the plots of land in the area known as 'Quercus Ubertis' was described as marshy meadowland, confirming that this area, in particular, was suitable for the pasturing of livestock. This land was bordered on one side by a road, on another by property belonging to 'Neri' or 'Nerio Ciacci' (sic), on another by property belonging to another 'outsider', the Sienese resident Neri di Guicciardo, and on a final side by property belonging to Albicino 'from Villa a Tolli' – presumably the Albicino di Giovanni recorded in the 1318 boundary document.[14]

All these individuals must also have realised that their political affiliations were different from those of neighbouring resident landowners associated with the commune of Sant'Angelo in Colle. Such a conflict of interests must at the very least have created an atmosphere of edginess, which would not have gone unnoticed by Sienese officials. At the very least, they must have paid attention to the identities of those landowners whose properties abutted land belonging to the residents of Villa a Tolli.

In this context, it is interesting to note that the seventh and eight demarcation points established between Sant'Angelo in Colle and Montalcino in the 1318 boundary document were recorded as the confines of land close to the designated eastern borders that was owned by a local woman from Sant'Angelo in Colle – Mita, wife of Minuccio di Banduccio. As we shall see, Mita was a wealthy woman in her own right. Indeed, according to the 1320 *Tavola delle possessioni*, Mita was the richest female in the early fourteenth-century village. Mita's land – a field close to the Tredine ditch on the eastern borders of Sant'Angelo in Colle's territory – was hemmed in by 'outsiders'. According to the 1320 *Tavola delle possessioni* Monna Mita's field was bordered on one side by a field belonging to Naldino di Nuto (an individual who is not mentioned in the *Tavola*, and who was thus presumably not a local resident). Naldino's field was in turn bordered by land belonging to Grati, or Gratio di Nuccio (also not mentioned in 1320 *Tavola delle possessioni*). On yet another side, Naldino's field was bordered by land belonging to the heirs of an individual referred to solely as Ciatis, or Ciatti, but who was most probably another resident of Villa a Tolli, and perhaps a relation of Nerio di Ciacci. According to the 1318 boundary document, the field belonging to the heirs of Ciatti provided a ninth demarcation point. This field ran at right angles to yet another field belonging to Naldino di Nuto, which was located within the *contrada fra le macchie*. One end of Naldino di Nuto's field was bordered by a road that connected Sant'Angelo in Colle with Villa aTolli. It was in this second field belonging to Naldino di Nuto, that a tenth boundary was fixed.

With neighbours such as these, Domina Mita may well have considered herself to be at the cutting edge. Moreover, for Mita, holding property on the confines of the territory must have presented a number of challenges. Not only was she surrounded by landowners with affiliations to another commune, and with interests that were no doubt contrary to those of the Sienese officials who controlled her own commune of Sant'Angelo in Colle. She was also, to all intents and purposes and despite being married, a lone female landowner in a male-dominated society. However, as we shall see in Chapter 5, Domina Mita's roots in such a society may well have been well established. It seems clear that by 1320 Domina Mita owned a vast amount of land, much of it apparently passed down by way of inheritance from her father, Piero Pecoraio. As discussion in Chapter 5 will attempt to show, Mita di Piero Pecoraio's ancestors could well have played a significant part in the affairs of Sant'Angelo in Colle, not least through their control of a broad swathe of land in the eastern territory but also through their ownership of a castellated farmhouse or tower there.

The final set of boundaries in the 1318 document was drawn up in the area to the north and north-west of Sant'Angelo in Colle. One is described somewhat tortuously as being fixed 'at right angles from the road towards a cross road at the top end of the roads leading from Sant'Angelo in Colle towards Villa a

Tolli and towards the territory of Montalcino'. At this point, reference was also made to the *contrada el piano dele maglie*, indicating that the land in the north-eastern part of the territory flattened out from the undulating scrubland of the *contrada fra le macchie* into a plain. The other demarcation point was drawn up in the vicinity of the wood of Montalcino and the nearby 'contrada del cerreta'. Once again, it becomes clear that land on the edges of Sant'Angelo in Colle's territory belonged to 'outsiders'. We learn, for example, that 'Chelis Feduccii' (Chele di Feduccio) and 'Perucci Diezonelli' (Peruccio di (?)Azzonelli) were joint owners of a stretch of woodland adjacent to the wood of Montalcino, and that their land was bordered at its lower end by property belonging to the commune of Sant'Angelo in Colle.[15] At least one of these two landowners, Chele di Feduccio, had connections with the commune of Montalcino, since he was recorded as being a resident of Villa a Tolli. 'Peruccio Diezonelli', the co-owner, was also possibly from Villa a Tolli. He was certainly not a resident of Sant'Angelo in Colle a couple of years later, since he does not figure in the 1320 *Tavola delle possessioni*.

It becomes clear from cross-references between the boundary document and entries in the 1320 *Tavola delle possessioni* that a number of residents of Villa a Tolli had interests on the western side of Sant'Angelo in Colle's territory. One landed possession along the demarcation line on this side of the village is described, for example, as belonging to the heirs of 'Feducci di Tolle'. The likelihood is that this group of individuals was related to Chele di Feduccio. If that were the case, members of the same family from Villa a Tolli would have exerted an influence on at least two of Sant'Angelo in Colle's borders. In fact, in tracing the borders between the two communes of Sant'Angelo in Colle and Montalcino in 1318 it becomes clear that residents of Villa a Tolli owned land to the east, north, north-west and west of Sant'Angelo in Colle's territory in the early fourteenth century. They thus presumably occupied a political niche as intermediaries not only between Montalcino and Sant'Angelo in Colle on the northern and north-western fringes of Sant'Angelo in Colle's territory, but also between Sant'Angelo in Colle and its own neighbour on its eastern and south-eastern borders, Castelnuovo dell'Abate.

It presumably did not go unnoticed by the Sienese that much of the terrain on the borders of their southern frontier castle lay in the hands of 'outsiders'. No doubt, they would also have noted that much of the land that was owned by residents of Villa a Tolli was bunched together. The presence of so many landowners answerable to the commune of Montalcino must have been unsettling. Far from being isolated and vulnerable on the less patrolled edges of the territory, such landowners may, in fact, have been engaged in territorial expansions that, over time, could have benefited the commune of Montalcino, rather than the Republic of Siena. As such they were a force to be reckoned with. Indeed, there may be a connection between this and the fact that other 'outsiders' – but this time from Siena – are recorded as owning property in the same areas as the residents from Villa a Tolli. According to the 1320 *Tavola delle possessioni*, several of the properties on the western side of Sant'Angelo in

Colle belonged to the wealthy Sienese citizen Neri di Guicciardo da Civitella. Indeed, it may be no coincidence that Neri di Guicciardo's lands on both the eastern and the western side of Sant'Angelo in Colle's territory were positioned in close proximity to those belonging to Villa a Tolli residents.

It is not improbable that the Sienese sought to balance such outside influence by persuading its own citizens to acquire land in the vicinity of that owned by the residents of Villa a Tolli. As at Castelfranco di Paganico, Sienese citizens may have been encouraged to invest in land in sensitive parts of the territory of Sant'Angelo in Colle, as well as assuming key administrative positions and acquiring property within the walls of the village itself. Surviving records concerning developments elsewhere indicate that such jostling and appropriation on the part of Sienese citizens was part of a deliberate policy of policing subject communes.

Tax records filed in respect of the city of Siena confirm that not only Sienese residents, but also Sienese institutions had already established footholds in a number of different parts of the territory of Sant'Angelo in Colle by the early fourteenth century. Not all of the pieces of land owned by these 'outsiders' were in the same place, although as we shall see it was often the case that land belonging to one Sienese 'outsider' bordered that of another. This would clearly have made sense if, as argued here, the sub-text was not only to establish a presence in the garrison's territory, but also to secure all borders.

According to the 1320 *Tavola delle possessioni*, the Sienese hospital of Santa Maria della Scala already possessed some 20 or so plots of land in the vicinity of Sant'Angelo in Colle, as well as at least one building inside the walls of the village which may have functioned as its first *grancia*, or clearing house.

Description of property	Location and description of neighbours or neighbouring property	Page no. or nos, ASS, *Estimo* 24
house	[next to Mutuis Orlandi[1] and Nardi (Nardellus Venture]	301v, 347v
land	Campo Guarnini (?Giovanni) [next to arable land belonging to Nardellus Venture]	347r
land	Collesorbi [next to fallow land with woodland belonging to Petrutius Bonanni]	376r
land	Fonte Collesi [next to partially fallow arable land belonging to Angelinus Guerre]	4r
land	Fossato Castellano [next to arable land belonging to the heirs of Bini]	184r
land	Fossechoi [next to arable land belonging to the heirs of Romaiuoli (?)Romanioli]	200v
land	Lamis Manti(?Manenti) [next to fallow arable land belonging to Landus Pepi]	267r
land	Maciaroti (?Maciareti) [next to arable land belonging to Naldus Jacomi]	351r

Table 1.1 Property belonging to the Sienese hospital of Santa Maria della Scala in and around Sant'Angelo in Colle as recorded in the 1320 *Tavola delle possessioni*[1]

land	Manganelli [one piece next to arable land belonging to the commune of Sant'Angelo in Colle; what was probably a second plot in the same area next to fallow arable land belonging to Landutius Giontarelli]	63r, 264r
land	Mori 'aterpi' [next to arable land belonging to Martinutuis Ensegne]	315r
land	Planeze [next to arable land belonging to Ser Tollus Gholli; what was probably a second plot in the same area next to fallow land and woodland belonging to Vanutuis Massaie]	408r, 440r
land	Poggio Peri [next to arable and woodland belonging to the heirs of Cecchi Pieri]	176r
land	Prete Schiace [next to fallow land belonging to the Commune of Sant'Angelo in Colle]	60r
land	Saporoia [next to vineyards belonging to Angelinus Bucci and Nardus Cambii, Maffuccia Bencivenne and Petrutius Bonnani; what was probably a second plot next to arable land belonging to Cecchinus Ghezzi; what may have been a third plot next to arable land belonging to the heirs of Nerii Rubei and to Mina Gianis and fallow arable land belonging to Lonardutius Johannis]	1v, 72r, 206r, 275r, 312r, 327r, 349r, 376v
land	Sesta [next to arable land belonging to the Heredes Altimanni]	194r
land	(Oliveto di Sesta) [next to arable land belonging to Landus Pepi]	266r
land	Torre Assonini [next to arable land belonging to Landus Gionte; what may have been a second plot next to a mixture of arable and woodland belonging to Naccinus Giordanelli; what may have been a third plot next to arable land belonging to Vannutuis Massaie]	272v, 355r, 441r
land	Tredine [next to fallow land belonging to the church of San Pietro; what may have been a second plot next to arable land belonging to Marrutuis Angelelli]	133r, 304r
land	(Piano Tredine) [next to arable land belonging to the Heredes Peruccii Assalti and to Ulivutius Johannis]	258r, 431v

Note to Table 1.1

1   Cross references between a number of entries in the 1320 *Tavola delle possessioni* do in fact confirm that only one structure was owned by the Sienese hospital of Santa Maria della Scala inside the walls at that date, and that this was positioned close to the water conduit. According to 'Mutuis Orlandi', his property was bordered on a second side by a road, on a third side by property belonging to 'Avitoli Aldobrandini' (?Ildibrandini), and on a fourth side by property inhabited by 'Nardi Ve(n)ture'. Avitoli Ildobrandini for his part (ASS, *Estimo* 24, fol. 6r) is recorded as owning property inside the walls that was bordered on one side by a road, on another by property inhabited by 'Mucci (Mutuis) Orlandi', and on a third side by property inhabited by 'Nardi Venture'. 'Nardellus' (sic) Venture's property is recorded as bordered on a second side by 'd(omi)ne Mite Pieri', and on a third side by

the water conduit. In the entry for the house inhabited by 'Mona Mita' (ASS, *Estimo* 24, fol. 330r) reference is made to two roads that bordered her property, to property owned by 'Nardi Venture', and to the water conduit.

Analysis

As the note to Table 1.1 shows, and despite the fact that different proprietors were named in respect of neighbouring structures, it seems likely that references to property belonging to the hospital of Santa Maria della Scala inside the walls of Sant'Angelo in Colle in 1320 concerned one and the same building. It seems likely that the land owned by the hospital in the surrounding territory was for the most part arable, with perhaps one or two lines of vines and a few patches of woodland.

The much smaller Sienese hospital of Mona Agnese is recorded as owning only three pieces of land in the territory of Sant'Angelo in Colle.[16] The Augustinian friars of Sant'Agostino in Siena for their part, whilst owning a huge amount of land in various parts of the Sienese *contado*, are also recorded as owning a number of properties inside and outside the walls of Sant'Angelo in Colle, including a large land holding with a building to the south-east, and a vineyard at 'planeti' (possibly, Pianezze, to the east of the village).[17]

But by far the largest Sienese landowner at Sant'Angelo in Colle in 1320 was Neri di Guicciardo. As well as acquiring arable land there, Neri di Guicciardo is also recorded as owning a large number of vineyards. According to Neri's own tax record, his agricultural land was scattered all over the territory of the southern garrison. Thus there were references to 'Agresta', 'Aiale', 'Asperio', 'Bagnolo', 'Campaie', 'Capratesis', 'Colle', 'Colle de Pantano', 'Collesorbi', 'Fonte Chinelli', 'Fonte Illato' (?Fontilatro), 'Fossati Merce Maiore', 'Fossati Porcis', 'Infernale', 'Infinilla', 'Iusteria', 'Lame Fornelle', 'Lama Parete', 'Lamasterino', 'Lame Corbole', 'Lamone', 'Lamore' (?'Lamone'), 'Lato', 'Leccio', 'Lubertinis', 'Macereti', 'Manganelli', 'Mareuchi' (?'Marrucca'), 'Montanina', 'Montegiano' (?'Monteiano'), 'Pescaia', 'Plano Orce', 'Plano Pantani', 'Plano Ripalette', 'Poggio Cancelli', 'Poggio Castiglione', 'Poggio Peschai', 'Prioracti', 'Pterosis', 'Puteo', 'Querceti', 'Quercis Uberti', 'Querciuolo', 'Ripatente', 'Roccheggiani', 'Saporoia', 'Sesta', 'Sitinus' (?Cetine, ?Citinale), 'Speltale' (?'Spuntale'), 'Stopielli', 'Sugarella', 'Torris Assonini', 'Trafossatella', 'Tredine', 'Val de Burlengnie (?'Brulenghi'), 'Valdemetata', 'Vallis Secche' and 'Vallo Gellese'.[18] By contrast, almost all of Neri di Guicciardo's vineyards were situated to the south and west of Sant'Angelo in Colle. Four of Neri's properties were at 'Collemattone'; three at 'Cigliori'; three at 'Capanne'; one at 'Fonterenza'; three at 'Ferrale'; one at 'Frabbiche' (or Fabbriche); one at 'Fontis delicate'; one at 'Romate'; one at 'San Biagio'; three at 'Saporoia'; one at 'Pianezze'; one in the area known as 'ospedale', and another outside the gate known as the 'Porta Maggiore'. The toponyms alone indicate Neri di Guicciardo's presence on the hills, in the valleys, amongst the marshland, near the springs of water, in the plain, close to the ditches and even in the woods.

A detailed consideration of Neri di Guicciardo's landed possessions in the territory of Sant'Angelo in Colle confirms that different parts of the terrain were favoured for particular kinds of cultivation. It becomes clear, for example, that a large number of vines were grown on the southern and south-western side of the village whilst there was, by contrast, a concentration of cereal crops to the east. Analysis of the rateable values of individual pieces of land owned by Neri di Guicciardo also opens up questions about the evaluation of land in the vicinity of the garrison. Logically, one would expect to find a direct relationship between the size of individual plots of land and their estimated values. This was indeed the case with many of the plots of arable land owned by Neri that were small, measuring only a few *staia*, and that were valued at less than one *lire*. However, it becomes clear that the price per *staio* could vary from one locality to another, and even within the same area. In such cases, the size of the plot of land was clearly not the only factor. Other factors such as the quality of the land, or its precise location and orientation may have been more important.

In some cases, the variations in value recorded in the 1320 *Tavola delle possessioni* are startling. One piece of arable and woodland measuring 46 *staia* in the area known as 'Renai de Rotta sui T(?r)edine' was estimated at 2 *lire* and 6 *soldi*, indicating a value of 1 *soldo* per *staio*.[19] By contrast, another plot of arable and woodland in the area known as 'Ficaiuolo' measuring six and a half a *staia* was estimated at 10 *soldi*, indicating a value of nearly 2 *soldi* per *staio*.[20] Similar variations are reflected in the evaluation of property owned by Neri di Guicciardo at Sant'Angelo in Colle. His plot at Poggio Peschaia, which measured 45 *staia*, appears to have been particularly valuable, being estimated at 116 *lire*, indicating a value of some 3 *lire* per *staio*. By contrast, that at Capanna was estimated at only just over 2 *lire* per *staio*. There were similar variations in the value of land owned by Neri di Guicciardo that was laid down to vines. Thus, one vineyard in the area known as 'Cilgliore' measuring something over half a *staio* was estimated at 11 *soldi*, whilst another in the same locality measuring over three and a half *staia*, was estimated at the much higher sum of 9 *lire* and 13 *soldi*.[21] Elsewhere, a vineyard measuring nearly one and a half *staia* in the area known as Capanna was valued at 2 *lire* and 13 *soldi*; whereas another at Ferrale measuring some five and a quarter *staia* was recorded as having a value of 26 *lire* and 12 *soldi*, representing a mark-up of some 300 per cent.[22]

There could have been any number of reasons for such variations, ranging from the quality of earth in individual plots, to the position of the land, the direction of the wind, the degree of sunlight, and even the length of time the land had been cultivated. All these factors could have been relevant in the planting, working and harvesting of cereal crops. But, given that the land itself was appropriate for the raising of crops, only the working of it would have been harder or easier (requiring more or less attention) as a result of the terrain being stony, shaded, on various levels, or having any number of other disadvantages. A number of small parcels of arable land scattered around the territory could in theory have yielded as much grain as a smaller number of larger plots. But in any event, the landscape surrounding medieval Sant'Angelo in Colle must have presented a patchwork of individual land holdings following infinite divisions of real estate through inheritance.

In the case of vineyards, certain conditions were prerequisite not only to the healthy growth of the plant itself, but also to the eventual yield and quality of the grapes. A south-facing, well-drained plot of land would always have been regarded as preferable, if not essential. While vines could obviously be grown on any plot of land, they were less likely to thrive away from the sun, and as a consequence the yield of fruit would have been small and the quality of wine poor. It is possible therefore that the differences in estimated value of the vineyards belonging to Neri di Guicciardo depended not so much on the size, but as to whether they were sited in better, or less propitious positions. On this basis, it would appear that the land in the vicinity of the area known as Ferrale was considered the best for vines. Of course, size may also have played its part. Neri di Guicciardo's land at Ferrale was considerably larger than plots containing vines at Cegliore and elsewhere. This may well have increased the overall value of the Ferrale vineyard, since there would have been economies in both the growing and the harvesting. Long lines of healthy vines established on well-drained, south-facing soil would clearly have yielded more, and better quality grapes than short lines established on less appropriate terrain.

While the selection of land in different parts of the territory of Sant'Angelo in Colle by Sienese 'outsiders' such as Neri di Guicciardo may thus have been prompted as much by the quality and position of the land as by political necessity, it may also have been influenced by the prospect of spin-offs from quite different factors. One such factor was the *transumanza*. This was the seasonal practice of moving large numbers of livestock down from the mountains to the lush low-lying Maremma meadows at the beginning of the winter season, and back again to the high pastures in the spring.[23] Tradition has it that land in the vicinity of the Sesta road was used for the *transumanza* from the high lands around Florence, Arezzo and Perugia. There were, in fact, three main *transumanza* routes down to the Maremma from Arezzo: one passing through Montepulciano; another through San Quirico; and a third through Cinigiano on the southern side of the Orcia River.[24]

Another three routes to the south of Siena passed through Paganico, Montepescali and Massa Marittima. This being the case, it seems unlikely that the Sesta road served as a *tratturro*, or main *transumanza* thoroughfare. If the Sesta road was involved at all, it is more likely that it was used as a *tratturello*, or cross-route. Sant'Angelo in Colle's position, north of the River Orcia and east of the Ombrone River could have served as a useful cross-transit point, with the additional prospect of hospitality along the way. Moreover, the land to the east of Sant'Angelo in Colle and south of the Sesta road would clearly have been attractive as a stopping off place during the long transit of herds of sheep and cattle, because of its lush meadows. It would also have been convenient for those driving livestock along the route from Arezzo that is known to have passed through Castelnuovo dell'Abate, before dipping down into the Orcia valley. Sant'Angelo in Colle could also have offered a limited amount of pastureland in the vicinity of the village, itself. As recently as the early twentieth century a number of plots of land abutting the track that skirts the village before forking off to meet the 'strada vicinale di Monteano' were still designated for such purposes (nos 210, 211, 213, 219 and 220 on the 1820 *Catasto* map).

Diagram 1.1
Transumanza routes
in the territory
around and to the
south of Siena

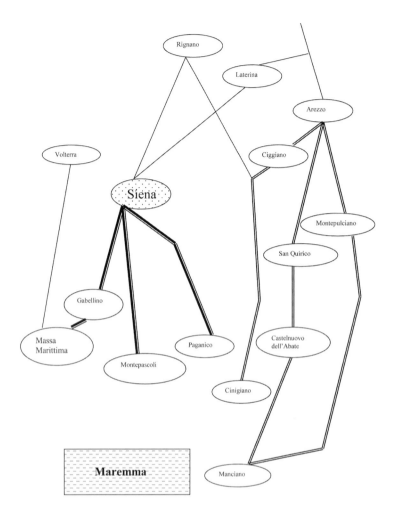

Such plots would have offered ideal grazing land not only for local livestock, but also for small groups of cattle and sheep driven along an east–west *tratturello* at the time of the *transumanza*. Their location close to the village walls would also have offered drovers anxious to stock up on victuals, as well as offloading cheese and milk, the rare comfort of bed and board, whilst knowing that their livestock were comparatively safe.

The financial spin-offs of the *transumanza* were complex and in many cases related. Clearly, money was to be made through the sale of dairy produce all along the route. On occasion, drovers also sold off individual animals.[25] Both transactions involved contact with centres of habitation. Both transactions no doubt also involved deviation from the main *tratturo*. In each case, also, individual drovers may have boosted local economies by purchasing goods for their own onward journey. But the practice of *transumanza* also prompted fiscal attention from cities with jurisdiction over wide areas of territory. By

Figure 1.1   Nineteenth-century *Catasto* map of Sant'Angelo in Colle and surrounding territory (detail) Archivio di Stato, Siena, *Catasto*, Mappa Montalcino, Sezione M, di 'Sant: Angelo in Colle', no. 32a

the early fourteenth century Siena was levying tax not only on the transport of livestock through its southern *contado*, but also on the sale of animals on the way down to the Maremma.[26] Levies on the use of land for pasture by herds of sheep, or droves of cattle in transit were also established at a relatively early date.[27] At the same time, certain exemptions were established in respect of local herds. On 14 March 1357/8 a deliberation reached by the *Concistoro* or 'Consiglio del Popolo' concerning Castel di Magliano, decreed that each head of family resident in that district should be able to maintain 20 *bestie grosse* (cattle) and 150 'delle minute' (goats and sheep) without having to pay any pasturing rights, so long as the livestock was their own.[28] The stricture that livestock should be locally owned is significant. Magliano is mentioned in the context of the transit of herds towards pastures in the vicinity of Albegna in the 1418 *Statuto della Dogana dei Paschi*.[29] The pastures of Albegna were in effect a gateway, since on 15 January of each year the lands there were officially opened to *transumanza* traffic, and from then on livestock could be put to pasture not only at Albegna, but also throughout the rest of the southern territory belonging to Siena.[30] Prior to that official opening there must have been a great massing of livestock in the vicinity of Albegna. The opportunities for saving and even evading tax through the mingling of livestock with that owned by local inhabitants in Magliano must thus have seemed attractive. That such practice had existed is reflected in the fact that it was deemed necessary to include specific stipulations in respect of local ownership in the

1418 statute. Other attempts to evade tax were probably made at different stages along the route, no doubt with mutual benefit.

Pastureland along a connecting *tratturello* such as the Sesta road – even if not used as a major transit route – could have constituted a rich source of revenue not only for the central Sienese government, but also for individuals owning land close to the *transumanza* routes. Both parties could in effect claim pasture 'levies'. While the Sienese officials collected monetary dues (according to the 1418 statute to be paid before the direction of livestock towards the pastures)[31], individual landowners along the way (such as Neri di Guicciardo) could hope to acquire payment through the right to pasture, as well as new livestock and fresh dairy produce (no doubt on occasion on the basis of the mutual benefits arising from the availability of pastureland). There seems little doubt that the practice of paying for the right to pasture was well established. As early as May 1222, the rector of Santa Maria della Scala was involved in discussion with Bernardino of Cinigiano about the rates he would charge for allowing the hospital's livestock to graze on his land.[32] While this livestock may not have been in transit towards the Maremma, the evidence of payment for the right to pasture is clear.

Quite apart from the seasonal influx of livestock caused by the *transumanza* and the financial opportunities this provided, ownership of pasture land was clearly advantageous, not only in terms of the individual's own livestock but also in terms of subletting to third parties. Pasturing was not necessarily limited, either, to areas of lush meadows. Agricultural land, when lying fallow, was also opened up for grazing.[33] Individual entries in the 1320 *Tavola delle possessioni* for Sant'Angelo in Colle indicate that at any one time a considerable percentage of the territory fell into that category. Where a system of rotation of crops was in operation, there was thus ample opportunity for the levying of pasture payment even in those situations where only a few plots of land were owned. For individuals such as Neri di Guicciardo, with his vast holdings of land, the potential recompense in each year was high.

As we shall see, Neri di Guicciardo, as well as owning large swathes of land in the vicinity of Sant'Angelo in Colle, also owned a considerable amount of property inside the walls of the village itself. Indeed, the location of a number of buildings belonging to Neri in the vicinity of the Sienese barracks suggests that he may have been intent on guarding his government's interests not only in land on the borders of the frontier castle's territory, but also inside the garrison itself. All in all, Neri di Guicciardo must have been well placed to control local events. Detailed consideration is given to the location of Neri di Guicciardo's property inside Sant'Angelo in Colle in Chapter 3, but first a word about the general character of the urban fabric and its immediate environs in the early fourteenth century.

Notes

1   In this context, see Giovanni Cherubini (ed.), *Signori, contadini, borghesi.*
    Ricerche sulla società italiana del Basso Medioevo (Florence, 1974), p. 275, where
    the author attempts a percentage assessment of the amount of agricultural,
    wooded and land laid out with vines existing in the vicinity of Prata and
    Montepescali. See also Roberto Farinelli and Andrea Giorgi, 'Radicondoli:
    società e territorio in una 'curia' attraverso la "Tavola delle Possessioni" ',
    in Costanza Cucini (ed.), *Radicondoli. Storia e Archeologia di un comune senese*
    (Rome, 1990), pp. 363–65, for an analysis of the value of different kinds of
    land in the vicinity of Radicondoli.

2   According to Ugo Ricci (*Sant'Angelo in Colle: Appendice* (typescript, 1989), p. 16)
    the ridge road between Montalcino and Sant'Angelo in Colle was constructed
    in 1777, and traced a course from the Porta Fortezza at Montalcino via the
    Chiesa di Osticcio to San Lazzaro, and then on past the Poggio della Croce
    in the vicinity of the Cappucins at Sargaiuolo, to Podere Casaccia and land
    belonging to the Cosatti and the Ciaia, before finally reaching the 'Chiusa', or
    dead end effected by property belonging to Maria Margherita Lucattini in the
    area known as Piano del Fontone. For the original documentation concerning
    the construction of roads in the vicinity of Montalcino during the late
    eighteenth century, see Archivio Storico del Comune di Montalcino (hereafter
    ACM), Archivio Preunitario (1361–1865), *Circondario dell' Ingegnere*, 1690,
    Campione delle strade della Comunità di Montalcino compilato l'Anno 1778
    dal provveditore di Strade Giuseppe Canali a forme del Nuovo Regolamento
    … Del 2 Giugno 1777 (hereafter *Circondario dell'Ingegnere*, 1690), [*Strade di S.*
    Angelo in Colle and *Strada della Villa a Tolli*]. Discussions were still continuing in
    respect of the development of the so-called 'Traversa dei Monti' during the early
    nineteenth century, see ACM, *Circondario dell'Ingegnere*, 1628, in a record dated
    29 November, 1823.

3   Luigi Donati and Letizia Ceccarelli, 'Poggio Civitella', in Alfio Cortonesi and
    Alba Pagani (eds), *Ilcinensia: Nuove ricerche per la storia di Montalcino e del suo*
    territorio (Rome, Manziana, 2004), pp. 15–36. For other considerations of early
    networks of transport in the vicinity of Sant'Angelo in Colle and Montalcino,
    see Elisabetta Mangani, 'L'orientalizzante recente nella valle dell'Ombrone',
    AION, Naples, 12 (1990), pp. 9–21. See also Stefano Campana, 'Ricognizione
    archeologica del territorio di Montalcino: risultati preliminari', *Ilcinensia: Nuove*
    ricerche: pp. 37–63, for a consideration of the main east–west and west–east
    transits established along the Orcia valley during the medieval period, in one
    direction towards the Maremma, and in the other, back up over the ridge of La
    Foce in order, eventually, to reach Chiusi.

4   See Thomas Szabò 'La rete stradale del contado di Siena. Legislazione statutaria
    e amministrazione comunale del Ducento', *Mélanges de l'École Francaise de Rome*,
    87 (1975), pp. 141–86 and 'Il tessuto viario minore e gli statuti della Valdorcia', in
    Alfio Cortonesi (ed.), *La Val d'Orcia nel medioevo e nei primi secoli dell'età moderna*,
    Atti del Convegno internazionale di studi storici, Pienza, 15–18 settembre 1988
    (Rome, 1990) (hereafter *La Val d'Orcia*), pp. 155–78. See also by the same author
    Comuni e politica stradale in Toscana e in Italia nel Medioevo (Bologna, 1992); and
    Donatella Ciampoli and Thomas Szabò (eds), *Viabilità e legislazione di uno Stato*
    cittadino del Duecento. Lo Statuto dei Viari di Siena (Siena, 1992); and Italo Moretti
    and Renato Stopani, *Romanico Senese* (Florence, 1981), and especially pages 15–18
    for the exact course of the nine principal roads south of Siena.

5   Roberto Farinelli and Andrea Giorgi, 'La "Tavola delle Possessioni" come

fonte per lo Studio del territorio: l'esempio di Castelnuovo dell'Abate', in Alfio
Cortonesi (ed.), *La Valdorcia nel Medioevo e nei primi secoli dell'Età moderna*, Atti del
convegno internazionale di studi storici, Pienza, 15–18 settembre 1988 (Rome,
1990), pp. 213–56 (238–9).

6   ACM, *Circondario dell' Ingegnere*, 1690 [*Strade di S. Angelo in Colle* and *Strada della
Villa a Tolli*].

7   ACM, *Circondario dell'Ingegnere*, 1693, no. 57.

8   ASS, *Estimo* 24, fol. 38r. The fact that no house inside the walls of Sant'Angelo
in Colle is recorded as belonging to Bernarduccio da Seggiano in the 1320 *Tavola
delle possessioni* might seem to imply that he was associated with the settlement
on the slopes of Monte Amiata across the river Orcia. He is, however, referred to
in the *Tavola delle possessioni* index as 'nunc de Sco Angelo i(n) Colle', indicating
that he had in fact transferred to the territory of Sant'Angelo in Colle.

9   Meaning within the sound of one's own bells.

10 ASS, *Estimo* 24, fol. 62r.

11 Ibid., fol. 9r.

12 Ibid., fol. 365r.

13 Ibid., fols 210r–210v.

14 Ibid., fol. 210r.

15 Ibid., fol. 88r.

16 Ibid., fols 117r (Pellentieri), 166r (Collesorbe) and 362r (Fossatellus alcoi).

17 ASS, *Estimo di Siena*, 109, fol. CXXVI (pencil no. 26).

18 Ibid., *Estimo di Siena*, 106, fols CLXXVI–CCI (pencil nos 50–75v) I am grateful to
Alessandra Severini and Ivalda Severini for their help in identifying and locating
many of the place names recorded in the 1320 *Tavola delle possessioni*. Further
consideration is given to Neri di Guicciardo and other Sienese citizens holding
property in and around Sant'Angelo in Colle during the early fourteenth
century in Chapter 6.

19 ASS, *Estimo* 24, fol. 50r.

20 Ibid., fol. 52r.

21 Ibid., fol. 51v.

22 Ibid., fols 54v and 57v.

23 Stephan R. Epstein, *Alle origini della fattoria toscana. L'ospedale della Scala di Siena
e le sue terre (metà '200 – metà '400)* (Florence, 1986), p. 58. Epstein suggests that
Santa Maria della Scala's *grancia* at Sant'Angelo in Colle (which according to
him was in the main involved in the rearing of swine) was positioned half-way
between Spedaletto and Grosseto along an east–west *transumanza* route. For the
origins and nature of the *transumanza* and, more specifically, *tratturi* or through
routes, established in Abruzzo, Molise, Campania, Puglia and Basilicata, see
Natalino Paone, *La Transumanza: Immagini di una civiltà* (Isernia, 1987). For a
survey of the *transumanza* in central Italy, see Danilo Barsanti, *Allevamento e
transumanza in Toscana. Pastori, bestiami e pascoli nei secoli 15–19* (Florence, 1987)
and Luchino Franciosa, *La transumanza nell'Appennino centro-meridionale* (Naples,
1951). According to the Sienese statute drawn up in respect of pasturing in

1418, it was an established practice that livestock came from the Casentino, the Mugello, Bologna, Lucca, Perugia, Camarino as well as several other localities outside Siena's borders. See ASS, *Dogana*, Paschi, 1, fol. 4v.

24 For *transumanza* routes south of Siena during the fourteenth century, see Giovanni Cherubini, 'Signori, contadini', p. 84 and Gabriella Piccinni, 'Ambiente, produzione, società della Valdorcia nel tardo medioevo', in *La Val d'Orcia*, pp. 33–58 (49).

25 For the practice of moving sheep from Cortona to the Maremma as early as the thirteenth century, see Laura Ticciati, 'Sulle condizioni dell'agricoltura del contado cortonese nel secolo 13', *Archivio Storico Italiano*, serie 5, 10 (1892), pp. 262–79. See also Giovan Battista Del Corto, *Storia della Valdichiana* (Bologna, 1971), p. 153.

26 See, for example, the discussion on 8 May 1332, during a meeting of the *Consiglio Generale* about the revenue that was to be gained from taxing sheep and 'other animals' on their way to the Maremma (ASS, *Consiglio Generale*, 111, old fol. 79v, new pencil pagination 80v). In this context, see also Gabriella Piccinni (ed.), *Il contratto mezzadrile nella Toscana medievale*, 3, *Contado di Siena 1349–1518* (Florence, 1992), p. 188. Piccinni notes that following the crisis in the countryside in the mid-fourteenth century a tax of 3 *denari* was levied on small animals sold by those transporting livestock to the winter pastures of the Maremma, and 4 *denari* for each animal simply transported through Sienese territory.

27 In this context, see Giovanni Cherubini, 'Proprietari, contadini e campagne senesi all' inizio del Trecento', in *Signori, contadini*, pp. 231–311, where the author considers the late fourteenth-century reform of tax on the sale of sheep. Cherubini also draws attention here to the Cerretani family of Stertignano in the Maremma who were prosecuted in 1404 for having sold sheep without paying the 5% tax to Siena. Their response was that they had been involved in such practice for decades and had on no occasion been subject to Sienese taxation. See also Ildebrando Imberciadori, 'Il primo statuto della Dogana dei paschi maremmani (1419)', in *idem*, *Per la storia della società rurale. Amiata e Maremma tra il 9 e il 20 secolo* (Parma, 1971), pp. 107–40. See also Giovanni Cherubini, 'Risorse paesaggio ed utilizzazione agricola del territorio della Toscana sud-occidentale nei secc. 14–15', in Centro Italiano di Studi di Storia e d'Arte, *Civiltà ed economia agricola in Toscana nei secc. 13–15. Problemi della vita delle campagne nel Tardo Medioevo*, Atti dell'ottavo Convegno Internazionale del Centro Italiano di Studi di Storia e d'Arte, Pistoia, 21–24 aprile 1977 (Pistoia, 1981), pp. 91–115 (112–15), reprinted in *Scritti toscani, l'urbanismo medievale e la mezzadria*, (Florence, 1991), pp. 219–39; and Ernestò Fiumi, 'Sui rapporti economici tra città e contado nell'età comunale', *Archivio storico italiano*, 114, fasc. 1 (1956), pp. 18–61.

28 ASS, *Manoscritti* C 10, fol. 30r. For the functions assumed by the *Concistoro*, see Andrea Giorgi, 'Il carteggio del Concistoro della Repubblica di Siena (spogli di lettere 1251–1374)', *BSSP*, 97 (1990), pp. 193–573.

29 ASS, *Dogana*, Paschi, 1, fol. 7r.

30 Ibid., fol. 5v.

31 Ibid., fol. 6r.

32 ASS, *Diplomatico in Caselle*, casella 39, 5 May 1222, *Archivio dello Spedale*.

33 Paone, *La Transumanza*, p. 22.

The Urban Fabric

2

Walls, Gates and Waterways

To modern eyes, Sant'Angelo in Colle appears to be a paradigm of medieval town planning, untouched by the ravages of time, and reminiscent of the portraits of hilltop towns in Ambrogio Lorenzetti's frescoes in the *Palazzo dei Nove* in Siena.[1] The urban fabric has, however, undergone several mutations since Sant'Angelo in Colle's glorious years as a Sienese *castello di frontiera*. Most significantly, the village has lost most of its surrounding walls. Only the north-eastern side of the village preserves the recognisable vestiges of an old circuit wall, pierced by an imposing portal.

This gateway is the most potent surviving symbol of Sant'Angelo in Colle's earlier strategic significance to the Republic of Siena. It is probably a mistake, however, to view medieval Sant'Angelo in Colle solely in terms of access from the north. The more important entrances to the village may originally have been on its southern and western sides. Guarded to the east by the Benedictine abbey of Sant'Antimo (under whose jurisdiction Sant'Angelo in Colle fell prior to its submission to Siena), and separated from settlements to the north and west by forest, Sant'Angelo in Colle must have felt relatively free from attack, except from feudal counts to the south and south-west.[2] It was in these directions, therefore, that the inhabitants of Sant'Angelo in Colle (and most especially when under the authority of the Republic of Siena, and thus able to turn to that source for funds for fortification of the village) must have felt the need to position lookouts in the form of fortified towers, and to erect fortified entrance gates overlooking the valley. One of the toponyms recorded in the 1320 *Tavola delle possessioni* for Sant'Angelo in Colle indicates that at least one of the gates into the village was reinforced with a wrought iron gate or portcullis, since reference was made to the 'Costa porta cancelli'.[3] The 1320 *Tavola delle possessioni* also contains references to the 'Poggio Cancelli'.[4] Given the reference to *costa*, or encircling slope, close to the *porta cancelli*, or gate of the portcullis or grate, it seems likely that this particular gate overlooked the Orcia valley. It must therefore have been positioned to the west, south or east. This, combined with the fact, that even now an area directly to the south of Sant'Angelo in Colle is referred to as 'Cancelli', would seem to confirm that there was indeed once a fortified gate on the southern side of the village.[5]

Figure 2.1   North-eastern portal, Sant'Angelo in Colle (external view)

There is now no trace of any gate other than that on the north-eastern side of the village, although records surviving from more recent periods confirm the existence of two gates – the 'Porta di Sant'Angelo' and the 'Porta di San Pietro'. That there were two gates in close proximity to each other on one side of the village by the end of the sixteenth century is also confirmed by a reference in an inventory of the possessions of the parish church of Sant'Angelo in Colle drawn up in 1587.[6] According to that record a small house outside the 'Porta a S. Pietro' and close to the church of the same *titulus* was bordered on one side by a cemetery and on another by 'un Porton vecchio del Castello', or old gate of the castle. It seems likely that this old gateway was still standing in the sixteenth century, although the fact that it is described as outside the gate of San Pietro indicates that it no longer assumed a defensive function. It may nevertheless once have marked the outer limit of an earlier circuit of walls surrounding the village.

As discussion in the following chapter will show, there is a degree of confusion about the location of a church outside the walls of the village that was dedicated to Saint Peter. As a result, there is also confusion about the original position of the gate of San Pietro. Although the small church to the south of Sant'Angelo in Colle is now dedicated to that saint, it seems that another structure to the north or north-east of the village carried the same *titulus* at a much earlier date. There is also evidence to suggest that by the early fourteenth century yet another church dedicated to Saint Peter was established inside the walls on the northern side of the village. Although it is generally argued that the Porta di San Pietro was positioned on the southern side of the village (no doubt because of its presumed proximity to the existing church with that *titulus*), the only church dedicated to Saint Peter and outside the walls in the sixteenth century was apparently positioned to the north of the village. There is some scope, therefore, for arguing that the one surviving gate at Sant'Angelo in Colle is the original Porta di San Pietro.

There seems little doubt, however, that at least one gate was positioned on the south side of the village at an early date. During the fourteenth-century Sienese officials did in fact refer to one of the gates of Sant'Angelo in Colle as facing Montenero to the south, on the other side of the Orcia River.[7] This gate, which must clearly have been positioned on the south side of the village, must also have overlooked the more distant towns of Casteldelpiano and Arcidosso on the northern slopes of Monte Amiata. Such a lookout would have provided an essential observation post, offering early warning of attack from the neighbouring mountain regions to the south, and from the marshy plains of the Maremma. There is also reference during the fourteenth century to the 'Contrada di Porta maie(?maria?maggiore)' and the 'Porta Maggiore', or main gate, itself, indicating that there was at one time yet another gate that was distinct both from the gate on the southern side of the village and from the Porta di San Pietro.[8] As we shall see in the next chapter, large parts of the village on the north-western side that were heavily fortified in the thirteenth and fourteenth centuries are now missing. It is possible, therefore, that the main gate to the village was originally located there. The fact that a vineyard belonging to Neri di Guicciardo is said to have been close to the Porta Maggiore would seem to confirm such an hypothesis since virtually all the vineyards owned by that Sienese 'outsider' in the vicinity of Sant'Angelo in Colle appear to have been situated to the west and south of the village.

The gate overlooking Montenero on the southern side of the village must have been erected at an early date, since it was recorded as already in a state of collapse by 1377.[9] Indeed, at that date, the Sienese *Consiglio Generale* was petitioned for funds by the inhabitants of Sant'Angelo in Colle in order that they might repair both the southern gate, and a piece of nearby wall that had fallen down. Given the path traced by the surviving stretch of wall on the north-eastern and south-eastern sides of the village, this southern gate could have been positioned on an upper level on, or near via Calcinaio, at the point where this road now crosses via del Paradiso, or in line with the outer circuit of walls that in part supports a number of houses on the eastern and south-eastern side of the village and in part stands free on the south-western side of via del Paradiso.

Figure 2.2
Proposed site of
southern gate

Nowadays, the via del Paradiso continues on and dips down steeply, and without obstruction to the site of what was (until recently) the public wash house, and to the church now known as San Pietro. Remains of the circuit of walls here appear to be of different, and perhaps more ancient construction than those elsewhere. It was perhaps at this level, therefore, that an old gate like that noted in the 1587 inventory was originally constructed.

The public washhouse on the southern side of the village (recently destroyed to make way for a private dwelling) was a relatively new build erected in the twentieth century. It is not marked on plans of Sant'Angelo in Colle drawn up in 1932. The position of this washhouse – outside the walls, but in close proximity to the village – may, nevertheless, mark the site of a much older structure. During the medieval and renaissance periods washing areas positioned on the fringes of urban fabrics were considered more hygienic, in that dirty water flowed away from, rather than through the built up area. In this way the local people avoided contaminating supplies of fresh drinking water inside the walls. Washhouses were thus for the most part sited just inside the walls at the lowest level of the village or town, or just outside the urban fabric in the immediate vicinity of one or other of the gates. The women of the town or village, and in particular those of the lower or serving classes who were mostly engaged in the fetching and carrying of water as well as the actual laundering of clothes, could thus go about their business in comparative safety.[10]

In the twenty-first century, the older women of Sant'Angelo in Colle recall that during the early years of the twentieth century, and before the construction of the modern washhouse near the present-day church of San Pietro, washing was carried out of the village on its western side, and down to the 'fonte pubbliche', or public washing place on the south side of the current entrance road to Sant'Angelo in Colle below the 'Podere Casello'.[11] At other times the women went even further to what was known as the 'fonte lontana', or distant fountain (also on the western side of Sant'Angelo in Colle), or to the 'fonte Ficaiuola' to the south-east.[12] All these sources of water survive, although the public wash place has clearly degraded over time. A stone inserted in its upper section implies that it was only constructed in 1897, but as we shall see, the *fonte pubbliche* did in fact exist at a much earlier date. Sadly, all that remains now are two sizeable basins of water. Any overhanging vault, additional troughs and external container walls that might have embellished this structure have long since disappeared. By contrast, the much smaller cisterns of the 'fonte lontana' and 'fonte Ficaiuola' are still covered by vaults, the latter carved out of the surrounding rock face.

A drawing of the site of the 'fonte lontana' and surrounding tracks dating to 1833 and recently unearthed in the communal archives at Montalcino, indicates that at that site, also, there was in addition a separate *abeveratoio*, or drinking trough, to the side of the main basin.[13]

It also seems clear from the accompanying annotations that the 'fonte lontana' was positioned on a through road connecting Sant'Angelo in Colle with Argiano. This road branched off from another thoroughfare on the north-western side of Sant'Angelo in Colle which, in one direction (where it is called via S. Angelo in Colle) gave direct access to the village, and in another direction (where it is called Via di Montalcino) led off towards Montalcino. The change of name occurs at the cross roads marking the site of the old Chiesa della Compagnia (now a private house belonging to the Lisini family). A further

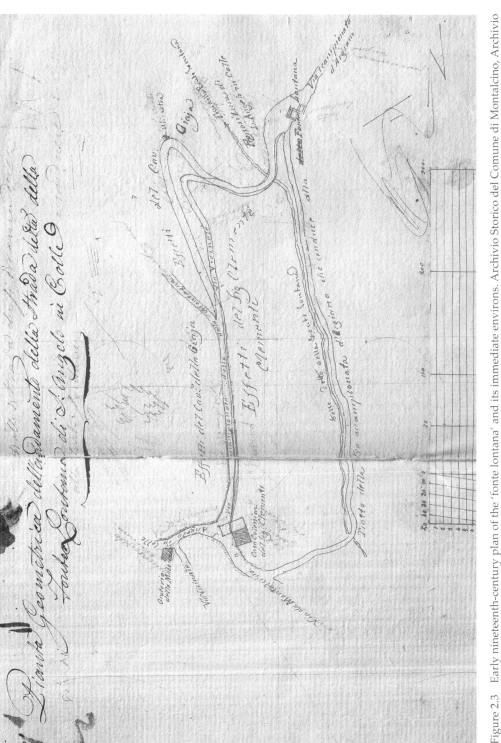

Figure 2.3   Early nineteenth-century plan of the 'fonte lontana' and its immediate environs. Archivio Storico del Comune di Montalcino, Archivio Preunitario (1361–1865), Ingegnere del circondario (1825–1850), Relazioni, rapporti, progetti e perizie, 1690 (1830–1833), folio 173, dated 24 July 1833

road, some distance to the north of the cross roads (called via vicinale in the 1833 drawing) branches off on the northern side of the via di S. Angelo. This, although now a cul-de-sac, originally connected with the ancient Sesta road, since the existing parallel road to the modern cemetery was constructed at a more recent date. Even until recently, a short-cut across to the Sesta road in the vicinity of what is now the Lisini Azienda at Casa Nuova (beginning at the end of the existing cul-de-sac) was regularly used by the inhabitants of Sant'Angelo in Colle.[14] In the medieval period, for anyone travelling to the village, either from Villa a Tolli, or along the Sesta road from Sant'Antimo, this would have been the most direct route to the village.

The cemetery road is not shown on the 1833 drawing. It thus seems likely that the original course of the road connecting the end of the Sesta road with Sant'Angelo in Colle branched off at the level of the cemetery and, following the contour of the hill, skirted round to join the old 'via vicinale'. This in turn offered access to the northern gate of the village by turning up the steep 'via Sant'Angelo in Colle' at the corner now marked by the entrance to a new public parking place.

The 1833 drawing is significant in a number of ways. It shows, for example, that the road connecting Sant'Angelo in Colle with Argiano opened out in front of the 'fonte lontana', presumably in order to provide a kind of *piazzale*, or gathering area, suitable for groups of washer women to congregate, and large enough also to accommodate herds of cattle. The drawing also clearly delineates the course of the 'fossa della fonte lontana', which runs along the eastern side of the Sant'Angelo in Colle/Argiano road. It seems clear from the course of this stream that the public fountain located on the current access road to Sant'Angelo in Colle could have been fed from the same source. The accompanying notes drawn up by the early nineteenth-century inspector of *viari*, or roads, are also significant for the references they make to other thoroughfares in the vicinity of Sant'Angelo in Colle. The inspector notes, for example, that the road branching off to the south of the village at the cross roads marking the site of the old church of the Compagnia was known as the 'via detta della Montagna', or the road known as the road of the mountain. This toponym indicates that the 'via detta della Montagna' had traditionally served as a transit route towards one specific mountain, the obvious candidate being Monte Amiata. This thoroughfare (which no doubt followed more or less the course of the existing road) must thus have circumvented Sant'Angelo in Colle before dipping down to cross the River Orcia to the east of Sant'Angelo Scalo, presumably by ford.[15]

There is also a reference to the 'fonte pubbliche' in the notes accompanying the 1833 drawing that makes it quite clear that this was regarded as a separate source of water serving a number of different functions. It seems likely, therefore, that the two large water basins still extant on the southern side of the current entrance road to Sant'Angelo in Colle were either already in place by the early nineteenth century, or that they replaced an earlier structure that had fallen into disrepair. There is support for such an hypothesis in the large uneven slabs of stone that still form part of the pavement immediately in front of the basins, as well as the right-hand supporting wall. The brick slab inscribed with the date 1897 may thus have been set in place following reconstruction work at the end of the nineteenth century. That said, there is in fact evidence to suggest that a public fountain was located outside the village as early as 1676.

According to the 1676 visit made by Bartolomeo Gherardini in his guise of 'Auditore Generale' in Siena for Grand Duke Cosimo III dei Medici, there was indeed only one public source of water in the vicinity of Sant'Angelo in Colle at that date.[16] From Gherardini's description it seems likely that this was the structure still referred to as the 'fonte pubbliche'. Gherardini noted that the public fountain had two sections, one for washing (the *lavatoio*) and the other for cattle (the *abbeveratoio*). This would seem to confirm that the public fountain of Sant'Angelo in Colle served a dual purpose (at least during the seventeenth century). Such duality was, of course, common practice, not only in more recent times, but also – as witnessed by many extant structures from the medieval period – at a much earlier date. Gherardini made no reference to any overhanging structure on Sant'Angelo in Colle's public fountain, but from the evidence of surviving fountains elsewhere, it seems likely that the two public water basins at Sant'Angelo in Colle were also covered. They may even have had a surrounding wall.

During the medieval period, a good source of water must always have been regarded as of prime importance. Its location was also extremely significant. In recent times at Sant'Angelo in Colle, the more distant 'fonte fenille' to the south of 'fonte lontana' was traditionally regarded as providing good drinking water, not only for the people living and working in the surrounding fields, but also for the inhabitants of the village itself. Drinking water was also traditionally collected from the 'fonte della Madonna' next door to the 'fonte puzzerla' (still extant in the form of a stand pipe), close to the 'fonte pubbliche' on the existing entrance road on the western side of the village. People still stop here, as they do at the 'fonte fenille', in the expectation that the spring water from both sources is untainted.

At least some, if not all of these courses of water may have existed in the medieval period, although few, if any of them would have been appropriate as sources of drinking water for those living inside the walls. Indeed, it seems likely that the many springs in the vicinity of Sant'Angelo in Colle originally served a variety of other purposes. Both the 'fonte lontana' and the 'fonte Ficaiuola', for example, as well as serving as watering places for livestock, could in addition have been where work was first carried out preparing and refining bales of cloth. Such merchandise was certainly included with other exports from Sant'Angelo in Colle transported through the clearing-house of Santa Maria della Scala at the end of the fourteenth century. While some refining of cloth may have been carried out in water troughs inside the village itself, the abundant source of clear spring water in close proximity to Sant'Angelo in Colle must have offered ample scope for activities of this

kind on the surrounding slopes. Indeed, prior to the investments made by
the Sienese hospital and the establishment of a grange inside Sant'Angelo in
Colle which may have contained appropriate spaces both for the housing of
livestock and for shearing and the processing of wool, it would no doubt have
been more practical to carry out such work outside the village.

For the women of the village in the medieval period intent on washing
private linen, the sites of the 'fonte lontana' and the 'fonte Ficaiuola' must,
however, have seemed rather too distant and unprotected. The steep incline
in either direction must, in addition, have seemed less practical in terms of
the transport of heavy loads of washing backwards and forwards from the
village. The location of both the 'fonte fenille' and the 'fonte della Madonna'
would likewise have presented significant drawbacks when drawing drinking
water, in the face of marauding companies of armed mercenaries who
habitually roamed the surrounding woods and fields. During those times it
was essential that drinking water was located in a safe site, not only for its
gathering by the inhabitants of the village, but also so that it was protected
from potential vandalism by hostile outsiders. The main source of drinking
water for Sant'Angelo in Colle during the medieval period must thus have
been located inside the walls. Even now, the sub-soil of the village is criss-
crossed by springs. It would thus have been relatively easy to acquire water
either through a system of wells sunk sufficiently deep to tap underground
springs, or in the form of open cisterns or fountains, filled in the main through
rainwater.

That a distinction was made between spring water and rain water in the
medieval period is clear from a record of 21 October 1317 included in the
archive of the *Consiglio della Campana* in Siena.[17] Reference was made there
to the source of 'buona acqua viva', or good flowing water in a spring, or
fountain just outside the walls near the Porta dell'Uliviera, in the vicinity
of the 'contrada dell'Abbadia Nuova'. It seems that this water (which was
described as 'very useful and necessary' both for the immediate district, and
for people elsewhere in the city as well as for others outside) was threatened
with contamination by the rain water which ran along the city's *fosso* –
literally a ditch, but in effect an open drain. According to the deliberations of
the *Consiglio della Campana*, it was essential that work should be carried out in
the vicinity of the Porta dell'Uliviera well so that water from the city's drain
should not penetrate and spoil it. The officials of the *Campana* were also aware
of various other threats to their precious spring water. In the same month of
October, consideration was given to the well in the cloister of the nuns of the
monastery of Santa Maria Novella that was fed from a spring, but which had
apparently dried up following work by the commune in the vicinity of Porta
Camollia.[18] This work, which had involved flattening the surrounding area
in order to make a field, had clearly disturbed the course of water flowing
underground. The Santa Maria Novella well was thus no longer useable, not
because the water had dried up, but because it had been diverted elsewhere.

In his description of Sant'Angelo in Colle in 1676 Gherardini noted that there were up to five private wells belonging to the local gentry inside the walls. Several, if not all of these still exist.[19] Of the private wells surviving in the gardens, orchards and courtyards of individual houses, at least one (that on plot 192 of the 1820 *catasto* map, an orchard situated on the western side of via Paradiso and facing via Cosatti) is so deep and capacious, that it is said to have saved the village from ruin in the twentieth century, when Sant'Angelo in Colle was threatened by a forest fire raging close to the walls.[20] Although there are no public fountains in the present-day village, the standpipe positioned close to the north-eastern end of the church of San Michele Arcangelo not only allows for the drawing up of piped water inside the old centre, but may also mark the site of an earlier source of spring water. The site of at least one other public cistern inside the walls is also clearly distinguishable in the raised terrace in front of the existing Trattoria del Pozzo. Residents of Sant'Angelo in Colle recall that the *pozzo*, or well, under this terrace – in effect a large open-air water tank – was used as a source of public water until well into the twentieth century. Although in the main fed by rainwater, this cistern was also serviced in times of scarce rainfall by horse-driven water carriers.[21] The date of construction of the Trattoria del Pozzo cistern is unclear, although – if the testimony of Gherardini is taken at face value – it seems unlikely that it predated 1676. Nevertheless, its position at the highest point of the village suggests that it may have occupied the site of a pre-existing well fed by an underground spring. In Gherardini's time this well may have been appropriated into a private orchard garden, rather than being open (as has more recently been the case) to the main square and thoroughfare.

In any event, it seems clear that some kind of public water system was established inside the walls of Sant'Angelo in Colle at an early date, since there are numerous references to a *corso d'acqua*, or water conduit in the 1320 *Tavola delle possessioni*. According to Duccio Balestracci and Gabriella Piccinni, there were numerous such water conduits in medieval Siena.[22] These structures, which were usually quite narrow and which in the thirteenth century were known as *cavine* or *treseppi*, usually followed a steep incline with along one side, a channel along which rainwater could flow. In many cases *cavine* and *treseppi* were established between houses, thus functioning in effect as open drains. In some ways, therefore, such conduits constituted a health risk. This may well have influenced the decision in 1309 to channel all such conduits in Siena underground, and to cover them with bricks. The water conduit at Sant'Angelo in Colle, which seems to have run above ground level, and to have penetrated several parts of the village, must have provided an essential source of water inside the walls during the early fourteenth-century. It may, indeed, have served a number of functions. While the upper reaches may have been reserved for the collection of water for personal use including washing and cooking, the lower parts of the conduit could have fed into a number of butts reserved as drinking water for animals, as irrigation systems for individual orchards, or to feed other troughs or cisterns reserved for the laundering of clothes. It is even possible that in one part of the village water channelled through the water conduit was used to assist in the treatment of animal skins and cloth.[23]

When Giovanni Antonio Pecci drew up a survey of Sant'Angelo in Colle in the eighteenth century, he specifically noted that the leaves of the copious *Lentischi* or *Sondala* plants in the vicinity of the village were used to treat animal skins.[24] It seems likely, therefore, that such a trade was well established by that date. It is also more than likely that the practice dated back to a much earlier period. In this context it is relevant that the road running at the lowest level on the eastern side of Sant'Angelo in Colle is called the 'via del Calcinaio', or road of the calcination, or lime-slating, indicating that in at least one part of this thoroughfare there were at one time troughs suitable for the washing and curing of animal hides.[25] The 'stradella ma(?n)gmeta', noted in the 1320 *Tavola delle possessioni* may well have been associated with such work, given the link to magnesium of lime. Nineteenth-century maps show that there was once a large open space in the vicinity of via del Calcinaio, on the site of one of the two small squares now known as the piazzette Palazzo Rosso. This may thus have been where animal carcases were assembled prior to undergoing cleaning and curing processes in adjacent troughs. The fact that a deep cistern still exists in the basement of Palazzo Ricci (plot no. 168 of the 1820 *catasto* map) would also seem to confirm that via del Calcinaio is an ancient toponym relating to a particular kind of activity carried out on the eastern side of the village.[26]

The existing topography of Sant'Angelo in Colle indicates how water inside the walls must have flowed. Regardless of the initial point of departure, surface water running in a system of conduits through the lower levels of Sant'Angelo in Colle must naturally have flowed down and out on the southern side of the village. In this way water from the *corso d'acqua* mentioned in the 1320 *Tavola delle possessioni* could have reached a public washing area in the vicinity of the site of the twentieth-century wash house and the present-day church of San Pietro. Such a site, positioned as it was in the shadow of the southern entrance gate, would not only have satisfied prevailing rules of hygiene, but would also have been conveniently near to the village, whilst at the same time being assured of protection by the adjacent fortified walls.

Troughs or ditches branching off from the main water conduit could also have pierced the walls of the medieval village to form a moat. Surviving plans of other urban fabrics, such as Pietrasanta in the vicinity of Lucca, show how internal water conduits flowed out through the town walls, to form just such defensive trenches.

Nineteenth-century maps of Sant'Angelo in Colle reveal a number of narrow alleyways at two different levels on the eastern side of the village. Several, if not all of these could have served to carry away rainwater as well as excess water from a main water conduit. Remains of one such 'run-off' ditch is still visible in the first of the two piazzette Palazzo Rosso. According to the 1820 *catasto* map of Sant'Angelo in Colle, this ditch originally formed part

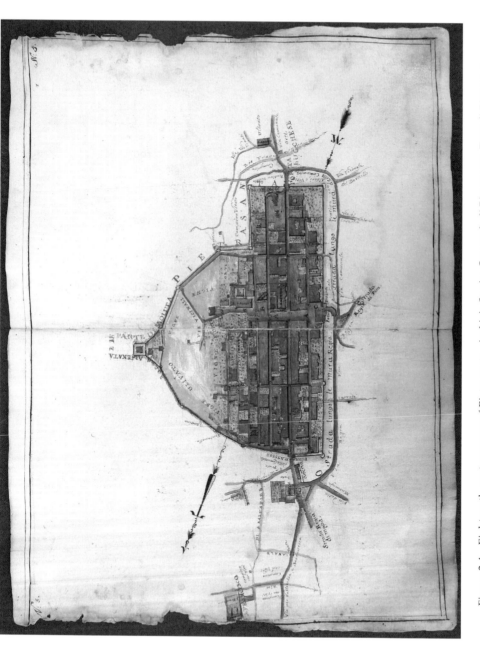

Figure 2.4 Eighteenth-century map of Pietrasanta. *Archivio Storico Comunale di Pietrasanta, Terra di Pietrasanta, Fondo della Comunità e Cancelleria, N. inventario provvisorio 207 Campione delle Strade situate dentro il Circondario di Pietrasanta e nei territorij soggetti alla sua Comunità, 1783 Ing. Carlo Mazzoni, Tavola n. 5*

of an alleyway which was bordered on one side by plots 118 and 115 and on the other, by plots 167 and 168 (see Diagram 2.1). Any *corso d'acqua* or *cavina* or *treseppo* following this course would have naturally drawn water down towards troughs positioned on the level of via del Calcinaio. Some alleyways, including the very obvious broader slope at the end of via Paradiso on the south side of the village, remain intact within the existing urban fabric. At times of copious rainfall it is easy to see how channels running alongside such alleys would fill with water creating rivulets of water abundant enough to fill trenches outside the walls and finally effect a moat, at least around the eastern and southern edges of the village.

We know that at least one trench or moat was already in existence on one side of Sant'Angelo in Colle as early as the fourteenth century, since there are references in the 1320 *Tavola delle possessioni* to an area known as 'carbonaia', a term commonly used in the medieval period to indicate an external ditch.[27] There are also references to the 'Costa Carbonelle', which appears to have been located in the vicinity of the church outside the walls that was dedicated to San Pietro.[28] Surviving documents from the medieval period reveal that such ditches and trenches were commonly used for defence. When the Government of the Fifteen elected several deputies to go to Colle Sabbatini in 1279, they made specific reference to the ditches and 'carbonarie' that were to form part of its fortifications.[29] It seems clear that the 'carbonaia' ditch at Sant'Angelo in Colle ran along beneath the steep bank known as the Costa Sant'Angelo on the south-west side of the village. There must thus have been a steep incline upwards between the ditch itself and the village above. Given its position and gradient, the slope to the south of the juncture of via del Paradiso and via Cosatti, would have been perfectly positioned for supplying water to the 'carbonaia' ditch. There is, moreover, further support for this in the fact that the slope is bordered at its southern end by one of the earliest stretches of wall.

The date of construction of the *corso d'acqua* at Sant'Angelo in Colle remains unclear. It is possible that it had its origins in a moat surrounding the first nucleus of the village that was fed naturally by rainwater. It is also possible that such a moat was filled by water from local springs on the hillside. A purpose-built water system may also have been introduced by the Sienese, following their take over of Sant'Angelo in Colle in the early thirteenth century. It may be relevant that at this period the Sienese, themselves, were in the process of constructing an elaborate network of water ways both above and below ground in Siena.[30] In fact, as early as 1251, members of the General Council under the Government of the Fifteen were considering ways of raising money on behalf of the *Opera del Condotto delle acque* in order to complete the city's *cannelle*, or water channels.[31] It is clear, also, that the *corso d'acqua* at Sant'Angelo in Colle was not just a mere trickle of water – drying with the summer heat and overflowing in the rainy season. Entries in the 1320 *Tavola delle possessioni* imply that the waterway was a permanent feature of the urban fabric, since there are numerous references to it when defining the limits of individual properties. It is also clear that, by the early fourteenth century, the conduit inside the walls was bordered on both sides by private dwellings.

Table 2.1
Property
described as
abutting the
corso d'acqua in
the 1320 *Tavola
delle possessioni*

Owner of property or tenant	Neighbouring properties and confines other than the water conduit (denoted as *)
Cenninus Cennis[1]	Road, *, Manovelli Ugolini
Ecclesia S(anc)ti Angeli	i[2] Road, heirs of Cichi Pieri, * ii[3] Road, road, *, Manovelli Ugolini
Finucius Ranuccini[4]	Manovelli Ugolini, road, road, *
Lonardutius Joahnnis[5]	Road, road, Mei Pepi, *
Martinus Berti[6]	Road, Ture Gui(?glie)ll(?m)i, medianti *, heirs of Blanchi, medianti *,Domina Duccie Gerini.[7]
Michus Genovesus[8]	i Road, road, Gemma Fanelli[9], * ii Road, Mini Joh(ann)is, La(n)dutii Berti, *
Mona Gioa[10]	Road, road, Fuccii Andeloni, *
Meus Pepi[11]	Road, Scolai Gianelli, Luna(r)dutii Joh(ann)is, *
Mona Mita Pieri[12]	Road, road, Nardi Venture, *
Mona Duccia Cioli[13]	Road, heirs of Blanc(?h)i, Bindi Accorsi, *
Nardellus Venture[14]	Road, ospedale S(anc)ti Ma(r)ie, D(omi)ne Mite Pieri, *
Scolariolus Gia(n)nelli[15]	Road, Folchini Joh(ann)is, Mei Pepi, *
Sozzus Ranucci[16]	Road, road, Manovelli Ugolini, *
Tinus di Montenere[17]	Road, Manovelli Ugolini, Guarnerutii Bruni, *
Vanutius q(uon)dam Berti Magri Ma(r)tini[18]	Road, Ture Gui(?glie)ll(?m)i, media(n)ti *, heirs of Blanchi, mediat(n)te*,d(omi)ne …. Duccie Gierini[19]
Ser Guccius Ser Francisci[20]	Cecchini Ghezzi, D(omi)ne Necche Nerii, *

Notes to Table 2.1

1 ASS, *Estimo* 24, fol. 85v, valued at 39 *lire*, 7 *soldi*.
2 Ibid., fol. 126v, valued at 14 *lire*, 13 *soldi*.
3 Ibid., fol. 129v, valued at 19 *lire*, 7 *soldi*.
4 Ibid., fol. 141v, valued at 33 *lire*, 7 *soldi*.
5 Ibid., fol. 275v, valued at 36 *lire*.
6 Ibid., fol. 283r, valued at 17 *lire*, 6 *soldi*, 6 *denari*. Described as half a house, the other half belonging to 'Vanutii Berti', presumably a sibling.
7 The reference to 'Domina Duccie Gerini' here may be an error, and intended instead to refer to 'Domina Duccie Cioli', whose entry in the 1320 *Tavola delle possessioni* contains a reference to a house and building plot inside the walls of the village that was bordered on one side by a road, on another by the heirs of 'Blanchi', on another side by property belonging to 'Bindi Accorsi' and on a fourth side by the water conduit, see *Estimo* 24, fol. 331r. There is confirmation of this in the fact that no record exists for a 'Domina Duccie Gerini', and that the heirs of 'Blanchi' for their part are recorded as owning a house that was bordered on two sides by a road, on a third side by property belonging to the commune of Sant'Angelo in Colle, and on a fourth side by property belonging to 'Domina Duccie Cioli' (see ASS, *Estimo* 24, 228r.) The double reference to the water conduit combined with 'medianti' would seem to imply that the water flowed along two courses in this area of the village.
8 ASS, *Estimo* 24, fols 287r and 287v, the first of which was valued at 110 *lire*, and the second at 40 *lire*.
9 This individual is not included in the 1320 *Tavola delle possessioni*.
10 ASS, *Estimo* 24, fol. 303r, valued at 39 *lire*, 7 *soldi*.
11 Ibid., fol. 325r, valued at 36 *lire*.
12 Ibid., fol. 330r, valued at 22 *lire*.
13 Ibid., fol. 331r, valued at 63 *lire*.
14 Ibid., fol. 347v, valued at 31 *lire*, 13 *soldi*.
15 Ibid., fol. 401r, valued at 47 *lire*, 7 *soldi*.
16 Ibid., fol. 410r, valued at 27 *lire*.

17 Ibid., fol. 416r, valued at 20 *lire*, 13 *soldi*.
18 Ibid., fol. 426r, valued at 17 *lire*, 6 *soldi*, 6 *denari*.
19 In the context of the reference to 'Domina Duccia Gierini', and 'mediante cursu', see footnote 7 above.
20 ASS, *Estimo* 24, fol. 451r, valued at 10 *lire*.

Analysis

On the basis of the recorded value of property abutting the water conduit in 1320, it would seem that most of the houses in this part of the village were of small to medium size. Only two, one of which belonged to 'Michus Genovesus' and the other to 'Domina Duccia Cioli', appear to have been of any significant size.

It seems unlikely, therefore, that the *corso d'acqua* at Sant'Angelo in Colle depended solely on the seasonal collection of rainwater. Most probably, it was fed by a spring, or from a well positioned high enough to provide a continual flow of water down through the lower parts of the village throughout the year. If devised by the Sienese, it is also possible that the flow of water was regulated by a sophisticated system of variations in level. Such an arrangement would have ensured running water in several parts of the village even during the dry summer months. There is little doubt that members of Siena's *Consiglio della Campana* were aware of the advantages to be gained in designing fountains and water systems on a number of different levels. When discussing the construction of the 'fonte della Pescaia' in Siena early in 1302, the officials of the Council not only referred to the length and height of the proposed fountain's perimeter walls, but also drew distinctions between the open and underground ditches and conduits which were to serve it. The Council also recommended that roads surrounding the 'fonte della Pescaia' should be lowered, 'accio chelacqua abbia piu pendente' (so that the water should have more of a slope).[32]

What happened in Siena was frequently copied elsewhere, and most especially in those communes that fell under its jurisdiction. An eighteenth-century drawing of the old 'fontana delle donne' at Montalcino and the adjacent complex known as the 'fonte buia', along with the water troughs and conduits in the vicinity of Santa Lucia and Sant'Agata, illustrates well how the *corso d'acqua* at Sant'Angelo in Colle may have been constructed so that it followed the lie of the land.[33]

Although only the main water cistern now remains, twentieth-century photographs show that the entire complex was still intact during the 1940s, and that the 'fonte delle donne' was at that time being used as a public wash house.[34] Both the surviving structure and the drawing offer valuable evidence of the ways in which the existing terrain and laws of gravity were harnessed to deliver water to various parts of Montalcino on it eastern and south-eastern sides. The eighteenth-century drawing gives no indication as to the age of the original complex. However, surviving reliefs on the *mensole*, or mensoles, of the arches of the main cistern, indicate that this part at least dates back to the medieval period. (This, despite an inscription dated 1523 on the façade of the existing 'fonte buia' structure.) From the eighteenth-century toponym, it seems likely that the 'fonte delle donne' had been reserved for women for some time, and most probably for the washing of personal linen. This may indeed have been its original function. There is support for this in the fact that this part of the complex was set apart from what appears to have been the main structure. The latter consisted of a large water cistern contained within a double-arched and vaulted building, and adjacent to this, three water troughs – defined variously in the eighteenth-century drawing as for the use of dyers, leather workers and horses. Information of this kind is particularly precious, since it shows how the water in the Montalcino complex served a number of quite diverse needs, thus throwing light on the ways in which such complexes functioned during the medieval period.

The construction and functioning of both the 'fonte delle donne' and 'fonte buia' clearly involved a complex system of water channels at different levels. Furthermore, both the 'fonte delle donne' and the main water cistern were originally enclosed within boundary walls. In the eighteenth century, the main cistern area was in addition edged at a higher level, by a parapet wall, with a separate flight of steps leading down to the 'fonte buia'. At that period, also, one large *bottino*, or water channel, was connected to the back of the main cistern of the 'fonte buia', and is shown running alongside the 'strada Butirone', before joining two other drainage systems that join it at right angles. On the other side of the 'strada Butirone', there is a smaller water conduit marked 'corso dell'acqua concia', presumably because this water was used for the treatment of cloth. Although clearly on a much smaller scale, the *corso d'acqua* at Sant'Angelo in Colle probably functioned in a similar way, with a central cistern feeding a system of water troughs, conduits and drainage ditches.

A scanty sketch of a stretch of walls in the top left hand corner of the eighteenth-century drawing labelled 'mura castellane' indicates that the fountain complex was at that date located inside the walls. But this was probably not always the case. Images of Montalcino under siege in the sixteenth century shows an inner circuit of walls around the Castelvecchio (the original nucleus of the town) immediately to the north of the 'fonte delle donne' and 'fonte buia' site.

It thus seems likely that when first constructed this complex was positioned outside the first circuit of walls.

Existing fountain structures at Bolsena and Acquapendente – albeit of much more recent date – offer further evidence of the ways in which water could be directed into various basins, cisterns and water conduits inside urban fabrics. The cistern fountain in the Piazza della Fontana at Acquapendente illustrates, in addition, how pipes inserted at an appropriate level in the walls of a water cistern could deliver water into a system of troughs that in turn drew off water to serve a wide area of the town.

Clearly, a similar system could have been developed in Sant'Angelo in Colle. The nature of the terrain surrounding the site of the Trattoria del Pozzo cistern there would have greatly facilitated the flow of water on the eastern and southern sides of the village. At the upper level (now slightly lower than the existing piazza del Castello), water could be collected and the cistern filled. At the lower level in front of the restaurant, in what is now known as

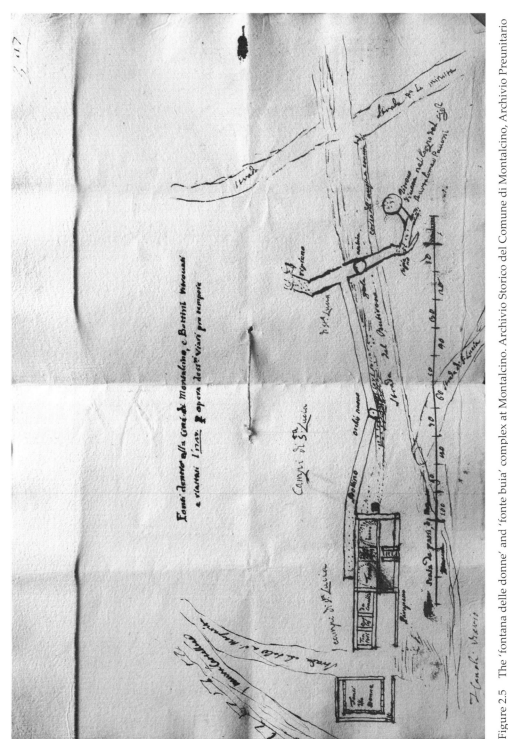

Figure 2.5 The 'fontana delle donne' and 'fonte buia' complex at Montalcino. Archivio Storico del Comune di Montalcino, Archivio Preunitario (1361–1865), Comunità di Montalcino fino al 1808, Acque e strade, 159, Ufficiali di acque e strade carteggi e atti, 1727–1813, no. 27

the 'piazzale del Pozzo', water issuing from spouts piercing at least one, if not two or three of the upper cistern's sides could then have fed a further system of troughs, or water conduits. The existing steep slope down to the restaurant from the piazza del Castello, and the lie of the land in the immediate vicinity of the restaurant itself could have made the piazzale del Pozzo an ideal site to position pipes or troughs serving a *corso dell'acqua*. Water collected in troughs at this lower level could then have been easily channelled along a number of conduits, one obvious contender being the present day via Cosatti.

If, as hypothesised here, the inner-most path of the *corso d'acqua* at Sant'Angelo in Colle ran along the original trajectory of a defensive structure in the form of a protecting ditch – which was later absorbed within the village's expanding urban fabric – it follows that its path as recorded in the early fourteenth century must have marked one side of the village's original boundaries. If this were the case, via Cosatti could have marked the outer limits of the early medieval village on its eastern and southern sides. It would also follow that the original wall enclosing the inner nucleus ran along the north-western side of the same road. In many ways medieval Sant'Angelo in Colle must have seemed a microcosm of its larger neighbour and protector, Siena. In hilltop towns, the only way to expand was downwards. Yet with each development away from the original, frequently fortified, nucleus on the summit of the hill, new boundary walls were needed to stitch the expanded urban fabric together, thus preserving it from attack. In parallel with this, new gates had to be erected to facilitate access and egress into and out of the expanded space. One need only look at seventeenth and eighteenth-century maps of Siena to appreciate the extent to which boundary walls criss-crossed the medieval city, bridging gaps as new buildings emerged, protecting water sources and encircling orchards as the population extended beyond pre-existing borders.[35] One surviving drawing records the eight different circuits of wall constructed in the city over the course of time.

Surviving records charting the urban development of Argiano (the hill-top hamlet to the south-west of Sant'Angelo in Colle) confirm how, at each step, new stretches of wall were built to enclose the enlarged community. By the late fourteenth century Argiano already had several circuits of walls. In 1391, the original nucleus of the *cassarum*, or castle complex, which was both castellated and flanked by a fortified wall, was set within a second circuit of walls which included two houses, three stables and half a *claustro* (literally a cloister, but more likely a kind of pen for keeping animals).[36] The *borgo*, or actual hamlet, was situated outside the castle, and thus presumably outside the inner circuit of walls. In effect, therefore, there were three distinct zones.

While Argiano may thus serve as a nearby example for the construction of walls resulting from the expansion of an original nucleus, Camigliano, a small hamlet to the west of Sant'Angelo in Colle appears to have mirrored the latter's growth in the middle years of the thirteenth century.[37] The population of both villages approximately doubled in size between 1212 and 1278. But things changed dramatically thereafter. The population of Camigliano, having

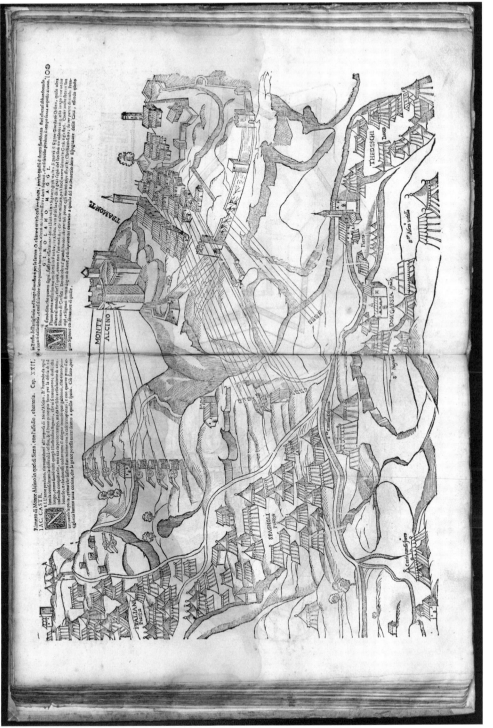

Figure 2.6   Sixteenth-century print of the Siege of Montalcino. Biblioteca Comunale degli Intronati, Siena, XXI bis A.17_100

Figure 2.7
Public fountain at
Acquapendente

expanded to about 150 souls – for the most part housed in quite modest
buildings, and with only one or two seigneurial abodes flanking the sides of
the main square – subsequently remained static.[38] By contrast, the population
of Sant'Angelo in Colle continued to grow.

Such growth must have stimulated a number of significant changes in the
village's urban fabric, not least through the need to provide new housing. Some of
the increased population could no doubt have been housed through the infilling
of previously open spaces, since the original nucleus most probably included
patches of open land for orchards and the safe grazing of sheep and cattle
inside the walls. But some, if not all, of this must have been filled in as a result
of the demographic surge between 1212 and 1225. The further expansion of the
population between 1225 and 1278 may thus have forced the village to extend
beyond its earlier boundaries. The much larger increase in population between
1278 and 1320 must have put further pressure on existing housing, resulting in
yet more appropriation of orchards and other open spaces, and perhaps leading
to yet another expansion beyond pre-existing walls. It was possibly around this
time, also, that a number of larger buildings were constructed on the northern
and eastern sides of the village, filling in previously vacant plots and imbuing the
village with an aspect of greater wealth and authority. It may not be coincidental
that it was during this period that the Sienese constructed a new barracks on the
site of the village's first *Palazzo Comunale*. The construction of the barracks may
have led to self-aggrandising investment inside the frontier castle by Sienese
residents intent not only on supporting the Government of the Nine, but also on
improving their own personal profiles. As we shall see in the next chapter, at least

Figure 2.8
Undated sketch
of the eight
circuits of wall
constructed at
Siena. Archivio
di Stato, Siena,
Stampe ASSI, n.
66. 'Otto circuiti
di muraglia
…', Teofilo
Gallaccini s.d.

one Sienese resident, Neri di Guicciardo, had acquired a considerable amount of property inside the walls of the village by 1320, much of it in the vicinity of the new barracks. He was thus both associated with the Sienese government and protected by it. As is argued in Chapter 3, Neri di Guicciardo's property in some ways also provided a buffer zone between the military and the local population.

Demographic growth at Sant'Angelo in Colle may well have resulted, therefore, in at least three distinct circuits of wall being constructed around the original nucleus of the village between the end of the first quarter of the thirteenth century, and the 1320s. On a very rough estimate, and if the urban fabric was developed in parallel with the increasing population, one might expect that the gap between the first and second set of walls would have been equivalent to a quarter of that established between the second and third circuits. As we shall see, the pathways of existing streets, and the remains of what are possibly very early entrances to the village would seem to support such a reconstruction. Even in the twenty-first century, the dramatic shifts in level between one part of Sant'Angelo in Colle and another, as well as the paths traced by its narrow alleys, offer striking evidence of the ways in which the village must have expanded during the early modern period. Indeed, the existing urban fabric would seem to confirm that several circles of wall were constructed outside the village's original nucleus. The inner core probably consisted of the old church of San Michele and a number of buildings positioned on the eastern side of the present-day via del Paradiso. An initial wall could thus have enclosed this area, sweeping down the via del Paradiso, following a south-eastern path along one side of the present via Cosatti, and completing its circuit in the vicinity of a *pozzo*, or cistern well near the present-day Trattoria del Pozzo.   Entrance to this original nucleus was possibly through a comparatively modest archway, remains of which may still be visible, in the wall running along the western side of via Cosatti.[40] In this context it may be relevant that an old arch used to span via del Calcinaio in the vicinity of plots 114 and 115. It is possible that this marked the site of a subsequent entrance to the village on its eastern side.

What was probably a second circuit of walls, constructed to contain the first notable expansion of Sant'Angelo in Colle in the thirteenth century, may by contrast have had an entrance on the western side, since there are traces of what appears to be a narrow gateway, half way up the alley that cuts off in front of the current site of the Monte dei paschi di Siena bank. Surviving stonework that juts out unevenly from the walls here, indicates that at one time this street was spanned by an archway on supporting posts. It seems that there was yet another gate on the south-western side of Sant'Angelo in Colle, since a nineteenth-century record concerning property owned in the village at that date by the hospital of Santa Maria della Croce in Montalcino refers to a building (number 142) in the square at the end of the immediately parallel alley as the 'casa della portaccia' (the house of the bad, or rotten gate).[41]

The 'casa della portaccia' presumably marked the limits of a new circuit of walls constructed to contain a further expansion of the village to the south-west. The use of the term 'portaccia' implies, however, that by the nineteenth century the gate itself was in disrepair, or had long since fallen down.

The inner western gate must have been built at a comparatively early date, since the buildings on either side of the street are amongst the oldest in the village. It is possible, therefore, that this gate formed part of a circuit of walls constructed beyond the first nucleus of Sant'Angelo in Colle some time before the middle of the thirteenth century. Such an expansion of the walls would have accommodated buildings constructed on the western and south-western sides of the via del Paradiso, the south-eastern and north-eastern sides of via Cosatti, and around the main square to the north-east, north and north-west. The *portaccia* referred to in the nineteenth-century map of property belonging to the hospital of Santa Maria della Croce was, by contrast, most probably linked to a further and possibly third circuit of walls. This circuit would have run along the present-day via della Piazzuola, crossing the via del Paradiso at its southern end, and continuing along the via del Calcinaio, before passing the present descent to the north gate, and circling back in front of the *Palazzaccio*.

The 1820 *catasto* map indicates a number of orchards along this latter trajectory, including the comparatively large (and combined) space on plots 192 and 190, and that surrounding plot 188 on the south-western side of the village, as well as another large open space on plot 160, immediately opposite the north gate. Whilst plot 160 has been built over, that in the vicinity of plot 188 remains open. The raised level of this in respect of the present-day via della Piazzuola gives the impression of a hanging garden, adding further support to the hypothesis that this part of the village was at one time bordered by a circuit wall.

Diagram 2.1 Proposed trajectory of initial circuit of walls at Sant'Angelo in Colle (traced over the 1820 *catasto* map of the village)[39]

The majestic cypresses flanking the existing entrance road to Sant'Angelo in Colle probably trace the line of yet a further circuit of walls. This may have been the ultimate line of defence established in the sixteenth century in the face of increasing Florentine aggression prior to the final conquest of the Sienese state. Remains of this wall to the height of several metres are still clearly visible between the northern gate and the *Palazzaccio*. A continuation of this circuit can also be traced on the eastern side of the village along the outer edges of plots 103, 105 and 106, reaching a height of five or so metres between plots 106 and 119, before being absorbed in the extension to the property of the Ricci family (on plot 120). Thereafter the walls falls away, but traces of the same circuit continue through plots 121, 123 and 124 to form the outermost supporting wall of the building on plot 125 and the garden of plot 126. The same wall continues on the outer perimeter of garden plots 128 and 130, underpinning once more the structures on plots 131 and 132, before completing a final sweep of the circuit at the present entrance to the village.[42]

Despite the reference to the destruction of the walls of Sant'Angelo in Colle shortly after 1280, it seems clear that the village contained a number of sections of wall in 1320, since many of the houses recorded in the *Tavola delle possessioni* for that year are described as being bordered on at least one side by 'le mura'. There were in addition at least two distinct areas outside the walls that were designated as orchard land (the 'costa Sant'Angelo' and the 'costa San Pietro'), but where there were also a number of shacks and hovels. Much of this seems to have changed during the course of the following decades. Indeed, surviving records reveal an increased activity in reparations and additions to the walls of Sant'Angelo in Colle financed by the Sienese government towards the end of the fourteenth century. In 1389, the *Concistoro* in Siena agreed that 48 *lire* (equivalent to the value of a medium-sized house in the village) should be spent constructing an extra 16 *canne* of wall.[43] No reason was given for this extension, but only a few years earlier (in 1380) the General Council had considered a request to fortify a palace that was sited

Figure 2.9
Possible remains
of an eastern
gateway in the
proposed initial
circuit of walls

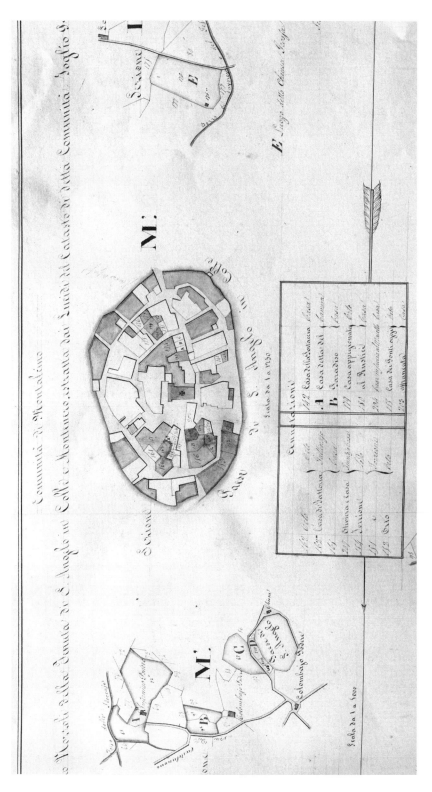

Figure 2.10 Nineteenth-century map of Sant' Angelo in Colle showing property belonging to the hospital of Santa Maria della Croce in Montalcino. Archivio Comunale, Montalcino, Ospedale, Atlante dei Beni stabili e livellari di proprietà dello spedale di S. Maria della Croce di Montalcino, XIX 31/44 (34)

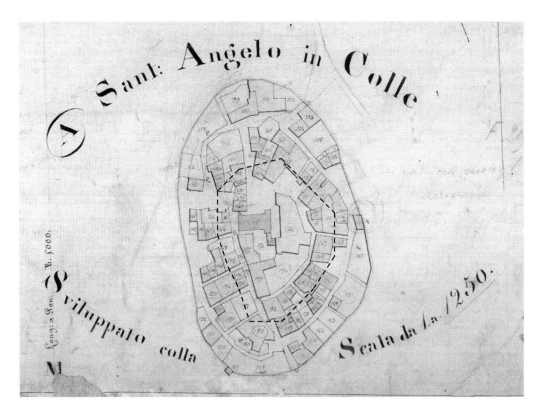

Diagram 2.2 Proposed second circuit of walls associated with a gateway on the western side of the village (traced over the 1820 *catasto* map)

near the walls of Sant'Angelo in Colle and which, at that date, was intended to function as the new *grancia* for the Ospedale di Santa Maria della Scala in Siena.[44] It seems clear that this was the building that had served at one time as the village's *Palazzo Comunale*, but which more recently had accommodated the Sienese barracks. Over time, it had, however, fallen into disrepair. The 16 extra *canne* of wall mentioned in 1389 may thus have been associated with the restoration of the old *cassero* – helping to secure the hospital of Santa Maria della Scala's newly-acquired property, and bringing the grange complex safely within the confines of the pre-existing urban fabric.

The remains of other complexes belonging to the hospital of Santa Maria della Scala indicate that it was normal to have not only a surrounding wall but also barbicans and corner towers.[45] According to Giuseppina Coscarella and Franca Cecilia Franchi ('Le Grance dello Spedale di Santa Maria della Scala nel contado senese'), each grange also contained its own church, and the *granciere*, or grange keeper, was responsible for the celebration of certain festivals there. Thus in many cases, as well as functioning as the secular headquarters and storage area in connection with local agriculture and trade, the grange also served as a point of religious reference. As already noted, it was also often the case that the grange assumed a charitable role in caring for the poor, accommodating pilgrims, helping the sick, baptising the new born and finding wet nurses for *trovatelli*, or orphans, who were laid at its door.

Proposed third circuit of walls

Hypothesised infill of walls to the north and north-east of the village following the construction of the third circuit of walls

Hypothesised further circuit of walls enclosing area known as Costa Sant'Angelo to the north-west and south-east of the village and additional extensions to the urban fabric on the north-east and south-eastern sides

Diagram 2.3 Proposed third circuit of walls associated with the 'casa della portaccia' (traced over the 1820 *catasto* map) with hypothesised further expansions in the area known as the Costa Sant'Angelo and elsewhere

Such diversity of function is well illustrated by the frescoes in the Pellegrinaio of Santa Maria della Scala itself.[46]

Stephan Epstein suggests that many of the granges established in the southern Sienese *contado*, essentially following the Cistercian matrix, in effect replicated in miniature the imposing central structure and administration of Santa Maria della Scala.[47] Granges constituted working businesses, whilst at the same time providing accommodation for the *granciere*, or grange master, and his family. Moreover, it was through the offices of the grange, that contracts were drawn up for the leasing of property belonging to the hospital, as well as the overseeing of local productions and husbandry, and the transport of goods both to other granges, and back to Siena itself. The grange master thus assumed the role and duties similar to those of modern factors.

Although Stephan Epstein maintained that Santa Maria della Scala's grange at Sant'Angelo in Colle was a relatively modest affair, reference to the fortification of the new complex in 1380 indicates that it was at the very least battlemented.[48] (Further consideration is given to the architectural form of the old *cassero*, and to the location of the gate referred to as the 'Porta Maggiore' in the following chapter.)

The dimensions and character of the one remaining tower block, the so-called 'Palazzaccio', would also seem to indicate that the new grange was a structure of some size. It also seems clear that the pre-existing barracks had themselves been fortified although possibly not when initially established on the site of the old town hall. In October 1380, when the Sienese were on the point of handing over the old *cassero* (which was specifically described as 'next to the walls') to the hospital of Santa Maria della Scala, reference was made to the fortification of the barracks some 40 years previously.[49] There may thus have been a period of time between 1280 and 1340 when the Sienese *cassero*, possibly merely established within the fabric of the old town hall rather than the result of a new build, was more like a secular palace than a military headquarters.

It seems likely, however, that the village walls themselves were fortified at a much earlier date, perhaps soon after Sant'Angelo in Colle was designated as a frontier castle in 1265. Like many other military outposts in the medieval period, the boundary walls of the village probably contained a number of towers – solitary observers of potential danger from the south, west, east and north. Such fortifications must necessarily have been reconstructed when displaced by new circuits of walls. Following the proposed path of the third circuit of walls at Sant'Angelo in Colle, we can identify a number of sites (including that of the *casa della portaccia*), where the size, shape and location of the ground plans would have been appropriate as lookout posts.[50] Nineteenth-century *catasto* maps show that the outermost circuit of walls (as defined at that time) had originally included at least one lookout tower to the south-west, on plot 129.[51] It seems likely that there were originally several more.[52] The walls of Montalcino sport the remains of four lookout towers even in the twenty-first century.[53] And several more towers were indicated by Giovanni Antonio Pecci when he made his sketch of the town around 1760.[54]

Sant'Angelo in Colle may thus at one stage have looked somewhat like Monteriggione, another frontier post, to the north-west of Siena. Such battlements and fortified towers were probably the norm. They not only served to protect towns and villages from attack, but also provided concrete evidence of allegiance. In financing the construction and reparation of walls in the subject commune of Sant'Angelo in Colle, the Sienese government succeeded not only in protecting its inhabitants, but also in confirming its own territorial claim to, and power over the village.

The position of the *Palazzaccio* on the north-western side of Sant'Angelo in Colle, and the existence of at least two other tower structures to the west and south-west prompts further speculation about access on the western side of the village during the medieval period. The present entrance road curving round on the north-western side of the village was constructed only in the mid-twentieth century. Before this, and even as late as the nineteenth century, Sant'Angelo in Colle was reached by way of the much older via di S. Angelo. As already noted, this road cut up over the hill to the north of Sant'Angelo in Colle, after forking off from the Sesta, Sant'Antimo and Castelnuovo del Abate road. There seems little doubt that during the early medieval period, the Sesta road offered the main access to Sant'Angelo in Colle from the north-east, avoiding the hills and thick forest that backed up towards Montalcino, but what of the continuation of this road, and possible access on the other side of the village? Nineteenth-century maps show how, prior to the construction of the 'Strada Traversa i Monti', Sant'Angelo in Colle – isolated from the north and north-west by forest – fitted snugly, like an egg, into a dog-leg of road, which branched off from an access point on the north-eastern side of the village (see Figure 1.1). One part of this road flanked the eastern and southern sides of the village, before zigzagging down to join the 'via di Montiano' (sometimes referred to as 'via di Monteano'), in order subsequently to pursue a southerly course towards the Orcia River. The other part of the dog-leg – on the western side – continued three-quarters of the way round the village, before cutting off in front of the *Palazzaccio*, and plunging down to meet the 'strada vicinale Fonte Lontano', and eventually joining up with the thoroughfare on the southern side of the village known as the 'via di Sant'Angiolo in Colle'. The stretch of road that in the nineteenth century hugged the perimeter of Sant'Angelo in Colle on its south-western side would seem to confirm that there was originally some kind of access to the village just south of the *Palazzaccio*.

As already indicated, the more recent toponyms 'strada di Sant'Angiolo' and 'strada vicinale di Fonte Lontano', most probably reflected names allotted at a much earlier date to thoroughfares leading to and from Sant'Angelo in Colle on its south and south-western sides. Although narrow and steep, these tracks would have been easily passable for those on foot or with oxen or mules. It is significant, also, that as late as 1833, the old 'strada di

Sant'Angiolo' still served as a thoroughfare connecting Sant'Angelo in Colle with Argiano. In the medieval period, this road could thus have provided an important transit route across towards the Orcia valley, and continuing via the ford in the vicinity of the confluence of the Orcia and the Ombrone to the more distant pasture lands of the Maremma. This same road could also have offered access to Sant'Angelo in Colle in the vicinity of the large public square on the western side of the village. Land workers could thus have disgorged the contents of their carts and panniers in an open space at (or just inside) a gate on the western side of the village, and returned down the hill to collect further produce, without entering, or passing through Sant'Angelo in Colle itself. In this context, it may be relevant to note that the road on the western side of the village that now lies within the existing outer perimeter is called 'la via della piazzuola'. This could indicate that the original function of this road was to transport people and goods backwards and forwards to the western square.

In some senses, the western side of Sant'Angelo in Colle would have been an ideal place for the delivery of produce gathered from the sun-drenched and well-drained southern slopes to the west and south. Given the various locations of gates proposed above, the road marked in nineteenth-century records as continuing around the south-eastern and south-western sides of Sant'Angelo in Colle would not only have effected a cut-through outside the walls for wagons, travellers on horseback and herds of animals being driven along an east–west *transumanza tratturello*, but would also have served local residents and land workers moving much shorter distances between one piece of the territory in the immediate vicinity of the village and another. For those wishing to bypass Sant'Angelo in Colle altogether, there was the cut up from the Sesta road that continued on past the old church of the Compagnia on the site of the present 'podere della Compagnia', and then dipped down steeply towards the Orcia River. This road also offered a transverse route that continued on down to Poggio alle Mura, and finally reached the River Orcia close to its confluence with the Ombrone. Such a cut through would have been an obvious route to take for those driving sheep and other livestock along the Sesta road on their way to the Maremma, and not wishing to enter Sant'Angelo in Colle itself.

This, then, was the basic framework of medieval Sant'Angelo in Colle under the Government of the Nine, as reconstructed on the basis of surviving records from the period, more recent surveys of the village dating to the sixteenth, seventeenth, eighteenth and nineteenth centuries, and the contemporary recollections of those who still live there.

An outer perimeter of walls – partially fortified by lookout posts – and punctured at one juncture by military barracks imposed upon the pre-existing town hall, with access and egress by way of at least two gates. Inside the fourteenth-century circuit of walls the urban fabric was crisscrossed by further sections of wall, and contained numerous narrow alleys on a number of different levels. Coursing along some of these alleys was an internal water system fed from a cistern in the highest part of the village which flowed out through the walls into a series of external ditches. In close proximity to the walls there was at least one public washing area, and at a slightly greater distance from the village several other sources of water serving a number of functions.

How, then, were the residents of Sant'Angelo in Colle accommodated during the early medieval period? As we shall see in the following chapter, a bird's eye view of the cheek-by-jowl existence of the 'angels on the hill' emerges from information contained within the 1320 *Tavola delle possessioni*. Individual entries in that document reveal much about the ownership of private houses, and the position of individual units of accommodation in terms of adjacent properties and fixed landmarks, such as the water conduit, public institutions and the village walls. In short, the 1320 *Tavola delle possessioni* for Sant'Angelo in Colle offers a unique opportunity to 'fit the parts together'.

Notes

1 For a recent analysis of the urban and rural scenes in the Lorenzetti frescoes in the Palazzo dei Nove, see Alberto Colli (ed.), *Ambrogio Lorenzetti: la vita del Trecento in Siena e nel contado senese nelle commitenze istoriate pubbliche e private: guida al Buon governo* (Siena, 2004). For an earlier analysis of the political and social implications of the frescoes, see Michael Baxandall, 'Art, Society and the Bouguer Principle', *Representations*, 12 (1985), pp. 32–43.

2 At the time of the oath of fealty to Siena on 15 July 1212, Sant'Angelo in Colle fell under the diocese of Arezzo, only later being placed under the ecclesiastical authority of Chiusi, see Ugo Ricci, *Sant'Angelo in Colle: Appendice* (Sant'Angelo in Colle, 1989), pp. 11 and 50. A number of castles that had previously been dependent on Sant'Antimo were handed over to Siena in 1212. But Sant'Antimo still apparently retained some rights over Sant'Angelo in Colle in 1216, since a papal bull drawn up on behalf of Onofrio III in December of that year records that the abbey still owned the church at Sant'Angelo in Colle, see Don Antonio Brandi, *Parrocchia di S. Michele Arcangelo in S. Angelo in Colle* (Sant'Angelo in Colle, 2004), p. 6. See also Odile Redon, *Uomini e comunità del contado senese nel Duecento* (Siena, 1982), p. 211, footnote 215. For an earlier reference to the links between Sant'Antimo and Sant'Angelo in Colle, see Don Antonio Brandi, *Parrocchia di S. Michele Arcangelo in Sant'Angelo in Colle* (Sant'Angelo in Colle, 1972), pp. 5–6. See also Emanuele Repetti, *Dizionario geografico fisico storico della Toscana* (6 vols, Florence, 1833–1846), 1, 1833, p. 86) for a suggestion that Sant'Angelo in Colle was at one time included in the parish of Santa Restituta. In 1462 Pope Pius II removed Sant'Angelo in Colle from the diocese of Chiusi and placed it under the diocese of Montalcino, see Don Brandi, *Parrocchia di S. Michele Arcangelo in S. Angelo in Colle* (Sant'Angelo in Colle, 2004), p. 8.

3 For references to the 'Costa porta cancelli', see Archivio di Stato di Siena (hereafter ASS), *Estimo* 24, fol. 401v.

4 For references to the 'Poggio Cancelli', see ASS, *Estimo* 24, fols 62r, 127r and 370r.

5 I am grateful to Stefania Fatorella Bindocci for drawing my attention to the area

to the south of the village that is still referred to as 'Cancelli'.

6 Archivio Vescovile di Montalcino (hereafter AVM), *Sant'Angelo in Colle*, Prepositura, 13, insert dated 1587, fol. 59r.

7 ASS, *Consiglio Generale*, 187, fol. 35v.

8 For a reference to the 'Contrada di Porta maie (?maggiore)' in the 1320 *Tavola delle possessioni*, see ASS, *Estimo* 24, fol.267v. For a reference to the 'Porta maggiore' in the context of a vineyard owned by Neri di Guicciardo, see his tax return in ASS, *Estimo di Siena*, 106, Terzo di Città, San Pietro in Chastelvecchio, 1318, pencil fol. no. 73v. See also ASS, *Estimo* 24, fol. 265v for what appears to be a reference to the 'contrada' of the Porta Maggiore.

9 See ASS, *Consiglio Generale*, 187, fol. 35v.

10 For a recent consideration of fountains and sources of water in and around Sant'Angelo in Colle, see Anabel Thomas, 'Cosa c'è dietro il nome? Le vecchie fonti di Montalcino e Sant'Angelo in Colle: acqua, località e toponomi', *Gazzettino e Storie del Brunello e di Montalcino*, 1 Anno No. 7, July (2007), pp. 14–16.

11 According to an assessment of the state of the roads in the neighbourhood of Sant'Angelo in Colle at the end of the eighteenth century, the *fonte pubbliche* were reached via a *cul-de-sac* that branched off from the main thoroughfare that cut up from the Sesta road, see Archivio Comunale di Montalcino (hereafter ACM), *Archivio Preunitario (1361–1865), Circondario dell' Ingegnere*, 1690, *Campione delle strade della Comunità di Montalcino compilato l'Anno 1778 dal provveditore di Strade Giuseppe Canali a forme del Nuovo Regolamento…. del 2 Giugno 1777 [Strade di S. Angelo in Colle]*. Presumably, it was this *cul-de-sac* that was subsequently lengthened to form the present entrance road to the village.

12 This structure still remains, albeit in a somewhat degraded state.

13 I am grateful to Bruno Bonucci for drawing my attention to this record. For the drawing of the fonte lontana, see ACM, *Ingegnere del Circondario*, 1690, foglio dated 24 July, 1833.

14 I am grateful to Alessandra Severini for this information.

15 According to Ilio Raffaelli, *Prima dell'Economia del Brunello. Montalcino: urbanistica, demografia, cultura e società dalle origini ai nostri giorni* (Montalcino, 2001), p. 169, another ford further to the west, close to the confluence of the Ombrone and Orcia rivers, was in operation in the early nineteenth century. According to the same source, the present bridge at Sant'Angelo Scalo was only constructed in the late 1870s.

16 ASS, *Manoscritti D 84, Visita fatta nell'Anno 1676 alle Città, Terre, Castella dello stato della città di Siena dall'Ill. Monsignore B. Gherardini, Auditore Generale in Siena per la A.S. di Cosimo III de' Medici Granduca VI di Toscana* (Eighteenth-century copy), fol. 75.

17 ASS, *Consiglio Generale*, 89, fols 163v–164v (new pencil pagination).

18 Ibid., fols 165v–166v.

19 Amongst those wells and cisterns surviving into the twentieth-first century and still in private possession are those situated in the courtyard of Palazzo Rosso (on plot no. 173), on plot no. 143, in the basement of Palazzo Ricci on plot no. 168, and on plot no. 192.

20 I am grateful to Giuliano Guerrini and Wanda de Merli for this information.

21   I am grateful to Wanda de Merli for this information.

22   Duccio Balestracci and Gabriella Piccinni, *Siena nel Trecento: assetto urbano e strutture edilizie* (Florence, 1977), p. 42.

23   For a recent exposition of such divisions, see my 'Cosa c'è dietro il nome?'.

24   ASS, *Manoscritti* D 67, *Memorie Storiche Politiche, Civili, e Naturali delle Città, Terre, e Castella, che sono, e sono state suddite alla Città di Siena. Raccolte dal Card. Gio(vanni) Antonio Pecci, Patrizio Sanese* (hereafter *Pecci*), fol. 85.

25   Annamaria Nada Patrone, 'Le Pellicce nel traffico commerciale Pedemontano del tardo medioevo', in *Cultura e società nell'Italia medievale: studi per Paolo Brezzi* (Rome, 1988), vol. 2, pp. 562–84, notes that animal hides were washed in calcinated water, giving rise to such toponyms as 'calcinarium' and 'via del calcinaio'. According to Patrone, the 'calcinarium' was often outside the walls, but always close to a flow of water. In that way local inhabitants would not only be distanced from the stench, but the smell itself could be diminished through being carried away from the urban fabric.

26   The remains of what was probably originally a *cavina* or *treseppo* of the original *corso d'acqua* have recently been unearthed at the side of the building that until a short while ago functioned as the village school (plot nos 175 and 175 bis on the 1820 *catasto* map of Sant'Angelo in Colle). I am grateful to the present owners, Luciana Andreini and Carmine Nutolo, for offering access to the site during restoration work.

27   See ASS, *Estimo* 24, fols 414r and 431r.

28   Ibid., fols 6r, 140r, 215r, 219r, 265r. I am grateful to Giuliana Guerrini for drawing my attention to the fact that there is still an area referred to as the 'carbonelle' to the north of village. In recent times, both *carbonaia* and *carbonella* have more commonly been adopted in the context of areas set aside for the making of charcoal.

29   ASS, *Consiglio Generale*, 23, fol. 7r. (new pencil pagination).

30   In this respect, see Roberta Ferri (ed.), *La memoria dell'acqua: I bottini di Siena* (Siena, 2006). See also Vinicio Serino (ed.), *Siena e l'acqua. Storia e immagini della città e delle sue fonti* (Siena, 1997); and Fabio Bargagli Petrucci, *Le Fonti di Siena e i loro acquedotti: note storiche dalle origini fino al 1555* (Siena, 1903 and Florence, 1906).

31   ASS, *Consiglio Generale*, 3, fols 7r–7v (new pencil pagination).

32   Ibid., 61, fols 62v–63v (new pencil pagination) [28 Feb, 1301/2].

33   ACM, *Archivio Preunitario (1361–1865), Lavori di acque e strade*, 159, *Ufficiali di acque e strade carteggi e atti 1727–1813, numero 27*, 'Fonti dentro alla città di Montalcino, e Bottini ritrovati e riattati l'1727 '. See, also, my 'Cosa c'è dietro il nome?'. For a discussion of the so-called 'Fonte di Porta di Fontebuia', see Bruno Bonucci, *Montalcino Pietre e storia* (San Quirico d'Orcia, 1999), pp. 26–28.

34   Bonucci, *Montalcino Pietre*, p. 28, fig. 15.

35   See Balestracci and Piccinni, *Siena nel Trecento*, pp. 20–26, for the expansion of the walls at Siena following the influx of newcomers after the thirteenth century. For a re-construction of the urban development at Siena, see Mario Ascheri, *Siena e la città-stato del Medioevo Italiano* (Siena, 2003), pp. 24–25.

36   Roberto Farinelli and Andrea Giorgi, *Camigliano, Argiano e Poggio alle Mura (secoli*

12–14), presented by Alfio Cortonesi (Siena, 1995), p. 14, note 20.

37 Ibid., pp. 14–19.

38 Ibid., p. 17. The house belonging to Ciampolo Gallerani, described as 'signore', or lord, of the castle in 1320, was valued at 141 *lire* 13 *soldi*. According to Farinelli and Giorgi, the *Arciprete*, or canon of the cathedral of Montalcino, by contrast was recorded as being accommodated in two houses belonging to the commune of Camigliano, one of which was valued at 80 *lire*, and the other of which was positioned above a 'domus cum furno' (presumably the old communal oven), which was valued at 150 *lire*. Other buildings ranged in estimated value from 5 to 50 *lire*. In the *Tavola delle possessioni* for Camigliano (ASS, *Estimo del Contado*, 80), the first of the buildings owned by the commune is in fact recorded as having a value of 60 *lire*.

39 ASS, *Catasto*, Mappa di Montalcino, Sezione M bis, di 'Sant: Angelo in Colle', no. 32a, (hereafter ASS, *Catasto*, Mappa Montalcino).

40 The infilling of stone and surrounding brick work here could also indicate that this aperture, if originally serving as an entrance to the first nucleus of the village, was subsequently adapted to serve a private dwelling. As Farinelli and Giorgi (*Camigliano, Argiano e Poggio alle Mura*, p. 18) note, evidence of such practice is still visible at Camigliano, where two doors in the curtain walls have been absorbed into later buildings. In this context, see Paolo Cammarosano and Vincenzo Passeri, *I castelli del Senese. Strutture fortificate dell'area senese-grossetana* (Siena, 2006), pp. 38 and 48, for similar portals at Buonconvento and Castelnuovo Berardenga. In the latter case there are also the remains of a subterranean passage that probably formed part of the original castle fortifications running from one side of the hill to another. If a similar arrangement existed at Sant'Angelo in Colle, the remains of the portal in via Cosatti could mark the end of just such a passageway on the eastern side of the original complex.

41 ACM, *Ospedale*, Atlante dei Beni stabili e livellari di proprietà dello spedale di S. Maria della Croce di Montalcino, XIX, 31/44 (34, 'Comunità di Montalcino, Pianta del livello Nozzoli della tenuta di S. Angelo in Colle e Montenero, estratta dei lucidi da Catasto di detta comunità).

42 It seems clear that one stretch of this outer wall was demolished as late as 1832. In August of that year, a request was made to erect a new building on a patch of land close to the walls that belonged to Donata della Ciaia, see ACM, *Ingegnere del Circondario di Montalcino*, 1690, no. 117. This plot is described as being on the south side of the village and in the vicinity of an olive press belonging to the della Ciaia. Following permission to erect the new structure, a nearby stretch of the village wall was dismantled and only a portion to the height of one and a half *braccia* was left to act as a kind of parapet, see ACM, *Ingegnere del Circondario di Montalcino*, 1690, no. 149.

43 ASS, *Concistoro*, 148, fol. 18.

44 Ibid., *Consiglio Generale*, 190, fol. 97r.

45 For a detailed analysis of the architectural characteristics of the hospital's granges, see Giuseppina Coscarella and Franca Cecilia Franchi, 'Le Grance dello Spedale di Santa Maria della Scala nel contado senese', *BSSP*, 92 (1985), pp. 66–92. See also Giuseppina Coscarella, 'Le Grancie dello Spedale di Santa Maria della Scala di Siena', in Giuseppina Coscarella and Franca Cecilia Franchi (eds), *La Grancia di Cuna in Val d'Arbia. Un esempio di fattoria fortificata medievale*

(Florence, 1983), pp. 7–9 (8–9).

46 For a recent consideration of the various functions assumed by Santa Maria della Scala itself, and an overview of bibliography, see Gabriella Piccinni and Laura Vigni, 'Modelli di assistenza ospedaliera tra Medioevo ed Età Moderna. Quotidianità, amministrazione, conflitti nell'ospedale di Santa Maria della Scala di Siena', in Giuliano Pinto (ed.), *La società del bisogno. Povertà e assistenza nella Toscana medievale* (Florence, 1989), pp. 131–74.

47 Epstein, *Alle origini della fattoria*, p. 36.

48 Ibid., p. 58.

49 ASS, *Consistoro*, 148, fol. 97v.

50 See, for example, ASS, *Catasto*, Mappa Montalcino, plot nos 191, 189 and 119.

51 I am grateful to Giuliano Guerrini for drawing my attention to this tower, the remains of which are still visible.

52 According to Giuliano Guerrini, a second tower was positioned on the south-western side of the village close to plot no. 132, and the remains of another tower close to plot no.121 on the south-eastern side of the village were still clearly visible in the mid-twentieth century.

53 Bonucci, *Montalcino Pietre*, p. 36.

54 ASS, *Manoscritti* D 70, fol. 201r, Giovanni Antonio Pecci, Map of Montalcino, *c.*1760.

3

Public Institutions, Key Buildings and Private Houses: Accommodating the Statistics and Locating the Structures

According to the 1320 *Tavola delle possessioni*, the early fourteenth-century village contained a considerable number of civic buildings (including a town hall, several other unspecified communal buildings, one public oven, and one public olive press) and at least one and possibly two charitable or public assistance bodies (one of which was the village hospital, referred to as the 'ospedale di Sant'Angelo', but which was possibly linked with another quite separate institution, known locally as the 'casa della misericordia'). There were in addition two churches inside the walls: one, the parish church, with the *titulus* of San Michele and the other, a church with the *titulus* of San Pietro. Just outside the walls there was another church of undefined *titulus* that belonged to the church of San Pietro, and slightly further away from the urban fabric, there was yet another church with the *titulus* of San Pietro that was under the jurisdiction of the parish church of San Michele. Surviving records from a slightly later period make reference to at least two shops, one of which is described in 1328 as belonging to 'magistri Bindi olim Bindi calzolarii' (master Bindo son of the deceased Bindi, shoemaker).[1] In a will drawn up on 5 June 1378 for Dominico di Giuntarello da Argiano further reference was made to the 'calzolaio' (shoemaker) of Sant'Angelo in Colle, as well as to the 'buttigaio', or 'bottegaio' (shopkeeper, possibly selling wine).[2] A document surviving from the last years of the fourteenth century also refers to a *speziale*, or spice merchant cum grocer, Guido di Dominici di Gabriello.[3]

It also seems that a hostelry or hotel was positioned on the outer limits of the village by the middle years of the fourteenth century. In November 1365 the villagers of Sant'Angelo in Colle apparently attempted to set such a building on fire but, when challenged by the landlord (Bartolomeo di Longaruccio), claimed that the real culprits were a company of mercenary soldiers fighting alongside John Hawkwood.[4] According to Bartolomeo di Longaruccio, the hotel, which was somewhat puzzlingly described as 'outside Montalcino', was inhabited by members of his own family, placed there specifically to 'defend Sienese territory'. Bartolomeo claimed that his relatives had personally witnessed the arson attack, and that the people of

Sant'Angelo in Colle should thus pay reparations for the damage. Other sources make specific reference, however, to the presence of John Hawkwood and his military company in the vicinity of Sant'Angelo in Colle.[5] The case thus remains open as to precise culpability.

That at least one hotel was positioned in close proximity to the walls of Sant'Angelo in Colle in the fifteenth century is confirmed by details recorded in an inventory of the furnishings and possessions of the parish church of San Michele drawn up in 1492.[6] According to that record, the parish church owned a kitchen garden located in the area known as the *carbonaia*, or ditch, of the 'mal albergo. 'riscontra' alla chiesa di S. Pietro confine muro castellano e il cimitero di detta chiesa' (bad hotel … next to or opposite the church of San Pietro and next to the wall of the castle and the cemetery of the said church). The wording here indicates that the hotel, which was possibly of dubious repute, was perched above part of the ditch or old moat of the village, and that it was in close proximity both to the walls of Sant'Angelo in Colle and to the church of San Pietro and its cemetery. The 1492 inventory also makes reference to a small house outside the village that was adjacent not only to the church of San Pietro but also to land owned by that institution. This small house was bordered on one side by the 'public road'. It follows that the church of San Pietro itself must have also been positioned in the vicinity of a public thoroughfare. As we shall see, it seems most likely that the old church of San Pietro (and thus the hotel also) was located in the north-eastern part of the village.

According to the 1320 *Tavola delle possessioni* there were also some 160 private dwellings or units of accommodation located inside the village walls. About 75 per cent of the some 120 individuals listed as owning such property appear to have been able-bodied men. A large proportion, if not all of these could have been heads of individual households. Even if one assumed a conservative position in assessing the number of children and other dependents associated with such heads of family, one would have to multiply 125 several times. Working on the basis of the comparatively low average of four individuals per household (including children, widows and aged dependents), and taking into consideration the unspecified number of individuals listed as heirs in the 1320 *Tavola delle possessioni*, as well as those others who seem not to have owned any property of their own inside the walls of the village, but who were nevertheless associated with Sant'Angelo in Colle through ownership of land there, it would seem that the early fourteenth-century population consisted of some 1,000–1,500, and possibly even as many as 2,000 souls.[7] There seems little doubt that in 1320 Sant'Angelo in Colle was thriving, if not bursting at the seams.

Accommodating the statistics

Logically, one would hope to set all the information contained in the 1320 *Tavola delle possessioni* concerning the various public institutions and private buildings into the context of the existing urban fabric of Sant'Angelo in Colle. In practice, this is not as straightforward as it might seem. Apart from revealing the large number of people living inside the walls in 1320, the *Tavola delle possessioni* for that year shows that the urban fabric itself was crammed full, with very little land left unused, and with many orchards and kitchen gardens pushed out beyond the existing circuit of walls. Indeed, it seems that the number of living units recorded was on the one hand too great to fit into the urban fabric as we now know it, and on the other, barely sufficient to house the estimated population of the early fourteenth-century village.

In reconstructing earlier demographics and topographies, the modern historian confronts numerous obstacles, not least because individual identities are hard to fix or chart from a distance; and in the case of built environments, many structures noted in earlier documents no longer exist, or have undergone reconstruction in a way that obscures their original orientation, aspect and even function.

Confronting medieval demographics

During the last few decades attention has turned increasingly to the problems involved in establishing urban medieval demographics, most significantly following the ground-breaking work carried out during the 1970s by Georges Duby and Jacques Le Goff on the general characteristics of the extended family in medieval Italy, and by David Herlihy and Christiane Klapisch-Zuber on the specific components of families as revealed by fifteenth-century Florentine *catasto* records.[8] English-speaking scholars such as Barbara Hanawalt and, more specifically in the field of Italian studies, Richard Ring, have carried out similar studies in the context of labouring families in the countryside.[9] Italian scholars such as Giuliano Catoni, Rinaldo Comba, Maria Ginatempo, Gabriella Piccinni and Giuliano Pinto have concentrated on contemporary Sienese statistics.[10] More recently, Rinaldo Comba and Irma Naso have been instrumental in drawing together a number of wide-ranging demographic and societal studies covering the entire five centuries of the early and later medieval period in Italy.[11] Of particular interest in the context of the reconstruction of the urban fabric and society of medieval Sant'Angelo in Colle, and likewise recently, Fabio Giovannini and Italo Moretti have considered birth, mortality and demography on the basis of the surviving archaeological evidence, and, specifically, architectural and urbanistic remains.[12] In Italy, the work of, on the one hand Giovanni Cherubini, and on the other, Alfio Cortonesi and their associated teams of researchers have also revealed a detailed and continuing interest in surviving statistics concerning the conditions of labour and societal functions of land workers in the Italian medieval countryside.[13] Recent findings were presented at the thirteenth 'Laboratorio Internazionale di Storia Agraria' held in Montalcino in September 2010, which was dedicated exclusively to the peasant family.[14] Papers presented on that occasion ranged in subject-matter form the idea or concept of the family itself,[15] to the role of peasant families in medieval politics,[16] the work of women[17] and the domestic spaces of the buildings in which land workers and their families lived.[18]

A common complaint in all such studies is the absence of comprehensive contemporary records, and the difficulties this presents when attempting to reconstruct medieval demographics and topographies. In their original study of Tuscans and their families published in 1978, Herlihy and Klapisch-Zuber pointed out that it was only after 1372 that the Florentine communal government stipulated that the sex and age of all members of individual families should be included in taxation records.[19] Prior to 1372 such information was hard to come by. This is not the only restricting factor. Herlihy and Klapisch-Zuber underline the difficulties associated in establishing the size of individual families, because such statistics that do survive record different figures for different areas and periods (pre- and post-Black Death). Herlihy and Klapisch-Zuber also record startling discrepancies within the individual areas themselves. For example, despite the average figure of 4–6 children per family cited by the Florentine chronicler Giovanni Morelli, one of his own Florentine contemporaries apparently gave birth to 20 children within the space of 24 years.[20] Herlihy and Klapisch-Zuber also draw our attention to the scarce documentation of births and deaths during the fourteenth and fifteenth centuries, on account of there being no regular registration of either.[21] During the same period, there were, moreover, few registrations of baptisms. Such information was more often than not included in private family memoirs, particularly in urban centres such as Florence. However, as Herlihy and Klapisch-Zuber point out, references to the affairs of the women folk in such families were often scarce, and the death of a female member of the family would obviously only have been recorded if she predeceased the individual making the record.

Establishing the overall size and demographic mix of the early-fourteenth century population of Sant'Angelo in Colle by reference to the individual entries in the 1320 *Tavola delle possessioni* alone is thus problematic. While there can be little doubt that there was something in the region of 1,000 souls in the early fourteenth-century village, there could have been very many more. It is often impossible, for example, to establish from individual entries in the 1320 *Tavola delle possessioni* such fundamental details as an individual's age or marital status. Moreover, even where a woman is referred to in terms of a living husband one can only draw the most general conclusions about her age, the only more-than-likely probability being that she had at least reached the age of puberty. Similar restrictions apply in those cases where the woman is referred to as a widow. As with those who were described as married, women who had been widowed might just as well have reached that state whilst comparatively young, as when having reached a mature or ripe old age. Indeed, in his *Medieval Households* published in 1985, David

Herlihy suggests that girls could be married as young as the age of 12, and might already be widowed by the time they were 15.[22] This is not the only area where the interpretation of surviving statistics is problematic. In those instances where a number of people were gathered together under the heading of heirs, all that can safely be said is that the individuals in question were the remaining members of a family group whose nominal head had died. Of their precise number, age and marital status, we often know nothing. Where only the head of the household is named, we can make an approximate guess as to the size of their family – four individuals per household being generally regarded as a conservative estimation. In practice, however, there could have been double that number. It was, for example, often the case (and especially in the countryside) that adult males, although holding property (most commonly land) in their own name, continued to live under the roof of an older married sibling, whilst themselves remaining unmarried.[23] There are also recorded instances of several married members of the same family living under the same rood. In the absence of more detailed documentation in the form of family memoirs, a thing rare amongst the peasantry and the lower working classes in such country urban areas as Sant'Angelo in Colle,[24] any assessment of the demographic mix is thus bound to be approximate.

Reconstructing medieval topographies

Reconstructing the early fourteenth-century urban fabric of Sant'Angelo in Colle on the basis of information contained in the 1320 *Tavola delle possessioni* alone is also a hazardous process. For one thing, the existing village has lost a number of its key landmarks, including virtually all of its communal offices. Thus, any attempt to reconstruct Sant'Angelo in Colle's early fourteenth-century built environment on the basis of cluster diagrams of individual buildings and their proprietors, but without reference to the village's key buildings or landmarks, inevitably results in a vacuum or a series of unlinkable spaces. In the absence of detailed tracking of the structural changes that have been made to the built environment over time, any reconstruction of the medieval village must thus at best be regarded as provisional.[25]

In the case of Sant'Angelo in Colle, we are nonetheless fortunate in having – in addition to the 1320 *Tavola delle possesioni* – a number of other references to the physical aspect of the early fourteenth-century village, as well as several other descriptions of Sant'Angelo in Colle dating to the seventeenth, eighteenth and nineteenth centuries. These throw light on some of the changes made to the built environment over time. They also help us to establish the location of key landmarks within the old centre of the village. This in turn allows us to link up cluster diagrams assembled on the basis of information contained within the 1320 *Tavola delle possesioni*.

A number of preliminary observations may thus be made about the difficulties encountered by the modern historian when attempting to reconstruct the topography of the early fourteenth-century village of Sant'Angelo in Colle.

The first observation worth making is that the rateable values of individual buildings included in the 1320 *Tavola delle possessioni* for Sant'Angelo in Colle indicate that the urban fabric at that time consisted in large part of small to medium-sized buildings. Just over a third of the dwellings listed fell in the middle to lower end of property values, being rated in the 30–70 *lire* bracket.

Table 3.1
Property inside
the walls of
Sant'Angelo in
Colle valued
at between 30
and 63 *lire* in
the 1320 *Tavola
delle possessioni*

Proprietor	Estimated value in		Page no.
	lire	*soldi*	
Angelino di Buccio	32	–	1r
Avitolo di Ildebrandino	38	7	6r
Beccha Tini	39	7	23r
Benvenuta Ghezzi	42	13	37r
Bindo di Accorso	42	13	17v
Bindo di Mergone	44	13	47r
Bindo di Raniero	40	–	25r
Cecchino di Cecco	35	7	93r
Cenne di Bartolo	40	–	90r
Cennello di Ugolino	38	–	98r
Cennino di Cenne	39	7	85v
Chele di Ruggiero	61	–	73r
Chonte di Ventura	42	7	77r
Church of Sant'Angelo (San Michele)	33	–	128r
Church of San Pietro	48	7[1]	134r
Cola di Giovanni	42	–	68r
Commune	38	13[2]	59v
	37	7	60v
	53	7	61r
Domenico di Brunaccio	38	13	112v
Finuccio di Rannuccino	33	7	141r
Folchino di Giovanni	40	–	143r
Giacopo di Micheluccio	35	7	155r
Giovannino di Rainaldo	42	–	251v
Grifuccio di Bruno	30	–	156r
Heirs of Blanco	40	–	228r
Heirs of Ghezzo	30	–	215r
Heirs of Pieruccio di Guiglielmo	30	–	179r
Heirs of Tura di Benincasa	45	12	229r
Heirs of Vive di Jacopo	39	7	212v
Hospital of Sant'Angelo	50	–	193r
Landuccio di Berto	33	–	263v
Lonarduccio di Giontarello	38	13[3]	278r
Lonarduccio di Giovanni	62	–	275r
Maffuccia di Bencivenne	43	–	312r
Maffuccino di Maffuccio	46	–	333r
Marruccio di Angelello	53	7	304v

Manno di Maffuccio	32	–	328r
Martino di Gianne	42	13	300r
Mencino di Orlando	31	7	326r
Meo di Pepe	36	–	325r
Mico Genovese	40	–	287v
Minuccio di Sozza	31	7	292r
Mona Duccia di Ciole	63 [4]	–	331r
Mona Gioia	39	7	303r
Mona Neccha di Ventura	48	–	332r
Muccio di Orlando	37	–	301v
Naccino di Giordanello	55	13	355r
Naccino di Nuccio	43	13	353r
Nardello di Ventura	31	13	347v
	31	13	347v
Nardo di Cambio	30	13	349r
Nenno di Raniero	47	–	340r
Nucciarello di Raniero	48	7	357r
Petruccio di Alamanno	39	–	390r
Petruccio di Bonanno	31	7	376v
Pietrino di Nerio	40	–	388r
	38	13 [5]	388r
Petruccio di Pepe	37	7	387r
Riccuccio di Guido	43	7	403r
Scholaio di Gianello	47	7	401r
Sozzo di Giacomo	38	13	405r
Vannuccio di Giovanni	39	7	438r

Notes for Table 3.1
1 Described as a house 'cum claustro' (with cloister or sheep pen).
2 Described as a house with an olive press.
3 Described as a 'casalinum' (or small house).
4 Described as a house 'cum platea' (with a building plot).
5 Described as a 'casalinum' (or small house).

Analysis of the 63 properties in this category

The largest group of middle size properties (39) were valued between 30 and 40 *lire*. Half as many again (18) were valued between 41 and 50 lire. A handful (3) were valued between 51 and 60 lire, and a further handful (3) that must have been verging on the larger size were valued between 61 and 63 lire.

Only about one eighth of the total number of living units were valued at higher figures, and were thus, presumably, larger.

Table 3.2
Property inside
the walls of
Sant'Angelo in
Colle valued at
over 70 *lire* in
the 1320 *Tavola
delle possessioni.*

Proprietor	Estimated value in		Page no.
	lire	*soldi*	
Berna di Ghezzo	100	–	31v
Bindo di Accorso	86	13	18v
Cecco di Tura	82	–	79v
Church of Sant'Angelo	135	–	126r
Commune	113	7 [1]	59v
	350	–	61r
Heirs of Cecco di Piero	150	–	172v
Heirs of Ser Francesco	76	13	167r
Heirs of Vivo di Jacopo	70	13	212r
Lando di Pepe	100	–	265r
Mico Genovese	110	–	287r
Mita di Tora	76	7	310r
Nino di Giovanni	102	8	342v
Paganello di Giovanni	125	–	380r
Ser Tollo di Gollo	80	–	407r

Note to Table 3.2
1 This property is described as a house combined with an oven.

Analysis of the sixteen properties in this category

This table shows that there were at least sixteen houses of some size with estimated values of between
70 and 100 *lire*. Eight properties were of exceptional size by comparison with the rest of the village, with
estimated values of between 100 and 150 *lire*. One very large building valued at 350 *lire* was owned by the
commune but was not apparently functioning as the *Palazzo Comunale* in 1320.

Forty or so other units were valued between 20 and 30 *lire.*

Table 3.3
Property inside
the walls of
Sant'Angelo in
Colle valued
at between 20
and 29 *lire* in
the 1320 *Tavola
delle possessioni*

Proprietor	Estimated value in		Page no.
	lire	*soldi*	
Betto di Romaiuolo	25	7	14r
Bindo di Accorso	21 [1]	–	17v
	23	7	17v
	28	13	18v
Bindo di Montenero	22	–	45r
Bosta di Micheluccio	24	13	42r
Casina di Altimanno	28	13	101r
Cecca di Guido	20	–	92r
Cecchino di Ghezzo	20	13	71r
Cecco di Bindo	21	7	84r
Church of Sant'Angelo	25	7	125v
	20	13	129v
	25	13	125v
Ciana di Guidarello	21	13	95r
Commune	21	7 [2]	61r
Domichello di Romaiuolo	22	–	109v
Domina Rosa wife of Fuccio	26	–	400r

Gano di Guglielmucci	28	13	149r
Gilio di Rannuccio	25	13	147v
Gratia di Ugolino	25	–	157r
Guarneruccio di Bruno	26	–	151r
Guiduccio di Tebaldo	29	13	159r
Heirs of Binozzio	24	13	232r
Heirs of Cecco di Piero	22	13 [3]	172r
	20	–	174r
Heirs of Franco	24	13	186v
Heirs of Guido Schifalorzo	26	7	217r
Heirs of Pieruccio di Guiglielmo	29	7	179r
Lonarduccio di Terno	21 [4]	–	277r
	27	13	277r
Maffeo di Januario or Gennaro	24	13	290v
Martinuccio di Martino	26	7	323r
Mino di ser Guillielmo	25	–	320r
Mita di Brunaccio	23	13	313r
Mona Mita di Piero	22	–	330r
Nuta di Sozzo	27	–	354r
Petruccio di Giovanni	27	13	383r
Petruccio di Pepe	23	7	387r
Petruccio di Piero	24	7	378v
	20	–	378v
Ristoruccio di Borgognone	21	7	398v
Sozzo di Rannuccio	27	–	410r
Tino di Montenero	20	13	416r
Tura di Guillelmo	27	13	413r
Vanne di Chele	28	13	433r
Vanuccio di Toro	20	–	442r

Notes to Table 3.3
1 Described as a 'plateam', or building plot.
2 Described as a 'casalinum', or small house.
3 Described as 'simul cum Viviano Ranuccio', possibly indicating that it was owned jointly with Viviano Ranuccio. However, no reference is made to any property inside the walls in the entry for Viviano Ranuccio in the 1320 *Tavola delle Possessioni*.
4 Described as 'unam quondam plateam' (what had been a building plot).

Analysis of the forty-six properties in this category

While the majority of these structures were described as a 'domus', or house, in one instance – in details recorded in respect of property owned by the commune – the term 'casalinum', or small house was adopted. The estimated value was not, however, significantly different. The same can be said for the two building plots. One conclusion to be drawn is that (as now) the evaluation of the property depended on overall square (rather than cubic) measurements.

Roughly 30 more units of accommodation fell in the much lower category of between 10 and 19 *lire.*

Table 3.4
Property inside
the walls of
Sant'Angelo in
Colle valued
at between 10
and 19 *lire* in
the 1320 *Tavola
delle possessioni*

Proprietor	Estimated value in			Page no.
	lire	*soldi*	*denari*	
Bindo di Accorso	14	7	–	18v
Cenne di Lactarino	19	7	–	91r
Church of Sant'Angelo	14	13	–	126v
	15	13	–	125v
	19	7	–	129v
Cignone di Benvenuto	18	–	–	99v
Commune	10 [1]	–	–	60v
	15	7	–	60v
Fuccio di Andelone	14	13	–	139r
Fatuiola Maffeo	15	–	–	145r
	16	1	–	145r
Guccio di Petruccio	16	13	–	153v
Heirs of Accorso	19	7	–	227r
Heirs of Cecco cavaliere	19	7	–	225r
Heirs of Cecco di Piero	14	7	–	172v
	14	13	–	173v
	15	7	–	172r
Heirs of Peruccio di Guillielmi	10 [2]	–	–	179r
Heirs of magister Puccio	12	–	–	231r
Lando di Gionte	18	–	–	272v
Marco di Johanelli	15	13		317r
Martino di Berto	17	6	6 [3]	283r
Mico Genovese	16	–	–	287r
Mideo di Fuccio	10	6	6 [4]	316r
Necca di Brunaccio	15	–	–	361r
Neruccio di Nolso	17	7	–	364r
Nino di Giovanni	14	7	–	343r
Novellina di Bino	16	13	–	368r
	19	7	–	368r
Ser Guccio di Ser Francesco	10	–	–	451r
Tura di Manno	18	13	–	453v
Vanuccio di Berto di magister Martino	17	6	6 [5]	426r
Vannuccio di Massaia	19	7	–	440r
Vina di Moreglio	17	7	–	443r

Notes to Table 3.4
1 Described as a 'casalinum', or small house.
2 Described as a 'casalinum', or small house.
3 Described as half a house. The other half is said to have belonged to Vanuccio di Berto – presumably Martino's brother.
4 Described as half a house. The other half is said to have belonged to the heirs of Nerio. No property inside the walls of Sant'Angelo in Colle is recorded in respect of these latter individuals in the 1320 *Tavola delle Possessioni*.
5 Described as half a house.

A mere handful – most of which were categorised as half houses – were valued at less than 9 *lire*.

Proprietor	Estimated value in			Page no.
	lire	*soldi*	*denari*	
Bella di Lamberto	9	13		46r
Church of Sant'Angelo	1 [1]			126r
Heirs of Cecco di Piero	1 [2]			172r
Heirs of Franco	7	13		187r
	3 [3]	10 [4]		186v
				187r
Giovanni di Gualtiero	6			253r
Lucarino di Ser Francesco	5	13	6 [5]	268v
Ser Guccio di Ser Francesco	5	13	6 [6]	451v

Table 3.5
Property inside
the walls of
Sant'Angelo in
Colle valued at
less than 9 *lire* in
the 1320 *Tavola
delle possessioni*

Notes to Table 3.5
1 Described as a 'casalinum', or small house.
2 Described as half of a 'casalinum', or small house.
3 Described as a building plot.
4 Described as a 'platea', or building plot.
5 Described as half a house.
6 Described as half a house.

Analysis of the eight properties in this category

On the basis of these details, it seems that – with the exception of the small house recorded in respect of the church of San Michele, and the half of a small house recorded in respect of the heirs of Cecco di Piero – there were very few really small structures inside the walls of the village in 1320. In the case of the properties owned by Lucarino di Ser Francesco and Ser Guccio di Ser Francesco, it seems that the two structures were contiguous and covered by the same roof.

While the overall picture that emerges is thus of a relatively modest built environment, the fact that some 20 or so buildings of some size already existed within what was a relatively small area indicates that early fourteenth-century Sant'Angelo in Colle also had a grander side.

Camigliano at the same date had surprisingly few buildings of any size. Details included in the *Tavola delle possessioni* of that community reveal that there were only one or two buildings (apart from property owned by the commune) that fell within the range of 50 to 80 *lire*.[26] A further handful fell within the bracket of 30 to 40 *lire*. But, for the most part, the urban fabric of early fourteenth-century Camigliano consisted of buildings valued between 20 and 30 *lire*.

The second, and perhaps more surprising, observation is that when comparing the existing old centre of Sant'Angelo in Colle with information furnished in the 1320 *Tavola delle possessioni* it appears that the urban fabric has shrunk. There are now far fewer buildings than the 100 or so individual units of accommodation referred to in the 1320 *Tavola delle possessioni*. There are also far fewer demonstrably large buildings. It is also clear that some of the key buildings noted in the early fourteenth-century *Tavola* are now missing. Inside the old centre, there is now only one church, no town hall, no hospital, and no public olive press.

It is, of course, inevitable that urban fabrics should change over time. Older buildings degrade; new buildings take their place. As will be revealed here, some of the changes wrought on the built environment at Sant'Angelo in Colle were the direct result of events such as wars, local rebellions and takeovers by outsiders. Other changes appear to have kept pace with the village's economic and political developments. As the economy of the village flourished in periods of peace, and particularly between the thirteenth and fourteenth centuries under the protection of the Government of the Nine, so the urban fabric expanded. As everyday conditions worsened during the fifteenth century, following drought, disease, a declining population and the inevitable accompanying poverty, so the built environment turned in on itself. When, in the sixteenth century, Sant'Angelo in Colle was relegated to a lesser level of importance as the power of Siena waned and that of Florence continued to rise, the entire fabric of the village seemed in danger of disintegration. Even so, the erstwhile frontier castle seems subsequently to have recovered some of its former prosperity. New patrons assumed responsibility for individual institutions inside the walls such as the parish church and the village hospital, and new proprietors established new homes inside the walls. As we shall see, such 'rebirths' could on occasion obscure earlier histories.

A number of key buildings noted in the 1320 *Tavola delle possessioni* were already missing by the late seventeenth century. When Bartolomeo Gherardini drew up his survey of Sant'Angelo in Colle in 1676 he noted that there were only six buildings of any size or significance there.[27] Three centuries earlier, there had been more than three times that number. Clearly, the old centre had already undergone considerable alteration. Gherardini's account throws light on some of those changes. Among the structures of substance noted by Gherardini in 1676 were a building belonging to the della Ciaia family; a building belonging to the heirs of Fausto Tolomei; another belonging to the Lucattini family from Arcidosso; another belonging to Giovanni Battista Cosatti; another belonging to the heirs of Fausto Forteguerri, and a final one belonging to the 'Prepositura', or parish. By cross-referencing with nineteenth-century *catastal* records, we can establish the location of some, if not all of these.[28] Gherardini made no reference to the old *Palazzo Comunale*, although he did note that the 'stanza del forno', or communal oven room, and the house of the hospital were still standing. He did, however, make notes about the size and (in one case) ownership of two buildings associated with what he identified as the *Palazzo di Giustizia*, or Palace of Justice. In 1676 Gherardini recorded that the building currently assuming that function was a mere 'casetta', or little house, and that the building that had previously served as the Palace of Justice had passed to the heirs of Alessandro della Ciaia. No precise reference was given as to the location of the small building currently serving as the Palace of Justice, or to any nearby structures. According to Gherardini, the original Palace of Justice was being used by the della Ciaia as a 'granaio', or grain storage. It seems likely, therefore, that it was a building of some size. In the twenty-first century the della Ciaia property (now owned by the Franceschi family) is a magnificent structure. It appears that it has assumed its present guise for at least 200 years. Ettore Romgnoli's eighteenth-century drawing of the *Palazzo della Ciaia* already shows the imposing and comparatively long façade for its somewhat narrow site adjacent to the church of San Michele Arcangelo.[29] Even if altered and enlarged by the della Ciaia when adopting it as a store house in the seventeenth century, the size of this building implies that the original Palace of Justice in Sant'Angelo in Colle must originally have dominated the village at its central point.

Given the numerous references to commune property in the 1320 *Tavola delle possessioni*, and in particular to an existing town hall, Gherardini's silence concerning such a structure is curious. An obvious conclusion is that the town hall no longer existed in any recognisable form by the seventeenth century. This would not be surprising, given what is now known of the history of the original structure. There seems little doubt that this was the building that was taken over by the Sienese to serve as a barracks, and that it subsequently functioned in a much altered form as the headquarters of the hospital of Santa Maria della Scala, before being abandoned in the fifteenth century. It also seems extremely likely that it underwent further change, and possibly even radical deterioration following the abandoning of the village during the conflict between Florence and Siena in the sixteenth century. It may, however, be significant that Gherardini, when contemporaneously discussing the urban fabric of Montalcino, likewise made no reference to a 'Palazzo Comunale', referring instead to the 'Palazzo di Giustizia' with its tall tower, and the 'Palazzo dei Priori'.[30] That there were clear distinctions between the two communal buildings is obvious from Gherardini's detailed account. According to Gherardini the 'capitani di giustizia', or officials of justice, were actually accommodated in the *Palazzo di Giustizia* along with the town's judge and notary. He also noted that the *Palazzo di Giustizia* contained five prisons, two of which were public, and the remaining three of which were 'segrete', or secret. By contrast, in the 'Palazzo dei Priori' there were neither prisons nor living accommodation. This was in effect the communal office where members of the administration gathered together for council meetings. It seems clear from this that the 'Palazzo dei Priori' served as the town hall. Had any such structure survived at Sant'Angelo in Colle, Gherardini must surely have made note of it.

Between the seventeenth and eighteenth centuries an element of uncertainty appears to have crept in concerning the site of the Palace of Justice in Sant'Angelo in Colle. When Giovanni Antonio Pecci drew up his *Memorie storiche, politiche, civili, e naturali delle città, terre, e castella, che sono e sono state suddite della città di Siena* between 1759 and 1761, he noted, like Gherardini, that the current Palace of Justice at Sant'Angelo in Colle was comparatively small ('angusto', or narrow). He also noted that the building was not very old. Like Gherardini, Pecci gave no clear indication as to the location of the building currently serving as the Palace of Justice. He did note, however, that it was generally thought that the original Palace of Justice was located on the site of the 'Torre', or tower (presumably the structure now known as the *Palazzaccio*).[31] One conclusion to be drawn from this is that the eighteenth-century chronicler Pecci confused the functions of what originally had been two quite separate structures: the one, the town hall serving as the administrative centre of the village which was indeed probably originally sited close to the *Palazzaccio*; and the other, the Palace of Justice, or law court, where legal issues would have been solved and where treasury matters may also have been considered, which was probably located (as Gherardini claimed) in the centre of the village close to the church of San Michele Arcangelo.

The third observation to be made is that while Bartolomeo Gherardini's account reveals that the seventeenth-century village was already a very different place from that indicated by entries in the 1320 *Tavola delle possessioni*, more drastic changes were to follow. It seems that the medieval village not only lost a proportion of its significant public buildings at an early date, but also a number of its larger buildings. The bank of more modest housing seems by contrast to have increased. In the eighteenth century Pecci noted, for example, that there were about 200 houses at Sant'Angelo in Colle – slightly more than the number recorded in the 1320 *Tavola delle possessioni*. Subsequently, there appears to have been a marked diminution. However, by the nineteenth century, only about 80 or so houses were recorded inside the old boundary walls of Sant'Angelo in Colle.[32] At the present time there are around 60. During the last 200 years alone, therefore, the village appears to have lost as much as a third of its eighteenth-century built environment.

By contrast, it seems that between the seventeenth and the nineteenth centuries a number of comparatively large structures were inserted into the urban fabric. During this period, also, several changes seem to have been made to pre-existing buildings, including the amalgamation of previously separate structures and complete new builds. While Gherardini noted only a handful of substantial structures in the seventeenth century, the ground plans of some 10 or so large buildings are clearly marked in the nineteenth-century 1820 *catasto* map for Sant'Angelo in Colle (in clockwise direction from the north, plot numbers 100, 101, 161, 165, 166, 115, 125, 188, 182, 193, 197, 155 and 156).[33] As we shall see, in at least one of these cases – the building on plot number 101 – it appears that several pre-existing structures were united behind one linking façade, thus obscuring the original aspects, and no doubt also the original functions of the individual units behind.

Some of the more drastic changes to the old urban fabric have occurred during the last 100 or so years. A number of buildings (including an open loggia) and open plots (including an orchard) originally situated on the western side of the main piazza (nos. 199, 200 and 201) were, for example, pulled down during the twentieth century in order to effect a larger public space in the vicinity of the church of San Michele Arcangelo. Elsewhere, reorganisation of the space in front of Palazzo Rosso (leading to the destruction of the building on plot no. 167) reduced the built-up environment, although at the same time providing more public open space. In other parts of the village, the filling in of open ground on plot nos 108, 132, 149, 154–6, 160, 173 bis, and partial alterations to plot nos 99, 121, 152 and153, as well as other changes in the area of plot nos 178, 179 and 183 have further distorted the old medieval nucleus. Many of the original *vicoli* (narrow alleyways) have in addition, been absorbed into private dwellings. Other changes have been made to the levels and layout of pre-existing streets and squares. Even the old cistern well in the Piazza del Pozzo is now virtually unrecognisable, having recently been filled in and converted into a restaurant terrace.

Such changes highlight some of the difficulties confronted by the modern historian when attempting to accommodate the topographical statistics of an earlier period. In the case of Sant'Angelo in Colle, without the supplementary information provided by later historians such as Bartolomeo Gherardini and Giovanni Antonio Pecci, and the more recent *catastal* maps of the nineteenth century, we might be able to conclude that the urban fabric had diminished in size during the intervening seven centuries, but we would not be in a position to chart how the built environment had expanded and diminished between any two fixed points in time. Nor would we be able to establish when, if at all, the function or aspect of a particular building had changed. As we shall see, questions concerning the ownership of property and the identity of individual proprietors, as well as the extent to which the various units of accommodation in the early fourteenth-century village were owned or rented presents further challenges to the modern historian intent on reconstructing the specifics of the medieval urban fabric.

Establishing the identities of individual property owners and reconstructing individual family units

While some of the details in the 1320 *Tavola delle possessioni* concerning the location and function of individual public institutions and private units of accommodation in the early-fourteenth century village raise questions about the extent of change in the urban fabric over time, close consideration of entries filed in respect of individual home owners reveals that many of the details furnished in the *Tavola* were themselves incompatible. Establishing whether or not an individual was the actual owner of the property, as opposed to being a temporary tenant is particularly challenging. The names of individual 'home owners' are sometimes subtly different; the precise amount of property held is often unclear. Confines of neighbouring buildings do not always tally, and it is on occasion difficult to establish whether an individual was local to Sant'Angelo in Colle, as opposed to being an 'outsider' from Siena or elsewhere. Uncertainties of this kind not only hinder attempts to establish the physical relationship between different units of accommodation, but also create problems when attempting to establish the precise location of key buildings and institutions such as the town hall and the hospital. All in all, this obstructs precise demographic analysis.

Addressing the anomalies

Some of the anomalies resulting from a comparison of individual entries in the 1320 *Tavola delle possessioni* may be explained in terms of human error.[34] While it was the case that professional *agrimensori*, or surveyors, and communal commissioners were charged with gathering and collating information for individual *Tavole* during the early fourteenth century, much of the detail for the preparatory *Tavolette* was inevitably furnished by the proprietors themselves, and through local testimonies. There were thus numerous ways in which such information could be flawed. Individual house owners may not always have known, for example, whether their neighbours rented or owned property adjacent to their own. In those cases where property was let out, the identity of the present tenant may not have been known or noted, the actual proprietor's name being instead included in the *Tavola delle Possessioni*.[35] In other cases, only the name of the tenant and not that of the owner may have been recorded. Numerous errors no doubt entered the system also, because individual house owners were not aware of, or failed to give their neighbour's full name. On occasion, the illegibility of an individual's handwriting must have compounded the confusion. All in all, there seems little doubt that the system was from the start seriously flawed. This is confirmed by surviving records. Even as early as 1319, the General Council in Siena was drawing attention to numerous inaccuracies in the *Tavole delle possessioni*.[36] One opinion was that too much value was placed on the representations of individual mayors in the communes of the *contado*. The implication was that such channels of communication were unreliable.

There seems little doubt that information concerning the amount of property owned was also on occasion deliberately withheld. It is a well-established fact that routine attempts were made to mislead tax officials during the medieval and Renaissance periods.[37] There were clearly a number of opportunities for obfuscation, for example, when siblings filed joint declarations. Where property was only partially declared, or where details of boundaries were left incomplete, there were bound to be disparities in the levying of tax. Where a number of properties were owned, and incomplete details were furnished by different members of the same family for the purpose of taxation, there was even greater scope for evasion. In such cases, at least one of the parties involved must have stood to gain from non-declaration, or under-evaluation of overall assets. A clear example of this in the 1320 *Tavola delle possessioni* for Sant'Angelo in Colle concerns property owned by two brothers, Guccio and Lucarinus (or Lucarino) di Ser Francesco. Both of these individuals apparently owned at least one half of a house inside the walls of Sant'Angelo in Colle. It is also clear that at least two of these half houses formed part of one and the same building, and were thus physically under the same roof. This much is clear from the declared boundaries.

The confines of one half-house belonging to Lucarino (which was valued at 5 *lire* 13 *soldi* and 6 *denari*) are recorded as two roads and a building belonging to Tura di Benencasa and Giovanni di Rainaldo.[38] The same entry also notes that the other half of this building belonged to Lucarino's brother, Guccio. In Guccio's entry (which is curiously inserted almost at the end of the 1320 *Tavola delle possessioni* after the section containing references to individuals whose names began with V) there is a reference to what appears to be exactly the same house, if it were not for the fact that Guccio, rather than Lucarino is recorded as the owner. At the same time, reference is made to the adjacent half building being owned by Guccio's sibling.[39] Thus far, information contained in the two records would seem to be compatible. However, details furnished in respect of another two half houses owned by Guccio and Lucarino are not so transparent. From the details furnished in respect of these and other nearby properties, it is clear that the two units (like the two half-houses recorded inside the walls) were accommodated under the same roof and were situated just outside the village on the Costa Sant'Angelo. For some reason, however, neither brother acknowledged this fact. There is no mention of their being neighbours on the Costa di Sant'Angelo, or to the living units there being physically connected.

One explanation for such an omission might be that Lucarino and Guccio had acquired property in their own right as they reached the age of majority, but that they had in addition taken over property previously belonging to their father whilst the latter was still living. If Ser Francesco was elderly and or unwell in 1320, such a move could have been both practical as well as financially advantageous for other members of the family. Ser Francesco for his part might have continued to live with one or other of his sons as a dependent. If assuming joint responsibilities for a family house inside the walls but at the same time accommodating the original proprietor, the brothers may have felt more obliged to declare the limits of their individual ownership. However, it seems more likely that Ser Francesco was already dead in 1320. As we shall see in Chapter 4, eight years after the drawing up of the 1320 *Tavola delle possessioni*, when Guccio di Ser Francesco drew up a sharecropping agreement with Nanni di Cenni, Ser Francesco was very definitely recorded as deceased. In the 1320 *Tavola delle possessioni* there is, moreover, an entry in respect of the 'heirs of Ser Francesco', which indicates that Ser Francesco was already dead at that date, or that he had died during the process of drawing up property details for the *Lira*.[40] The latter, combined with the fact that one of the sons may have reached the age of maturity around the same time might explain why the entry for Guccio di Ser Francesco seems to have been included as an afterthought, out of alphabetic order and towards the end of the *Tavola delle possessioni*.

The 1320 *Tavola delle possessioni* also contains a separate entry for a Domina Becca di Ser Francesco, indicating that Guccio and Lucarino had a sister who at that date was in a position to file her own independent tax declaration.[41] As we shall see, the affairs of Becca di Ser Francesco were very definitely linked with those of Guccio and Lucarino. Cross-referencing between several of the entries in the 1320 *Tavola delle possessioni* would also seem to confirm that all three individuals, including the so-called 'heirs of Ser Francesco' were members of the same extended family clan. Details concerning Domina Becca's ownership of property and land in and around Sant'Angelo in Colle indicate that she, like her brothers, was engaged in her own game of obfuscation in respect of the Sienese tax officials. According to her entry in the *Tavola delle possessioni*, Becca di Ser Francesco owned no living accommodation inside the walls and only one piece of land in the territory beyond (at Ficaiuoli).[42] This property was recorded as an orchard cum kitchen garden measuring just over half a *staio*, valued at the comparatively high sum of 6 *lire* and 17 *soldi*. Apart from an individual named as Mico di Genoa, neighbouring landowners to Becca's property are recorded on two remaining sides as the heirs of Cecco di Piero. In the entry for Mico di Genoa, however, there is a reference to worked land at Ficaiuoli that was bordered on one side by a road, on another by Domina Becca di Ser Francesco, and on two other sides by land belonging to Luca (sic) di Francesco.[43] It would seem from this that Becca and Luca owned neighbouring plots of land. Such contiguity between individuals with the same patronym would on most occasions indicate a family relationship. One would normally conclude, therefore, not only that Becca and Luca (?Lucarino) were siblings, but also that their contiguous properties at Ficaiuoli resulted from divisions of land following the death of an earlier member of the family. It is curious, however, that in Becca's own entry no reference was made to Luca or Lucarino di Ser Francesco, or for that matter to any other identifiable members of the same family. As we shall see in the next chapter, at least one piece of land at Ficaiuoli was owned not by Lucarino, but by Lucarino's brother, Guccio. Might the reference to Luca in Mico di Genoa's entry thus be a slip of the pen? Or did all these individuals hold individual plots of land in the same area?

A number of other inconsistencies emerge in the context of land held by Becca di Ser Francesco. Despite the reference to only one piece of land at Ficaiuoli in her own entry in the 1320 *Tavola delle possessioni*, Becca seems in fact to have owned at least one other piece of land in the territory of Sant'Angelo in Colle. In the entry for Mico di Genoa, Becca is also referred to in the context of land abutting worked land belonging to Mico in the area known as Pantano.[44] Other individuals with land next to this property are recorded as Sozzo di Giacomo and the heirs of Cecco di Piero. Could the reference to Ficaiuoli in Becca's entry thus be a slip of the pen for Pantano? It seems not. Once again, cross-reference with other entries in the 1320 *Tavola delle possessioni* throws light on some of the apparent inconsistencies. For example, Guccio di Ser Francesco, in his entry is recorded as owning land at Pantano.[45] His land was likewise said to border land belonging to the heirs of Cecco di Piero. Guccio's land at Pantano must therefore have been in the vicinity of, if not next to land belonging to Becca in the same area. We are thus able to show not only that Becca's own entry was incomplete, but that she owned two plots of land in close proximity to terrain belonging to what were probably her siblings – Guccio and Lucarino. Further cross-checking reveals a number of links between property held inside the walls of Sant'Angelo in Colle by the childen and 'heirs of Ser Francesco'.

The group of individuals referred to as the 'heirs of Ser Francesco' in the 1320 *Tavola delle possessioni* are recorded as owning a house inside the walls of the village, which appears to have been located in close proximity to property belonging to at least one of the three putative siblings, Becca, Lucarino and Guccio. The property belonging to the group of heirs is described as bordered on two sides by a road, on another side by Domina Nuta di Ghezzo, and on a final side by property belonging to Bindo di Accorso. Domina Nuta di Ghezzo's property is recorded rather as abutting property owned by an individual named as Cecchino di Ghezzo.[46] Given the apparent physical proximity of those two properties, and the fact that both Nuta and Cecchino had the same patronym, it seems likely that these two individuals were siblings. Perhaps, like Guccio and Lucarino, they were sharing a family house, jointly passed on to them by way of inheritance. There are a number of other connecting threads. Cross checking between other entries in the 1320 *Tavola delle possessioni* would seem to confirm that the living house recorded in respect of the heirs of Ser Francesco was close to, if not adjacent to one owned by Guccio di Ser Francesco, given that the house declared as under the sole ownership of the latter was described as abutting property belonging to Cecchino di Ghezzo.[47] Perhaps, like Domina Nuta and Cecchino, these individuals were not only related but also in effect accommodated under the same roof in adjacent properties. If the proposed relationship between Becca and Guccio is correct, Becca may also have been accommodated in the same complex.

Unless by some extraordinary coincidence two individuals with the name Ser Francesco were associated with the early fourteenth-century village of Sant'Angelo in Colle, it must surely be the case that the group referred to as the 'heirs of Ser Francesco' in the 1320 *Tavola delle possessioni* was part of the same family as Becca, Guccio and Lucarino. However, while there is evidence to suggest that the latter three individuals were siblings, and thus the direct beneficiaries of Ser Francesco, those gathered under the general denomination of 'heirs' could have consisted of a quite disparate group, including spouses related through marriage, as well as aunts, uncles, cousins, and other dependents such as underage children, spinsters and widows. This might explain why the entry for the 'heirs of Ser Francesco' included references to two pieces of land, neither of which can be associated with any of the terrain mentioned in the context of Guccio or his brother Lucarino or Becca.

Detailed analysis of the information concerning various members of Guccio, Lucarino and Becca di Ser Francesco's family confirms some of the many ways in which individual entries in the 1320 *Tavola delle possessioni* for Sant'Angelo in Colle can be shown to be incomplete records of situations on the ground. In the case of this family clan, at least three of its members also appear to have recognised that there were a number of advantages to be gained in glossing over the precise circumstances of the family's affairs, when it came to the levying of tax on family property.

In the most extreme cases, several individual members of the same family might hope to evade tax altogether. This was particularly the case where a number of individuals filed group declarations as heirs, and where some, if not all of them were under age. Tax liability depended in large part upon the age of the individual whose property was being assessed.[48] For those under the age of majority (18 years), or in the twilight of their days (70 and over), there were specific exemptions. It must thus have been in the interest of many heirs to declare their patrimony as a group, to age slowly whilst young and to appear to deteriorate rapidly the more advanced they were in years, for in that way they were more likely to benefit from age-related exemptions. With joint declarations it was clearly easier also to smudge information about individual ages, about which individual lived where, and, in particular, how different properties handed down by way of inheritance were divided up. In this context, it is significant that about 50 of the entries in the 1320 *Tavola delle possessioni* for Sant'Angelo in Colle are filed under the category of heirs.

Where women were the owners of land or living accommodation, there were further complications. While often barred from buying property in their own name, women nonetheless frequently acquired land, houses and even entire institutions such as hospital complexes through legal transactions carried out on their behalf by male representatives or relatives.[49] In many cases the woman's name did not initially appear on the deeds. Thus, a woman might hold property over a considerable period of time, but would not necessarily be identified as the owner of the property when it came to compiling information for the purpose of taxation. In addition, while a woman might be endowed with land and property as part of a dowry agreement, such assets were frequently amalgamated with those of her spouse, and effectively managed and declared by him.[50] According to the pact agreed at the time of her marriage, a widow might stand to forfeit dowry property on the death of her husband, thus never, herself, being recognised as the rightful owner. Even in those cases where buildings and land reverted to the woman's family on the death of her husband, she, as owner but now widowed and often once more dependent on her natal relations, was unlikely to assume responsibility for such assets. On occasion, the dotal property was reallocated following a subsequent marriage contract, thus further confusing the issue of ownership. Domestic traditions concerning the rights of women to purchase property in the medieval period must thus have seriously complicated the work of those attempting to draw up accurate records for the purpose of taxation. Not the least problem must have been establishing current ownership, and thus individual liabilities.

There is yet another aspect that merits consideration when attempting to explain the apparent inconsistencies in documents such as the 1320 *Tavola delle possessioni* for Sant'Angelo in Colle. It seem likely that in filing separate returns, spouses – like siblings, and groups of heirs – also sought on occasion to diminish their overall tax payments by filing incomplete details and by being less than transparent about the ownership and use of individual pieces of property. We can trace one such example by comparing the entries for Mona Mita di Piero and Minuccio di Banduccio in the 1320 *Tavola delle possessioni* for Sant'Angelo in Colle.

There are, in fact, two entries for Mita di Piero.[51] This is puzzling, if only because in one entry there is reference to a property which might have served as living accommodation, whereas in the other, no mention at all is made of property inside the walls of the village. In the first entry there are references not only to agricultural, or worked land (some of which had been left uncultivated and some of which contained vines), but also to a building in the area known as 'Tori (?torre) Sassonini' referred to as a 'quondam castellare', or ruined castle or fortified farmhouse. The second entry (which contains the further information that Mita was the daughter of Piero now deceased, and that she was currently married to Minuccio di Banduccio) refers to a number of other pieces of worked land, as well as a large amount of woodland, and a relatively small house inside the walls of Sant'Angelo in Colle. Mita's husband, Minuccio di Banduccio, for his part, is recorded as owning only a kitchen garden, or orchard.[52] No mention is made in Minuccio di Banduccio's entry of his marital status. The potential for confusion and obfuscation where details clarifying the marital status of an individual were withheld is obvious. In the absence of separate entries for Mita and the reference to her current husband, one might well have assumed that Minuccio di Banduccio was a bachelor, and that he had no home to live in inside the walls. Cross-referencing between the various entries allows us to establish a quite different picture. Although declaring no living accommodation of his inside the walls, there seems little doubt that both Minuccio and his wife had access to a unit of accommodation belonging to Mita. This was clearly a somewhat modest dwelling, with a rateable value of only 22 *lire*, but it must have been considerably larger than the half-houses noted in the 1320 *Tavola delle possessioni* that were valued at 10 *lire* or less.

The fourth and last observation about the difficulties encountered by the modern historian when attempting to reconstruct the topography of early fourteenth-century Sant'Angelo in Colle concerns the amount of accommodation available and the various ways in which members of the local population were accommodated within it. How was this thriving population physically accommodated within the urban fabric? How many families lived inside a single building? How many of the units were owned by their inhabitants as opposed to being rented, either from other locals or from 'outside' proprietors?

The most glaring anomaly arising from the 1320 *Tavola delle possessioni* is the apparent discrepancy between the number of housing units available in the early fourteenth-century village and the estimated size of the population at that date. While this may in part be explained by various kinds of human error and obfuscation in the drawing up of details for the purpose of taxation (as outlined above) it may also partly be due to the fact that a reading of the 1320 *Tavola delle possessioni* in isolation offers only a partial picture of the extent of the village's living accommodation in the early fourteenth century. A number of other contemporary records indicate that there were several more structures in the medieval village than those recorded in the 1320 *Tavola delle possessioni*. Some houses owned by Sienese 'outsiders' were not, for example, specifically recorded in the 1320 *Tavola delle possessioni*, but rather referred to in the details of the confines of properties belonging to local residents. The fact that property belonging to Sienese 'outsiders' was not included in the *Tavola* should cause no surprise. Such information would normally have been included in returns filed in Siena, and should thus be comparatively easy to trace. However, even then, as we shall see, it is not always easy to establish a complete picture. Real problems arise when individuals recorded in the *Tavola* for Sant'Angelo in Colle are not clearly identified as Sienese citizens, and when no specific information is given about the commune in which they were officially registered. Without such detail, there is no way in which any cross-referencing can be made. That said, there seems little doubt that property belonging to Sienese 'outsiders' considerably swelled the number of units of accommodation available in early fourteenth-century Sant'Angelo in Colle. What is less easy to establish is whether or not such property was let out to local residents, or reserved for their own private use.

There is yet another factor that could have had a bearing on the apparent discrepancy between the amount of accommodation available and the estimated size of the population. According to the 1320 *Tavola delle possessioni*, at least 150 individuals and groups of heirs listed there did not in fact own any property inside the walls.

Table 3.6   Individuals recorded as owning no property inside the walls of Sant'Angelo in Colle in the 1320 *Tavola delle possessioni,* but who nevertheless owned land in the vicinity of the village (Arranged here in alphabetical order)[1]

Name and origin of proprietor	No. of plots	Description and position of terrain	Approx. size in *staia*	Overall patrimony in lire soldi denari			Page no.
Albicino da Villa i Tolli	1	agricultural, or worked land [Poggio]	8 and 1/2	7	2	-	9r
Amideo di Puccio	3	1/2 piece of uncultivated agricultural, or worked land; 2 pieces of agricultural, or worked land [Valle ?Puabni, Iusterna, Colle]	23; 6, 13 and 4/5	28	11	6	10r
Andreolo di Credi da Villa i Tolli	1	½ piece of uncultivated land [S. Biagio]	2 and 1/3	5	3	6	8r
Angelino di Franco	2	1 piece of agricultural, or worked land; orchard, or kitchen garden with *casalino,* or small, isolated house [Pianete, ?or Pianese, San Piero]	2 and 2/3; 2/3	24	8	-	3r
Avitolo di Duccio	1	agricultural, or worked land [Trofie]	20	7	2	-	12r
Bartolino di Ghezzo	4	1 piece of uncultivated agricultural, or worked land; the rest agricultural, or worked land [Fonterenza, Val Brulenghe, Montanina]	16; 2/3, 4, 5 and 1/3	61	13	-	28r
Becchina di Berto	1	agricultural, or worked land [Speltale or Spuntale]	10	20	-	-	27r
Becchina di Lento	1	agricultural, or worked land containing vines and woodland [Cappane]	4 and 1/2	13	10	-	43r
Bernaduccio di Pietro	4	2 pieces of wooded agricultural, or worked land; the rest agricultural, or worked land [?Magnietaia, Torre Asinino, or Torre Assonino; Quatrata, Poggio Vanuccio]	60, 13 and ½; 18, 5	169	9	-	40r
Bernarduccio da Seggiano, 'now of Sant'Angelo in Colle'	4	3 pieces of agricultural, or worked land; 1 piece of agricultural, or worked land on which was a palace, a 'domo cappanna' or country house, and a mill [Quercia Umberti, or Uberti, Poggio, Vignale; Tredine]	1; 3 and 1/4, 4 and 1/3; 23	153	15	-	38r
Berto di Ser Raniero da Montalcino	1	uncultivated agricultural, or worked land [Sitini]	6 and 4/5	4	11	-	50r
Bindo di Benincasa	1	uncultivated agricultural, or worked land [Ficaioli]	3 and 3/4	11	5	-	49r
Bindo di Gratia	1	agricultural, or worked land with vineyard [Monte Combole]	5	46	13	4	55r

Binduccio di Berto	1	agricultural, or worked land [Ferrale]	4 and 7/10	34	9	-	44r
Binduccio di Boncambi	1	agricultural [Speltale or Spuntale]	14 and 1/5	21	6	-	30r
Bino (or Bindo) di Lambertino	1	vineyard [Saporoia]	1 and 1/3	11	5	-	54r
Bino di Raniero	11	4 pieces of agricultural or worked land; 3 vineyards, 2 pieces of agricultural, or worked land with olives; 1 orchard, or kitchen garden; half of a piece of agricultural, or worked land with a hut [Fonte Delicato, Aiale, Romata (x2); Saporoia (x2), Romata; Fabriche, Pianese; Costamori; Romata]	7/10, ½, 3 and ½, 4 and ¼; 9/10, 3 and 1/5, 6 and 1/3; 1, 1/3; 1/5; in all, 8	161	6	6	34r
Caselle, or Casella da Montalcino	1	agricultural, or worked land [Vignale a Sesta]	10 and 2/3	30	-	-	104r
Casino di Bino (or Bindo)	5	1/3 of a piece of agricultural, or worked land and wood;1 piece of wooded agricultural, or worked land; half share in 1 piece of uncultivated agricultural or worked land; 1 piece of agricultural, or worked land; 1 piece of agricultural, or worked land with hut [Campaia or Campare; Capraia; Valle ?Pivani; Sesta]	in all, 38; 1 and 2/3; in all, 23; 4 and 2/5; 4	59	8	4	66r
Cecca di Bonone (Bonono?)	1	half share of agricultural, or worked land with vineyard [Pianese]	in all, 8 and 1/2	34	-	-	102r
Cecco di Giovanni	7	4 agricultural, or worked land; 1 agricultural, or worked land with hut; 2 pieces of land with vineyards [Ubertini, Prioratti, Poggiuolo Albinelli, Fonte Latro; Romata; Fabriche, Ferrale]	4 and 2/5, ½, 4 and ½, 2; 6 and 4/5; 2 and 1/2, 1 and 1/3	137	19	-	82r
Cecco di Nuccio	4	1 piece of land with vineyard; 1 agricultural, or worked land; 1 piece of woodland; 1 piece of worked land with wood [Capanne; Frailla; Usinella (x2)]	4/5; 4 and 1/5; 9; 16	29	11	-	87r
Chele di Ferrante	3	2 pieces of agricultural, or worked land; 1 piece of land with vineyard [Poggio di Castiglione, Trafossatella; Saporoia]	2, 24 and 1/3; 1 and 1/5	42	10	-	89r
Chele di Freduccio da Villa i Tolli	1	agricultural, or worked land [Capanne]	1 and 3/4	9	12	-	88r
Chino (or Ghino) di Bonaiuto	4	3 pieces of uncultivated agricultural, or worked land; one piece of agricultural, or worked land including a vineyard and hut [Piano Cornelli, Collesorbi, or Collesorbe, ?[2]; Sitini]	54,18, 14 and 9/10; 6	113	13	-	78r

Ciatto di Nuccio da Villa i Tolli	1	agricultural, or worked land [Magienta or Magneta]	14	11	13	-	103r
Ciellina di Niccoluccio	1	vineyard [Fonte Delicate, or Delicata]	2 and 1/3	14	16	-	96r
Cola (or Cole) di Marzuolo	1	vineyard [Pianese]	1 and 1/20	6	13	-	106r
Cola (or Cole) di Michele	1	agricultural, or worked land [Roccagiane]	5 and 3/4	5	5	-	97r
Cola (or Cole) di Micheluccio	1	agricultural, or worked land [Spedale]	1/5	2	3	-	105r
Domina Cellina, widow of Micheluccio	1	agricultural, or worked land [Saporoia]	2 and 4/5	21	7	6	259r
Domina Nuta, wife of Ciaffi (or Ciatto [?di Nuccio?)	2	vineyard; 1 piece of uncultivated land [Ferrale; Cappanelli]	100 and 1/10; 1 and 1/10	13	19	-	360r
Domina Rosa di Piero pecoraio	1	uncultivated wooded land [Collesorbe]	6	1	18	-	116r
Domina Tessina di Peruzzo	1	agricultural, or worked land [Fenilla]	9	15	-	-	420r
Dominico di Guido	1	agricultural, or worked land with wood [Fossatello del Cuoio]	6	3	16	-	118r
Drudo di Cenno	1	agricultural, or worked land [Pellentieri]	10	7	-	-	117r
Figlio di Lunardo	3	2 pieces of land with wood; 1 agricultural, or worked land [Costa Carbonelle, Campo Giovanni; Colle Mattone, or Collemattone]	4, 3; 3 and 1/5	27	-	-	140r
Gerino di Gregorio	1	vineyard [Agliori]	2/5	2	-	-	150r
Ghino di Filippuccio	2	1 piece of agricultural, or worked land with vineyard; 1 piece of agricultural, or worked land [Colle Mattone, or Collemattone; Campo Giovanni]	4 and ½; 27	74	14	-	152r
Giannello di Credi da Villa i Tolli	5	3 pieces of agricultural, or worked land; half of a piece of agricultural, or worked land; 1 vineyard [Poggio Arne, Magnieta, or Magienta (x2); Tredine; Pianese]	9, 15, 10; in all, 3; 2 and 3/4	47	10	-	160r
Gianni di Lamberto	2	1 piece of agricultural, or worked land; 1 piece of land used as orchard, or kitchen garden [Saporoia; Costa Sant'Angelo]	3/4; 1/8	4	16	-	162r

Giannino di Accorso	1	agricultural, or worked land, serving as an orchard, or kitchen garden [Costamorri]	1/5	1	12	-	163r
Giovanni di Rainuccio	1	agricultural, or worked land [Sassonini]	3	3	15	-	254r
Giovanni di Vitale	1	uncultivated land [Collesorbi, or Collesorbe]	25	12	10	-	250r
Guido di Vanne	2	½ piece of agricultural or worked land; 1 piece of agricultural or worked land with vines [?[3]; Fonte delicato]	3 and ½; 4 and 2/3	21	18	-	161r
****Heirs of:							
Altimanno	5	1/3 of a piece of uncultivated land with wood; 1 piece of uncultivated land; 1/3 of a piece of uncultivated land; 1 piece of agricultural, or worked land; 1 piece of uncultivated agricultural, or worked land [Pretesciace; Pieve a Sesta; Preteschiace; Sesta; Poggio Vannuccio]	20;7; in all, 31; 2 and 1/3;43	71	15	8	194r
Becca 'fratessa'	1	agricultural, or worked land [Manganelli]	2	2	-	-	241r
Benavento (Bencivenne)	1	half a piece of agricultural, or worked land [Marrucha] (Other half belonged to the heirs of Ventura)	in all, 25	5	-	-	245r
Berta di Martino	1	wooded agricultural, or worked land [Costa Carbonelli]	2 and 1/2	1	3	-	219r
Berto dimagistro Martino	3	vineyard; 2 pieces of wooded agricultural, or worked land [Pianezze, ?or Pianese; Vallocchi (x2)]	1 and 1/10; 3 and 4/5, 27	33	19	-	234r
Bindo di Rannuccio	3	1 piece of uncultivated land; 1 piece of agricultural, or worked land; 1 piece of worked land with vineyard [San Biagio; Pianese; Fossato Castellano]	1 and ½; 1 and ½; 3	17	13	6	191r
Bino (or Bindo)	1	agricultural, or worked land [Fossato Castellani, or Castellano]	1 and 1/8	1	3	-	184r
Bino (or Bindo) di Giacomino	1	agricultural, or worked land [Campo Giovanni]	3 and 2/3	5	2	-	190r
Bino di Rannuccio	4	orchard, or kitchen garden; 1 piece of uncultivated worked land; 2 pieces of agricultural, or worked land [San Piero; Sitini; Macereta, Scopielle]	1/10; 3 and 1/3; 2, 4	8	5	6	183r
Bino (or Bindo) di Tassino	2	1 piece of agricultural, or worked land with orchard, or kitchen garden and hut; 1 piece of agricultural, or worked land [Aiale; Colle Mattone, or Collemattone]	1; 6 and 4/5	45	3	-	182r

Borgognone	3	2 pieces of agricultural, or worked land; 1 piece of land serving as an orchard, or kitchen garden [Colle, Aiale; Costamorre, or Costamorri]	8 and 3/5, 2 and ½; 1/10	11	3	-	244r
Brunaccio	1	'ortale', or orchard [San Piero]	3	-	6	-	185r
Cenni (or Cenno)	2	agricultural, or worked land [Collesorbi, or Collesorbe, Tredine]	14, 1 and 1/2	11	7	6	166r
Cenni (or Cenno) di Gratia	2	agricultural, or worked land [Preteschiace, Piano a Sesta]	3, 1 and 4/5	4	13	-	199r
Cianni (or Ciane) da Villa i Tolli	1	agricultural, or worked land [Magnieta]	47	39	3	-	236r
Ciante da Villa i Tolli	1	agricultural, or worked land [Pieve a Sesta]	4	3	7	-	235r
Ciolo	1	agricultural, or worked land [Colle Mattoni, or Collemattone]	1	1	10	-	220r
Cremonese	1	agricultural, or worked land serving as an orchard, or kitchen garden [Costa San Piero]	1/20	-	6	-	246r
Domina Becca	3	half a piece of agricultural, or worked land with wood; 1 piece of uncultivated land; half a piece of uncultivated land with wood [Caprarese (x2); Quercete]	in all, 19 and ½;9; in all, 30	14	11	9	203r
Fatio della Villa (?Villa i Tolli)	1	agricultural, or worked land [Rivulgare]	6	10	-	-	214r
Fiduccio (or Feduccio) da Villa i Tolli	3	2 pieces of agricultural, or worked land; 1 piece of land with vineyard [Magnienta, Lampereta; Pianezza, or Pianese]	5 and 1/5, 9; 1 and 2/5	19	10	-	226r
Gianne (or Gianni, or Giane) di Orlando	1	half a piece of wooded agricultural, or worked land [Fossatellis, or Fossatello]	in all, 11 and 1/2	4	16	-	257r
Gianne (or Gianni, or Giane) di Uguiccione	1	agricultural, or worked land with wood [Capine, ?or Capanne]	4	1	13	-	221r
Giovanello	1	half a piece of agricultural, or worked land used as vineyard [Planezzis, or Pianese]	8 and 1/2	34	-	-	233r
Giovanni di Appare	2	1 piece of uncultivated agricultural, or worked land; 1 piece of agricultural, or worked land with olives [Montegianni; Ficaiuoli]	5; 3/5	17	13	-	168r
Giovanni di Giacomino	1	agricultural, or worked land [Campo Giovanni]	3 and 3/5	5	2	-	170r

Guadagno	1	agricultural, or worked land [Manganelli]	13	13	-	-	240r
Guido di Accolone	2	1 piece of uncultivated and wooded agricultural, or worked land; 1 piece of uncultivated scrub land [Pietre Schiate, or Preteschiace; Tredine]	11 and 4/5; 1 and 1/2	5	2	6	256r
Letto di Sabatino	1	agricultural, or worked land [Lato]	6	3	12	-	224r
Maffuccio	1	agricultural, or worked land with olives [Ficaiuoli]	2/5	3	7	-	192r
Micheluccio	2	wooded land; 1 piece of agricultural or worked land [Termine; Lameparte, ? or Lameparete]	6; 3	5	1	-	223r
Mino di Argomento	2	1 piece of uncultivated agricultural, or worked land; 1 piece of agricultural, or worked land [Preteschiate, or Preteschiace; Poggio Banduccio, or Vanuccio]	9; 1 and 1/5	8	10	-	202r
Muccio	1	woodland [Agresta]	37	21	12	-	196r
Naldo di Jacopo	5	3 pieces of agricultural, or worked land; 1 piece of land serving as an orchard, or kitchen garden; 1 piece of uncultivated land [Sitini, Fernaccioli, Vallocchi; San Piero; Poggio delle Campanelle]	7 and 7/10, 1 and 1/5, 1 and 1/4;1/20; 2	36	2	-	169r
Nerio	2	1 piece of agricultural, or worked land; 1 piece of agricultural, or worked land serving as a vineyard [Saporoia]	1 and 9/10; 3 and 1/5	37	7	-	242r
Nerio di Fabro	1	agricultural, or worked land [Speltale]	3 and 3/5	12	-	-	208r
Nerio di Orlando da Villa i Tolli	8	agricultural, or worked land [Pieve a Sesta (x2); Quercia Uberti (x3), tanis, Poggio Vannucci, or Vannuccio (x2)]	3 and ¾, 1 and ½, 1 and 4/5, 4 and ½, 4 and ½, 6, 5 and ½, 8	32	4	6	210r
Nerio di Rubeo	5	3 pieces of agricultural, or worked land; 1 piece of uncultivated agricultural, or worked land; 1 piece of agricultural, or worked land with wood [Lama, or Lame Fornelli (x2), Saporoia; Migliarine; Serpielli]	15, 12, 5 and 7/10; 4 and 1/5; 2 and 1/8	37	4	-	206r
Nerio di Soffia (or Soffie) da Villa i Tolli	1	half a piece of uncultivated land [San Biagio]	in all, 2 and 3/10	3	6	-	209r
Nerio di Tassino	1	agricultural, or worked land [Pianneze, or Pianese]	9	48	-	-	239r
Nerio di Ventura (or Venture)	3	1 piece of wooded agricultural, or worked land; 2 pieces of land used as orchard, or kitchen garden [San Biagio; Costa San Piero, Costamorri]	13 and ½; 1/10, 1/20	25	10	-	238r

Nigro da Montalcino	1	1 piece of agricultural or worked land with wood [Sugarella]	46	69	-	-	205r
Nuccio di Brunaccio	1	agricultural, or worked land [Cappanne, or Capanne]	2 and 1/5	5	10	-	222r
Nuti (or Nutio) di Delafante (or della fante)da Villa i Tolli	3	2 pieces of agricultural, or worked land; 1 piece of uncultivated agricultural, or worked land [Poggio Aine, or Arne, Vignali a Sesta; Pianerze, or Pianese]	44, 2 and 2/5; 14 and 7/10	59	5	-	237r
Peruccio di Assalto	1	agricultural, or worked land [Piano Tredine]	1 and ½	17	6	-	258r
Piero di Pecoraio	1	agricultural, or worked land with wood [Sopra Castello]	15	5	-	-	243r
Ranucetto	1	agricultural, or worked land [Rubiaio]	10	2	10	-	248r
Romaniolo	5	½ a piece of agricultural or worked land with woodland; 1 piece of uncultivated agricultural or worked land; 1 piece of uncultivated land; 1 piece of agricultural or worked land; 1 piece of agricultural or worked land [Preteschiace; Preteschiace; Capratese; Aqua Vivola; Fossechoi]	In all, 11 and 4/5; 3 and 9/10; 15 and ½; 7 and ½; 5	28 6	11		200r
Toro, or Torre	1	uncultivated land [Fonte Chinelli]	1	-	5	-	247r
Ventura	5	1 piece of uncultivated agricultural, or worked land; 2 pieces of agricultural, or worked land; 1 piece of land serving as orchard, or kitchen garden; one half of a piece of agricultural, or worked land [Logo; Pozzo del Pantano, Greppo di Lato; Costamori, or Costamorri; Marruca]	7; 7 and 1/5, 6; 1/10; in all, 25	17	17	-	165r
*************							
Lando (or Landi) di Guadagno	1	agricultural, or worked land [Finilla]	7	9	18	-	280r
Landuccio di Duccio	1	vineyard [Colle Mattoni, or Collemattone]	1 and 3/5	16	-	-	270r
Landuccio di Giontarello	3	2 pieces of uncultivated agricultural, or worked land; 1 orchard, or kitchen garden [Fonte Collese, Manganelli; Lubertine]	9 and 3/10, 3; 1/7	14	16	6	264r
Lonarduccio di Benvegnati	1	piece of woodland [?Bocerano ?Ibcerano]	10	4	3	-	271r
Lonarduccio di Vecce, or Vucci	2	agricultural, or worked land [Montannina, or Montanina, Campo Giovanni]	13, 6	23	13	-	279r
Marco di Giovanelli, or Giovanello	1	uncultivated agricultural, or worked land [Capratesi]	19 and ½	8	9	-	302r

Martinello di Guidarello	2	agricultural, or worked land [Val di Brubenga, or Brulenga, Collemattone]	3 and ¾, 2 and 3/5	11	14	-	306r
Menchino di Ghezzo	6	5 pieces of agricultural, or worked land; 1 piece of agricultural, or worked land with hut [Citinale (x2), Montanina (x2), Speltale; Montanina]	5 and 4/5, 2 and ½, 10 and 2/5, 2 and 4/5, 1 and 9/10; 4 and 3/10	39	1	6	297r
Menchino di Lamberto	1	wooded agricultural, or worked land [Fossato Rivolgare]	4	6	13	-	307r
Mina di Gianni, or Gianne	1	agricultural, or worked land [Saporoia]	1 and 1/5	5	7	-	327r
Mina di Maffuccio	1	agricultural, or worked land [Collemattone]	4 and ½	39	-	-	311r
Mino di Giovanni	3	2 pieces of agricultural, or worked land; 1 piece of agricultural, or worked land with hut [Caprofico, Finilla; San Giovanni]	6, 17; 9	63	10	-	308r
Minuccio di Banduccio	1	orchard, or kitchen garden [Costa Sant'Angelo]	1/10	2	9	-	295r
Mita di Nerio	3	2 pieces of agricultural, or worked land; one piece of agricultural, or worked land serving as an orchard, or kitchen garden [Lama Fornelle, Lama Parete; Aie (?) Burle Larie (?)]	4, 4; ¼	10	7	-	314r
Mon(n)a Becca di Petrino	1	vineyard [Fabrica]	2 and 1/4	17	7	-	338r
Mon(n)a Becca di Ser Francesco	1	piece of land serving as an orchard, or kitchen garden [Ficaiuoli]	1/2	6	17	-	296r
Mon(n)a Giacomina di Sozzo	1	agricultural, or worked land serving as a vineyard [Saporoia]	3 and ½	26	17	-	337r
Mon(n)a Lucia di Guido	2	1 vineyard; 1 agricultural, or worked land serving as a vineyard [Fonte Delicata (x2)]	1 and ½; 4/5	7	14	-	322r
Mon(n)a Mita di Baldiccione	1	orchard, or kitchen garden [Ficaiuoli]	½	5	12	-	298r
Mon(n)a Mita di Minuccio	2	1 piece of agricultural, or worked land; 1 piece of agricultural or worked land with wood [Poggio di Cappanelli; Iusterna]	3 and 1/5; 6 and 7/10	7	13	-	334r and 335r
Mon(n)a Scolaia	6	half a piece of uncultivated and wooded agricultural, or worked land; 2 pieces of agricultural, or worked land; 2 half pieces of agricultural, or worked land; half a piece of scrubland [Collesorbe; Monteiano, Vignalis, or Vignale a Sesta; Aqua Viva, Planezze, ?or Pianese; Canale]	10 and 2/5; 7/10, 4/5; 6 and 1/4, 1 and 1/5; 23	18	18	6	284r

Mutia di Gionti	1	agricultural or worked land [Torre Assonino]	7 and 1/2	4	2	6	336r
Naldo di Giacomo	1	agricultural or worked land [Maciareti]	2 and 1/2	1	12	-	351r
Narduccio di Giovanni	1	agricultural or worked land [Manganelli]	3 and 1/2	10	10	-	371r
Necchina di Tura	1	agricultural or worked land with wood [Greppus de lato]	6	2	16	-	359r
Nerio di Dietavive	5	4 pieces of agricultural or worked land; 1 orchard or kitchen garden	1 and 1/6; 3; 2 and ½; 4 and 1/10; 1/3	56	7	-	362r
Novellino di Ventura	2	agricultural, or worked land [Querce Alfilo, Ficaiuoli]	3, 2	13	5	-	346r
Nuccio di Credi da Villa i Tolli	2	half a piece of land; 1 piece of uncultivated land [Tredine; Planezze, ?or Pianese]	in all, 3, 1/2	3	5	-	366r
Nuccio di Massaio	1	agricultural, or worked land [Poggio Cancelli]	2	1	7	-	370r
Nuccio di Sanni	1	agricultural, or worked land [Lame Combole]	2 and 3/10	2	2	-	372r
Nuta di Nuccio	1	half a piece of agricultural, or worked land [Fonte Delicata]	in all, 3 and 1/2	4	2	-	358r
Nuto di Ventura	2	1 piece of agricultural, or worked land; 1 piece of uncultivated agricultural, or worked land [Aqua Viva; Petrosi]	1 and 3/5; 2 and ½	3	14	-	352r
Paolo di Nerio di Rubeo	1	half a piece of wooded agricultural, or worked land [Cappanelli]	in all, 6 and 2/5	3	4	-	391r
Petrino di Nerio[4]	3	1 piece of agricultural, or worked land; 1 piece of land 'cum arboribus', or planted with trees (possibly fruit and/or nut); half a piece of wooded agricultural, or worked land [Fossato Castellani; Sitini; Cappanelli]	1; 1 and 7/10; in all, 6 and 2/5 (other ½, brother Paolo (di Neri di Rubeo)	8	6	-	382r
Petruccio di Ciane, or Cianno da Villa i Tolli	1	uncultivated agricultural, or worked land [Poggio Arne]	16	13	7	-	393r
Petrucciuolo di Salite, or Saliti	2	vineyard; agricultural or worked land [Colle Mattone, or Collemattone; Montanina]	1 and 1/5; 11 and 7/10	25	14	-	394r
Pietro di Bindo da Montalcino	2	1 piece of agricultural, or worked land; 1 piece of agricultural, or worked land with wood [Sugarella; Pietra Rudinella]	11; 6	26	10	-	386r
Pia di Farolfo	1	agricultural, or worked land gone to scrubland [Vallocchi]	17 and ½	64	4	-	392r

Ristoruccio di Vitale	5	vineyard; agricultural, or worked land; wooded agricultural, or worked land; 2 pieces of uncultivated agricultural, or wooded land [Saporoia; Trafossatello; Fossato Capraia; Capraia; Collesorbe]	½; 9; 17; 8 and ½, 41	114	17	-	395r
Salito di Orlando	1	wooded agricultural, or worked land [Fossatello Alcoi]	11 and ½	4	16	-	411r
Scolaiuolo di Bononno da Montalcino	2	agricultural, or worked land [Bagnuolo; Dell Olmo]	27, 7	277	-	-	415r
Ser Francisco and brother Nierio, sons of Cecco di Piero	1	agricultural, or worked land [Sitini]	1 and 1/10	3	13	-	255r
Sozzino di Sozzo	1	agricultural, or worked land [San Biagio]	1	4	10	-	412r
Sozzo di Mainetto	1	uncultivated woodland [Fernicioli]	5 and 1/3	4	10	-	409r
Sozzo di Meldi	1	agricultural, or worked land [Montegiano]	5 and ¼	22	-	-	404r
Tessina di Lascia	1	agricultural, or worked land [Planezze, ?or Pianese]	2 and ¼	7	2	-	417r
Tino di Maffuccio	1	agricultural, or worked land [Poggio Manicii]	c. 4 and ½	5	19	-	418r
Torazzuolo di Toro	1	agricultural, or worked land [Lame Corbole, or Corboli]	16	14	13	-	421r
Tura di Martino	1	vineyard; half of a small house on Costa Sant'Angelo [Ficaiuolo]	1/10; in all, 1/20	1	4	-	414r
Tura di Morello	2	1 piece of agricultural, or worked land serving as vineyard with hut; 1 piece of wooded agricultural, or worked land [Planezza, ?or Pianese; Torre Assonino, or Assonini]	2 and 2/5; 14	25	8	-	419r
Turello di Giannino	2	2 pieces of land serving as orchard, or kitchen garden [Costamoro (x2)]	c. 1/10, c. 1/10	1	4	-	422r
Turello di Leto	1	land serving as orchard, or kitchen garden [Costamoro]	c. 1/10	-	14	-	423r
Ulivezio (?Uliveccio) di Giovanni	8	orchard, or kitchen garden; 1 piece of wooded agricultural, or worked land; 5 pieces of agricultural, or worked land; 1 piece of agricultural, or worked land with hut [Costa Sant'Angelo; Macerete; Tredine, Cappanna, or Capanna, Piano Tredine, Iusterna, San Biagio; Tredine]	c. 1/10; 2 and ½; c. 2 and 1/10, 1 and ½, 1 and ½, 1 and ¼, c. 1 and ¾; 2 and 1/4	30	8	6	431r

Vanne di Gherardo da Villa i Tolli	3	2 pieces of agricultural, or worked land; 1 piece of uncultivated agricultural, or worked land ['Subtus stradella magnieta', or underneath the road, or track to Magnieta]	7, ½; 35	32	19	-	445r
Vannuccio di Cremonese	1	agricultural, or worked land [Piano Sesta]	2 and 2/5	1	16	-	435r
Vannuccio di Ensengni, or Insegne	1	agricultural, or worked land [Saporoia]	c. 2 and ½	14	9	-	447r
Vannuccio di Rainero	2	half of a piece of agricultural, or worked land with a hut; 1 piece of agricultural, or worked land [Romate; Valle]	in all, 8; 3/5	25	10	6	444r
Vesi di Mico	1	uncultivated agricultural, or worked land [Capraia]	15	15	-	-	428r
Villano di Bruno	1	agricultural, or worked land [Piannezza, ?or Pianese]	5 and 4/5	15	9	-	446r
Vinitiana, wife of Guidarello	1	agricultural, or worked land with 'cappana', or hut [Bagnuolo]	c. 1	9	10	-	448r
Vinuccio di Ciampolo	6	1 uncultivated piece of agricultural, or worked land with wood; 2 pieces of agricultural, or worked land; 1 piece of agricultural, or worked land serving as a vineyard; 1 piece of uncultivated agricultural, or worked land; wooded land [Lamone; Speltale, Colle Mattone, or Collemattone; Colle Mattone, or Collemattone; Val di Brulengha; Campo Giovanni]	12; 2 and 3/5, 2 and ½; 2; 1 and ½; 3	35	19	6	436r
Viviano di Ranuccio	7	half of a piece of scrubland; orchard, or kitchen garden; 1 piece of agricultural, or worked land with olives; 2 pieces of agricultural, or worked land; vineyard; 1 piece of agricultural, or worked land serving as a vineyard [Piano Cornelli; Costa Sant'Angelo; Fossato Castellano; Sistini, Salsore; Saporoia (x2); Saporoia]	28; c. 1/20; ½; 4 and ¾, 3; 1 and 4/5; 1 and ¾	50	18	-	429r

Notes to Table 3.6

1 As already noted, *Estimo* 24 is not strictly alphabetical, individual entries for the most part being ordered in alphabetical sections according to the first letter of the individual's first given name. In the case of women (whose entries are shown here in bold italic), the original record distinguishes between Domina and Mon(n)a, placing these individuals, respectively under D or M, and irrespective of their actual name. These distinctions have been respected in the order adopted in this table. Several women are not given any title. These are inserted here (as in *Estimo* 24).

2 No reference was made to the location of the third piece of worked land, which was referred to by a separate hand in the Ta*vola*.

3 The location of this half piece of land is not given.

4 Although no living accommodation is declared in respect of this individual, he seems in fact to have owned property inside the walls, since he is described as a neighbour in the entry for property belonging to Gratia di Ugolino.

This can be explained in a number of ways. Some of those listed as having no living accommodation inside Sant'Angelo in Colle may have lived in shacks or hovels on surrounding land, or on orchard and kitchen garden land immediately adjacent to the walls. Others (like Becca di Ser Francesco) may have been accommodated in houses belonging to relations. Others may have lived in rented or tied premises in the countryside, as part of a system of *mezzadria*, or sharecropping.[53] Arrangements of this kind would clearly have eased pressure on the number of units of accommodation inside the walls. Where individuals lived in houses and shacks outside the walls of Sant'Angelo in Colle, or as *mezzaiuoli* in premises owned by someone else, it would have been quite legitimate that they should claim they owned no living accommodation of their own. Many other individuals could in fact have lived inside the walls, but on a rental basis in property that was neither their own, nor that of any related family member.

Where individuals lived in rented accommodation it seems likely that the responsibility for declaring such property would have fallen not on them, but on the actual owners.[54] It is in this context that references in the 1320 *Tavola delle possessioni* to multi-ownership of property by both local inhabitants of Sant'Angelo in Colle and Sienese 'outsiders' are particularly relevant. Those with local knowledge would have been in a particularly strong position to rent out units of accommodation. But 'outsiders', too, and especially those who were in a position to provide local employment would have been well-placed to engage in the letting business. Surviving tax records indicate that some of these 'outsiders' would also have owned enough property to lay one of the units of accommodation aside for their own personal use.

Table 3.7 Property inside the walls of Sant'Angelo in Colle owned by Siennese 'outsiders' between 1318 and 132

Proprietor	Description of property and declared boundaries	Estimated value in	
		lire	*soldi*
Andrea di Boncambio[1]	Building plot: road, road, commune, water conduit	21	7
	Orchard with olives and almond trees: Ser Guccio di ser Francesco, Manovello di Ugolino, road, Fuccio di Andolone	1	7
Friars of Sant'Agostino[2]	House: road, Lando di Pepi,[3] Lando di Pepi	90	-
	House: road, road, Domina Benvenuta di Ghezzo,[4] road	15	-
Gano di Lambertino[5]	House: road, Manovello di Ugolino, Fuccio Andelmi	15	-
Heirs (Cione and Nigi) of Baldiccione[6]	House: road, hospital of Santa Maria,[7] Neri di Guicciardo[8]	24	13
	House: road, Finuccio di Ranuccino, 'mediante curso' (?and in the middle, the water conduit),[9] Manovello di Ugolino,[10] Neri di Guicciardo	36	13
Heir of Maestro Fei and Niccoluccio, his son[11]	Half of a house with a building plot: road, road, Avitolo di Ildobrandino,[12] water conduit	15	10
	Half of a house:[13] road, road, Nardo di Ventura,[14] Muccio di Orlando[15]	5	-

Lando di Domino Meo di Tolomeo[16]	House: road, road, heirs of Micheluccio[17]	100	-
Manovello di Ugolino[18]	Land with a house built on it in the area known as 'Castello': road, road, 'domina Cina'[19]	35	-
	Land with a house built on it: road, Finuccio di Ranuccio[20], Cennino di Cenno	12	-
	Land with a house built on it: road, Gianni di Lambertino[21], Sozzo di Ranuccio[22]	7	7
	House: road, ?road, church of Sant'Angelo, 'this church'[23]	10	13
	House: road, road, Angnoluccio di Guerre[24]	70	-
	House: road, Tino di Montenero,[25] Muccio 'di d(i)c(t)i Castri'	28	-
Meo di Bonfiglio[26]	House: road, Ristoruccio di Toro,[27] Bindo di Raniero[28]	35	-
	House ('casa cum interiori):[29] road, Ristoruccio, Bindo di Raniero	100	-
Neri di Guicciardo da Civitella[30]	Building plot: road, castle wall, Cenno di Bartolo	-	10
	'Casalinum', or small house: heirs of Cecco, road, property belonging to the Commune[31]	-	5
	House: road, road, property belonging to the Commune	-	10
	House: road, road, Cecchina di Guido[32]	10	-
	'Casalinum', or small house: road, road, property belonging to Neri himself	10	-
	Building plot: road, road, heirs of Petruccio Guillielmi	-	10
	House: road, Lonarduccio di Giovanni, property belonging to Neri himself	15	-
	House: road, heirs of Vivo,[33] Domina Mita di Tora	18	-
	House: road, road, property belonging to the Commune, Gano di Guigliolmuccci	7	-
	House: Angelo di Buccio, road, Landuccio di Giontarello[34]	8	-
	Building plot: road, road, Chele di Ruggiero[35]	-	5
	House: road, road, road, Chele di Ruggiero	15	-
	House: road, Petruccio di Piero,[36] property belonging to Neri himself	15	-
	House: castle walls, road, heirs of Franco[37]	18	-
	House with building plot: Petruccio di Piero, road, property owned by Neri himself	20	-
	House: road, road, heirs of Franco	10	-
	House: road,road, heirs of Franco	15	-
	House: road, road, Giacomino di Micheluccio	30	-
	House: road, road, Naccio di Nuccio[38]	160	-
	House: road, road, property belonging to the Commune	90	-
	House: road, water conduit, Ser Tollo di Gollo 'mediante cursu'[39]	15	-
	Building plot: Conte di Ventura, heirs of Baldiccione,[40] road	1	13
	Building plot: road, heirs of Cecco cavaliere,[41] Tura di Manno	1	13

Niccoluccio di Mandriano[42]	House: road, Viviani Burnacci[43]	15	-
	House: road, Nerio[44] di Ranerio, Becca Tini	27	-
Baldera di Bencivenni[45]			
Filippo di ser Niccolaio Buonsignori[46]			
Naddo di Bernardino da Valcortese[47]			

Notes to Table 3.7

1   Archivio di Stato di Siena (hereafter ASS), *Estimo* 102, Terzo di Città`, Incontri, 1328, fols 88r–89r, new pagination.

2   ASS, *Estimo* 109, Terzo di Città`, Santa Agata (hereafter *Estimo* 109), fols 23r–26v, new pagination.

3   According to the entry drawn up in respect of property owned by Lando di Pepi in the 1320 *Tavola delle Possessioni* for Sant'Angelo in Colle, the one property owned by him inside the walls (valued at 100 *lire*) was bounded by property belonging to the parish church, a road, and property belonging to Neri di Guicciardo (see ASS, *Estimo* 24, fol. 265r). In records drawn up in respect of property owned by Neri di Guicciardo inside the walls of Sant'Angelo in Colle, there is no reference to Lando di Pepi (see ASS, *Estimo* 106, Terzo di Città`, San Pietro in Chastelvecchio, 1318 (hereafter *Estimo* 106), fols 50r–75v, new pagination). Reference is, however, made to Lando di Pepi as the owner of land abutting a vineyard belonging to Neri di Guicciardo in the area known as 'otra(?oltre) Porta Maiore', see *Estimo* 106, fol. 73v.

4   According to Benvenuta di Ghezzo's entry in the 1320 *Tavola delle Possessioni* for Sant'Angelo in Colle, her house (valued at 42 *lire* and 13 *soldi*) was bordered on one side by a road, on another by property belonging to the heirs of Ser Francesco and on a third side by property belonging to Bindo di Accorso, see *Estimo* 24, fol. 37r.

5   ASS, *Estimo* 138, Terzo di Camollia, Sant'Andrea a Lato la Piazza, 1318, fols 287r–287v.

6   Ibid., *Estimo* 108, Terzo di Città`, Porta all'archo, 1320 (hereafter *Estimo* 108), fols 231v–237r, pagination on bottom left-hand side of page. (New pencil pagination, fols 249r–254r, top right-hand side of page. All entries concerning Sant'Angelo in Colle on pages 249v–252r, new pagination, are cancelled out.)

7   There does not appear to be any reference to this property in the 1320 *Tavola delle Possessioni* drawn up for Sant'Angelo in Colle. It seems likely, however that it belonged to the Sienese hospital Santa Maria della Scala, given that *Estimo* 108 was drawn up in respect of Sienese residents. References within such a document would most likely have concerned local institutions, unless specified otherwise.

8   Records drawn up in respect of property held by Neri di Guicciardo inside the walls of Sant'Angelo in Colle make no reference to the hospital of Santa Maria, although a building plot owned by Neri and valued at 1 *lire* and 13 *soldi* is described as bordered on one side by the heirs of Baldiccione, see ASS, *Estimo* 106, fol. 63r, old pagination.

9   According to the entry for Finuccio di Ranuccino in the 1320 *Tavola delle Possessioni* for Sant'Angelo in Colle, one of the houses owned by him inside the walls of the village was bordered on one side by Manovello di Ugolino, on two other sides by road, and on the fourth side by the water conduit, see *Estimo* 24, fol. 141v. Neri di Guicciardo for his part is said to have owned a house within the walls valued at 15 *lire* that was bordered on one side by the water conduit, on another side by property belonging to Ser Tollo di Goglio and on the third side, the 'mediante cursu', see *Estimo* 106, fol. 63r, new pagination.   It is possible that the terms 'cursus aqua' and 'mediante cursu' were reserved for different parts or differing degrees of flow of the water conduit. But the latter term may also have been used to describe one particular section, perhaps one that traversed the middle of the urban fabric.

10 In records concerning property held inside the walls of Sant'Angelo in Colle by Manovello di Ugolino, there is no reference to the heirs of Baldiccione, although one piece of land with a house described as 'built on it', and valued at 12 *lire* is said to have been bordered by property belonging to Finuccio di Ranuccino, see *Estimo* 108, fol.685, old pagination.

11 ASS, *Estimo* 139, Terzo di Camollia, Sant'Andrea a Lato la Piazza, 1318, fols 150r–153v, new pagination bottom left of the page.

12 No reference is made to these individuals in details concerning the one piece of property owned by Avitolo di Ildibrando inside the walls in the 1320 *Tavola delle Possessioni*.

13 The other half of this property is said to belong to 'the hospital'.

14 No reference is made to Nardo di Ventura in the 1320 *Tavola delle Possessioni*. In an entry concerning property belonging to Nardello di Ventura, there is however a reference to a house valued at 31 *lire* and 13 *soldi* which was bordered on one side by a road, on another by property belonging to the 'hospital of Santa Maria', on another side by property belonging to Mita di Piero, and on a fourth side by the water conduit, see *Estimo* 24, fol. 347v.

15 In the entry in the 1320 *Tavola delle Possessioni* in respect of the house owned by Muccio di Orlando inside the walls, bordering properties are said to have been owned by Avitolo di Ildibrando, Nardo (sic) di Ventura and 'the hospital of Santa Maria', see *Estimo* 24, fol. 301v.

16 ASS, *Estimo* 129, Terzo di San Martino, San Cristofano allato la Chiesa, 1318, fols CCCXV–CCCXVII.

17 The entry for the heirs of Micheluccio in the 1320 *Tavola delle Possessioni* contains no reference to property owned by them inside the walls of Sant'Angelo in Colle.

18 ASS, *Estimo* 108, cc. 683r-685r, old pagination. The fact that Manovelli di Ugolino's property inside the walls of Sant'Angelo in Colle is described in terms of houses built on plots of land may indicate that this Sienese outsider had acquired previously unoccupied areas of the village, and had subsequently arranged for houses to be built on them. In this context it may be significant that the house and land bordering property owned by Ciana di Guidarello was close to a stretch of wall in the area known as 'Castello'. That area presumably encompassed the fortified Sienese barracks. The Via del Castello still exists and cuts up from Via Calcinaio into the main square between plots 158 and 156. Property owned by Manovelli di Ugolino in that part of the village may thus have provided a buffer between the new commune area and local residents. It may also be that Manovelli di Ugolino acquired land close to the new military barracks that had been confiscated from local residents.

19 According to the 1320 *Tavola delle Possessioni* (*Estimo* 24, c. 95r), a female resident, Ciana di Guidarello, owned a house valued at 21 *lire* and 13 *soldi* that was bordered on one side by a road, on another by property belonging to Chele di Ruggiero, and on the third side by property belonging to Manovello di Ugolino. It seems likely, therefore, that the Cina referred to in *Estimo* 108 was a shortened version of Ciana di Guidarello. Chele di Ruggiero, for his part, is said to have owned a house valued at 61 *lire* that was bordered on one side by a stretch of wall ('murus d(i)c(t)i castri'), on another by a road, and on a third side by property belonging to Ciana di Guidarello (see *Estimo* 24, c. 73r).

20 According to the entry for Finuccio di Rannuccini in the 1320 *Tavola delle Possessioni* (*Estimo* 24, c. 141v), one of the two houses owned by that individual inside the walls that was valued at 33 *lire* and 7 *soldi* was bordered on one side by property belonging to Manovello di Ugolino, on two other sides by roads, and on the fourth side by the water conduit. The house owned by Manovello di Ugolino's other neighbour, Cennino di Cenno, was likewise, said to be bordered on one side by the water conduit (see *Estimo* 24, c. 85v).

21 Presumably the Gianni di Lamberti included in the 1320 *Tavola delle Possessioni* (*Estimo* 24, c. 162r), although details recorded in respect of this individual make no reference to property owned inside the walls of Sant'Angelo in Colle.

22 According to the 1320 *Tavola delle Possessioni*, this individual's house was bordered on two sides by roads, on a third side by property belonging to Manovello di Ugolino and on a fourth side by the water conduit (see *Estimo* 24, c. 410r).

23 According to details furnished in respect of San Michele in the 1320 *Tavola delle Possessioni* two pieces of church property were bordered by property owned by Manovello di Ugolino: one, valued at 19 *lire* and 7 *soldi*, and another slightly larger property valued at 20 *lire* and 13 *soldi* (see *Estimo* 24, fol. 129v). The smaller of the two buildings was bordered on two sides by a road, on another by the water conduit, and on the last side by the property belonging to Manovello. The larger structure was bordered on one side by a road, on another by property belonging to Bindo di Accorso and on the third side by property belonging to Manovello di Ugolino. It thus seems clear that Manovello's property was contiguous with, or wedged in between the two buildings belonging to the church.

24 According to the 1320 *Tavola delle Possessioni*, this individual was called Angelinus.

25 According to the 1320 *Tavola delle Possessioni*, Tino di Montenero's property abutted the water conduit, see *Estimo* 24, fol. 416r.

26 ASS, *Estimo* 143, Terzo di Camollia, La Magione del Tempio, 1318 (hereafter *Estimo* 143), 227r–229v, old pagination.

27 No individual of this name is included in the 1320 *Tavola delle Possessioni* for Sant'Angelo in Colle.

28 Details furnished for property owned by Bindo di Raniero inside the walls of Sant'Angelo in Colle in the 1320 *Tavola delle Possessioni* contain no reference to adjacent property owned by Meo di Bonfiglio, but refer rather to property owned by Neri di Guicciardo and Pietro Ranieri, see *Estimo* 24, fol. 25r. Details furnished in respect of property held inside the walls by Neri di Guicciardo make no reference either to Meo di Bonfiglio, or to Ristoruccio di Toro or to Bindo di Raniero, see ASS, *Estimo* 106, fols 50r–75v, new pagination.

29 ASS, *Estimo* 143, fol. 228v. The first two entries on this page (including the description of this house, and a reference to worked land in Percena) are struck through. Given the duplicate references to Ristoruccio and Bindo, it seems likely, however, that Meo di Bonfiglio had at one time owned two contiguous properties inside the walls of Sant'Angelo in Colle.

30 ASS, *Estimo* 106, cc. 50r-75v, new pagination.

31 No individuals of this name are included in the 1320 *Tavola delle Possessioni*, but according to the entry for the heirs of Cecco di Piero (c. 171v), they owned a house valued at 15 *lire* and 7 *soldi* that was bordered on two sides by a road, and on the third side by property belonging to Neri di Guicciardo.

32 In the 1320 *Tavola delle Possessioni* this individual is named Cecca.

33 No individuals of this name are included in the 1320 *Tavola delle Possessioni*, but according to the entry for the heirs of Vivo di Jacopo (c. 212r), they owned a house valued at 39 *lire* and 7 *soldi* that was bordered on one side by a road, on another by property belonging to Lonarduccio di Terno and on a third side by property belonging to Neri di Guicciardo. In the entry for Lonarduccio di Terno (c. 277r) reference is made to neighbouring property that belonged not to the heirs of Vivo di Jacopo, but to the heirs of Vivo di Argiano.

34 This individual is not recorded as owning any property inside the walls of Sant'Angelo in Colle in the 1320 *Tavola delle Possessioni*.

35 According to Chele di Ruggiero's entry in the 1320 *Tavola delle Possessioni* (c. 73r) the property abutting that belonging to Neri di Guicciardo was likewise a building plot (valued at 11 *soldi*).

36 According to the 1320 *Tavola delle Possessioni* (c. 378v), Petruccio di Piero owned two houses abutting property belonging to Neri di Guicciardo, one valued at 24 *lire* and 7 *soldi*, the other at 20 *lire*.

37 According to the 1320 *Tavola delle Possessioni* (c. 186v), the heirs of Franco owned four properties inside the walls that abutted property belonging to Neri di Guicciardo. Two of these were building plots (valued respectively at 3 *lire* and 10 *soldi*). The two houses were valued at 24 *lire* and 13 *soldi* and 7 *lire* and 13 *soldi*. Both building plots were said to abut the walls of the village on one of their sides, but that valued at 3 *lire* was also apparently adjacent to the 'palatuim comunis Senarum', or structure serving as the Palazzo Comunale of the Republic of Siena, on another.

38 This individual is named as Naccinus in the 1320 *Tavola delle Possessioni*.

39 According to Ser Tollo di Gollo's entry in the 1320 *Tavola delle Possessioni* (*Estimo* 24, fol. 407r), his house inside the walls was bordered on two sides by a road, and on the third side by property belonging to Vanuccio di Giovanni. However, a piece of worked land lying fallow sited on the 'podium castillionis', or hill of the castle, is described as bordered on one side by property belonging to Neri di Guicciardo (see fol. 407r). Neighbouring proprietors on the other two sides of Ser Tollo's land were said to be Bosta di Micheluccio and the Commune. In Bosta's entry (*Estimo* 24, fol. 42r), no reference was made either to land in the area of the 'hill of the castle' or to Ser Tollo di Gollo, but a house belonging to Bosta inside the walls was said to be bordered on one side by property belonging to Jacopino di Micheluccio, on another, by property belonging to Neri di Guicciardo, and on a third side by a road. Jacopino (or Jacopus) for his part is also said to have owned a house that was bordered on one side by property belonging to Neri di Guicciardo (see *Estimo* 24, fol. 155r). In the entry for the Commune (*Estimo* 24, fol. 58r) reference is made to a plot of worked and wooded land in the area known as 'poggio di castiglione' that was bordered on one side by other property belonging to the Commune of Montalcino, on another by a road, and on the third side by property belonging to Neri di Guicciardo. It seems likely, therefore, that the so-called 'hill of the castle' was located inside or near the existing walls of the village in 1320. It also seems that the 'mediante cursu' flowed through part of this area. See footnote 9 above for various interpretations of the term 'mediante cursu'.

40 According to records furnished in respect of the Sienese heirs of Baldiccione (ASS, *Estimo* 108, fol. 249v, new pagination), those individuals owned two houses inside the walls of Sant'Angelo in Colle that abutted property belonging to Neri di Guicciardo. One of the houses belonging to the heirs of Baldiccione (valued at 24 *lire* and 13 *soldi*) was said to be bordered on a second side by a road, and on the third side by property belonging to the hospital of Santa Maria. The other house (valued at 36 *lire* and 13 *soldi*) was said to be bordered on a second side by a road, on a third side by Finuccio di Ranuccio and the 'mediante curso, and on a fourth side by property belonging to the Sienese resident Manovello di Ugolino. Of the two properties recorded as owned by the heirs of Baldiccione, it seems likely that the larger one abutted Neri di Guicciardo's building plot, since details furnished in respect of Manovello di Ugolino (ASS, *Estimo* 108, fol. 685r, old pagination) refer to land upon which a house had been built which was bordered on one side by property belonging to Finuccio Ranuccio, and on another by property belonging to Cennino di Cenno. This is confirmed by the fact that the entry for Cennino di Cenno (see *Estimo* 24, fol. 85 v) refers to neighbouring property as belonging to Manovello di Ugolino. Cennino di Cenno's house was also bordered on one side by the water conduit.

41 According to the entry for the heirs of Cecco 'cavaliere' in the 1320 *Tavola delle Possessioni* (fol. 225r), their house inside the walls was bordered on one side by a road, on another by Cenello di Ugolino,

and on a third side by Giovanni di Rainaldo and the 'mediante cursu aque'. No mention is made of Neri di Guicciardo as the owner of neighbouring property. In details furnished for Giovanni di Rainaldo, there is no mention of either the heirs of Cecco 'cavaliere' or of Neri di Guicciardo.

42 ASS, *Estimo* 104, Terzo di Citta`, San Quiricho in Chastelvecchio, 1318, fols 264r–265v, new pagination.

43 This individual is not included in the 1320 *Tavola delle Possessioni*, although there are a number of references to individuals holding the same patronym, including 'Dominichus', Mita, Neccha and the 'heirs of Brunacci'. In none of the details furnished in respect of property held by those individuals is there any reference, however, to property owned by Niccoluccio di Mandriano.

44 Nerio di Ranerio is not included in the 1320 *Tavola delle Possessioni*, but an entry for Nennus, or Nenno di Raniero, describes a house inside the walls valued at 47 *lire* which was bordered on one side by a road, on another side by property belonging to Riccuccio di Guido, and on the third side by property belonging to Niccoluccio di Mandriano, see *Estimo* 24, fol. 340r.

45 According to the *Sconpartimento delle Parrocchie e Contrade della Citta di Siena, fatto Terzo per Terzo, nell Anno 1318 in occasione della Lira o Presta imposta su' Beni Stabili Esistenti nella Citta e Territorio Sanese* (ASS, *Manoscritti* C46, fol. 108) (hereafter *Sconpartimento delle Parrocchi*) property owned by this individual at Sant'Angelo in Colle was recorded in *Estimo* 108 on fol. 9. Although Baldera's name is included in the index to that volume, pages with the old pagination of IX–XVIIII are now missing.

46 According to the index of *Estimo* 109 (fol. 126), this individual had some property at Sant'Angelo in Colle, but the relevant page appears to be missing in the surviving register.   It may be significant, however, that Filippo di Niccolaio Buonsignori is recorded (*Estimo* 109, fol. CXXIII, old pagination) as owning the whole of the 'castrum' and 'curiam' of Montenero.

47 According to the *Sconpartimento delle Parrocchie* (fol. 352) property owned by this individual at Sant'Angelo in Colle was recorded in *Estimo* 93, Nobili del Chontado, fol. 315. In the existing volume there are missing pages between fols 303 and 362.

Analysis of the forty-three properties in this category:

Many of the properties declared in respect of these Sienese outsiders were described as building plots or plots of land upon which houses had been built. From details furnished in respect of these, it also seems that a large number of the building plots were located in the vicinity of the water conduit. Some of them were also said to abut the existing walls of the village. This would seem to support the argument that parts (if not all) of a pre-existing circuit of walls, but also parts of the urban complex in the vicinity of that circuit were destroyed or appropriated following the late thirteenth-century Ghibelline insurrection. It would also seem to support the hypothesis that the water conduit marked the path of an earlier circuit of walls.

Most of the houses owned by these Sienese outsiders were small, but in a handful of cases at least one structure of some size was also recorded. In the case of Lando di Domino Meo di Tolomeo, only one large house (valued at 100 *lire*) inside the walls seems to have been owned. While a case may be constructed for sub-letting where a number of smaller properties were also owned, it seems more likely that Lando di Domino Meo di Tolomeo reserved the property he owned inside the walls of the village for his own personal use.

Several of the houses owned by Sienese 'outsiders' in the early fourteenth-century village were clearly substantial structures. One house belonging to Lando di Meo di Tolomeo, for example, must have been one of the largest in the village, since it was valued at 100 *lire*.[55] Another belonging to Meo di Buonfiglio was probably much the same size, since it, likewise, was valued at 100 *lire*.[56] A slightly smaller structure valued at 90 *lire* is recorded as belonging to the Augustinian friars of Sant'Agostino.[57] Yet another, again probably of slightly smaller dimensions because valued at 70 *lire*, was owned by Manovello di Ugolino.[58] Another, the largest of the properties recorded in respect of a resident of Siena, a house with an estimated value of 160 *lire*, is recorded as belonging to Neri di Guicciardo.[59] Of all the Sienese 'outsiders' recorded as owning property in this southern frontier castle, Neri di Guicciardo seems the most likely individual to have played a significant role in renting out living accommodation. According to his own tax return in 1318, he owned over 20 houses and building plots inside the walls of Sant'Angelo in Colle. These ranged in value from a few *soldi* to well over 100 *lire*. In at least three cases it is clear that the structures abutted other property belonging to Neri. Elsewhere it emerges that several properties while not contiguous, were at least clustered together.

It is inconceivable that Neri di Guicciardo retained all this property for his own personal use or that it remained uninhabited, when demand for accommodation inside the village must have been so great. Equally, it seems unlikely that members of Neri's family, or familiars engaged on personal family business on his behalf could have made use of all of the 20 or so properties inside the walls recorded as belonging to him. The obvious conclusion must be that some, if not all of the property belonging to Neri di Guicciardo at Sant'Angelo in Colle was let out. If this were the case, Neri di Guicciardo's combined holdings must have set him apart not only as an 'outsider' of great wealth, but also as a potentially powerful landlord who could influence daily life in the village through the offer of work on his land, and the provision of accommodation both on the land, and within the village. The fact that Sienese 'outsiders' like Neri di Guiccardo, Lando di Meo di Tolomeo, Meo di Buonfiglio and Manovello di Ugolino invested in property inside the walls of Sant'Angelo in Colle must have made a considerable impression on local inhabitants. As the owner of a large amount of land outside the walls as well as of numerous properties inside Sant'Angelo in Colle itself, Neri di Guicciardo, in particular, must have been regarded as a member of the local elite, if not the village's leading figure. There can have been little doubt about the power and influence of these Sienese 'outsiders', both individually and as a group. If, in addition, assuming the role of landlords in letting out some of the property they acquired, they must also have influenced the lives of local residents in an immediate and practical manner. Indeed, for some of the inhabitants, existence inside the walls of Sant'Angelo in Colle may have depended upon their being able to afford the rent on living accommodation belonging to an absentee Sienese landlord.

There is yet another way whereby apparent discrepancies between the size of the urban fabric and the number of people needing to be accommodated inside the walls of the early fourteenth-century village may be explained. During the medieval and renaissance periods buildings were often divided into several units of accommodation so that members of the same clan could occupy separate quarters whilst remaining in close physical proximity under the same roof.[60] Cluster diagrams based on details of property furnished on behalf of a number of local inhabitants in the early fourteenth-century village suggest that the joint living houses established by Guccio and Lucarino di Ser Francesco and other members of their family were not exceptional. Cross-reference between individual entries in the 1320 *Tavola delle possessioni* also indicates that joint living houses and different parts of the same building served, on occasion, as accommodation for a number of individuals who were not related.

The overall size of the buildings divided up in this way could vary. Some multi-tenancing appears, for example, to have been established within relatively substantial structures. Although a proportion of the larger properties recorded in the village no doubt functioned as single units of living accommodation for the local elite, it becomes clear that in some cases the owner of a substantial home effected subdivisions within it in order to accommodate close relations, as well as extended members of the same clan. Individual entries in the 1320 *Tavola delle possessioni* also show that it was often the case that autonomous, but contiguous living units belonged to individuals who were not only related to each other, but were also recorded as having comparatively high patrimonies.

Accommodating a number of different households under one roof could obviously be effected in several different ways. In many cases individual units were positioned on different floors. In others, the units of accommodation could be positioned side by side on the same level. Yet others might be arranged in such a way that they were both partially above and partially below neighbouring units. Heads of households might thus claim contiguity with other heads of households, even though individual units of accommodation were not precisely adjacent. In such circumstances, not only the homeowners, but also the tax officials must have faced considerable problems when trying to furnish and establish accurate details about the confines of individual living units. It must have been comparatively easy to name neighbours to the sides, front and back. It would have been far more difficult to give an accurate account of adjacent property partly above, partly below, or partially to the side or back. Such complicated arrangements might explain why details furnished by one head of a household in one entry in the 1320 *Tavola delle possessioni* for Sant'Angelo in Colle do not always tally with those of another, even when there is some degree of certainty that the two properties were, in fact, contiguous.

In the last analysis we should remember that medieval households were crowded affairs. There can be little doubt that even comparatively small premises would have commonly accommodated many more individuals than is now normally the case. Thus many of those declaring no accommodation of their own may in reality have lived with relatives who did hold property inside the walls, and in some cases several related branches of the same family may have lived in a single unit of accommodation, the responsibility for which rested with the most senior member or the nominated head.

Establishing the locations of key buildings and public institutions

If an assessment of the conditions of home ownership and the ways in which individual households were accommodated within the medieval urban fabric is taxing, establishing the location of the individual buildings themselves is even more challenging. While cluster diagrams assembled from details contained in the 1320 *Tavole delle possessioni* help establish in broad terms the relationship between different households, it is difficult to pinpoint the position of individual buildings within the village itself without some fixed point of reference, such as the town hall, the water conduit, or one of the village's two churches. A particular obstacle resides in the fact that entries in the 1320 *Tavole delle possessioni* concentrate on ownership, rather than function. While we may hypothesise that Neri di Guicciardo's multiple ownership of property resulted in his being able to let some of his accommodation to non-property owners inside the fourteenth-century frontier castle, in the absence of more precise information about the function of each building, we can only hypothesise about what kind of property was let out, and the degree of home-letting Neri di Guicciardo might thus have been involved in. Some of the buildings owned by Neri may, for example, have been left empty. Some may have been given over to storage, or used as offices. We cannot even be certain which, if any of the buildings Neri di Guicciardo used as his own living accommodation. Similar problems arise when attempting to establish which of the several buildings listed as belonging to the commune actually served as the town hall in 1320, and which – if any – functioned rather as subsidiary offices and storage spaces. Lack of specific details concerning the function of individual buildings belonging to key entities and public institutions also hinders any attempt, for example, to position ecclesiastical property in relation to individual church structures.

The parish church of San Michele Arcangelo and the church of San Pietro inside the walls

It is generally argued that the existing church of San Michele Arcangelo arose from a much earlier and considerably smaller edifice on the same site.[61] Some maintain that there is proof of the first church in the remains of an arched window still visible on the wall facing the piazza.[62] Others argue that a small inscribed stone inserted on the exterior of the north-facing wall and above the existing doorway there, which bears the date 1321 refers to work recently carried out on the church fabric, thus confirming that a second church was erected on the site of an earlier building early in the fourteenth century.[63] It seems unlikely, however, that this was this stone's original position. It is both too small and displayed at too high a level for its inscription to be easily legible from the ground. As a commemorative inscription it would thus have been unimpressive. While it is possible that some work was carried out on the structure of a pre-existing church during the third decade of the fourteenth century, and that such efforts were commemorated in the surviving stone, archival evidence presented here indicates that a far more radical restoration, if not complete rebuild took place at a slightly later date. As we shall also see, work on the fabric of the church of San Michele Arcangelo during the fourth decade of the fourteenth century was funded in large part by a local resident, Giovanni di Paganello.

While it is likely that the first church of San Michele was located on or near the site of the existing church of San Michele, no records survive in confirmation of this. Nor can we be sure that the new church followed the lines and orientation of the pre-existing structure. It is generally argued that the old church of San Michele was small, as was often the case with Romanesque *pievi*. However, the only concrete information that survives is that the building was large enough to accommodate the commune's consuls and other members of the community of Sant'Angelo in Colle when they gathered together in July 1212, to offer a formal oath of loyalty to the Sienese government. The space inside the old church must thus have been large enough to house some or all of the heads of household of the existing 87 *fuochi*, or families. It must also presumably have been large enough to accommodate officials brought from Siena as witnesses to the act of allegiance from the newly subject commune.

Other factors hinder consideration of the location of the second of the two religious entities listed in the 1320 *Tavola delle Possessioni*, the church of San Pietro.[64] For one thing, no such structure is now visible inside the walls. (As already noted, although a church with that *titulus* still exists, it is actually positioned outside the village, on its southern side.) For another thing, surviving documents despite referring to a church with the *titulus* of San Pietro outside the walls indicate that this structure was located not on the southern side of the village, but to the north or north-east. The situation is further complicated by the fact that the twentieth-century church of the Madonna del Rosario di Pompei (located close to the *Palazzaccio* and inside the existing perimeter of walls on the northern side of the village) has on occasion been referred to as 'detta anche di S. Pietro'.[65] Nevertheless, there seems little doubt that a church with the *titulus* of Saint Peter had been established inside the walls of Sant'Angelo in Colle by the early fourteenth century, since this entity was included in the 1320 *Tavola delle possessioni*. Of the material structure of both this and the church of the same *titulus* to the north of the village, there is, however, now no trace. According to the entry in the 1320 *Tavola delle possessioni*, the church of San Pietro owned a number of properties in the territory of Sant'Angelo in Colle, including a 'small' church (of undefined *titulus*) 'outside the walls' of the village.[66]

One church dedicated to Saint Peter and outside the walls of the village was certainly in existence by the early thirteenth century, since a papal bull issued by Onorius III in 1216, noted that such an entity was at that date united with and under the jurisdiction of the parish church of Sant'Angelo in Colle.[67] Other documents indicate that this was the church that was located to the north of the village. Initially, Don Antonio Brandi believed that it was this church that was recorded as handed over by Pope Pius II to the authority of the Cathedral of Montalcino in 1462.[68] At a later date, however, Don Brandi came to the conclusion that it was the present-day church of San Pietro on the southern side of the village that was (albeit only temporarily) allocated to the diocese of Montalcino.[69] Other chroniclers have suggested that it was the church inside the walls that was handed over.[70] As we shall see, such distinctions have a significant bearing on our analysis of surviving works of art associated with the Sant'Angelo in Colle. As we shall also see, reconsideration of surviving records concerning the church of San Piero outside the walls – whether on its northern or its southern side – is extremely relevant when attempting to establish the location, embellishment and history of the entity with that *titulus* inside the walls.

An attempt is made here to disentangle some of the complex threads of argument.

Although some maintain that references to the church of San Pietro in earlier records concerned the present church of that *titulus* outside Sant'Angelo in Colle on its southern side, there are a number of reasons why this cannot be. The present church of San Pietro apparently only acquired that *titulus* at a relatively recent date. According to a pastoral visit of 1765, the church on the southern side of the village was in the eighteenth century known as the church *'della Misericordia' Beatae Mariae Virginis*.[71] During a slightly later pastoral visit to the village in 1778 what was presumably the same structure was referred to once again not as San Pietro but as the church of the 'Vergine Maria detta della Misericordia'.[72] The hypothesis raised here is that the church with the present *titulus* of San Pietro outside the walls should more realistically be identified with the structure of undefined *titulus* that was recorded in the entry for the church of San Pietro inside the walls in the 1320 *Tavola delle possessioni*.

By contrast, it seems more likely that the church with the *titulus* of San Pietro described in the early thirteenth century as being outside the walls of Sant'Angelo in Colle was located to the north of the village. In such a location it would have been close to the old thoroughfare cutting up from the Sesta road, and close also to a parcel of land known as late as the nineteenth century as the 'Campo di San Pietro' on the north-eastern side of Sant'Angelo in Colle.[73] 'Campo di San Pietro' seems in fact to have been an ancient toponym since there are references in the 1320 *Tavola delle possessioni* to the 'contrada', or area 'known as San Pietro'.[74] There is a reference to the field itself in a list of the land belonging to the parish church of San Michele that was included in the inventory of that entity's possessions drawn up in 1492.[75] It is significant, also, that when Ippolito Borghesi conducted a pastoral visit to Sant'Angelo in Colle in 1618, he referred to the 'ecclesiam S. Petri positam extra limina dicti castri' (the church of San Pietro outside the walls of this castle) as being located on the eastern side of the village.[76] Borghesi noted that this church had only one altar, and that at that time it was embellished with an 'iconam satis vetustam' (or venerable painting).

According to a pastoral visit in 1680, the same church was situated close to the farm known as the 'podere Casella'.[77] There are, in fact, two farms in the vicinity of Sant'Angelo in Colle that might qualify in this respect. Both are situated to the north of the village: the podere Casello, close to the modern entrance road to the village, and the podere Casella, which is closer to the new cemetery. Of the two, it seems most likely that the farm in the vicinity of the cemetery was the closest to the church of San Pietro, since it also borders the area referred to in the early nineteenth century as the 'luogo delle Casella S. Piero'.[78] There is further confirmation that the church of San Pietro outside the walls of Sant'Angelo in Colle was positioned close to podere Casella, in the reference in 1672 to a 'luogo' or area 'detto di S. Pietro', known as San Pietro, that was close not only to the 'strada maestra', or main road, but was also bordered on one side by 'il Ferralino'.[79] This last can be no other than the podere Ferralino, which is positioned to the south west of the existing cemetery. In a slightly later inventory dated 1693, reference was made in the context of the same property to the 'Campo S. Piero'.[80] On the basis of all these facts, there can be little doubt that the church of San Pietro which was under the jurisdiction of the parish church of San Michele was not only located outside the walls of Sant'Angelo in Colle on its north-eastern side, but was also half a mile or so from the urban fabric. As such, it would have been some distance away from a church with the same *titulus* inside the walls.

Establishing the precise location of the church inside the walls is hampered not only by the fact that the building itself no longer exists (at least in any obvious form), but also by the fact that although it is mentioned in records post-dating the 1320 *Tavola delle possessioni*, no clear picture emerges of its position within the urban fabric. It seems likely, however, that the church was close to, if not contiguous with other property owned by San Pietro inside the walls. According to the 1320 *Tavola delle possessioni*, the church owned a building with a cloister that abutted the walls.[81] There is no reference, however, to the church building itself, or to its precise location. This should not necessarily surprise us. In the entry for San Michele in the 1320 *Tavola delle possessioni*, there is no specific reference, either, to the location or rateable value of any church structure with that *titulus* inside the walls. In countless other contemporary tax records, we find details of land and property owned by individual churches, but no reference to the church building itself. This can be explained in a number of ways. In the case of religious institutions, the church building was normally exempt from taxation. There was thus no need to make any specific mention of its size or location in tax returns.[82] In any event, such information was probably deemed unnecessary, not only because of tax exemptions, but also because church structures were such obvious landmarks within individual urban fabrics. There could be no mistaking the function or position of a church building. It was thus not necessary to record its boundaries. In the case of the church of San Pietro inside the walls of Sant'Angelo in Colle, reference was probably made to the church without *titulus* outside the walls because that structure was a subsidiary asset, and thus liable to taxation.

Given the details recorded in the entry for the church of San Pietro in the 1320 *Tavola delle possessioni* for Sant'Angelo in Colle, the most likely location for the church itself must have been on a plot adjacent to or contiguous with the declared house and cloister. This property was apparently bordered on one side by a section of the early-fourteenth century circuit of walls, and on two other sides by roads. Relatively few such 'cornered' sites in the modern village would appear to offer sufficient space for the accommodation not only of a church but also an adjacent house and cloister. The two most likely candidates are those numbered in the 1860 *catasto* map of Sant'Angelo in Colle as plots 100 and 101 to the north-east, and in the vicinity of plot 143 on the north-western side. Of these, the former two seem the most likely, not least because of the amount of space available there. The building on plots 100 and 101 now belongs to the Lisini family, but at the beginning of the twentieth century, both this complex and the adjacent plot of land on which the church of the Madonna del Rosario (which, as we may remember, has on occasion been referred to as 'detta anche San Pietro') was constructed belonged to the Clementi family.[83] The original borders of this property must thus have extended over much of the northern side of the village. There would clearly have been ample space here for both the church and the house and cloister recorded in the 1320 *Tavola delle possessioni*.

Plot 143 is by comparison somewhat cramped, and for a number of other reasons that are outlined below, would not seem to be the most obvious site for either the church or its adjacent property. That said, the plot adjoining plot 143 does at first sight seem an attractive possibility because of what appears to be the remains of a cloister courtyard adjacent to the existing building there. However, in such a position the church of San Pietro inside the walls would have been virtually on the doorstep of the parish church of San Michele. Plot 143 also seems too far inside the existing outer boundaries to conform to the description in 1320 of the house and cloister belonging to San Pietro being bordered on one side by the village walls. It is also relevant that the term 'chiostro', or cloister, was not only adopted in a religious context during the medieval period. This term was in fact often coined to describe an inner pen for the accommodation of animals. Thus, not only religious buildings, but also ordinary dwellings inside the walls of a village, as well as properties in the countryside, might be described as possessing a 'cloister'. Clearly, such pens would not necessarily have conformed to the religious prototype of walls pierced by arches, not least because as such they would have offered scant protection to the animals housed inside. The fact that a courtyard with a well and vestiges of what could have been the surrounding walls of a 'chiostro' or pen still survive on plot 143 is thus in itself not that significant. There are, moreover, several other buildings in Sant'Angelo in Colle that have similar inner courtyards. One or two buildings also reveal the vestiges of arches (sometimes in sequence) on their outer walls. One such example is the building on plot 104, close to the north-eastern gate. It is significant that this structure faces plots 101 and 100 across the steep entrance slope that joins via del Calcinaio. It also occupies a corner site. Moreover this building is one of the few remaining structures in the village that is both 'cornered' by roads whilst at the same time backing onto a surviving stretch of the outer circuit of walls.

Given the changes made to the urban structure under the authority of the Sienese government, and the numerous expansions of the village between the thirteenth and fourteenth centuries, as well as later alterations made to pre-existing buildings in a more recent period, it is possible that an original church dedicated to saint Peter and inside the walls had already been destroyed by the time of the 1320 *Tavola delle possessioni*, and that only the adjoining complex of house and cloister was still intact. One would, however, expect some mention to be made of this in the 1320 *Tavola*. And, in any event, such an hypothesis seems weak, given that the eighteenth-century chronicler Giovanni Antonio Pecci spoke of 'un antica chiesa di S. Pietro, che ancora in parte si dice S. Pietro vecchio, che fu assegnata dal Pontefice Pio II l'anno 1464 in parte di dota alla Cattedrale di Montalcino', when describing the buildings inside Sant'Angelo in Colle.[84] On the basis of this evidence, the old church of San Pietro must still have been standing in the fifteenth century.

Further evidence that there were two churches inside the walls of Sant'Angelo in Colle in the fifteenth century resides in surviving records concerning the *Compagnia della Concezione*, a local lay confraternity. According to a record dating to 1483 that company's members used to gather together on the eve of all feasts associated with the Virgin (except that of her immaculate conception) in order to form a procession and visit 'the two churches of the castle'.[85] In the light of this, it seems clear that in the eighteenth century Pecci was making a distinction between the church of San Pietro inside the walls that was no longer standing, and the church with the same *titulus* that was outside the village and that was still functioning. It also seems clear that it was in the latter church that in the previous century Pier Giovanni della Ciaia had wished to be laid to rest, since he stipulated in 1651 that he should be buried in the church of San Pietro 'fuori le mura di Sant'Angelo in Colle' (outside the walls of Sant'Angelo in Colle).[86]

What then, can be established about the site of the old church of San Pietro inside the walls, given the scant surviving documentary evidence and the numerous ways in which the medieval urban fabric has changed? The reference in 1492 to the 'carbonaia' of the 'mal albergo' abutting both the walls of the village and the church and cemetery of San Pietro would seem to confirm that the entire church complex of San Pietro inside the walls was still standing at the end of the fifteenth century. It also seems likely, given the description of the adjacent 'orto' belonging to the parish church, that the church of San Pietro overlooked a steep area given over to orchards and kitchen gardens. A number of entries in the 1320 *Tavola delle possessioni* do in fact refer to the area, or 'contrada' of San Pietro, as well as to the 'Costa San Pietro' in the context of the location of kitchen gardens, or orchards.[87] Combined together, such references indicate that the old church of San Pietro inside the village was not only situated close to, if not abutting, one stretch of the walls, but also overlooked kitchen gardens on the Costa San Pietro and at least one stretch of the village ditch or moat bordering that part of the village which was known as the 'Contrada di San Pietro'.

Neither of the sites earmarked in the existing urban fabric as possible locations for the church of San Pietro inside the walls would appear to correspond exactly with details furnished in the 1320 *Tavola delle possessioni*. However, given the evidence outlined above, somewhere in the vicinity of plots 100 and 101 would seem to be the most likely.

The fact that plots 101 and 100 are located in close proximity to the building on plot 104 – a mere stone's throw away on the other side of the north-eastern gate – also strengthens the hypothesis that the old church of San Pietro was located in this part of the village. It is also relevant that plots 101 and 100 are bordered by a surviving stretch of the outer circuit of walls and overlook the steep incline on the northern side of the village. When approaching the village, the Lisini building effectively towers above the current entrance road that skirts Sant'Angelo in Colle on its northern side. The path traced by the road at this point (at a considerably lower level) may in effect follow if not reflect the external ditch, or 'carbonaia'. Thereafter, it ascends the steep gradient of the hill before reaching the tower of the *Palazzaccio* on the western side of the village. Even here, the ground is several metres lower than plots 101 and 100. On the basis of topography alone, plots 101 and 100 would thus seem to relate well to the location of the church of San Pietro inside the walls as described in the late fifteenth century.

The obvious question is, if the church complex of San Pietro inside the walls was still standing at the end of the fifteenth century and if it was located in the vicinity of plots 101 and 100, why is there apparently no trace of it now? One answer may be that the church building was destroyed or left in parlous condition before, or following the abandoning of the village and the siege of Montalcino during the sixteenth century. Another possibility is that the church was deconsecrated and subsequently amalgamated with other structures to form a private building. This might well have been the course of events, if it was indeed the old church of San Pietro inside the walls that was allocated to the cathedral of Montalcino by Pius II in the mid-fifteenth century. That transfer was apparently in part motivated by the fact that the congregation of the church of San Pietro had dwindled to a size that was no longer viable in the context of the upkeep of the church fabric. Without individuals willing to donate money towards such upkeep and the every day needs of the clergy, there was likely to be a rapid decline of both. Transferred back to the care of the parish of Sant'Angelo in Colle after a comparatively brief period under the jurisdiction of the cathedral of Montalcino, the church of San Pietro probably fared little better. In this context it may be significant that when Francesco Bossi visited Sant'Angelo in Colle in 1576 he made reference to a church dedicated to Saint Peter that was in poor condition.[88] It is possible therefore, that the church with the *titulus* of San Pietro inside the walls finally deteriorated beyond repair some time during the last years of the sixteenth century. In this context, it is relevant that Gherardini made no reference to a church dedicated to Saint Peter inside the walls in his record of Sant'Angelo in Colle in 1676.[89] It may not be coincidental, therefore, that the existing building belonging to the Lisini family is thought to date from the late seventeenth or early eighteenth century.

Figure 3.1
Façade of
Palazzo Lisini,
Sant'Angelo
in Colle

Given the evidence of much earlier constructions visible in the existing façade, there seems little doubt that the Palazzo Lisini derives from a reconstruction project during which numerous changes were made to a pre-existing structure or a number of structures on the same site.[90] Might this originally have been the site of a church? There are a number of factors that would support such a hypothesis. There are, for example, vestiges of several arches on the street side of the present building, as well as what appears originally to have been a tower-like structure wedged between two parts of the existing façade. Detailed consideration of both the internal spaces and the ground plan drawn up of the building at a later date adds further support to the argument that an entire church complex originally existed on this site.

Embedded within internal spaces of the existing building is a long nave-like structure placed at right angles to the road and stretching back towards the outer circuit of walls. At its far end, this space narrows internally on each side to a single, centrally positioned aperture. Aerial photographs and exterior views strengthen the argument that this part of the building may once have served as a church (the façade of which opened onto via del Calcinaio, and the apse end of which overlooked the walls and steep ditch on the northern edge of the village). Not only is there a single stretch of roof, which appears

Figure 3.2   Aerial view of the northern section of Sant'Angelo in Colle, including Palazzo Lisini

to trace the boundary lines of the internal nave-like space, but at a lower level the centrally positioned aperture would make particular sense if it originally served as an apse window, marking the canonical east end of a church.

Traces of the tower-like structure in the central part of the existing façade may thus be all that is left of the 'campanile', or bell tower of the old church of San Pietro inside the walls. On the basis of the ground plan of the existing building, and plans drawn up in respect of the village during the nineteenth century, such a tower would have flanked the façade of the church on the right-hand side. On the basis of this reconstruction, also, one would have to argue that the 'Costa San Pietro' and 'Contrada di San Pietro' were on the northern side of the village. The proposed north-eastern location of the church with the *titulus* of San Pietro outside the walls – close to the 'Campo San Pietro' and the 'Podere la Casella' – would in any event tend to support such a proposition. However, this would clearly have a bearing on the name traditionally allotted to the northern gate. The prevailing view is that this was the main gate to the village and that it was known as the Porta Sant'Angelo. On the basis of the above reconstruction this is probably incorrect. If the church of San Pietro inside the walls was indeed positioned on plots 100 and 101, the nearby gate must surely have been known as the 'Porta San Pietro'. The original Porta Sant'Angelo may, by contrast, have been positioned in closer proximity to the 'Costa Sant'Angelo', which – as already noted – was located on the south-western side of the village.

The Palazzo Comunale and the visual impact of the Sienese barracks

While the case remains open as to the original location of the church of San Pietro inside the walls, there is a greater consensus of opinion as to the position of the old town hall. Despite this, there are once more a number of conflicting theories. Some claim that the old town hall stood on the site of the palace associated with the Tolomei family on the north-eastern side of the village (in via del Calcinaio, on plot 161).[91] Others are of the opinion – perhaps on the basis of Pecci's belief that the Palace of Justice was positioned on the site of the old tower – that the town hall was positioned on the site of the present-day Franceschi building, on plot 166.[92] Most, however, maintain that the old town hall was situated on the north-western side, close to the *Palazzaccio*.[93] Given the details furnished for the commune in the 1320 *Tavola delle possessioni*, and the cluster diagram assembled from property in the vicinity of the structure functioning as the town hall in the early fourteenth century, it seems that this was indeed the case.

Cluster Diagram 3.1 shows that at least three, and possibly six, communal properties were situated in close proximity to each other on one side of the village. One of the properties, a comparatively large structure valued at 53 *lire 7 soldi*, and abutting a building plot owned by Neri di Giucciardo, was bordered on at least two sides by roads, one of which appears to have bordered a considerably larger communal structure valued at 350 *lire*. This building,

Cluster Diagram 3.1 Property belonging to the commune of Sant'Angelo in Colle in 1320 identifiable as in the vicinity of the old and new town halls

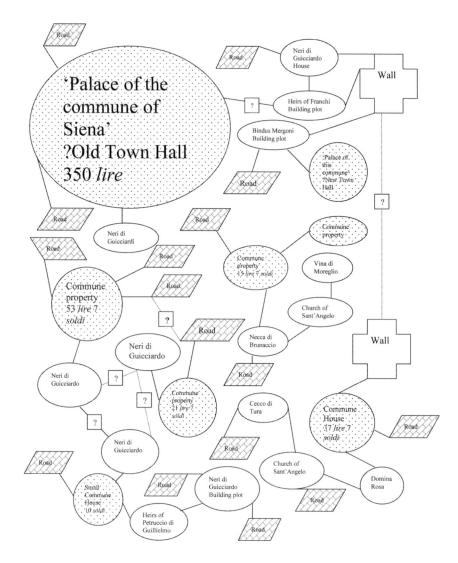

tentatively identified here as occupying the site of the original town hall, was positioned close to the village wall. On at least two sides, it was separated from the walls by empty building plots, one belonging to the heirs of Franchi, another to Bindus Mergoni. It seems likely that it was also bordered on a third side by another building plot belonging to Neri di Guicciardo.

In the 1320 *Tavola delle possessioni* entry for the commune itself, there are a number of references to communal property ranging in value from 10 *soldi* to 350 *lire*.[94] Somewhat confusingly, four of these buildings are described as abutting property belonging to Neri di Guicciardo, but no reference is made to the building plot belonging to the heirs of Ser Franchi, or to the other individual who is also recorded as owning property abutting the old town hall, Bindus Mergoni.[95] Only one building, which must have been of modest to medium proportions (given its estimated value of 37 *lire* and 7 *soldi*) is described as adjacent to the walls. A neighbour on one side of this building is named as Domina Rosa – presumably the Domina Rosa wife of Futio, whose own property is described as bordered on one side by a road, on another by property belonging to the church of Sant'Angelo, and on another, by property belonging to the commune.[96] The entry for Domina Rosa does not, however, refer to the function of the adjoining communal property.

Somewhat puzzlingly, none of the buildings recorded as belonging to the commune in its own entry in the 1320 *Tavola delle possessioni* are identified as functioning as the town hall. Another curious fact is that the largest property (that valued at 350 *lire*) is described merely as 'a house'. Logically, this structure would have been the most appropriate structure to house the original town hall, if only because of its apparent size. However, a number of other entries in the 1320 *Tavola delle possessioni* contain clear references to a building that at that period was functioning as the town hall. It seems clear from these that this structure was not only close to the walls, but was also bordered by building plots.

The 1320 *Tavola delle possessioni* does in fact contain a number of references to what appear to be empty building plots, many of which seem to have been positioned close to the village walls. These building plots were for the most part of modest dimensions. One plot belonging to Chele di Ruggerio, for example, was valued at only nine *soldi*.[97] Another, that belonging to the heirs of Ser Franchi was valued at three *lire*. This was the plot that on one side abutted the commune building valued at 350 *lire*, and on another side backed on to a stretch of wall.[98] A number of other empty plots are likewise described as being close to property owned by the commune. One or two of them seem to have been virtually surrounded by commune buildings. For example, the building plot recorded as owned by Neri di Guicciardo in Cluster Diagram 3.1, appears to have been bordered on at least three sides by property belonging to the commune (including the structure tentatively identified here as the original town hall). It is possible that open land close to the walls and in the vicinity of the largest commune structure in 1320 had either at one time been built upon and the structures subsequently dismantled, or had not yet been filled. It is also possible, however, that these plots were all that remained of buildings razed by the Sienese when they established their new military barracks on the site of the village's old town hall in 1282. This would clearly have been politically expedient if the owners of such property had been involved with the recent Ghibelline rebellion. It may also have been deemed appropriate at this date to isolate the official buildings of the commune from the populace. There is certainly evidence of such practice at a slightly later date, when in April 1345, the decision was taken to purchase a number of houses in the vicinity of the new Sienese 'cassero' and the 'Porta Cittadina' at Grosseto.[99] According to this record, once purchased, those buildings were to be demolished. The reference to the 'Porta Cittadina' is significant, if only for the implication that the new barracks at Grosseto had been positioned close to the main entrance to the town. If the same course had been adopted at Sant'Angelo in Colle during the 1280s, the new *cassero* there may likewise have been sited close to the main entrance. If that were the case, it would seem likely (as already hypothesised) that the main gate, or at least the main gate of the Sienese barracks was on the western side of the village. It would also seem likely that this was the gate that was referred to in contemporary records as the 'Porta Maggiore'.

There seems little doubt that the site of the *Palazzo Comunale*, like that of the *Palazzo di Giustizia*, changed over time. The designation of a comparatively small building for the town hall under the village's new regime as a subject Sienese commune could, for example, have resulted from a deliberate attempt on the part of the Sienese to reign in the villagers' civic pride, following continued unrest at Sant'Angelo in Colle. Even if not affected in the early thirteenth century, a change of site must surely have been necessary once the Sienese military had established itself on the site of the old town hall. The building functioning as the town hall in 1320 may thus have been all that remained of an original and possibly much larger complex that was either dismantled or appropriated by the Sienese when first gaining control of Sant'Angelo in Colle early in the thirteenth century, or when subsequently constructing their own barracks on the site of the old town hall. Cluster Diagram 3.1 presents a number of possibilities. One small commune building valued at 15 *lire* and 7 *soldi*, for example, appears to have bordered the building plot belonging to Bindus Mergoni, and thus to have been in close proximity to the much large structure valued at 350 *lire*. Another comparatively small commune building valued at 21 *lire* and 7 *soldi* appears not only to have abutted Neri di Guicciardo's building plot, but also to have bordered the somewhat larger commune propery valued at 53 *lire* and 7 *soldi* (which likewise abutted Neri's building plot, and which was probably also close to the largest commune property, although perhaps divided from it by a road).

When set against the present-day village, only one area seems compatible with Cluster Diagram 3.1: the area on the north-western side of the village around the *Palazzaccio*. While Palazzo Tolomei on the eastern side of the village may have been close to an older and inner circuit of walls, there is no way in which it, or any of its surrounding buildings could be described as bordered by three roads. Moreover, that particular building appears to post-date the fourteenth century. The *Palazzaccio* site is the only area where there is a matching pattern of wall, roads and open spaces. It is also the only part of the village that has been consistently associated with the old *Palazzo Comunale*. Moreover, there was ample space here for other offices dealing with communal affairs. The large site extending back from the *Palazzaccio* towards the present-day church of the Madonna del Rosario, could have accommodated several such buildings. Prior to the fourteenth century, this area may thus have been dominated by an imposing structure serving as the village's original town hall, just as the area around the old nucleus of the *pieve*, or principal church of San Michele may at one time have been dominated by the Palace of Justice.

As in many other urban fabrics, different spaces within the subject commune of Sant'Angelo in Colle must have carried different political charges.[100] While no surviving records provide us with precise information as to what parts of the walls were demolished by the Sienese following the Ghibelline rebellion, and whether the stretch of land known as the 'Costa Sant'Angelo' was amongst those parts of the village that were destroyed, we know that the Sienese government proceeded with particular care when selecting the site for their new *cassero*. This indicates that the location of that symbol of military power was as important to the Sienese authorities as the structure itself. The position finally chosen, on the site of the village's old town hall, was highly significant. In establishing themselves in an area where matters of local importance had previously been discussed in an atmosphere of at least partial independence, the Sienese were very obviously reaffirming and stamping their own central authority over the whole village. That the Sienese were aware of the significance of positioning the new military complex where once local laws had prevailed, is confirmed by events elsewhere, and in particular by their treatment of the counts of Montorsaio in 1255. On 18 March of that year, the General Council in Siena decreed that the counts of Montorsaio should be barred from returning to their land, and that instead certain masters of the craft should be sent to Montorsaio to design the *cassero* which was to be built at the foot of the pre-existing tower there.[101] Thus the previous owners were not only divested of their possessions, but the authority of Siena was literally stamped upon their erstwhile symbol of power, the tower.

The new military complex at Sant'Angelo in Colle no doubt constituted an imposing visual addition to the thirteenth-century urban fabric, most particularly after its fortification in 1340. Remaining structures at Montelaterone (to the south of the River Orcia), and elsewhere, indicate that the *cassero* at Sant'Angelo in Colle could have consisted of a tower structure (possibly divided up on different floors into a number of individual units of accommodation), which was in turn connected to and protected by an inner circuit of walls.[102] Further areas for the use of the military may have been constructed in the remaining internal spaces of the tower, as well as on adjacent plots. That the new barracks was a complex of some size seems likely, given the remains of the *Palazzaccio* – more a large rectangular block, than a slender tower. In keeping with other military structures of the time, the new barracks at Sant'Angelo in Colle may also have been approached via a fortified gateway. The rough aperture in the north-western wall of the existing tower has by tradition been accepted as marking the original position of such a gateway, despite the fact that the structure itself was barely visible above ground level by the eighteenth century.[103] As it stands, the structure known as the *Palazzaccio* is the result of a restoration project carried out in the twentieth century. The present building can thus only be regarded as an approximate reconstruction of part of the fourteenth-century urban fabric, although it no doubt follows in large part the ground plan of the pre-existing tower. Moreover, it is likely that the original tower was accessed not on the ground floor, but at an upper level. This does not, however, preclude the possibility that there was once a fortified gateway in this part of the village.

If the fortress at Montelaterone is anything to go, by the new *cassero* at Sant'Angelo in Colle would have been physically separated from the rest of the village by dint of its own circuit walls.[104] This was certainly the case at Argiano where (as already noted) the fortified 'cassarum' was not only flanked by a fortified wall and another circuit of walls, but was quite separate from the *borgo*, or town itself in 1391.[105] Such an arrangement would inevitably have set up a conflicting dialogue, possibly even challenging an earlier fortified nucleus inside the village. At Montelaterone, the fortified *Palazzo Vescovile*, or Bishop's Palace, in the lower part of the town that was associated with the nearby Abbadia San Salvatore, and which constituted a visual representative of that abbey's power, was one of the first buildings to be destroyed following the Sienese takeover.[106]

That some kind of fortified structure was located in the centre of Sant'Angelo in Colle and at the summit of the hill is confirmed by the fact that the central square is still known as the 'Piazza Castello'. Remains of a fortified nucleus in close proximity to the church of San Michele were also apparently still visible in the early twentieth century.[107] At that date, the Piazza Castello contained a quadrangular orchard surrounded by the remains of ancient walls.[108] The shape of this, combined with the square's name, suggests that there may once have been a *castellare*, or fortified tower in the centre of the village. There is further evidence of this in the fact that one of the alleys opening onto the Piazza Castello is still known as the 'via Costa Castellare'. If a Palace of Justice had indeed existed at the centre of the old fortified nucleus of Sant'Angelo in Colle during the thirteenth century, the Sienese might have wished to diminish its significance, either by dismantling it, or by establishing a second symbol of authority elsewhere. There would certainly have been ample reasons for so doing following the attempted coup by the Ghibelline faction in 1280. The establishment of the new Sienese military barracks on the site of the old town hall must have seemed a neat solution.

Plans of other medieval towns, such as Montecchio and Castelfiorentino, illustrate how the insertion of fortified buildings following military takeovers or the assumption of feudal rights confronted, and to some extent also dwarfed adjacent urban fabrics.[109]

At Castelfiorentino, the so-called 'casseretto', or little barracks, the property of the marquises of Monte Santa Maria, who also had feudal rights elsewhere including at Montecchio, is virtually enclosed by its own circuit of walls and crowned at the south-east corner by its own tower. Even now, the ruined castle complex and the remaining tower appear to confront the *Palazzo Pretorio* (the equivalent of the local magistrate's court), across a south-east diagonal.[110] By contrast, at Montecchio the complex of the so-called 'cassero overo roccha', dominates the *Palazzo di Giustizia*, or law court, inside the walls, whilst at the same time protecting the main gate by being positioned in close proximity

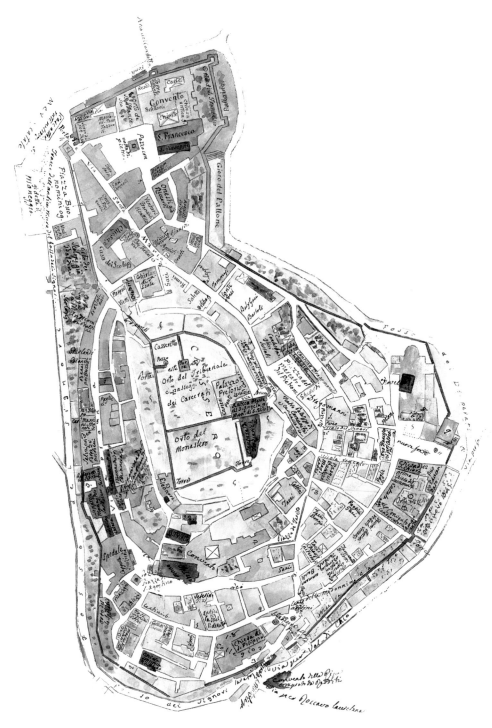

Figure 3.3   Nineteenth-century plan of Castelfiorentino. Biblioteca Comunale di Castiglione
Fiorentino, Rielaborazione (A. Vanni Desideri 2008) della pianta Fondo Ghizzi, ms. 512

to it. Indeed, the inordinately high tower of the barracks at Montecchio not only looms over other buildings in the town, but at the same time creates a separate and fortified aspect to anyone approaching the walls. Fourteenth-century Sant'Angelo in Colle may have presented a similar aspect, with private dwellings abutting an outer circuit of walls, but dominated at one point by the large fortified structure that contained the Sienese barracks.

Comparison with the fortified *cassero* at Montelaterone (which was constructed around 1262) offers insights about the possible architectural form of the barracks at Sant'Angelo in Colle.[111] It seems that the sides of the former were irregularly disposed, probably because of the lie of the land in the upper part of the town. The tower at Montelaterone was higher than the walls, and the entrance on the first floor level of the south-eastern side of the tower was reached by a *botola*, or circular vent, with stairs then leading down on the inside to the courtyard. A very similar shaped aperture to that surviving at the upper level of the tower at Montelaterone pierces the north-western side of the *Palazzaccio* tower at Sant'Angelo in Colle. This would seem to confirm not only that the *Palazzaccio* was indeed originally accessed from that side (the window serving as a lookout), but also that the original tower formed part of a larger complex. At Montelaterone, at least one building was inserted at the lower level between the tower and the surrounding walls on its south-eastern and south-western side. Armed men were also billeted on the ground floor, whilst the *castellano*, or captain of the castle was accommodated together with his family on the first floor. However, according to Franza and Nanni, the fortified complex at Montelaterone was abandoned at an early date, and thereafter there was progressive filching of the external masonry. There can be little doubt, however, that when first constructed the Sienese *cassero* at Montelaterone affected an imposing presence. Not only did its tall tower overlook the adjacent urban fabric, but its own fortified walls protected it from both internal and external attack. A very similar situation could have been created at Sant'Angelo in Colle.

In any event, it seems clear that the area around the new barracks at Sant'Angelo in Colle was politically charged. The 1320 *Tavola delle possessioni* shows that a number of Sienese citizens owned property in close proximity both to the existing town hall and to the new barracks. As a group, these individuals must have created a secure zone between the Sienese officials and military and the rest of the village, even in the absence of walls around the barracks themselves. In this respect, Neri di Guicciardo emerges as a key player. Most, if not all of his property, was in some way adjacent either to the barracks or to the new town hall. Neri di Guicciardo thus not only established his own power base in the shadow of, and protected by the Sienese military but was also well placed to monitor the local affairs of the village through proximity to the offices of the commune.

The new barracks at Sant'Angelo in Colle must also have sent a politically charged message to anyone approaching the frontier castle. Given the position of the present-day *Palazzaccio* and the evidence of other surviving medieval urban fabrics, it seems likely that the new *cassero* was positioned in line with or close to pre-existing fortifications, perhaps along and above the remains of an earlier wall. For those approaching from the north, south or west, therefore, the new barracks would not only have confirmed that the frontier castle was well fortified, but also have advertised that Sant'Angelo in Colle was under the protection of an incumbent Sienese military. Potential rebels, whether from outside, or within, would have received due warning.

The communal olive press

Confirmation that both the barracks and the new town hall were sited in the vicinity of the *Palazzaccio* also emerges from cluster diagrams associated with the early fourteenth-century communal olive press.

This indicates that much of the official communal business of making oil was carried out on the western side of the village. Until recently, there were at least four olive presses in Sant'Angelo in Colle, one opposite the old *Palazzaccio* (in the vicinity of plot 207), two belonging to the Franceschi and the Azienda il Poggione (plots 113 and 147/8), and a further one in private hands on the southern side of the village (plot 125). At least two of these presses date back to the seventeenth century. When Bartolomeo Gherardini drew up his description of Sant'Angelo in Colle in 1676 he referred to five presses, noting that they were in private hands, and that they belonged to the heirs of Alessandro della Ciaia; the heirs of Fausto Tolomei; the Lucattini and to the Forteguerri. The 1820 *Tavolo indicativo* confirms that there were still five olive presses in the village, and cites their locations as on plots 147, 148, 140, 133 and 125.[112] It seems likely that these were the same presses as those identified by Gherardini two centuries previously. According to the 1820 *Tavolo indicativo*, the first two olive presses belonged to the della Ciaia family; that on plot 140 to the Clementi; that on plot 133 to the Ciacci Santi di Antonio. That on plot 125 is described as being jointly owned by Margherita Chiaromanno, a member of the Lucattini family, and Donato della Ciaia.

Of the two olive presses currently belonging to the Franceschi, that in the vicinity of plots 147 and 148 would seem to be the most likely site for the communal olive press recorded in 1320, although both plots 133 and 140 were also well situated on the western side of the village. The press just across the road from the *Palazzaccio*, on plot 207, seems not to have formed part of the medieval urban fabric. Recorded in an early nineteenth-century survey of property belonging to the Montalcinese hospital of Santa Maria della Croce in Sant'Angelo in Colle, this building appears to be of relatively recent construction, although parts of its surrounding walls are clearly old.

Although on quite separate sites from the group of properties including the town hall and the barracks, plots 147, 148, 140 and 133 would, nevertheless, have been close enough to effect a kind of continuation of the communal business quarter. In many ways this would also have been a practical solution, given the existence of the outside road curling round from the

Cluster Diagram 3.2
Property in
the vicinity of
the communal
olive press at
Sant'Angelo in
Colle in 1320

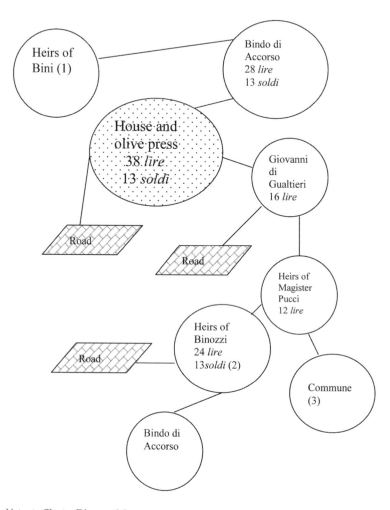

Notes to Cluster Diagram 3.2

1 No property inside the walls of Sant'Angelo in Colle in respect of a group of heirs of this name is
   recorded in the 1320 *Tavola delle possessioni*, but see Cluster Diagram 3.4, footnote 4.
2 In details furnished in respect of property held inside the walls by Bindo di Accorso, no reference is
   made to these heirs, but see Cluster Diagram 3.4, footnote 4.
3 In details furnished in respect of property owned by the Commune inside the walls, no reference is
   made to their heirs.

south, and finishing halfway up the western side of the village in the vicinity
of the *Piazzale*. These would have been ideal sites for the delivery of olives:
close enough to the village walls and the protection of lookout towers, but
without having to broach the main part of the village itself. The press on plot
125 would have been similarly protected, being close to a gate (that proposed
at the crossing between via del Paradiso and via del Cosatti), although it would
obviously have been further away from the commune district. However, as we
shall see from discussion in Chapter 6, plot 125 (consisting of a house and a
press) may well be the same as that acquired some time between 1320 and 1335

by a local inhabitant, Giovanni di Paganello. Plot 125 thus seems an unlikely candidate for the site of the communal olive press, at least at the later date.

In fact, the cluster diagram constructed in respect of the boundaries of the communal olive press as recorded in the 1320 *Tavola delle possessioni* supports the hypothesis that the press was located in the vicinity of plots 147 and 148. On this site, the press would have been bordered on one side by a small property belonging to Giovanni di Gualtiero on plot 150, 149 or 144. Giovanni's property would in turn have been bordered by an equally small structure belonging to the 'heirs of magister Pucci'. In its turn, that property would have been bordered by a much larger building belonging to the heirs of Binozzi, or Binoccio. Yet another somewhat larger structure belonging to Bindus or Bindo di Accorso would have bordered the press and property belonging to the heirs of Bini, but without abutting the property belonging to Giovanni di Gualtiero or the 'heirs of magister Pucci' or the heirs of Binozzi, or Binoccio. Details furnished in respect of the heirs of Bini in the 1320 *Tavola delle possessioni* refer only to a piece of worked land in the area known as the 'Fossato Castellani', or ditch of the castle.[113]

The communal oven

According to recent records, the village oven was in the nineteenth century located on plot 116 on the eastern side of the village, adjacent to the proposed course of the early fourteenth-century water conduit and in close proximity to the communal water cistern.[114] Also positioned on the eastern side of the village at that date was a granary on plot 103, close to the northern gate. The same source records another granary on the western side of the village on plot 136, in close proximity to the Ciacci Santi olive press on plot 133. It is extremely difficult to establish whether or not any of these structures assumed the same function in the early fourteenth-century village, although the cluster diagrams assembled from details recorded in the 1320 *Tavola delle possessioni* do reveal that the early fourteenth-century communal oven was bordered on two sides by a road, and on a further side by property belonging to Andrea di Boncambio, an individual not included in the list of local inhabitants, but who elsewhere is identified as a Sienese citizen.[115]

In his own tax return filed in Siena, Andrea di Boncambio described his property in the southern frontier castle as a building plot, bordered on one side by property belonging to the commune of Sant'Angelo in Colle, on two further sides by a road, and on the fourth side by the water conduit. This would seem to support the hypothesis that plot 116 marked the ancient site of the communal oven. This would have made sense, also, if the main granary storage was also situated on the eastern side of the village. However, the confines recorded in the 1320 *Tavola* could also relate well to plot 191 on the south-western side of the village.[116] There is further support for this being the site of the earlier communal property in the fact that an old oven still exists on that site, and was in public use until recently.

Cluster Diagram 3.3 Property in the vicinity of the communal oven at Sant'Angelo in Colle in 1320

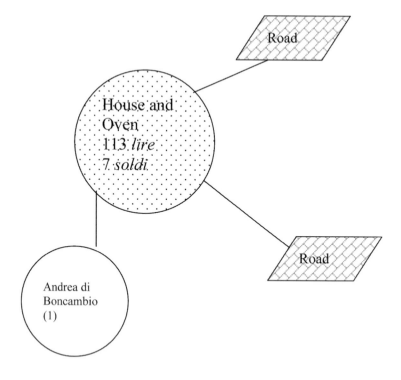

Note to Cluster Diagram 3.3

1 In 1318, Andrea di Buoncambio, a Sienese resident, was recorded as owning several pieces of land in the vicinity of Sant'Angelo in Colle (at least one of which included a *capanna*, or shack), as well as a *platea*, or building plot, and a piece of orchard land containing olives and almond trees inside the walls (see Archivio di Stato, Siena, *Estimo* 102, Terzo di Città, Incontri, 1318, fol. 92). The building plot, which is said to have been bordered on one side by the water conduit, is recorded as abutting property belonging to the commune. Andrea di Buoncambio may in fact have been connected with Sant'Angelo in Colle by birth, as the 1320 *Tavola delle possessioni* contains an entry for a Binduccius (Binduccio) Boncambi (di Buoncambio), who at that date is recorded as owning only one piece of worked land outside the walls in the area known as Speltale (*Estimo* 24, fol. 30r). Given the similar patronyms, it is possible that Binduccio and Andrea were siblings, and that the family property at Sant'Angelo in Colle had been divided between them. It is also possible that for the purpose of taxation Andrea shouldered the main burden of property held in and around the village.

The village hospital, the hospital and 'domus' of the Misericordia, and Santa Maria della Scala's first 'office' in Sant'Angelo in Colle

As with many of the other key buildings that no longer exist in the twenty-first century, establishing the original location of the *ospedale di Sant'Angelo*, or old village hospital of Sant'Angelo in Colle, is no easy matter.[117] The hospital is listed as an independent entity in the 1320 *Tavola delle possessioni*.[118] However, the *Tavola* itself presents a number of problems, if only because it contains a number of references to a second entity in close proximity to the village hospital which appears to have had a separate identity, and yet to have served likewise as a charitable institution. This second building is sometimes referred to as the *domus,* or office of the Misericordia, and sometimes as the hospital of the Misericordia itself. Further complications arise from the fact that a third building belonging to the 'hospital of Santa Maria' is cited in a different part of the village close to the water conduit. This building, which was described as the *domus* of the Sienese hospital of Santa Maria della Scala, appears to have been functioning during the first half of the fourteenth century as yet another kind of 'welfare centre'. As we shall see, this office not only served for the drawing up and witnessing of local wills, but, like the *ospedale di Sant'Angelo,* may also have housed and cared for the sick of the village.

The village hospital itself is said to have owned only one property inside the walls of the village, the building serving as the hospital. According to the entry in the *Tavola,* the hospital building was bordered on one side by property belonging to Nancio di Jordanello; on another by a road; and on a third side by property belonging to Riccuccio di Guido. In the entry for Nancio di Jordanello the adjoining property is, however, referred to not as the village hospital but as the hospital of the Misericordia.[119] In Riccuccio di Guido's entry the same property is described not as the hospital, but as the *domus,* or house of the Misericordia.[120] On the basis of this information one would have to conclude that there were two separate, but adjacent properties serving a similar charitable function. One of the two buildings was clearly that described in the 1320 *Tavola delle possessioni* as the *ospedale di Sant'Angelo;* the other building appears to have served both as the headquarters, or office, and the hospital of an institution known as the 'Misericordia'. There is, however, a problem, in that there is no separate entry for the hospital of the Misericordia in the 1320 *Tavola delle possessioni* for Sant'Angelo in Colle. One explanation might be that this was an outside institution, associated (like the hospital of Santa Maria della Scala) with Siena. However, it seems more likely that the Misericordia was a local institution, since no reference is made to Siena in any of the *Tavola* entries where it is cited. It could be that it was a charitable organisation associated in some way with the parish church of San Michele. One of the eight buildings owned by San Michele – a *casalinum,* or small house valued at a mere 1 *lire* – is in fact described as bordered on one side by a road, on another by property belonging to Landi di Pepe and on its final side by property belonging to the 'hospital of the Misericordia'.[121] But it seems more likely that it was associated with the village hospital itself, since details recorded in a number of entries in the *Tavola delle possessioni* indicate that the Misericordia *domus* was adjacent to the structure serving as the village hospital. There is no suggestion in the 1320 *Tavola* that the village hospital was divided into two sections, one serving as an office, and the other housing the wards and associated hospital spaces. The adjacent building may thus indeed have served as a hospital office. That being the case, references to the *domus* and hospital of the Misericordia may in fact have concerned the whole complex of the *ospedale di Sant'Angelo.* It is also possible that the term 'Misericordia' was deliberately adopted in order to reflect the charitable nature of the village hospital, as one aspect of its varying functions. In effect, such a term would have advertised the fact that this was not only the place were the local sick were housed and cared for, but that it was also an institution that offered hospitality and charity to passing travellers.

Attention focuses here on the possibility that the medieval village hospital of Sant'Angelo in Colle functioned on a number of different levels.[122] There seems little doubt that the hospital building was of a reasonable size, being valued at 50 *lire* (equivalent to two and a half small houses).[123] Such a structure would clearly have contained enough space for the accommodation of a considerable number of people. Even if functioning primarily as a hospice, devoted in the main to offering hospitality to passing trade, the village hospital clearly had the potential to offer some degree of medicinal and welfare care. It may even (and perhaps in imitation of institutions in Siena and elsewhere) have operated as a clearing house for *trovatelli* – the term allotted to orphans and abandoned babies.

From its overall recorded patrimony of 73 *lire* 19 *soldi* 6 *denari*, it seems clear, however, that the village hospital was not particularly well endowed in the early fourteenth century. Of the five pieces of land (including worked land, vines and woodland) recorded as in its possession in 1320, only one – a piece of agricultural land in the area known as 'lame parete' – was of any size, measuring seven and a half *staia*. In order to function efficiently the hospital must have had to rely on local endowments or revenue generated from travellers passing through the village. As we shall see in Chapter 7, the hospital did indeed attract considerable endowments during the second quarter of the fourteenth century. Prior to that date, the institution may have faced considerable difficulties, not least because it seems to have functioned independently from the other main centre of charity in the medieval village, the parish church, and to have been physically separated from it. Two centuries later, it seems that the village hospital no longer existed as an independent entity, since sixteenth-century records describe the hospital as being dependent on the church of San Michele.[124] At that date, also, it was known as the 'Ospedale di Sant'Antonio'.

No records survive to pinpoint the site of the sixteenth-century hospital, although it has been suggested that it was positioned on the site of the present day Franceschi building.[125] The hypothesis is raised in Chapter 7 that the hospital of Saint Anthony developed out of the earlier village hospital, and that it was only the *titulus* of the hospital that changed, the building itself remaining on the original site. While the renamed hospital could obviously have been moved to a different site, it would seem more likely that it continued to operate within the original complex, if only for practical reasons.

So, how, then, to go about reconstructing the original site of the earlier *ospedale di Sant'Angelo*? Details furnished in the 1320 *Tavola delle possessioni* indicate that a possible site for the original hospital complex was to the south of the parish church, and in close proximity to a transverse route running east–west through the original nucleus of the village. When set against the existing urban structure of Sant'Angelo in Colle, the cluster diagram derived from references in the 1320 *Tavola delle possessioni* to property in the vicinity of the hospital of the Misericordia, the *domus* of the Misericordia and the *ospedale di Sant'Angelo* fits well with a site on the western side of the village, and in relatively close proximity but not contiguous to the church of San Michele.

The first point to be made is that all of the buildings in Cluster Diagram 3.4 appear to have been bordered on one side by a road, indicating a linear arrangement. It also seems that the individual buildings were linked together, as if in one continuous stretch. An obvious location for such a series of interlocked properties would have been along the lower reaches of via Paradiso, and perhaps spilling over onto what is now a large open garden space (on plot 194) that forms part of the Franceschi property (on plot 166).

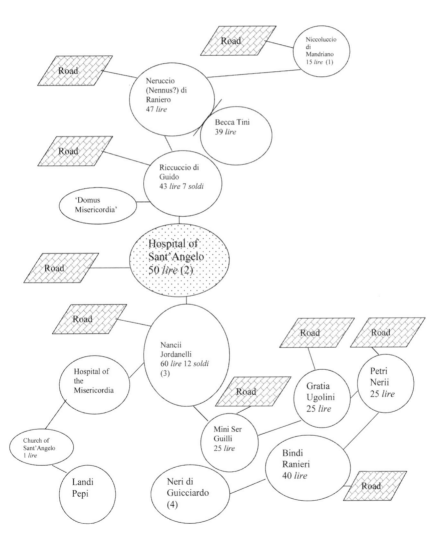

Cluster Diagram 3.4 Property in the vicinity of the village hospital of Sant'Angelo in Colle in 1320

Notes to Cluster Diagram 3.4

1   According to details furnished in respect of Niccoluccio di Mandriano, one of the houses owned by him inside the walls of Sant'Angelo in Colle was on one side bordered by the joint properties of Nerio di Raniero and Becca Tini (see Archivio di Stato (hereafter ASS), Siena, *Estimo* 104, Terzo di Città, Santo Quiricho in Chastelvecchio, 1318, fol. 264v, new pagination). In the entry for Becca Tini in the 1320 *Tavola delle possessioni* for Sant'Angelo in Colle, however, only Niccoluccio di Mandriano is recorded as the owner of adjoining property. There is no separate entry for Neruccio Ranieri in *Estimo* 24, although two entries refer respectively to Nerius (or Nennus) and Nucciarellus Ranieri. In the entry for Nennus (sic) there is a reference to a house valued at 47 *lire* that was bordered on one side by a road, and on another by property belonging to Niccoluccio di Mandriano.

2   According to details furnished in respect of the hospital of Sant'Angelo, the hospital building was bordered on one side by Nancio di Giordanello, on another by a road, and on a third side by Riccuccio di Guido.

3   According to details furnished in respect of Naccino di Giordanello, property owned by him inside the walls abutted on one side property belonging to the hospital of the Misericordia.

4   Details furnished in respect of property owned by Neri di Guicciardo inside the walls of Sant'Angelo in Colle in 1318 make no reference to Bindi Ranieri (see ASS, *Estimo* 106, Terzo di Città, San Pietro in Chastelvecchio, 1318, fols 50r–75v, new pagination).

Interestingly, the fairly substantial building on plot 193 was only divided into three separate sections at a comparatively recent date. In the Leopoldine *catasto* map of 1820 it is shown as one large L-shaped construction adjacent to the 'Casa Canonica', or priest's house. It is perhaps significant also that a connecting corridor is known to have run through two and possibly three sections of that building.[126] The same corridor continued into a vaulted area that at one time skirted the site of the cemetery of San Michele Arcangelo. It may originally have continued through to via Cosatti and out through the proposed gateway there. For any hospital complex – whether serving travellers (who may already have been suffering from a contagious disease, or already be seriously ill), or caring for the sick of the local community – availability of a number of interconnecting spaces that allowed for quarantine areas, as well as proximity to a cemetery would clearly have been an advantage, if not a practical necessity. There can be little doubt that it would also have been convenient to have an internal link between the different sections of the hospital complex. Such a link would have allowed hospital officials to transport sick patients into infirmaries or isolation spaces, and eventually out to a cemetery in the event of death.

There is some doubt about the date of construction of the cemetery on the eastern side of San Michele Arcangelo. According to Don Brandi, it only became operational from the end of the sixteenth century.[127] Prior to this, it seems that there was another, rather small cemetery outside the walls, in the area known as 'Campo di San Pietro', close to Podere la Casella.[128] As we have seen, reference was made to this site in an inventory of property belonging to the parish of Sant'Angelo in Colle that was drawn up in 1492.[129] When Francesco Bossi visited Sant'Angelo in Colle in 1576 in the guise of 'Visitatore Apostolico', he referred to a cemetery close to a church with the *titulus* of San Pietro, although it is not clear from his description whether he was referring to a church inside or outside the walls, and whether the cemetery in question was on the north or south side of the village.[130]

A number of bones were in fact discovered in the vicinity of the present church of San Pietro when the Villa Baldi was being constructed on the south-western side of the village during the twentieth century.[131] Other bones have also been discovered underneath the Piazza Castello on the north-western side of the parish church, indicating that this may have been the site of yet another cemetery. It is possible, therefore, that the cemetery on the eastern side of San Michele Arcangelo served not the church but the hospital complex, and that it was only appropriated for use by the parish church after the foundation of the hospital of Sant'Antonio in the sixteenth century.[132]

What, then of the other possible hospital complex, the originala *domus* of Santa Maria della Scala that was located close to the water conduit? The first point to be made is that the several references to the 'hospital of Santa Maria' in the 1320 *Tavola delle possessioni* quite clearly concerned the Sienese institution of Santa Maria della Scala and not the *ospedale di Sant'Angelo in Colle*.[133] It may be significant in this context that Palazzo Rosso (on plots 170, 171 and 172) and with one side facing onto via Cosatti has traditionally been referred to as 'the hospital building'.[134] This understanding may, however, have derived from the fact that the neighbouring structure on plot 175 (that until recently functioned as the village school house) was recorded in the nineteenth century as belonging to the hospital of Santa Maria della Croce in Montalcino.[135] It is possible, therefore, that the Santa Maria della Scala 'hospital building' was in fact that on plot 175. That said, and if the trajectory of the water conduit as reconstructed here is correct, the Santa Maria della Scala property could have been located on plot 170 or 175. In any event, and regardless of the exact position of the property belonging to Santa Maria della Scala, there seems little doubt that Santa Maria della Scala's original *domus* functioned as a kind of headquarters, but not yet as a full-blown *grancia* during the first half of the fourteenth century. It was in the *domus* that a will was drawn up on behalf of Ser Meo (?Pomeo) di Berto di Salimbeni in December 1340.[136] Since the will was apparently drawn up on site, it is possible that Ser Meo was ill, or even on his deathbed. That being the case, the *domus* could have served both as an office and as a kind of hospice. There are certainly no references during the first half of the fourteenth century to the hospital having a *grancia* in the village. By contrast, around the middle of the century we begin to find references to the Sienese hospital's *granciere*, or head of grange, at Sant'Angelo in Colle.[137]

According to the 1320 *Tavola delle possessioni*, Santa Maria della Scala owned only one building inside the walls of the village in 1320. In the absence of the hospital acquiring further property in the village after 1340, it seems likely that the original *domus* fronting the water conduit on the eastern side of the village was the building that was subsequently turned into the hospital's first grange at Sant'Angelo in Colle. The original *domus* building presumably underwent radical change shortly after 1340, since the new complex must have been used not only for official hospital business, but also for the storing of local produce and the housing of animals. In such a position, on the eastern side of the village, the grange would have been well placed to receive animals driven into the village through a north-eastern gate from the eastern pastures. Access from the western side of the village would have been less convenient. The decision to occupy the site of the Sienese barracks towards the end of the fourteenth century may thus have been influenced not only by the increased business of the hospital of Santa Maria della Scala in and around Sant'Angelo in Colle, but also by the fact that the construction (or reconstruction) of the northern gate offered more convenient access on the northern side of the village.

Clearly, fitting the parts of medieval Sant'Angelo in Colle together is a complex matter, even when dealing with easily recognisable public structures. Accommodating individual households within the urban fabric presents even greater challenges. It is, however, possible to construct a number of cluster diagrams for several different pockets of housing inside the walls of the village, while at the same time establishing links between them. These help to establish a broader picture of the overall distribution of households in the early fourteenth century village, as well as the relationship between public and private spaces at that period. They also throw light on individual patterns of ownership of property.

A number of preliminary findings are summarised here. First, micro-clusters based on living accommodation recorded in the 1320 *Tavola delle possessioni* for Sant'Angelo in Colle reveal that some local residents not only owned several properties, but that the houses themselves were positioned in different parts of the village. It thus seems unlikely that such properties housed extended family groups. More probably, they were used to accommodate a number of quite separate households on a letting and rental basis. One multiple property owner was the village treasurer, Bindo di Accorso. The cluster diagram based on Bindo di Accorso's holdings inside the walls indicates that most, if not all of his property was bordered by different neighbours.

In one instance, for example, a building belonging to Bindo is described as being bordered by property belonging to the church of San Michele Arcangelo; in another, that it was adjacent to property belonging to the commune. Yet another property, described as a *platea*, or building plot, was recorded as bordered on one side by a stretch of wall.

A second finding arising from a consideration of micro-clusters of living accommodation in the early fourteenth-century village is that there were a number of empty building plots and derelict buildings in and around Sant'Angelo in Colle in 1320. This prompts further questions about the available space inside the walls following the various demographic expansions of the thirteenth century. It also throws light on the demolition ordered by the Sienese government following insurrection in the village around 1280. Most significantly, the existence of ruined or derelict structures outside the existing circuit of walls indicates that rather than expanding its boundaries at the end of the thirteenth century, the village may in fact have been drawn in.

Bindo di Accorso was not the only one to declare ownership of a *platea* in the 1320 *Tavola delle possessioni*. Monna Gemma di Accorso, who was probably Bindo's sister, is also recorded as owning a building plot.[138] In the

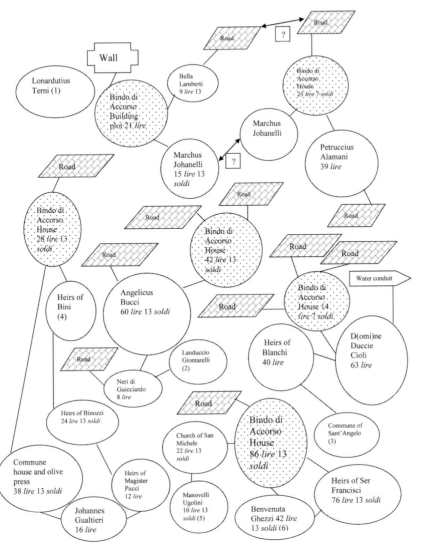

Cluster Diagram 3.5 Property inside the walls of Sant'Angelo in Colle belonging to Bindo di Accorso in 1320

Notes to Cluster Diagram 3.5

1 No reference is made to Bindo di Accorso as the owner of adjacent property in the context of either the house valued at 27 *lire* 13 *soldi*, or the building plot valued at 21 *lire* which was recorded under the name of Lonardutuis Terni in *Estimo* 24.

2 No house is declared in respect of this individual in *Estimo* 24.

3 There is no reference in the context of property held by the commune inside the walls of Sant'Angelo in Colle to the 'heredes Blanchi'.

4 No property inside the walls of Sant'Angelo in Colle is declared in respect of any heirs of this name in *Estimo* 24. It is possible, therefore, that Bindo di Accorso's property abutted that belonging to the heirs of Binozzi.

5 Manovelli (Manovello) Ugolini (di Ugolino), a Sienese resident, was recorded as owning a considerable amount of land in the vicinity of Sant'Angelo in Colle, as well as six houses inside the walls of the village itself (see Archivio di Stato, Siena, *Estimo* 108, Terzo di Città, Porta all'archo, 1320, fols 683r–687v, old pagination). One of the houses, which was valued at 10 *lire*, 13 *soldi*, is said to have been bordered on one side by property belonging to the parish church, and on another by further property belonging to the same entity. It seems clear, therefore, that the largest property owned by

Bindo di Accorso was positioned in the vicinity of property belonging to the church of San Michele, if not the church itself. Given Bindo's professional role as village treasurer, it is also possible that the largest of his properties served a dual purpose, both as a living house and as an office. Given Bindo's function, one might also expect such an office to be positioned close to, or inside one of the communal buildings. Given its recorded proximity to church property, it also seems likely that Bindo's property was located within the old nucleus of the village, perhaps contiguous to the old Palace of Justice, or even forming part of that structure.

6 In the entry recorded for the heirs of Ser Francisci (Francesco) in *Estimo* 24 this individual is referred to as 'd(omi)ne nute Ghezzi'.

case of Gemma di Accorso, the wording 'quandam plateam cum quo(?n) dam casalino in costa S(an)c(t)i Angeli' (what used to be a building plot with what used to be a small house on the Costa Sant'Angelo) also reveals that she owned the remains of a small house adjacent to her building plot. It is unclear whether that property was still standing in 1320, or whether it was a complete ruin. However, as we shall see, the significant point was that her property was located on the Costa Sant'Angelo, in other words outside the existing perimeter of walls. This, combined with the fact that many of the village's kitchen gardens were likewise located outside the walls in the same area, would seem to indicate that the outer limits on this side of the village had been drawn in some time before 1320. Entries elsewhere in the 1320 *Tavola delle possessioni* indicate that there were a number of other derelict buildings or ruins in and around the early fourteenth-century village. In several cases it also becomes clear that, like the plots belonging to Bindo di Accorso and his sister Gemma, they were close to the walls.

The fact that the shrinkage of the urban fabric appears to have occurred in the Costa Sant'Angelo area is significant, since entries in the *Tavola delle possessioni* and more recent records indicate that this area was on the south-west side of the village. Indeed, this area is still known as the Costa Sant'Angelo. At its southern limit the 'Costa Sant'Angelo' abuts the road that now leads down to Sant'Angelo Scalo. Nowadays, this is a comparatively large expanse of steeply inclined brush land, interspersed now and then by small vegetable plots and pens containing chickens. While such unprotected terrain may have been appropriate for orchards and possibly even vines or olive groves in the medieval period, it was hardly the right place for kitchen gardens, which were normally located inside the walls. This was sensible, both from the point of view of security, but also for the practical ease of gathering fresh produce. With an expanding population, such plots were, however, on occasion filled in. At the same time, pre-existing walls were pushed out to provide new secure spaces for the erection of further buildings and for the accommodation of local husbandry. As a result, what had served as a moat outside the walls was often appropriated to serve as a new internal road, or to make way for the building of new houses.

However, it was certainly not always the case that settlements outgrew their initial perimeters. In many instances small towns and hamlets were forced to draw in their defences, in order to establish a safer centre. In such circumstances erstwhile living accommodation, building plots and kitchen gardens could be left stranded on the wrong side of the walls. In this context it is significant that Mona Gemma's ruined property is described as being on the Costa Sant'Angelo. There seems little doubt, either, that prior to 1320 a number of other properties were scattered about on the Costa Sant'Angelo. Moreover, some of these were clearly still standing at the time of the 1320 *Tavola delle possessioni*. It is possible, therefore, that the whole of the Costa Sant'Angelo area was at one time enclosed by an outer circuit of walls.

References to empty building plots, ruined houses and kitchen gardens in the vicinity of Costa Sant'Angelo in the *Tavola delle Possessioni* certainly indicate that the village had shrunk within narrower boundaries by that date. But what were the factors that led to the mix of ruined buildings, empty building plots and buildings that were still standing in 1320? An hypothesis raised here is that it was the built-up area on the Costa Sant'Angelo that suffered the main brunt of Siena's wrath following the Ghibelline insurrection in the village at the end of the thirteenth century.

The Sienese may have chosen this symbolic point, close to the original gateway to the village and facing potential invaders from the south for the meting out of their punishment: destroying pre-existing fortifications and any houses in the vicinity that might have been regarded as safe havens for potential rebels. This might also explain why the Sienese chose to erect their new military headquarters on the western side of the village. During reconstruction work at Sant'Angelo in Colle following the demolition work in the village, the Sienese may also have chosen to establish a new stretch of wall on a different circuit, leaving the Costa Sant'Angelo outside the fortified centre, as an example to those who might think of questioning the authority of the Republic of Siena in the future. Such humiliation of subject communes and warnings to potential enemies were common.

A third observation that can be made on the basis of micro-clusters of living accommodation in the early fourteenth-century village concerns the surviving stretches of wall. While hypotheses concerning damage to buildings on the slopes surrounding Sant'Angelo in Colle inevitably remain hypothetical, a number of cluster diagrams deriving from entries in the 1320 *Tavola delle possessioni* add strength to the proposed reconstruction here of the old nucleus of the village around the church of San Michele on the summit of the hill, and the stretches of wall that enclosed it. In particular, they provide support for the hypotheses raised here concerning the trajectory of the first circuit of walls around that nucleus, and the location of an ancient gateway in via Cosatti. They also throw light on the course traced by the water conduit and the location of private properties abutting it. Details furnished in respect of a fairly small building belonging to the church of San Michele, referred to here as Property A, provide a particularly useful case study.

According to entries in the 1320 *Tavola delle possessioni*, Property A, which was valued at slightly less than 20 *lire*, was bordered on two sides by a road, and on another side by the 'corso d'acqua'.[139] It was also apparently contiguous with properties belonging to Bindo Accorso and to Manovello di Ugolino. The properties belonging to these two individuals were said, in turn

Cluster Diagram 3.6 Property in the vicinity of Property A, a small building belonging to the church of San Michele in 1320

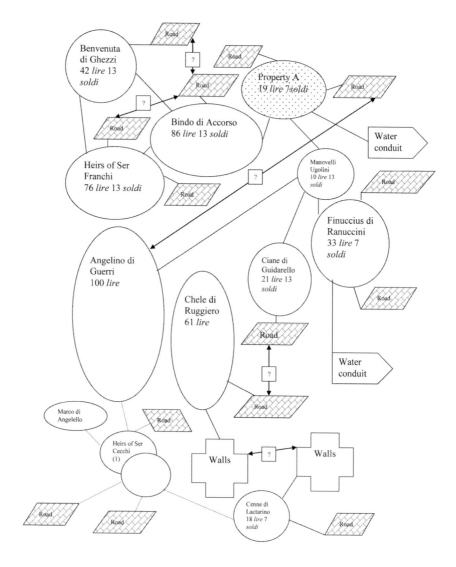

Note to Cluster Diagram 3.6

1 There is some confusion over this property, since according to the entry for the heirs of Cecco di Piero in the 1320 *Tavola delle possessioni* for Sant'Angelo in Colle, one of the several houses owned by them inside the walls of the village (described as half a 'casalinum' and valued at 1 *lire*) was bordered on two sides by a road, and on a third side by property belonging to Cenne di Lactarino – see *Estimo* 24, fol. 172r; and another, valued at 150 *lire*, was bordered on one side by a road, on a second side by property belonging to Marco di Angelello, and on a third side by property belonging to Angelino di Guerri – see *Estimo* 24, fol. 172v.

to abut a number of other houses close to the village walls. One of Manovello di Ugolino's neighbours, Finuccio di Ranuccini, appears to have looked out onto the same stretch of the water conduit mentioned in the context of Property A. A neighbour of Manovello di Ugolino, Angelino di Guerri, looked out onto what was probably one of the same roads mentioned as bordering Property A. Thus far, Property A would seem to fit in well with a site on the northern side of via Calcinaio. However, one of Angelino's neighbours, Ser Cecchi, owned property abutting that of Cenne di Lactarini that appears to have abutted another stretch of walls. Another of Manovello di Ugolino's neighbours, Ciane di Guidarello, in his turn, abutted property belonging to Chele di Ruggerio, which, like the building belonging to Cenne di Lactarino, was likewise bordered by a length of wall. Assembled together, such details indicate that Property A was comparatively close to at least one section of the village's walls. The problem lies in identifying the particular stretch of walls in question. Given the proposed reconstruction of the original nucleus of the village outlined in the previous chapter, and the fact that Property A belonged to the church of San Michele, it is possible that at least some of the references to walls in Cluster Diagram 3.6 related to a surviving stretch along via Cosatti. If this were the case, Property A as well as being close to a stretch of the water conduit running along via Cosatti, must presumably also have overlooked private dwellings on the eastern and south-eastern side of this flow of water. These, as well as fronting up to the old nucleus of the village, must on their other sides have abutted more recent stretches of wall, perhaps even that circuit that is still partially visible along the present-day via Calcinaio.

Thus reconstructed, it seems that different parts of the early fourteenth-century village had clearly definable characteristics. The northern and north-western sections of the village were in large part reserved for the Sienese military, for commune offices, and for properties in the hands of private Sienese citizens. On its western fringes, the village appears to have been dominated by a number of olive presses and a large open square which could have served multiple functions, including the threshing of corn, space for the delivery of produce from the countryside and the assembling of livestock. The south-western and inner western side of the village was probably dominated by the hospital complex. The eastern side of the village appears by contrast to have been where a variety of water-dependent trades were practised. A large square here (in front of Palazzo Rosso) may also have served as an assembly space for sheep prior to shearing, and for assembling animal hides before their transfer to nearby washing troughs. It was possibly in this area, also, that many of the workers involved in the leather and cloth trades were accommodated. Houses on the western side of the village may, by contrast, have been reserved for land workers.[140]

The following chapters consider the varying lifestyles and fortunes of a number of Sant'Angelo in Colle's inhabitants during the early fourteenth century, from those holding little, if any property, to those who might best be described as a middle-class elite. As we shall see, there were a number of clearly-defined societal groups in the medieval village. As we shall also see, many of these groups were interlinked. It becomes clear that while the inhabitants of Sant'Angelo in Colle may have been forced at an early stage to bend their knees to officials of the Republic of Siena, they also continued to draw strength from their own close-knit society and the several extended family clans there.

Notes

1 See Giuliano Pinto and Paolo Pirillo (eds), *Il Contratto di Mezzadria nella Toscana Medievale, I, Contado di Siena, sec. 13 –1348* (Florence, 1987), p. 207, no. 157.

2 Archivio di Stato di Siena (hereafter ASS), *Diplomatico di Montalcino*, Busta 34 bis, no. 166.

3 ASS, *Diplomatico in caselle, casella* 1141, 20 July 1396, *Archivio dello Spedale*.

4 Andrea Giorgi, 'Il carteggio del Concistoro della Repubblica di Siena (spogli di lettere 1251–1374)' *BSSP*, 97 (1990), pp. 193–573 (under that date). Vincenzo Passeri (*Documenti per la Storia delle Località della Provincia di Siena* (Siena, 2002), p. 308) maintains that Bartolomeo di Longaruccio's house (sic) was indeed situated at Montalcino.

5 Neri di Donato, 'Cronaca senese' in *Chroniche senesi, Rerum Italicarum Scriptores,* (eds), Alessandro Lisini and Fabio Iacometti (Bologna, Zanichelli, 1931–39).

6 Archivio Vescovile di Montalcino (hereafter AVM), *Sant'Angelo in Colle*, Prepositura, 131, fol. 2v.

7 In this context it is worth bearing in mind Herlihy and Klapisch-Zuber's findings in respect of Prato (*I toscani e le loro famiglie*, (Bologna, c.1988, p. 269), where they estimate that between 1371 and 1372 children under the age of 8 constituted 38% of the total population.

8 See Georges Duby and Jacques Le Goff (eds), *Famiglia e parentela nell'Italia medievale* (Bologna, 1981) and David Herlihy and Christiane Klapisch-Zuber, *Les Toscans et leurs familles* (Paris, 1978). English translation, *Tuscans and their families: A study of the Florentine catasto of 1427* (New Haven, Conn., 1985) and Italian translation, *I toscani e le loro famiglie* (Bologna, c.1988). See also David Herlihy, *Medieval Households* (The President and Fellows of Harvard College, 1985), Italian translation, *La famiglia nel Medioevo* (Rome and Bari, 1989), and Christiane Klapisch-Zuber, 'Fonti e metodi per la storia demografica del tardo Medioevo: nascità e morte nelle famiglie fiorentine', in Daniela Romagnoli (ed.), *Storia e storie della città* (Parma, 1988–9), pp. 147–55.

9 Barbara A. Hanawalt, *The Late Medieval Peasant Family* (New York and London, 1985) and Richard Ring, 'Early Medieval Peasant Households in Central Italy', in *Journal of Family History*, 2 (1979), pp. 2–25. See also, Paolo Galetti, 'La donna contadina: figure femminili nei contratti agrari italiani dell'alto medioevo', in Maria Giuseppina Muzzarelli, Paola Galetti and Bruno Andreolli (eds), *Donne e lavoro nell'Italia medievale* (Turin, 1991), pp. 41–54.

10 See, for example, Giuliano Catoni and Gabriella Piccinni, 'Famiglie e redditi nella Lira Senese del 1453' in Rinaldo Comba, Gabriella Piccinni and Giuliano Pinto (eds), *Strutture familiari, epidemie, migrazioni nell'Italia medievale* (Naples,

1984), pp. 291–304; Maria Ginatempo, 'Per la storia demografica del territorio senese nel Quattrocento: problemi di fonti e di metodo', *Archivio Storico Italiano*, 142 (1984), pp. 521–32 and 541–47, and eadem, *Crisi di un territorio. Il popolamento della Toscana senese alla fine del Medioevo* (Florence, 1988).

11   Rinaldo Comba and Irma Naso (eds), *Demografia e società nell'Italia medievale: secoli 9–14* (Cuneo, 1994).

12   Fabio Giovannino, *Natalità, mortalità e demografia dell'italia Medievale sulla base dei dati archeologici* (Oxford, 2001) and Italo Moretti, 'La demografia medievale attraverso le testimonianze architettoniche e urbanistiche', in Carlo A. Corsini (ed.), *Vita, morte e miracoli di gente comune: appunti per una storia della popolazione della toscana fra 14 e 20 secolo* (Florence, 1988), pp. 37–50.

13   See, for example, Giovanni Cherubini (ed.), *Signori, contadini, borghesi. Ricerche sulla società italiana del basso-medioevo* (Florence, 1974); 'Gli archivi per la storia locale dell'età medievale', in Giovanni Parlavecchia (ed.), *Gli strumenti della ricerca storica locale, Archivi e biblioteche*, Atti del Convegno di studio, Castelfiorentino-FI, 14 giugno 1984 (Pisa, 1988), pp. 59–64; and Alfio Cortonesi, Gianfranco Pasquali, and Gabriella Piccinni (eds), *Uomini e campagne nell'Italia medievale* (Rome and Bari, 2002).

14   Entitled 'La Famiglia Contadina nell'Europa Medievale e Moderna', this conference was organised by Alfio Cortonesi, Danilo Gasparini, Michael Matheus, Massimo Montanari, Gabriella Piccinni and Giuliano Pinto under the auspices of the Associazione centro di studi per la storia delle campagne e del lavoro contadino.

15   Tiziana Lazzari, 'L'idea di famiglia' and Giuliano Pinto, 'La famiglia Contadina nella storiografia'.

16   Jean Pierre Devroey, 'La famiglia contadina nei polittici altomedievali'.

17   Gabriella Piccinni, 'Il lavoro delle donne'.

18   Paola Galetti, 'Gli spazi della casa contadina'.

19   Herlihy and Klapisch-Zuber, *I toscani e le loro famiglie*, 1988, p. 69.

20   Ibid., p. 269.

21   Ibid., p. 272.

22   David Herlihy, *La Famiglia nel Medioevo*, Italian translation, *La famiglia nel Medioevo* (1989), p. 134.

23   See Gabriella Piccinni, 'La campagna e le città (secoli 12–15)', in Alfio Cortonesi, Gianfranco Pasquali, and Gabriella Piccinni (eds), *Uomini e campagne nell'Italia medievale* (Rome and Bari, 2002), pp. 123–189 (163).

24   For a notable exception, see Duccio Balestracci, *La zappa e la retorica. Memorie familiari di un contadino toscano del Quattrocento* (Florence, Salimbeni, 1984).

25   While Roberto Farinelli and Andrea Giorgi's reconstruction of medieval Castelnuovo dell'Abate is meticulous in many respects (see their 'La "Tavola delle Possessioni" come fonte per lo Studio del territorio: l'esempio di Castelnuovo dell'Abate', in Alfio Cortonesi (ed.), *La Valdorcia nel Medioevo e nei primi secoli dell'Età moderna*, Atti del convegno internazionale di studi storici, Pienza 15–18 settembre, 1988 (Rome, 1990), pp. 213–56), they offer few words of caution. Indeed, their reconstruction would seem to be an open and shut case. See, also these authors' 'Radicondoli: società e territorio in una "curia"

attraverso la "Tavola delle Possessioni" ', in Costanza Cucini (ed.), *Radicondoli: storia e archeologia di un comune senese* (Rome, 1990), pp. 353–91 and 461–64.

26 ASS, *Estimo di Siena*, 80.

27 See Don Antonio Brandi, *Notizie relative a Argiano – Poggio alle Mura – S. Angelo in Colle Tratte dalla Visita fatta nell'anno 1676 dall'Ill.mo Sig.re Bartolomeo Gherardini*, undated typescript transcription, p. 7. See also ASS, *Manoscritti D 84, Visita fatta nell'Anno 1676 alle Città, Terre, Castella dello stato della città di Siena dall'Ill. Monsignore B. Gherardini, Auditore Generale in Siena per la A.S. di Cosimo III de' Medici Granduca VI di Toscana* [eighteenth-century copy] (hereafter Gherardini), pp. 72–80.

28 See ASS, 1820, *Catasto, Tavola indicativa*, which identifies the local parish as the owner of the large building on plot no. 197; the della Ciaia as the proprietors of buildings on plot nos 166, 170, 171 and 193, and the Cosatti as the owners of the buildings on plots 175, 180, 181. Presumably, the Tolomei palace on plot 161 is also one of the buildings singled out by Gherardini, as is also no doubt the very large building on plot 165, now owned by the Ricci family. A member of the Lucattini family, Margherita Chiaramanni, is recorded in the 1820 *Tavola indicativa* as owning plot 168, which forms part of another large property now owned totally by the Ricci. This building seems originally to have occupied plots 168, 167 and 179. The same member of the Lucattini family also appears to have been the joint owner with a member of the della Ciaia family of another fairly substantial structure, the building on plot 125, which also contained an olive press. The Clementi, predecessors of the Lisini, are also recorded as the owners of the substantial property on plot 101. No reference is made in the 1820 *Tavola indicativa* to property owned by the heirs of Fausto Forteguerri, although reference is made to possessions handed down by them.

29 Biblioteca Comunale degli Intronati, Siena, *Disegni*, Armadio 1, C.II.3, Ettore Romagnoli, 'Vedute dei Contorni di Siena', no. 64 ('Palazzo dei Signori della Ciaia nel castello di S. Angelo in Colle presso M. Alcino').

30 Gherardini, pp. 2–3.

31 ASS, *Manoscritti, D 67, Memorie storiche politiche, civili, e naturali delle città, terre, e castella, che sono, e sono state suddite della città di Siena. Raccolte dal Cavaliere Gio(vanni) Antonio Pecci, Patrizio Sanese* (hereafter *Pecci*), fol. 86.

32 ASS, *Catasto*, Mappa di Montalcino, Sezione M bis, di 'Sant. Angelo in Colle', no. 32a.

33 Ibid.

34 Giovanni Cherubini ('Proprietari, contadini e campagne senesi all' inizio del Trecento', in idem (ed.), *Signori, contadini, borghesi, Ricerche sulla società Italiana del basso-medioevo* (Florence, 1974, p. 236) maintains that the process of gathering individual details in a series of preliminary *tavolette* and *tavole*, before assembling all the information in the final *Lira* must inevitably have resulted in inaccurate transcriptions.

35 Such a situation could have developed, for example, in respect of a house inside the walls of Sant'Angelo in Colle which is recorded as belonging to the Sienese citizen Neroccio di Martino di Civitella in 1348. According to his will which was drawn up in December of that year, Neroccio intended that this property should be left to the Sienese hospital of Santa Maria della Scala, even though it was at that time rented out at an annual rent of 30 *lire* to Domenico di Donato. See ASS, *Diplomatico in caselle, casella* 900, 16 December, *Archivio dello Spedale*. Neroccio

made no reference to Domenico di Donato's origins, although one might expect him to have been a resident of Sant'Angelo in Colle. In fact, the surviving documentary evidence suggests that he was not, since he is not listed in the 1320 *Tavola delle possessioni* for Sant'Angelo in Colle. Nor is there apparently any reference to his father Donato in that record. Apart from the annual rent, it seems that there was an obligation on the part of Santa Maria della Scala to celebrate in perpetuity an annual mass in Neroccio's name in the church of Sant'Agostino (presumably in Siena). If Santa Maria della Scala was unwilling to accept the legacy under the conditions laid down in his will, Neroccio stipulated that the property in Sant'Angelo in Colle should be left (with its existing encumbrances) to the Casa della Misericordia in Siena. The potential misunderstandings in terms of the drawing up of details for the purpose of taxation of such a property are well illustrated in this one will alone.

36 William M. Bowsky, *Le finanze del Comune di Siena 1287–1355* (Florence, 1976), p. 127.

37 Ibid., pp. 108–10, where Bowsky notes that Sienese citizens holding property in the *Masse* or in the *contado* on occasion declared such assets to the commune in which they were located, where they, themselves, were immune from local taxes. Further evasion of tax was effected through fraudulent contracts with third parties, effectively hiding such possessions from the eyes of the central government in Siena. Bowsky also notes the practice whereby property was apparently handed over to a religious or charitable institution, or where an individual became a member of a confraternity that was exempt from tax, whilst in reality continuing to live a lay life, enjoying the use of his or her property, and avoiding having to pay tax.

38 ASS, *Estimo* 24, fol. 268v.

39 Ibid., fol. 451v.

40 Ibid., fol. 167r.

41 Ibid., fol. 296r.

42 Ibid.

43 Ibid., fol. 286v.

44 Ibid., fol. 288r.

45 Ibid., fol. 174r.

46 Ibid., fol. 71r.

47 Ibid., fol. 451r.

48 See Enrico Fiumi, 'L'Imposta diretta nei comuni medioevali della Toscana', in *Studi in onore di Armando Sapori* (2 vols Milan, 1957), pp. 329–53 (338–39).

49 This was particularly the case in Florence, one of the least advantageous places to be born a woman in the medieval period insofar as personal liberties and independence were concerned. See my consideration of Ginevra dei Bardi's foundation of the hospital of Sant'Onofrio in Florence in *Art and Piety in the Female Religious Communities of Renaissance Italy: Iconography, Space and the Religious Woman's Perspective* (New York, 2003), pp. 165–68. In this context, see also Samuel K. Cohn, Jr., *The cult of remembrance and the Black Death. Six Renaissance cities in central Italy* (Baltimore and London, 1992). For a recent bibliographical survey of the social and legal position of women in medieval

and early RenaissanceTuscany, see Gianna Lumia-Ostinelli, 'Le eredità delle donne: i diritti successori femminili a Siena tra Medioevo ed età moderna', in Silvia Colucci (ed.), *Morire nel Medioevo. Il caso di Siena*, Atti del Convegno di Studi, 14–15 novembre 2002, Università degli Studi di Siena, Dipartimento di Archeologia e Storia delle Arti, Dipartimento di Storia, con il patrocinio della Accademia dei Fisiocritici Onlus, *BSSP*, 110 (2003), pp. 318–40. See also Gabriella Piccinni, 'Per uno studio del lavoro delle donne nelle campagne: considerazioni dell'Italia medievale', in Simonetta Cavaciocchi (ed.), *La Donna nell'Economia secc. 13–18*, Atti della 'Ventunesima Settimana di Studi', Prato, 10–15 aprile 1989, (Prato, 1990), pp. 71–81 (73, footnote 7).

50 See Christiane Klapisch-Zuber, *La famiglia e le donne nel Rinascimento a Firenze*, (Rome, 1995). In this context, see ASS, *Curia del Placito*, 1296, 1, fols 4v–13v, which lays out the specific restrictions concerning women's dowries and rights of succession.

51 ASS, *Estimo* 24: fols 309r and fols 330r–330v.

52 Ibid., fol. 295r.

53 In this respect, see Maria Ginatempo, 'Il popolamento della Valdorcia alla fine del medioevo (15–16 secolo)', in Alfio Cortonesi (ed.), *La Val d'Orcia nel Medioevo e nei primi secoli dell'età moderna*, Atti del Convegno internazionale di studi storici, Pienza, 15–18 settembre 1988, (Rome, 1990), pp. 113–53 (127–28, 133, footnote 60 and p. 139). See also Gabriella Piccinni, 'I mezzadri davanti al fisco. Primi appunti sulla normativa senese del '400', *Cultura e società nell'Italia medievale. Studi per Paolo Brezzi* (Rome, 1988), pp. 665–82; and *Seminare, fruttare, raccogliere: mezzadri e salariati sulle terre di Monte Oliveto Maggiore, 1374–1430* (Milan, 1982). See also Giuliano Pinto, 'Dimore contadine e infrastrutture agricole', in Giuliano Pinto (ed.), *La Toscana nel tardo medioevo. Ambiente, economia rurale, società* (Florence, 1982), pp. 225–246. See Chapter 4 for a detailed discussion of the system of *mezzadria* in respect of the medieval village of Sant'Angelo in Colle.

54 For the opportunities in terms of the evasion of tax where property was concerned, see footnote 37 above.

55 ASS, *Estimo di Siena*, 129, Terzo di Camollia, San Cristofano allato la chiesa, 1318, fol. CCCXVII.

56 Ibid., 143, Terzo di Camollia, La Magione del tempio, 1318, fol. 228v (old pagination).

57 Ibid., 109, Terzo di Città, Santa Agata, 1318, fol. 25v (new pagination).

58 Ibid., 108, Terzo di Città, Porta all'archo, 1320, fol. 687v (old pagination).

59 Ibid., 106, Terzo di Città, San Pietro in Chastelveccio, 1318, fol. 61r (new pagination).

60 In this respect see Duccio Balestracci and Gabriella Piccinni, *Siena nel Trecento: assetto urbano e strutture edilizie*, (Florence, 1977), p. 131, where the authors draw attention to an extreme case of multi-tenancing involving a member of the Tolomei family in the ownership of 1/192 of Palazzo Tolomei in Siena. While this extraordinary fraction no doubt evolved on paper as a result of dividing up property in respect of the acknowledged inheritance, rather than reflecting any real physical divisions, it nevertheless helps to focus our attention on what were occasionally extremely complex living arrangements.

61 Don Antonio Brandi, *Parrocchia di S. Michele Arcangelo in S. Angelo in Colle* (typescript, Sant'Angelo in Colle, 1972) (hereafter Brandi, 1972), p. 12. See also Don Antonio Brandi, *Montalcino, terra di chiese, conventi e cappelle* (typescript, Sant'Angelo in Colle, 1994), p. 33.

62 Ugo Ricci, *S. Angelo in Colle nella storia e nella vita del contesto Senese e Toscano* (typescript, Sant'Angelo in Colle, 1989), p. 32.

63 Brandi, 1972, p. 33. The inscription reads 'MCCCXXI Tempore D.M. Prepositi De Domo Contis Guiduccio Operaio'.

64 The location of this church was first discussed in my 'La Festa della Madonna della Misericordia', *Gazzettino e Storie del Brunello e di Montalcino*, Anno 3, 38 (2010), pp. 16–17; 39, pp. 16–17 and 40: pp. 18–19. For an earlier consideration of the location of churches with the *titulus* of San Pietro in the territory of Sant'Angelo in Colle and confusions arising from the change of *tituli* of some of these churches, see Ugo Ricci, *S. Angelo in Colle nella storia e nella vita del contesto Senese e Toscano* (typescript, Sant'Angelo in Colle, 1985) (hereafter Ricci, 1985), pp. 28, 36, 40, 51, 68–71 and 84. See also Don Antonio Brandi, *Parrocchia di San Michele in S. Angelo in Colle* (typescript, Sant'Angelo in Colle, 2004) (hereafter Brandi, 2004), pp. 51–52.

65 Ricci, 1985, p. 8.

66 ASS, *Estimo* 24, fols 132r–137r.

67 Brandi, 1972, p. 28. This may explain why a late fifteenth-century inventory drawn up for the church of San Michele contains details of furnishings 'for the altar of San Pietro', see Brandi, 1972, p. 21. For the inventory itself, see AVM, *Sant'Angelo in Colle*, Prepositura, 131, fol. 2v.

68 Brandi, 1972, p. 13, where 1464 rather than 1462 is noted as the date of handover.

69 Brandi, 2004, p. 16.

70 ASS, *Pecci*, fols 86–87.

71 Ibid., fol. 17.

72 Ricci, 1985, p. 71.

73 See AVM, *Sant'Angelo in Colle*, Prepositura, 131, sheet dated 26 November 1816, where there is a reference to the 'giardino luogo annesso denominato le caselle e S. Piero e colle apezzamenti di terreno … un campo' (adjacent garden in the area known as the 'caselle and San Pietro'). On the verso of the same sheet, there is a further reference to the 'giardino. luogo della Casella S. Piero' (garden in the place of the 'Casella San Pietro').

74 ASS, *Estimo* 24, fols 132r, 169r and 183r.

75 AVM, *Sant'Angelo in Colle*, Prepositura, 131.

76 Ricci, 1985, p. 68.

77 Ibid.

78 AVM, *Sant'Angelo in Colle*, Prepositura, 131, sheet dated 26 November1816, see footnote 73, above. In this context, it may be relevant that the 1492 inventory drawn up in respect of property belonging to the parish church of San Michele referred not only to a small house outside Sant'Angelo in Colle that was 'next to the church of San Pietro', but also to 'Il poderuccio di San Pietro' (Brandi, 1972,

p. 21). The farm now known as 'Podere la Casella' could thus have developed from the latter structure.

79   AVM, *Sant'Angelo in Colle, Prepositura*, 131, (first register – inventory dated 1672, fol. 3r).

80   Ibid., fol. 88.

81   ASS, *Estimo* 24, fol. 134r.

82   For the exemption from tax of religious institutions, see Bowsky, *Le finanze*, pp. 108–9. Religious institutions were even exempt from tax levied on livestock owned by them. See, for example, the distinctions laid down by the *Concistoro* in March 1364 in respect of the tax of two florins per each pair of oxen in the district of San Quirico a Osenna that was to be levied from individual owners, with the exception of 'luoghi pii', in order to build the walls and fortress there. (ASS, *Manoscritti*, C10, under that date and Deliberazioni del Concistoro e del Consiglio del Popolo, 35, fol. 27v [*Archivio del Riformagione*].

83   Ricci, 1985, p. 88.

84   *Pecci*, fols 86–7. Ricci for his part (Ricci, 1985, pp. 50–51) maintains that it was the church of San Pietro outside the walls that was placed under the authority of the Cathedral of Montalcino in the mid-fifteenth century. As we shall see it was this church also that was described by Bossi in 1576 as being in a poor condition.

85   Brandi, 1972, p. 37.

86   See Don Antonio Brandi, 2004, pp. 63–66.

87   In this context see in Table 3.6, the entries for the heirs of Bino (or Bindo) di Rannuccio, the heirs of Brunaccio, the heirs of Naldo di Jacopo, the heirs of Nerio, or Nero di Ventura, or Venture, and the heirs of Cremonese.

88   Brandi, 2004, p. 16.

89   See Gherardini, p. 75, where Gherardini notes that inside the walls, there was only one church, the 'pievana', or parish church.

90   I would like to thank the Lisini family for furnishing me with plans of Palazzo Lisini, and for allowing access to that site.

91   I am grateful to the late Signora Maria Gentile Lisini Baldi for this information. According to Don Brandi (Brandi, 2004, p. 63), however, the Tolomei building on Via del Calcinaio was only erected in 1580.

92   I owe this information to Giuliano Guerrini. See ASS, *Manoscritti* D84, fol. 72, for Gherardini's opinion that the 'Palazzo di Giustizia' was originally located on plot 166.

93   Pecci himself indicated the site of the 'tower' as the original location of what he identified as the Palace of Justice, no doubt as a result adding strength to subsequent claims concerning the original position of the town hall.

94   ASS, *Estimo* 24, fols 58r–63v.

95   Ibid., fol. 47r.

96   Ibid., fol. 400r.

97   Ibid., fol. 73r.

98   Ibid., fol. 186v.

99   ASS, *Manoscritti*, CI, fol. 400v, under that date.

100   In this respect, see Marvin Trachtenberg, *Dominion of the eye: urbanism, art and power in early modern Florence* (Cambridge, 1997).

101   ASS, *Consiglio Generale* 4, fol 45v.

102   For the sienese *cassero* at Montelaterone, see Vincenzo Bacciarelli, 'Castellum de Montelatroni cum omnibus aecclesiis et capellis, muris et fossis atque munitionibus' and Michele Nucciotti, 'Insediarsi "all'estero". L'edificazione del cassero senese di Montelaterone (1262–1266) e la prima politica amiatina del comune di Siena', in Vincenzo Bacciarelli and Paolo Pacchiani (eds), *Montelaterone: Storie, religione ed arte di un'antica cella del Montamiata* (Rome, 2006), pp. 25–102 and 179–90. See also, Nello Nanni, Il Cassero Senese di Montelaterone: Una Tappa contrastata nell'espansione Cittadina', *Amiata Storia e Territorio*, anno 13 marzo, 38/39 (2002), pp. 9–15; and Michele Nucciotti, 'Il cassero senese di Montelaterone: L'Indagine Archeologica', *Amiata Storia e Territorio*, anno 13, marzo, 38/39 (2002), pp. 19–23. For other military constructions erected by the Sienese during the thirteenth and fourteenth centuries, see Arnaldo Verdiani-Bandi, *I castelli della Val d'Orcia e la Repubblica di Siena* (Siena, 1996). See also Giuseppe Morganti, 'Il Castello della Ripa d'Orcia', in Carlo Avetta (ed.), *'Tintinnano'. La Rocca e il territorio di Castiglione d'Orcia*, (San Quirico d'Orcia, 1988), pp. 161–71. Ricci (Ricci, 1985, pp. 119–20) suggests that the *Palazzaccio* at Sant'Angelo in Colle may have been similar in architectural form to the 'Rocca', or fortress of Tentennano (sic). The urban fabric of Ripa d'Orcia is also not dissimilar in shape and form from that at Sant'Angelo in Colle. In this context it is significant that one side of the castle courtyard at Ripa d'Orcia coincides with the outer perimeter wall.

103   ASS, *Pecci*, fol. 86.

104   For a consideration of the defensive system of walls at Montelaterone, including a reproduction of the plan of the town according to the Leopoldine *Catasto* of 1823 and a reproduction of the nineteenth-century drawing of the town made by Romagnuoli, see Nanni, 'Il Cassero senese di Montelaterone', pp. 12 and 13.

105   Roberto Farinelli and Andrea Giorgi, *Camigliano, Argiano e Poggio alle Mura (secoli 12–14)*, presented by Alfio Cortonesi (Siena, 1995), p. 14, footnote 20.

106   Nucciotti, 'Insediarsi', p. 182, footnote 7. See also Nanni, 'Il Cassero senese di Montelaterone', p. 12, and p. 11, footnote 30 for a reference in 1293 to the 'cassero vecchio, cioe della curia dell'abate'.

107   Ricci, 1985, pp. 12–13.

108   Don Antonio Brandi, *Parrocchia di S. Michele Arcangelo in S. Angelo in Colle* (typescript, Sant'Angelo in Colle, 1991), p. 8. Brandi notes that the present square was constructed during the 1930s.

109   See Andrea Sandrini, Pianta e veduta del castello di Montecchio, 1600 (Archivio di Stato, *Possessioni Piante* 434) in Gabriella Orefice, Castiglion Fiorentino (Arezzo), Atlante storico delle città Italiane. Toscana 4 (Rome, Bonsignori Editore, 1996), p. 34.

110   For the history of Castelfiorentino, see *Storia di Castelfiorentino* (Castelfiorentino, 1994).

111 In this respect, see Gabriele Franza and Nello Nanni, 'Il cassero senese di Montelaterone: Le caratteristiche architettoniche e i Cuteri del Restauro', *Amiata Storia e Territorio*, anno 13, 38/39 marzo (2002), pp. 16–18.

112 ASS, *Catasto*, Montalcino, Mappe del Catasto sezione M bis, *Tavola indicativa dei Proprietari e delle Proprietà respettive*, 2 Montalcino da F' a D' (hereafter *Tavola indicativa*).

113 Ibid., *Estimo* 24, fol. 184r.

114 Ibid., *Catasto, Tavola indicativa* .

115 Ibid., *Estimo* 24, fol. 59v. See Table 3.6, footnote 1. As Table 3.6 shows, Andrea di Boncambio also owned an orchard with olives and almond trees at Sant'Angelo in Colle which was bordered on one side by property belonging to Ser Guccio di ser Francesco, on another by property belonging to Manovello di Ugolino, on another by a road, and on a final side by property belonging to Fuccio di Andolone.

116 This would in turn open up the possibility that the proposed trajectory of the water conduit running along present-day via Cosatti extended further to serve the western side of Sant'Angelo in Colle.

117 Ugo Ricci (Ricci, 1985, p. 72) suggested that the hospital's 'house' may have been located on plot 166, later adopted by the Ciaia.

118 ASS, *Estimo* 24, fols 193r–193v.

119 Ibid., fol. 355r

120 Ibid., fol. 403r.

121 Ibid., fol. 126r.

122 There is a more detailed consideration of this in Chapter 7.

123 ASS, *Estimo* 24, fol. 193r.

124 According to records surviving in the family archive of the Brogioni (see ASS, *Ospedale* 1183), the village hospital was far better endowed in the sixteenth century than during the medieval period. The most obvious reflection of this was the fact that it owned property inside the walls of the village that was quite separate from the hospital building. One of the properties belonging to the hospital in 1574 was a house that was positioned in close proximity to the 'Ecclesie maioris', in other words the parish church of San Michele. This building was bordered on two sides by roads and on another by property belonging to a local resident, Bartolomeo di Giuliano, and on a final side by an olive press belonging to Cesare di Tolomeo. By this date, the hospital also owned another house close to the Porta di San Pietro, which was bordered on one side by commune property, on another side by a house that had previously belonged to an individual referred to solely as Ciatti, and on a final side by a house belonging to Francesco di Capuccio. No reference was made to the location of the hospital building itself, although the *casa*, or house of the hospital was said to have been used as a school (see Brandi, 2004, p. 32). It is possible, therefore, that this building was located on plot 175, which still functioned as the village schoolhouse at the end of the twentieth century. It should, however, be noted that neither Gherardini nor Pecci recorded the location of the village hospital in their descriptions of Sant'Angelo in Colle. Nor were any connections drawn between that institution and the village school.

125 For the possible location of the sixteenth-century hospital on the site of the present-day Franceschi building, see Ricci, 1989, p. 65.

126 I am grateful to Gastone Ferretti for this information, and for showing me the remains of a connecting door in this corridor on plot 193.

127 Brandi, 1991, p. 10.

128 Brandi, 1972, p. 13.

129 Ibid., and Ricci, 1985, p. 51.

130 Brandi, 1991, p. 9. (Don Brandi appears to assume that this cemetery was on the south side of the village in proximity to the present church of San Pietro.)

131 Ibid.

132 As we shall see in Chapter 8, such a course of events may have had a bearing on the iconography of an early fourteenth-century fresco positioned on the southern wall of San Michele.

133 See the entries for Mona Mita Pieri and Nardellus Venture, ASS, *Estimo* 24, fols 330r and 347v.

134 I am grateful to Gina Martini for this information.

135 See the nineteenth century *Atlante dei Beni stabili, liberi e livellari di proprietà dello spedale di S. Maria della Croce di Montalcino*, Archivio Comunale di Stato di Montalcino, *Ospedale di Santa Maria della Croce*, XIX, 31/44 [no. 34, *Comunità di Montalcino. Pianta del livello Nozzoli della tenuta di S. Angelo in Colle e Montenero estratta dei lucidi da catasto di detta comunita*], no. 180.

136 ASS, *Diplomatico di Montalcino*, Busta 35 bis, no. 126. According to this record, the will was witnessed in the *domus* of Santa Maria della Scala at Sant'Angelo in Colle.

137 Biblioteca Comunale degli Intronati, Siena, *Manoscritti* B. VI. 20, new pagination fol. 34r.

138 ASS, *Estimo* 24, fol. 294r.

139 Ibid., fol. 129v.

140 For a survey of the arrangement of such zones elsewhere in the Sienese *contado* during the early modern period, see Duccio Balestracci, 'Approvvigionamento e distribuzione dei prodotti alimentari a Siena nell'epoca comunale. Mulini, mercati e botteghe', *Archaeologio medievale*, 8 (1981), pp. 127–54.

Aerial view of Sant'Angelo in Colle. Photograph by Andrea Rabissi

View of Sant'Angelo in Colle from the north. Photograph by Andrea Rabissi

Palazzaccio, Sant'Angelo in Colle. Photograph by Andrea Rabissi

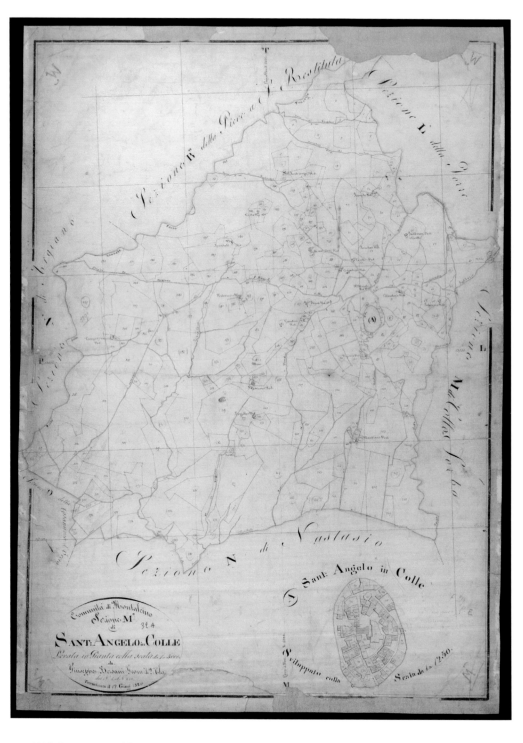

1820 *Catasto* map of Sant'Angelo in Colle and its environs. *Archivio di Stato, Siena, 'Catasto, Mappa di Montalcino, Sezione M bis, di "Sant:Angelo in Colle", no. 32a'. Courtesy of Archivio di Stato di Siena*

Eighteenth-century drawing of land and fields belonging to the Lucattini in the vicinity of Sant'Angelo in Colle. *Archivio di Stato, Siena, Biblioteca Vecchia, n. 18. 'Pianta delle terre in questione promosse dal signor Cavaliere Lucattini a Sant'Angelo in Colle ai nobili signori della Ciaia e Cavalier Pecci secondo l'accesso al quale c.' Courtesy of Archivio di Stato di Siena*

Attr. 'Master of 1346', *Madonna and Child*. Chiesa della Madonna del Rosario, Sant'Angelo in Colle. *Su concessione del Ministero per i Beni e le attività culturali. Foto Soprintendenza B.S.A.E di SIENA & GROSSETO*

Martino di Bartolomeo, *Archangel Michael and Saint John the Baptist. Museo Civico e Diocesano d'Arte Sacra di Montalcino, nos. 14–15PN. Photograph by Andrea Rabissi. Courtesy of Museo Civico e Diocesano d'Arte Sacra di Montalcino*

Attr. Ambrogio Lorenzetti, *Saint Paul and Saint Peter. Museo Civico e Diocesano d'Arte Sacra di Montalcino, nos. 12–13PN. Photograph by Andrea Rabissi. Courtesy of Museo Civico e Diocesano d'Arte Sacra di Montalcino*

Part II

SOCIETY AND
SOCIETAL VALUES

The People

4

The Homeless, the Dispossessed, the Poor and the 'Mezzadria'

Before becoming embroiled in Siena's military affairs early in the thirteenth century, Sant'Angelo in Colle probably functioned like a miniature version of a bustling market town, serving as a stopping off place for travellers and trades people, but essentially quietly engaged with its own curved ploughs and the seasonal fruits of its orchards and market gardens.[1] The changing seasons regulated different agrarian activities from furrowing the earth for growing corn and creating pastures for sheep and cows, and from tending the vines and olives for the production of wine and oil, to the rooting out of acorns for the feeding of the pigs. Once drawn under the Sienese yoke, the pace of life must have quickened with the influx of strangers from the city, the construction of more dwellings inside the walls and the establishment of new patterns of leasing and renting. Despite this, it seems that Sant'Angelo in Colle continued to depend in large part on age-old rhythms of agricultural life.

A minority of the village's residents, as professionals, would of course have been involved in the daily transactions of the village – as merchants overseeing local business and as lawyers drawing up legal documents. Others, as officials of the commune (and often outsiders), would have managed communal finances, establishing law and order through the drawing up and enforcing of local regulations and statutes. As such, they would ultimately have been answerable to Siena and, closer to hand, the Sienese military garrisoned inside the village itself. But for the majority of the inhabitants, life must have consisted of hard labour in the surrounding fields and woods.

Quite apart from the *nullatenenti*, those with no property at all to their names, personal details filed in the 1320 *Tavola delle Possessioni* for Sant'Angelo in Colle imply that a substantial number of the local inhabitants were poor, with patrimonies of less than 20 *lire*.[2]

Table 4.1 Patrimonies of less than 20 *lire* as recorded in the 1320 *Tavola delle possessioni*[1]

	lire	*soldi*	*denari*
Andreolus Credis	5	3	6
Albiccinus de Villa a Tolle	7	2	-
Avitolus Ducci	7	2	-
Becchina Berti	20	-	-
Becchina Lentti	13	10	-
Bella Lamberti	9	13	-
Bindus Bene(n)case (Benincase)	11	5	-
Bertus Ser Ranerii	4	11	-
Bertus (actually Binus) Lambertini	11	5	-
Chola (Chele) Freduccii	9	12	-
Cenne Lactarini	19	7	-
Ceccha Guidi	20	-	-
Ciellina Niccholucci	14	16	-
Chola Michaelis	5	5	-
Chola Micchelucci	2	3	-
Chola Marzuoli	6	13	-
D(omi)na Rosa Pieri pecoraio	1	18	-
Drudas (Drudus) Cennis	7	-	-
Dominichus Guidi	3	16	-
D(omi)na Nuta uxor Ciaffi	13	19	-
D(omi)na Tessina Peruzzi	15	-	-
Dadus Valchericci (Valcherini)	3	16	-
Gerinus Gregorii	2	-	-
Giannos (Gani) Lamberti (Lambertini)	4	16	-
Gianinius Accorsi (Accorsi)	1	12	-
Heredes Venture	17	17	-
Heredes Cennis	11	7	6
Heredes Johanis Appare	17	13	-
Heredes Janis Jacomini	5	2	-
Heredes Banducci	14	7	4
Heredes Bini Ranuccii	8	5	6
Heredes Bini	1	3	-
Heredes Brunaccii	6	-	-
Heredes Bini Jacomini	5	2	-
Heredes Bindi Ranuccii	17	13	6
Heredes Maffuccii	3	7	-
Heredes Cennis Gratie	4	13	-
Heredes Mini Argomenti	8	10	-
Heredes D(omi)ne Becche	14	11	9
Heredes Cecchi Franchi	16	15	-
Heredes Nerii Fabri	12	-	-
Heredes Nerii Sossie di Tolle (Villa a Tolle)	5	3	6
Heredes Fatii de la Villa	10	-	-
Heredes Berto(e) Martini	1	3	-

Heredes Cioli	1	10	-
Heredes Gian(n)is Uguiccionis	1	13	-
Heredes Nuti Brunacci	5	10	-
Heredes Micchelutii	5	1	-
Heredes Leti Sabbatini	3	12	-
Heredes Feduccci di Villa a Tolle	19	10	-
Heredes Accorsi	19	18	-
Heredes mag(ist)ri Puccii	12	-	-
Heredes Ciantis di Villa a Tolle	3	7	-
Heredes Guadagni	13	-	-
Heredes Becche fratesse	2	-	-
Heredes Peri pecorai	5	-	-
Heredes Borgognonis	11	3	-
Heredes Benaventis (Bencivenis)	5	-	-
Heredes Cremonesis	-	6	-
Heredes Tori	-	5	-
Heredes Ranuccetti	2	10	-
Heredes Guidi di Colona (Accolone)	5	2	6
Heredes Giannis Orlandi	4	16	-
Heredes Perucci Assalti	17	6	-
Iohanes Vitalis	12	10	-
Johaninus Rainucci	3	15	-
Landutuis (Landuccio) Giontarelli (Juntarelli)	14	16	6
Landutuis Duccii	16	-	-
Lonarduccius (Lonardelli) Benvegnate	4	3	-
Landus Guadagni	9	18	-
Mon(n)a Scholai	18	18	-
Mon(n)a Gem(m)a Accorsi	2	7	-
Minutius Bandacci (Bandutii)	2	9	-
Mon(n)a Beccha Ser Francisci	6	17	-
Mon(n)a Mita Baldiccionis	5	12	-
Marchus Johanelli	8	9	-
Martino(?e)llus Guidarelli	11	14	-
Menchinus Lamb(er)ti	6	13	-
Mita Nerii	10	7	-
Mideris (Mideus) Fuccii	10	6	6
Mo(?e)ldina Guidarelli	13	7	-
Mon(n)a Lucia Guidi	7	14	-
Mina Giannis	5	7	-
Mon(n)a Mita Minucci[2]	3	4	-
	4	9	-
Mutia Gionte	4	2	6
Mon(n)a Becca Petrini	17	7	-
Novolhinus (Novellinus) Venture	13	5	-
Naldus Jacomi	1	12	-
Nutus Venture	3	14	-
Nuta Nuccii	4	2	-

Necchina Ture	2	16	-
Neccha Brunacci	15	-	-
Nerituis (Nerutuis) Nolsi	17	7	-
Nenus (Nerius) Ciantis de Villa a Tolle	2	6	-
Nuccius Credis di d(e)c(t)a Villa	3	5	-
Nuccius Massai(?n)e	1	7	-
Nardutius Johanis	10	10	-
Nutius Sanne	2	2	-
Nerius Guadagni	3	12	-
Petrinus Nerii	8	6	-
Pagolus Nerii Rubei	3	4	-
Petrutuis Ciani di Villa a Tolle	13	7	-
Sozzus Mainetti	4	10	-
Salitus Orlandi	4	16	-
Sozzinus Sozzi	4	10	-
Ser Franciscus et Ser Nere q(uon)dam Cecchi Pieri	3	13	-
Tura Martini	1	4	-
Tessina Lasie (Lascie)	1	2	-
Tinus Maffucci	5	19	-
Torazzuolus Tori	14	13	-
Turellus Jan(n)ini	1	4	-
Turellus Leti	-	14	-
Vese Michi	15	-	-
Van(n)utuis Cremonosis (Cremonesis)	1	16	-
Van(n)utuis Tori	20	-	-
Vina Morelli (Moregli) (Meglioregli)	19	19	-
Villanus Brunus	15	9	-
Van(n)utius Insegne (Ensegne)	14	9	-
Vinitiana uxor Guidarolli (Guidarelli)	9	10	-

Notes to Table 4.1

1   The Latinate form of names as they appear in the index to *Estimo* 24 is retained here for easy cross-reference to page numbers.

2   There are two different entries for this individual in *Estimo* 24.

At first sight it also seems that more than half of the population might best be described as *fuori casa*, or homeless.[3] However, as this chapter will attempt to show not all those recorded as having no property inside the walls should be classed as poor or homeless; indeed, several are recorded as having patrimonies of over 100 *lire*.

Landowner	Patrimony in		
	lire	soldi	denari
Bartolinus Ghezzi	111	13	-
Binus Ranerii	159	4	6
Bernarduccius de Seggiano	153	15	-
Bernaduccius Pietri	119	9	-
Cecchus Johannis	137	19	-
Ristornectus (Ristorucciius) Vitalis	114	17	-
Scolauiolus Buonomi de Mo(n)te alcino	277	-	-

Table 4.2 i   Those owning no property inside the walls but who nevertheless had patrimonies of over 100 *lire* as recorded in the 1320 *Tavola delle possessioni*

Amideus Pucci
Binus Ranerii
Casinus Bini
Cecchus Johannis
Giannollus Credis di Villa a Tolle
Heredes Venture
Heredes Naldi Jacobi
Heredes Alteman(n)i (Altimanni)
Heredes Romanuioli
Heredes Nerii Rubei
Heredes Nerii Orlandi di Villa a Tolle
Mon(n)a Scholai
Menchinus Ghezzi
Neri Dietavive (Diotavive)
Ristornectus (Ristorucciius) Vitalis

Table 4.2ii Those owning no property inside the walls but who nevertheless owned five or more pieces of land as recorded in the 1320 *Tavola delle possessioni*

Note to Table 4.2

1   The Latinate form of names as they appear in the index to *Estimo* 24 is retained here for easy cross-reference to page numbers.

Some of the same individuals appear also to have owned considerable amounts of land. It is also relevant that not all of the individuals recorded as owning no living accommodation in 1320 were locals. Several of them were clearly outsiders, and thus had no real need of living accommodation inside the walls of Sant'Angelo in Colle. Berto di ser Raniero, Casella, Nigro, and Scolaiuolo di Bononni, for example, are described as from Montalcino; and Andreolo di Credi, Chele di Freduccio, Ciatto di Nuccio, Giannello di Credi, Nerio di Soffio, Nerio di Orlando, Fiduccio (?Feduccio), Cianti, Cianno, Nerio di Cianti, Nuccio di Credi, Petruccio di Cianno, and Vanne di Gherardo were, by contrast, residents of Villa i Tolli. A number of other individuals had connections with other nearby communes, or were residents of Siena. As already indicated, although it might have been politically expedient for Sienese residents to own property associated with this southern frontier castle, it may have been just as advantageous to establish a presence in the countryside surrounding Sant'Angelo in Colle.

But what conclusions can be drawn about those members of the local population who are recorded as owning land but no living accommodation inside the walls? Some of the apparently homeless people were women, but the majority were men. As already noted, it was more commonly the case that women owned no property in their own right during the early modern period. More often than not, it was also the case that women were accommodated within their natal families prior to marriage, moving away to a husband's home when married and returning to their previous home when widowed. In the case of women, therefore, one would not normally expect to find references to ownership of living accommodation. Omissions of that kind are more puzzling in the context of the male inhabitants of early fourteenth-century Sant'Angelo in Colle.

One possibility is that some of the men of the village scratched a living in *capanne*, or shacks, erected in their kitchen gardens and orchards, or on patches of worked and woodland in the countryside outside the village. According to the 1320 *Tavola delle possessioni*, a large number of buildings, including shacks and farmhouses of various sizes, were scattered around the early fourteenth-century village. Some of these structures were owned by Sienese outsiders, but many others belonged to the inhabitants of the village, themselves.[4]

Table 4.3 Land in the vicinity of Sant'Angelo in Colle containing built structures ranging from shacks to houses (i) belonging to local residents (according to the 1320 *Tavola delle possessioni*

Name of owner, or owners	Description and location of terrain	Approximate measurement in *staia*	Estimated value in *lire soldi denari*			Page no.
Angelino di Franco from Sant'Angelo in Colle	Orchard with *casalino*, or small house in the area known as San Piero	3/5	6	4	-	3r
Angelino di Guerri	Land with vineyard and *domo*, or house in the area known as Capanne	8 and 3/5	107	17	-	4r
Berna di Ghezzo	Agricultural land with a *capanna*, or hut in the area known as Aiale	2 and 1/5	9	7	6	31r
Bernarduccio da Seggiano, 'now of Sant'Angelo in Colle'	Agricultural land on which was a palace, a house, a *capanna*, or hut, and a mill in the area known as Tredine	23	145	6	-	38r
Bino, or Bindo di Raniero	Half of a piece of Agricultural land with a *capanna*, or hut in the area known as Romata	Whole piece of land measured 8	22	8	6	34r
Bindo di Mergone	Agricultural land with kitchen garden and *capanna*, or hut, in area known as Usinilla	108	185	7	-	47r
Casino di Bino	Agricultural land with hut, in contrada Tredine (also known as Canale, or Canalis)	4	9	-	-	66v
Cecchino di Ghezzo	Agricultural land with *capanna*, or hut, in area known as Saproia	3 and 4/5	30	9	-	71v

Cecco di Giovanni	Agricultural land with *capanna*, or hut in area known as Romate	6 and 4/5	40	-	-	82r
Cecco di Tura	Agricultural land with *capanna*, or hut in area known as Romate	3 and 2/5	14	3	-	79v
Cenni di Bartolo	Agricultural land with *capanna*, or hut in area known as Lame S..ino	15	40	15	-	90r
Chino (?or Ghino) di Bonaiuto	Agricultural land including a vineyard and *capanna*, or hut, in area known as Sitini	6	32	13	-	78r
Dominchello di Ramaiuolo	Agricultural land with *capanna*, or hut in area known as Greppo	5	13	7	-	109r
Heirs of Bino (or Bindo) di Tassino	Agricultural land with kitchen garden and *capanna*, or hut in area known as Aiale	1	4	7	-	182r
Heirs of Pieruccio di Guiglielmo	Agricultural land with *capanna*, or hut in area known as Pantani	12	56	5	-	178r
Giovanni di Gualterio	Agricultural land with vineyard and a *capanna*, or hut in area known as Collemattone	7	67	13	-	253r
Giovanni di Rainaldo	*Ortale*, or kitchen garden, cum orchard with *casalino*, or small house on the Costa Sant'Angelo	1/5	11	7	-	251r
Landuccio di Berto	Kitchen garden with *casalino*, or small house in the area known as Costa (probably Costa Sant'Angelo)	1/10	-	15	-	263v
Mona Necca di Niggozante	*Ortale*, or kitchen garden, with orchard with *domo*, or house in the area known as San Pietro	1/20	12	-	-	281r
Menchino di Gezzo	Agricultural land with *capanna*, or hut in area known as Monteiano	4 and 3/10	5	7	6	297r

Mico di Genovese	Kitchen garden with *casalino*, or small house in the area known as San Pietro	Less than 1/10	5	3	-	286r
	Agricultural land with *capanna*, or hut in area known as Monteiano	4/5	8	16	-	288r
	Agricultural land with *capanna*, or hut in area known as Tavoleta	36	91	17	-	288v
Mino di Giovanni	Agricultural land with *capanna*, or hut in area known as San Giovanni	9	16	13	-	308r
Minutio di Sozzo	Agricultural land with *capanna*, or hut in area known as Monteiano	2 and 1/5	10	13	-	292v
Nardo di Cambio	Agricultural land with *capanna*, or hut in area known as fonte Chinelli	19	34	3	-	349r
Nenno di Raniero	kitchen garden with *casalino*, or small house in the area known as San Pietro	2/5	4	3	-	340r
Nino di Giovanni	Agricultural land with a vineyard and house at Collemattone	7 ½	67	10	-	342v
Petruccio di Piero	Agricultural land with *capanna*, or hut, and a kitchen garden in area known as Valle	7	15	5	-	378v
Scholaio di Gianelli	Agricultural land with *capanna*, or hut in area known as Sitini	5	16	7	-	402r
Ser Guccio di Ser Francesco	Mixed orchard and kitchen garden with *capanna*, or hut on the Costa di Sant'Angelo	3/20	1	4	-	449v
Tura di Guigli, or Guilli	Agricultural land with *capanna*, or hut in contrata Rocchigiane	4 and 4/5	22	12	-	413r
Tura di Manno	Agricultural land lying fallow with *capanna*, or hut in area known as Cappanelle	8	17	7	-	453v
Tura di Morello	Agricultural land serving as vineyard with hut	2 and 1/5	7	14	-	419r
Ulivezio (?Uliveccio) di Giovanni	Agricultural land with *capanna*, or hut in area known as Tredine	2 and ¼	7	1	-	431v

Vannuccio di Rainero	Half of a piece of Agricultural land with *capanna*, or hut in area known as Romate	Whole plot measured 8	22	13	6	444r
Vinitiana, wife of Guidarello	Agricultural land with *capanna*, or hut in area known as Bagnuolo	1	9	10	-	448r

Name of owner, or owners	Description and location of terrain	Approximate measurement in *staia*	Estimated value in			Table 4.3 ii. Belonging to Sienese non residents
			lire	*soldi*	*denari*	
Andrea di Buoncambio[1]	Agricultural, or worked land with vines and a *capanna*, or hut in area known as Saproia	5 and 1/3	21	18	-	
Friars of Sant'Agostino[2]	Agricultural, or worked land with two houses and a *claustro*, or cloister/ cum pen in the area known as San Giovanni	233	566	-	-	
Heirs of Baldiccione[3]	Agricultural, or worked land with 'quondam' (?what was once) *capanna*, or hut in area known as Cappanelle	3 and 1/5	12	5	-	
Manovello di Ugolino[4]	'cappannate' (?occupied by a number of *capanne*, or huts) land that was worked and consisted of fields in the area known as Poggio Peschaia	11	33	7	-	
Neri di Guicciardo[5]	Agricultural, or worked land with a house and woodland in area known as Capanne	68	143	-	-	
	Agricultural, or worked land with vines and a *capanna*, or hut in area known as Saporoia	3	12	10	-	
	Agricultural, or worked land with a *capanna*, or hut in area known as Poggio Peschaia	42	116	-	-	
Niccoluccio di Mandriano[6]	Agricultural, or worked land with a *capanna*, or hut in area known as Fabriche	26	56	-	-	
	and Agricultural, or worked land with a *capanna*, or hut in area known as Bagnuolo	14 and 1/2	16	2	-	

Notes to Table 4.3ii
1   ASS, *Estimo* 102, Terzo di Città, Inchontri, 1318, fol. 88r, new pagination.
2   Ibid., 109, Terzo di Città, Santa Agata, fol. 26v, pencil pagination bottom left.
3   Ibid., 108, Terzo di Città, Porta all'archo, 1320, fol. 232v, pagination bottom left.
4   Ibid., fol. 687r, old pagination.
5   Ibid., 106, Terzo di Città, San Pietro in Castelvecchio, 1318, fols 57r, 66r and 73v, pencil pagination top right.
6   Ibid., 104, Terzo di Città, Santo Quiricho in Chastelvecchio, 1318, fol. 264v, new pagination.

Some of the buildings were clearly large enough, also, to accommodate at least one extended family group. There was thus a considerable supply of living accommodation outside the walls of the village. Several of those listed in the 1320 *Tavola delle Possessioni* as being without living accommodation inside Sant'Angelo in Colle were thus in a position to live outside the walls of the village in their own properties. Others may have been tenant landworkers, or sharecroppers, living in rented premises in the village itself or on land outside.

Although it is generally argued that sharecropping was only fully developed in southern Tuscany at a later date, material considered here indicates that a system of *mezzadria* was established in the territory of Sant'Angelo in Colle as early as the first half of the fourteenth century.[5] For many *mezzaiuoli*, or sharecroppers, life consisted of a series of temporary employments, with numerous upheavals for the family, as work places changed or individual contracts lapsed.[6] Most itinerant sharecroppers owned neither land nor living accommodation, and were thus entirely dependent on the renewal of existing contracts, or offers of similar work elsewhere. For these individuals, there was no fixed home. They were, in effect, 'nullatenenti'.

For the more fortunate, however, there were regular contract renewals and even agreements carried over from one generation to another, where sons and other heirs continued the work of older relations. It was also often the case that individual sharecroppers contemporaneously worked a number of pieces of land belonging to different owners.[7] Surviving *mezzadria* contracts indicate that land workers very often supplemented their incomes by taking responsibility for, and working land belonging to others, as well as looking after their own land. On occasion they also gained access to living accommodation belonging to landlords who not only sought able-bodied hands to work their land, but who also hoped to increase their yields by accommodating such workers on the land itself.

As we shall see, far from being dispossessed, some of the individuals recorded in the 1320 *Tavola delle possessioni* as owning no property inside the walls of the village, seem in fact to have been involved in the quite profitable process of managing their own land as well as that belonging to someone else. One such individual was Neri di Dietaviva. In December 1306, Neri di Dietaviva, 'detto Villabruno', agreed to work 'a mezzo', or for half-share, an orchard 'in the district of Sant'Angelo in Colle' which belonged to 'Meo di Ugo da Siena'.[8] Meo's orchard, which was apparently planted with fruit trees, was described as being in the vicinity of the 'Via Carraie' – a topononym that, as already suggested, indicates an area criss-crossed by cart and wagon tracks. This area (which, from cross reference with entries in the 1320 *Tavola delle possessioni* was apparently also known as 'Costamorri' or 'Costamori') probably hugged the walls of Sant'Angelo in Colle on its eastern side. In 1306 Neri not only agreed to work Meo di Ugo's land well, but also to look after his trees. In addition, and at his own expense, Neri agreed to deliver to Meo half of all the fruit garnished from Meo's orchard.

In terms of financial gain, there seems little doubt that Neri's recompense was in kind rather than in cash. It also seems clear that Meo di Ugo was an absentee landlord, since contemporary records show that his own living house was in Siena. It is possible, however, that Meo's family originally came from Sant'Angelo in Colle, and that the holdings there had been passed down to him by way of inheritance. Resident in the Terzo di San Martino in the area of Spada forte in Siena, it seems that Meo di Ugo was an individual of comparatively modest means. His overall patrimony of some 230 *lire* was mostly accounted for by the value of the half house owned by him in Siena.[9] Meo's two pieces of land at Sant'Angelo in Colle were the only land owned by him outside Siena. At the end of the second decade of the fourteenth century Meo di Ugo's property at Sant'Angelo in Colle was recorded as one piece of worked land and wood in the area of Greppo measuring 10 *staia* and valued at 2 *lire* and 10 *soldi*, and the piece of land serving as an orchard which Neri Dietavive had agreed to work. The orchard measured just over half a *staia* and was valued at 3 *lire*. Significantly, it was also described as being bordered on one side by property belonging to Neri Dietavive. Such proximity may well have persuaded Meo to turn to Neri to work his orchard and maintain his fruit trees during his absence. Indeed, the *mezzadria* agreement of 1306 may thus have arisen as much from Meo di Ugo's need of a local retainer, as from any pressing need on Neri Dietavive's part. From Neri's point of view, tending Ugo's orchard would have merely involved the extension of work no doubt carried out on a daily basis around Neri's own trees and kitchen garden.

It does not appear, either, that Neri was desperately in need of sharecropping work. In 1320, in addition to the orchard on the Costamori, Neri Dietavive owned four pieces of worked land (measuring in total some 11 *staia*) with an overall value 10 times that of the land belonging to Meo.[10] Neri's own orchard land seems, moreover, to have been rated at a higher rate per *staio* than that of his Sienese neighbour. According to the 1320 *Tavola delle possessioni*, Neri's plot of land (which abutted on one side the land belonging to Meo di Ugo, on two others a road, and on a final side land belonging to Turelli Pieruzzi) measured just over a third of a *staia*, and was valued at 11 *lire* and 18 *soldi*.[11] Despite being smaller, Neri's orchard was thus deemed almost a third more valuable than that belonging to Meo di Ugo. In 1320, Neri di Dietavive's overall patrimony was, however, recorded as 50 *lire*, less than a quarter of that recorded in respect of Meo di Ugo. Even so, Neri was certainly not one of the poorest residents of Sant'Angelo in Colle at that date. Yet he apparently owned no living accommodation inside the walls of the village. Nor do any of the surviving records contain any reference, either, to a shed or shack on any of Neri's declared pieces of land. The surviving *mezzadria* agreement of 1306 implies that Neri di Dietavive gained nothing from the deal with Meo di Ugo other than produce from Meo's land. Where, then did Neri (who, 14 years later, owned a little bit of land which no doubt earned a little bit of income in kind, but who himself was apparently still homeless) spend his nights? Accommodation in someone else's property seems the only logical answer.

One possibility is that Neri di Dietavive was still living with his parents in 1306. There is no reference to Neri's marital state in either the 1320 *Tavola delle possessioni* or the sharecropping agreement drawn up with Meo di Ugo. Had Neri's father still been alive in 1320, Neri might well have still been living in the family home. But it is also possible, as the example of Mona Mita and her husband Minuccio di Banduccio illustrates, that Neri di Dietavive was married (if not in 1306, then at least by 1320), and that he had access to living accommodation within the walls of Sant'Angelo in Colle through property owned by his wife. It is also possible that Neri already had access to living accommodation at the time of his agreement with Meo di Ugo through another sharecropping engagement on someone else's land. One further possibility is that Neri di Dietavive was renting accommodation inside the walls of Sant'Angelo in Colle, and thus not required to submit details of that property in the 1320 *Tavola delle possessioni*.

As already noted, many local residents were recorded as owning more than one property inside the walls of Sant'Angelo in Colle in 1320, and must thus have been able to assume the role of landlord to homeless land workers. It was certainly not the case either, that sharecropping agreements were signed solely between local residents and absentee landlords. At least two surviving records concerning affairs at Sant'Angelo in Colle refer to a system of *mezzadria* that was established between local members of that community. In one of the cases, it also seems clear that the sharecropper was to have access to accommodation on the land he was to work as part of the contractual agreement.

The first record, a contract dated 16 July 1328, concerns a sharecropping agreement drawn up between Nanni di Cenno and Guccio 'del fu Francesco'. The latter individual can most probably be identified with the Guccio di Ser Francesco, who was discussed in the previous chapter, along with other putative members of his family clan. As we shall see, Guccio was a professional man, if not already in 1320 then at least in 1328.

According to the surviving record, a contract 'a mezzo' for the period of three years was agreed between Nanni di Cenno 'da Sant'Angelo in Colle' and the notary, Guccio del fu Francesco, likewise 'from Sant'Angelo in Colle'.[12] According to this contract Nanni di Cenni agreed to work two pieces of land belonging to Ser Guccio. One of the pieces of land (in the area known as Ficaiuoli) is said to have contained a *capanna*, or shack. The other plot, another piece of worked or agricultural land, was positioned in the area known as Monteiano. The wording of the 1328 contract implies that Nanni di Cenno was to be allowed to use the shack on Guccio's land at Ficaiuoli, and possibly even to live inside it, since it was agreed that Nanni should not only preserve and maintain the land there but also the 'capanna' positioned on it.[13] Nanni agreed to work the land conscientiously, as well as to sow seed and to harvest crops at the appropriate time. He was also charged to 'use' good labourers and 'conductoris', (contractors, or hired hands). In addition, Nanni agreed to divide the fruits of the land equally with his employer, and to transport all relevant goods to Guccio's house in Sant'Angelo in Colle. At the end of the three-year period Nanni was to hand back both the uncultivated land and the shack.

One curious fact is that Nanni di Cenno was not included in the list of inhabitants in the 1320 *Tavola delle possessioni*, despite the fact that he was described as 'of' Sant'Angelo in Colle in the 1328 sharecropping agreement. It is possible that in 1320 Nanni had not yet reached the age of maturity. If this were the case, he could still have been living in the family home, and thus not have featured for purposes of tax. Two individuals named Cenne or Cenno (Cenno di Bartolo and Cenno di Lactarino) are in fact included in the 1320 survey.[14] However, there is nothing in either of the entries furnished in respect of those two individuals to indicate any connection with Ser Guccio di Ser Francesco or his land. Another possibility is that in 1320 Nanni di Cenno was not yet independent of a number of heirs, and was thus included under the name of that group for the purpose of taxation. One group of heirs with a similar patronym, the 'heredes Cennis Graties', is indeed included in the 1320 *Tavola delle possessioni*.[15] It seems from their entry that these individuals were abjectly poor, their entire patrimony being estimated at a mere 4 *lire* and 13 *soldi*. They are recorded as owning only two relatively small pieces of worked land: one, measuring just over three *staia*, in the area known as 'Preteschiace'; and the other, measuring just under two *staia*, near Sesta, in the area known as 'Piano a Sexte'. There is no reference to any unit of accommodation either inside or outside the walls of the village. Members of this family clan may thus have been forced to seek sharecropping deals, not only in order to make ends meet, but also in order to have somewhere to live. However, as with Cenno di Bartolo and Cenno di Lactarino, there is no evidence of any connection with Ser Guccio di Ser Francesco. Of Nanni di Cenno, there is no other obvious trail in the 1320 *Tavola delle possessioni*.

It is, however, possible (and perhaps more likely) that in 1320 Nanni di Cenno was involved in a sharecropping agreement elsewhere. By 1328 he may thus have been an experienced *mezzaiuolo*. He may even have achieved the status of steward or factor. The wording of the 1328 contract, both in the particulars of the work expected from Nanni, the extra hands he was to employ and in the extent of land placed in his care would seem to indicate that Nanni was already established in the field of sharecropping. It is also clear that Guccio di Ser Francesco was happy to invest him with considerable authority.

By contrast with the paucity of information concerning Nanni di Cenno's background and family, it turns out that we know a great deal about his employer. As noted in the last chapter, Guccio di Ser Francesco owned a considerable amount of property both inside the walls and in the countryside around Sant'Angelo in Colle in 1320.[16] He was also a comparatively wealthy man. In 1320, Guccio's overall patrimony was estimated at 336 *lire* and 9 *soldi*. He was also part of an extended local clan, with at least two siblings, Becca and Lucarino. Despite owning a number of pieces of land, Becca was the least well endowed of the three siblings. Guccio, for his part, not only owned more land but was also clearly richer than Lucarino, and thus probably the oldest brother. (In 1320 Lucarino di Ser Francesco owned seven pieces of land as opposed to the 20 recorded for Guccio, and is said to have had a patrimony of 208 *lire* and 5 *soldi*.)[17] While not the richest men in the village, such patrimonies reveal that both Guccio and Lucarino were relatively comfortable. By comparison with the overall patrimony of 50 *lire* recorded in respect of Neri di Dietavive, both brothers were extremely well heeled. As a practising notary, Guccio di Ser Francesco must also have acquired a certain social cachet, and been regarded as a respectable representative of the village's middle class.[18]

According to the 1320 *Tavola delle possessioni*, Guccio's landed possessions consisted of agricultural land, as well as worked land with woodland, worked land with vineyards and worked land with olives. In addition, he owned a number of orchards and kitchen gardens, including some that also contained olives or vines. At least one area owned by Guccio was laid out solely to vines. For the most part, the individual plots of land were of modest dimensions, ranging from between one or two, to eight or nine *staia*. A notable exception was a portion of worked and wooded land at Cerrete, which measured 35 *staia*. Many of the pieces of orchard and kitchen garden owned by Guccio, and especially those located close to the walls on the Costa di Sant'Angelo and on the Costa di San Piero measured less than one *staia*. One of these – a plot measuring little more than a tenth of a *staio* on the Costa di Sant'Angelo – which was described as an 'ortale' (probably a mixture of an kitchen garden and an orchard), and which was bordered on one side by a road, on two other sides by land belonging to Manovello di Ugolino, and on a fourth side by land owned by the heirs of Banducci, contained a *casalino*, or small house or shack. Curiously, and particularly in the light of details contained in the 1328 sharecropping agreement with Nanni di Cenno, none of the pieces of land recorded as belonging to Guccio at Ficaiuoli are said to have contained a shack. Once again, it becomes clear that information contained in individual entries in the 1320 *Tavola delle possessioni* was on occasion incomplete.

This was not the only discrepancy. In the case of property owned by Guccio di Ser Francesco at Ficaiuoli, it is curious, for example, that no mention is made of either his brother Lucarino or his sister Becca as owning any land in the vicinity. By contrast, in the entry drawn up for Lucarino in the 1320 *Tavola delle possessioni*, reference was made to a piece of worked and woodland at Ficaiuoli of considerable size (measuring eighteen *staia*), that is definitely recorded as bordering another piece of land in the same area belonging to Guccio.[19] Moreover, despite the apparent detail in the recording of land owned by Ser Guccio di ser Francesco in the 1320 *Tavola delle possessioni*, entries furnished in respect of some of the individuals who are said to have owned land bordering Guccio's property do not always tally with the information contained in Guccio's own entry. According to Lando di Pepe, for example, his plot of ground at Ficaiuoli was bordered, not on one, but on two sides by land belonging to Ser Guccio di Ser Francesco. Likewise, in the entry for the heirs of Banduccio, the kitchen garden cum orchard land owned by them at Ficaiuoli (which measured about one fifth of a *staio*) was described as bordered, not on one, but on two sides by land belonging to Ser Guccio di Ser Francesco, despite the fact that in Guccio's own entry we are told that his plot (a much larger piece of land measuring nearly two and a half *staia*) was bordered on only one side by the heirs of Banduccio.[20] According to Guccio's entry, his piece of land was in addition bordered on two sides by roads, and on a fourth side by land owned by the heirs of Cecco di Piero. The entry for the heirs of Cecco di Piero concerning their land at Ficaiuoli (which likewise consisted of worked land and olives, and which was about twice as large as Guccio's neighbouring plot, measuring about four and a third *staia*), recorded, however, that their plot was bordered on two sides by Guccio's property.

Such discrepancies may in part have arisen from the fact that the land around Sant'Angelo in Colle was partitioned into a number of disparate parts. Many of these plots were also put to a variety of uses, although – as the examples of worked land and olives owned by Guccio di Ser Francesco and others at Ficaiuoli show – it was also often the case that a patchwork of plots belonging to a number of different people was carved out of land laid out to one common purpose. It seems that irrespective of the use to which such land was put, some of the plots were large, some small. In addition, many plots, rather than being set side by side, appear to have looped around each other. Clearly, the larger the piece of land, the easier it would have been for it to curve around several sides of a neighbouring piece of property. Defining how many sides of an irregularly shaped plot of land abutted terrain belonging to neighbouring landowners must on many occasions have depended on individual perspectives. That the land itself was frequently put to a variety of uses must also have presented a challenge to notaries charged with drawing up the details of individual sharecropping agreements. That difficulties of this kind persisted even in more recent times is reflected in the detailed drawing made of land held by the Lucattini family during the eighteenth century (see Colour plate 5).

It seems clear that Nanni di Cenno was to involve himself in a number of different activities following his agreement to work for Guccio di Ser Francesco in July 1328. Apart from an undertaking to plant and harvest crops, reference was also made to the 'fructubus omnibus dictarum arborum' (the yield of each of the said trees), without, however, specifying the actual species of tree. It seems likely that Nanni di Cenno was in the main hired to help care for Guccio di Ser Francesco's olive trees, but no doubt also to be involved in the gathering of the olives and perhaps even the production of olive oil. Ficaiuoli was clearly an area deemed particularly appropriate for olive groves. Of the six pieces of agricultural land owned by Guccio in the area of Ficauioli, five are said to have contained olives. One of the five is also referred to as 'tere ortati', or orchard land. The land at Monteiano, a comparatively small plot measuring just under two *staia*, was by contrast described merely as 'tere laborati', or worked land.[21] It seems that the plot at Ficaiuoli that Nanni di Cenno was charged with working not only consisted of worked or agricultural land with olives, but was also the largest piece of land owned by Guccio in that area.[22] At nine *staia*, it was nearly 30 times the size of a neighbouring plot belonging to Lando di Pepe, which measured only a third of a *staio*, but which was laid out with olives.[23]

Despite inconsistencies in the description of the confines of individual pieces of land and the identities of individual owners, there can be no doubt that Guccio di Ser Francesco owned a considerable amount of property in various parts of the territory of Sant'Angelo in Colle by the time of the 1320 *Tavola delle possessioni*. In some areas, such as the Costa di Sant'Angelo and Ficaiuoli, he owned multiple plots of land. Why Guccio chose to enter into a sharecropping agreement on only two pieces of his land remains a mystery. It was certainly not the case that these were the only two areas containing labour-intensive plots, nor was it the case that they were both of considerable size. Two other pieces of agricultural land owned by Guccio at Pantano were considerably larger (measuring respectively 17½ and 8 *staia*). These and the several other pieces of arable land owned by Guccio, in such diverse areas as Capraia, Macerete and the area known as 'Fossato Castellani', as well as two plots containing vines at Infernale and Ferrale must all have made demands on Guccio's time and energy.

One possibility is that Guccio di Ser Francesco entered into a number of sharecropping agreements, not only because of conflicts arising as a result of his professional life, but also because of the sheer practical necessity of tending what was a considerable amount of landed property. It seems likely that as a legal man busily engaged in the affairs of Sant'Angelo in Colle, Guccio would at some point have needed to subcontract care of some, if not all, of his landed property. Maintaining his several olive groves and vineyards must have been of prime importance. But the several plots of land given over to kitchen garden and orchard must also have required constant attention. Extra responsibilities imposed upon Guccio through inheritance of land following the death of his father may finally have stretched his capabilities to the limit. Thus in 1328, if not before, Guccio may have been forced to relieve himself and his family from the mounting pressures of their landed properties.

While the sharecropping agreement with Nanni di Cenno appears to be the sole document to have survived concerning the working of land owned by Guccio di Ser Francesco in the territory of Sant'Angelo in Colle, several other contracts could have been drawn up in respect of other plots of land in

Guccio's possession. Guccio may even have subcontracted care of some of his land to other members of his extended family. Indeed, such a pattern could have been established long before the sharecropping agreement drawn up with Nanni di Cenno. Details inserted in a will drawn up in 1335 on behalf of another professional man, Giovanni di Paganello – who appears to have assumed the role of village notary previously held by Guccio di Ser Francesco – indicates that at least one such arrangement was established in Sant'Angelo in Colle during the early fourteenth century.

Attention focuses in particular on two provisions inserted in Giovanni di Paganello's will that appear to have been motivated by, and related to the working of Giovanni's land. According to these provisions, Minuccia, the daughter of Cecco di Giovanni, was to receive 10 *lire* for clothing and her brother Giovanni was to receive one of Giovanni di Paganello's own white oxen.[24] The latter provision in particular suggests that Giovanni di Paganello and Giovanni di Cecco di Giovanni had been involved in some kind of sharecropping agreement. While it was an established practice that *mezzaiuoli* should receive a loan, or (in part payment for their work) tools with which to work the land, it was also frequently the case that their employers offered to underwrite the cost of a beast of burden. Giovanni di Paganello's gift may thus have been motivated by a desire to honour a sharecropping contract that had not formally lapsed at the time of his will. The fact that Giovanni di Paganello also left money for the clothing of Giovanni di Cecco's sister Minuccia would seem, however, to imply that the relationship between these three people amounted to something more than a business agreement between the two men. Details furnished in the 1320 *Tavola delle possessioni* for Sant'Angelo in Colle do in fact reveal that all three individuals were members of the same extended family clan. It thus seems that responsibility for working at least some of Giovanni di Paganello's landed possessions had been passed on to his own relatives.

Although Giovanni di Paganello made no reference in his will either to a family connection or to any kind of sharecropping agreement with members of Cecco di Giovanni's family, it emerges that he and Giovanni di Cecco were closely related on his father's side. Details furnished in the 1320 *Tavola delle possessioni* allow us to piece together a nexus of associations, not only between Giovanni di Paganello's father, Paganello di Giovanni, and other members of the older generation of the family, but also between Giovanni di Paganello and his own contemporaries. It becomes clear, for example, that Giovanni di Paganello's father Paganello di Giovanni had at least three brothers: Nino, Cecco and Lonardutio, or Lonarduccio. Cecco di Giovanni was thus Giovanni di Paganello's paternal uncle, and Cecco's children Giovanni and Minuccia were Giovanni di Paganello's first cousins. Individual entries in the 1320 *Tavola delle possessioni* also indicate that there was an imbalance between the relative financial states of the different members of this extended family clan. As we shall see in the discussion of the male elite of Sant'Angelo in Colle in Chapter 6, the patrimony of Giovanni di Paganello's father Paganello was considerably larger than that of his sibling, Cecco.

There is no question, however, that Cecco di Giovanni should be positioned amongst the poor or dispossessed of early fourteenth-century Sant'Angelo in Colle. According to the 1320 *Tavola delle possessioni* Cecco's patrimony amounted to 137 *lire* and 19 *soldi*.[25] Cecco also appears to have owned several pieces of land at that date. Five pieces of arable, or agricultural land are recorded in various parts of the territory of Sant'Angelo in Colle, and on the largest of these – a plot measuring some seven *staio*, and valued at 40 *lire* – there was a *capanna*. Cecco is also recorded as owning two quite small vineyards. He could barely be classified, therefore, as impoverished. Yet Cecco di Giovanni was one of those individuals who are recorded in 1320 as owning no property inside the walls of Sant'Angelo in Colle. Yet again, therefore, the question arises as to where Cecco di Giovanni and his family actually lived. It is possible, given the availability of a shack outside the village, that Cecco had no need of living accommodation inside Sant'Angelo in Colle itself. Another possibility, however, is that Cecco di Giovanni was responsible for working someone else's land as well as his own, and that in so doing, he gained access to living accommodation owned by his employer. Consideration is given here to the possibility that Paganello di Giovanni, and subsequently his son Giovanni di Paganello, provided that facility.

In this context, it is significant that both Paganello di Giovanni and Cecco di Giovanni owned arable land close to each other, in the area known as Poggiuolo Albinelli. Details furnished in the 1320 *Tavola della possessioni* reveal that in each case there was also a common confine in land belonging to a third brother, Nino di Giovanni.[26] Perversely, in Nino di Giovanni's own entry there is no record of his holding land at Poggiuolo Albinelli.[27] Reference is made, by contrast, to a plot of worked land belonging to Nino at Tavoleta, which was bordered by land belonging to Cecco di Giovanni. Reference is also made to a piece of worked land at Trafossatella that was bordered by land belonging to Paganello di Giovanni. It seems from this that the three siblings were each responsible for working plots of land in close proximity to each other. The likelihood is that the individual plots had previously been joined together, and that they had subsequently been divided up by way of inheritance. In such situations and if only for practical reasons, different members of the same family clan must on occasion have assumed a number of joint responsibilities for working inherited land. This must particularly have been the case where one sibling aspired to a professional life. In 1335 Giovanni di Paganello had already been working as the village notary at Sant'Angelo in Colle for a number of years. As we shall see, he had also considerably increased the patrimony he had received from his father. It is not unlikely, that a by-product of this was the need for extra assistance in working the land that Giovanni then owned. As with the agreement drawn up between Guccio di Ser Francesco and Nanni di Cenno, when it came to working Giovanni di Paganello's own landed possessions, a sharecropping contract with a member of the local population may have seemed a practical solution. There would have been a number of practical advantages also, if such an agreement were drawn up with members of Giovanni di Paganello's own family. These individuals would not only have been on hand to carry out work on Giovanni's land whilst toiling on their own adjacent plots; as blood relations, they must also have been deemed particularly trustworthy. In effect, at minimum cost and inconvenience, there was maximum profit for the whole clan. Giovanni di Cecco may thus have been engaged to work part or all of the land acquired by Giovanni di Paganello following the death of Giovanni's father Paganello. Giovanni di Cecco may even have been following in the footsteps of his own father Cecco, in carrying forward a contract originally agreed between Cecco and Giovanni di Paganello's father. As we shall see, Paganello di Giovanni was not only one of the richest men in 1320, but he also owned a large amount of property. He and his son Giovanni in his turn were thus well placed to offer both employment and accommodation to other members of the family.

While records in respect of sharecropping in the vicinity of Sant'Angelo in Colle imply that working the land and gathering its produce was a key preoccupation, other documents show that the care of livestock constituted an equally important part of everyday activities in the vicinity of the early fourteenth-century village. These records also throw light on the different kinds of agreement that were drawn up between absent or distanced owners and the individual or individuals chosen to look after livestock such as sheep and goats.[28] One such document records that in December 1328, Giuntinus, or Giuntino 'olim Pannochia' (son of the deceased Pannochia) 'of Sant'Angelo in Colle' agreed to look after 220 sheep and goats belonging to two residents of Montalcino: Daddo di Brunicello and Pietro di Naldo.[29] Giuntino promised to tend this livestock for the period of two years at his own expense. He also agreed not to sell or pass on any of the sheep or goats to anyone else without the express permission of their owners. Giuntino was to deliver any produce from the livestock (including wool and cheese) to Montalcino, where it was to be divided between the two owners. Giuntino finally promised that neither he, nor any of his relatives would commit any fraud or maltreat the livestock.

Neither Giuntino nor his father Pannocchia was included in the list of individuals holding property in and around Sant'Angelo in Colle in 1320. Yet they were clearly recognised as members of that community at the time of the 1328 contract. Such an omission may be explained in a number of ways. As shepherds and/or goatherds, Giuntino and Pannocchia may not have had any fixed abode. Indeed, the nature of their work must have imposed a peripatetic life style. It is possible, also, that they acquired grazing rights, rather than owning land in their own right. They may thus have been categorised as *nullatenenti*, even though they were in fact engaged in meaningful employment. Like sharecroppers working the land, shepherds must often have had to move from one place to another in search of work, as short-term contracts expired.[30] In the normal course of events they must also have needed to move from one area of pasture to another, according to the needs of individual livestock. They also needed to stick close to their livestock, looking after them by day, and at night-time probably sleeping in close proximity to them in rudimentary shacks or stone shelters. Under such circumstances, one would not expect to find any reference to a shepherd or a goatherd in a document drawn up specifically for the purpose of taxation of land owned or living accommodation.

That said, Giuntino di Pannocchia was clearly not the only shepherd or goatherd associated with the early fourteenth-century village of Sant'Angelo in Colle. Nor does it seem that all such individuals were poor or without property. One surviving record not only reveals the identities of another local family involved in the pasturing of goats on behalf of a third party during the early years of the fourteenth century, but also throws light on arrangements made for their living accommodation. According to a record of 27 November 1308, Donna Buonafemmina, 'widow of Assalto' and Assaltino 'son of the deceased Petruccio' of Sant'Angelo in Colle, agreed on that date to sell a house inside the walls of the village to Fra Renaldo (or Ranaldo) of the order of Saint Augustine in Siena.[31] On the same day the same individuals entered into a rental agreement with Fra Ranaldo for a period of one year in the same property. At the same time, Donna Buonafemmina and Assaltino agreed with Fra Ranaldo that they should look after 40 goats for the period of one year, and on an equal share basis. Pasturing of the livestock was to be at Donna Buonafemmina and Assaltino's expense. On re-consigning the goats at the end of the year's contract, Donna Buonafemmina and Assaltino were to be paid 100 *soldi*. No mention was made of the way in which they might be accommodated following the expiry of this agreement.

This record is interesting not least for the light it throws on the involvement of women as goatherds. Clearly, this kind of work was not the province of men only, whether young, able bodied, or elderly. Nor was it only young women who were employed. Donna Buonafemmina was clearly already elderly, not because she was described as a widow, but because Assaltino her grandson was already old enough to be included in the contract. It seems in fact that Donna Buonafemmina's own son Petruccio had already been dead for some years at the time of the 1308 contract.

The deal arranged between Fra Ranaldo and Donna Buonafemmina and her grandson is also illuminating in terms of the extent to which business transactions during the early modern period not only involved third parties, but also frequently depended on the passing on of previous liabilities or debts: a fact often not revealed by the survival of one sole record. The 1308 record is significant for the light it throws on the complex nature of such agreements. Often what on the surface appeared to be a simple and one-off transaction, was in fact linked to and motivated by a number of other, apparently unrelated factors. As we shall see, the agreement with Donna Buonafemmina and her grandson involved a number of complex and interrelated financial calculations.

On the face of it, Buonafemmina and Assaltino in assuming responsibility as goatherds not only stood to gain in kind, benefiting from half of the produce from the livestock (including milk, cheese and wool), but also financially from the sale (if allowed, and even if not, then clandestinely) of any new animals born to the herd. They were also to be paid a lump sum for their labours at the end of the year. At the same time, and as a result of the sale of the family house inside the walls of Sant'Angelo in Colle, Buonafemmina and Assaltino obtained a large amount of ready money. Moreover, they were not left homeless, since the terms of the sale allowed them to continue to live in their property, albeit paying an annual rent. In the short-term Buonafemmina and Assaltino clearly stood to gain financially. The selling price of the house was recorded as 34 *lire*. The annual rent was to amount to 40 *soldi* – the equivalent of 2 *lire*. At the end of the year they were thus left with over 30 *lire* in hand – potentially the equivalent of 15 years' rent. In addition, at the end of their year as goatherds they were to receive a further 100 *soldi* – the equivalent of the combined salaries of two low-grade workers in the city, and more than enough to cover both the cost of future rent and their own living expenses. The cost of pasturing the animals was not recorded, but the immediate monetary advantages of this deal must have been obvious. Moreover, the combined terms of the sale of the house and the agreement concerning the pasturing and care of the goats meant that short-term outgoings were relatively low. On paper, it would seem that problems could only have arisen at the end of the year's contract, if the agreements concerning the care of the livestock and the renting of the family home were not renewed. If that were to happen, Buonafemmina and Assaltino could find that they were homeless, and, in the absence of further employment, unable to find accommodation elsewhere. This may indeed have been a common situation where individuals lurched from a state of comparative financial security to one in which they were forced to draw on their existing assets (in many cases in the form of living accommodation and or land), in order to cover ongoing living expenses, pay off outstanding debts and/or support new initiatives. In the case of Buonafemmina and Assaltino there were, in addition, a number of other associated issues.

Although the surviving record concerning the business transactions between Fra Ranaldo and Donna Buonafemmina and Assaltino might appear to have offered immediate financial advantages to the grandmother and her grandson, their situation was in reality deeply compromised by previous events. It appears that Buonafemmina and her family had been in financial difficulties prior to 1308 as a result of an earlier loan taken out by Buonafemmina and her son, Petruccio. A record dated 2 February 1305 refers to a sum of 24 *lire* that had been lent (but which had not apparently been repaid) to Petruccio di Assalto, his wife Gemma and his mother Buonafemmina by Nerio di Guicciardo and Ciampolino di Ciardino di Tiaro da Civitella di Ardinghesca.[32] According to this record, Nerio (presumably the Neri di Guicciardo who assumed such a high profile in the affairs of Sant'Angelo in Colle during the early fourteenth century) and Ciampolino invested Fra Ranaldo 'of the order of Saint Augustine in Siena' with full powers to resolve the issue. In the meantime Fra Ranaldo is recorded as repaying the outstanding debt. Fra Ranaldo in his turn thus needed to extract the outstanding sum of 24 *lire* from Petruccio di Assalto and his family. The 1308 transaction was in all probability connected with this.

The circumstances surrounding the previous loan remain unclear. It is not impossible, however, that Petruccio and his family had agreed to work land belonging to Neri di Guicciardo and his business partner Ciampolino, or that they had already been involved with the care and pasturing of livestock belonging to the Augustinians in Siena. The fact that the money was lent not only to Petruccio, but also to his wife and mother, would seem to favour the hypothesis that several members of the family had already been engaged as shepherds and/or goatherds by at least one of the parties named in the documents. If this were the case, the sheep or goats may have belonged not to the Augustinians in Siena but to the two Sienese 'outsiders', although the loan of 24 *lire* could have been required to cover the costs associated with the care and pasturing of the flocks. In any event, the debt was clearly long standing, since Petruccio di Assalto is already described as dead in 1300. It also seems likely that he left behind a number of other debts. According to a record dated 29 July 1300, Buonafemmina (already a widow) and Assaltino (already described as 'son of the deceased Petruccio') had resorted to the sale of a piece of land at Sesta to the convent and friars of Sant'Agostino in Siena.[33] The fact that this land was sold, rather than left to the religious community in Siena in the form of a legacy indicates that Petruccio's heirs needed money. The fact that the land was purchased by the Augustinians may also explain why Fra Ranaldo of the same order was subsequently drawn into the dispute arising from the outstanding debt to Neri di Guicciardo and Ciampolino. The sale of the land at Sesta may even have been a disguised form of repayment of a previous loan. Petruccio's assets in the form of landed property may in fact have been considerable. Even if the land at Sesta was the only plot inherited by Petruccio's heirs, it was in itself a considerable asset, since it was apparently sold for the comparatively high sum of 100 *lire*. It must thus either have been an extensive plot, or prime arable or pasture land.

Ownership of a large plot of land at Sesta must have invested Petruccio di Assalto and his family with considerable status. Entries in the 1320 *Tavola delle possessioni* concerning land at Sesta refer for the most part to comparatively small plots of arable land measuring around 6 *staia* and ranging in value between 3 to 11 *lire*.[34] A few, and clearly much larger plots are, however, recorded as valued between 30 and 90 or so *lire*.[35] One, a piece of arable land lying fallow that belonged to the Pieve at Sesta and measured 65 *staia* was estimated at the extraordinarily high value of 477 *lire*.[36] Nearby, a piece of arable land that was about a third of the size was recorded at less than a quarter of that value, at 94 *lire*.[37] Perhaps significantly, this latter plot was recorded as being bordered on one side by land belonging to Fra Ranaldo. The same individual is mentioned as a neighbour of arable belonging to Lando di Pepe in the adjoining area known as the 'Oliveto di Sesta'.[38] It seems from this that not only the Augustinian community but also one of their officials, Fra Ranaldo, were well established in the eastern part of Sant'Angelo in Colle's territory by the end of the second decade of the fourteenth century.

A further somewhat curious conclusion to be drawn from such details is that uncultivated arable land to the east of the village was on occasion valued at a higher rate than land that was being worked. There may have been sound ecological and economic reasons for this. There can be little doubt that there were powerful arguments in favour of operating a rotation system, not least from the point of view of not overworking the land and ploughing back richness into the earth. Land lying fallow also opened up possibilities for the pasturing of livestock, with all the associated benefits in kind. From a purely practical point of view, also, the manure produced by sheep, cows and goats in turn enriched the ground, preparing it for future cultivation. Pasturing thus constituted an essential part of agricultural life. Petruccio di Assalto and his family, far from being dispossessed or miserably poor, may thus have contributed significantly to the village's prosperity through the ownership of a large strip of pastureland on the eastern side of the territory. Nevertheless, natural setbacks, such as inclement weather, illness and simple overstretching of available funds could inhibit the repayment of loans. Outstanding debts could, in turn, have wide ranging consequences.

The fact that in 1308 (and in the wake of the failure to repay the previous loan) Petruccio's heirs resorted to the sale of a house inside the walls of Sant'Angelo in Colle whilst at the same time undertaking to look after livestock that presumably belonged either to Fra Ranaldo or to the Augustinian community is surely no coincidence. This may have been the only way in which the family could pay off the earlier debt. It was no doubt a neat solution also for Fra Ranaldo, for in that way he regained some of the money he had paid on the family's behalf to two of Petruccio's creditors in the form of rent. At the same time he was able, as agent of the Augustinian community in Siena, to tie the family into a contractual obligation concerning the welfare of either his own livestock or that belonging to the Sienese community of Sant'Agostino. In one sense the grandmother and the grandson would pay off the debt through their own toils. It is even possible that the goats were pastured on the same plot of land at Sesta that Petruccio's family had been forced to sell in 1300. If that were the case, Buonafemmina and Assaltino may also have avoided having to pay pasture levies, since both the land and the livestock would have belonged to the same religious entity. Quite apart from this, with the sale of the family house Buonafemmina and her grandson would have acquired a sum of money that could cover the debt paid on their behalf by Fra Ranaldo, whilst at the same time leaving the family with a chunk of money for their immediate expenses.

Many other individuals associated with Sant'Angelo in Colle may have found themselves in similar circumstances, at one time owning property inside the village, but being forced to sell it to cover the repayment of debt, but nevertheless retaining some rights over the property through rental agreements. Contemporaneously, they could have entered into arrangements concerning the pasturing and care of livestock on land that likewise may once have belonged to them, but was then sold to a third party in similar resolution of outstanding debts.

One other surviving contract dealing with the pasturing of livestock in the vicinity of Sant'Angelo in Colle appears, by contrast, to have concerned a resident who not only possessed land of his own, but also owned property inside the walls of the village. This record is also significant for the light it throws on the obligations and responsibilities assumed by the respective parties. On 22 March 1322/3, in the presence of two witnesses from Montalcino – Ser Guillielmo Fructi and Ser Accursio di Ser Maffeo – Minuccio di Sozzo 'of Sant'Angelo in Colle' agreed to a contract of two years with Binduccio di Bindo and Bonino Scholaiuolo concerning the pasturing and care of a huge number of sheep and goats.[39] The entire consignment consisted of 118 sheep and rams, and 37 goats and billy goats. Binduccio and Bonino had contributed two-thirds of the livestock, and Minuccio the remaining third. According to the agreement, which was drawn up by the Montalcinese lawyer, Ser Griffo di Ser Paolo, the onus for caring for the livestock was to fall on Minuccio di Sozzo. He was also to take 50 per cent of the proceeds. The other 50 per cent was to be shared equally between Binduccio and Bonino. It was agreed that Minuccio di Sozzo should pasture the livestock in any of the pasturelands owned by him, but he was on no account to subcontract the pasturing to a third party. By the terms of the same agreement Minuccio was also expected to look after the livestock and protect them in every way from 'all people'. Such stipulations were no doubt included not only to ensure that Minuccio assumed responsibility for the watering and feeding of the livestock, but also so that he should make every effort to safeguard the sheep and goats against animal predators as well as protecting them from human marauders.

Although specific reference to Sant'Angelo in Colle is made in the case of Minuccio di Sozzo, no such explanations are given in respect of Binduccio di Bindo and Bonino Scholaiuolo. In fact, it seems likely that at least one, if not both of those individuals were resident in Montalcino in 1323. Binduccio di Bindo is certainly described as a citizen of Montalcino in January 1327/8 when he is referred to in the context of a debt owed by him and Binduccio di Nerio of Sant'Angelo in Colle to the Sienese citizen, Lando di Tolomeo.[40] And several years before the agreement drawn up with Minuccio di Sozzo, a Binduccio Bindi was referred to as 'sindaco', or mayor, of Montalcino.[41]

Minuccio di Sozzo for his part does appear in the 1320 *Tavola delle possessioni* for Sant'Angelo in Colle.[42] According to his entry there, he owned six pieces of land in the vicinity of the village, as well as a modestly sized house (valued at 31 *lire* and 7 *soldi*) inside the walls. His overall patrimony in 1320 was estimated at 149 *lire* and 13 *soldi*. Like Petruccio di Assalto, Minuccio di Sozzo was thus clearly neither dispossessed nor poor. His land, a mixture of agricultural, vineyards and terrain lying fallow, ranged in size from small plots measuring two to three *staio*, to a much larger one at Montegiano that covered an area of

23 *staio*, and was estimated at the relatively high sum of 51 *lire* and 7 *soldi* – virtually a third of Minuccio's entire patrimony. Significantly, this latter plot was described as partially worked and partially fallow. Such terrain would clearly have offered opportunities for the pasturing of a comparatively large flock of sheep and herd of goats. This could well have influenced Binduccio and Bonino in their choice of Minuccio di Sozzo as a partner in the business of rearing livestock in the vicinity of Sant'Angelo in Colle. There must have been many other situations where partially worked land, or terrain lying fallow offered similar opportunities. Indeed, business partnerships in this field may have depended as much on the availability of uncultivated land for pasturing, as the personal needs or financial circumstances of the individual assuming the role of shepherd.

The agreement drawn up between Minuccio di Sozzo and Binduccio di Bindo and Bonino Scholaiuolo is also significant in the context of the political climate. In 1323 Montalcino and its citizens were not finally drawn within the Sienese net. In effect, therefore, Minuccio di Sozzo could have been seen as fraternising with the enemy. Nor was this agreement the only one of its kind drawn up between residents of the two communes before the people of Montalcino were offered full Sienese citizenship in 1361. In October 1353 Pietro 'del fu Neri di Cacciato' (son of the deceased Neri di Cacciato) of Montalcino drew up an agreement with Vannuccio 'of Sant'Angelo in Colle', whereby the latter agreed to look after a house with a vineyard and land as well as two olive groves in the vicinity of the southern frontier castle.[43] Clearly, business transactions continued between the two centres despite the uneasy relationship existing between Siena and Montalcino during the first half of the fourteenth century.

To conclude. While internal family arrangements, formal share cropping contracts and various transactions concerning shepherding and pasturing may thus account for some of the apparently homeless of Sant'Angelo in Colle in 1320, it seems clear that such divisions of labour were not necessarily fuelled by the socio-economic circumstances of the various individuals. Practical factors such as a continuing farming activity within one branch of a family, ownership of contiguous plots, or merely the availability of land itself could be equally influential. The lack of reference to living accommodation may also have resulted from an individual's age or sex. As Table 3.6 shows, a considerable number of those recorded as owning no property inside the walls of Sant'Angelo in Colle were defined as heirs. While they may thus have inherited a family home, they may not yet have reached the age of maturity, and may thus have figured in the *Tavola delle possessioni* only in terms of their deceased relation. It is also relevant that several of those recorded as owning no living accommodation in the 1320 *Tavola delle possessioni* for Sant'Angelo in Colle were women. Some of these may have had access to living accommodation within their natal families. Others may have lived with spouses. Some of them could have become involved in sharecropping agreements drawn up by their male relatives, and thus have been accommodated in premises belonging to an employer.

But as the example of Donna Buonfemmina has shown, it would be a mistake to dismiss women as playing little part in the life or welfare of early fourteenth-century Sant'Angelo in Colle. Quite apart from working the land, or curing and storing its produce, it seems that many *contadine*, or peasant women, became involved in the processing of wool and weaving, and thus the working of cloth.[44] Gabriella Piccinni also makes the significant point that it was the women who were mostly engaged in making cheese.[45] Cloth and cheese, as we have seen, formed a significant part of the produce assembled in the *grancia* of Santa Maria della Scala towards the end of the fourteenth century, before onward transit from Sant'Angelo in Colle to Siena. Quite apart from transactions drawn up between such individuals as Fra Ranaldo and the family of Petruccio di Assalto, the extensive business activities of the Sienese grange may thus have brought particular benefits to the women of Sant'Angelo in Colle. While those individuals may have been involved in cheese making and the spinning of yarn for decades, and even centuries before the foundation of the Sienese grange in the village, such activities must by necessity have been limited to a fairly local market. With the investment in land in the vicinity of Sant'Angelo in Colle, and the establishment of the Sienese hospital's first *domus* inside the walls, that local market was set for diversification and development. In the face of the increasing involvement of Santa Maria della Scala and the physical expansion of its headquarters in Sant'Angelo in Colle towards the of the fourteenth century, the market for such local goods clearly expanded exponentially.[46]

Although individual peasant women associated with early fourteenth-century Sant'Angelo in Colle probably received little money for their pains or their produce, and should thus most naturally be placed in the category of 'the poor', and in many cases also of 'the dispossessed', their work was nevertheless hugely important. Not only did they contribute to the continued well-being of the local population, but as members of a female work force associated with the hospital of Santa Maria della Scala they helped to maintain citizens in Siena. Thus, while it was no doubt the norm that the women of the village, and in particular those associated with the working of the land, or the pasturing of livestock were regarded as having little social significance, many of them may in fact have contributed significantly to the village's finances. Their labours, as much as those of their menfolk, must have influenced the village's ability to pay the dues levied from them as a subject commune.

As we shall see, one or two of the women associated with the early fourteenth-century village of Sant'Angelo in Colle not only appear to have held land in their own right, but also to have owned the family house. The next chapter will attempt to show that, far from being dispossessed or poor, these women had sufficient assets to contribute independently to the welfare of the village. Moreover, being sufficiently rich in their own right, they must also have acquired a considerable profile in local affairs.

Notes

1 For the production of wine and olive oil in the territory of Montalcino during the early modern period, with associated bibliography, see Alfio Cortonesi, 'La vita e l'olivo nelle campagne di Montalcino (secoli 13–15)', in Alfio Cortonesi (ed.), *La Val d'Orcia nel medioevo e nei primi secoli dell'età moderna*, Atti del Convegno internazionale di studi storici, Pienza, 15–18 settembre 1988 (Rome, 1990), pp. 189–212.

2 For a survey of the social structure of communities in the Sienese *contado* under the government of the Nine, see Andrea Barlucchi, *Il 'Contado' Senese all'epoca dei Nove', Asciano e il suo territorio tra Due e Trecento* (Florence, 1997), p. 49 and especially Appendix VII, pp. 295–301. According to Barlucchi, it was commonly the case for about 30% of the population to have patrimonies of between 100 and 500 *lire*. It was also more often than not the case that some 60% fell in the category of having patrimonies lower than 100 *lire*. Those with patrimonies of between 500 and 1,000 *lire* amounted, if at all, to some five or seven percent of the population, whereas those with patrimonies of over 1,000 *lire* rarely rose above three or four percent. See also Giovanni Cherubini, 'Proprietari, contadini e campagne senesi all' inizio del Trecento', in *idem* (ed.), *Signori, contadini, borghesi. Ricerche sulla società Italiana del Basso Medioevo* (Florence, 1974), pp. 241–42, 248, 252 and 286–87 for a consideration of patrimonies recorded for Sienese residents and institutions during the same period, and a comparison between these and those recorded for peasant proprietors. According to Cherubini, most of the patrimonies recorded in respect of Sienese residents exceeded 200 *lire*, although in the area around San Donato di sotto, where there were a large number of craftsmen, the average patrimony was in the region of 177 or 178 *lire*. In this context, an insight into average working salaries and the cost of daily necessities is offered by Silvana Balbi di Caro and Gabriella Angeli Bufalini, in *idem*, 'Uomini e Monete in terra di Siena', in *La Collezione Numismatica della Banca Monte dei Paschi di Siena* (Pisa, 2001), pp. 30–133. Street workers engaged in the construction of a street in the borgo S. Maria in Siena in 1324 could expect, for example, to receive a daily salary ranging between 4 and 12 *soldi*. The highest annual salary a low-grade worker might therefore expect to receive would have been in the region of 40 or 50 *lire*. Balbi de Ciao and Bufalini also consider the cost of bread and the average percentage of salary that might have to be expended on this very basic daily necessity. From this, it emerges that a low grade worker, particularly in times of poor crops, might have had to spend as much as a quarter of his annual earnings solely in order to provide himself and his family with enough grain.

3 See Table 3.6.

4 A detailed consideration of the part played by absentee Sienese landlords in the early fourteenth century village follows in Chapter 6.

5 In his 'Un contratto per Siena: la mezzadria poderale', in Lucia Bonelli Conenna and Ettore Pacini (eds), *Vita in villa nel senese: dimore, giardini e fattoria* (Siena, c.2000), pp. 403–36 (409–10), Mario Ascheri cites evidence showing that a system of sharecropping was already established in medieval Tuscany a century earlier. He also refers to legislation drawn up in 1256 regarding the behaviour and conduct expected from the *mezzaiuolo* in looking after property belonging to other individuals.

6 For *mezzadria* and terms of contract during the medieval period, see the

extended bibliographical reference in footnote 22 of the Introduction. See also, Lucia Brunetti, 'L'Ospedale di monna Agnese di Siena e la sua Filiazione Romana', *Archivio della Società romana di storia patria*, 126 (2003), p. 40, and especially footnote 11, for the way in which institutions such as the Sienese hospital of Monna Agnese worked individual properties.

7   In this respect, see Gabrielle Cortonesi and Margherita Fontani, *Storia di un antico castello 'Suvvicille'*, Pro Loco Soviculle, (Siena, 2006), pp. 112–14. In one agreement drawn up in January 1262/3 some 13 or so plots of arable land, vineyards and olive groves in the vicinity of Sant'Angelo in Colle, as well as a farm house were handed over for management over a period of 10 years to Domenico di Cieto and his family.

8   See Giuliano Pinto and Paolo Pirillo, *Il Contratto di Mezzadria nella Toscana Medievale*. I, *Contado di Siena, sec. XIII-1348* (Florence, 1987), pp. 115–16, no. 67.

9   Archivio di Stato di Siena (hereafter ASS), *Estimo di Siena* 120, fol. CXXXVI, new no. 98.

10 ASS, *Estimo* 24, fols 362r–362v, where Neri's patrimony is estimated at 56 *lire* and 7 *soldi*.

11 Ibid., fol. 362v.

12 Pinto and Pirillo, *Il Contratto di Mezzadria*, pp. 207–8, no. 157.

13 While the term *capanna* seems to have been adopted in the context of quite rudimentary structures, it seems likely that it was also used on occasion (and perhaps in a deliberate attempt to avoid higher taxation) to describe a building that was closer to a farm house than a shack. In this context, see Gianfranco di Pietro, 'Per la storia dell'architettura della dimora rurale: alcune premesse di metodo', *Archeologia Medievale*, 7 (1980), pp. 343–61, and Maria Serena Mazzi, 'Arredi e masserizie della casa rurale nelle campagne fiorentine del 15 secolo', *Archeologia Medievale*, 7 (1980), pp. 137–52.

14 ASS, *Estimo* 24, fols 90r and 91r.

15 Ibid., fol. 199r.

16 Ibid., fols 449r–51v.

17 Ibid., fol. 268v.

18 For the function and local standing of such individuals in medieval society, see Barlucchi, *Il 'Contado' Senese all'epoca dei Nove*, pp. 134–37.

19 ASS, *Estimo* 24, fol. 268r.

20 Ibid., fol. 180r.

21 Ibid., fol. 449r.

22 Ibid., fol. 450v.

23 Ibid., fol. 266v.

24 ASS, *Diplomatico in Caselle, casella* 784, 28 March 1335, *Archivio Spedale*.

25 ASS, *Estimo* 24, fols 82r–83v.

26 Ibid., fols 380v and 82v.

27 Ibid., fols 342r–344v.

28 For the involvement of the Hospital of Santa Maria della Scala, and in particular the role assumed by the *grancia* of Sant'Angelo in Colle in the pasturing and rearing of sheep and goats, see Stephan R. Epstein, *Alle origini della fattoria toscana. L'ospedale della Scala di Siena e le sue terre (metà '200 – metà '400)* (Florence, 1986), pp. 91–98.

29 ASS, *Diplomatico di Montalcino*, Busta 37 bis, no. 106.

30 For a number of agreements concerning pasturing and the care of sheep and goats in the early medieval period, see Viviana Persi, *Il registro del notaio senese Ugolino di Giunta Parisinus Latinus 4725 (1283–1287) alle origini dell'archivio della Casa misericordia di Siena* (Siena, 2008), nos 1, 17, 32, 100, 108, 164.

31 Archivio di Stato di Firenze, *Diplomatico 45, Montalcino*: S. Agostino, no. 22.

32 Ibid., no. 21.

33 Ibid., no. 14.

34 See, for example, ASS, *Estimo* 24, fols 19r and 20v.

35 Ibid., fols 104r, 124r and 176v.

36 Ibid., fol. 385r.

37 Ibid., fol. 197r.

38 Ibid., fol. 266r.

39 Archivio Storico del Comune di Montalcino (hereafter ACM), *Fondi diversi, Archivi di Particolari, Ser Griffo di ser Paolo*, Imbreviature 3–4 (hereafter *Griffo di ser Paolo*), (3), fols 74r–74v.

40 ACM, *Griffo di Ser Paolo*, 4, fol. 66v.

41 ASS, *Diplomatico*, 40 (Comune di Montalcino, (spoglio parziale) *Diplomatico*, 29 November 1243 – 14 February 1408), 11 January 1310.

42 ASS, *Estimo* 24, fols 292r–292v.

43 ACM, *Ospedale Santa Maria della Croce*, 154.

44 In this context, see Gabriella Piccinni, 'Per uno studio del lavoro delle donne nelle campagne: considerazioni dell'Italia medievale', in Simonetta Cavaciocchi (ed.), *La Donna nell'Economia secc. 13–18*, Atti della 'Ventunesima Settimana di Studi', Prato, 10–15 aprile 1989, (Prato, 1990), pp. 71–81 (73). See also Giovanni Cherubini, 'Proprietari, contadini e campagne senesi all' inizio del Trecento', in idem (ed.), *Signori, contadini, borghesi. Ricerche sulla società Italiana del Basso Medioevo* (Florence, 1974), p. 40.

45 Piccinni, 'Per uno studio del lavoro delle donne', p. 75. For the production of cheese during the medieval period, see Irma Naso, 'La Produzione casearia europea in un trattato del tardo medioevo', in *Cultura e società nell'Italia medievale: studi per Paolo Brezzi* (2 vols, Rome, 1988), 2, pp. 585–604.

46 In this context it is also worth noting that the production of cheese could also have been boosted in September and May of each year by the transit of herds of livestock along *transumanza* routes in the vicinity of Sant'Angelo in Colle. See Natalino Paone, *La Transumanza, Immagini di una civiltà* (Isernia, 1987), pp. 46–47. Such passage may also have boosted the local population of shepherds. According to Giuliano Guerrini, as late as the twentieth century, several of those involved in the seasonal driving of livestock along

the Orcia to the Maremma sought permanent jobs as shepherds in and around Sant'Angelo in Colle, once the *transumanza* was completed. In doing so they may well have been following previous traditions and patterns of employment.

5

Widows, Wives, Spinsters and Daughters: Poor Relations or Women with Prospects?

Attention turns in this chapter to a number of property-owning women in early fourteenth-century Sant'Angelo in Colle, in an attempt to establish which, if any, of the female members of the population might best be classified as 'women with prospects', as opposed to 'poor relations'. Nearly 50 entries in the 1320 *Tavola delle possessioni* for Sant'Angelo in Colle – some one sixth of the entries recorded there – were filed in respect of women.[1] In some cases it is clear that the woman was married. Thus, there are references to Domina Nuta 'uxor Ciaffi', Domina Rosa 'uxor Futii', Domina Rosa di Piero 'uxor Minutii Banduccii' and Vinitiana 'uxor Guidarelli'.[2] In one instance, that of Domina Cellina, it also becomes clear that the woman had been married but was at that date widowed, since her entry contains a reference to her dead husband, Micheluccio.[3] In the majority of cases, however, no reference was made to the woman's marital state. It would seem from this that the early fourteenth-century population consisted of a considerable number of property-owning spinsters who had reached the age of maturity, but who had not yet engaged in matrimony, or had long since been widowed.[4]

Few of the patrimonies declared in respect of women in the 1320 *Tavola delle possessioni* are large, most falling between less than 10 and 50 or so *lire*. Moreover, where a living house was declared, its value often tended to fall at the lower end of the scale. More than a third of the properties listed in respect of women were valued at less than 20 *lire*.

Proprietor	Lire	soldi	denari
Beccha Tini (Cini)	86	7	-
Becchina Berti	20	-	-
Berna Ghezzi	178	18	6
Benvenuta Ghezzi	42	13	-
Bosta Michelucci	78	5	6
Becchina Lentti	13	10	-
Bella Lamberti	9	13	-
Ceccha Guidi	20	-	-

Table 5.1 Patrimonies declared in respect of the women of Sant'Angelo in Colle in the 1320 *Tavola delle possessioni*[1]

Ciana Guidarelli	21	13	-
Ciellina Niccholucci	14	16	-
Ceccha Bononis	34	-	-
D(omi)na Rosa Pieri pecoraio	1	18	-
D(omi)na Nuta uxor Ciaffi	13	19	-
D(omi)na Rosa uxor Futii	270	17	-
D(omi)na Tessina Peruzzi	15	-	-
D(omi)na Cellina uxor d(omin)i Micchelutii	21	7	6
Fatuiola Maffei (Maffuccii)	57	13	-
Gratia Ugolini	187	1	-
Mon(n)a Neccha nigozzantis	128	16	-
Mon(n)a Scholai	18	18	6
Mon(n)a Gem(m)a Accorsi	11	7	-
Mon(n)a Beccha Ser Francisci	6	17	-
Mon(n)a Mita Baldiccionis	5	12	-
Mon(n)a Gioia	50	12	9
Mita Tora (Torrci)	123	18	-
Mina Maffutii	39	-	-
Maffuccia Benciven(n)is	97	14	-
Mita Brunacci	27	8	-
Mita Nerii	10	7	-
Mo(?e)ldina Guidarelli	13	7	-
Mon(n)a Lucia Guidi	7	14	-
Mina Giannis	5	7	-
Mon(n)a Mita Pieri	318	2	3
Mon(n)a Duccia Cioli	63	13	-
Mon(n)a Neccha Venture	54	-	-
Mon(n)a Mita Minucci[2]	3	4	-
Mon(n)a Mita Minucci	4	9	-
Mutia Gionte	4	2	6
Mon(n)a Jacomina Sozzi	26	17	-
Mon(n)a Becca Petrini	17	7	-
Nuta Sozzi	27	-	-
Nuta Nuccii	4	2	-
Necchina Ture	2	16	-
Neccha Brunacci	15	-	-
Novellaria (Novellina) Bini	75	19	6
Pia Farolfi	64	4	-
Tessina Lasie (Lascie)	7	2	-
Vina Morelli (Moregli) (Meglioregli)	19	19	-
Vinitiana uxor Guidarolli (Guidarelli)	9	10	-

Notes to Table 5.1

1 The Latinate form of names as they appear in the index to *Estimo* 24 is retained here for easy cross-reference to page numbers.

2 There are two entries for Mona Mita, see *Estimo* 24, cc. 334r–335r.

Proprietor	Lire	soldi	denari
Beccha Tini (Cini)	39	7	-
Berna Ghezzi	100	-	-
Benvenuta Ghezzi	42	13	-
Bosta Michelucci	24	13	-
Bella Lamberti	9	13	-
Ceccha Guidi	20	-	-
Ciana Guidarelli	21	13	-
D(omi)na Rosa uxor Futii	26	-	-
Fatuiola Maffei (Maffuccii)[2]	16	13	-
	15	-	-
Gratia Ugolini	25	-	-
Mon(n)a Neccha nigozzantis[3]	12	-	-
	4	17	-
Mon(n)a Gem(m)a Accorsi[4]	11	7	-
Mon(n)a Gioia	39	7	-
Mita Tora (Torrci)	76	7	-
Maffuccia Benciven(n)is	43	-	-
Mita Brunacci	23	13	-
Mo(?e)ldina Guidarelli	13	7	-
Mon(n)a Mita Pieri	22	-	-
Mon(n)a Duccia Cioli[5]	63	13	-
Mon(n)a Neccha Venture	48	-	-
Nuta Sozzi	27	-	-
Neccha Brunacci	15	-	-
Novellaria (Novellina) Bini[6]	19	7	-
	16	13	-
Vina Morelli (Moregli) (Meglioregli)	17	7	-

Table 5.2   Recorded value of living houses declared on behalf of the female residents of Sant'Angelo in Colle in the 1320 *Tavola delle possessioni*[1]

Notes to Table 5.2

1   The Latinate form of names as they appear in the index to *Estimo* 24 is retained here for easy cross-reference to page numbers.
2   This individual owned two properties, one of which is described as bordered on one side by the walls of the village.
3   One of these properties is described as an 'ortale cu(m) domo' (an orchard with a house) in the 'loco S(an)c(t)i Petri'. The other is described as a 'casalinu(m)' (small house) on the 'costa S(an)c(t)i Ang(e)li'.
4   This property is described as 'qua(n)da(m) platea(m) cu(m) quodam casalino' (an erstwhile building plot with an erstwhile small house) on the 'costa S(an)c(t)i Ang(e)li'.
5   Described as 'domu(m) cu(m) platea' (house with building plot).
6   One of these two properties is said to have bordered property belonging to Monna Gemma Accorsi, and the other to have bordered property belonging to Fatuiola Maffei. No reference is made to Novellina in the entries for Monna Gemma or Fatuiola.

If such properties constituted the only living accommodation, it would appear that a sizeable number of single women in the early fourteenth-century village – whether spinsters or widows – lived in fairly modest circumstances, if not actually on the borderline of poverty. In fact, the majority of the women listed in the 1320 *Tavola delle possessioni* seem not to have possessed any living accommodation of their own, even though in some instances they are recorded as owning several pieces of land. While their individual patrimonies may have indicated that they were women with prospects, their actual physical state must therefore have been one of dependency.

The initial conclusion to be drawn from a consideration of the women of Sant'Angelo in Colle as revealed by entries in the 1320 *Tavola delle possessioni* is that most of them were in effect poor relations, living for the most part in property inside the walls that belonged to other people – namely husbands, fathers, brothers, sons and other male relatives – or (as previous discussion has indicated) in property rented out to them inside the walls by neighbours or absentee landlords. Some women belonging to land-working families may also (as previous discussion has also indicated) have lived in family properties outside the walls of the village, or in properties belonging to their sharecropping landlords.

It quickly becomes clear, however, that although individual entries in the 1320 *Tavola delle possessioni* may provide an insight into the financial circumstances of the female residents of early fourteenth-century Sant'Angelo in Colle, they only offer a partial picture. There must have been many women in Sant'Angelo in Colle – including young girls, spinsters, wives, widows and aged women – who were in fact consigned to obscurity because they owned no living accommodation or land, and were thus not included in a document drawn up for the purpose of taxation of property. In those cases where a married woman had no property of her own to declare, there was obviously no reason why her name should be included in the 1320 *Tavola delle possessioni*, since her husband would have been identified as owner of the family's real estate, and thus the individual to be noted for the purpose of taxation. Many spinsters sheltered within the confines of their natal families and owning no real estate would in the same way have been excluded from such records as the *Tavole delle possessioni*. Likewise, a widow, unless able to maintain an independent existence or remaining within the orbit of her deceased husband's family, would in all likelihood have had to rejoin her natal family, and thus fallen into the same category as the married woman with no real estate or the female not yet independent.

This does not mean that individual units of living accommodation or landed property remained unaccounted for. As already noted, it was sometimes the case that when a woman's husband died, she relinquished property previously held for her by her spouse by passing it on to surviving heirs on her husband's side of the family. Where a house or plot of land had originally formed part of the woman's dowry, ownership often also reverted to her own natal family. It was then that family's responsibility not only to protect the widow and her property, but also to file relevant details of her patrimony in their own tax declarations. On occasion, the widow was able to retain control of property previously held by her and/or her husband. This was particularly the case when there were no heirs on her husband's side to dispute her claims. In such cases, the widow might also continue to live independently in what was previously the family home, albeit often in reduced circumstances. The same could apply if a woman inherited property directly from her father.

Although it was generally the case that family possessions were passed down through the male line, there is evidence in at least one instance in the 1320 *Tavola delle possessioni* for Sant'Angelo in Colle of property being handed down to a daughter. Detailed consideration is given here to one such instance, that involving Mita di Piero. The fact nevertheless remains, that where an unmarried woman acquired property through inheritance, her name would not have been included in the *Tavola delle possessioni* until or unless she had reached the age of majority and/or was semi-independent of her natal family, under the care of some third party. In many instances the woman's identity and in particular the precise details of property owned by her could remain hidden under the general title of 'heir', or indeed under the name of a male relative. Establishing the precise number of women in the early fourteenth-century village is thus virtually impossible for the modern historian. Quite apart from the impediments outlined above, aged women (whether widows or spinsters) would necessarily have been confined to the shadows of their fireside places, whereas immature girls (being exempt from taxation until they reached the age of majority, and certainly not in any position to own property of their own as minors) must have flitted unrecorded from one space to another in any number of households, defying even perhaps at that period any attempts at an accurate census of the population.

Despite the obvious gaps in the 1320 *Tavola delle possessioni*, a number of points can, nevertheless, be made. It was not the case that all unmarried women in the early fourteenth-century village lived in mean little houses. At least a handful of the spinsters of the early fourteenth-century village appear to have owned houses inside the walls that were far from small. Mona Duccia di Ciole, or Ciolio, for example, is recorded as owning a house valued at 63 *lire*, 13 *soldi*.[5] Mona Necca di Ventura, for her part, owned a house valued at 48 *lire*.[6] Another apparently unmarried woman, Maffuccia di Bencivenne, owned what was probably a similarly sized house to that of Mona Necca di Ventura, since it was valued at the only slightly lower figure of 43 *lire*.[7] Another spinster, Benvenuta di Ghezzo, declared what must have been only a slightly smaller house than those owned by Necca and Maffuccia, since hers was valued at 42 *lire*, 13 *soldi*.[8] Slightly further down the scale, but nevertheless still within the category of a reasonably sized building, we find a reference to a house belonging to Mona Gioia that was valued at 39 *lire*, 7 *soldi*.[9] None of the properties listed in the range of 30 or 50 or so *lire* can have been particularly small. That belonging to Mona Duccia di Ciole must have been fairly substantial. A number of other women are recorded as owning even larger houses. Mita Tora, for example, appears to have owned one of the larger houses in the village, since it was valued at 76 *lire* 7 *soldi*.[10] Mita Tora also owned a considerable amount of worked agricultural land as well as a vineyard. Berna Ghezzi appears to have owned an even larger house that was valued at 100 *lire*.[11] Some of the other women also possessed several plots of land in the surrounding countryside. Becca di Cino (or Tino), for example, as well as owning a house valued at nearly 40 *lire*, was also the owner of three pieces of worked agricultural land, and a vineyard.

It was certainly not the case, therefore, that all the women in the early fourteenth-century village fell into a category of poverty or dependency. Moreover, while most of the patrimonies listed for women in the 1320 *Tavola delle possessioni* were comparatively modest, a number stand out as being above the average. Becca di Cino's recorded patrimony was, for example, 85 *lire*, 6 *soldi*.[12] Maffuccia di Bencivenne's patrimony was even higher, at 97 *lire*, 14 *soldi*.[13] Mita Tora's recorded patrimony was higher again, at 123 *lire*, 18 *soldi*. Four other women (Berna Ghezzi, Gratia Ugolini, Domina Rosa, wife of Futii and Mona Mita Pieri, wife of Minutii Banducci) are recorded as having patrimonies of between 178 and 318, or so *lire*. In such cases it seems inappropriate to speak of 'poor relations'. These were clearly individuals of some means, and, as such, not only capable of an independent existence, but also 'women with prospects'. As we shall see, a number of women seem not to have been reduced to a state of dependence either, even when married. Indeed, one or two of them clearly enjoyed considerable social status in their own right.

The two wealthiest women in the early fourteenth-century village were Domina Rosa, wife of Futio (or Fuccio) and Mona Mita di Piero, wife of Minuccio di Banduccio. Domina Rosa's patrimony was in the region of 270 *lire*, Mona Mita's, around 318 *lire*. Interestingly, both Rosa and Mita are recorded as owning houses in their own right. In at least one case, also, the husband seems not to have been socially equal to his wife, since his recorded patrimony was considerably lower. The identity of Domina Rosa's husband is not entirely clear. Only one man listed in the 1320 *Tavola delle possessioni* for Sant'Angelo in Colle carries the name Futio or Fuccio: Fuccius Andelonis. This individual is recorded as owning a piece of land with vines in the area known as Ferrale and an orchard with olives on the Costa di Sant'Angelo. His overall patrimony was 78 *lire* and 15 *soldi*.[14] Fuccius, or Fuccio di Andelone, also owned a small house inside the village walls. This structure, which was valued at 14 *lire* and 13 *soldi* is recorded as being bordered on one side by property belonging to Domina Gioia; on another by a road; and on a third side by property belonging to Gianni Lambertini. In none of the references to neighbouring property, is there any mention to Domina Rosa. According to Domina Rosa's entry, her house, which was valued at 26 *lire* was bordered on one side by road, on another by property belonging to the church of San Michele, and on a third side by property belonging to the commune.[15] It is possible, therefore, that Rosa di Fuccio's husband was not a resident of Sant'Angelo in Colle, and that Rosa's name was only included in the 1320 *Tavola delle possessioni* because of her own personal association with the village through ownership of property there.

By contrast, there seems little doubt that Mita di Piero's husband, Minuccio, was a local man. In the second of the two entries for Mita in the 1320 *Tavola delle possessioni* she is very definitely described as 'daughter of the deceased Piero' and currently the wife of Minuccio di Banduccio 'of Sant'Angelo'.[16] Mita's overall patrimony in this second entry was assessed at 237 *lire* and 3 *soldi*. In the first entry filed in Mita's name her overall patrimony was declared as 80 *lire*, 19 *soldi* and 7 *denari*.[17] As will become clear in the analysis of patrimonies recorded in respect of the male population in the next chapter, Mita di Piero's combined assets placed her on equal footing with some of the wealthier men in the early fourteenth-century village. She was in fact richer than the village notary of the period, Guccio di Ser Francesco, and Paganello di Giovanni, father of Giovanni di Paganello, village notary during the 1330s. On this basis alone, Mita di Piero must have been regarded as a leading member of the local society, even though she was apparently married to someone who was virtually penniless, and despite the fact that they were both apparently living in a rather small house.

The example of Mona Mita di Piero, even if an exception, would seem to contradict prevailing assumptions not only about the ownership of property by married women, but also about their perceived social status during the early modern period in Italy. Far from being penniless and dependent, Mita, even without her inherited property had a claim to some 14 or so *staia* of arable land, much of which also contained vines. As an heir, Mita experienced a threefold increase in her patrimony. She also gained control of over 10 times as much worked land and an area of woodland, the size of which was equalled only by that recorded in respect of the commune, the church of San Michele and the parish of Sant'Angelo in Colle.

Proprietor	Estimated size of plot in *staia* **and** *tabule*		Page number in ASS, *Estimo* 24
Avitolo di Ildibrandino	1		6r
Bernarduccio di Pietro	68		40r
Betto di Romaiuolo	38		15r
Bindo di Accorso	7 18 2 29	25 50	18r 20r 20v
Casino di Bino	38 1	 60	66r
Cecco di Bindo	9		84r
Cecco di Nuccio	9 16		87r
Cennino di Cenno	7		85r
Chele di Ruggiero	5		73r
Cola di Giovanni	17		68r

Table 5.3
Woodland declared in respect of local proprietors in Sant'Angelo in Colle, including the exceptional example of Mona Mita di Piero[1]

Comune di Sant'Angelo	100		58r
	40		
	46		
	400		
	38		58v
	6		
	60		
	20		59r
	16		60r
	7		61v
	2		62v
	3		
	1105		63r
Conte di Ventura	58		77r
Domenico di Brunaccio	8		113r
Domenico di Guido	6		118r
Donna Rosa di Piero Pecoraio	6		116r
Ecclesia di Sant'Angelo			
Ecclesia di Sant'Angelo	65		121r
	29		
	2		122r
	14		122v
	10		123v
	40		124v
	6		125r
	225		128r
Ecclesia di San Pietro	8	30	132v
	3		133v
Figlio di Lunardo	4		140r
	3		
Finuccio di Rannuccino	28		141r
Gratia di Ugolino	40		157r
Heirs of Altimanno	20		194r
Heirs of Banduccio	3		180r
	7	50	
Heirs of Berto di magistro Martino	27		234r
Heirs of Berto di Martino	2		219r
Heirs of Cecco di Franco	11		203v
Heirs of Cecco di Piero	8		176r
	23		
Heirs of Donna Becca	19	50	203r
	30		
Heirs of Franco	22		187v
	2		188v
	7		189r
Heirs of Gianni di Orlando	11	50	257r
Heirs di Gianni di Uguiccione	4		221r
Heirs of Guido di Colona	11	80	256r
Heirs of Guido di Schifalorzo	9		217r
	10		217v

Heirs of Micheluccio	6		223r
Heirs of Muccio	37		196r
Heirs of Nerio di Rubeo	2	15	206v
Heirs of Nerio di Ventura	13	50	238r
Heirs of Nigro di Montalcino	40		205 r
Heirs of Peruccio di Guillielmini	7		178r
Heirs of Piero Pecoraio	15		243r
Heirs of Romaiuolo	11	80	200r
Heirs of Ser Francesco	12 6		167r
Lando di Pepo	1	85	266v
Lonarduccio di Benvegnato	10		271r
Lucarino di Ser Francesco	4 18	80	268r 268v
Maffeo di Gennario	7	25	290r
Manno di Maffuccio	1 16 23	50	328r 328v 329r
Martinuccio di Martino	15		323r
Menchino di Lamberto	4		307r
Mino di Ser Guillelmi	75		320r
Mona Gioa	19 30	50	303r
Mona Mita di Minuccio	6	70	335r
Mona Mita di Piero	235		330r
Mona Necca di Venture	9		332r
Mona Scolaia	10	40	284r
Naccino di Giordanello	10		355r
Necchina di Tura	6		359r
Nino di Giovanni	8	60	342r
Novellina di Bino	1 8 6 9	50 85	367r 367v
Nucciarello di Ranerio	17		357r
Ospedale di Sant'Angelo	5	50	193r
Paolo di Nerio di Rubeo	6	40	391r
Parrocchia di Sant'Angelo	120 110 22 9	 50	374r 374v
Petrino di Nerio	6	40	382r
Petruccio di Bonanno	90 14 3 22		376r
Petruccio di Piero	10	50	379r
Pietro di Bindo da Montalcino	6		386r
Ristoruccio di Borgognone	5	72	397r

Ristoruccio di Vitale	17		395r
Salito di Orlando	11	50	411r
Scolaio di Giannello	66		401v
	13		402v
Ser Guccio di Ser Francesco	35		449r
	2	80	451r
Sozzo di Giacomo	56		405r
Sozzo di Mainetto	5	30	409r
Tura di Manno	6		453r
Tura di Morello	14		419r
Ulivuccio di Giovanni	2	50	431r
Vannuccio di Massaio	2		440v
	10		441r
Vinuccio di Ciampolo	12		436r
	3		436v
Viviano di Mende	38		424r
	20		

Note to Table 5.3

1 All in all some three thousand and seventy *staia* of land in the territory of Sant'Angelo in Colle was
   given over to trees in 1320. However, not all of the plots recorded in the 1320 *Tavola delle possessioni*
   consisted of pure woodland. Some are recorded as also containing arable land (as, for example, the
   areas known as Campaia, [?Campane or ?Capraia], Campo Giovanni, Capanne [?Capine], Capanelli,
   Costa Carbonelle, Fossatellus del Cuoio [?Fossatello Alcoi], Fossato Capraia, Fossato Rivolgare,
   Macerete, Pietra Rudinella, San Biagio, Serpielli, Sitini, Sopra Castello, Torre Assonino, Usinilla,
   and Vallocchi). Others consisted of a mixture of arable land and vines (as, for example, in the areas
   known as Cappane, Colle Mattoni, Ferrale, Fontedelicata, Fossato Castellano, Monte Combale,
   Pianese[?Pianezza], Saporoia and Sitini). The 1320 *Tavola delle possessioni* also contains references
   to plots of uncultivated or fallow arable land which contained woodland (at Collesorbe, Lamone
   and Prete [?Pietre] Schiace), and even 'uncultivated wooded land' (at Collesorbe, Pietre Schiace and
   Quercete). Virgin woodland is also recorded in the areas known as Agresta, Bocerano [?Vocerano],
   Campo Giovanni and Termine.

Particular attention is paid here to Mita di Piero, not only because we can be
certain about her husband's identity and her married state in 1320, but also
because information contained within the 1320 *Tavola delle possessioni* and in
other surviving documents from the period encourages further speculation
about Mita's natal family and the circumstances of her marriage to Minuccio
di Banduccio.

There seems little doubt that Mita di Piero was the same individual as that
referred to in the 1318 boundary document in the context of her holding land
on one of the borders established between the two communes of Sant'Angelo
in Colle and Montalcino. It also seems likely that Mita was the sister of Rosa di
Piero Pecoraio, whose will of 1328 underpins the discussion of patterns of piety
in early fourteenth-century Sant'Angelo in Colle in Chapter 7. As will become
clear, Rosa di Piero Pecoraio, like her sister, was married to a local man from
Sant'Angelo in Colle. Unlike her sister, however, Rosa was probably already
widowed by 1320. Unlike her sister, also, Rosa is not included in the 1320 *Tavola
delle possessioni* for Sant'Angelo in Colle. She may thus either have returned to
her natal home, or have moved away from the village. It is perhaps significant
that despite her local associations with Sant'Angelo in Colle, Rosa di Piero

seems to have directed most of her charity towards religious foundations in Montalcino when drawing up her will in 1328. Indeed, it becomes clear that she favoured one particular religious order there, and that she was in addition concerned to promote the well-being of that order's female religious. It is possible therefore, that when widowed Rosa left Sant'Angelo in Colle in order to join a religious order in the nearby commune of Montalcino. As we shall see in Chapter 7 she was nevertheless conscious of certain obligations to religious life in Sant'Angelo in Colle, since she also left money to the church of San Michele.

Consideration of the personal circumstances of these two sisters offers a perspective not only on links between Sant'Angelo in Colle and Montalcino during the early fourteenth century, but also on the patterns of piety established by the former commune's women. While no testamentary details have so far surfaced in respect of Mona Mita di Piero, there seems little doubt that she was financially well off, and – like her sister, Rosa – was in a position to patronise religious and charitable institutions. The question arises why Mita, despite being the richest female in the village, was apparently married to a pauper. From his own entry in the 1320 *Tavola delle possessioni*, it seems that Minuccio di Banduccio's assets amounted to a mere 2 *lire* and 9 *soldi*.[18] If this was really the case, Minuccio di Banduccio must not only have sponged off his wife by living in her house inside the walls of Sant'Angelo in Colle, but also – owning virtually no land himself – to have benefited almost entirely from the fruits of Mita's own extensive lands in the countryside around the village.

The fact that two entries were included in the 1320 *Tavola delle Possessioni* in respect of property owned by Mita di Piero prompts a number of other hypotheses. The most likely scenario is that the first entry records property in Mona Mita's possession prior to her father's death, and that the second entry – where specific reference is made to Mita's deceased father and to her current husband – records the property inherited by Mita, which not only increased her own personal patrimony, but by law also benefited her husband. If this were the case, it seems likely that Mita's father Piero had only recently died, perhaps even during the drawing up of records for the 1320 *Tavola delle possessioni*. Some of the family possessions may thus have passed to Mita as one of Piero's surviving independent heirs. The fact that the 1320 *Tavola delle possessioni* also contains an entry for the heirs of Piero di Pecoraio, and that land owned by that group is recorded as being bordered by land belonging to Mita di Piero, adds strength to this hypotheses.[19] It would also seem to confirm that Piero di Pecoraio had only recently died. This could explain why details of property to be passed on to Minuccio di Banduccio as a result of his marriage to Mita were recorded in an entry under the name of his wife.

There seems little doubt that Mita had been married to Minuccio di Banduccio at least two years prior to the drawing up of the 1320 *Tavola delle possessioni*, since in the 1318 boundary document reference was made to land belonging to 'Mita di Piero, wife of Minuccio di Banduccio'. It is nevertheless significant that while reference was made to Mita di Piero's husband in that document, the officials responsible for drawing up the boundary record recognised Mita, and not her husband, as the owner of the land. Whatever the explanation of the two entries for Mita di Piero in the 1320 *Tavola delle possessioni*, it seems clear that Mita herself had already assumed a position of some standing by the time of the 1318 boundary document, in so far as ownership of land was concerned.

The fruits of Mita's land before, but particularly following the death of her father must have brought her considerable wealth. Her main income probably came from the sale of wood, and/or the rearing and slaughtering of pigs. As Table 5.3 shows, with terrain measuring some 235 *staia*, Mita – as a private individual –controlled a large percentage of the woodland owned by the local residents and commune of Sant'Angelo in Colle. From the details contained in other entries in the 1320 *Tavola delle possessioni*, it seems clear that many of Mita's neighbours owned plots of woodland measuring less than 10 *staia*. A number of other individuals owned slightly larger tracts of woodland, a handful being in possession of wooded areas covering upwards of 50 or so *staia*. But few could compare with the overall size of Mita di Piero' terrain. Only Petruccio di Bonanni, or Bonanno, stands out, as owning three plots of woodland measuring in total 117 *staia*. But even this was only half the size of the woodland owned by Mita.

Mita's personal wealth may also have stemmed in part from the production and sale of wine, for she is recorded as owning land partially laid down to vines in the *contrade* of Collemattoni and Piannezza. In all measuring slightly less than 12 *staia*, the combined value of these two vineyards was considerable. Estimated at between 6 and 7 *lire* per *staia*, Mita di Piero's vineyards notched up a combined value of 79 *lire* and 14 *soldi*. Mita could in addition have received revenue from the sale of crops such as hay and wheat, since she owned a mixture of cultivated and uncultivated land near her woodland in the *contrada* of 'Miglianni', as well as arable land in the areas known as 'Pianezze', 'Marrucca'.[20] The land at Miglianni was bordered on one side by land belonging to Neri di Guicciardo and on another by water, variously described as the 'Fossato Tredine' and 'the ditch'. It was thus presumably ideal for 'grass' crops. It is not impossible, either, that some of Mita's woodland was on occasion used for the pasturing of cattle, although the lush meadows to the east and south-east of Sant'Angelo in Colle would have offered the most appropriate grazing. It was in fact there, in the area known as the 'Pian d'Orcia' next to the Orcia River, that Mita held some 50 *staia* of land. With an estimated value of 50 *lire*, the land in 'Pian d'Orcia' seems to have been the most valuable piece of Mita's real estate in terms of square metres. Significantly, as at Miglianni, Mita's land at 'Pian d'Orcia' seems once again to have confronted the same Sienese neighbour, since we learn from the 1320 *Tavola delle possessioni* that the land was bounded on one side by the River Orcia; on another side by a ditch; and on a third side by land belonging to Neri di Guicciardo.

All in all, Mita di Piero's portfolio was impressive. Not only did she own a large amount of valuable terrain, but much of her land was also sited in strategic positions within the territory itself. According to the 1318 boundary document, the Tredine ditch defined part of Sant'Angelo in Colle's southern borders. The River Orcia clearly defined another extreme. It thus seems that Mita, and/or earlier members of her family had established a strong presence on both the south and the south-eastern sides of the village – traditionally the areas most vulnerable to attack. It may be no coincidence, therefore, that in all but one instance the Sienese outsider Neri di Guicciardo is recorded as holding land adjacent to properties owned by Mita. Neri di Guicciardo may in effect have been facing up to one of the more notable individuals of the early fourteenth-century population. Mona Mita for her part may have felt that proximity of this kind placed her under the constant scrutiny of the reigning authorities.

Consideration of the financial circumstances of Mita di Piero on the basis of information contained within the 1320 *Tavola delle possessioni* presents us with a number of conflicting pictures. On the basis of her landholdings Mita was clearly a woman with prospects. Her marriage, by contrast, appears to have offered her few advantages, whether financial or social. Yet Mita was obviously not a poor relation. Nor, if the testamentary stipulations of her sister Rosa are anything to go by, did Mita occupy an inferior social position within the society of the early fourteenth-century village. There is, moreover, evidence that Mita's family had at one time established a power base in the territory outside Sant'Angelo in Colle, since in the first of Mona Mita's two entries in the 1320 *Tavola delle possessioni* there is a reference to a 'quoddam castellare' (ruined castle) at 'Tori sassonini', or Torre Assonini. It seems likely that this was on the site of the present podere la Torre, on the northern side of the Sesta road, and to the north-west of Sesta itself. The fact that Mita di Piero, or more likely her ancestors had at one time possessed a castle or fortified farmhouse on the eastern side of Sant'Angelo in Colle could indicate that the family once wielded considerable power in the neighbourhood. Against this background, it seems almost inconceivable that Mita would have formed an alliance with an individual whose only asset was a small orchard valued at less than 3 *lire*, when Mita's own patrimony was valued at over 100 times that amount. It is tempting to argue that such inconsistencies resulted from an attempt to avoid tax. However, in the absence of further documentary evidence, it would seem impossible to deny Minuccio di Banduccio's comparative poverty. That said, such an imbalance could be explained in a number of other ways. Minuccio di Banduccio's union with Mita di Piero may, for example, have had a political dimension to it in that it was designed to compromise or restrict the prestige of a previously powerful local clan.

In 1320 the fortified farmhouse belonging to Mita clearly offered no practical defence against potential intruders from the east, since it was described as a ruin. In an earlier period, however, it may have assumed a significant role in the defence of the village on its eastern side. If it was indeed positioned on the site of the present podere la Torre, it not only overlooked the Sesta road, but (as a result of its elevated position) was also a perfect lookout for the south-eastern stretch of the Orcia valley. Following the submission of Sant'Angelo in Colle to Siena in the early thirteenth century, a fortified structure in this position could, however, also have served as a point of resistance against those assuming power inside the village. In any event, it would no doubt have been in the interests of the Republic of Siena that local powers in the surrounding territory should either be crushed or co-opted to the Sienese cause. Had the Sienese government decided on the former, the castellated building belonging to Mita's ancestors might well have been destroyed, and/or the family forced to retreat within the walls of the newly established subject commune. Had the Sienese opted for co-opting the family, they might have allowed Mita's ancestors to maintain possession of their landed property in the territory of Sant'Angelo in Colle but only on the basis that they lived inside the village, where they could be kept under close observation. It is of course also possible that the family's misfortunes dated from a more recent period. Mita di Piero's family may, for example, have been implicated in the Ghibelline-inspired rebellion of 1280. In the aftermath of this, the family's fortified base in the countryside could have been dismantled, or left to go to rack and ruin, and the marriage prospects of female members deliberately restricted. It may have been decided, for example, that Piero di Pecoraio's daughters should marry beneath their social rank, in order to reduce the overall power base of the family, as well as to stem future challenges from other potential rebels. This would certainly not have been the first or only example of this kind of social engineering in the early modern period.[21]

In any event, there can be little doubt, that in the context of personal wealth alone, Mita di Piero stood head and shoulders above her nearest rival, Rosa, the wife of Fuccius, or Fuccio. While the identity of Rosa's husband remains uncertain, there can be little doubt that she, too, occupied a position of some significance in early fourteenth-century Sant'Angelo in Colle. Significantly, and by comparison with Mita di Piero Pecoraio, Rosa di Fuccio appears to have owned very little land. Her real estate in 1320 consisted of only three arable plots, one of which was described as partly uncultivated. One of the pieces of land – that recorded as at Lama Corboli – was, nevertheless, extensive, measuring nearly 90 *staia*, and with an estimated value of 205 *lire* and 7 *soldi*. Moreover, Rosa's land at Lama Corboli was estimated at more than twice the value per square metre of the land owned by Mita di Piero at Pian d'Orcia. It was also almost twice the size of Mita di Piero's patch.

Given its toponym, it seems likely that Rosa's land at Lama Corboli – like that at Pian d'Orcia belonging to Mita – served as pasture. Given that Rosa owned no woodland, it also seems likely that her revenue came in the main from the growing of crops and the pasturing of cattle. From the latter, she might also have produced cheese, and in part benefited from the proceeds of the curing and onward sale of animal hides. It seems clear that Rosa, the wife of Fuccio, and Mita, the wife of Minnuccio, were women with independent means, despite being bound in matrimony. As such they must both have formed part of the social elite in the early fourteenth-century village of Sant'Angelo in Colle. Whilst at least one of them may have found their circumstances compromised by marriage, neither of the women can be categorised as poor. Perhaps in the final analysis, Mita di Piero and Rosa, wife of Fuccio should be considered as exceptions to the rule. That said, they nevertheless become eligible for consideration as potential benefactors for the embellishment of the fabric (a topic discussed in Chapter 8). But first, a consideration of how the riches of Mita and Rosa and their fellow sisters (both wed and unwed) compared with those of their men folk.

Notes

1 Appendix I.

2 Archivio di Stato di Siena (hereafter ASS), *Estimo* 24, fols 360r, 400r, 330v and 448r.

3 Ibid., fol. 259r.

4 The latter was, for example, probably the case for Novellina Bindi, see *Estimo* 24, fols 367r–368r. In her own entry no reference is made to Novellina's marital state. However, in an entry for Vanuccio di Massaia (fol. 440v) there is a reference to Novellina 'uxor olim bindi raynucii' (Novellina the widow of Bindo Rainuccio) as the owner of adjacent property in the 'contrada' of Pianezze. While there is no reference to Vanuccio in the context of land owned at Pianezze in Novellina's own entry, he is referred to in the context of two pieces of land owned by Novellina at Torre Assonino (fols 367r and 367v). It seems likely that it was one and the same woman (Novellina Bindi) who was recorded in the context of these various pieces of land, and that some time before the drawing up of the 1320 *Tavola delle possessioni* she had been widowed. There is further confirmation of this in the fact that there is also an entry in the 1320 *Tavola della possessioni* for the heirs of Bindo di Rannuccio' (fol. 191r). Vannuccio di Massaia does in fact refer to these individuals as the owners of adjacent land in the area known as 'Quercia Magiore' (fol. 440v), although this fact is not acknowledged in the entry for the heirs themselves.

5 ASS, *Estimo* 24, fol. 331r.

6 Ibid., fol. 332r.

7 Ibid., fol. 312r.

8 Ibid., fol. 37r.

9 Ibid., fol. 303r.

10 Ibid., fol. 310r.

11 Ibid., fol. 31v.

12 Ibid., fols 23r–23v.

13 Ibid., fol. 312r.

14 Ibid., fol. 139r.

15 Ibid., fol. 400r.

16 Ibid., fols 330r–330v.

17 Ibid., fol. 309r.

18 Ibid., fol. 295r.

19 Ibid., fol. 243r.

20 In this context, see Giovanni Cherubini, 'Risorse, paesaggio ed utilizzazione agricola del territorio della Toscana sud-occidentale nei secoli 14–16', in *Civiltà ed economia agricola in Toscana nei secc. 13–15: problemi della vita delle campagne nel tardo Medioevo*, Atti dell'ottavo Convegno internazionale del centro italiano di studi di storia e d'arte, Pistoia, 21–24 aprile 1977 (Pistoia, 1981), pp. 91–115. See also, Gabriella Piccinni, 'Ambiente, produzione, società della Valdorcia nel tardo Medioevo', in Alfio Cortonese (ed.), *La Val d'Orcia nel medioevo e nei primi secoli dell'età moderna*, Atti del Convegno internazionale di studi storici, Pienza, 15–18 settembre 1988 (Rome, 1990), pp. 33–58; and Gabriella Piccinni, *Seminare, fruttare, raccogliere: mezzadri e salariati sulle terre di Monte Oliveto Maggiore, 1374–1430* (Milan, 1982).

21 For a consideration of social engineering during the early modern period through restrictions placed on marriage between certain families, see Christiane Klapisch-Zuber, 'Relazioni di Parentela e vita politica a Firenze nel 14 secolo', in *eadem* (ed.), *La Famiglia in Italia* (New Haven, *c.*1991), pp. 233–54.

The Male Elite: Sienese 'Outsiders', Seven Rich Locals and Two Exceptionally Wealthy Clans?

When set beside the patrimonies recorded in respect of the inhabitants of other small towns and villages in the southern Sienese *contado*, those entered in the *Tavola delle possessioni* for Sant'Angelo in Colle indicate that there were several wealthy men in the early fourteenth-century village, even though not all of them would appear to fit into the top five or seven percentile, as identified by Andrea Barlucchi.[1] In 1320, there were at least seven individuals and at least two groups of heirs in Sant'Angelo in Colle whose assets placed them in a category well above other members of the local population at that date.

	lire	soldi	denari
Chiesa di Sant'Angelo	1357	18	3
Heirs of Cecchi Pieri (Cecco di Piero)	877	2	4
Michus Genovesis (Michele da Genova)	809	1	-
Bindus Accorsi (Bindo di Accorso)	733	9	-
Lonardutuis Johan(n)is (Lonarduccio di Giovanni)	620	4	-
Ninus Johan(n)is (Nino di Giovanni)	539	1	-
Landus Pepi (Lando di Pepe)	537	13	-
Chiesa di San Pietro	422	3	7
Ser Guccius Ser Francisci (Ser Guccio di Ser Francesco)	336	9	-
Heirs of Vive Jacobi (Vivo di Giacomo)	328	5	6
Paganellus Johan(n)is (Paganello di Giovanni)	310	5	-

Table 6.1 Patrimonies declared in respect of the men and institutions of the village in the 1320 *Tavola delle possessioni*: Seven Rich Locals and Two Exceptionally Wealthy Clans?[1]

Note to Table 6.1
1 The Latinate form of names as they appear in the index to *Estimo* 24 is retained here for easy cross-reference to page numbers.

Analysis

In 1320 the parish church of San Michele stood head and shoulders above both the second religious entity, the church of San Pietro, and the seven or so individuals and two groups of heirs whose patrimonies ranged from just over three hundred to nearly nine hundred *lire*. Michele da Genova, or Genoa, was clearly the most highly endowed individual, no doubt in part as a result of the high value of 110 *lire* placed on one of the properties he is said to have owned abutting the water conduit (See Table 2.1). But, as Table 6.2 in this chapter will show, Michele da Genova's house was not the largest structure in the early fourteenth century. A number of other properties ranging in value between 113 *lire* and 350 *lire* must have been larger.

In this context alone, it seems reasonable to describe them as a male elite. A word of caution is, however, necessary. By comparison with patrimonies recorded in respect of residents in Siena, even the highest figures recorded in the 1320 *Tavola delle possessioni* for Sant'Angelo in Colle can appear modest.[2] Moreover, even the partial assets declared in respect of land and living accommodation owned by Sienese 'outsiders' in and around Sant'Angelo in Colle between 1318 and 1320 cast some of those identified here as the male elite into shadow.

Table 6.2 Patrimonies of Sienese 'outsiders': Assets of Sienese residents in respect of property and/or land held in the 'corte' or territory of Sant'Angelo in Colle between 1318-1320

Proprietor	Value of possessions in		
	Lire	*soldi*	*denari*
Cione e Nigio di Baldicione[1]	365	5	5
Andrea di Nerio di Beccherini[2]	38	-	-
Baldera di Bencivenne[3]			
Gianni di Bencivenne[4]	5	16	6
Tofano di Benentende[5]	13	9	-
Naddo di Bernardino da Valchortese[6]			
Andrea di Buoncambio[7]	56	15	-
Meo di Buonfiglio[8]	124	9	-
Heirs of Maestro Fei and Niccoluccio 'suo figliuolo'[9]	183	19	6
Heirs of Franco[10]	29	14	-
Neri di Guicciardo da Civitella[11]	2351	16	-
Gano di Lambertino[12]	54	16	-
Niccoluccio di Mandriano[13]	346	13	2
Ghino di Mino di Cinigiano[14]	24	6	-
Lando di Maestro Meo di Tolomeo[15]	100	13	-
Mei di Ugo[16]	5	10	-
Manovello di Ugolino[17]	354	13	-

Notes to Table 6.2

1 ASS, *Estimo* 108, Terzo di Città, Porta all'archo, 1320 (hereafter *Estimo* 108), old page no. CCXXXVIII, new pencil pagination 249. These heirs owned some twenty-one plots of land in the territory of Sant'Angelo in Colle consisting of a mixture of woodland, field and worked, or agricultural land (variously containing woodland, vineyards, vineyards and wood, olives, marshland and fallow areas). They also owned two comparatively modest houses inside the walls, one valued at 24 *lire* and 13 *soldi*, the other at 36 *lire* and 13 *soldi*. According to *Estimo* 108, their overall patrimony was 7293 *lire*, 13 *soldi* and 8 *denari*. They were thus seriously rich. Their house inside Siena was alone valued at 433 *lire*, 6 *soldi* and 8 *denari*. The statistics in Table 6.2 are drawn from *Estimo* 108, cc. 231v–237r. A number of other references to property held at Sant'Angelo in Colle in cc. 249v–252r of the same register are cancelled out.

2 ASS, *Estimo* 99, old page no. CXXXVIIIv, new no. 56v. Andrea di Nerio owned only one piece of land in the territory of Sant'Angelo in Colle. This plot, which was in the area known as 'fonte dellamo' (?fonte allomo), measured 6 *staia*, and was described as 'tere vineate' (land laid down to vines). He was nevertheless an individual of considerable wealth, owning several properties in and around Lucignano and elsewhere. His living house in the popolo di San Giovanni in Siena was valued at 266 *lire*, 13 *soldi* and 4 *denari*, and his overall patrimony was recorded as 3141 *lire*.

3 According to the 'Sconpartimento delle Parrocchie e Contrade della Città di Siena, fatto Terzo per Terzo, nell'Anno 1318 in occasione della Lira o Presta imposta sui Beni Stabili Esistenti nella Città e Territorio Sanese' (ASS, *Manoscritti* C46, c. 108, under Terzo di Città, Porta all'arco, c. 9), Baldera di Bencivenne was one of the Sienese 'outsiders' who owned property at Sant'Angelo in Colle. This individual is not, however listed in the relevant register (ASS, *Estimo* 108), but ten pages (old page nos. IX-XVIIII) are now missing. It seems likely that Baldera di Bencivenne's details were included amongst those. It also seems likely that Gianni di Bencivenne (who likewise owned property at

Sant'Angelo in Colle and is included in *Estimo* 108) was a sibling, although there is nothing in Gianni's entry to indicate any such relationship.

4 ASS, *Estimo* 108 verso of old page no. CXXI, top right pencil no. 109, lower left 111v. Gianni di Bencivenne owned four plots of land in the vicinity of Sant'Angelo in Colle, two of which were described as agricultural, one as worked land including an orchard with olives, and a third plot that was laid out as a kitchen garden and shared with the heirs of Baldiccione.

5 ASS, *Estimo* 108, old page no. CCXXVI, top right no. 236, lower left no. 218. According to this entry, Tofano owned only one piece of land in the territory of Sant'Angelo in Colle. This was described as agricultural land in the area known as Bagnuolo. However, in what appears to be a duplicate entry elsewhere (ASS, *Estimo* 104, old page no. 417, new no. 416), an individual of the same name is recorded as owning a further three plots of agricultural land at Sant'Angelo in Colle, as well as one plot lying fallow in the area known as San Biagio. The total value of those possessions was 16 *lire* and 6 *soldi*. According to this latter entry, Tofano di Benentende, a grocer, or spice merchant, did not own a house in Siena, and the holdings at Sant'Angelo in Colle constituted his only assets.

6 According to the 'Sconpartimento delle Parrocchie e Contrade della Città di Siena, fatto Terzo per Terzo, nell'Anno 1318 in occasione della Lira o Presta imposta sui Beni Stabili Esistenti nella Città e Territorio Sanese' (ASS, *Manoscritti* C46, c. 352, under 'Nobili del Chontado', c. 315) Naddo di Bernardino was one of the Sienese 'outsiders' owning property at Sant'Angelo in Colle, but there is no entry for this individual in the relevant register (ASS, *Estimo* 93). There are, however, at least forty missing pages in this register, between old page nos 303 and 362. It seems likely therefore that Naddo di Bernardino's details were included there.

7 ASS, *Estimo* 102, Terzo di Città, Inchontri, 1318, old page no. LXXXXII, lower left 88. Andrea di Buoncambio owned eleven plots of land in the vicinity of Sant'Angelo in Colle, as well as a 'platea', or building plot inside the walls. Half of the plots of land were described as agricultural, in one case including brushland, and in another including woodland and partly lying fallow. One plot in the area of San Biagio was virgin woodland; another at Saporoia (which also included a 'cappana', or shack) included vines. Andrea also owned an 'ortale' or kitchen garden cum orchard inside the walls of the village containing olives and almond trees. According to the entry in *Estimo* 102, Andrea owned no land elsewhere.

8 ASS, *Estimo* 143, Terzo di Camollia, La Magione del Tempio, 1318, old page no. 227, lower left 228. Some of the entries in the pages concerning Meo di Buonfiglio in *Estimo* 143 are cancelled out, including several pieces of land at Sant'Angelo in Colle. There are also two separate compilations. Additional notes indicate further assessments of this individual's assets in 1321 and 1323. Despite this, it seems clear that in 1318 Meo di Buonfiglio owned a number of plots of agricultural land at Sant'Angelo in Colle, including some that also contained vines; one piece that was partially fallow and another that was laid out to kitchen garden. At that date, Meo also owned a comparatively modest house inside the walls. His main asset, however, seems to have been a house with land and vineyards in the territory of Pozzecchi that was valued at 3850 *lire*. His comparatively modest assets at Sant'Angelo in Colle are in that context misleading.

9 ASS, *Estimo* 139, Terzo di Camollia, Sant'Andrea a Lato la Piazza, 1318, (old page nos. 226-242) but in respect of Sant'Angelo in Colle, page nos. CCXXVI-CCXLII. All of the thirty or so possessions in and around Sant'Angelo in Colle, are however crossed out. An additional note dated 1323 makes reference to the hospital of Santa Maria della Scala. It is possible therefore, that Maestro Fei's possessions at Sant'Angelo in Colle were willed to that Sienese institution. Much of the land (which included worked land, olive groves, vineyards, fallow land, and meadowland) was located on the eastern side of the village. Nine of the plots seem to have been either owned jointly or divided between Maestro Fei's heirs and the hospital of Santa Maria della Scala. The Sienese institution also owned one half of one of the properties belonging to these heirs inside the walls of Sant'Angelo in Colle. All in all, there seem to have been close links between Santa Maria della Scala and the heirs of Maestro Fei. It is possible that (like Domina Buonafemmina and her grandson Assoltino, see Chapter 4) the heirs of Maestro Fei had disposed of part of their patrimony in order to cover debts.

10 ASS, *Estimo* 129, Terzo di San Martino, San Cristofano allato la Chiesa, 1318, c. CCCXXV, lower left, pencil no. 324. These possessions, consisting of three plots of agricultural land, two of which were in the area known as Lamone, seem to have been the only property owned by this group of heirs outside Siena. They also owned what was probably a comparatively large house and piece of land inside Siena that was valued at 140 *lire*. Their overall recorded patrimony was 150 *lire*, 4 *soldi*. Another group with the same patronym (and thus possibly related) is listed in the 1320 *Tavola delle possessioni* for Sant'Angelo in Colle (*Estimo* 24, cc. 186r–189r) with a much higher patrimony of 290 *lire* and 17 *soldi*. According to the entry in *Estimo* 24, the heirs of Franco resident in Sant'Angelo in Colle owned some twenty or so pieces of mostly agricultural land (some of which contained brushland or woodland, and two of which also contained vines). Their land was positioned in various parts of the territory, including in one case a plot lying fallow and containing woodland in the area known as Lamone. Inside the walls they also owned two building plots and two small houses. Both

of the building plots abutted the walls. One is said also to have abutted the 'palatiu(m) comu(n)is Sen(arum)', or Sienese town hall.

11 ASS, *Estimo* 106, Terzo di Città, San Pietro in Chastelvecchio, 1318, old page no. CLXXVI, new pencil no. 50 top right. According to this record, Neri di Guicciardo's considerable patrimony outside Siena consisted solely of land and houses in the vicinity of and inside the walls of Sant'Angelo in Colle. Neri owned some one hundred and eighty-six plots of land ranging from pasture and marshland to vineyards and agricultural land (that on occasion also contained fallow sections, woodland, olives, and vines and sometimes a mixture of several of these) in various parts of the territory. Inside the walls of the village he owned twenty-three houses and building plots. The combined value of his possessions in and around the village must have singled him out as one of the richest individuals associated with Sant'Angelo in Colle during the early fourteenth century.

12 ASS, *Estimo* 138, Terzo di Camollia, Sant'Andrea a Lato la Piazza, 1318, old page no. CCLXXXVII, new no. 287 (new no. lower left 286). According to this record, all of Gano di Lambertino's possessions outside Siena were at Sant'Angelo in Colle, including a small house inside the walls and eleven assorted plots of land, one or two of which abutted each other. One plot of agricultural and wooded land in the vicinity of the river Orcia is said to have measured 130 *staia*, yet its overall value was only 7 *lire* and 5 *soldi*. Most of the other plots measured between 3 and 5 *staia* and were valued at relatively low rates.

13 ASS, *Estimo* 104, Terzo di Città, Santo Quiricho in Chastelvecchio, 1318, old page no. 257, new pencil no. 264. Eight of the thirteen plots of land owned by this individual in the territory of Sant'Angelo in Colle were described as agricultural; two others (one in the area known as Collemattone, the other in the area known as 'fonte allomo') were laid out with vines; a couple other plots close to the walls served as kitchen gardens and orchards, and a final plot at Collemattone lay fallow. Niccoluccio also owned two houses inside the walls of the village.

14 ASS, *Estimo* 108, old page no. in pencil 527, top right 544, lower left 509. The three pieces of land owned by this individual are described as 'campie', or fields. One of them, in the area known as Quarrata, is also described as wooded.

15 ASS, *Estimo* 129, c. CCCXV, described as 'poitas in castro m(o)ntiscalcini' (?'podesta', or mayor of Montalcino). Lando is said to have owned one piece of worked land measuring just over two *staia* and what must have been a house of some size inside the walls, since it was valued at 100 *lire*. According to the entry in *Estimo* 129, Lando's overall patrimony was 5409 *lire*, 8 *soldi* and 8 *denari*. He was thus an individual of considerable wealth, perhaps the richest outsider in early fourteenth-century Sant'Angelo in Colle. He may also have been the first member of the Tolomeo family to form a relationship with the village.

16 ASS, *Estimo* 120, old page no. CXXXVI, new no. 98, upper right. According to this record, Meo di Ugo's two plots of land at Sant'Angelo in Colle (consisting of a mixture of worked and woodland at Greppo and a kitchen garden cum orchard on the 'costamori') were the only possessions he held outside Siena. In the city, however, he owned half of a house that was valued at 225 *lire*. Once again, it seems that the value of assets in and around Sant'Angelo in Colle does not accurately reflect the financial circumstances of the proprietor. It is possible that such cases resulted from an individual in the city inheriting possessions from a poorer relative in the country.

17 ASS, *Estimo* 108, old page no. 683, new no. 660 upper right, new no. 643 lower left. All of Manovello di Ugolino's property outside Siena was at Sant'Angelo in Colle. Of the thirty-six plots of land listed in *Estimo* 108, at least three seem to have contained a built structure of some size, since the term 'domo' was adopted. It also seems clear that a large amount of Manovello di Ugolino's land consisted of fields. This 'outsider' in particular must thus have been in a good position to let out land for pasture. His overall patrimony of 662 *lire*, 19 *soldi* and 9 *denari* included a house and building plot in Siena valued at 308 *lire*, 6 *soldi* and 9 *denari*.

As Table 6.2 shows, even the partial assets of some of these 'outsiders' exceeded the total patrimonies recorded in respect of the wealthier members of the local population. In one case, the partial assets amounted to more than 2,000 *lire*, a figure that was over twice as much as the highest patrimony recorded for the wealthiest group of inhabitants in Sant'Angelo in Colle (let alone a single person) during the same period.

Consideration is given here to the financial profiles of both the Sienese 'outsiders' and a number of local inhabitants, in an attempt to establish how such individuals may have affected everyday life within the subject commune of Sant'Angelo. Attention focuses in particular on patterns of ownership of both land and living accommodation and the extent to which the combined value and function of these could be said to establish certain individuals as elite members of the early fourteenth-century society.

Some light has already been thrown on the ways in which the Sienese created power bases or points of surveillance inside the walls of subject communes through the positioning of strategic new buildings and through investment in property close to key institutions such as the communal offices. In this way the periphery was secured and at the same time a watchful eye was cast over internal affairs. Some mention has also been made of the patterns of land tenure established by Sienese 'outsiders', and the ways in which these might have helped to reinforce the political *status quo*. There is little doubt that 'outsiders' like Neri di Guicciardo had the capacity to wield considerable power and influence inside the subject commune of Sant'Angelo in Colle. There is sufficient evidence, also, to indicate that he may not only have influenced the livelihoods of local residents through the letting out of property, both in the countryside and within the walls of the village, but also through employment of land workers in sharecropping agreements, or with contracts to take care of livestock. One could thus argue that at least some of the Sienese 'outsiders' established in the vicinity of Sant'Angelo in Colle in the early fourteenth century played a key part in maintaining the fabric of society there. No documents have, however, so far surfaced in direct confirmation of this. Indeed, as we shall see in the last two chapters, those documents that do remain concerning patterns of patronage and piety in the early fourteenth-century frontier castle illustrate the significant part played by the local residents rather than their Sienese masters. It is nonetheless clear that several of the Sienese 'outsiders' associated with Sant'Angelo in Colle in the early fourteenth century had considerable assets, and were thus well placed to contribute both to the social welfare of the village and the embellishment of the urban fabric.

Of the 17 Sienese 'outsiders' known to have owned land and property in and around Sant'Angelo in Colle during the early fourteenth century, the one who had the most impressive portfolio of land and property was clearly Neri di Guicciardo. In 1318, the value of Neri's assets in and around Sant'Angelo in Colle alone amounted to 2,351 *lire*.[3] As already noted, this individual owned land in a number of different areas around the village. Clearly, the use to which such land was put must not only have affected Neri di Guicciardo's own personal fortunes, but also those of the individual landworkers or shepherds and goatherds employed to work on it. Much of Neri's land was agricultural, or arable, but he also owned a considerable number of olive groves, vineyards and pieces of woodland. Not all of Neri's land was cultivated at any one time. Of the 180 or so small plots of land recorded as owned by him in 1318, some one in seven are also described as being partially uncultivated, or lying fallow. This could indicate that Neri was operating a system of crop rotation at Sant'Angelo in Colle and that he was seriously engaged in the business of agriculture there. But the fact that Neri was in possession of a large amount of fallow land must also have allowed for the pasturing of livestock, including cows, sheep and goats. As already suggested in Chapter 4, one such arrangement may well have involved Petruccio di Assalto, the individual named in the context of an outstanding loan to Neri in the early years of the fourteenth century.

Small plots of land like those acquired by Neri di Guicciardo would clearly have been ideal for handing over to local landworkers to tend as sharecroppers. On one unusually large piece of worked land, however, there was also a reference to a 'domo', or house.[4] This land, which measured 68 *staia* and was valued at 143 *lire*, was in the area known as 'Capanne'. On two other plots, one combining vines at Saproia and the other, agricultural land in the area known as Podio, or Poggio Peschaia, there were references instead to a 'capanna', or shack.[5] Neri di Guicciardo thus had the means to install local foremen, if not whole family groups, on at least three plots of land belonging to him in the vicinity of Sant'Angelo in Colle. The fact that the building at Capanna is described as a house rather than a shack also indicates that it could have served as living accommodation for Neri di Guicciardo himself. Its rateable value implies that it was a building of some size. It may even have been large enough to accommodate not only a foreman and a group of sharecroppers, but also Neri di Guicciardo and his own family. Even if not established permanently at Sant'Angelo in Colle, Neri di Guicciardo could clearly count on having living accommodation on the land, when visiting the village. But, as we now know, he also owned a considerable amount of property inside Sant'Angelo in Colle itself, including a house that was apparently even larger than the building at Capanne.

None of the other Sienese citizens recorded as owning property in the territory of Sant'Angelo in Colle in the early fourteenth century had such impressive profiles as Neri di Guicciardo. Yet several of them owned a number of pieces of land there, as well as more than one house inside the walls of the village itself. At least one of these, Lando di Maestro Meo di Tolomeo, was also considerably wealthier than Neri. A number of the Sienese 'outsiders' other than Neri di Guicciardo were thus well placed to engage in systems of sharecropping and the sub-letting of property inside the walls of Sant'Angelo in Colle. Niccoluccio di Mandriano, for example, is recorded as owning 13 pieces of land as well as two houses inside Sant'Angelo in Colle itself.[6] Another 'outsider', Manovello di Ugolino, whose overall patrimony (including a house of some size in Siena) was declared as 662 *lire*, 19 *soldi* and 9 *denari*, appears to have owned 36 pieces of land around Sant'Angelo in Colle (with estimated values ranging from 1 *soldo* to 64 *lire* and 17 *soldi*), as well as several houses inside the village ranging in value from 7 to 70 *lire*.[7] On three pieces of land owned by Manovello there was, in addition, a building described as a 'house'. The comparatively low overall values of these possessions – 35 *lire*, 12 *lire*, and 7 *lire* and 2 *soldi* respectively – indicate, however, that all three built structures were quite small. It also seems likely that at least two of the properties were positioned inside the existing walls of the village since (unusually) no overall measurements were recorded for the individual plots of land. A somewhat curious formula of words was also adopted in the context of their location: 'in curia sive in castro predicto' (in the said parish or castle), with no reference to any particular 'contrada' (as was normally the rule when describing plots of land outside the walls).

The huge range of estimated values recorded in respect of land owned by Manovello di Ugolino may be explained by the fact that he appears to have owned every kind of terrain (apart from woodland), from simple field to kitchen garden, arable land, olive groves, vineyard, scrubland and land lying fallow. Some of the plots of land with the lowest estimated value were described as 'campie', or fields. There were also great variations in the size of the individual plots. Many of Manovello's fields were comparatively small, measuring on average between one and two *staia*. Nevertheless, he did own one unusually large field at Poggio Pescaia. This plot measured 11 *staia* and had an estimated value of 33 *lire* and 7 *soldi*. It seems, in addition, that this field had some kind of shack or shacks on it, since the plot was described as 'terra cappannate e campie' (land with shacks and fields). Manovello's field at Poggio Pescaia was bounded on one side by land belonging to Neri di Guicciardo, very likely the plot already noted as containing another 'capanna'. It seems clear, therefore, that both Neri di Guicciardo and Manovello di Ugolino were in a position to offer some rudimentary form of accommodation in the area of Poggio Pescaia.

A number of other Sienese 'outsiders', among them Niccoluccio di Mandriano, could offer similar facilities, although as we shall see the size of the individual shacks varied considerably. Some, though probably very simple, were clearly more suited than others for semi-permanent accommodation. Others could only have offered temporary shelter. Three of the pieces of land owned by Niccoluccio di Mandriano were described as laid down to orchard or kitchen garden, two as agricultural land mixed with vines, the rest as arable plots – one lying fallow and another described as partially fallow.[8] Two of Niccoluccio's plots of agricultural land – one, a piece measuring 14½ *staia* at Bagnuolo, and another measuring 26 *staia* in the area known as 'Fabbriche, or Fabbrica'– is also said to have contained a 'capanna', or shack. It seems likely that the building at Bagnuolo was a fairly modest structure, since the overall value of the plot was recorded as 16 *lire* and 2 *soldi*. Even if the land at Bagnuolo was valued at the comparatively low rate of half a *lira* per *staio*, the shed on it could only have been worth some nine or so *lire*. Had the value of the land been greater, the shack must have been worth even less, and thus to have been even more rudimentary. The shack at Fabbrica, by contrast, may have been considerably larger. The overall value of the plot of land there (including the building on it) was recorded as 56 *lire*. If the land at Fabbrica was likewise valued at half a *lira* per *staio*, the 'capanna' there could have been worth some 40 or so *lire*, and thus have had the dimensions of a medium-sized house. If that were the case, the shack at Fabbrica (like property owned by Neri di Guicciardo) could have been used by local land workers engaged by Niccoluccio di Mandriano to work as sharecroppers.

Comparing the recorded value of various pieces of land belonging to Sienese 'outsiders' in the vicinity of Sant'Angelo in Colle with their individual patrimonies results in some surprising findings. Although the estimated value of individual plots belonging to Niccoluccio di Mandriano was, on average, higher than that recorded in respect of land owned by Neri di Guiccardo, Niccoluccio's overall patrimony of 346 *lire*, 13 *soldi* and 2 *denari* was much lower than that of either Neri di Guicciardo or Manovello di Ugolino. By comparison with both of those 'outsiders', Niccoluccio di Mandriano's holdings in the countryside must have been considered rather small beer. Yet, as we shall see, Niccoluccio di Mandriano's patrimony was comparable to several of those recorded in respect of the local male elite in Sant'Angelo in Colle. As such, one might expect him to have assumed a certain profile within the local society. It seems unlikely, however, that Niccoluccio di Mandriano established himself on a permanent basis inside the walls of Sant'Angelo in Colle. Although he possessed two houses inside the walls of the village, they must have been comparatively modest dwellings, since one was valued at 15 *lire*, and the other at 27 *lire*. Comparison with the estimated value of many other units of housing in the village indicates that Niccoluccio's property in Sant'Angelo in Colle was similar to those inhabited by people not abjectly poor, but nevertheless at the lower end of the social scale. As an 'outsider' with a comparatively high patrimony (even if not equalling that of the much richer Neri di Guicciardo), Niccoluccio di Mandriano would surely have wished to make a more obvious statement about his social standing, if acquiring living accommodation inside the walls of the subject commune for his own use. It seems more likely, therefore, that Niccoluccio's houses at Sant'Angelo in Colle served as an investment, perhaps being let out to local landworkers.

So far, no firm evidence has emerged of sharecropping arrangements drawn up between Sienese landowners and local inhabitants of Sant'Angelo in Colle during the early fourteenth century. There is, however, evidence that at least one or two of the Sienese 'outsiders' owning property in and around the village offered financial assistance to members of the local population in the form of loans. An entry in the records of the Montalcinese notary Ser Griffo di Ser Paolo of 7 January 1327/8 notes, for example, that Binduccio di Nerio of Sant'Angelo in Colle and Binduccio di Bindo of Montalcino owed 'Lando domino Meo di Tolomeo' of Siena the sum of 12 florins.[9] This debt was to be paid back within six months. Given Binduccio di Bindo's involvement several years earlier with another inhabitant of Sant'Angelo in Colle, Minuccio di Sozzo, it is possible that the debt owed to Lando di Tolomeo was associated with the tending of that individual's holdings in the same territory. It is also possible, however, that Lando had been approached because of his known wealth. According to tax records drawn up in 1318 Lando di Tolomeo owned a house of some size inside the walls of Sant'Angelo in Colle, but only a small piece of agricultural land in the area known as 'aie burle'.[10] His overall patrimony in 1318 was recorded as 5,409 *lire*, 8 *soldi* and 8 *denari*. As Table 6.2 shows, Lando di Tolomeo was in effect one of the richest 'outsiders' to invest in the southern frontier castle. Like Neri di Guicciardo, he would have been an obvious person to turn to when seeking a loan. It is, of course, possible that Lando had also increased his holdings in the southern frontier castle by 1328.

This in turn could have resulted in the necessity of hiring local help, and a sharecropping arrangement involving Binduccio di Nerio and Binduccio di Bindo. But, in the absence of further documentary evidence, such speculation and the hypothesis that the majority of Sienese 'outsiders' associated with Sant'Angelo in Colle during the early fourteenth century were absentee landlords remains unproved.

Nevertheless, there can be little doubt that as a group these Sienese 'outsiders' owned a considerable amount of property in and around the subject commune, and in that way established a noticeable presence. There is, moreover, evidence to show that they tended to cluster together. Eight of the plots belonging to Manovello di Ugolino (including that at Poggio Pescaia) are said to have abutted property belonging to Neri di Guicciardo. Five of the plots recorded as owned by Niccoluccio di Mandriano also abutted property belonging to Neri. Amongst these were the two pieces of arable land at Bagnuolo and Fabbrica. Four of the eleven pieces of land owned by another Sienese 'outsider', Andrea di Buoncambio, are similarly described as abutting property owned by Neri di Giucciardo.[11] One of Andrea's holdings, a plot of worked land including vines at Saproia that measured nearly five and a half *staia* and that was valued at 21 *lire* and 18 *soldi*, also contained a 'capanna'.

In records concerning the holdings of other Sienese 'outsiders' such as Giovanni di Bencivenne,[12] Gano di Lambertino,[13] Lando di Meo di Tolomeo,[14] Meo di Bonfiglio,[15] Tofano di Benentende,[16] the heirs of Franco,[17] the heirs of Baldiccione,[18] and the heirs of Maestro Feo and his son Niccoluccio,[19] similar clustering patterns emerge, with references not only to Neri di Guicciardo as the owner of neighbouring land, but also to other members of the same Sienese clique. In some ways this was inevitable. There was only so much land available in the territory and Neri di Guicciardo, in particular, seems to have owned a considerable amount of it. One would thus expect his name, at least, to crop up regularly in descriptions of the boundaries of individual pieces of land. However, the fact that many Sienese 'outsiders' acquired land in close proximity to each other must not only have strengthened their individual positions but also raised their collective profile. In effect, through their combined holdings, these 'outsiders' established a separate power base, even though individually working each of their plots with a view to their own personal gains.

It is perhaps a mistake, though, to regard all the land owned by Sienese 'outsiders' in the vicinity of early fourteenth-century Sant'Angelo in Colle in terms of territorial politics. It is significant that several of the 'outsiders' are recorded as only owning land at Sant'Angelo in Colle. Reference has already been made to one such individual – Meo di Ugo – the sharecropping employer of Neri di Dietavive. Others recorded as being in a similar position were Tofano di Benintende, Andrea di Buoncambio, the heirs of Maestro Fei, Manovello di Ugolino and Gano di Lambertino. It is possible, therefore, that some of these individuals had family ties with Sant'Angelo in Colle, and that they acquired land there by way of inheritance. Some of them may even have come from the village, and only relatively recently been established in Siena. Andrea di Buoncambio, for example, could have been the brother of Binduccio di Buoncambio, one of the individuals listed as a resident of Sant'Angelo in Colle in the 1320 *Tavola delle possessioni*.[20] Somewhat curiously, Andrea owned only a 'platea', or building site, and 'orto' planted with olives and almond trees inside the walls of the village.[21] Binduccio di Buoncambio for his part apparently owned no property inside the walls. According to Binduccio's entry in the 1320 *Tavola delle possessioni*, he owned only a piece of worked land at Speltale, valued at 21 *lire* and 6 *soldi*.[22] Perhaps these two were all that remained of a family clan originally established in Sant'Angelo in Colle, Andrea in the meantime having moved away to Siena. Had Andrea and Binduccio been brothers, and had Andrea subsequently moved away and their joint assets been divided, it might have been considered sensible that the one who remained should have access to the land, in order to secure his own livelihood. Binduccio might also have profited from the olives and almond trees that formed part of his brother's inheritance. There may even have been a tacit agreement that Binduccio should tend the kitchen garden during his brother's absence. Similar divisions and arrangements may have been agreed between the heirs of Maestro Fei and Maestro Fei's son, Niccoluccio, although in that case the real estate was considerably larger. All in all, that group jointly owned some 30 pieces of land around Sant'Angelo in Colle, as well as two houses and what used to be a building plot inside the walls of the village itself.[23]

In any event, whether originally from Sant'Angelo in Colle, or newly attracted to it following its takeover by Siena, these Sienese 'outsiders' were in several cases men of considerable wealth and social standing. As such they would not only have had the funds to commission and underwrite artistic projects at Sant'Angelo in Colle, but would also have been familiar with current fashions at the centre. Even if not directly responsible for the commissioning of works of art inside Sant'Angelo in Colle, they would thus have been in a unique position to offer advice as to the best artist available for the job, as well as the most recent or appropriate painting, sculpture or architectural structure to reflect. At the very least, they must have injected new perspectives into the early fourteenth-century village of Sant'Angelo in Colle as a result of being able to transfer their first-hand experience of contemporary trends in the city to the frontiers of the Sienese *contado*.

What then, of the financial circumstances of the local male elite of Sant'Angelo in Colle itself? The highest patrimony recorded in the 1320 *Tavola delle possessioni* for Sant'Angelo in Colle was that of the commune, at 2,007 *lire* 15 *soldi* and 6 *denari*.[24] This figure was some 30 per cent higher than that recorded in respect of the parish church of San Michele, at 1,357 *lire* 18 *soldi* 3 *denari*.[25] This in turn was almost double that of the richest group of people in the village in 1320, the heirs of Ser Cecco di Piero. As already noted, the percentage of individuals in the Sienese *contado* under the Government of the Nine with patrimonies of between 500 and 1,000 *lire* fluctuated somewhere between 7 and 8 per cent of the population. The heirs of Ser Cecco, with assets of nearly 900 *lire*, must thus have been regarded as seriously rich, both by the

Sienese 'outsiders' and by the local residents. Their overall patrimony was double that recorded in respect of Sant'Angelo in Colle's second church, San Pietro. It was also nearly three times higher than that recorded in respect of another member of the male 'elite' – Paganello di Giovanni.[26]

Apart from the heirs of Ser Cecco, two other individuals – Bindus, or Bindo di Accorso and Michele da Genoa – are recorded as having the next highest patrimonies (in the region, respectively of 700 and 800 *lire*). A further handful of men – including Giovanni di Paganello, Ser Giovanni di Ser Francesco, Lando di Pepe, Nino di Giovanni, and Lonarduccio di Giovanni – had assets of between some 300 and some 600 *lire*. A second group of heirs who may likewise have been regarded as comparatively well off – the relatives of Vivo di Giacomo – are recorded as having a joint patrimony of just over 300 *lire*. Other entries in the 1320 *Tavola delle possessioni* reveal that the combined assets of individuals who were clearly siblings, albeit operating independently, fell into the same category. Details furnished in respect of the Romaiuoli brothers Bectus and Dominichellus, each of whom are recorded as owning their own house inside the walls of the village, as well as 10 or so plots of land in the territory beyond, provide an interesting example.[27] While independently owning several different pieces of land, these brothers also had joint possession of four plots, two in the area known as Tredine, one in the area known as 'Piano a Sexte', and one at Capraia. The combined value of these four pieces of land alone was 60 *lire*, 11 *soldi*. The sum of the brothers' joint patrimonies amounted to over 250 *lire*. While clearly not in the league of either the heirs of Vivo di Giacomo or those singled out here as the male elite of the village in 1320, as a family unit Bectus and his brother were thus comparatively well off. Significantly, neither of their houses could have been structures of any size or significance, valued respectively at 25 *lire*, 7 *soldi* and 22 *lire*. As we shall see, although it is clearly legitimate to conclude that there was a direct correlation between the amount of land owned and the overall wealth (and thus social position) of any single individual, a number of other factors, such as the value of property owned inside the walls, or an individual's professional qualifications could be equally influential in deciding whether he formed part of the social elite.

According to the 1320 *Tavola delle possessioni*, Bindo di Accorso – the second highest endowed individual in the early fourteenth-century village – was the owner of a considerable amount of land in the vicinity of Sant'Angelo in Colle, as well as several houses inside the walls.[28] Of the five houses and one building plot described in Bindo di Accorso's entry, one seems to have been of substantial size, being valued at 86 *lire*. The other four ranged in value from 14 *lire* 7 *soldi* to 42 *lire* 13 *soldi*. For sheer quantity of property owned, Bindo di Accorso must have been considered as one of the leading local lights in the early fourteenth-century village, apart from the heirs of Cecco di Piero. With an overall patrimony of some 730 *lire* Bindo's only other rival in wealth was Michele da Genoa. For the rest, he stood head and shoulders above the other male inhabitants of the village. As we shall see, there are good reasons for concluding that his professional duties inside the village also positioned him within the ranks of the elite.

Bindo di Accorso's country possessions consisted in the main of arable land, combined in several cases with woodland and vines. The plots of arable land were for the most part comparatively small, ranging in size from one to eight or nine *staia*, but one piece of land combined with woodland in the area known as Asperio is recorded as measuring 18 *staia*, and a separate piece of arable land held in the area known as Ripatecta was slightly larger at 20 *staia*. Neither piece of land was recorded as having a particularly high value, the combined arable and woodland plot at Asperio being estimated at 11 *lire*, and that at Ripatecta being estimated at 16 *lire* and 13 *soldi*. There were, nevertheless, distinctions in value between individual plots. A third piece of combined arable and woodland owned by Bindo di Accorso in the area known as Caprarese, measuring 29 *staia*, was estimated at 16 *lire* and 17 *soldi*. The land at Caprarese was thus valued at a lower rate than that at Asperio, despite the fact that both plots consisted of the same mixture of arable and woodland. There is little indication that Bindo's land yielded olives, and thus oil. Nor do the comparatively small sizes of individual plots of land combined with vines indicate that Bindo was seriously involved in the production of wine. However, ownership of so many plots of arable land clearly offered considerable opportunities for the growing of crops, and subsequent revenue from grain and flour. Bindo's land may also have served for the pasturing of both local animals and those driven through the area as part of a seasonal *transumanza*.

This individual's professional life is also significant. Surviving records show that Bindo di Accorso was intimately concerned with the affairs of Sant'Angelo in Colle in his professional guise as 'camerlengo', or village treasurer. As such, he would have been involved with all matters of monetary exchange, including taxation, local business transactions, and personal debt.[29] In this guise, Bindo must also have become involved with other members of the legal profession, including no doubt the village notary Ser Guccio di Ser Francesco. There was certainly physical proximity between two of the houses belonging to the families of Bindo di Accorso and Ser Francesco, since details furnished in the 1320 *Tavola delle possessioni* show that the heirs of Ser Francesco were the proprietors of a fairly substantial house (valued at 76 *lire* and 13 *soldi*) that was adjacent to the largest property owned by Bindo.[30] As earlier discussion has shown, the heirs of Ser Francesco were also established in close proximity to at least one of the properties belonging to the three siblings Guccio, Lucarino and Becca. At the very least, therefore, some form of neighbourhood association, if not alliance, must have been established between the families of Bindo di Accorso and Ser Guccio di Ser Francesco. In fact, as we shall see, several of the individual men credited with having the highest patrimonies in 1320 not only owned adjacent properties but were also related.

Cross-reference between individual entries in the 1320 *Tavola delle possessioni* shows, for example, that two wealthy siblings – Paganello and Nino di Giovanni – owned contiguous properties inside the walls of the village.[31] In addition, both of these buildings seem to have been of some size, since their rateable values were recorded as 125 *lire* and 100 *lire* respectively. It also becomes clear that one of the seven houses recorded in respect of another group of the village elite – the heirs of Cecco di Piero – albeit of somewhat modest size, was adjacent to the large house belonging to Paganello di Giovanni.[32] Another house belonging to the heirs of Cecco di Piero (again rather small, being valued at 14 *lire* and 13 *soldi*) was said to have abutted property belonging to Michele da Genoa.[33]

One significant conclusion to be drawn from a consideration of the highest patrimonies recorded in respect of the male population of Sant'Angelo in Colle in 1320 is thus that several of those individuals identified as belonging to the village's male elite were established in close proximity to each other. Moreover, several of the properties in question were structures of some size. With the exception of Lonarduccio di Giovanni and the heirs of Vivo di Jacopo, or Giacomo, all those recorded as having high patrimonies in 1320 appear to have owned at least one large building inside the walls. There seems little doubt that the size of the house in which an individual lived would have played a significant part in advertising, if not reflecting his or her social standing. Indeed it was possibly the case that the size of living accommodation owned was considered more significant than the ownership of land. Paganello di Giovanni, for example, whilst owning comparatively little land, was in possession of a house inside the walls that was valued at the considerable sum of 125 *lire*. As we shall see, Paganello di Giovanni's family also assumed a central position in the affairs of Sant'Angelo in Colle, not least through the professional duties as village notary assumed by Paganello's son, Giovanni.

A number of other individuals may have assumed positions of influence in Sant'Angelo in Colle as a result of their professional status, rather than the size of their real estate inside or outside the village walls. Several entries in the *Tavola delle possessioni* include, for example, the prefix 'Ser' – a title that implies both education and social standing. Significantly, not all such individuals are recorded as having large patrimonies, although in some cases it is clear that they owned rather large houses. It is worth noting, for example, that although the heirs of Ser Francesco had apparently inherited quite a substantial house, and appear to have had rich neighbours, their recorded patrimony was actually rather low. Although the title 'Ser' no doubt indicated some social rank (at least for Ser Francesco, the head of the family), and the size of the inherited living accommodation (and possibly even its location) would seem to imply an elevated social position, the overall patrimony of 85 *lire* and 1 *soldi* recorded in respect of the heirs of Ser Francesco would seem to imply the opposite.[34] In fact, the entry for the heirs of Ser Francesco in the 1320 *Tavola delle possessioni* shows that the inherited house inside the walls constituted their main asset. In the countryside beyond, they owned a comparatively large piece of land in the area known as Collesorbi, that was partly covered by wood and partly uncultivated, but which was estimated at the surprisingly low sum of 6 *lire*. They are also recorded as owning a further 6 *staia* of woodland in the area known as Canale, that was valued at the not much higher sum of 11 *lire* and 8 *soldi*. That said, and as we have already seen, the entry for the heirs of Ser Francesco in the 1320 *Tavola delle possessioni* probably only partially reveals their actual position within the early fourteenth-century society of Sant'Angelo in Colle. In fact, these individuals probably belonged to a much larger and prosperous clan that included the three siblings, Guccio, Lucarino and Becca di Ser Francesco. They thus had strength by association. The combined patrimonies of Guccio and Lucarino amounted to over 500 *lire*.[35] Clustered together within the walls of Sant'Angelo in Colle, the individual members of Ser Francesco's family must in fact have affected a powerful social presence, irrespective of the variations in their individual patrimonies.

Thus far, and if the guiding principle is taken to be the extent of land and property owned, as well as an individual's overall financial circumstances, it would seem that early fourteenth-century Sant'Angelo in Colle was dominated by a handful of wealthy clans. There were, however, two notable exceptions, Bindo di Accorso and Michele da Genoa. Bindo di Accorso's patrimony, twice that of Mita di Piero, must have set him in a social bracket well above that of the richest women in the village, as well as many of the well-to-do men. Bindo's rival in wealth, Michele da Genoa, may well have been regarded as occupying an even higher social niche, since his patrimony was recorded as just over 809 *lire*.[36] Michele da Genoa was clearly the richest single man living in the early fourteenth-century village.

In 1320 Michele da Genoa owned three houses inside the walls of Sant'Angelo in Colle, as well as 18 plots of land in the countryside beyond. One of these (a plot at 'Sitine'), which appears either in part or totally to have been left uncultivated, was valued at 184 *lire* and 3 *soldi*. This comparatively high sum may partly be explained by the size of the plot, since it measured some 85 *staia*. Another piece of arable land in the area known as Pantano seems to have been even more valuable, since it was estimated at 110 *lire*, despite apparently measuring only 33 *staia*. The other plots owned by Michele da Genoa were on the whole rather modest in size, and consisted for the most part of arable land, kitchen garden and vineyards. On each of three pieces of arable land there was, in addition, a *capanna*, or shack. For Michele, therefore, there were several opportunities not only to engage in sharecropping contracts but also to accommodate *mezzaiuoli* in buildings on his land. Strangely, and despite his great wealth and apparent potential for influence through sharecropping agreements, no records have as yet surfaced concerning Michele da Genoa, other than the entry for him in the 1320 *Tavola delle possessioni*.

With Paganello di Giovanni, another of the individuals identified as a member of the male elite in 1320, we are more fortunate. Moreover, as previous discussion has shown, it seems that at least one of the sharecropping agreements drawn up in the context of land in the vicinity of Sant'Angelo in Colle involved a number of relatives of Paganello di Giovanni. Paganello di Giovanni is singled out here for particular consideration, not only because of the links that can be drawn between his family and the practice of *mezzadria* in the early fourteenth-century village, but also because, unlike Michele da

Genoa, we can establish a great deal about his own personal circumstances as well as those of several members of his extended family clan.

There seems little doubt that Paganello di Giovanni was already a man of means by 1320. In terms of wealth alone, his standing in early fourteenth-century Sant'Angelo in Colle must have been equal to that of Ser Guccio di Ser Francesco. Both men clearly qualify for inclusion in the male elite of the village, albeit at the lower end of the scale. Although not recorded as a professional man in the 1320 *Tavola delle possessioni*, it seems likely that Paganello was associated with the law through at least two other members of his family. Surviving records reveal that a Giovanni di Paganello, referred to here as Giovanni di Paganello 'senior', was involved with the affairs of central government in Siena as early as February, 1260.[37] The hypothesis is raised here that Giovanni di Paganello 'senior' was the father of Paganello di Giovanni, and that he may have been the first member of the family to acquire real estate in and around Sant'Angelo in Colle as part of a move by the Sienese government to colonise its subject commune. Evidence in support of this hypothesis is considered in greater detail in the Chapter 7. As that chapter will show (regardless of the presumed relationship between Giovanni di Paganello 'senior' and Paganello di Giovanni and any association the former may have had with Sant'Angelo in Colle during the thirteenth century), there can be little doubt that Paganello's own son, Giovanni di Paganello, not only inherited his father's real estate in and around the village, but also remained at Sant'Angelo in Colle until his death some time between 1335 and 1336. It is also clear that Giovanni di Paganello followed the law – even if not in the footsteps of his putative grandfather, Giovanni di Paganello 'senior'. Surviving documents show that Giovanni di Paganello served as the village notary of Sant'Angelo in Colle from at least the mid 1320s. There seems little doubt, therefore, that he, like his father, occupied a special niche within the early fourteenth-century society of Sant'Angelo in Colle.

According to the 1320 *Tavola delle possessioni*, Paganello di Giovanni's landed property consisted of nine pieces of terrain and a *casalinum*, or small house, just outside Sant'Angelo in Colle, as well as a large house inside the walls with a recorded value of 125 *lire*.[38] The value of Paganello's house inside the village was topped only by two others: one valued at 150 *lire* which belonged to the heirs of Cecco di Piero, and another, valued at 135 *lire*, which belonged to the church of Sant'Angelo (see Chapter 3, Table 3.2). The apparent size of Paganello di Giovanni's living accommodation in Sant'Angelo in Colle strengthens the hypothesis that he was one of the leading figures in the early fourteenth-century village, even though his declared patrimony in the 1320 *Tavola delle possessioni* ranked ninth. It seems, in addition, that Paganello was one of a number of well-heeled siblings established in Sant'Angelo in Colle, and that this group – like the heirs of Ser Cecco and the heirs of Ser Francesco – formed a clan of some influence.

Cross-referencing between other entries in the 1320 *Tavola delle possessioni* reveals that Paganello di Giovanni's house was bordered on one side by property belonging to his brother, Nino.[39] Nino's house, like that owned by Paganello, seems to have been a structure of some size, since its value was recorded as 100 *lire*. Other property owned by Nino di Giovanni inside the walls was equally substantial. The overall value of the three houses declared as owned by him in 1320 was 214 *lire*. Of the two siblings, Nino was clearly the wealthiest. His total patrimony – recorded at some 540 *lire* – was almost twice that of his brother Paganello, and placed him in sixth position in the rank of wealthy men. The combined visual impression of the two adjacent houses owned by Paganello and his brother Nino must have been impressive.

The two brothers also seem to have owned a number of neighbouring plots of land. In fact, they appear to have owned adjacent land in two different locations – one in the area known as 'Tra Fossatella' and the other at 'Poggiuolo Albinelli'.[40] A number of other individuals bearing the same patronym as Paganello and Nino, and who were in all probability their siblings also appear to have owned land with common borders.

Table 6.3 Ownership of contiguous property inside the walls, or of plots of land in the vicinity of Sant'Angelo in Colle, by Paganello di Giovanni and other members of his family[1]

Property	Paganello	Nino	Vanuccio	Lonarduccio	Cecchino	Folchino
Living house inside walls	@	@				
Poggiuolo Albinelli	@	*				
Poggiuolo Albinelli		*			@	
Costis		@			*	
Tavoleta		@			*	
Trafossatella	@	@				
Trafossatella		@		*		
Ferrale		@	@			
Pantano		*		@	*	
Pantano			@	*		
Campo Giovanni		@				@

Note to Table 6.3

1 @ denotes the individual from which details concerning contiguity of land have been taken. * denotes the individual who is said to have owned contiguous property.

Analysis

It is clear from this table that there were considerable inconsistencies between details furnished in individual entries. Nino di Giovanni, for example, seems not to have declared his ownership of land at Poggiuolo Albinelli despite the fact that he is mentioned as a neighbour to what were possibly two separate plots of land in that area belonging to Paganello and to Cecchino. Nino for his part declared land at Costis that was said to border land belonging to Cecchino. Details recorded for the latter individual make no mention of this. Nino is also said to have had a plot of land at Trafossatella that bordered land belonging to Lonarduccio. No mention is made of such a plot in Lonarduccio's entry. Lonarduccio for his part is said to have owned land at Pantano that was bordered by plots belonging to Nino and Cecchino. This is not verified by the entries for either of those individuals, but according to Vanuccio's entry his land was bordered by property belonging to Lonarduccio. Apart from the two living houses declared inside the walls by Paganello and Nino, there is consistency in only three instances: concerning land at

Ferrale belonging to Nino and Vannuccio; land at Campo Giovanni belonging to Nino and Folchino, and land at Trafossatella belonging to Paganello and Nino. There seems in particular to have been a lack of transparency concerning land held at Pantano, where four of the brothers appear to have had holdings.

Lunardutio, or Lonarduccio, di Giovanni, for example, is recorded as owning a piece of land in the area known as 'Pantano', which is described as abutting on one side land owned by Nino di Giovanni, and on another, land belonging to Cecco di Giovanni.[41] Cecco di Giovanni for his part is said to have owned land at Poggiuolo Albinelli that was bordered on one side by terrain belonging to Nino di Giovanni.[42] That land in turn was close to land belonging to Paganello di Giovanni. Thus, three individuals with the same patronym – Paganello, Nino and Cecco – owned three separate, but contiguous plots. Cross-referencing in the 1320 *Tavola delle possessioni* indicates that a number of other individuals belonged to the same family. Indeed, on the basis of patronym alone, Paganello di Giovanni could have had as many as 11 or so siblings.

Paganello di Giovanni (dead by February 1332)

*Son of Giovanni {?Giovanni di Paganello 'senior'}

*Sibling of Nino, Vanuccio, Lonarduccio (?dead before or in February 1332), Cecchino, Folchino, {?Narduccio, ?Mino,?C(?h)ola and ?Clerice}

*Father of Giovanni

Giovanni di Paganello (dead by November 1336)

*Married ?first to ?Lagia
            married to Broccola by March 1335

*Father of   Mina (?daughter of Lagia)
                  Giovanni (son of Broccola)

*Brother of Marco and Becca

Table 6.4
Proposed
Genealogy for
the family of
Paganello di
Giovanni[1]

Note to Table 6.4
1 The proposed relationship between these individuals arises from the fact that they not only all have the same patronym, but in several cases are also recorded as owning contiguous living accommodation, and or plots of land. In those cases where no contiguous land is recorded in *Estimo* 24 individual names are inserted within brackets.

Such an extended family would clearly have led to complex divisions of land and living accommodation for the purpose of inheritance. It was frequently the case that buildings (like land) were divided up between various members of the same family over time, most often as a result of changing circumstances within the family itself, such as the coming of age of a younger member, or death of the head of the household. Many such divisions involved the services of a notary and the drawing up of a formal document noting the change of ownership. It was no doubt sometimes the case, however, that such formalities were dispensed with, particularly where land was concerned, and when an erstwhile minor came of age, and took to working land previously tended by a grandfather, a father, an uncle, or a sibling. There must have been many situations, also, where an older member of the family was still alive, but where a younger member of the clan was in fact shouldering the responsibilities. Individual families may also have established working agreements as to the division of labour, without recourse to formal testaments. As already indicated in Chapter 4, it seems likely, for example, that some of the members of Paganello di Giovanni's extended family were more concerned than others with the working of the land. Cecco di Giovanni was not the only one of the family who owned no property inside the walls of the village. At least one other family member, Lonarduccio di Giovanni, was recorded in the 1320 *Tavola delle possessioni* as being in a similar position. Yet, on the face of it, Lonarduccio was richer than both Paganello and Nino, having a declared patrimony of some 620 *lire*.[43] Perhaps Lonarduccio, like Cecco's son Giovanni, spent much of his time working the family's landed possessions, and in recompense was accommodated on the land or in one of the houses inside the walls recorded as belonging to one or other of his brothers.

A number of surviving documents confirm the close relationship between the siblings of this particular family, as well as throwing light on the links between the older and younger generations. They also reveal how some members of the family assumed particular responsibilities for the family's overall estate. One such record concerns the division of land held within the family following Lonarduccio's death. According to a record drawn up by the Montalcinese notary Ser Griffo di Ser Paolo on 28 February 1332, Lonarduccio di Giovanni was dead, and his widow Rosa had reached a number of important decisions concerning her husband's nephew, Giovanni di Paganello.[44] Most significantly, Rosa is said to have wanted to relinquish any claim she might have had on her dowry property. One conclusion to be drawn from this is that Lonarduccio di Giovanni had died childless, and that all of his male siblings had predeceased him. (Giovanni's own father, Paganello, is in fact recorded in the 1332 record as already deceased.)

The responsibility for dealing with Rosa's dowry land appears to have fallen on Giovanni di Paganello 'junior'. While this could indicate that a particularly close relationship had existed between Lonarduccio and Paganello – perhaps because they were the two oldest siblings – it is also possible that Giovanni di Paganello was selected because he was the oldest independent male heir of the next generation, and perhaps the only surviving male in the family in 1332. Giovanni di Paganello may indeed have been the only direct male heir. No reference is made in the 1332 record to Rosa's subsequent intentions, but the fact that she was relinquishing dowry property to her deceased husband's nephew, and that no reference was made at that time to any children of her own, must indicate that she was either returning to her own natal family, or seeking refuge in a religious foundation. As the next chapter will show, at least two other local women, Cora, widow of Ristoruccio di Borgognone and Rosa di Piero Pecoraio, widow of Neri, or Nerio di Griffo, seem to have opted for association with a religious order following the death of their husbands.

According to the document drawn up by Ser Griffo di Ser Paolo in February 1332, Giovanni di Paganello was declared heir to half of Lonarduccio's property. On the basis of this, he was to take possession of a vineyard at 'Celglolo', which was bordered on one side by land belonging to Neri di Guicciardo and on another side by land belonging to Andrea di Chele, as well as an orchard, or kitchen garden, on the 'Costa di Sant'Angelo', which was bordered on one side by road, on another by the same Neri di Guicciardo, and on a third side by land belonging to the hospital of Santa Maria della Scala in Siena. Since neither the vineyard nor the orchard was recorded as in the possession of Lonarduccio di Giovanni in 1320, one conclusion must be that Lonarduccio was not at that date married to Rosa, and that these two plots of land were the ones that came into Lonarduccio's possession as part of his wife's dowry.

Giovanni di Paganello for his part seems only to have enjoyed these legacies for a short time, for only a few years after the death of his uncle, he, himself, is recorded as drawing up his own testamentary stipulations, and by 8 November 1336 he also was dead.[45] At that point questions must once more have been raised about the division of Giovanni's accumulated assets. Consideration of Giovanni di Paganello's testamentary stipulations throws further light on the dates at which Paganello di Giovanni's siblings had died, and what heirs – if any – survived. A telling point is that at the time of drawing up his hand-written will in 1335, Giovanni di Paganello seems only to have looked to the younger generation of the family. In particular, Giovanni's legacies seem to have been directed towards the children of only two of his father's brothers – Nino and Cecco di Giovanni.

One of Giovanni di Paganello's stipulations was that on his death his cousin Lunardo di Nino (the son of his paternal uncle, Nino) should receive a property abutting one of Giovanni's own houses in Sant'Angelo in Colle. It is possible that the building in question rightfully belonged to Lunardo since it appears to be the same structure described in the 1320 *Tavola delle possessioni* as valued at 100 *lire* and belonging to his father Nino di Giovanni.[46] Some time before 1335, this building must, however, have passed to Giovanni di Paganello. It is possible that Nino's son Lunardo had either not been born – Nino's wife being pregnant at the time of Nino's death – or was considered too young to inherit the family house. As we shall see, Giovanni di Paganello's second wife was also probably pregnant at the time of his drawing up his 1335 will, since Giovanni constructed a number of contingency plans in the event of the birthing, successful or otherwise, of that child. As discussion in Chapter 7 will show, Giovanni di Paganello was aware not only of the dangers to the mother in child birth, but also of the possibility that the child itself might be still-born, or might not subsequently survive. In the event, both Giovanni di Paganello's newborn heir Giovanni and his wife survived him, and the child was given in care to Giovanni di Paganello's brother, Marco. It is not impossible, therefore, that Lunardo di Nino's father or indeed both his mother and his father had died whilst Lunardo was still a baby, and that he, by consequence, was left under the protection of his cousin, Giovanni. This could explain why a house belonging to Nino was handed over to Giovanni di Paganello, but was subsequently destined to return to Lunardo.

It is worth remembering in this context the various hypotheses that were raised in Chapter 4 concerning the living accommodation available to Giovanni di Paganello's paternal uncle Cecco di Giovanni. The stimulus for those hypotheses was the fact that Cecco di Giovanni's branch of the family appears not to have owned property inside the walls of Sant'Angelo in Colle. One conclusion drawn was that Cecco di Giovanni could have been accommodated in property belonging to Giovanni di Paganello in the countryside around Sant'Angelo in Colle. Consideration was also given to the possibility that members of Cecco's extended family were accommodated in one of the several buildings owned by other members of the clan inside the walls. Entries drawn up in respect of the brothers Guccio and Lucarino di Ser Francesco and other members of their extended family in the 1320 *Tavola delle possessioni* confirm that such sharing of living accommodation would not have been an exception in the early fourteenth-century village. The stipulations in Giovanni di Paganello's will would seem to confirm that in certain circumstances property inside the walls belonging to one member of the family could be made available to another member of the clan, although probably on the condition that it should subsequently revert to the original owner or surviving members of his immediate family.

The fact that a house belonging to Nino di Giovanni was at one time handed over to his nephew, Giovanni di Paganello but, according to the latter's will, was destined subsequently to be returned to Nino's own son Lunardo following Giovanni's death, opens up a number of possibilities in the context of the living accommodation used by Cecco di Giovanni and his family. Might Cecco di Giovanni, for example, have acquired the rights to property belonging to Nino, the wealthiest of the siblings, rather than from his less wealthy brother Paganello, or from that individual's son, Giovanni di Paganello? So far, no documentary evidence has surfaced to clarify or confirm any of these hypotheses. On the basis of existing documents, there seems little doubt, however, that different members of this extended family clan assumed a number of different responsibilities for each other's assets.

Giovanni di Paganello appears in fact to have considerably increased his father's holdings in the 15-year period between the 1320 *Tavola delle possessioni* and the drawing up of his own will. In 1320 Paganello di Giovanni is recorded as owning one house inside the walls of Sant'Angelo in Colle, a little shed on what was probably a kitchen garden or orchard close to the walls of the village, five pieces of arable land, one piece of worked land which included vines, a separate vineyard and a kitchen garden or orchard on the 'Costa San Piero'.[47] In 1335 Giovanni di Paganello appears not only to have acquired several more properties inside the walls of Sant'Angelo in Colle, but also to have been in possession of a considerable number of pieces of land in the countryside beyond. Amongst other assets, Giovanni di Paganello mentioned a second vineyard in the area known as Cegliore; a further two pieces of worked land in Pantano with quite different neighbours from those cited in connection with land in the same area recorded as belonging to his father Paganello in 1320; a piece of land near the Fossa Tredine; a piece of land at Querce Uberti; a house inside the walls of Sant'Angelo functioning as an olive press, which was bordered on one side by the village's water conduit; a second house, apparently in the same area (because of reference once more to the 'corso d'aqua'), and yet another house next to a 'chiostrorello', or courtyard/cum pen which was likewise owned by him. By 1335, Giovanni di Paganello appears therefore not only to have considerably increased the family's overall assets, but also to have established two local businesses – one based on the practice of law, and the other concerning the processing of local olives.

The building inside the walls of Sant'Angelo in Colle recorded as combining a house and an olive press must have been one of Giovanni di Paganello's more significant acquisitions. The obvious conclusion to be drawn is that Giovanni di Paganello was by that date intent on producing olive oil. It is, however, curious that none of the land recorded in respect of Paganello di Giovanni in the 1320 *Tavola delle possessioni* appears to have contained olive groves. Nor were any of the plots apparently acquired by Giovanni di Paganello between 1320 and 1335 described as containing olive trees. If Giovanni's press was producing olive oil, it must have been from olives cultivated on other individuals' land.

Giovanni di Paganello's ownership of the press at Sant'Angelo in Colle may thus have placed him in a powerful position to control local business. Collecting, processing and finally pressing olives no doubt required, even if only at certain times of the year, a considerable work force. While individual landowners might be responsible for the initial gathering of the olives, once delivered to a press inside the walls, such produce was presumably handed over to a number of other individuals for the further stages necessary to producing the olive oil itself. By 1335, Giovanni di Paganello may thus have been viewed not only as an individual of some wealth, and a public official of some local significance, but also as an important local employer. All this must have combined to place Giovanni di Paganello in a prime position as a potential local benefactor and patron. As we shall see in the following chapter, Giovanni did in fact play a significant part in the construction and embellishment of at least two key buildings in the early fourteenth-century village: the church of San Michele Arcangelo and the church of San Pietro.

Notes

1 For an analysis of patrimonies in the Sienese *contado*, see Chapter 4, footnote 2. According to Barlucchi, individuals with patrimonies of between 500 and 1,000 *lire* generally represented the top 5–7% of the population.

2 In this respect see Giovanni Cherubini, 'Proprietari, contadini e campagne senesi all' inizio del Trecento', in idem (ed.), *Signori, contadini, borghesi. Ricerche sulla società Italiana del Basso Medioevo*, (Florence, 1974), pp. 231–311 (p. 248).

3 Archivio di Stato di Siena (hereafter ASS), *Estimo di Siena*, 106, Terzo di Città, San Pietro in Chastelvecchio, 1318, fols 50r–75v.

4 Ibid., fol. 57r.

5 Ibid., fol. 66r and fol. 73v.

6 Ibid., *Estimo di Siena*, 104, Terzo di Città, Santo Quiricho in Chastelvecchio, 1318, fols 264r–265v (old number 257 ff.)

7 Ibid., *Estimo di Siena*, 108, Terzo di Città, Porta all'archo, 1320, fols 683r–687v.

8 Ibid., *Estimo di Siena*, 104, Terzo di Città, Santo Quiricho in Chastelvecchio, 1318, old page number 257, new pencil pagination 264.

9 Archivio Storico del Comune di Montalcino (hereafter ACM), *Fondi Diversi, Archivio dei particolari, Ser Griffo di Ser Paolo* (hereafter *Ser Griffo di Ser Paolo*), 4, fol. 66v. Binduccio di Nerio was not included in the 1320 *Tavola delle possessioni* for Sant'Angelo in Colle, although given his patronym he could have been a member of one of several groups of heirs included in that list.

10 ASS, *Estimo di Siena*, 129, Terzo di San Martino, San Cristofano allato la Chiesa, 1318, fol. CCXVII.

11 Ibid., *Estimo di Siena*, 102, Terzo di Città, Inchontri, 1318, fols 88r–89r (old number LXXXXII ff.).

12 Ibid., fol. 109 (old number CXXI).

13 Ibid., *Estimo di Siena*, 138, Terzo di Camollia, Sant'Andrea a Lato la Piazza, 1318, fols 286r–287v.

14 Ibid., *Estimo di Siena*, 129, Terzo di San Martino, San Cristofano allato la Chiesa, 1318, fols CCCXV–CCCXVII.

15 Ibid., *Estimo di Siena*, 143, Terzo di Camollia, La Magione del Tempio, 1318, fols 227r–229v.

16 Ibid., *Estimo di Siena*, 194, fol. 416 (old no. 417).

17 Ibid., *Estimo di Siena*, 129, Terzo di San Martino, San Cristofano allato la Chiesa, 1318, fol. CCCXXV.

18 Ibid., *Estimo di Siena*, 108, Terzo di Città, Porta all'archo, 1320, cc 231v-236v (old number CCXXXVIIII ff.).

19 Ibid., *Estimo di Siena*, 139, Terzo di Camollia, Sant'Andrea a Lato la Piazza, 1318, (hereafter *Estimo* 139), fols CCXXVI–CCXLII.

20 Ibid., *Estimo* 24, fol. 30r.

21 Ibid., *Estimo di Siena*, 102, Terzo di Città, Inchontri, 1318, fols 88r–89r (old number LXXXXII ff.).

22 ASS, *Estimo* 24, fol. 30r.

23 Ibid., *Estimo di Siena*, 139, fols 150r–153v (old number CCXXVI ff.).

24 Ibid., *Estimo* 24, fol. 63v.

25 Ibid., fol. 130r.

26 Ibid., fol. 381r. Details recorded in the *Tavola delle possessioni* for Camigliano during the same period (ASS, *Estimo del Contado*, 80) reveal that only one individual – Giovanni di Mende – had a patrimony to equal that of the upper echelon at Sant'Angelo in Colle. At just under 600 *lire*, Giovanni di Mende's patrimony was in line, for example, with that of Giovanni di Paganello's wealthier brother Nino. It is significant, however, that Giovanni di Mende was not specifically recorded as a resident of Camigliano. In addition, part of Giovanni di Mende's entry, including the details of his overall patrimony and a reference to a house valued at 22 *lire* and 13 *soldi*, were crossed out in the *Tavola delle possessioni* register. Details furnished in respect of this individual are thus not entirely reliable. However, even in the neighbouring commune of Castelnuovo dell'Abate to the east of Sant'Angelo in Colle, there were only a handful of individuals whose patrimonies of between 300 and 500 *lire* could match those of the wealthier members of the community at Sant'Angelo in Colle in the early fourteenth century. (See ASS, *Estimo del Contado*, 56). For the most part, patrimonies recorded in respect of Castelnuovo dell'Abate were lower than 100 *lire*, and many fell within the bracket of 10 to 20 *lire*. Only one individual, Nerio di Bonifiglio, stands out from the rest, with a recorded patrimony of over 1,000 *lire* (ASS, *Estimo* 56, fol. 278). But Nerio himself seems not to have owned a house inside the walls of Castelnuovo dell'abate.

27 ASS, *Estimo* 24, fols 14r–15r and 109r–110r.

28 Ibid., fols 17r–21v.

29 In small communes, the village treasurer also on occasion assumed some of the duties of the local 'notaio', or lawyer, see Andrea Barlucchi, *Il 'Contado' Senese all'epoca dei Nove'. Asciano e il suo territorio tra Due e Trecento* (Florence, 1997), pp. 137–40.

30 ASS, *Estimo* 24, fol. 167r.

31 Ibid., fol. 380v and fol. 343r.

32 Ibid., fol. 172v.

33 Ibid., fol. 173v.

34 Ibid., fol. 167r.

35 Ibid., fols 268r and 451v.

36 Ibid., fols 286r–288v.

37 ASS, *Manoscritti* B41, no. 586.

38 ASS, *Estimo* 24, fols 380r–381r.

39 Ibid., fol. 380r.

40 Ibid., fols 380v and 381r.

41 Ibid., fol. 276r.

42 Ibid., fol. 82v.

43   Ibid., fol. 276r.

44   ACM, *Ser Griffo di Ser Paolo*, 4, fol. 161v.

45   According to the codicil included in the 28 March 1335 will drawn up by Giovanni di Paganello. (See ASS, *Diplomatico in Caselle*, *casella* 784, 28 March 1335, *Archivio Spedale*.)

46   ASS, *Estimo* 24, fol. 343r.

47   Ibid., fols 380r–380v.

Civic Awareness

7

Piety, Charity and Social Welfare

If personal wealth and professional status were the key components in establishing an individual's position in society, they must also have had a part to play in the development of his or her civic awareness. There can be little doubt that several, if not all, of the individuals discussed in the last chapter were well placed to influence affairs in the early fourteenth-century village. The same can be said for at least two of the women discussed in Chapter 5. Some of these individuals must also have been predisposed to support charitable and religious institutions, not only through financial support during their own lifetimes, but also in legacies and testamentary stipulations drawn up to ensure their spiritual well-being in the after life.

An attempt is made in this chapter to assess the patterns of piety and charity in Sant'Angelo in Colle under the Government of the Nine. In particular, consideration is given to the distinctions that were drawn between local institutions and those further afield. Clearly a number of factors could influence the choice of institution deserving support. As we shall see, in some cases a family connection with a particular institution was the deciding factor. It is also clear that individual testators were often anxious to place their spiritual eggs in many baskets. Surviving records indicate that it was quite normal to leave a number of legacies to different institutions. Attention focuses here on the key factors influencing selection of individual institutions.

Samuel K. Cohn Jr. has dominated enquiries in this field since the late 1980s.[1] Initially embarking on a ground-breaking consideration of the testamentary legacies of Sienese citizens between the thirteenth and early nineteenth centuries, Cohn opined that individual choices might embrace lifelong, even multigenerational attachments, as well as pre-existing commitments to friends and family.[2] He also suggested that personal legacies involved the dual perspective of the testator's own faith, as manifested in his donation of property and the ensuing honour attached to his family, and the more general matter of the well-being of his own soul in the afterlife.[3] Noting that parish churches and monasteries were the traditional focus points for piety and donations, Cohn suggests that monastic communities were in the lead during the last part of the thirteenth century.[4] This trend was, however, reversed at the end of the following century, when neighbourhood churches began to eclipse both the monasteries and the hospitals.[5]

There can be little doubt that that which was local was best placed to attract attention. There may also have been historical reasons why a local institution should figure regularly in testamentary stipulations. It is not surprising, for example, that the important local monastic institution of Sant'Antimo routinely featured in the legacies of residents of both Sant'Angelo in Colle and Montalcino during the early fourteenth century. Something more distant would clearly have been less familiar, although if rich and influential it would no doubt have been better placed to attract attention. The Sienese hospital of Santa Maria della Scala must surely have fallen into such a category. However, it is probably a mistake to underestimate the political dimensions of medieval piety. Consideration of the patterns of legacies in respect of Santa Maria della Scala in wills drawn up for residents of Sant'Angelo in Colle and Montalcino during the thirteenth century and early fourteenth century indicates that much could depend on events on the ground, and that the power of the individual institution was not necessarily the deciding factor. Testamentary stipulations drawn up on behalf of residents of Montalcino, and most noticeably those notarised prior to Montalcino's final subjugation to Siena in 1361, appear, for example, to have concentrated almost exclusively on local institutions. Of the numerous wills drawn up on behalf of residents of Montalcino by the local lawyer Ser Griffo di Ser Paolo between 1318 and 1332, only one or two contain any mention of Siena, and those that do appear to have been dictated by individuals either already associated with Siena by birth, or through marriage, or who themselves were 'outsiders'.[6]

In the general context of legacies to hospitals, Cohn suggests that the first half of the thirteenth century witnessed a gradual rise that remained relatively stable, albeit with minor variations until about 1325.[7] Thereafter, and contrary to traditional assumptions concerning the impact of the Black Death in 1348, there was a noticeable dip in legacies to hospitals, with an upward trend only after the renewed outbreak of plague in 1363. With specific reference to Santa Maria della Scala, Cohn notes how the development of that institution's holdings reflected such trends in the rapid expansion of its patrimony during the early fourteenth century, followed by a period of virtual stagnation and a renewed and aggressive expansion between 1385 and 1400. Indeed, Cohn suggests that by the latter date Santa Maria della Scala had achieved a near monopoly, at the expense of many smaller local hospitals, including those attached to monasteries. Prior to the second half of the fourteenth century, Cohn argues that the various independent hospitals inside Siena, as well as those scattered around in the suburbs and countryside and associated with neighbourhood churches and powerful families, were favoured almost as much as Santa Maria della Scala.[8] Between the outbreak of the Great Plague and the end of the fourteenth century, there was, however, an exponential rise in bequests to Santa Maria della Scala, and by the fifteenth century it was attracting more than two thirds of all endowments made to hospitals.

Coining the phrase 'civic Christianity', Cohn suggests that the fifteenth century witnessed a greater trend towards social responsibility and public charity, as well as a taste for 'ceremonial magnificence', frequently manifested in 'lavish ecclesiastical building programmes'.[9] On the face of it somewhat anachronistically, Cohn describes medieval wills as 'contemporary opinion polls'.[10] Yet, as we shall see, the contents of wills discussed in this chapter vividly reflect the personal circumstances of the individual testators, whilst at the same time indicating much about their sense of political correctness, their familial aspirations and their traditional, indeed sometimes ancient bonds of affection and respect. Moreover, it becomes clear that individual testators drawing up their wills around the time of the Great Plague were already engaged in raising civic awareness, as well as being intent on contributing to the embellishment of ecclesiastical and charitable institutions. As we shall also see, these patterns of piety and charity indicate that the testators concerned were already intent on what Cohn would describe as 'a cult of remembrance'. There is little doubt, for example, that they 'sought to leave a mark'.[11] Nor, in at least one case, could one deny that the testator sought to manipulate the actions of surviving family members in maintaining property over several generations, and thus preserving the family's name and honour.

From surviving records concerning Sant'Angelo in Colle, it appears that land and property acquired by Santa Maria della Scala in the vicinity of the village was on occasion sequestered, rather than bought or received as a result of a voluntary endowment. There are numerous examples of such practice where the original owner or community defaulted on the repayment of loans, or was perceived as a potential threat to the Sienese government. Before the final concord of 1361, both the individual inhabitants of Montalcino and the town itself must often have fallen into the latter category.

By contrast, and in line with Cohn's findings, during the last few decades of the fourteenth century, the hospital of Santa Maria della Scala appears not only to have figured on several occasions in testaments drawn up by residents in Montalcino, but also to have benefited from a number of generous legacies. Thus, on 24 June 1370, Giovanni di Montalcino and his wife Cecca petitioned to become oblates of the Sienese hospital, donating all of their possessions to Santa Maria della Scala, including a house in Montalcino.[12] A decade later on 12 June 1380, Tuccino di Andrea, named the hospital of Santa Maria della Scala as his 'erede universales', or universal heir.[13] The testator insisted, however, that this role should only be assumed by the Sienese institution if they were willing to recognise a number of stipulations within his will. If they were unwilling to do so, or if it became clear that the contents of the will were not being recognised, the role of universal heir was to revert to the convent of Sant'Agostino in Montalcino. A caveat of this kind suggests that Tuccino di Andrea entertained a number of doubts about the Sienese hospital.

On occasion, it also becomes clear that a testator in Montalcino was predisposed to favour a Sienese institution because of a family connection. Thus, when on 4 May 1398 a certain Donna Andrea 'daughter of Guicciardo

da Siena' ratified the decision made by Dolso di Ser Bavando of Montalcino
to donate one of her possessions at Sant'Angelo in Colle to Santa Maria della
Scala, she herself is revealed as being already connected with Siena on her
father's side.[14] At other times, a testator, in moving away from his or her
birthplace, may have felt less obliged to recognise institutions in their home
town when it came to drawing up their will. When, on 27 June 1348 Moresco
di Cenno – described as 'of Montalcino' but at that date living in the castle of
Magliano – drew up his will, he stipulated, for example, that two houses and
a piece of land in the territory of Magliano should be left, not to any institution
in Montalcino, but to Santa Maria della Scala in Siena.[15] He also laid down
that if his wife Preziosa wished to join Santa Maria della Scala as an oblate,
the hospital should grant her the usufruct of the property at Magliano on the
understanding that it would be returned to them after Preziosa's death. On
22 August 1391, Simona, daughter of Franceschino di Montalcino, and widow
of Guccio di Andrea Molli, likewise left all her possessions in the Castello di
Torrita and its district, not to any religious or charitable institutions in the
town where her father had been born, but to Santa Maria della Scala. Simona
also stipulated that the Sienese hospital should assume the role of ultimate
heir in the context of a house in Siena, in the event of two other individuals
already allocated that role in her will dying without children or descendants.
Simona also seems to have been set on involving the Sienese institution in
considerable monetary expense, since she asked that Santa Maria della Scala
should amongst other things be responsible for paying the *lira*, or tax levied
on the entire community of Torrita.[16]

    In many ways the pattern outlined here is what one should expect. The
residents of Montalcino, political pawns in the ongoing conflict between Siena
and Florence throughout the thirteenth century, must have been hard pressed
to identify which of the two super powers was most likely to be in control of
their lives at any one time. For testators, choosing whether to endow a Sienese
or a Florentine religious community or charitable foundation may have
amounted to a hazardous 'hedging of bets'. Siding with the wrong power
could have disastrous consequences. At the very least, any property or land
underwriting the spiritual service sought could, for example, be expropriated
by 'hostile' forces; at the worst, it could be destroyed. Any endowment made
to Florence prior to that city's defeat by Siena in the Battle of Montaperti in
1260 must clearly have been at risk, given that the year after their resounding
victory the Sienese are said to have forced the people of Montalcino to destroy
their urban fabric as punishment for their alliance with the wrong side.[17] That
the destruction of Montalcino was thorough is recorded in the town statutes
drawn up for Siena in 1262, where reference is made to the demolition, even,
of buildings belonging to the Damianite nuns of Montalcino, a community
of Franciscan female religious.[18] Small wonder, therefore, that surviving
testamentary stipulations drawn up on behalf of Montalcino citizens prior
to the mid-fourteenth century appear to have concentrated on local hospitals
and religious communities.

However, as we shall see, political constraints were not the only factors influencing testators' legacies during the thirteenth and early fourteenth centuries. Pre-established traditions were often just as influential in shaping patterns of piety and charity on the ground. If political expediency was the only factor in deciding where to leave property and money, one might expect that the inhabitants of Sant'Angelo in Colle (by contrast with the people of Montalcino) would have felt constrained to endow Sienese charitable institutions or religious communities following the first oath of fealty to Siena in 1212. Yet surviving evidence indicates that the villagers did not immediately turn towards Siena. There is indeed evidence to suggest that despite their newly established political allegiance, residents of Sant'Angelo in Colle were as likely to turn their attention to nearby Montalcino, as to endow Siena's principal institutions. At first sight, this might seem strange, given that Montalcino was not yet firmly under the Sienese yoke and thus presumably still regarded as a potentially hostile commune. Nor was there any formal alliance at that date between Sant'Angelo in Colle and Montalcino. It seems, however, that a complex nexus of relationships had been established between Sant'Angelo in Colle and Montalcino over time. Quite apart from the physical proximity of the two communes and the opportunities this must have given for contact through trade, religion and education, it seems likely that individual families forged bonds through marriage. While the Sienese takeover of Sant'Angelo in Colle must have driven a forceful wedge between the two communities, pre-established family connections would have been hard to sever. In fact, when writing about the early relationship between the two centres, the eighteenth-century historian Giovanni Antonio Pecci suggested that the renewed oath of fealty to Siena in 1225 was forced on the people of Sant'Angelo in Colle precisely because the Sienese government suspected that their subject commune was too friendly with the neighbouring commune of Montalcino.[19] Such anxieties may well have persuaded the Sienese to select Sant'Angelo in Colle as its main base in the continuing battle against Montalcino. Thus, as with childhood friends sent out to battle in the school boxing ring, the people of Sant'Angelo in Colle were thrown into the fray against individuals they may very well previously have considered as business partners and even friends and relations.

As we shall see, surviving testamentary stipulations indicate that the inhabitants of the newly subject commune of Sant'Angelo in Colle were at first not much troubled about social welfare in Siena, when it came to the dispensing of property or monetary endowments. Only towards the end of the thirteenth century does there seem to have been an increased interest, for example, in the affairs of Santa Maria della Scala. It is not unlikely that this resulted from the establishment of the first headquarters of the hospital in the village around that time. But it may also have been in some way influenced by the re-establishment of order in Sant'Angelo in Colle following the Ghibelline rebellion of 1280 to 1281. It may also be relevant that early in 1298 the abbot of Sant'Antimo, Fra Benedetto, decreed in a statement issued in the church of

Sant'Egidio in Montalcino, that an indulgence of 40 days should be offered to all those who made donations to the Sienese hospital.[20] While the residents of Montalcino may not have been much inclined to respond positively to such a proposition, the people of Sant'Angelo in Colle, with their long-established relationship with Sant'Antimo, and by now firmly under the Sienese yoke, may have been more compliant.

The earliest surviving record detailing the donation of land in the vicinity of Sant'Angelo in Colle to the hospital of Santa Maria della Scala dates to 5 September 1292.[21] According to this document, the land which was in the area known as 'Ferrale' had been left to Santa Maria della Scala by Giovanni di Federigo, a resident of Sant'Angelo in Colle.[22] The wording in the document is, however, open to a number of interpretations, since reference is made not only to the Sienese hospital 'taking possession' of land left to them in Giovanni di Federigo's will, but also to certain obligations they had in respect of Giovanni's widow Benvenuta. It is possible that Giovanni di Federigo had willed the land at Ferrale to Santa Maria della Scala at an earlier date, but that during his lifetime (and subsequently, during that of his widow) he had reserved the right to enjoy the usufruct of that holding. Provisions of this kind were common.

Straightforward endowments in the form of land were clearly beneficial to any institution (whether charitable or religious), not only because the produce (including livestock, grain, fruit, nuts, oil, wine and wood) could contribute to everyday needs, but, through onward sale, such holdings could also help maintain financial stability. Individual institutions were no doubt anxious to attract as many endowments of this kind as possible. At one and the same time they helped with the running costs and enhanced the capital value of the institution as a whole. However, a common arrangement involved the owner retaining the fruits, or usufruct, of the land during his or her lifetime. Frequently, the understanding was that the land should be bequeathed to the institution on the death of the beneficiary of the usufruct. In addition, it was also often understood that the institution would be responsible for the benefactor's health and well-being whilst he or she was still alive.

While in the main consisting of the donation of money, land or other property, it was also common practice for a potential benefactor to offer him or herself in personal service to the selected institution. This may indeed have been what happened to Benvenuta, the widow of Giovanni di Federigo. Clearly, such service could be mutually advantageous, although in the short-term it was likely to benefit the benefactor rather more than the institution. However, on occasion, the benefactor offered him or herself in a semi-religious role as a 'commesso' or 'commessa' or secular oblate.[23] Agreements of this kind often resulted in the owner of the land becoming a resident of the institution he or she endowed. In such cases the institution not only had to wait to benefit from the fruits of the land, but could also be tied into a lengthy period of responsibility for the welfare of the individual benefactor. Not all of those who committed themselves to the institution they endowed were single, infirm or old. While by far the most applications came from widows, on many occasions apparently able-bodied couples (often without children and thus no heirs to dispute their joint patrimony) opted to endow an institution with all their goods in exchange for a life within that institution's walls.[24]

Surviving records imply that at least some of the land and property owned by Santa Maria della Scala in the territory of Sant'Angelo in Colle by the beginning of the fourteenth century had been donated, rather than purchased. By the end of the second decade of the fourteenth century, Santa Maria della Scala appears, indeed, to have established a significant presence in and around the subject commune of Sant'Angelo in Colle.[25] One document dated 1 July 1320, refers, for example, to several pieces of land that the hospital had acquired as a result of testamentary stipulations laid down by a local resident of the village, Giovanni di Rainaldo.[26] As we have seen, the 1320 *Tavola delle possessioni* contained a number of references to land outside the village as well as to at least one property inside the walls that belonged to 'the hospital of Santa Maria'. If all this property did indeed belong to Santa Maria della Scala, it would seem that the hospital owned nine or so pieces of land in various parts of the territory, from Prete Schiace, Manganelli and Saproia to the east, to Plano Tredine and Torris Assoni to the east and north-east, and Poggio Peri and Planezze in the north.

Santa Maria della Scala continued to expand its holdings at Sant'Angelo in Colle during the first third of the fourteenth century. In June 1327, the hospital bought a piece of agricultural land (including a vineyard) in the area known as 'Capanne', from Mino 'il cherico' (the cleric), son of Giovanni di Sant'Angelo.[27] In February 1328/1329, the hospital acquired 'ogni ragione' (all the benefits and rights) that Antonio di Mino Tolomei had previously enjoyed from a piece of land in the vicinity of Sant'Angelo in Colle, as well as a 'capanna', or shack that had previously belonged to Niccolò di Galgano di Puccio (Fuccio?).[28] A few years later, in November 1333, Ristoruccio di Borgognone and his wife Cara, both residents of the village, endowed the hospital with a house and three vineyards in Ceglioli, Pianeggi and Fontedelicata.[29] Following Ristoruccio's death on 5 December 1333, his widow assumed the title of 'oblata' at Santa Maria della Scala, donating all her remaining possessions to the hospital.[30] It is possible that Ristoruccio, while clearly expectant of the spiritual rewards for himself and his wife following endowment of several parcels of land to the Sienese hospital, may also have anticipated that his wife Cara might benefit from an association with Santa Maria della Scala in the event of his predeceasing her. The speed with which Cara transported her own person and her property to the Sienese hospital following Ristoruccio's death does indeed suggest meticulous forward planning. In all likelihood, Cara was already intent on transferring away from Sant'Angelo in Colle and establishing herself inside the walls of the Sienese institution at the time of the original endowment. In opting for a life of service to the hospital of Santa Maria della Scala, Cara no doubt hoped to be taken care of, not only as a widow, but also as she became increasingly fragile during her later years. For their part, and as discussion below will show, the officials of Santa Maria della Scala may have hoped to call upon Cara, as an oblate, to help in the everyday chores of the hospital. In any event, the hospital would finally have stood to benefit from the fruits of Ristoruccio and Cara's estate.

Despite the Sienese hospital's obvious presence in and around the village, Santa Maria della Scala was by no means the only point of reference for charitable donations from residents of Sant'Angelo in Colle, either in the late thirteenth century, or during the latter years of the Government of the Nine. While some testators clearly directed their minds (and charity) towards the centre of government and various Sienese coffers, there was also, as the following case studies show, a well defined and quite separate interest in local affairs. The testamentary stipulations of two individuals associated with the early fourteenth-century village – Rosa di Piero Pecoraio and Giovanni di Paganello – are examined in detail here in an attempt to show that while Sienese institutions were certainly not ignored, local religious and charitable concerns (including institutions in the nearby commune of Montalcino) appear to have exerted just as great if not more influence on the people of Sant'Angelo in Colle.[31]

A number of general points can be made at the outset. Both Rosa di Piero Pecoraio's will of 1328 and that drawn up by Giovanni di Paganello in 1335 reflect links forged with nearby Montalcino. They also illustrate the various ways in which individual testators in Sant'Angelo in Colle sought to endow different religious orders in the neighbouring commune, despite being subject to Siena. Most of Rosa di Piero's attention was directed to the Franciscan community of San Francesco in Montalcino. Giovanni di Paganello, by contrast, appears to have favoured the Augustinian friars of Sant'Agostino in the same town, although he did stipulate that the convent of San Francesco should receive two *staio* of good oil (further evidence of his being involved in the production of oil by that date). To Sant'Agostino, he left an entire vineyard.

Rosa di Piero Pecoraio's will contains an unusually large number of stipulations concerning individual members of the community of San Francesco in Montalcino. It seems likely, therefore, that she had forged a particularly close association with the friars there. She was apparently on first name terms with several of the brothers, stipulating that money should be left to friar Niccolo di ser Paulo (?Paolo) and friar Giovanni Canofilo (elsewhere Ganofilio). One of the witnesses to Rosa's will was another friar, Manente Manni Ciampole. Other documents confirm that both friar Manente and friar Ganofilio were attached to San Francesco.[32] Niccolo di ser Paulo (?Paolo) was very likely a member of the same community. There is, in addition, evidence that at least one member of Rosa's own family had already joined the Franciscan community on the Poggio del Castelvecchio, since reference is made to her son, 'frate' Giovanni, immediately after a stipulation that the friars of San Francisco should conduct a sung mass on Rosa's behalf following her death. Confirmation that Giovanni was indeed attached to San Francesco resides in the 15 September 1328 will of one of Rosa's daughters, Lagia, who stipulated that money should be left to 'John of the order of *frati minori*, my brother'.[33] Rosa's other daughter, Binda, had apparently predeceased her mother, since Rosa stipulated that money should be left to the son of Ser Donato and his wife Domina Binda, 'ol(im) fil(ia)' (once, or previously, her daughter). This, combined with the proximity in date of the two surviving wills drawn up for Rosa and Lagia, suggests that all three women may have been struck down by the same illness. However, although a grandson survived, it seems that Rosa felt a stronger impulse to concentrate on the welfare of her son's adopted religious community.

Perhaps not surprisingly, given her sex and widowed state, Rosa seems also to have been interested in the welfare of Montalcino's female religious. As we shall see, she left money to a group of women known as the 'fratesse', or female friars, as well as to the 'mantellate' – probably a group of Third-Order secular, but mantled women. It is tempting to suggest that when widowed, Rosa – like Cara, wife of Ristoruccio di Borgognone – decided to offer personal service to a religious order by becoming a *commessa*, or secular oblate, although no reference is made to this in the surviving will. Rosa may even have joined one of the two groups of female religious in Montalcino that was associated with San Francesco, although as we shall see, she had already been widowed for several years at the time of drawing up her will. That said, Rosa's will confirms that she was anxious to establish that continued support should be given to the Franciscans in Montalcino, and in particular to the community of 'frati minori' after her death. Indeed, as the following transcript shows, the first stipulation in Rosa's will was that she herself should be buried in the church of the conventual Franciscan friars:

On the twenty second of August, in Montalcino, in the year of our Lord 1328 … domina Rosa Pieri, widow of Neri di Griffo and of sound mind … wishes her body to be buried on the site of the *frati minori* of Montalcino … She also leaves 10 *soldi* to the *fratissis* of Montalcino for their necessities … She further leaves to the *fraternita laudinus* of the *frati minori* 10 *soldi*, and to the *mantellatoris* of the *beati fra(n)cisci* of Montalcino 5 *soldi* … and to the 'Massarius sive op(e.?)arius(?)' of the parish church of Sant'Angelo in Colle a candle worth 40 *soldi* … and to the convent of the *frati minori* of Montalcino, 40 *soldi* for a sung mass … and to her son friar Giovanni, 25 *lire* for his needs …[34]

Rosa seems to have been resident in Sant'Angelo in Colle several years before the drawing up of her surviving will, since there is an entry under her name in the 1320 *Tavola delle possessioni*.[35] By that date Rosa was already widowed. Her patrimony was small, consisting of only one piece of wooded land in the area known as Collesorbi, which was valued at 1 *lire* and 18 *soldi*. No reference was made in 1320 to any living accommodation owned by Rosa inside the walls of Sant'Angelo in Colle. It is possible, therefore, that she had returned to her natal family following the death of her husband. Given that Rosa's father Piero Pecoraio appears also to have been dead in 1320, or to have died during the drawing up of the *Tavola delle possessioni*, it is also possible that Rosa, even if only for a short period of time, was living with one of her siblings, or with another part of her extended family inside the walls of the village. It nevertheless seems likely that some time between 1320 and 1328 Rosa sought refuge in Montalcino, for it was here, and with the services of the local Montalcinese notary, Ser Griffo di Ser Paolo, that she drew up her will in 1328.[36] Although thus apparently turning her back on what may have been her birthplace, Rosa di Piero was nonetheless careful not to exclude Sant'Angelo in Colle from her will, even though her legacy in respect of the village's parish church was small.

It may be relevant that Rosa di Piero was not particularly well endowed (at least according to the entry drawn up for her in the 1320 *Tavola delle possessioni*). Yet it seems that she was associated with one of the more powerful families of early fourteenth-century Sant'Angelo in Colle. As we have seen, Rosa's sister Mita di Piero Pecoraio not only owned a considerable amount of land on the eastern borders of the territory, but also possessed the ruins of a fortified tower or farmhouse that may once have served as a kind of feudal seat. While Rosa appears to have had little money of her own, and must thus have been considered a 'poor relation', Mita by contrast was one of the wealthiest women in the village. Rosa di Piero Pecoraio's testamentary stipulations thus provide insights not only to the patterns of piety adopted by local women in a subject Sienese commune, but also to the ways in which women of a specific class may have been inclined to dispose of their wealth. It is probably fair to say that in the case of Rosa di Piero Pecoraio, we witness the charitable instincts of a member of the female elite, even though she herself was not wealthy. Indeed, it is argued here that Rosa di Piero's will throws further light on the expectations of such a woman when once widowed and disenfranchised. In particular, it invites speculation on the ways in which widowed women sought solace through association with religious communities.

Rosa di Piero's reference to the female friars as 'of Montalcino' confirms that they were attached to a religious community in the neighbouring commune. Yet it seems that these women had also established a connection with Sant'Angelo in Colle several years before the drawing up of Rosa's will. The monastery of the 'fratesse' was in fact included in an independent entry in the 1320 *Tavola delle possessioni* and is recorded as already owning land in the vicinity of the village. It also becomes clear that Rosa di Piero was not the only inhabitant of Sant'Angelo in Colle to show interest in the 'fratesse' of Montalcino. It seems that at least one of the residents of early fourteenth-century Sant'Angelo in Colle had joined the 'monastero delle fratesse' several years before the drawing up of Rosa di Piero Pecoraio's will, since there is an entry in the 1320 *Tavola delle possessioni* to the heirs of Becca, 'fratessa'.[37] According to this entry the 'female friar' Becca had owned three pieces of worked land in the area known as Manganelli, which – by 1320 – had reverted to her heirs. Becca's heirs for their part made no reference to any property inside the walls. One possibility, therefore, is that Becca had been widowed and had been obliged to leave the house in which she had lived as a married woman, returning to her natal family and taking with her the pieces of land offered to her husband at the time of her marriage. Another possibility is that Becca had already endowed the female friars with a living house, prior to joining that community, although there is no reference to any such property owned by the 'fratesse' inside the walls of Sant'Angelo in Colle in the 1320 *Tavola delle possessioni*. It is also possible that Becca, like Cara, the widow of Ristoruccio di Borgognone, took land with her to the community of the 'fratesse' when first being widowed, but with the proviso in her case that such land should revert to her heirs on her death.

The female friars of Montalcino had clearly acquired several pieces of land in the vicinity of Sant'Angelo in Colle by the early fourteenth century.[38] According to their entry in the 1320 *Tavola delle possessioni* the community owned three pieces of arable land containing olive trees in the area known as Ficaiuoli, although their patrimony there was modest. The three plots at Ficaiuoli, which had an overall value of three *lire* and four *soldi*, were apparently clumped together, and were bordered on one side by a road, on another, by land belonging to the heirs of Cecco di Piero, and on the remaining two sides, by land belonging to Manovello di Ugolino.[39] The female friars' land must thus have been close to, if not adjacent to land owned by Guccio di Ser Francesco and his sister Becca.

It would be tempting to associate Becca, the sister of village notary Ser Guccio di Ser Francesco, with Becca the female friar, if it were not for the fact that no religious title was included in Becca di Ser Francesco's own entry in the 1320 *Tavola delle possessioni*. It may nevertheless be no coincidence that the female friars of Montalcino are recorded as owning land in Ficaiuolo. In 1320 Becca di Ser Francesco was recorded as owning land both at Ficaiuoli and at Pantana. Becca's two male siblings also owned land at Ficaiuoli, and, as we have already seen, several of their plots had common boundaries. Becca and her two brothers had no doubt inherited land at Ficaiuoli from their father Ser Francesco, and what had originally been a much larger plot that had then been divided up between the three siblings. The fact that the female friars owned land in close proximity to that belonging to Becca and her brothers thus opens up a number of possibilities. It does not seem to be stretching the limits of hypothesis too far to suggest, therefore, that Ser Francesco's family had already endowed the female friars of Montalcino with some of their land at Ficaiuolo.

As we shall see, both the 'fratesse' and the 'mantellate' were almost certainly attached to the Franciscan order in Montalcino. But, in any event, the details of Rosa di Pecoraio's will confirm that at least one of the groups endowed by her was associated with the Franciscan order, since she refers to the *mantellate* as of the 'blessed Franciscans'. A Franciscan association for the *fratesse* also seems likely, since surviving references frequently mention them in the same breath as the church of San Francesco, the conventual complex established by *frati minori conventuali* in the area of Montalcino known as the 'Poggio', or hill, of Castelvecchio.[40] Thus, Rosa di Piero's concern for the friars of San

Francesco, although in part fuelled by the fact that her own son was a member of that community, may also have been prompted by her own relationship with the town's female religious. Rosa's will thus provides a point of reference both for the position assumed by the female friars and the mantled women of Montalcino during the fourteenth century, and for the conditions of their relationship with the Franciscan Order.

In this context, a brief digression to consider the origins of the Franciscan order in Montalcino seems in order. There seems little doubt that a flourishing community of both male and female Franciscans was established in Montalcino by the early fourteenth century. Indeed, surviving records show that their individual institutions attracted a considerable number of endowments and promises of active service, both from local residents in Montalcino and from individuals living outside the territory of Montalcino. Interestingly, Rosa's endowments seem to have come at a specific turning point in the affairs of both the *fratesse* and the *mantellate*. Rosa may thus have acted not only as a champion of the Franciscans, but also as a lobbyist for its female branch.

Surviving archival material referring to the religious men and women of Montalcino during the early modern era includes a number of references to the town's female religious. It seems that the terms 'fratesse' and 'mantellate' were reserved for different kinds of female religious, since Fucciarini di Guido, when drawing up a codicil to his will in January 1327/8, noted that a fellow citizen of Montalcino – Piazza di Giunta – intended his daughter Mita to 'be married' *mantellata sive fratessa'* (either as a mantled woman or as a female friar).[41] Another document dated 8 January 1409, indicates that the *fratesse* and the *mantellate* may not only have been associated with the same order, but also with the same religious community, since reference is made to the 'filie', or daughters of San Francesco, who belonged to the 'ordine minore'.[42] It is possible that the female friars were more closely associated with the Second Order than their mantled, and probably Third Order sisters. In any event, the term *fratesse*, which clearly derives from *frate* rather than *suora*, probably indicates that the female friars of Montalcino adopted a fairly rigid discipline. On at least one occasion, they are, in fact, described as *mo(n)ialibis overo fratissis*.[43] Where these women were actually housed is unclear, although it seems that the female friars were at one time established outside the walls of Montalcino. The earliest reference to the *fratesse* as a distinct group outside Montalcino dates to the late thirteenth century.[44] A record dated 24 October, 1298, refers to an area outside Montalcino known as the *Domus*, or *Casa delle Fratesse* (the house of the female friars), confirming that this community of female religious was not only originally established outside the walls of Montalcino, but that they still owned some kind of monastic complex in the surrounding countryside at that date.[45] Further reference was made to the area known as the 'casa delle fratesse' in October 1310.[46]

Given her decided interest in the Franciscans, it is curious that Rosa's will contains no reference to the group of Clarissans, or Second Order Franciscans of San Damiano who are known to have established an independent presence in Montalcino some time before 1260. By the second half of the thirteenth century, these women were apparently living in reduced circumstances without a fixed monastic complex. According to Sienese statutes dating to 1262, the monastic complex of the 'Clarisse di San Damiano' in Montalcino had been destroyed, along with many other buildings inside and outside the walls, as part of the Sienese punishment of Montalcino following the 1260 battle of Montaperti.[47] Despite this, the Damianites had clearly survived as a religious group, since the Sienese authorities voiced concern about their welfare, noting that they had been made homeless unjustly. No precise indication survives as to the original site of the monastery of the Clarissans, but the 1262 statutes refer to it as having been 'in', rather than 'prope' (or near), Montalcino, indicating that this group of religious women had originally been established inside the walls.

A hypothesis raised here is that the problems of the Damianites were resolved by their being annexed to the Franciscan friars in Montalcino, perhaps being housed in what was in effect a double community complex consisting of both male and female religious. It also seems quite probable that at the same time another, and quite separate group of religious women from outside the walls was likewise brought under the protection of the Franciscan community on the Poggio del Castelvecchio. The amalgamated community of religious women may then have assumed the overall title of 'female friars'. This could explain the absence of references to the Damianites in documents post-dating 1262. It may also explain why Rosa di Piero Pecoraio made no specific reference to the Damianites, despite her obvious bias towards the Franciscan Order. However, the question remains where such women, and indeed where the friars themselves were accommodated.

The early history of the 'frati minori' is comparatively well documented. It seems that a group of Franciscan friars had formed a coherent community on the Poggio del Castelvecchio by the end of the second decade of the thirteenth century. According to the eighteenth-century Franciscan chronicler Padre Piero Bonaventura Bovini, Saint Francis came to Montalcino in 1218 and vested some 1,300 male and female citizens of the town as Tertiary Franciscans.[48] At almost the same time, a group of *frati minori conventuali* assumed responsibility for the complex of San Marco (which included an old 'ospizio', or hospital) on the Poggio del Castelvecchio, and established a male community there. Towards the end of the thirteenth century, the friars also gained possession of the nearby parish church of San Michele Arcangelo. Fra Bovini maintained that both the church and the hospice of San Marco were handed over personally to Saint Francis, when the saint first arrived in Montalcino in 1217 or 1218.[49] Bovini noted that the 'ospizio' – which he described as an ancient institution – was founded some time between the end of the twelfth century and the beginning of the thirteenth century, and was originally run by Benedictines.[50] The building itself consisted of one large room, a number of other smaller spaces, and an orchard. According to Bovini's contemporary, Tullio Canali, however, the people of Montalcino held Saint Francis and the newly vested

Franciscans in such affection, that they personally interceded with the abbot of Sant'Antimo in the question of accommodation, even offering the use of their own private houses.[51] In the end, the Benedictines of Sant'Antimo stepped in with the offer of both the church and hospice of San Marco. It is not impossible, however, that the Franciscans had first congregated in a private house inside Montalcino, and that they only moved to the Poggio del Castelvecchio when it became clear that their initial premises were too small.[52]

There seems little doubt that following the visit of Saint Francis, the newly vested townspeople of Montalcino would have been fired with enthusiasm for the emergent new order. Some of them must also have wished to establish a Franciscan community on a more formal basis. The recasting of the Franciscan rule in 1221, and its confirmation by Pope Honorius III in 1223, would have provided an extra stimulus for just such action. As lay tertiaries, many of those vested by Saint Francis could, of course, have continued to live in their own homes, no doubt in some cases donning the Franciscan habit. There is, in fact, some evidence to suggest that many individuals did just this, since in 1284 abbot Simone of Sant'Antimo decreed that 'quei non sono iscritti al terz(a) ord(in)e di S(an) Francesco, non possino vestire il d(ett)o Abito' ('those who are not officially registered as members of the Third Order of Saint Francis, cannot wear the Franciscan habit').[53] The implication was that prior to 1284 a number of citizens had adopted religious habits without signing up formally to the Franciscan Rule. But these individuals may never have intended joining a conventual complex. By contrast, the friars who subsequently congregated on the Poggio del Castelvecchio, may have established a community immediately after being vested by Saint Francis. One thing is clear. In 1285, Don Simone, abbot of Sant'Antimo, ratified an agreement that the Franciscan friars on the Poggio del Castelvecchio should have possession of the church of San Michele Arcangelo to the south of San Marco, together with its surrounding orchard and contiguous house.[54] As we shall see, possession of the church of San Michele Arcangelo by the male members of the order may have had repercussions for the accommodation of their female religious.

The precise date of handover of the church of San Michele Arcangelo is unclear. According to one document dated 13 September 1286, the complex had not yet been consigned to the Franciscan friars, despite papal agreement to the handover. It seems that the handover of the church had been blocked by the clergy of San Salvatore in Montalcino, who claimed that San Michele Arcangelo belonged to them. After a number of delays, the entire complex of San Michele Arcangelo was, however, handed over to the Franciscan friars.[55] Bovini implies that the friars transferred their living quarters to the new complex shortly after acquiring possession of it.[56] At the same time, plans for the destruction, or dismantling, of both San Marco and San Michele Arcangelo, in order to construct a large new church with the joint *titulus* of San Francesco and San Marco, were already in hand.

With the transfer to the San Michele Arcangelo complex, the old 'ospizio' of San Marco must have fallen vacant. This site could have offered an ideal solution for the accommodation of the dispossessed Damianites, and any other religious women seeking a place of greater safety inside the walls of the town. Thus housed, in close proximity to the *frati minori conventuali*, it might also have seemed logical to refer to these women as the female friars, or 'fratesse' of Montalcino.

Some sources indicate that building work on the new complex of Santi Francesco e Marco began in 1287.[57] Indulgences were certainly being offered to those who endowed building work for the friars as early as 1272.[58] The new church was, however, only finally finished some time after 1335.[59] By this date, the church of San Marco had been displaced by the construction of the new east end of Santi Francesco e Marco, and the remains of the church of San Michele Arcangelo had been incorporated into the new southern transept, to form the chapel of the Annunziata. On completion of the new conventual complex, only one other building, the 'ospizio di San Marco' remained standing, surrounded by a large square.

Surviving archival material shows that the female friars of Montalcino were involved in building work of their own during the final years of construction of Santi Francesco e Marco. In particular, they were building their own new monastic church. It is argued here that if the *fratesse* were indeed first established in the hospice of San Marco (following the move of the *frati minori* to the church and surrounding complex of San Michele Arcangelo), they would in some senses have been dispossessed as a result of the decision to construct the new church of Santi Francesco e Marco. They would have needed to carry out building work of their own, if only to provide themselves with a new place of worship, following the destruction of the church of San Marco. Such work would most naturally have been carried out in close proximity to the female friars' existing premises. If the hypothesis that the *fratesse* were at one time established in the hospice of San Marco is correct, the new church and, indeed, the entire new monastic complex, must have been contiguous to the new church and conventual buildings of Santi Francesco e Marco. This may well explain why the two projects are often mentioned in the same breath in surviving documents. In any event, building work on the female friars' new monastic complex must have been well advanced by 1320, given that reference is made to the 'monasterio delle fratesse' in the *Tavola delle possessioni* of Sant'Angelo in Colle for that year.[60]

Further reference was made to the new monastic complex of the *fratesse* in the will of a Montalcino resident, Mina, daughter of the deceased Griffo di Montevarchi, and wife of Lao di Vanni di Giuseppe.[61] Like Rosa di Piero Pecoraio, Mina wished to be buried on the site of the *frati minori* of Montalcino. In addition, she left 5 *soldi* to the 'locum', or site, of the *fratesse*. Other benefactors followed. In December, 1335, Daddo di Brunicello – rector of the Casa della Misericordia – stipulated in his will that money should be left not only for the completion of the new church of San Francesco, but also for work 'i(n) op(er)e loci mon(asteru)m fratessam de mo(n)tal(cin)e (on the works in the monastery of the Fratesse of Montalcino).[62]

Several other individuals played their part in steering the female friars' building works forward. In March 1336, Capello di Bartolomeo, resident in Montalcino, left money for continuing work on the church of the *fratesse*.[63] And in February 1337, Nera, wife (?widow) of Daddo di Brunicello, left money to the *fratesse*, not only for general 'opere', but, more specifically, for their dormitory.[64] A record of November 1343 refers, in addition, to 'suora' Angela, abbess of the monastery of Montalcino.[65] Without any specific *titulus*, we cannot be sure that this reference concerns the monastery of the *fratesse*. Nevertheless, it is clear that, as the new church of Santi Francesco e Marco rose on the sites of the old churches of San Marco and San Michele Arcangelo, the *fratesse* of Montalcino put the finishing touches on their own monastic complex. There can be little doubt, either, that Rosa di Piero Pecoraio, a widow from Sant'Angelo in Colle, was not only aware of developments within the community of female friars in Montalcino, but was also sufficiently concerned to edge this project forward through her own financial support.

In the absence of further documentation, it is impossible to judge how close Rosa di Piero Pecoraio herself was to the female religious she endowed. For the same reason, it might seem that little more can be said about the way in which these religious women in Montalcino carried out their daily business, and what kind of existence Becca 'fratessa' from Sant'Angelo in Colle led. However, a case is presented here that surviving documentation concerning the sister community of San Francesco in Siena can throw light on the life led by the female friars of Montalcino and the services they offered to their Franciscan brothers on the Poggio Castelvecchio during the fourteenth century.

According to the pastoral visit made by Cardinal Francesco Bossi in 1575, both male and female religious were established in the conventual complex of San Francesco in Siena in the sixteenth century. While the men were accommodated in the front of the building, the women were housed in quarters to the rear.[66] Bossi refers to the women's area as the 'Monastero delle Monache di S. Francesco'. But he also refers to the same site as the 'Monastero delle Mantellate', implying that Second-Order and Third-Order women lived cheek by jowl on the same site. The women themselves provided Bossi with a very detailed account of their present circumstances and their early history.

According to this, the female religious of the Franciscan community in Siena had been associated with the friars there from at least the end of the thirteenth century, and well before the completion of the large new church of San Francesco, which, like the church of Santi Francesco e Marco in Montalcino, was under construction in the early fourteenth century. Other surviving documentary evidence indicates that the Sienese female religious were initially accommodated in close proximity both to their Franciscan brothers, and to the Porta Ovile and the church of San Pietro, which was used as the friars' spiritual base before the construction of the new church of San Francesco. This much is clear from a surviving document dating to either the 1290s, or the early years of the fourteenth century. In this document, reference is made to a Miranda, '*mantellata*', and a letter she had sent to Vanni in Città della Pieve (then Castello della Pieve), which had been brought to him from Siena by a Franciscan friar.[67] Vanni's reply was addressed to 'Madonna Mira(n) da mantelata in Siena, avile da la porta de' frati minori' (Madam Miranda, mantled female religious in Siena at the Ovile gate of the Franciscan friars).[68]

According to Bossi in the sixteenth century, 16 religious women were living in very confined and run-down quarters at the side of San Francesco, 14 being professed, and 2 as novices. Bossi also referred to a serving woman and another woman who had been accepted, but who had neither entered the community, nor presented the promised entrance dowry of 200 florins. Two of the most senior women (Suora Beatrice, the prioress, and Suora Battista) told Bossi that they had promised to observe 'la Regola delle Continenti di S. Francesco', but according to their own rule, which had been confirmed by Pope Nicholas IV. It would seem from this that the *mantellate* of San Francesco in Siena were following the rules and regulations approved by the papal bull 'Supra Montem', of 1289, which maintained that religious women abiding by the three rules of poverty, chastity and obedience, were not obliged to live strictly enclosed lives. But the women told Bossi that they neither offered vows of poverty, chastity or obedience, nor observed *clausura*, but went in and out of their monastic complex with the permission of their *Ministra* (or Mother Superior), and according to their every day needs. In this respect, they seem to have adopted an independent stance similar to that established by members of the Secular Third Order. At the time of Bossi's visit the *mantellate* apparently asserted their independence by professing solely in the presence of their own *Ministra*. The women claimed that the same practice had been observed at an earlier date, when they were, in their words, 'sotto li Frati' (under the authority of the friars), although at that time the ceremony of profession was witnessed in addition by the community's male confessor. In this context, it may be relevant to note the papal bull issued by Boniface VIII on 5 April, 1298, which stipulated that the affairs of the Second-Order nuns of Santa Chiara in Siena should be governed by the order of *frati minori*.[69] Perhaps the *mantellate* of the Porta Ovile were placed under the authority of the friars at the same date.

In any event, the reference to being 'sotto li Frati' offers firm evidence that the sixteenth-century female religious of San Francesco had developed from a group of women that had, at one time – probably early in its history – been subjected to a more rigid internal discipline. This may also explain why, in two surviving documents from the early modern period, reference is made to the 'fratelle' of Siena: Donna Teodora, daughter of the deceased Cristoforo Tolomei, refers in her will of 20 May 1295, to her sister Vitadio 'monaca dell'Ordine delle fratelle'.[70] A decade later, in December 1311, Donna Nella, widow of Ugo di Iacopo, refers simply to the 'Fratelle'.[71] The link between this term and 'fratesse' is clear. In each case, the female religious is indicated, and in each case an association with the friars is implied.

It seems clear, in fact, that both 'fratelle' and 'fratesse' were adopted freely during the thirteenth and early fourteenth centuries, but increasingly less thereafter. This suggests that the terms were reserved for religious women associated with the Franciscan Rule during the early stages of its development: in other words, before the development of a distinct hierarchy of First, Second and Third Orders, each with their own set of rules and regulations, and each offering varying degrees of access and enclosure. Consideration of the Franciscan female religious in early modern Siena thus supports the hypothesis raised here, that the *fratesse* of Montalcino were associated with the Franciscan friars, and that their internal discipline was similar to, if not the same as the Damianite Clarissans.

It seems likely that the female religious of San Francesco in Siena remained under the authority of the friars until at least 1444, when Pope Eugenius IV issued a bull stipulating that the 'sorelle', or sisters, of the Third Order of Saint Francis in the city of Siena should be freed from all obligations to their Franciscan brothers.[72] Interestingly, it seems that this papal bull was specifically intended to remove the possibility of scandal arising from the close proximity of male and female religious. From Bossi's description, it is clear that the women of San Francesco were very far from being physically enclosed, or decently separated from lay society. Not only could the women look out on the world, but the world could look in at them. Bossi describes the women's premises as consisting, on the upper floor, of a long, cramped, corridor that terminated in two wired windows. From these windows the women could watch religious and civic processions and other ceremonies celebrated in the square below. Another window looked down onto the road leading to the Fonte d'Ovile. A door at the end of the same corridor opened onto the city walls, which in turn supported the houses of the lay community. Bossi was clearly uneasy about this, noting that a number of the roofs of nearby buildings abutted the said corridor, offering easy access to the monastic complex. In an additional note, Bossi records that it had been the custom for 'scolari' or male pupils to be housed in these adjacent premises. The women for their part insisted that this was no longer the case, no doubt wishing to avoid accusations of impropriety, or closer inspection of what may have been scandalous arrangements. These were not the only elements of the women's accommodation that would have caused displeasure and unease to the papal visitor. Many of the larger rooms, according to Bossi, had windows looking out onto the public Piazza San Francesco, and some of these were close to the ground, allowing the women to have conversations with anyone who passed by.

By the sixteenth century, the female religious of San Francesco had established what amounted to an open house. Prior to the most recent papal bull, both men and women had been allowed to enter the area beyond the first door of the monastic complex. Many women subsequently moved freely beyond, and up to the nuns' church and throughout the rest of the complex. At times these female visitors stayed on to eat and even sleep side by side with their religious sisters. In addition, women on the brink of marriage were allowed to stay in the community during Holy week and on feast days around Easter. Fathers and brothers were also allowed in the upper part of the complex, but only on the community's Feast Day, and, on occasion, to visit sick relations.

However, despite all these signs of independence, the women were apparently still physically yoked to their Franciscan brothers. Bossi reports that they were obliged to supply their brothers with linen in the form of sheets, covers and pillows for sick friars, and, also, to attend to the needs of the *Ministro* (or Father Superior), when he came to visit. The women also had to cook for the convent's sick. Nor were such duties carried out in the privacy of their own quarters. The women explained that half of the friars' conventual complex had been put at their disposal in order to affect these tasks. Not only did the women enter the male quarters, then, but the friars, it seems, also visited the premises of their sisters. The women were clearly not happy. 'We have always served and still serve, and during these last two months we have had to make 'orzata' and other things for one sick patient and we are kept busy doing these things, and while often the brothers themselves come to collect laundry and food, we would like to be freed from this obligation. We can barely make ends meet; we get some funds from our relatives, but the conventual friars give us nothing, and the little that we receive is spent on our animals and on building work.'[73]

Although apparently content to remain accommodated within, or next to the male conventual complex, the female religious of San Francesco were clearly anxious to exercise greater control both over their own work, and over any financial rewards such work might bring. The remarkable thing is the extent to which these women were in bondage to their Franciscan brothers (even towards the end of the sixteenth century), in a relationship that was based on servitude without pay. No wonder their monastic complex was cramped and in need of repair.

Bossi's record reveals much about the symbiotic relationship established between male and female religious in the Sienese community of San Francesco. Although ostensibly occupying separate premises, the women in fact had daily contact with their Franciscan brothers. As well as moving in and out of the friars' conventual complex, the women also established regular contact with members of the lay community. However, despite such freedom of movement, they were abjectly poor. They were, moreover, responsible for the upkeep of their own monastic complex and their own living expenses, even though they had for a long time been forced to work without pay for their male brothers. Apart from occasional charity from their relations, the Sienese female religious of San Francesco had no apparent independent means, no land, no property, and presumably few, if any, endowments. In this respect, their Franciscan sisters in Montalcino must have been more fortunate. They had not only attracted endowments of land and money at an early stage, but by the beginning of the fourteenth century had also accrued enough capital to construct their own independent monastic complex, and thus presumably carry on their own religious life comparatively independently. Nevertheless, for Becca, the female friar from Sant'Angelo in Colle, daily life in her chosen community may have been very similar to that outlined by Cardinal Francesco Bossi in the sixteenth century. Rosa di Piero Pecoraio, for her part, emerges as one, in a long line of both male and female benefactors, who contributed to the independent status of the female friars of Montalcino. Ironically, such legacies, in loosening the bonds between these women and their erstwhile male protectors, may have helped to consign the female friars of Montalcino and the links between them and the early fourteenth-century residents of Sant'Angelo in Colle to the margins of monastic history.

What, then of the second testator considered in detail here, Giovanni di Paganello?

By contrast with Rosa di Piero, Giovanni di Paganello, although also endowing a religious institution in Montalcino, was at the same time ready to lay down conditions that would benefit charitable foundations much further afield: in Siena. Giovanni di Paganello's testamentary arrangements allowed for a certain amount of flexibility in the dispersal of his wealth. Much hung, it seems, on his having a legitimate male heir at the time of his death. Giovanni di Paganello was prepared to distribute his money between several institutions and relations in the event of dying without having a living heir; however, such largesse was to be diminished if the opposite were the case. In some senses this is what one might expect. Giovanni di Paganello would naturally have wanted to make adequate provisions for any heir or heirs that survived him. But, as the following discussion will attempt to show, a number of other factors (including pre-existing patterns of piety and service established within Giovanni di Paganello's own family) may also have contributed to the testamentary caveats included in his will.

In the case of this second testator, it is relevant not only that we are once more dealing with an individual who was associated with one of the leading families of Sant'Angelo in Colle, but also that the testator was male. It is also significant that Giovanni di Paganello was a professional man. His testamentary stipulations thus offer insights not only to the preoccupations of the male elite of Sant'Angelo in Colle, but also to the mindset of those who were closely involved in the everyday affairs of the village as a result of their legal position and expertise. As village notary, Giovanni di Paganello was essentially the second in command, if not the principal official in the village. It is perhaps not so surprising therefore, that he was considerably more generous than Rosa di Piero, when anticipating what funds should be allocated to various local institutions. Whilst Rosa was content (and possibly constrained) to offer a comparatively small amount of money to cover the cost of wax in the church of San Michele Arcangelo, Giovanni appears to have been prepared to assume responsibility for the whole fabric. The hypothesis is raised here that such munificence depended not so much on the fact that Giovanni di Paganello was a man, but on the fact that he had achieved a position of considerable influence in the village by 1335. Giovanni di Paganello was clearly embedded within the social fabric of the village not only as a result of his considerable assets, but also as a result of his professional work there. Rosa di Piero, by contrast, was widowed, possessed comparatively few assets, and may already have left the village by the time of her will. While Giovanni di Paganello was clearly still in the thick of things, Rosa's horizons had shrunk. Distinctions of this kind must surely have had a bearing on the pattern of piety each individual adopted.

The testamentary stipulations included in Giovanni di Paganello's will of 28 March 1335, while preoccupied in part with Montalcino, indicate that Giovanni, unlike Rosa di Piero Pecoraio, was particularly interested in building projects in his own village. While Rosa di Piero made only a passing and general reference to one of the churches in the village, it seems that Giovanni di Paganello was prepared to underwrite the cost of repairs to the parish church, as well as to contribute to similar work in the second church of San Piero. While no particular sum of money was stipulated in this context, it seems that Giovanni was prepared to pay all that was necessary for the completion of work on each of those sites. Giovanni also asked that a plot of land (in the area known as Pantano) should go to the village hospital of Sant'Angelo. In addition, Giovanni stipulated that a vineyard in the area known as Cegliro should be left to the friars of Sant'Agostino in Montalcino.[74] A second plot at Pantano was instead designated to the hospital of Santa Maria della Scala.[75] Yet another plot of land in the area known as Fracino was to go to the hospital of Monna Agnese in Siena.

As we have already seen, Giovanni di Paganello also included a number of 'lasciti' for various members of his close and extended family in Sant'Angelo in Colle. Thus, as well as legacies to his nephew and niece, Giovanni left the house with an olive press to his brother Marco, and another house to his sister Becca. Giovanni also named as his overall heir his daughter Mina (presumably born to his first wife Lagia) and 'any heirs yet to be born'. In the event of any such heirs dying before reaching the age of maturity, Giovanni stipulated that his universal heirs should be considered as the convent of Sant'Agostino in Montalcino, the hospital of Sant'Angelo in Colle and the hospital of Monna Agnese in Siena. Without a legitimate heir, Giovanni appears to have anticipated a tripartite agreement, benefiting one religious order and two hospitals. Significantly, in the event of Giovanni di Paganello's heirs dying prematurely, the larger hospital of Santa Maria della Scala would lose out, the sole Sienese hospital to benefit from such a situation being the much smaller 'Ospedale di Monna Agnese'.

According to an additional note added to Giovanni di Paganello's will by the notary 'Giovanni di magister Martinelli' in November 1336, it seems that Giovanni was indeed survived by a son, another Giovanni. This child must have been born shortly after the drawing up of Giovanni di Paganello's will in March 1355, indicating, as already suggested, that Broccola, Giovanni di Paganello's second wife, must already have been pregnant at the time of her husband's will. Broccola certainly survived her son's birth, since reference was made in November 1336 to the repayment of dowry money to her. Giovanni di Martinelli's note was, however, essentially concerned with the executive duties that were to be assumed by Giovanni's brother, Marco di Paganello, in respect of the male child Giovanni. It seems that the continuing well being of this child deprived both the Augustinian friars of Montalcino and the local hospital of Sant'Angelo in Colle, as well as the Sienese hospital of Monna Agnese, of a considerable amount of land and property.

The caveats in Giovanni di Paganello's will are most naturally explained in terms of his own personal hopes for the future. At the time of drawing up her will, Rosa di Piero's world was no longer expanding. Widowed, with one daughter already having predeceased her, another possibly on the brink of death, and a son who had relinquished all claims on the world in joining a religious order, Rosa must have been predisposed to look inwards and consider her own immediate needs. Giovanni di Paganello, it seems, was still looking forward. Not only did he already have an apparently healthy heir in the form of a female child, Mina, from a previous marriage, but he had also remarried, and his new wife was of childbearing age, and pregnant. This, combined with what we know of his professional standing, and his accumulated assets both inside the walls of Sant'Angelo in Colle and in the countryside beyond, must have encouraged him to look to the future, and even beyond his own demise towards the continuation of the family's various business enterprises and an increasing prosperity. There was much still to be played for in terms of the family's local standing and Giovanni di Paganello's own posthumous fame.

In the event of his not being survived by any adult male or female heirs, Giovanni di Paganello must have foreseen that the patrimony he had accumulated would be dispersed. The stipulation that two thirds of Giovanni's assets should be divided equally between the hospital of Monna Agnese in Siena and his own local hospital at Sant'Angelo in Colle, rather than with Santa Maria della Scala is, at first sight, curious. But, as the following discussion will attempt to show, Giovanni di Paganello's own background and personal circumstances at the time of drawing up his will may have predisposed him to favour, if at all, the smaller Sienese institution.

Quite apart from this, there is evidence to suggest that other members of Giovanni di Paganello's family were involved with the 'Ospedale di Monna Agnese' long before Giovanni set about drawing up his will. Whilst acknowledging the difficulties involved in the reconstruction of medieval genealogies, where individuals without high or aristocratic status were for the most part referred to solely in terms of their patronyms (as opposed to a given and continuing family name), it seems at least possible that the late thirteenth-century Sienese notary Giovanni di Paganello (identified here as Giovanni di Paganello 'senior') was the father of the Paganello di Giovanni recorded as a resident of Sant'Angelo in Colle in the 1320 *Tavola delle possessioni*. It is relevant that Paganello's son, Giovanni di Paganello 'junior' also followed the law, and, while specifically involved in the legal affairs of Sant'Angelo in Colle as the village notary, was at the same time involved with the central Sienese government. Indeed, one of the earliest surviving records concerning the legal activities of Giovanni di Paganello 'junior' covers the transmission of land and property outside the walls of Sant'Angelo in Colle to the Sienese hospital of Santa Maria della Scala, in 1328.[76]

Surviving records show that Giovanni di Paganello 'senior' likewise played an active part in the political affairs of Siena. He was also involved with the affairs of the hospital of Monna Agnese. In particular, he assumed a central position in disputes between communes in the southern Sienese *contado*.[77] Thus, during negotiations with representatives of the Guelf party in the castle of Arcidosso in September 1280 (in an attempt to reach a peaceful agreement with Ghibelline exiles), Giovanni di Paganello 'senior' is referred to as 'notarius, sindicus et actor et spetialis nunctius parties guelfe civitatis et comitatis senensis ad infrascripte faciende spetialiter constitutus' – in other words, acting specifically on behalf of the Guelph central government.[78] In the same month, when the *podestà* and governors of Siena ratified the peace concluded between the Guelf and Ghibelline factions, Giovanni di Paganello 'senior' was recorded both in his professional guise of notary, and as a witness.[79] In the course of 1280 he was called upon to act as procurator by leading Sienese families such as the Forteguerri, the Montanini, the Piccolomini, the Salimbeni, the Rossi, the Baronci, the Malavolti, the Accarigi, the Del Mancino, the Tolomei and the Rinaldini, in numerous attempts to establish peace between the Guelfs and the Ghibellines.[80] Giovanni di Paganello 'senior' was also mentioned on several occasions around this time in the context of affairs at Sant'Angelo in Colle, principally acting as witness.[81] There is evidence of his involvement, also, in the political affairs of the Government of the Nine in the following decade. In June 1294, for example, he acted as notary, Sienese citizen and 'sindico' on behalf of the Commune of Siena when ratifying the conditions of submission drawn up in respect of Montepulciano.[82] It is clear from this that Giovanni di Paganello 'senior' was not only closely involved with the southern Sienese 'contado', but also had contact with Sant'Angelo in Colle several decades before the inclusion of Paganello di Giovanni in the 1320 *Tavola delle possessioni*.

Perhaps more significantly, Giovanni di Paganello 'senior' is also recorded towards the end of the thirteenth century as acting on behalf of the newly-founded 'spedale di Monna Agnese' in Siena. This association may have had particularly poignant undercurrents for Giovanni di Paganello 'junior'. The hospital of Santi Gregorio e Niccolo in Sasso in Siena – better known as 'l'ospedale di Monna Agnese' – was founded some time before 1275 by Agnese, daughter of Affrettato.[83] It quickly gained recognition as a refuge for pregnant and single women. In some ways it was a forerunner of the modern shelter. Already between 1275 and 1276, the commune of Siena was making a regular payment to the 'ospedale' of Monna Agnese towards the purchase of cloth and bread for the poor and infirm housed within the hospital's walls.[84]

And in 1278, some three years after its foundation, the hospital was granted extraordinary concessions, following a petition sent by Monna Agnese to the 36 priors governing Siena.[85]

Giovanni di Paganello 'senior' is named as the notary responsible for drawing up the 1278 petition in which Monna Agnese called upon the city for help in the purchase of a house, in order to care for more than 40 people.[86] Such involvement at this crucial moment in the development of the hospital may well have fostered a special relationship between the family of Giovanni di Paganello 'senior' and the new Sienese institution. If Giovanni di Paganello 'senior' was indeed the father of Paganello di Giovanni, his connection with the hospital of Monna Agnese could in turn have influenced the testamentary stipulations of Paganello's own son Giovanni. Giovanni di Paganello 'junior' may indeed have been intent on continuing an association with the hospital that had been established within his own family two generations earlier.

The Ospedale di Monna Agnese continued to attract exceptional attention throughout the final years of the thirteenth century. Specific indulgences were offered in respect of the hospital as early as the papacy of Benedict X (between 1290 and 1303).[87] And in November 1292, less than 20 years after its foundation, the Ospedale di Monna Agnese was granted immunity from all communal taxes.[88] This exemption from tax was clearly regarded as an important moment in the development of the hospital, since copies were made of the original act of immunity as late as the sixteenth century.[89]

There could, finally, have been an even more poignant motive behind Giovanni di Paganello's decision to favour the hospital of Monna Agnese, in the event of his heirs dying before reaching the age of maturity. The earliest of the copies of the dispensation granting immunity from all community taxes confirms that Monna Agnese's original intention was to help those infants whose mothers had died in childbirth.[90] In many cases these motherless children were subsequently delivered as orphans to the hospital of Santa Maria della Scala.[91] The Ospedale di Monna Agnese was thus concerned with the protection if not salvation of motherless children. As already indicated, when Giovanni di Paganello drew up his will in March 1335, he already had one 'motherless' child, and his current wife Broccola was pregnant. Although Broccola survived the birth of her child, it may be that the mother of Giovanni's other child, Mina, had not. Giovanni di Paganello's decision to endow the hospital of Monna Agnese may thus have been motivated as much by that hospital's declared function and his own personal experiences and anxieties, as by any family connections or pre-existing patterns of piety.

In any event, Giovanni di Paganello 'junior' was certainly not the first resident of Sant'Angelo in Colle to endow the hospital of Monna Agnese in the early fourteenth century. According to the 1320 *Tavola delle possessioni*, the hospital already owned three pieces of land in the vicinity of the village: one at 'Pellentieri', another at 'Collesorbi' and a third at 'Fossatellus Alcoi'.[92] This comparatively young hospital foundation had thus already established links with the southern Sienese '*contado*'. This may have been due in part to the association formed with the much larger and more influential hospital of Santa Maria della Scala. In effect, there was a symbiotic relationship between the two. Thus, the influence exerted by Monna Agnese's hospital on patterns of piety in such centres as Sant'Angelo in Colle may have grown in parallel with that of Santa Maria della Scala.

Surviving records concerning the affairs of the hospital of Monna Agnese in the fifteenth century contain details of land held in a number of areas in the southern Sienese *contado*. Thus, there are references to land owned at Villa a Sesta, Camigliano, Lucignano and Buonconvento. There are also references to 'la casa a camilgliano' – indicating that the hospital owned a house inside the village of Camigliano itself.[93] It seems that the hospital of Monna Agnese also owned an olive press and a 'grancia' inside Camigliano, and that it continued to draw revenue from these until well into the seventeenth century.[94] During the first half of the fifteenth century, there were also increasing endowments to the hospital from residents of Montalcino.[95] The hospital also drew on the legal services of a local notary there. In entries covering the hospital's finances between 1432 and 1434, the Montalcinese lawyer Ser Lazzaro was paid for services rendered to Matteo di maestro Nofrio da Montalcino in respect of 34 florins the latter had promised to the hospital of Monna Agnese, in connection with the purchase of a house in Montalcino.[96] It also seems clear that the 'Ospedale di Monna Agnese' acquired property in Montalcino at a comparatively early date. In 1437 Ambrogio and his brothers (sons of Giovanni di Montalcino) are recorded as purchasing a house that had previously belonged to Niccolo di Camino (or Comino), and which, before that, had belonged to the hospital of Monna Agnese.[97] The hospital seems also to have established a number of business relationships inside Montalcino. Thus, in 1442 payments were recorded in respect of Marciano of Montalcino for the spinning of linen yarn, presumably for use in the clothing and bedding of the hospital inmates in Siena.

None of the property in the 'corte' of Sant'Angelo in Colle described as belonging to the hospital of Monna Agnese in 1320, or earmarked by Giovanni di Paganello in 1335 as destined for that institution (regardless of the survival into maturity of any of his heirs) was, however, recorded in a list of the hospital's possessions drawn up in 1541.[98] Indeed, surviving records indicate that this property may have been sold off at a much earlier date, since no mention is made of Sant'Angelo in Colle in recorded yields from land owned by the hospital of Monna Agnese drawn up for the years 1432–4.[99]

Despite this, some links were maintained between the hospital of Monna Agnese and Sant'Angelo in Colle well into the fifteenth century. One surviving record indicates, indeed, that the hospital was operating a system of *mezzadria* there as late as the middle of the fifteenth century. The document in question records that on 12 May 1441, one roman gold florin was received from Caterina d'Antonio da Sant'Angelo in Colle in final payment for a mule consigned to her by the hospital of Monna Agnese.[100] Caterina was presumably using this mule either to work land belonging to the hospital, or to transport goods from the land to the hospital complex in Siena. The fact that the mule had originally been bought by the hospital of Monna Agnese indicates further that Caterina was working on their behalf.

Such ebb and flow in the possession of land in and around Sant'Angelo in Colle was no doubt in large part due to the changing financial circumstances of the hospital of Monna Agnese itself. But it may also have reflected the waning significance of Sant'Angelo in Colle, and, by contrast, the greater prominence of other more recent conquests by the Sienese. Archival material considered here suggests that during the latter years of the Government of the Nine, the inhabitants of Sant'Angelo in Colle became increasingly interested in their own local concerns. Thus, local charitable and religious institutions were bound to receive a larger proportion of the bequests that were made.

Giovanni di Paganello's desire to underwrite the expenses of reconstruction and/or restoration of the old parish church of San Michele at Sant'Angelo in Colle as well as that of the other church inside the walls of the village, San Piero, bears witness to this trend. At least one other individual, Ser Longo di Ser Tuccio (?Duccio, ?Guccio), also appears to have played a leading role in the upkeep of local institutions in Sant'Angelo in Colle during the last years of the Government of the Nine. In fact, according to the will drawn up for Ser Longo in 1348, he not only wished to be buried in the parish church of San Michele, but also left money for the embellishment of the fabric there. At the same time, Ser Longo, like Rosa di Piero Pecoraio, appears to have been particularly concerned with the welfare of the Franciscan community in nearby Montalcino. A detailed consideration of Ser Longo's will follows in the next and final chapter. As will become clear, attention focuses in particular on the role this individual may have played in the embellishment of key buildings in the early fourteenth-century village. But, as a case study, ser Longo di Ser Tuccio's will also encourages more general speculation about the artistic influence exerted by the city of Siena, its institutions and its residents on the urban fabrics of its subject communes. More specifically, Ser Longo's will stimulates discussion of the iconography of works of art that were associated with charitable and religious institutions during the medieval period, raising questions about patronage, self-fashioning and the sense of place. Last, but not least, in considering the decorations of the village hospital and parish church of San Michele in Sant'Angelo in Colle, Chapter 8 aims to provide a conclusion to the history of Sant'Angelo in Colle, 'castello di frontiera' under the Government of the Nine.

Notes

1   See Samuel K. Cohn Jr., *Death and property in Siena 1205–1800: Strategies for the afterlife* (Baltimore and London, *c*.1988); *The cult of remembrance and the Black Death. Six Renaissance cities in central Italy* (Baltimore and London, 1992), and 'Last Wills: Family, Women and the Black Death in Central Italy', in idem, *Women in the Streets. Essays on Sex and Power in Renaissance Italy* (Baltimore and London, 1996), pp. 39–56. See also Thomas Kuehn, *Law, Family and Women. Toward a Legal Anthropology of Renaissance Italy* (Chicago, 1991).

2   Cohn, *Death and Property*, 1988, p. 1.

3   Ibid., p. 4.

4   Ibid., p. 32.

5   Ibid.

6   Archivio Storico del Comune di Montalcino (hereafter ACM), *Archivio Preunitario (1361–1865), Fondi Diversi, Archivi di Particolari: Ser Griffo di Ser Paolo* (hereafter *Ser Griffo di Ser Paolo*), nos 3 and 4.

7   Cohn, *Death and Property*, 1988, p. 17.

8   Ibid., p. 21.

9   Ibid., p. 17.

10   Ibid., p. 15.

11   Cohn, *Cult of Remembrance*, 1992, p. 18.

12   Archivio di Stato di Siena (hereafter ASS), *Diplomatico in Caselle, casella* 1019, 24 June 1370, *Archivio dello Spedale*.

13   Ibid., *casella* 1074, 12 June 1380, *Archivio dello Spedale*.

14   Ibid., *casella* 1145, 4 May 1398, *Archivio dello Spedale*.

15   Ibid., *casella* 893, 27 June 1348, *Archivio dello Spedale*.

16   Ibid., *casella* 1127, 22 August 1391, *Archivio dello Spedale*.

17   ASS, *Manoscritti* C21, fol. 73r.

18   Lodovico Zdekauer, *Il Constituto del Comune di Siena dell'Anno 1262* (Milan, 1897), (reprinted Arnoldo Forni, 1983) no. 90, p. 46.

19   ASS, *Manoscritti* D 67, *Memorie Storiche Politiche, Civili, e Naturali delle Città, Terre, e Castella, che sono, e sono state suddite alla Città di Siena. Raccolte dal Card. Gio(vanni) Antonio Pecci, Patrizio Sanese*, fol. 88.

20   ASS, *Diplomatico in Caselle, casella* 406, 3 March 1298/9, *Archivio dello Spedale*.

21   Ibid., *casella* 342, 5 September 1292, *Archivio dello Spedale*.

22   According to the nineteenth-century 'spoglio' relating to this document, Giovanni di Federigo's land was located in the area known as 'Serrule'.

23   In this context, and for some further consideration of the tax benefits associated with the endowment of religious and charitable institutions with land and property, see Stephan R. Epstein, *Alle origini della fattoria Toscana: L'ospedale della Scala di Siena e le sue terre metà '200–metà '400* (Florence, 1986), pp. 47–55 and Giuliano Catoni, 'Gli oblati della Misericordia. Poveri e benefattori a Siena

nella prima metà del Trecento', in Giuliano Pinto (ed.), *La Società del bisogno. Povertà e assistenza nella Toscana medievale* (Florence, 1989), pp. 1–17; and Maura Martellucci, 'Dio li perdoni; ch'egli è stato un buono rettore', *BSSP*, 110 (2003), pp. 452–88, and especially 456, note 9. Reference was made on various occasions to abuses in relation to the exemption of tax enjoyed by religious institutions. On 31 January 1290/91, the General Council in Siena elected several deputies with the brief to stem the flow of cases whereby members of lay society offered their possessions to churches and other religious organisations in order to avoid taxation on them. See ASS, Spoglio *Manoscritti* CI, fol. 155r. The point was made that such individuals frequently regained possession of such property under rental contracts. As leesors, they did not pay tax. Nor, as landlords, did the religious establishments. Clearly, a considerable amount of revenue was being lost in this way, since several references were made to the abuse of tax in the context of endowments throughout the 1290s.

24   Not all such would-be benefactors were welcome. On at least one occasion, it becomes clear that an endowment had been denied, on the basis that the individual concerned was undesirable.

25   See Chapter 1, Table 1.1.

26   ASS, *Diplomatico in Caselle*, casella 641, 1 July 1320, *Archivio dello Spedale*. For details of property owned by Giovanni di Rainaldo in the vicinity of Sant'Angelo in Colle, see ASS, *Estimo* 24, fol. 251r.

27   ASS, *Diplomatico in Caselle*, casella 712, 4 June 1327, *Archivio dello Spedale*. It seems likely that this individual is the same as Mino Conti, described in June 1348 as 'parish priest' of the church of San Michele (see Chapter 8 footnote 3).

28   ASS, *Manoscritti* B42, c. 173r.

29   ASS, *Diplomatico in Caselle*, casella 772, 28 November 1333, *Archivio dello Spedale*.

30   Ibid., *casella* 773, 5 December 1333, *Archivio dello Spedale*.

31   For Rosa di Piero's will of 22 August 1328, see ACM, *Ser Griffo di Ser Paolo*, 4, fol. 102r. For Giovanni di Paganello's will, see ASS, *Diplomatico in Caselle*, casella 784, 28 March 1335, *Archivio Spedale*. Rosa di Piero's will was first discussed by this author in a chapter entitled, 'Le fratesse e le mantellate terziarie della corte di Montalcino nel basso medioevo', in Mario Ascheri and Vinicio Serino (eds), *Prima del Brunello. Montalcino Capitale Mancata* (San Quirico d'Orcia, 2007), pp. 59–90.

32   ACM, *Ser Griffo di Ser Paolo*, 4, fol. 104r, in the 17 September 1328, will of Landino di Piero.

33   Ibid., fol. 103v.

34   Free translation by Anabel Thomas.

35   ASS, *Estimo* 24, fol. 116v.

36   It is significant that a separate entry in the 1320 *Estimo* (fol. 243r) refers to three pieces of worked land including woodland owned by the 'heirs of Piero pecchorai' and valued at five *lire*. This would seem to confirm the connection between Sant'Angelo in Colle and Rosa di Piero's natal family. By contrast, no reference is made either to Nero di Griffo, Rosa's erstwhile husband, or to any of his heirs.

37 ASS, *Estimo* 24, fol. 241r. Becca's terrain was bordered by land belonging to Lonarduccio di Giovanni, Neri di Guiccardo and the church of San Pietro.

38 Ibid., fols 171r–176v.

39 Curiously, in the entry for the heirs of Cecco di Piero, no reference was made to the *fratesse*, see ASS, *Estimo* 24, fols 171r–176v. Nor is there any mention of these women in the details filed in respect of land owned by Manovello di Ugolino.

40 San Francesco developed from an earlier church complex with the *titulus* of San Marco. For the history of San Marco and its expansion into the later church of Santi Francesco e Marco, see Don Antonio Brandi, *Chiesa e Convento di S. Francesco in Montalcino* (typescript, Montalcino, 1967) (hereafter *San Francesco*). See also, ACM, *Fondi aggregati*, Convento di San Francesco (hereafter *Conv. San Francesco*), 10 (*Campione* dated 1642) and 11 (*Campione* dated 1750, which was collated by Padre Bovini).

41 ACM, *Ser Griffo di Ser Paolo*, 4, fol. 65v.

42 ASS, Comune di Montalcino, *Diplomatico* (hereafter *Montal. Dip.*), Busta 34 bis, no. 196.

43 ACM, *Ser Griffo di Ser Paolo*, 4, fol. 176r in the will of Domina Flora, wife of Ser Bandi di Nardo, dated 8 March 1334.

44 ASS, *Montal. Dip.*, Busta 33, no. 55, in the will of Donna Oglente, widow of Martinuccio Ildebrandino, dated 5 October.

45 Ibid., Busta 37, no. 28.

46 Ibid., Busta 32, no. 157.

47 Bruno Bonucci, *Dalla Val di Starcia si vede Montaperti'* (Siena, 1998), p. 73. For the 1262 statute, see Zdekauer, *Il Constituto del Comune di Siena*.

48 Brandi, San Francesco, p. 7. In page 4 of a typescript inserted into Bovini's *Campione*, the date of Saint Francis's visit is given as 1217.

49 ACM, *Conv. San Francesco*, 11, fol. 5.

50 Ibid., fol. 1.

51 Tullio Canali, *Notizie Istoriche della Città di Montalcino in Toscana*, transcribed by Don Antonio Brandi from the original manuscript in the Biblioteca Comunale, Montalcino, (typescript, 1966), p. 54. See also, ACM, *Conv. San Francesco*, 11, typescript, fol. 4.

52 This might explain why two records concerning transactions of land and property dating to the late twelfth century were included in the archives of San Francesco, see ACM, *Conv. San Francesco*, 11. If these holdings were handed over to the Franciscans, prior to their being established at San Marco, it would have been appropriate for the friars to have some kind of record concerning previous ownership of such property. Bovini suggests, however, that the friars found these records when they took over the San Marco complex.

53 ACM, *Conv. San Francesco* 10, fol. 178v.

54 Brandi, *San Francesco*, pp. 7–8.

55 Archivio del Seminario Arcivescovile, Montearioso, Siena, *Pergamene del Convento di S. Francesco di Montalcino* (hereafter ASAS, *Pergamene*), 4.

56   ACM., *Conv. San Francesco*, 11, fol. 8. Bovini suggests that the friars transferred to the complex of San Michele Arcangelo as early as July 1285.

57   Brandi, *San Francesco*, pp. 9–10.

58   ACM, *Conv. San Francesco*, 10, fol. 176r. Further indulgences were offered on 30 November 1288, 'a coloro che aiuteranno i Frati Minori di Montalcino a costruire la chiesa e il convento' (to those who in the future will help to construct the church and conventual complex of the Franciscan friars), see ASAS, *Pergamene* parchment carrying that date.

59   Brandi, *San Francesco*, p. 9.

60   ASS, *Estimo* 24, fol. 299r.

61   ACM, *Ser Griffo di Ser Paolo*, 4, fols 165r–165v.

62   Ibid., fol. 184r. This will was drawn up in the sacristy of San Francesco. An earlier will possibly dating to 1329 (see page 5 of typescript notes inserted in ACM, *Conv. San Francesco*, 11) contained a similar stipulation concerning the completion of San Francesco. In a codicil dated 4 March 1334/5, Daddo once again desired that the church of San Francesco, in particular, should be speedily completed, noting that building work had begun in 1297 (see ACM, *Conv. San Francesco*, 10, fol. 2v.).

63   ACM, *Ser Griffo di Ser Paolo*, 4, fol. 191v.

64   ASS, *Montal. Dip.*, Busta 35bis, no. 99.

65   Ibid., Busta 33bis, no. 191.

66   Biblioteca Comunale degli Intronati, Siena, Ms A.VIII.51, fols 122r–124r.

67   ASS, *Conventi*, (*San Francesco*), 1734, III, B, 6: *Lettera di Vanni a Mira(n)da mantellata*. See Mahmoud Salem Elsheikh, 'Testi senesi dello Duecento e del primo Trecento', *Studi di Filologia Italiana*, 29 (1961), pp. 112–44 (133–36).

68   Elsheikh, *Lettera di Vanni*, p. 135.

69   ASS, *Diplomatico in Caselle*, casella 394, 5 April 1298, *Archivio di San Francesco a Siena*.

70   ASS, *Diplomatico Tolomei*, no. 39 (Registi del Mazzo numero 4, dal 1286 al 1299). Several decades later, there is another reference to *Fratelle* in the 12 December 1311 will of Donna Nella, widow of 'Ugo di Iacopo, che si chiamava Ugo Trollio', see ASS, *Diplomatico Tolomeo*, no. 67 (Registi del Mazzo numero 6, dal 1311 al 1319).

71   Ibid., no. 67.

72   ASS, *Diplomatico in Caselle*, casella 1274, 31 August 1444, *Archivio di San Francesco*.

73   Free translation by Anabel Thomas.

74   This vineyard was not recorded as belonging to Paganello di Giovanni in 1320, nor does it appear under the assets of Paganello's brother Lonarduccio.

75   Once again, according to the 1320 *Tavola delle possessioni*, Giovanni's father Paganello owned no land at Pantano. However, as already noted, Giovanni was subsequently designated heir to his paternal uncle, Lonarduccio di Giovanni, see ACM, *Ser Griffo di Ser Paolo*, 4, fol.161v. In 1320 Lonarduccio, is recorded as owning eight pieces of worked land and vineyards, one of which was valued at 40 *lire* and 17 *soldi*, and was situated in Pantano, see ASS, *Estimo* 24, fol. 275r. It

seems likely, therefore, that the land Giovanni di Paganello chose to donate to the hospital of Sant'Angelo and to the hospital of Santa Maria della Scala in 1335 came from his uncle rather than his father.

76   ASS, *Manoscritti* B42, no. 3198.

77   *Il Caleffo Vecchio*, (eds) Mario Ascheri, Alessandra Forzini, Chiara Santini (5 vols, Siena, 1931–1991) (hereafter *Caleffo Vecchio*), vol. 3. See also ASS, *Manoscritti*, B41, no. 586 for a reference to the agreement notarized by Giovanni di Paganello in February, 1260, concerning land in the territory of Bibbiena. During the second half of the 1270s Giovanni di Paganello was also much involved with the affairs of Massa, see *Caleffo Vecchio*, Giovanni Cecchini (ed.), vol. 3, nos. 880 and 883–95, pp. 1066–1068 and 1072–1101.

78   Ibid., no. 905, p. 1126.

79   Ibid., no. 909, p. 1134,

80   Ibid., nos 914, 915, 925–930 and 939, pp. 1156–1160, 1179–1195 and 1227–1230.

81   ASS, *Biccherna* 79 (in a register dated January 1281–June 1281), fol. 9r.

82   *Caleffo Vecchio*, Giovanni Cecchini (ed.), vol. 3, no. 992, pp. 1387–1393.

83   For the history and development of this institution, see Lucia Brunetti, 'L'Ospedale dei SS Gregorio e Niccolo in Sasso di Siena detto di Monna Agnese 1275–1446: Nascità, consolidamento e organizzazione di un'ospedale femminile per poveri, infermi e partorienti', Università degli Studi di Siena, Anno Accademico 2001–02; and idem, 'L'ospedale di Monna Agnese di Siena e la sua Filiazione Romana', *Archivio della Società romana di storia patria*, 126 (2003), pp. 37–67; and idem, *Agnese e il suo ospedale, Siena, secc. 13–15* (Pisa, 2005). See also, Patrizia Turrini, Religiosità e spirito caritatevole a Siena agli inizi della reggenza lorense: luoghi pii laicali, contrade e arte,' part 1, *Annuario dell'Istituto Storico Diocesano Siena* (1994–95), pp. 9–128 (120–8).

84   Brunetti, 'L'ospedale di Monna Agnese di Siena e la sua Filiazione Romana', p. 38, note 6.

85   Ibid.

86   Brunetti, 'L'ospedale di Monna Agnese di Siena e la sua Filiazione Romana', pp. 11–12.

87   ASS, *Manoscritti* B23, n.229. See also, Brunetti, 'L'ospedale di Monna Agnese di Siena e la sua Filiazione Romana', p. 39, note 8.

88   For one of several copies made of this exemption from tax, see ASS, *Monna Agnese* 13, fol. 747 (pencil 137), 'Donna Agnese, Ordini, Cartecipazioni e Descritti dall'anno 1292–1656', Reg N.I, fol. 28r.

89   ASS, *Monna Agnese* 13, 747 (pencil 137), fols 28r and fols 30r–30v.

90   Ibid., fol. 28r.

91   In this context, see Maura Martellucci, 'I bambini di nessuno. L'infanzia abbandaonata al Santa Maria della Scala di Siena (secoli 13–16)', *BSSP*, 108 (2001), pp. 9–221.

92   ASS, *Estimo* 24, fols 117r, 166r and 326r.

93   ASS, *Estimo del Contado*, 80, fols 37r, 56r, 43r, 77r, 78r, 79r, 90v. For other property owned by the hospital in the vicinity of Camigliano, see ASS, *Monna Agnese*, 5,

'Donna Agnese, Documenti e Memorie dal 1401 all'anno 1601', Reg B no V, fol. 6r.

94 Alfio Cortonesi, *Poggio alle Mura e la bassa Val d'Orcia nel medioevo e in età moderna*, (Poggio alle Mura, 1996), pp. 89–102.

95 ASS, *Monna Agnese*, 98, fols 56r, 59v and 61r.

96 Ibid., fols 51v, 78r and 91v.

97 Ibid., fol. 33r.

98 ASS, *Monna Agnese*, 13, 'Le Rischapate', no. 743, fol.747 (pencil 137).

99 ASS, *Monna Agnese*, 98. It seems clear that endowed land, as well as on occasion continuing to be used by the original owner, was also frequently sold off within decades, if not years of the original endowment. According to a surviving record from1283, a large number of possessions at Montenero and in the 'curia' and 'districtus' of Sant'Angelo in Colle were offered to the monks of Abbadia San Salvatore on Monte Amiata by Ingnilranucci (or Inghiramo) di Gualtierocti of Montenero and his wife Jacomina in exchange for the couple's acceptance as oblates within the Cistercian order (see ASS, *Chronicle of Abbadia San Salvatore*, 5, fols 87r–87v.). However, according to the 1320 *Tavola delle possessioni* for Sant'Angelo in Colle, no property either within or outside the walls belonged to the Cistercian monks at that date.

100 ASS, *Monna Agnese*, 98, fol. 52v.

8

Embellishing the Fabric

On 16 June 1348 Ser Longo, son of the deceased Ser Tuccio (?Duccio, ?Guccio) and resident of Sant'Angelo in Colle, apparently lay on his death bed, for on that day a number of worthies gathered together in his house to witness his will.[1] Amongst the throng were Giovanni, rector of the church of San Michele, Francesco di Alessandro, a doctor from Montalcino, and Cianello di Petruccio from Seggiano. Also present were Angelo di Franco, Domenico Banduccio, Viviano di Angiolino (all described as 'from Sant'Angelo in Colle'), Nerio di Nanni from Villa a Tolli and one other individual, Meo, who was described as 'living' in the village, but who was not necessarily a resident. This was clearly an impressive gathering of individuals, and alone would suggest that Ser Longo was a person of some standing. As we shall see, the size of the different endowments stipulated in Ser Longo's will confirm that this was indeed the case. But references to the individual characters themselves within the text of the will indicate that there is a further story to be told.

The fact that a doctor from Montalcino was amongst the group of witnesses gathered at Ser Longo di Guccio's bedside suggests, for example, that Ser Longo may have been obliged to draw up a will as a result of a sudden and life-threatening illness. Furthermore, the details of the will itself suggest that Longo was perhaps not the only member of the family to be struck down. Individual asides within the will imply that Ser Longo's wife, Tessa, was pregnant but, like her husband, ill. That Ser Longo was on the point of an untimely death, and that other members of his family were threatened with the same fate, is also confirmed by several other caveats. Ser Longo stipulated, for example, that 50 *lire* should be allocated to his sister Margherita, and 100 *lire* to his other sister Francesca, but that in the event of their dying and their having no heirs, the money was to be spent instead on masses for his and their souls. Ser Longo also asked that in the event of his wife Tessa giving birth to a live male heir money should be paid to the church of San Michele, in thanksgiving. But, in the event of the death of such an heir Ser Longo decreed that his own mother Gemma should become his universal heir. Should Tessa give birth to a female heir, Ser Longo stipulated that the sum of 300 golden florins should be paid to the hospital of Santa Maria della Scala in Siena, no doubt by way of insurance for such a daughter's future as a prospective bride, but possibly also to cover the possibility of her being left an orphan. In the event of neither a son nor a daughter being born alive or reaching the age of maturity, Ser Longo again asked that his mother Gemma should become his universal heir. On Gemma's death the role of universal heir was to pass to Santa Maria della Scala. In the event of Gemma predeceasing Ser Longo's wife, and Tessa, herself subsequently dying, Ser Longo wished that Santa Maria della Scala should inherit all his assets, and that Friar Francesco di Giovanni of the 'frati minori', together with three other individuals (Giovanni di Vitale, Andrea di Chele and Naccio di Jordanello) should act as his executors.

There seems little doubt that, whether in the shorter, or the longer term, the Sienese hospital of Santa Maria della Scala was to benefit from Ser Longo di Ser Guccio's testamentary stipulations. In itself, this would not have been unusual. Nor would it have been strange, in terms of the patterns of piety established in both Sant'Angelo in Colle and Montalcino during the late thirteenth century. But, as we shall see, in the case of Ser Longo, the involvement of officials from the Sienese hospital in managing Ser Longo di Ser Guccio's estate may well have been significant also in the context of embellishments ordered by the testator both in Montalcino and in his own village.

Given the date of the drawing up of Ser Longo's will, it seems more than likely that both he and possibly his wife and sisters, also, had been struck down by the plague. The fact that more than one reference was made to responsibilities that were to be assumed by Ser Longo's mother, Gemma, in the event of the death of other members of the family, is in itself unusual. At the very least, it implies that Gemma, who had been married to Ser Longo's father, was not only still healthy, but also comparatively young, and in a position to command the family's affairs. No reference is made in the will to Gemma's current marital state, although the fact that Ser Longo refers to her as 'mater mea' (my mother), rather than in terms of his deceased father could indicate that Gemma had remarried.

Ser Longo's family was clearly associated with the professional class of the early fourteenth-century village, since the testator is described as 'Longo, son of the deceased village notary'. It seems likely therefore, that Longo had followed in the footsteps of Guccio di Ser Francesco, and Giovanni di Paganello in assuming responsibility for the legal affairs of Sant'Angelo in Colle. Longo does not figure, however, in the list of property owners in the 1320 *Tavola delle possessioni* for Sant'Angelo in Colle. His residency in Sant'Angelo in Colle may thus have post-dated 1320 – perhaps in the wake of Giovanni di Paganello's death some time between March 1335 and November 1336.

Irrespective of the date of their arrival in Sant'Angelo in Colle, there can be little doubt that Ser Longo and his family (like the families of Giovanni di Paganello and Ser Guccio di Ser Francesco before him) were regarded as belonging to the local elite. Apart from the prestige that went hand in hand with being representatives of the law and in particular the role of village notary, the family must also have acquired a certain profile in local affairs through the ownership of land and property in the territory of Sant'Angelo in Colle. According to his will, Ser Longo was the owner of at least two houses: one, a living house inside the walls and another, on a piece of worked land in the area known as Ferrale. On this same plot there was also a shack. It also seems that Ser Longo owned a second piece of worked land in Ferrale, as well as a piece of land given over to olives in the area known as Romiale. This latter, Ser Longo stipulated was to remain in the possession of his mother, Gemma. After Gemma's death, the olive grove at Romiale was to be appropriated to serve the needs of the poor of Sant'Angelo in Colle.

Ser Longo's will also contains a number of stipulations concerning generous monetary endowments to religious orders, indicating once more that he was a comparatively rich man. It seems clear that Ser Longo was set to become an important local benefactor, not only in his own village, but also in the nearby commune of Montalcino and surrounding territory. To the Augustinian friars of Sant'Agostino in Montalcino, Ser Longo left the considerable sum of 10 florins, in order that they should pray for his spiritual welfare after his death. Money was also to be given to the abbey of Sant'Antimo and to Friar Ranieri of the Guglielmite order. In particular, it seems that Ser Longo di Ser Guccio (like Rosa di Pecoraio before him) had a special affinity for the Franciscan order. Although he was clearly anxious to ensure the well-being of his soul in a variety of ways and through a number of different agencies, it was above all the Franciscans that Ser Longo wished to endow. Casting freely, he left 10 *lire* to the Franciscans of Montalcino so that the friars there should pray for his soul; to the Franciscan community at San Processo on the slopes of Amiata, he left another 10 *lire*, and yet a further 10 *lire* was left to the group of Franciscan friars established at Colombaio, close to Montalcino. Ser Longo seems to have been especially concerned that the Franciscans of Montalcino should be well clothed, since he stipulated that the 'frati minori' there should receive an annual payment of 10 florins in perpetuity to cover the cost of their 'indumenti'. Even more significantly, Ser Longo stipulated that 150 *lire* – equivalent to three times the annual salary of a manual worker at that period – should be left to the 'frati minori' in Montalcino to cover expenses involved in the construction and embellishment of a chapel and pulpit in the church of San Francesco itself.[2] He specifically requested, moreover, that the chapel should be furnished with a 'paramento', or hanging, and a 'pianeta', or altar cloth, as well as a chalice. Such stipulations would seem to confirm not only that Ser Longo di Ser Guccio was wealthy, disposed to endow the Franciscan order, and concerned with the particulars of his legacies, but also more generally that there were strong links between Sant'Angelo in Colle and Montalcino even during the last years of the Government of the Nine.

Other stipulations within the 1348 will show that Ser Longo was deeply concerned about local welfare within his own village. Indeed, he stipulated that 50 items of clothing, or tunics (each of which should value 40 *soldi*), were to be left to the poor of Sant'Angelo in Colle. (Whether these were to be distributed separately, or to be issued within the precincts of the village hospital is not clear.) Apart from clothing, Ser Longo's will also included a stipulation that the sum of 150 *lire* – the same amount he had laid aside for the construction and embellishment of the chapel in the church of San Francesco in Montalcino – should be allocated to the disadvantaged of his own local population. The will also contained a number of references to sums of money (ranging in value from 50 *lire* to 200 florins) that were to be paid to various members of Ser Longo's family, with the inference in at least one of the cases that such money was then to be distributed among the poor of Sant'Angelo in Colle. Other stipulations indicate that income was to be generated for the relief of the poor from Ser Longo's own land holdings.

To the village hospital 'of San Michele' Ser Longo left a piece of land in the area known as Collemattone, so that the officials of that institution should pray for his soul. He also endowed the representatives of two churches in Sant'Angelo in Colle in expectation that they too should carry out the same services. To Ser Giovanni, rector of San Michele, Ser Longo left 40 *soldi*, and to Ser Nuccio, rector of the church of San Pietro, 20 *soldi*. To Domino Mino Contis (di Conti), the parish priest of San Michele, Ser Longo left the comparatively large sum of three gold florins.[3]

There is an unexpected significance in the detail of the wording concerning Ser Longo's legacies to Ser Giovanni, Ser Nuccio and Domino Mino. Reference to the two rectors of Sant'Angelo in Colle, one responsible for the church of San Michele, and the other for the church of San Pietro confirms that both institutions were still functioning inside the walls of the village around the middle of the fourteenth century. The fact that the parish priest of San Michele is named as Mino and that he is said to have belonged to the Conti family, is also significant in the context of the small inscribed stone inserted above the door on the north side of the present church of San Michele Arcangelo. According to Don Antonio Brandi, the parish priest in 1321 was Marco di Conti.[4] The details of Ser Longo's will in this respect are thus somewhat puzzling. It is of course possible that two members from the same family held the office of parish priest at San Michele over the course of several decades. But, it was more commonly the case that those holding religious office were endowed for life. Thus, a parish priest would usually remain in office until his death.

The fact that Mino di Conti was recorded as parish priest of San Michele in 1348 does not, however, preclude the possibility that another member of his family had been engaged in a similar role prior to that date. In those cases where a particularly wealthy or powerful local clan held sway, it would have been in everyone's interest to keep the position of parish priest within the family. It is possible therefore that a parish priest named Marco was succeeded by a brother or nephew named Mino some time after 1321 and before the drawing up of Ser Longo's will in 1348. There is in fact some support for such a course of events in the reference on 4 June 1327 to Mino the cleric, son of Giovanni da Sant'Angelo in Colle.[5] According to this record the hospital of Santa Maria della Scala had bought a piece of agricultural land including vines belonging to Mino in the area known as Capanne. While no reference was made to Conti as a family name, the fact that Mino was described as a member of the clergy in 1327, rather than the 'proposto', or parish priest, is significant. He may only have assumed the latter position some time after June 1327.

The small inscribed stone now positioned above the north door of the church may thus indeed have been associated with another member of the Conti family, who held the office of parish priest prior to Mino. In any event, and more importantly, the details of Ser Longo's will reveal that the parish priest of San Michele in 1348 was still a member of the Conti family. That family must thus have been associated with the parish church for upwards of three decades. There seems little doubt that the rector of San Michele, Ser Giovanni, had also been associated with Sant'Angelo in Colle for several decades, since reference was made in the 1320 *Tavola delle possessioni* to land owned by Giovanni, 'the cleric'.[6] By 1348, Ser Giovanni must thus not only have reached what would at that period have been perceived as old age, but as rector must also have been regarded as a significant and long-standing representative of the local population. As we shall see, this may have had a bearing on the embellishment of the urban fabric generally, and in particular on the iconography of decorations carried out inside the church of San Michele.

The differential in the stipulated legacies to the village's two rectors would seem to confirm that Ser Nuccio, the rector of San Pietro, and the institution itself – at least in Ser Longo's opinion – were of less consequence than Ser Giovanni and the parish church of San Michele. There is confirmation of this in the overall patrimony recorded for the church of San Pietro in the 1320 *Tavola delle possessioni*.[7] At just over 420 *lire*, the patrimony of San Pietro was less than a third of that recorded in respect of San Michele. There may be further confirmation of the different roles assumed by the two rectors in the early fourteenth-century village in the fact that Ser Giovanni was chosen to be one of the witnesses present at the drawing up of Ser Longo's will and Ser Nuccio was not. Ser Giovanni's presence could, however, have been due to a number of other factors.

It seems that Ser Longo was anxious not only to ensure his own spiritual welfare after death by leaving money to the rector of San Michele, but also that he and his family should continue an association already established with the parish church. Despite the stipulation that money should be left to the Franciscan friars of Montalcino in order that a chapel should be erected in his name in the church of San Francesco there, Ser Longo stipulated that his own body should be buried in the church of San Michele 'et ibi mea eligo sepultura' (and there I elect, or have elected my tomb). Other details within the will confirm that Ser Longo already owned a chapel inside the parish church, since reference was made to the sum of six *lire* in the context of an annual provision of wax for illumination 'i(n) cappella mea que est in d(i) c(ta) Eccl(e)sia' (for my chapel that is in the said church). This chapel may also have been made available to other members of Ser Longo's family. Ser Longo was also clearly interested in the general furnishings of the new church, since he stipulated that three gold florins should be spent on the production of a missal for use in religious celebrations there.

The variety of stipulations contained in Ser Longo's will indicates that he was in many ways following in the footsteps of Giovanni di Paganello. In 1335, Giovanni di Paganello, while endowing the Augustinians of Montalcino, had also made arrangements for the bestowal of oil to the Franciscans in the same town. He had also left a number of legacies to other religious institutions (including Sant'Antimo), as well as making considerable provisions for the charitable and religious institutions in his own village. As we have seen, he was not only ready to provide land to ensure the well-being of the local hospital in Sant'Angelo in Colle, but was also prepared to underwrite the expense of building work in both of the village's two churches. There are, however, a number of subtle differences in the stipulations drawn up by these two testators.

Giovanni di Paganello appears to have been concerned about the construction or restoration of the parish church. Ser Longo seems by contrast to have been particularly interested in its internal spaces and the ways in which it might be embellished. One conclusion to be drawn from a comparison of the two wills, therefore, is that building work in progress (or not yet begun) at the time of Giovanni di Paganello's will in 1335 was well advanced, if not completed by 1348, when Ser Longo set about deciding how to allocate his own not inconsiderable assets. Another conclusion to be drawn is that in 1348 Ser Longo and his family were set to become (if they were not already established as such) significant patrons of the new parish church. This family may indeed have been the first, not only to underwrite the expenses of new decorations in San Michele, but also to erect a family chapel inside the reconstructed fabric.

Ser Longo's will thus provides us with a point of departure for an analysis of the embellishment of the fabric, and in particular consideration of surviving fourteenth-century decorations in the church of San Michele. As we shall see, it also prompts speculation about various religious rites celebrated inside the parish church on behalf of the village hospital. In particular, it triggers a number of questions about the decoration of the 'Ospedale di Sant'Angelo' itself, as well as the various ways in which that institution's affairs were administered.

Although entries in the 1320 *Tavola delle possessioni* indicate that the two institutions were independent of each other, and although Ser Longo himself appears to have distinguished between the two sets of officials when specifying individual endowments, the details of his will indicate that there were already close links between the hospital and the parish church in the early medieval period. Indeed, it seems likely that the two were closely entwined. There seems little doubt either, that Ser Longo assumed a significant role in the affairs of both institutions. Apart from the clothing and monetary payments set aside for the poor of Sant'Angelo in Colle (some of whom may have been housed in the village hospital, or have sought the services of the 'Casa della Misericordia'), Ser Longo stipulated that the hospital 'of San Michele' should benefit from a third of the fruits of the land owned by him at Collemattoni.

The details of these endowments are significant, not only for the light they throw on Ser Longo's benevolence towards his own local population and his own local hospital, but also for the reference to the hospital's *titulus*. While most surviving records refer only to the 'hospital of Sant' Angelo', Ser Longo's will reveals that the hospital carried the same *titulus* as the parish church. This alone confirms that the clergy of San Michele must have felt especially obliged to involve themselves in the spiritual welfare of the hospital, placed (as we now know it was) under the protection of the same patron saint.[8] The shared *titulus* must also have played a part in determining how and where such spiritual care was practised. It seems likely, for example, that any observance in respect of the hospital that was carried out inside the parish church itself would have taken place at an altar dedicated to the Archangel Michael, or in front of imagery including the figure of that saint. The most likely site for such observance, given the *titulus* of the parish church, must surely have been either in the proximity of, or at the high altar.

In this context, it is significant that according to a pastoral visit made in 1618, the church of San Michele contained at least one image of Saint Michael – a frescoed figure that was displayed in the high altar area.[9] According to the early seventeenth record, this figure of the patron saint of both the parish church and the hospital was painted on the back wall, immediately behind the high altar. Some have assumed that this was an oversize image of the Archangel Michael, but there is nothing in the early seventeenth-century pastoral record to support such a theory. Indeed, the fact that no reference is made to the dimensions of the frescoed figure rather indicates that it was a normal size. Of the age or artistic style of the fresco, there is no mention. However, as we shall see, the existence of such a figure in the vicinity of the high altar may be significant in the context of establishing one of the original sites at which religious observance was carried out on behalf of the village hospital.

Although both Giovanni di Paganello and Ser Longo di Ser Guccio made financial provisions for the upkeep of the hospital's fabric and for its continued well being, neither made any reference to a specific altar serving the hospital inside the church of San Michele. Nor did either of them stipulate specific legacies in respect of the embellishment of the hospital's internal spaces. Of the physical state of the hospital complex of San Michele during the last years of the Government of the Nine, and the way in which its affairs were managed, we know virtually nothing. No documents other than the surviving wills of Giovanni di Paganello and Ser Longo di Ser Guccio appear to throw light on the affairs of the hospital during the fourteenth century. By contrast, a more detailed picture emerges from records drawn up by Francesco Piccolomini when he visited the village in May 1573. At that date, a new village hospital (dedicated to Saint Anthony Abbot and run by Friar Galiatinus, the rector of the parish church of San Michele Arcangelo) was clearly functioning under the auspices of the parish church. Moreover, religious observations were clearly being carried out in the hospital's name at an altar on the north wall of San Michele closest to the entrance to the church.[10]

The same records show that the hospital fabric was in a state of acute degradation by the late sixteenth century. Francesco Piccolomini noted that the internal spaces of the existing hospital were badly furnished in so far as beds and bed linen were concerned. Indeed, Francesco Piccolomini opined that the place was 'fit for dogs rather than humans'.[11] The general state of the place, in his opinion was appalling ('pessimum'). Three years later, in 1576, conditions inside the hospital were apparently little better, since the Apostolic visitor Francesco Bossi stipulated that the spaces reserved for the sick and for pilgrims at Sant'Angelo in Colle should be made decent ('decenti') and that the hospital building should be appropriately furnished within six months.[12] Of internal decorations, Bossi made no mention.

On the basis of archival material that has so far surfaced, there appears to be no way of establishing whether the new hospital of Sant'Antonio was established inside the premises of the pre-existing hospital of San Michele, or whether the two institutions occupied completely different sites. But even if the hospital of Sant'Antonio had sprung up within the confines of the older hospital of San Michele, any embellishment of the fabric carried out in the time of Giovanni di Paganello or Ser Longo di Ser Guccio must surely have been destroyed or have been in poor condition by the sixteenth century. That said, it is significant that when Francesco Piccolomini made reference to the hospital's altar inside the parish church of San Michele, no mention was made of any similar structures or decorations inside the hospital complex itself. It seems likely, therefore, that by the sixteenth century the internal spaces of the village hospital were bare. This is hardly surprising, given the village's recent history and the abandonment of Sant'Angelo in Colle prior to the siege of Montalcino. That said, an attempt is made here to reconstruct the embellishments of the earlier medieval complex.

Most pastoral visits of the sixteenth and later centuries tend to stress the poverty and disrepair of hospital complexes, noting, if anything, not the internal decorations, but the filthy pallets, insufficient bed coverings and frequent absence of hospital personnel. The embellishment of the fabric is virtually unrecorded. At an earlier date, however, the situation seems to have been very different. John Henderson's studies concerning the administration of hospital complexes and the embellishment of their internal spaces during the medieval and early renaissance periods have immeasurably changed our understanding of how such institutions looked and functioned in early modern Italy.[13] From contemporary accounts it would seem that at least some early hospital complexes were not only centres of medical care, but also visually splendid. Many hospitals, and especially those established in the vicinity of Florence and Siena were also clearly held in high regard. Leon Battista Alberti referred, for example to the 'splendide case di cura' that had been established at great expense and where any citizen or visitor could find everything possible at the service of his health.[14]

The first question, therefore, is whether there were ever any decorations inside the village hospital of Sant'Angelo in Colle. In some cases it may possibly have been more convenient to display painted altarpieces or three-dimensional works commissioned on behalf of a hospital, or to site an altar owned and endowed by such an entity not within the hospital complex itself, but in a neighbourhood church instead. This must particularly have been the case where the hospital had established a close association with a local religious entity, either as a result of physical proximity, or by dint of having a common titular saint.

Recent research into the administration of early hospital complexes throws considerable light on the connections that were established between charitable and religious entities.[15] It seems, for example, that it was common practice for local clergy to visit hospitals in their parish, in order to offer the holy sacraments to the impoverished, the weary, the sick and the dying. There is also confirmation in such studies of the practice whereby clergy officiated in front of an altar or altars set up within the spaces of the individual hospital complexes. But all was not paradise in those splendid houses of healing, even during the early renaissance. According to one commentator, Buoncompagno da Signa, the hospital of San Giovanni Battista in Florence served disgusting food and rotten wine, and contained fetid pallets for the poor inmates whose constant lamentations prevented rest or sleep.[16] Even at that date, upkeep, rather than the embellishment of the fabric was the source of constant anxiety. Where there were restricted funds for the maintenance of an institution – as was possibly the case with the village hospital at Sant'Angelo in Colle prior to the legacies of Giovanni di Paganello and Ser Longo di Ser Guccio in the fourteenth century – any votive images adopted or commissioned in its name must have been fairly basic, if funded by the hospital authorities themselves. Surviving documents charting the development of Monna Agnese in Siena, for example, reveal a desperate need of funds just to expand the hospital building only a few years after its foundation. This, despite the fact that the hospital had been established on a central site in the shadow of the Duomo, and that almost from its inception it received glowing reports as a result of its protection and nurturing of women in childbirth. Funding for the continued well-being and upkeep of little-known hospital complexes in rural areas must necessarily have depended in large part on the legacies of well-intentioned local benefactors.

Against such a background, the grandiose series of fifteenth-century frescoes in the 'Pellegrinaggio', or general ward of the hospital of Santa Maria della Scala in Siena might seem to be unusually splendid painted testimonies to the wealth and significance of that particular city institution: lavish exceptions to what were normally cramped, bare and miserable spaces of charity. There is, however, evidence to show that at least one of the hospital buildings in Montalcino, Santa Maria della Croce, was embellished with a number of frescoes at an early date. It also becomes clear that the internal spaces of the same institution contained numerous painted artefacts, including decorated beds and chests for linen. Analysis of this hospital complex provides a base from which to consider not only the decoration of internal spaces of medieval hospitals in general, but more specifically the embellishment of the medieval hospital of San Michele in Sant'Angelo in Colle.

The hospital of Santa Maria della Croce seems to have begun life under the simple title of 'Casa di San Lorenzo', apparently because it was established close to the parish church of that *titulus* on the northern edge of Montalcino.[17] The same may very likely have been the case for the village hospital of Sant'Angelo in Colle: giving rise to the name 'Casa della Misericordia', or 'Casa di San Michele'. In this context it may be significant that references to the structure abutting the hospital building in the 1320 *Tavola delle possessioni* adopted the term 'domus' or 'casa'.

The date of the foundation of the 'Casa di San Lorenzo' in Montalcino is unclear. The eighteenth-century historian, Tullio Canali, suggested that a hospital complex already existed on that site in the early eleventh century.[18] But the earliest surviving reference to the hospital in the context of testamentary endowments dates to July 1280.[19] Two other hospitals, that of Santa Lucia (better known as the Misericordia) and the Ospedale of Fra Manente, were established inside the walls of Montalcino by the end of the thirteenth century.[20] Four more hospitals were established in and around Montalcino by 1332; a couple more followed shortly thereafter.

Although there are no documentary references to a village hospital in Sant'Angelo in Colle prior to 1320, it is tempting to argue that it, too, was founded some time between the thirteenth and the fourteenth centuries. Its probable location within the old nucleus of the urban fabric, close to an original east–west route through the village would, in fact, imply a much earlier foundation. Given that the parish church of San Michele, if not the whole village was at an early date under the jurisdiction of the monks at Sant'Antimo, it is also possible that the 'Casa della Misericordia' and the adjoining 'Ospedale di San Michele' originally functioned as resting places for travellers with business at the nearby monastery. If that were the case, the hospital complex at Sant'Angelo in Colle might very well have been founded as early as the eleventh century, and possibly even earlier. Even during the fourteenth century, the hospital's position on a north-south axis – close to the southern gate and fronting what was no doubt the main thoroughfare through Sant'Angelo in Colle – must have made it a convenient stopping off place.

Some of the hospital institutions in Montalcino certainly functioned as resting places rather than as centres for the care of the sick. Indeed, it seems that the hospital of San Bartolomeo della Strada outside the walls of Montalcino on the road leading east to Buonconvento, as well as another nearby hospital complex were reserved solely for travellers and pilgrims.[21] At least part of the complex at Sant'Angelo in Colle may thus have been reserved for a similar purpose. Indeed, it may initially have been as much involved with the needs of travellers as with those struck down by poverty or ill health. It may even have been virtually self-sufficient through such travellers' payments for board and lodging. This in turn could have resulted in sufficient funds, and even endowments for the embellishment of the fabric. However, the upkeep of even newly established institutions was clearly a hazardous business.

Surviving records show that the funding of the various hospital complexes in Montalcino following their original foundation was frequently patchy and inadequate. Several institutions folded early through lack of funds. Others were merged with larger complexes as they faced increasing financial difficulties. By the mid-fifteenth century only four hospitals remained in Montalcino: that known as the Misericordia associated with the church of Santa Maria Maddalena, that of San Cristoforo, that newly established under the title of Santa Maria delle Grazie following the failure of the Guglielmite community of the same *titulus*, and that of San Lorenzo – by then known as Santa Maria della Croce.

Virtually nothing now remains of the old hospital of Santa Maria della Croce. Modern commune buildings occupy the site of the original hospital complex and only a few fragmented columns displayed in an internal courtyard survive to testify how a grandiose loggia inserted into the original façade once looked.[22] Of the early fifteenth-century frescoed paintings within the façade loggia (documented as the work of the local artist, Domenico Mettifuoco di Montalcino), there is now no trace.[23] Nothing remains, either, of the decorations in the spaces behind the façade. However, two inventories surviving from the fifteenth century show that both the external and the internal spaces of the hospital were by that date quite lavishly decorated. The earlier of the two inventories dated 28 August 1483, and in private possession, has been transcribed by Don Antonio Brandi.[24] The later inventory, dated 15 July 1498 (and apparently covering the period up to 12 March 1504), is unpublished and remains in the archive of Santa Maria della Croce, now part of the communal archive in Montalcino.[25]

Individual entries in the two inventories indicate that much of the hospital complex of Santa Maria della Croce was embellished with fresco paintings by the late fifteenth century. In many ways, therefore, the hospital complex in Montalcino seems to have mirrored the larger and more politically significant hospital of Santa Maria della Scala in Siena. Most significantly, it appears that different kinds of embellishment were reserved for different parts of the hospital complex. Perhaps not surprisingly, it seems that distinctions were made between those spaces that were reserved for the inmates, or patients, and those that were occupied by hospital officials. In effect, and as one might expect, there were considerable differences between the embellishment of public and private areas. The 1483 inventory refers to at least one room as the 'camera dipenta', implying that it was completely covered with fresco paintings, possibly including narrative scenes.[26] Other rooms with names such as the 'Camera di cottimello (probably some kind of crab apple or quince) and the 'Camera de Trombetti (trumpets?)' seem to have been decorated with natural or abstract motifs. Common to both inventories are numerous references to 'lettiere dipinte', or painted beds, and to painted and decorated chests ranging from 'forzieri' to 'goffani' ('cofani') and 'cassoni'.

Without further detail, it is impossible to establish what these particular pieces of furniture looked like. However, recent studies by Lucia Sandri and Duccio Balestracci indicate that there was a degree of uniformity in the internal furnishings of hospitals in the territories of Florence and Siena during the early modern period.[27] Sandri refers in particular to the painting in red of hospital furniture and the placing of donors' coats of arms on bed ends in the hospital of San Matteo in Florence. Sandri's analysis of San Matteo also reveals that space was left for prayer around an altar set up inside that hospital complex, including seats for the friars to hear confession, and 'panche da predica', or benches for praying.[28] Sandri also notes that the women's ward included an altar decorated with various sacred objects, a crucifix, candlesticks and painted panels. While such paintings may, for the most part, have depicted images of the Virgin and Child, others may also have included the figures of saints. As we shall see, Sandri's findings are particularly relevant in the context of two extant panels associated with Sant'Angelo in Colle and tentatively identified here as having originally embellished the old village hospital.

A very similar picture concerning the embellishment of medieval hospitals in Italy emerges from Alfredo Liberati's consideration of decorations inside the hospital complex of Santa Maria della Scala in Siena. According to a number of documents published by Liberati at the beginning of the twentieth century, the hospital complex of Santa Maria della Scala contained a vast range of painted artefacts by the middle of the fourteenth century.[29] Indeed, it becomes clear that the internal spaces of the hospital were filled with a variety of decorated artefacts ranging from painted beds, to painted bed coverings, and from painted signs of the hospital to be affixed to property left to it, to painted coats of arms for individual rectors. These furnishings were placed in a number of different spaces ranging from the infirmary and wards, to the 'spezeria' (or dispensary), the 'pellegrinaio' (or room of the pilgrims, often also designated as a general ward), the 'scrittoio' (or study cum office), hospital chapels, and even the pharmacy. Indeed, it not only seems that the hospital fabric had been thoroughly embellished at a comparatively early date, but also that both wall decorations and individual painted artefacts within the hospital complex were kept in good condition through constant renovation. Liberati cites a large number of now little-known painters who were apparently employed on a regular basis at the hospital, if not in the production of new artefacts, then in the restoration and refreshing of older decorations.

Interestingly, the documents published by Liberati indicate a uniform and slightly austere painting of ward furniture at Santa Maria della Scala, with only an occasional addition of the colour red or green. By contrast, the inventories of the hospital of Santa Maria della Croce in Montalcino show that more elaborate decoration was reserved for those spaces used by hospital personnel. Thus, the 1498 inventory contains a reference to 'una lettiera bella dipinta', or beautiful painted day bed, that had been consigned to the new rector Frater Andreonico and his wife Juliette.[30] The 1483 inventory entry for the painted chamber next to the 'sala principale' (or refectory) on the upper floor of the hospital refers also to a painted vault above the 'lettiera' there.[31] In the 'camera di Frate Giovanni' – most probably the private room of an earlier rector – there was yet another painted bed, but this one was described as rather old, perhaps confirming that it was no longer in use.[32] These, and other beds positioned in other rooms at Santa Maria della Croce, appear to have been quite separate from the 15 'small' beds which were possibly little more than pallets, and which are described in 1483 as being in the 'pellegrinaio'. Although the public ward may thus have been comparatively plain, there seems little doubt that the more private areas of the hospital were well furnished, and on occasion even lavishly embellished.

In both inventories of the hospital of Santa Maria della Croce there are also a number of references to paintings of the Virgin Mary, although there are few precise references to individual iconographies.[33] The 1483 inventory indicates that there were at least two such paintings in the fifteenth-century hospital. One was displayed in a painted chamber next to the 'Sala Principale', or refectory. Another was recorded as in the 'Camera di Frate Giovanni'. In a room beside the kitchen, there was also a 'tavoletta da Madonna col tabernacolo' – presumably a Madonna and Child set within a small tabernacle. And, in the so-called 'Camera del Vetturale' (presumably the room of the coachman), reference was made to 'Una Madonna dipenta da camera' – presumably another small-scale painting. In the hospital chapel there was also a large painted altarpiece displayed above the altar there ('una tavola grande a l'altare bella'), as well as two small painted panels depicting the Crucifixion and the Madonna and Child in the company of a number of saints.

The fact that reference was made to 'uno quadro di Madonna dipento' in the 'Camera del Vetturale' and that no specific mention was made of the Christ child may be significant. While it is possible that the reference to the Virgin was intended to include the presence also of her child, Alessandra Gianni, in recent research into the foundation and development of the hospital of the Misericordia in Siena, reaches the conclusion that there were a large number of depictions of the 'Madonna della Misericordia', or Virgin of Mercy, in hospital and lay confraternity spaces in early renaissance Siena.[34] Gianni suggests that the imagery of the standing Virgin of Mercy without her child provided visual evidence of the works of charity or 'misericordia' practised by hospital and other charitable institutions during the early modern period. In this context she draws attention to the image of the *Madonna della Misericordia* that was painted during the first half of the fourteenth century in the church of San Pellegrino alla Sapienza, (adjacent to the Casa della Misericordia), fragments of which survive in the depot of the Pinacoteca in Siena.[35] Gianni also points out that the iconography of the Madonna della Misericordia or 'del Manto' was used on occasion for the covers of the 'biccherne', or account books, of Santa Maria della Scala – in other words, in the internal spaces of the hospital itself.[36] Gianni offers no firm evidence that hospital authorities selected images of the Madonna della Misericordia in preference to other depictions of the Virgin. That said, a number of images of the Madonna della Misericordia inside the complex of Santa Maria della Scala, both in the form of early Biccherna covers, and in large-scale frescoes of the Virgin with outspread mantle would seem to support the hypotheses Gianni proposes.

What conclusions can then be drawn about decorations in the early fourteenth-century hospital complex of San Michele in Sant'Angelo in Colle, and the artists called to work there? Clearly, much must have depended on the size of the hospital complex, as well as the amount of money it had at its disposal. That there was scope for embellishment of the fabric, is clear, since the early fourteenth-century hospital building was a structure of some size. Valued at 50 *lire*, it must have occupied 5 times the space of some of the smaller buildings in the village, and by the same token it must have been as much as 10 times the size of some of the half houses recorded in the 1320 *Tavola delle possessioni*.[37] At least some of the internal spaces of the hospital complex in Sant'Angelo in Colle must also have been furnished, even if only with beds and chests. Within the spaces of the late fifteenth-century hospital complex of Santa Maria della Croce there were, for example, at least seven chests inlaid with intarsia work (two of them also containing painted panels). Further reference was made to a 'gaffanaccio' (or long chest for holding hospital documents), to several other chests of unspecified form and size, and to at least one coffer that was described as 'new', along with 11 other types of chest (two of which were described as for storing bread), and a number of other undefined boxes.

Much clearly depended on the financial circumstances of the institution at any one moment, as well as the number of endowments it attracted. By the fifteenth century the hospital of Santa Maria della Croce in Montalcino had considerably increased its wealth, having absorbed land and property that had previously belonged to other institutions. The fifteenth-century hospital building in Montalcino also appears to have been a structure of some size, since it is described as occupying three floors. According to surviving records, there were in the region of 20 internal spaces in the entire hospital complex. These included the refectory, the 'pellegrinaio', various antechambers, the 'room of the women', some store rooms, the 'room of Fra Giovanni', the 'camera del Pane', or bread room, the 'camera del Vetturale', a 'scrittoio', a chapel, various corridors and staircases, a loggia, a cellar, stables, the lower level 'piazza' or square, and at least two kitchens. While the hospital complex at Sant'Angelo in Colle may have been divided up in a similar way, it must have been on a much smaller scale. However, at the very least, it must have contained a general ward, a refectory and kitchen area, and a number of storage spaces, as well as connecting corridors and a room or rooms reserved for hospital officials.[38] Some of the internal spaces of the hospital complex in Sant'Angelo in Colle may also have been painted with frescoes – perhaps, as at Santa Maria della Croce, with narrative scenes, or with symbols of vegetables or fruits. The hospital officials no doubt also enjoyed the use of painted beds, chests and votive images, some of which must have been funded by outside benefactors, and thus have included their names or coats of arms. Some may even have included images of specific donors.

Given its *titulus* prior to the sixteenth century, one would expect that many of the images produced on behalf of the village hospital in Sant'Angelo in Colle during the medieval and renaissance periods must have included the figure of the Archangel Michael. Given Sant'Angelo in Colle's status as a subject Sienese commune, it also seems likely that decorations produced for both the parish church and the village hospital would have reflected recent artistic developments in Siena. As we shall see, a number of painted artefacts datable to the fourteenth century and associated with Sant'Angelo in Colle do in fact indicate knowledge of, if not direct influence from the work of contemporary Sienese artists.

In a recent publication Diana Norman stresses the influence of Sienese artists and Sienese iconography in the *contado* of Siena under the Government of the Nine.[39] She also offers persuasive evidence of the spread of artistic compositions and styles through deliberate repetition in the religious spaces of churches and chapels outside Siena, of earlier 'high profile' images such as Duccio di Buoninsegna's *Maestà*. Norman also draws attention to the physical presence of leading Sienese artists such as Bartolo di Fredi in centres such as Montalcino during the latter part of the fourteenth century. According to Norman, Bartolo di Fredi's presence in Montalcino stimulated a series of commissions of art works reflecting current developments in Siena. Hospital decorations in the early fourteenth-century hospital of San Michele in Sant'Angelo in Colle may have reflected just this kind of osmosis. Moreover, potential benefactors in Sant'Angelo in Colle, like Giovanni di Paganello and Ser Longo di Ser Guccio, anxious to endow their local institutions and searching for artistic guidance in the embellishment of those fabrics, would not have had to look far before encountering the most recent art works of leading Sienese artists.

Particular consideration is given here to the activities of the Lorenzetti brothers, and the influence these artists may have had on the embellishment of both the parish church of San Michele and the church inside the walls dedicated to Saint Peter. Both Pietro and Ambrogio Lorenzetti are known to have carried out work for sites in the vicinity of Sant'Angelo in Colle. Attention focuses here on the work of Pietro. Only a few years before the drawing up of Ser Longo's will in 1348, Pietro Lorenzetti (or a close follower) seems to have formed a close relationship with the community of Castiglione del Bosco to the north-west of Sant'Angelo in Colle, since Pietro's artistic style has been recognised in fresco work in the church of San Michele there.[40]

According to the accompanying inscription, the painting of the *Annunciation to the Virgin between Six Standing Saints* on the altar wall of San Michele was

Figure 8.1   Attr. Pietro Lorenzetti, Annunciation to the Virgin with Six Saints Fresco dated 1345, Pieve of San Michele, Castiglione del Bosco

completed in 1345. Several years prior to the work at Castiglione del Bosco, Pietro Lorenzetti also appears to have painted portable panels for Castiglione d'Orcia and Montichiello.[41] For any artist intent on embellishing the fabric of Sant'Angelo in Colle during the same period, there was thus ample evidence of Pietro Lorenzetti's expertise in both fresco and painted panel work in the vicinity. Ambrogio Lorenzetti for his part had produced a huge painted altarpiece of the *Virgin and Child enthroned between the seated figures of Saint Peter and Saint Paul* for the parish church of Santi Pietro e Paolo in nearby Roccalbegna.[42] Evidence of the Lorenzetti brothers' artistic style, if not actual examples of their autograph work, were thus clearly visible in various parts of the southern Sienese *contado* several years before the drawing up of Ser Longo's will in 1348. When Ser Longo was on his death bed, the frescoes in the church of San Michele at Castiglione del Bosco, may well have been regarded as the most up-to-date and sophisticated example of Sienese artistic expertise in the region. The fact that this imagery was also produced for a church with the same *titulus* as the parish church in Sant'Angelo in Colle, must have been of particular interest to the clergy of San Michele. Indeed, the hypothesis is raised here that the embellishment of the *pieve* at San Michele in Castiglione del Bosco directly influenced decorations carried out in the parish church at Sant'Angelo in Colle.

While the present parish church of San Michele Arcangelo probably reflects more or less accurately the lines and orientation of the fourteenth-century structure that replaced the original, much smaller church of San Michele, little remains of its earlier embellishment. There are now only a couple of frescoes dating to the fourteenth century. The earliest, a much damaged *Sacra Conversazione* (or Holy Conversation) depicting the Virgin and Child in the company of three (and at one time four) saints (including, on the Virgin's left-hand side, two figures identified as Saint John the Baptist and Saint Anthony Abbot, and on her right-hand side a figure traditionally identified as Saint Stephen), is attributed to an anonymous artist active during the first half of the century. This fresco, which had been covered by whitewash and which is displayed on the south wall of the church close to the altar of Carlo Borromeo was only rediscovered in the second half of the nineteenth century.[43]

The second fresco, which is located on the south wall above the organ, is a mutilated composition including the figure of a male saint identified as *Saint Leonard*. Like the *Sacra Conversazione*, it is attributed to an unknown fourteenth-century artist, but one who was active towards the end of the century.[44]

Both of these frescoes have been severely damaged. It is, moreover, clear that the *Sacra Conversazione* was already in a damaged state when it was covered over. Photographs taken prior to recent restoration work show clear evidence of existing *lacunae*, as well as the chiselling and hammering of the surface commonly effected in the course of preparing the surface of pre-existing decorations for new layers of 'arriccio', or plaster, prior to carrying out new fresco painting, or to applying a top layer of whitewashing.[45]

Figure 8.2　Unknown fourteenth-century artist, Sacra Conversazione fresco, Parish church of San Michele Arcangelo, Sant' Angelo in Colle

In the case of the *Sacra Conversazione*, the entire central part of the Virgin's face and upper torso is missing. The Christ Child's body seems also to have been damaged or distorted, perhaps through later restoration. There is in addition extensive damage to the lower part of the figures of Saint John the Baptist and Saint Anthony Abbot. As already noted, only one saint is now discernible on the Virgin's right-hand side, and even there, a large part is missing from the central part of that figure's body. Of what was presumably the figure of a fourth saint on the Virgin's far right-hand side, nothing now remains, apart from a small area of greenish paint in the lower part of the

Figure 8.3 Unknown fourteenth-century artist, Saint Leonard fresco, Parish church of San Michele Arcangelo, Sant'Angelo in Colle

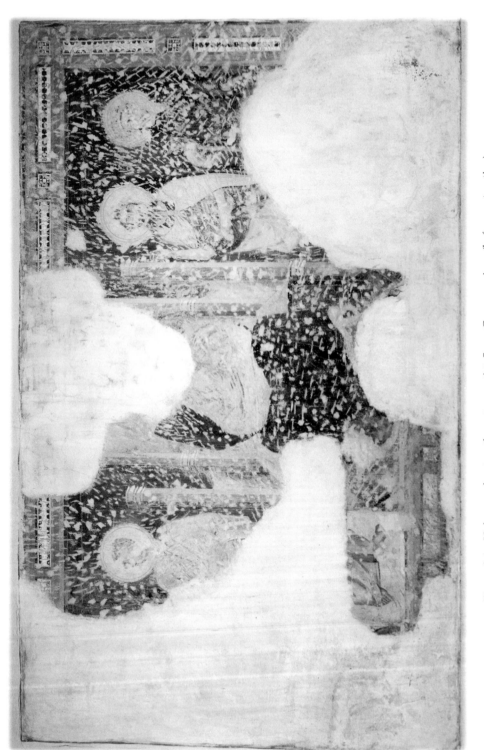

Figure 8.4   Unknown fourteenth-century artist, Sacra Conversazione (before restoration) fresco, Parish church of San Michele Arcangelo, Sant'Angelo in Colle

existing fresco. According to Don Antonio Brandi, much of the damage to the *Sacra Conversazione* resulted from the construction of a small connecting door between the church and the adjacent cemetery, and the later positioning of a baptismal niche in this part of the church.[46]

The second fresco, which depicts *Saint Leonard* standing under an arch, appears instead to have been damaged by the construction of the pulpit. As is the case with the surviving *Sacra Conversazione*, essential parts of the original composition of the *Saint Leonard* fresco are now missing. Although the upper part of the figure of *Saint Leonard* is comparatively well preserved, the whole of the lower part of his body has been destroyed. It is also clear that *Saint Leonard* originally formed part of a larger composition, since the remains of a second arched compartment are visible on his upper right-hand side. Moreover, in that section, the arch seems to have sprung from a lower level than that framing the figure of the saint. This was commonly the case when a narrative scene, or image of the Virgin and Child, was flanked by standing saints. It seems likely, therefore, that the *Saint Leonard* figure once formed part of a *trompe-l'oeil* triptych or polyptych. Given the surviving details, it seems reasonable to suggest that at least one other figure of a saint on the other side of a missing central image was originally included to balance the figure of *Saint Leonard*. It is virtually impossible to establish whether there were further flanking figures. It is, however significant that the position and gaze of a small spandrel figure inserted above and to *Saint Leonard*'s right encourages the viewer to look to their right, as if not only to initiate contact with *Saint Leonard*, but also to extend their gaze further to the right. The fact that there is no balancing small figure in the spandrel above *Saint Leonard*'s left shoulder could indicate, therefore, that *Saint Leonard* was flanked by another saint on his left-hand side. The remaining triangular-shaped ground of fictive variegated marble in the spandrel above *Saint Leonard*'s left shoulder could thus have bridged the gap between two arches framing two standing figures of saints in the original fresco.

It is significant that *Saint Leonard* is depicted in the black habit of the Augustinian Hermits. There seems little doubt that this order had developed a particular veneration for Saint Leonard by the fourteenth century.[47] It was thus common not only for Saint Leonard to be painted in Augustinian space, but also that he should be depicted as a member of the Augustinian order. However, the inclusion of a saint so vested in the embellishment of a parish church apparently unconnected with the Augustinian order prompts a number of questions.

The most obvious explanation for the Augustinian habit of *Saint Leonard* in the parish church of Sant'Angelo in Colle is that a community of Augustinian Hermits had been established in, or near the village by the end of the fourteenth century, and that they were in some way responsible for the commissioning of the fresco. This does indeed seem to have been the case. As already noted, several entries in the 1320 *Tavola delle possessioni* for Sant'Angelo in Colle contain references to Fra Ra(i)naldo, or Renaldo 'of the Augustinian order' as the owner of a number of pieces of land in the territory. As we have also seen, this same individual played a key part in the purchase and subsequent sale of property and land in and around the frontier castle over a number of years.[48] Fra Ranaldo also seems to have acted on behalf of the Augustinian community in Siena over the purchase of property in Montalcino as early as 1297. On 10 February, 1297, for example, Tavena, son of the deceased Deo di Tolomei of Siena, is recorded as selling to Fra Ranaldo a house and kitchen garden in Montalcino. On that occasion, Fra Ranaldo was also referred to as prior of the hermit friars of the order of Saint Augustine in the province of Siena.[49] He thus emerges as a high-ranking official within the Augustinian community. As discussion in Chapter 4 has shown, the Sienese community of Sant'Agostino also had direct dealings with a number of the inhabitants of Sant'Angelo in Colle during the first decade of the fourteenth century, most notably in the context of the pasturing and care of livestock. Quite apart from that, it seems clear that Sant'Agostino held property both inside the walls and in the vicinity of the village by the time of the drawing up of the Sienese *Lira* towards the end of the second decade.[50] One of the two houses owned by the Sienese Augustinians inside the walls of Sant'Angelo in Colle was also clearly a structure of some size as it was valued at 90 *lire*. In addition, and perhaps most significantly, there is evidence to show that Sant'Agostino owned a large amount of land to the south-west of Sant'Angelo in Colle, which may also have housed a conventual complex. This holding certainly contained a number of buildings, and its overall recorded value of 566 *lire* was unusually high. In this context it is relevant that in an early eighteenth-century compendium of papers concerned with the affairs of the Augustinian community in Siena we find a reference to a record of 1276 in which mention was made of the church of Santa Maria Interata 'near to the castle of Sant'Angelo in Colle'.[51] All these factors combined could have resulted in the establishment of an altar inside the parish church of San Michele Arcangelo with specific Augustinian iconography. One conclusion, therefore, must thus be that the figure of *Saint Leonard* is all that remains of an altar decoration commissioned in the name of local Augustinians, who had been established in the vicinity of Sant'Angelo in Colle for at least a couple of hundred years.

As we shall see, there may also have been a political dimension to such a presence inside the principal church of Sant'Angelo in Colle. Diana Norman's extensive researches in connection with the Augustinian church of San Leonardo al Lago, a few kilometres to the west of Siena, prompts her to speculate about the relationship between the central Sienese government and the Augustinian Hermits during the fourteenth century.[52] Norman also reminds us of the close association established between the Sienese hospital of Santa Maria della Scala and the Augustinian Hermits. She suggests that Santa Maria della Scala may have played a significant role, not only in commissioning the painting of the chancel at San Leonardo al Lago, but also in influencing the details of individual scenes there. As ever, there were political angles to the relationship between central government, its chief hospital institution and the religious community of the Augustinian Hermits. Norman argues that in establishing close links with the latter, the Sienese were better placed both to control and to administer their subject territories in the southern *contado*. She also suggests that the disposition of the order's principal rural hermitages closely reflected Siena's territorial expansion towards the Maremma.

In one sense, therefore, the Augustinian Hermits emerge as the chief guardians of subject communes in the southern *contado*. Given the patterns of influence outlined above, it seems likely that decorations produced for the religious spaces of the Augustinian Hermits in the southern Sienese *contado* would, moreover, have influenced the embellishment of nearby urban fabrics, especially where there was an established Augustinian connection. But in any event, given the links established between the Augustinian Hermits, Sant'Angelo in Colle, the hospital of Santa Maria della Scala and the hermitage church of San Leonardo al Lago, it is not unlikely that the latter site would have been singled out as a point of reference, had the artist responsible for painting the *Saint Leonard* fresco in Sant'Angelo in Colle been encouraged to take inspiration from recently executed decorations produced for the Augustinian order.

No records survive as to the identity of the artist involved in the production of the *Saint Leonard* fresco. However, it is generally agreed that the fresco was produced some time during the last quarter of the fourteenth century – in other words shortly after the completion of decorations in the chancel of San Leonardo al Lago, and at roughly the same time as the hospital of Santa Maria della Scala was consolidating its position in the new grange at Sant'Angelo in Colle. It is also generally agreed that the chancel area at San Leonardo was reserved for the religious observances of the Augustinian Hermits and no others. As such, any embellishments there would have held particular significance for Augustinians elsewhere. Thus, in considering the iconography and style of the *Saint Leonard* fresco at Sant'Angelo in Colle, particular attention is paid here to the frescoed images of the *Life of the Virgin* that were painted in the chancel area of San Leonardo al Lago some time between 1360 and 1370.[53]

However, it is also possible that the artist who painted the fresco at Sant'Angelo in Colle was encouraged to take note of an altarpiece at San Leonardo al Lago which, in the early seventeenth century, was described as containing the figure of the *Virgin and Child framed by Saints John the Baptist, Augustine, Leonard and Agostino Novello*.[54] This latter image is considered first. Although no traces of the San Leonardo al Lago altarpiece now remain, it seems likely that it was produced some time during the first half of the fourteenth century, since eighteenth-century records attribute it to Simone Martini or Lippo Memmi.[55] Reference was made in the seventeenth century to the altarpiece being displayed in a subterranean chapel below the church of San Leonardo. Norman suggests that this was the site of the original twelfth-century oratory and subterranean grotto-chapel. Any altarpiece displayed on that site must thus have been imbued with particular significance, for it was from this point that the subsequent community developed. For this reason, if for no other, the iconography of the altarpiece at San Leonardo al Lago may have been replicated or reflected in images produced on behalf of Augustinian hermits elsewhere. It is not impossible, therefore, that the fresco at Sant'Angelo in Colle was an attempt to replicate the image at San Leonardo al Lago.

It is significant that the fresco at Sant'Angelo in Colle appears originally to have depicted a fictive triptych or polyptych, and that one of the saints included in the composition also figured at San Leonardo al Lago. The positioning of the figure in the fresco at Sant'Angelo in Colle is also relevant. According to the seventeenth-century description of the altarpiece at San Leonardo al Lago, the two figures of Saint Augustine and Saint Leonard were positioned on either side of the Virgin and Child. In the fresco fragment remaining in the church of San Michele Arcangelo in Sant'Angelo in Colle, the figure of *Saint Leonard* appears to have assumed a similar position in close proximity to the central image. That the artist responsible for painting the fresco with Saint Leonard at Sant'Angelo in Colle was drawing inspiration from an older style of painting is in fact indicated in the rather old-fashioned depiction of the background curtain, looped up at regular intervals to individual points in the surrounding architecture. Such details were common in early fourteenth-century painting. Given the incomplete state of the *Saint Leonard* fresco now, and the absence of any earlier descriptions of it, one can only speculate on the identity of the other figure or figures included in the composition. However, if this fresco was commissioned by a local branch of the Augustinian order, and with the specific intention that it should embellish an altar in the parish church of Sant'Angelo in Colle associated with that, it must surely have included the figure of the order's founding saint, Augustine. Thus far, the links drawn between the two sites would seem valid.

As for the identity of the artist responsible for the fresco of *Saint Leonard*, the overall artistic style and composition indicates that an individual in the circle of Taddeo di Bartolo or Martino di Bartolomeo may have been involved. Some links can also be drawn with the frescoed figures of *Saint Catherine of Alexandria* and an *Unidentified female saint* in the church of Sant'Agostino in Montalcino, that have been attributed to Bartolo di Fredi and dated to the late 1380s.[56] In particular, there are similarities in the conjunctions between the head and neck of each of the three figures. There are also similarities in the way in which in each case a single line describes the outline of the nose and carries up into the arch of the eyebrow. Given the proposed dating of the *Saint Leonard* fresco, and what is known of Bartolo di Fredi's activities in nearby Montalcino during the same period, there would be good reasons for suggesting a link with that artist. However, Martino di Bartolomeo also seems to have established a link with Sant'Angelo in Colle, when painting the altarpiece that included the figures of *Saint Michael* and *Saint John the Baptist*, which in the early nineteenth century was recorded as in the church of San Michele at Sant'Angelo in Colle, and which is now displayed in the Museo

Civico e Diocesano at Montalcino. Given its iconography and the positioning of the two saints, there are good reasons for supposing that this altarpiece (which is thought to have been painted some time during the first decade of the fifteenth century) was commissioned to embellish a space dedicated to Saint Michael. Clearly, both the parish church and the village hospital at Sant'Angelo in Colle would have qualified. Moreover, if Martino di Bartolomeo (or an artist working in his circle) was responsible for producing an altarpiece for either of the two entities dedicated to Saint Michael at Sant'Angelo in Colle, he could very easily have been engaged to execute fresco work in the same area.

What then, of the supposed links between the Saint Leonard fresco and the images of the *Life of the Virgin* in the chancel area of San Leonardo al Lago? While there is uncertainty about the artist responsible for the altarpiece displayed in the subterranean chapel of San Leonardo al Lago, it is generally agreed that the chancel frescoes there were painted by Lippo Vanni. This individual (who belonged to the second generation of Sienese artists following in the wake of Duccio, Simone Martini and the Lorenzetti brothers) not only produced work for the *Palazzo Pubblico* and the churches of San Francesco and San Domenico in Siena, but, more significantly, is also documented as being engaged in 1345 to embellish a number of liturgical books, as well as an antiphonary and lectionary, for the hospital of Santa Maria della Scala.[57]

Given the several references to the hospital of Santa Maria della Scala in Ser Longo's will, and the testator's desire that the Sienese institution should finally become his universal heir, it would not have been unnatural for officials from Santa Maria della Scala to have been interested in Ser Longo's testamentary stipulation that a new missal should be produced for the church of San Michele at Sant'Angelo in Colle. Moreover, the three gold florins stipulated in Ser Longo's will must have allowed for the production of a fairly sumptuous missal.[58] That being the case, it would surely have been deemed appropriate to commission the services of an individual known to be experienced in the art of illumination, rather than to turn to the no-doubt less expensive skills of a local artist. (Although the artistic influence would in all likelihood have been much the same, if the missal were eventually produced by a local artist.) Presumably, the authority for selecting the artist for the new missal lay in the hands of the clergy of San Michele. However, had the parish priest (or even the rector, Ser Giovanni) turned to the hospital of Santa Maria della Scala for guidance, Lippo Vanni must surely have been brought to their attention. This artist thus emerges as a very likely source of artistic style and inspiration for the embellishment of San Michele in the wake of Ser Longo's will.

Given the fragmentary nature of the existing fresco of *Saint Leonard*, and in the absence of any surviving documentary evidence, it is now virtually impossible to establish the circumstances of its commission. However, it seems most likely that the figure of the saint was intended either to represent the commissioning body (as argued here, a local Augustinian community), or in some way to have been relevant to the building or space in which it was located. The position of the *Saint Leonard* fresco, at the far end of the southern wall of the church San Michele Arcangelo and close to the high altar, implies a link either with the high altar itself and its surrounding area, or with a space beyond the confines of the church, on its south-eastern side. Traditionally, the area outside the main body of the church, but in the vicinity of the high altar was reserved for use as a sacristy, and for the storing of religious furnishings and vestments. On occasion, however, such areas also accommodated private funerary chapels. The *Saint Leonard* fresco could thus have marked the transition of space between one such chapel and the main body of the church. However, no surviving records describing the internal furnishings of the parish church refer to a funerary chapel in the sacristy area. Moreover, the way in which the figure of Saint Leonard is represented in the fresco at Sant'Angelo in Colle encourages another interpretation.

Quite apart from his association with the Augustinian order, Saint Leonard was often included in decorations associated with prisons and enclosure.[59] While no surviving documents refer to the existence or location of a village prison at Sant'Angelo in Colle, it was often the custom that such a structure was established within the walls of an existing tower or castle. An obvious place for the prison at Sant'Angelo in Colle must thus have been inside the walls of the fortified 'Palazzaccio'. However, evidence presented here indicates that prior to the end of the thirteenth century that site was occupied by the old *Palazzo Comunale*, and that by the late fourteenth century, the Sienese 'casserone' or 'palazzo' on the site of the 'Palazzaccio' had been consigned to the hospital of Santa Maria della Scala for development as a fortified grange. At that date, therefore, any space within the old 'cassero' that had served as a prison must have been forfeited. The Palace of Justice seems, however, to have survived intact on a separate site, since – even though they do not appear to agree about its precise location – both Gherardini in the seventeenth century, and Pecci in the eighteenth century make reference to it. As already noted, Gherardini claimed that the original Palace of Justice had been located close to the church of San Michele on the site of the building that, in the seventeenth century, was being used by the Ciaia family. When describing the Palace of Justice in Montalcino, Gherardini had also noted that the building there contained living accommodation for officials, as well as a number of prisons.

The Palace of Justice at Sant'Angelo in Colle must presumably have contained some area in which to detain miscreants, even if only temporarily. It may even have housed a formal prison in which to accommodate wrong-doers on a more permanent basis. Given the degree of autonomy offered to the commune of Sant'Angelo in Colle as early as 1266, in terms of being able to elect their own *podestà* or mayor, it also seems likely that some form of public prison was established in the village by the second half of the thirteenth century, if not before. The Palace of Justice would have been an obvious public building to serve such a purpose. If the original *Palazzo di Giustizia* was indeed located in close proximity to the east end of the parish church of San Michele, as argued by Gherardini, it is moreover quite possible that there was a physical communication between the two structures in the form of a connecting passage-way. The *Saint Leonard* fresco could thus have marked the dividing line between the religious space of the church and the presence and judgement of God, and the lay space of the Palace of Justice and the secular authority of the judiciary. In this context it is significant that the traditional symbol of Saint Leonard, the handcuffs, are not only given unusual prominence in the *Saint Leonard* fresco by being centrally positioned, but are also unusually large. Such prominence would seem not only to remind the viewer of Saint Leonard's own martyrdom, but also to offer a warning. In effect, such a detail could have reflected the manacled state of those led to incarceration beyond the confines of the parish church, perhaps after having confessed their sins before the image of *Saint Leonard*. Such practice of public confession in front of a painted image just prior to, or immediately following judgement, was well established in the medieval and early renaissance periods.[60] At Sant'Angelo in Colle, the fact that the saint himself was vested in Augustinian robes may also have reflected the judicial authority assumed by the Augustinian Hermits there.

What, then, can be established about the circumstances governing the commissioning of the earlier fresco of the *Sacra Conversazione*? Consideration is given here to the possibility that this image was one of the first pieces of fresco decoration commissioned to embellish the new church of San Michele, following its reconstruction some time between the fourth and fifth decades of the fourteenth century. At the same time, an attempt is made to link the iconography of the fresco with stipulations laid down in Ser Longo di Ser Guccio's will of 1348. But first, a word about the chronology of the new church construction, and the implications this may have for the embellishment of the fabric.

Very often, where changes were made to an older structure or when a building was completely rebuilt (as was possibly the case with the church of San Michele at Sant'Angelo in Colle), reconstruction work commenced at the canonical east end, around the high altar. As is well known, it was thus commonly the case that a new high altarpiece was the first piece of decoration to be commissioned following major building work. Clearly, the commissioning of a new high altarpiece or any wall decoration to be positioned at the east end of the new church of San Michele must have post-dated the decision to renovate or completely reconstruct the old church. On the basis of archival material presented here, that project, although perhaps under discussion for a number of years, probably only began to take concrete form during the fourth decade of the fourteenth century. That being the case, the frescoed figure of the archangel Michael on the back wall of the church could only have been put in hand towards the end of the 1330s or even during the following decade, when most of the building work appears to have been finished. Fresco work positioned further away from the high altar must have been carried out later. On the basis of this, the fresco of the *Sacra Conversazione* could only have been painted around the middle of the century, if not slightly later.

Although much damaged and possibly distorted through restoration, the *Sacra Conversazione* does indeed indicate that the artist responsible for painting it was responding to artistic developments of the fourth decade of the fourteenth century.[61] There are similarities, for example, between the standing figures in the *Sacra Conversazione* and the saints positioned against flat backgrounds and within carefully decorated borders on the altar wall of the church of San Michele in Castiglione del Bosco (see Figure 8.1). The spindly nature of the architecture in the Castiglione del Bosco fresco is also reflected in the somewhat curiously upended structures that make up the Virgin's throne in the fresco at Sant'Angelo in Colle. But the broader treatment of drapery, combined with the slightly elongated proportions of the figures in the *Sacra Conversazione*, indicate that the artist who carried out the fresco in the church of San Michele Arcangelo was also aware of developments in the second generation of Sienese painters. On the basis of this, the *Sacra Conversazione* fresco could not have been carried out until the end of the 1340s.

The original iconography of the *Sacra Conversazione* is not immediately clear: partly because of its much restored state, but also partly because (as we shall see) at least one of the surviving figures has been significantly altered. Quite apart from the obvious *lacunae* and later reconstructions carried out by restorers, there is the fundamental problem that the composition is shorn of one of its principal figures. The degraded condition of the surviving fresco even before its restoration also hampers identification of the figure standing on the Virgin's right-hand side. In its present state, this third saint is not easily identifiable on the basis of either his facial characteristics or the details of his clothing. It seems unlikely, however, that he was intended (as claimed by some) to depict Saint Stephen. That deacon saint is normally depicted vested in a dalmatic and with two stones – the symbols of his martyrdom – positioned at either side of his head. The figure on the Virgin's right-hand side in the *Sacra Conversazione* fresco appears, by contrast, to be dressed in a toga draped over bare flesh. There is no sign either of stones on his head, or in the vicinity of his feet, although his left foot appears curiously deformed, indicating that some other details may have been lost, or misunderstood in later restoration work. A patch of what appears to be original green paint close to this figure's right foot may, however, help in reconstructing the original composition. Given its position, and shape, it is tempting to suggest that this small area of green is all that remains of the dress of a kneeling donor figure. However, while such a hypothesis is attractive, it seems more likely that the area of green paint in the vicinity of the unidentified saint's right foot is all that remains of a dragon's tail, and that the missing figure in the *Sacra Conversazione* fresco must thus have depicted the Archangel Michael.

Tentative confirmation that this was indeed the case emerges from a consideration of the identities of the other saints included in the *Sacra Conversazione*. Further support for such a hypothesis emerges from details in Ser Longo di Ser Guccio's will, as well as what has now been revealed about the patterns of piety established through the legacies of other testators in the early fourteenth-century village. Given what is now known about Giovanni di Paganello and the support he stipulated in respect of building work at San Michele, a case could, for example, be made for the *Sacra Conversazione* having been produced in response to Giovanni's testamentary legacies of 1335. This would explain the inclusion of the figure of Saint John the Baptist in a privileged position on the Virgin's left-hand side in the surviving fresco. While Giovanni di Paganello made no specific reference to the embellishment of the new church in his will, an altar dedicated to his patron saint could nevertheless have been erected in his name after his death, perhaps even in celebration of the safe birthing of his son – like him, named John. Yet, on the basis of the presumed chronology of building work on the new church, and the artistic style of the *Sacra Conversazione* itself, a date in the mid to late 1330s would seem too early, both for the commissioning and for the execution of that fresco. There is, in addition, no reference at any date in surviving documents to an altar dedicated to Saint John the Baptist inside the parish church of San Michele.

Given the presumed date of execution of the *Sacra Conversazione* some time during the fifth decade, a stronger case can be made for the inclusion of the figure of Saint John the Baptist at the request of Ser Giovanni, the rector of San Michele at the time of Ser Longo di Ser Guccio's 1348 will. By the same token, one could argue that Ser Longo di Ser Guccio himself was a likely candidate for involvement in the project. The fact that the rector of San Michele was called in to witness the contents of Ser Longo's will does indeed indicate a close relationship between the two. At the very least, Ser Giovanni must have assumed responsibility for the execution of key stipulations laid down by Ser Longo, such as where the deceased testator should be buried. Both these individuals are considered here in the context of the circumstances surrounding the commissioning and execution of the *Sacra Conversazione* fresco. First, Ser Giovanni: given his role as rector, it would have been natural for Ser Giovanni to be involved in plans for the furnishing and decoration of the new parish church. At the same time, he would most probably also have deemed it appropriate that his own patron saint should be included in any new embellishments, and that this figure should, moreover, be placed close to the figures of the Virgin and Child. Ser Giovanni must also have played a prominent role in the execution of any new decorations, assisting in such practical matters as ensuring the church itself was open for work, and that the ongoing work was protected during the artist's absence. But Ser Longo, the second candidate, emerges as the most likely overall patron for the project, not only on the basis of the date of his will, but also because of his personal interest in the parish church and the affairs of the parish. The implications of this are considered below.

If Ser Longo had been associated with the commissioning of the *Sacra Conversazione*, one would expect to find some reference to him or his patron saint within the composition. There are a number of details that suggest this was indeed the case. As it stands, the saint on the far right of the composition appears to depict the Augustinian saint Anthony Abbot. There seems little doubt, however, that this figure was originally intended to depict the Franciscan saint Anthony of Padua. Not only is the figure tonsured and his face that of a young man, but the habit in which he is clothed is clearly Franciscan. At a later date, a relatively clumsy attempt was clearly made to alter the position of this figure's hands, so that he should seem to hold a stick in his right hand, and trail a lead in the other (perhaps attached to a bell, or looped around Saint Anthony Abbot's traditional symbol, a wild boar, or pig). Depicted in this guise, the figure on the far right-hand side of the *Sacra Conversazione* is recognisable as the Augustinian hermit Saint Anthony Abbot, even though little attempt was apparently made to alter his Franciscan clothing, or change his face into that of an older man. The fact that a figure depicting Anthony of Padua was originally included in the image of the *Sacra Conversazione* adds support to the hypothesis presented here that the fresco was associated with Ser Longo di Ser Guccio, not least because of Ser Longo's obvious partiality towards the Franciscan order. But this is not all. Saint Anthony of Padua would also have been relevant in the context of Ser Longo's concern about social welfare in the early fourteenth-century village. Indeed, the numerous references in Ser Longo's will to the conditions of the poor in Sant'Angelo in Colle, must surely have favoured the inclusion of Saint Anthony of Padua in any decorations commissioned in his name.

How then, might the original iconography of the *Sacra Conversazione* have reflected its intended function and focus for religious observation? Saint Anthony of Padua's role both in feeding the hungry and in protecting the poor would clearly have rendered him a suitable figure to include in any image associated with the village's main charitable organisation, the village hospital. Thus, once more, we can trace a link between the iconography of the surviving fresco and the testamentary stipulations of Ser Longo di Ser Guccio's will. Quite apart from the clothing that Ser Longo stipulated should be distributed among the poor, very likely through the auspices of the hospital, the testator also asked that officials associated with the hospital should pray for his soul, and that payment for such prayers should be realised from the piece of land at Collemattone left to them by Ser Longo in his will.

The combined presence of Saint John the Baptist and Saint Anthony of Padua in the original fresco of the *Sacra Conversazione* could thus have reflected the involvement of the rector of the church and one of the village hospital's chief benefactors, Ser Longo di Ser Guccio. But what of the circumstances that might have stimulated such a commission?

According to his will, Ser Longo was prepared to set aside a further sum of money for the parish church of San Michele Arcangelo in the event of his wife giving birth to a live male heir. In giving birth to a son, Ser Longo's wife Tessa, or another member of the family, may thus have honoured Ser Longo's testamentary intentions by offering money to the church authorities which, in turn, might then have set about commissioning a new fresco. Such a course of events would most naturally have resulted in the inclusion of one or more donor figures within the completed image. Thus, the hypothesis initially raised here in the context of the surviving patch of green paint in the fresco of the *Sacra Conversazione*. But there are a number of reasons why this patch of paint should not be construed in terms of a donor figure. First and foremost is the fact that the positioning of the patch of paint so far away from the central figure militates against its representing a kneeling donor with arms raised in reverence towards the Virgin and Child. It is, moreover, positioned both too low in the composition and too far from the third saint to be seen as directly associated with that figure. The shape of the remaining patch of green is also incompatible with such a figure depicting a male donor. The conclusion would thus have to be that this is all that remains of a kneeling female. In itself, this does not present a problem, since there seems little doubt that Ser Longo was dead by 16 December 1348. Reference was made at that date to a piece of land at Fonterenza that was bordered on one side by land belonging to Ser Longo's 'heirs'.[62] Further reference was made to land owned by the 'heirs'of Ser Longo in the area known as Ferrale in the following year.[63] At least some members of Ser Longo's family had clearly survived him. However, it is the colour green that remains an obstacle to the hypothesis. Had Ser Longo (as we now know) died shortly after drawing up his will, and Tessa survived him, she must surely also have been depicted as a widow dressed in black weeds in any decorations carried out in her name or in that of her defunct husband. Thus, even if the small remaining patch of green paint had originally formed part of a kneeling donor figure, it is unlikely that it can be associated with Ser Longo's widow. The same argument applies if the kneeling figure was intended to depict Ser Longo's mother Gemma, unless she, in the meantime, had remarried (a possibility already canvassed at the beginning of this chapter). Gemma was certainly destined to assume significant responsibilities in the event of outliving both her son, her daughter-in-law, and any progeny from their marriage. It is also possible that one or other of Ser Longo's two sisters survived both him and his wife, and that it was one of them who was responsible for commissioning the *Sacra Conversazione* in Ser Longo's name. No mention is made of the marital state of either of these individuals in Ser Longo's will, which suggests that they were still spinsters in 1348. There was thus no question that either of them should be depicted in widow's weeds, if, following Ser Longo's death, one or other of them became involved in a project to commission new decorations for the parish church.

Setting aside the various hypotheses concerning the inclusion of a donor figure in the fresco of the *Sacra Conversazione*, a question still remains about the identity of the saints positioned on the Virgin's right-hand side. As we shall see, establishing the identity of these two figures assists interpretation of the remaining patch of green paint. Logically, the saint closest to the Virgin and Child must have had some special significance for the original patron. Ser Longo's preferred saint would surely have been Longinus, if only because of the link between his own name Longo (deriving from the Greek for spear) and the lance of the Roman centurion.[64] It was, however, rare for this saint to be depicted as a single figure, whether on panel or in fresco. Longinus was most commonly included amongst the crowd in scenes of the Crucifixion. Had the fourteenth-century artist responsible for painting the *Sacra Conversazione* been asked to include Longinus in the composition, he may thus have been uncertain how to proceed. In this context, it may be relevant that the unidentified saint in the *Sacra Conversazione* appears to be dressed in a toga. Although Saint Longinus was traditionally depicted in military attire, at least one image from the seventeenth century shows his nude body enveloped in a flowing toga. Representing Saint Longinus in the guise of a Roman clad in a toga would clearly have distinguished him from any other soldier saint, such as the Archangel Michael. If the third figure was indeed intended to depict Saint Longinus, there may also have been a more general intention to make reference to the suffering of Christ through the wound pierced in his side. This would have been particularly relevant if, for example, the *Sacra Conversazione* had been commissioned in association with the village hospital at Sant'Angelo in Colle.

What case can then be made, that the *Sacra Conversazione* was not only commissioned on behalf of Ser Longo di Ser Guccio, but that it was intended to serve religious observations in the name of the village hospital? Given what has been argued earlier in the context of the location of the original hospital complex, the position of the hospital cemetery, and the adjacent site of the parish church, it would have been logical for any decoration carried out in the name of the village hospital in the church of San Michele Arcangelo to be positioned at the interface between the church and the hospital. The location of the *Sacra Conversazione* on the south wall of San Michele would seem to satisfy just such a brief. This was the most obvious place, also, to position an interconnecting door. Indeed, the door between the church and the cemetery that subsequently caused such damage to the *Sacra Conversazione* may have replaced a much smaller aperture that offered access not only to the adjacent burial ground, but also to the original hospital complex. Ser Longo's involvement in the affairs of both the hospital and the parish church could thus have been acknowledged through the inclusion of Saint Anthony of Padua and Ser Longo's own patron saint in an image that bridged the two worlds of the church and the hospital.

The identity of the fourth and missing saint in the *Sacra Conversazione* would then be the only remaining missing part of the puzzle. The hypothesis is raised here that this figure depicted the titular saint of both the hospital and the parish church, the Archangel Michael, and that it is the remains of a dragon's tail that we now see in the patch of green paint. Given the location of the fresco inside the church of San Michele, it would obviously have been appropriate for the titular saint to be included somewhere in the composition. This was certainly the case in the fresco decorations carried out in the high altar area of the church of San Michele Arcangelo at Castiglione del Bosco, where the Archangel Michael is included in a central position close to the Virgin Annunciate. Significantly, in that composition, both the curving neck and twisted tail of Saint Michael's dragon are positioned in such a way that they abut, and indeed in the case of the tail invade adjacent spaces. Given the proposed reconstruction so far, the only position the Archangel Michael could logically have occupied in the *Sacra Conversazione* in the church of San Michele at Sant'Angelo in Colle would have been on the Virgin's far right-hand side, adjacent to the figure tentatively identified here as Saint Longinus. If that was the case, the remaining patch of green paint, while perhaps distorted in shape during later restoration work, could quite credibly be all that remains of a dragon's tail. Thus reconstructed, the *Sacra Conversazione* would have included references not only to the original patron (in the figure of the saint standing on the Virgin's right-hand side and the figure of Saint Anthony of Padua on the far right-hand side of the composition), and to at least one other individual involved in the execution of the work (in the figure of Saint John the Baptist), as well as to the titular saint of both the space in which the fresco was located, and the institution in whose direction it beckoned the viewer, the village hospital beyond the south wall of San Michele.

To conclude. Changes to the original iconography of the fresco of the *Sacra Conversazione* clearly hamper reconstruction of the circumstances under which it was commissioned. A number of points can nevertheless be made. In its present state, damaged and repainted, there seems little doubt that the *Sacra Conversazione* no longer faithfully reflects its original iconography. It seems clear that over time the fresco has assumed at least two different guises: one in which a Franciscan saint played a significant role, and another in which precedence was given to a saint more commonly associated with the Augustinian order. While questions could be raised as to whether or not recent restoration work has faithfully followed earlier intentions, there seems little doubt that a deliberate attempt was made at some point to shift the emphasis from the unidentified saint on the Virgin's right-hand side to the two saints on her left. The hypothesis is raised here that this shift in emphasis followed the emergence of the new village hospital dedicated to Saint Anthony Abbot. More precisely, consideration is given to the possibility that the *Sacra Conversazione* fresco, although first serving religious observations in the name of the village hospital with the *titulus* San Michele, was subsequently re-fashioned to serve the new hospital complex under the titulus of Sant'Antonio Abate.

The date at which the *titulus* of the village hospital of Sant'Angelo in Colle changed is not known. It is clear, however, that when the Brogioni family assumed responsibility for the complex in the late sixteenth century it was already dedicated to Saint Anthony Abbot. There seems little doubt either that a hospital altar already existed inside San Michele a year before the Brogioni assumed responsibility for the hospital of Saint Anthony Abbot, since reference was made to such a structure in Francesco Piccolomini's 1573 pastoral visit. However, although Francesco Piccolomini recorded that the hospital's altar was close to the entrance of the parish church on the northern wall, he made no reference to any embellishment of the altar table. This may be explained in a number of ways.

By the last quarter of the sixteenth century, the urban fabric of Sant'Angelo in Colle must have been in a parlous state following Siena's defeat by the Florentines. Indeed, there seems little doubt that the preceding decades marked something of a nadir in the village's fortunes. First abandoned by the villagers themselves, and then attacked and pillaged by hostile forces advancing towards Montalcino, both the buildings and their interiors must have been in a sad state. Only with the emergence of new patrons such as the Brogioni was there any hope of renovation and renewal. The Brogioni, who had already been put in charge of the parish church at the beginning of the sixteenth century may, however, have been hard pressed to make ends meet by the time they assumed responsibility for the village hospital. This may have resulted in their appropriating and reworking pre-existing decorations, rather than incurring the expense of commissioning new works. It is possible, for example, that a decision was taken to rework the *Sacra Conversazione* fresco, in order to provide a new focus for religious observation on behalf of the renamed hospital of Saint Anthony Abbot. If, in addition, the hospital of Saint Anthony Abbot had arisen on the site of the old hospital of San Michele, it might have seemed logical to make changes to the existing iconography of a fresco that in effect constituted an entrance to that complex.

Transforming the figure of Saint Anthony of Padua into that of Saint Anthony Abbot must have seemed an obvious course of action. But other changes may have seemed equally appropriate. Ideally, if the fresco were to represent the threshold of the renamed hospital the Christ Child should bestow his blessing on Saint Anthony Abbot. In its pre-existing state, the Christ Child appears to have concentrated his attention on the two figures positioned on the Virgin's right-hand side (one of which was no doubt intended to represent the original patron, and the other of which may have represented the hospital's titular saint). In terms of the new hospital, such an emphasis would have needed to be changed. Surviving paintwork around the figure of the Christ Child does indeed indicate that a number of alterations were made to this part of the fresco. The Virgin appears originally to have held her child close to her, balancing his buttocks on her left thigh. In such a position the child would naturally have directed his gaze towards the saints on the Virgin's right-hand side. In the fresco's existing state, the child's body is depicted lifted up and turning away from his mother. The viewer's gaze follows. The fact that the pose of the Christ Child appears to have been changed so that he turns away from the two saints on the Virgin's right-hand side, gesturing instead towards the figures on the Virgin's left, is significant. Such a change of direction would clearly have satisfied the new iconographical demands arising from the change of *titulus* of the village hospital.

So much for the surviving works of art in fresco inside the parish church that date to the fourteenth century. What then of the surviving portable works of art from the same period, that are likewise associated with Sant'Angelo in Colle? Establishing the circumstances under which these images were produced, including the locations in which they were first displayed is extremely difficult. Despite Sant'Angelo in Colle's comparatively small size it seems that several of the painted panels associated with the village were, over time, positioned on several different sites. One painting of the *Madonna and Child* was apparently displayed in three separate churches in the space of less than 200 years. There is also evidence, that individual altarpieces were at different times assembled out of a number of disparate parts. In attempting to reconstruct the histories of these images, we are thus missing both the specificity of space and the homogeneity of the original artefact.

Only one portable work of art associated with Sant'Angelo in Colle and datable to the fourteenth century now remains in the village. This is the half-length image of the *Madonna and Child* known locally as the *'Madonna della Misericordia'*[65] (see Colour Plate 6). This painting, which has been variously attributed to Duccio, Lippo Memmi and the Lorenzetti workshop, has more recently been designated as the work of the 'Maestro di Sant'Angelo in Colle' or the 'Maestro di 1346'.[66] The prevailing opinion is that the panel was painted by a local artist, rather than by one of the more famous individuals operating from Siena, thus the prevailing attribution to the Master of 1346. This individual is credited with painting frescoes in the cloister of San Francesco in Montalcino, as well as the triptych of the *Madonna and Child flanked by Saint Augustine and Saint John the Baptist* now displayed in the Museo Civico e Diocesano in Montalcino, which comes from the Augustinian church of Santi Filippo e Giacomo.[67] Also displayed in the same museum and attributed to the same artist is a panel of the *Madonna and Child*, which at one time was displayed in the church of the Natività di Maria a Salti in San Giovanni d'Asso.[68] If all of these works were indeed painted by the same individual, the 'Maestro di 1346' must have been active over a wide area, not only producing work for Montalcino and Sant'Angelo in Colle, but also receiving commissions from a number of other nearby towns and villages. The fact that this artist is also presumed to have been active around the time that Giovanni di Paganello and Ser Longo di Ser Tuccio were intent on patronising local religious and charitable institutions at Sant'Angelo in Colle, encourages further speculation as to his role in the embellishment of the urban fabric there.

The *'Madonna della Misericordia'* has had a chequered history. It is now displayed above the altar in the twentieth-century church of the Madonna del Rosario in Sant'Angelo in Colle. Prior to this, it was displayed on at least two other sites in the village. In the eighteenth century it was recorded in a church outside the walls. A hundred years later it was described as being displayed on a number of occasions inside the parish church of San Michele Arcangelo.[69] This is a painting that has not only been moved from place to place, but has also been damaged, almost to the point of destruction. Indeed, it seems that there is comparatively little left of the original paint surface. Any attempt to place the *'Madonna della Misericordia'* in the ambit of one of the several important Sienese workshops of the early fourteenth century on the basis of its paintwork alone is thus hazardous. From the point of view of its composition, there seems little doubt, however, that the artist responsible for this work was familiar with products from the workshops of the Lorenzetti brothers. The pose of the child, in particular, is close to that in Ambrogio Lorenzetti's painting of the *Maestà* in Massa Marittima. But that the Sant'Angelo in Colle *Madonna and Child* was painted by Ambrogio Lorenzetti himself seems unlikely, if only because the overall pose of the two figures seems somewhat stilted – as if painting to a formula, rather than as a result of inspired artistry.

While there is documentary evidence for the association of the *'Madonna della Misericordia'* with Sant'Angelo in Colle during the last 300 years, there are a number of conflicting views about its original provenance. One body of opinion argues that the panel was not originally commissioned for Sant'Angelo in Colle at all, but was brought to the village some time during the eighteenth century.[70] There is some support for this view in the fact that a reference was made in 1760 to a new altarpiece that had apparently only just been set in place in the church of San Pietro outside the walls of the village.[71] This, it seems, was the painting of the *Madonna and Child* now displayed in the church of the Madonna del Rosario. One hypothesis raised in the context of the eighteenth-century reference to the painting is thus that the panel was brought to Sant'Angelo in Colle when Francesco Maria Tozzi assumed the role of parish priest of San Michele in 1754.[72] However, it has also been suggested that the panel of the *Madonna and Child* was from the beginning intended for a church space at Sant'Angelo in Colle, and in particular for the church with the *titulus* of San Pietro that was recorded as outside the walls of Sant'Angelo in Colle in the early thirteenth century.[73] Accordingly, it has been argued that the panel of the *Madonna and Child* was assigned to the cathedral of Montalcino when that diocese assumed responsibility for a church at Sant'Angelo in Colle with the *titulus* of San Pietro in the middle of the fifteenth century.[74]

The view that the painting of the *Madonna and Child* was newly arrived in Sant'Angelo in Colle in the middle of the eighteenth century was at first championed by Don Antonio Brandi. In doing so, Don Brandi relied in part on the fact that details in a pastoral visit of 1765 revealed that the church on the south side of the village was at that date known as the church of the Misericordia, because of the painting of the *Madonna and Child* that had 'for some years' been displayed on its high altar.[75] Of the church dedicated to Saint Peter to the north of the village, and the church of the same *titulus* inside the walls, Don Brandi made no mention. His initial conclusion was thus that the painting must have come from outside the village. Subsequently, Don Brandi was reluctant to make further enquiries into the earlier history of the *'Madonna della Misericordia'*, maintaining that it was useless to proceed along a path where no answers could be given to the hypotheses raised.[76] Renewed consideration of the available documentary evidence does, however, provide a number of possible solutions to previously unanswered questions. In particular, it provides a framework whereby the *'Madonna della Misericordia'* – rather than being produced for a completely different location, or being transported away from the village some time during the fifteenth century and only returning there two centuries later – could in fact have been originally produced for one of the churches at Sant'Angelo in Colle and have remained in the village throughout.

But first, a word about the panel's more recent history. There seems little doubt that by 1765 this painting of the *Madonna and Child* was positioned on the high altar of the church now known as San Pietro on the southern side of the village. Despite the reference in the 1765 pastoral visit to the 'Chiesa della Madonna della Misericordia', it seems that from the late eighteenth century onwards this church was more often than not referred to locally as the 'Chiesa della Compagnia', because of its use by the 'Compagnia della Madonna della Misericordia' (after the foundation of that company in 1793).[77] According to the 1765 record the *Madonna and Child* panel was already known locally as the 'Madonna della Misericordia'.[78] It seems clear, therefore, that the reference to the 'Chiesa della Madonna della Misericordia' derived not from the established *titulus* of the small church on the southern side of the village, but from the fact that the painted image had recently been set up on the altar there. This, combined with the subsequent title 'Chiesa della Compagnia' which likewise depended on local events, would seem to add support to the hypothesis raised here that the church to the south of the village is the same as that recorded without *titulus* amongst property belonging to the church of San Pietro inside the walls in 1320.

In 1849 the decision was taken to restore both the fabric of the church on the south side of the village and the painting on its high altar. It seems likely that the *'Madonna della Misericordia'* was removed from the church before restoration work of the structure began. The first stage of restoration of the church was completed by January 1850, but two years later, no conservation work had apparently been carried out on the panel of the *Madonna and Child*, since reference was made at that date to yet another attempt to repair the painting. Clearly, such action was long overdue. In 1852 the *'Madonna della Misericordia'* was described as in a state of complete degradation ('in stato di assoluto deperimento'). It was shortly afterwards repaired by the Sienese restorer, Domenico Monti.[79] According to some sources, the painting was moved out of the Chiesa della Madonna della Misericordia in 1877 and subsequently displayed in the parish church of San Michele, where it remained for several years.[80] According to other sources, the painting of the *'Madonna della Misericordia'* was already displayed in San Michele before 1869.[81] It is in fact possible that the painting never returned to the church outside the walls after the decision to restore that fabric in 1849. In any event, some time during the first decade of the twentieth century, the painting was moved once again and set up above the altar in the purpose-built church of the Madonna del Rosario.[82] Some sources maintain that the *'Madonna della Misericordia'* was once more displayed in San Michele in 1933, but this must only have been a temporary arrangement, since the painting was clearly associated with the church of the Madonna del Rosario throughout the second half of the twentieth century, and is still displayed there now.[83]

What case can then be made for the image of the *Madonna and Child* or so-called *'Madonna della Misericordia'* being originally produced to embellish a religious structure in Sant'Angelo in Colle some time around the middle of the fourteenth century? A number of points can be made. When Giovanni Antonio Pecci drew up his record of Sant'Angelo in Colle in the eighteenth century, he noted (like Gherardini in the previous century) that only one church structure (that of the *pieve*, or San Michele) was still standing inside the walls. Pecci noted, however, that the village had once contained 'un antica chiesa di San Piero', an old church of San Pietro, which was still sometimes referred to as 'San Pietro vecchio'.[84] It was this church, according to Pecci, that was placed under the authority of the cathedral in Montalcino during the fifteenth century. (Pecci also referred to the church of San Pietro outside the walls that was under the authority of the parish church, without, however, indicating its precise location.)[85] Pecci's reference to the old church of San Pietro inside the village, combined with information contained in the 1320 *Tavola delle possessioni*, and other documentary evidence considered here would thus seem to provide irrefutable evidence that there were indeed two churches inside the walls of Sant'Angelo in Colle in the early fourteenth century. The panel now known as the *'Madonna della Misericordia'* could have been produced to embellish either of these two structures.

The most likely site is the parish church of San Michele, although as we shall see, the *'Madonna della Misericordia'* was at one time assembled together with two other painted panels that may originally have been produced for San Pietro Vecchio. There is in fact some support for the theory that the *'Madonna della Misericordia'* was associated with San Michele in the record drawn up by Ippolito Borghesi during his pastoral visit to the village in 1618. According to this, the embellishment of the high altar table in San Michele consisted of an 'icona assai antica' (or rather old icon).[86] At the same time Bishop Borghesi noted that the altar table itself was in no fit state for the celebration of mass, and ordered that such practice should be discontinued forthwith.[87] Previous readings of this record have resulted in the assumption that the high altar area of San Michele was embellished with only one image, a fresco of Saint Michael. The wording of Borghesi's report has even persuaded some to conclude that the figure of Saint Michael noted on the back wall of the church was one and the same as the image on the high altar itself.[88] The wording of the 1618 record would seem to imply, however, that there were two separate images in the area of the high altar: one, a painting of Saint Michael on the wall (without doubt a fresco) and another, an icon, (without doubt a wooden panel) on the altar table itself:[89]

The use of the term *icona* in the 1618 record indicates that the altarpiece on the high altar table of San Michele was not only old, but was also painted on a gold ground. In all likelihood the term icon was also adopted because the iconography of the high altarpiece appeared to follow Byzantine prototypes, where the Virgin held her child in a close embrace, whilst engaging the viewer with her eyes. The *'Madonna della Misericordia'* would seem to fit both such criteria. If in addition the *'Madonna della Misericordia'* formed part of an altarpiece originally commissioned to embellish the new church of San Michele, the overall format would no doubt have been typical of a number of fourteenth-century polyptychs that were produced in the shops of Duccio, Ugolino-Lorenzetti, Francesco di Segna and other individuals associated with the first generation of Sienese artists. These for the most part depicted a three-quarter length Virgin and Child in the company of saints – ranging in number from at least four to six. In this context it is significant that in a record dating to the last third of the sixteenth century, there is a detailed description of the high altar furnishings of San Michele which includes a reference to 'due altri quadri antichi a piramide dorati' (two other old paintings with pyramidal gables and gold grounds).[90] According to this inventory, which was witnessed by the parish priest Asciano Borghesi, each of the two panels contained the images of three saints. It is possible, therefore, that the panel of the *'Madonna della Misericordia'* is all that remains of a polyptych consisting of the Virgin and Child in the company of six saints, and that this polyptych was the 'icona assai antica' noted by Ippolito Borghese as on the high altar of San Michele in 1618. If this were the case, it also seems likely (given the *titulus* of the parish church), that one of the six figures included in that altarpiece represented Saint Michael. However, in the absence of further documentary evidence, all that can safely be said about the embellishment of the high altar table of San Michele in the early seventeenth century is that the table itself was in a bad state, and its decoration included an old gold ground painting. There is, nevertheless, sufficient evidence to suggest that several years prior to that, the high altar was embellished with at least two gold back panels each of which contained the figures of three saints. The likelihood is that there was also a central panel depicting the Virgin and Child.

The fact that the fabric of San Michele Arcangelo was in poor condition in the early seventeenth century may, however, be significant when attempting to reconstruct the earlier history of the embellishment of the church's high altar. A number of changes were certainly made around this time. Indeed, it has been suggested that the degraded state of the church noted by Ippolito Borghesi in 1618 was the prime reason for the replacement of the pre-existing altar table by an ornate structure in the Baroque style.[91] It is possible that the whole of the east end of the church was refreshed shortly after the pastoral visit of 1618. At that date, even if not before, any decorations that were regarded as old-fashioned, or in too deteriorated a state were no doubt removed. This could have resulted in the original high altarpiece, or at least its central part, being taken off the altar table and set up elsewhere, there being no other space deemed appropriate for it. One obvious place to display an image of the Virgin and Child hitherto positioned on the high altar of the parish church would have been the church of San Pietro outside the walls that had been under the jurisdiction of the church of San Michele since at least the thirteenth century.

Thus, one possible course of events is that the *'Madonna della Misericordia'* was originally produced as the central panel of a polyptych commissioned for the high altar of the newly refurbished parish church of San Michele some time during the fifth decade of the fourteenth century; that it remained on that site until the seventeenth century; that it was removed from the high altar of San Michele some time after 1618; that it was subsequently sheered of its lateral panels and removed to the church of San Pietro to the north of the village; and that some time before 1765 it was repositioned inside the small church now known as San Pietro on the south side of the village. Such a course of events might explain why eighteenth-century records refer to the *'Madonna della Misericordia'* as being 'recently set up in the church of San Pietro', apparently investing that fact with significance. In any event, such a complex course of events would by no means have been unusual, it often being the case that older works of art were dismantled, refashioned, and even reassembled with other unrelated parts, following removal from their original or previous sites.[92]

Further consideration is given in this context to the format and content of the two painted panels of saints attributed to Martino di Bartolomeo which are thought originally to have formed part of a triptych, and which – like the *'Madonna della Misericordia'* – are recorded as displayed inside the parish church of San Michele in the nineteenth century[93] (see Colour Plate 7). Reconstructing the format of this altarpiece is compromised by the fact that the central panel was at some time in the comparatively recent past removed, and now appears to be lost. There seems no doubt, however, that the central image depicted a Madonna and Child, since the nineteenth-century record describes the altarpiece as a triptych consisting of the saints John the Baptist and the Archangel Michael flanking the Virgin. It also seems clear from the positioning of the two small figures of the *Angel Gabriel* and the *Virgin Annunciate* facing each other in the gables of the two panels of the saints that this was their original position, flanking the central image of the Virgin. (It would clearly have been inappropriate for the gazes and gestures of Gabriel and Mary to be interrupted or diverted through the inclusion of further figures in intervening gables.) There is little doubt, therefore, that Saint Michael was placed in the privileged position on the Virgin's right-hand side. This indicates that the altarpiece was not only originally painted for an institution dedicated to Saint Michael, but also that it was set up in a prime position within that institution's space. An obvious site would have been the high altar table of San Michele. Indeed, such an altarpiece might well have been described by Ippolito Borghesi in the early seventeenth century as an 'icona assai antica'. Moreover, the fact that the altarpiece included the image of the titular saint might also explain the somewhat confusing wording of the 1618 pastoral record. However, as we shall see, there are a number of reasons why this was probably not the case.

An alternative hypothesis raised here is that the altarpiece including the figures of the *Archangel Michael* and *Saint John the Baptist* was originally intended for display inside the hospital of San Michele, before that institution changed its title some time between the fifteenth and sixteenth century. Although the positioning of the two paintings clearly indicates that they were destined to embellish an altar or structure dedicated to the Archangel Michael, neither of the two panels is compatible with the late sixteenth-century reference in the context of the embellishment of the high altar of San Michele to 'two panels of pyramidal shape, each containing three figures of saints'. Moreover, since none of the surviving records for San Michele make reference to any other area dedicated to Saint Michael apart from the obvious site of the high altar itself, the implication must be that the two panels attributed to Martino di Bartolomeo were originally produced for a different altar in a different space. There are in addition a number of other factors that would appear to favour an original position in the hospital of San Michele as opposed to inside the parish church.

In its original form, the altarpiece must have seemed unusually tall, at least in its lateral parts. This could have been deliberate, if the surrounding space was restricted. The two side panels together measure 97 centimetres in width. Combined with a central panel, the resulting width of the altarpiece must have been in the region of 150 or so centimetres. When enclosed within a frame, it would have been at least 15 or so centimetres wider. As we shall see, such an altarpiece could not have fitted comfortably on either of the two altar tables that survive inside the church of San Michele Arcangelo. One of these, that presently serving as the high altar, which was found inside the seventeenth century baroque structure when that was dismantled in the twentieth century, is just 165 centimetres wide.[94] This altar table was presumably the one that was positioned in the parish church following reconstruction work during the fourteenth century. Even at a conservative estimate, the three panels combined would barely have fitted. With hardly a centimetre clear on either side, such an embellishment would have appeared cramped and ill at ease with the surrounding space. A second and much narrower altar measuring 115 centimetres in width, which is thought to have served as the original high altar in the earlier church of San Michele, could not even have housed the two panels of the saints.[95] Displayed within a smaller space and on a somewhat wider altar table, such an altarpiece would have affected a much more commanding presence. A hospital chapel, or even a hospital ward, could have provided just such a space.[96] One final point: there is some evidence to suggest that Martino di Bartolomeo's altarpiece may originally have consisted of more than three panels, since the outer edges of both surviving panels contain gouged holes that may originally have served to attach further elements of the same altarpiece. Rather than being designed as a triptych, it may thus originally have been a polyptych. As such, it would certainly not have fitted on even the larger of the two surviving altar tables in San Michele.

As with the 'Madonna della Misericordia', in the absence of further documentation no firm conclusion can be reached about the original position of the Martino di Bartolomeo altarpiece. It may be significant, however, that the three panels associated with this artist remained together over the course of four centuries. When recorded inside the parish church in the nineteenth century, no reference was made to the 'tripytch' being cut down, nor was there any suggestion that it had been assembled from other surviving fragments. It seems likely, therefore, that it had either remained in its original location, or that it had been recently transferred to San Michele from a nearby and associated site. If originally produced for a space inside the hospital of San Michele, such an altarpiece could have remained *in situ* until that institution changed its *titulus*, or was constructed on a different site. In either case, it would have seemed logical to transfer the altarpiece into the main body of the church following the change in *titulus* of the hospital. At that point, and there being no other altar table on which to display the altarpiece inside San Michele, it could have been placed in storage, one possible area being the sacristy. It could then have remained in the parish church untouched, unnoticed and unrecorded until the nineteenth century.

The '*Madonna della Misericordia*', by contrast, is known to have been displayed on a number of different sites. Moreover, no conclusions can be drawn about its original location from its iconography. It may be no coincidence, however, that the painting was recorded in the nineteenth century as flanked by two panels depicting the figures of Saint Peter and Saint Paul.[97] Displayed in such company, one could argue that the '*Madonna della Misericordia*' was at one time displayed in a church with the *titulus* of San Pietro or San Paolo. However, the fact that these three paintings were assembled in triptych form in the nineteenth century does not, in itself, prove (as many have claimed) that the '*Madonna della Misericordia*' was originally intended to be displayed alongside the figures of Saint Peter and Saint Paul. Nor does it constitute firm evidence that the '*Madonna della Misericordia*' originally formed the central part of a triptych. Indeed, as already argued, the artistic style and assumed date of the panel would indicate rather that it originally formed part of a polyptych. That said, the association of these three panels in the nineteenth century prompts further hypotheses.

The extant panels of *Saint Peter and Saint Paul,* like the panel of the '*Madonna della Misericordia*', have had a chequered history[98] (see Colour Plate 8). Nothing is known of their location prior to the nineteenth century and the year 1869, when it seems that they were removed from the parish church of San Michele and placed in the collection of the Pinacoteca in Siena.[99] At a later date they were moved once again, this time to what was then known as the Diocesan Museum in Montalcino. They are currently displayed in the renamed Museo Civico e Diocesano d'Arte Sacra in Montalcino. That the interior of the church of San Michele was where these two panels were originally positioned is open to question. Given their iconography, it seems more likely that they were associated with the embellishment of a church with the *titulus* of San Pietro or San Paolo. Attention focuses here on the possibility that the two panels originally formed part of an altarpiece that first adorned one of the two churches with the *titulus* of San Pietro that are known to have existed in and around Sant'Angelo in Colle during the medieval period. Consideration is given first to the church of San Pietro outside the walls on the northern side of the village.[100]

There seems little doubt that the church of San Pietro outside the walls was an ancient foundation, since we know that it was placed under the authority of the parish church of San Michele as early as 1216. It also seems clear that the clergy of San Michele were not only responsible for religious observation in San Pietro, but also for the care of the church structure and its internal furnishings. Reference to the furnishings of the altar of San Pietro in an inventory drawn up for the church of San Michele in 1492 indicates that the parish clergy continued as guardians of the church outside the walls for several hundred years. Indeed, there is evidence to show that they were still responsible for an altar dedicated to Saint Peter as late as the seventeenth century, since an inventory drawn up for San Michele in 1672 refers not only to the 'altar of San Pietro', but also to four other altars, apart from the high altar itself.[101] It also seems clear that furnishings used during religious observation in San Pietro were kept in the mother church, since in an inventory of the parish church drawn up in May 1674, reference was made to three 'davanzali', or altar coverings, for 'the altar of Saint Peter'.[102] In 1676, the pastoral visitor Gherardini for his part noted that the church of San Pietro outside the walls was not only still under the jurisdiction of the parish church, but was also still being officiated by the parish priest and his chaplain.[103] Gherardini also made reference to the Chiesa and Compagnia della Concezione. Of the small church of undefined *titulus* to the south of the village, and of a chapel on the north side of the village known as the 'Cappella della Madonna delle Nevi', and referred to on occasion as the chapel of the 'Madonna delle Grazie',[104] that had been recorded in a pastoral visit a century earlier, Gherardini made no mention.

Although references to the 'altare di San Pietro' in seventeenth-century records might appear to imply that the altar was inside the parish church, it seems clear that by the eighteenth century there were only four altars in San Michele (apart from the high altar itself), and none of these are recorded as carrying the titulus of San Pietro. In 1751 two of the four lateral altars were identified as the altar of the Rosary and the altar of the Crucifixion; the other two (on the north wall) were recorded as being under the authority of the Order of Saint Stephen.[105] One of the altars (that immediately to the left on entering San Michele) was said to have previously been dedicated to Saint Anthony Abbot.[106] Of Saint Peter, there was no mention.

In fact, information included in an inventory of San Michele drawn up in 1672 and in a pastoral visit to the village in 1680 appears to confirm that the 'altare di San Pietro' was positioned inside the ancient church of San Pietro outside the walls. According to the 1672 record, the clergy of San Michele were responsible for celebrating the feast of the titular saint Peter (but none other) in the church of that titulus.[107] According to the 1680 pastoral visit, the only church with the titulus of San Pietro existing at Sant'Angelo in Colle at that date was located in the vicinity of 'podere Casella'. It seems clear, therefore, that references to both the altar of Saint Peter and the celebration of the feast of the titular saint concerned the church under the authority of San Michele, which was outside the walls.

By the end of the seventeenth century, the clergy of San Michele had thus been officiating in the church on the northern side of the village for over 400 years. However, surviving documents indicate that there was an abrupt change of affairs during the following century. Indeed, it seems that by the mid-eighteenth century the church of San Pietro outside the walls was in a state of acute degradation. That it was already much deteriorated at least a century or so earlier, is indicated in a loose leaf inserted after the 1492 inventory of furnishings inside San Michele. According to that record, which probably dates to around the middle of the sixteenth century, the church was already in danger of collapse.[108] The parlous state of the church of San Pietro may, in the end, have inhibited any form of religious observation there. In this context, it is significant that in an inventory taken of San Michele in 1751, there was for the first time no reference to the altar of Saint Peter. It is possible, therefore, that the parish church had relinquished, or was in the process of relinquishing its responsibility for the church of San Pietro during the middle of the eighteenth century. In this context, it is significant that in a note written in 1743 by the parish priest of San Michele, Asciano Borghese, reference was made to proposed restoration work at the church of San Pietro.[109] Indeed, according to this note, Asciano Borghese had been given permission by Bishop Borgognini to demolish the church of San Pietro, and to use the site on which it stood for the construction of a new cemetery. Specific reference was made to the demolition of a small room next to the house known as 'la Casella'. There seems little doubt, therefore, that the church in question was that on the northern side of the village, and that discussions were already under way for the demolition of the church complex in the vicinity of Podere La Casella. As ever, there are a number of conflicting pieces of evidence. According to Giovanni Antonio Pecci, the church of San Pietro was still standing and still under the authority of San Michele during the period that he was drawing up his record of Sant'Angelo in Colle between 1759 and 1761.[110] It is possible, therefore, that there was some lapse in time between the cessation of religious observation in the church of San Pietro, and the abandonment and destruction of the fabric itself.

In any event, there were obviously good reasons why, at least from the sixteenth century onwards, portable and particularly perishable furnishings associated with religious celebrations in the church of San Pietro outside the walls should be stored in a place of greater safety. This could explain why the two panels of *Saint Peter* and *Saint Paul* were in the end displayed inside San Michele. That said, the altar table of San Pietro (with perhaps its altarpiece attached) was certainly still *in situ* inside the church of San Pietro during the sixteenth-century, since reference was made at that date to a 'tabulas ligneas valoris aureorum decem pro servitio Ecclesia' (a wooden table, or panel worth 10 gold [?florins] for the service of the church).[111] The fact that the term *tabulas* rather than *icona* was used should probably be construed in terms of reference to the high altar table, rather than its embellishment. Yet, the comparatively high value placed on this 'table' (over three times the amount of money stipulated by Ser Longo di Ser Guccio in 1348 for the production of a decorated missal) must indicate that it was a relatively elaborate structure.

In this context it is also significant that when Ippolito Borghesi conducted his pastoral visit of Sant'Angelo in Colle in 1618, he noted that the church of San Pietro had only one altar, and that it was embellished with an 'iconam satis vetustam', 'a rather old icon, or image'.[112] Once again, the terminology would seem to imply a gold back painting of some age. No mention was made of the iconographical content of the high altar 'icon' in the seventeenth century pastoral visit, but any altarpiece displayed in such a location must surely have contained some reference to the titular saint, Peter.[113] One candidate must be the surviving panel of *Saint Peter*. The near-frontal pose of *Saint Peter* and the fact that he appears to stare straight out, as if personally engaging the viewer, would certainly seem to imply that the space in which this panel was originally displayed was directly associated with that particular saint. As we shall see, it also seems likely that this panel was originally positioned adjacent to a central image of the Virgin and Child.

Consideration of a number of intact fourteenth-century polyptychs from the early Sienese school indicates that the figures of Peter and Paul were often positioned one at either side of the Virgin and Child. Paul is commonly positioned on the Virgin's right-hand side. However, when a polyptych formed part of the embellishment of a high altar table, and when the titular saint of the church was Peter, that saint assumed the more privileged position on the Virgin's right-hand side. One such example is the polyptych of the *Virgin and Child enthroned between Saints Vincent, Peter, Paul and Lawrence*, attributed to Luca di Tommè which was originally painted for the church of San Pietro at Venano in Gaiole in Chianti, and which is now displayed in the Pinacoteca Nazionale in Siena.[114] If the two surviving panels of *Saint Peter* and *Saint Paul* now displayed in Montalcino had originally functioned as part of a high altarpiece in a church with the *titulus* of San Pietro, one might expect a similar arrangement. However, the pose of *Saint Paul* with his sword over his right shoulder and his head turned towards his left shoulder must surely indicate that he, too, was positioned to the right-hand side of a central image of the Virgin and Child. Moreover, holes gouged in the right-hand side of the panel of *Saint Paul* indicate that it was attached on that side to another panel.[115] Matching holes are visible on the left-hand side of the panel of *Saint Peter*. It seems likely, therefore, that the two panels were originally positioned side by side within the same altarpiece. If that were the case, one would expect them to have been balanced by another two saints on the other side of a central image of the Virgin and Child. Of any such panels, there now seems to be no trace. While plausible, the hypothesis that the surviving paintings once formed part of a polyptych must thus remain unproved.

No documentary evidence survives either to confirm the circumstances under which such an altarpiece was commissioned. However, on the basis of the iconography of the surviving two panels, and the gaze of *Saint Peter* himself, a working hypothesis must be that the altarpiece was produced for a church with the *titulus* of San Pietro. The fact that Saint Paul is included might also indicate that the patron responsible for the funding of the work favoured that particular saint. There seems little doubt either that the two panels were produced some time during the fourteenth century. Indeed it has generally been claimed that they were produced in the circle of the Lorenzetti brothers. A number of details within each panel are, however, closer to the style of a later generation of artists. While the artistic style of both saints, and in particular the figure of *Saint Paul* shows the influence of the Lorenzetti workshop, there is much to suggest a later hand. In particular, there are similarities with paintings produced by artists formed during the second generation of fourteenth-century Sienese masters. The hypothesis is raised here that the panels of *Saint Peter* and *Saint Paul* were produced some time during the second half of the fourteenth century. If they were indeed produced in the ambit of the Lorenzetti brothers, there is a case for arguing that their present somewhat ambiguous artistic style depends upon the intervention of a less refined follower of that workshop, or that it results from later restoration.

Consideration is given here to the latter possibility and that such restoration was carried out at a comparatively early date, perhaps as a result of a decision to 'refresh' an older altarpiece, or as a result of the original altarpiece being dismantled, or moved to a new site. Attention focuses in particular on the transitional style of the second half of the fourteenth century that informed and influenced the work of Bartolo di Fredi and his workshop. But, first a word about Bartolo di Fredi himself and his association with the southern Sienese *contado* communes, and in particular, Montalcino.

It is a well-known fact that Bartolo di Fredi was active in painting both frescoes and panel paintings destined for religious spaces in and around Montalcino during the 1380s.[116] However, in 1360 he is also documented as making a journey 'in Maremma e montagne per disegnare le tere del chomune'.[117] That he was directed towards the southern part of Siena's territory and with the particular brief to make drawings of those lands in the Maremma and the mountainous areas that Siena already owned must open up the possibility that Bartolo di Fredi visited Montalcino (and perhaps Sant'Angelo in Colle also) as early as the seventh decade of the fourteenth century. He was certainly involved with Montalcino by 1376.[118] Church authorities in Sant'Angelo in Colle would no doubt have been aware of some, if not all, of Bartolo di Fredi's activities there. It is not impossible, either, that Bartolo di Fredi was called upon to carry out work in one or other of

Sant'Angelo in Colle's two churches. He may also have become involved in decorations for the newly reorganised *grancia* of Santa Maria della Scala.

If Bartolo di Fredi, or members of his workshop were called to Sant'Angelo in Colle for a specific commission to embellish the urban fabric there, they might also have been asked to refresh some of the earlier decorations in the village, or to produce new works to embellish, or even take the place of pre-existing paintings. Such practice was widespread. As discussion in this chapter has shown, artefacts in the interior of the hospital of Santa Maria della Scala were regularly repaired and refreshed. Many examples elsewhere show that renovation and restoration were common in both lay and religious space throughout the medieval and renaissance periods.[119] Often, such 'refreshing' was necessitated by the vicissitudes of time. But on numerous occasions, earlier images were reworked and repainted in order to emphasise their original and/or continuing significance. As Cathleen Hoeniger has shown, one particular part of a much earlier image was often 'refreshed' with the express intention that the power of the original image should be preserved. Cult images were indeed among those decorations most commonly and continually repainted.

Analysis of the surface of the two panels of *Saint Peter* and *Saint Paul* does not, however, indicate any significant interventions.[120] Although much worn, both the composition and the paint surface seem to be original.[121] However, several details indicate that these panels could not have been produced, as hitherto claimed, by an artist working in the inner circle of the Lorenzetti brothers' workshop. The covering with cloth of the two saints' left hands is, in particular, reminiscent of later artists (Bartolo di Fredi amongst them), as is also the bulbous treatment of Saint Peter's nose. Comparisons can also be drawn with the facial characteristics of the figure of *Saint Augustine* in an altarpiece painted by Bartolo di Fredi which is now displayed in the church of Sante Fiora e Lucilla at Torrita di Siena, but which was most probably originally produced for the church of Sant'Agostino in Montalcino in the 1390s.[122] There are, in particular, similarities in the treatment of the wrinkles above the bridge of the nose and across the forehead in the figure of *Saint Augustine* and that of each saint in the two surviving panels associated with Sant'Angelo in Colle. That this was a characteristic of a later generation of artists is clear from a consideration of a number of other figures painted by Bartolo di Fredi and members of his workshop. Similar pronounced wrinkle lines are, for example, evident in the faces of *Saint Paul* and *Saint Peter* – two of four panels of standing saints – now displayed in the Museo Civico e Diocesano d'Arte Sacra in Montalcino.[123] These figures were produced in 1381 for one of the choir chapels of the church of San Francesco in Montalcino. Similar facial characteristics (including both the bulbous nose and the pronounced forehead wrinkles) are also evident in the painted fragment of a figure of *Saint John the Evangelist* attributed to Bartolo di Fredi, which is now in a private collection.[124] The way in which Saint Paul's index finger curls over the hilt of his sword in one fluid curve in the Sant'Angelo in Colle panel also occurs in Bartolo di Fredi's *oeuvre*, one example being the aforementioned figure of *Saint Paul* painted for the church of San Francesco in Montalcino. Another such detail can be seen in the left hand of *Saint Augustine* in the altarpiece now displayed in the church of Sante Fiora e Lucilla in Torrita di Siena.

Similar motifs also occur in works produced in the circle of Bartolo di Fredi. Thus, in an image of *Saint Paul*, now in a private collection under the attribution of the 'Maestro della Madonna di Palazzo Venezia', there are similarities not only in the treatment of the fingers of the right hand and the covering of the left hand with drapery, but also in the marked furrowing of the saint's brow.[125] There are similarities also in the treatment of the figure of *Saint Peter*, now in the Robert Lehman Collection in New York, which is likewise attributed to the circle of the 'Maestro della Madonna di Palazzo Venezia'.[126] Not only do we find the same covering of the left hand by drapery, but the solid depiction of the fingers of the Robert Lehman Collection saint's bared right hand, as well as the highlighting of his knuckles are particularly close to comparable details in the two panels associated with Sant'Angelo in Colle. There are similarities, also, in the decided downturn of Saint Peter's moustache in the Lehman Collection image. Most significantly, two panels depicting the full-length standing figures of *Saint Peter* and *Saint Paul* displayed in the church of Saint Louis en l'Ile in Paris, seem almost to replicate the same two figures of saints in the two panels associated with Sant'Angelo in Colle. Although previously attributed to Luca di Tommè, Cesare Brandi did not hesitate to attribute the two panels in Paris to Bartolo di Fredi.[127] A coincidence of this kind must surely add support to the hypothesis that Bartolo di Fredi or his workshop was at one point involved with the affairs of Sant'Angelo in Colle.

However, once again it is impossible to prove such a hypothesis without further documentary evidence, and it, like several others raised here, must remain in the realm of informed speculation. That said, and regardless of questions of attribution, a possible course of events canvassed here is that the images of *Saint Peter* and *Saint Paul* associated with Sant'Angelo in Colle, while at a later date displayed in the church of San Pietro outside the walls of the village, originally formed part of the high altar embellishment of the church with the *titulus* of Saint Peter inside the walls of Sant'Angelo in Colle. A hypothesis raised in this context is that the two panels became associated with religious observance in the church of San Pietro outside the walls to the north of the village, when the church of San Pietro Vecchio fell into disrepair. In that way, they would have remained under the authority of the parish church of San Michele until some time around the middle of the eighteenth century.

Why and under what circumstances the church of San Pietro inside the walls disappeared remains unclear. All that can safely be said is that it was no longer standing in the seventeenth century, when Bartolomeo Gherardini made his pastoral visit to Sant'Angelo in Colle. However, if Giovanni Antonio Pecci's conclusions during the following century are correct, the church known as San Pietro Vecchio was still standing in the fifteenth century, since it was that structure – according to the eighteenth-century chronicler – that was transferred to the authority of the cathedral in Montalcino during the papacy of Pius II. That transfer seems to have been due to the lack of a sufficient congregation, and thus potential benefactors prepared to contribute to the upkeep of the church fabric. It seems likely, therefore, that San Pietro Vecchio was already in a degraded state by 1464.

The inevitable question is why and how the second church at Sant'Angelo in Colle had reached such a state. Archival material recently unearthed in the State Archives in Siena does in fact reveal that the church of San Pietro was already in a poor state by 1322.[128] According to this new record, both the church and the 'house' of San Pietro were in danger of collapse at that date. Indeed, the damage was so grave that Ser Tura di Gualtieri, the rector of the church, had decided – with the permission of Abbot Talomeo (sic) of Sant'Antimo – to sell a piece of land belonging to the church in order to fund restoration work on the walls of the tribune. The sale had been ratified in the church of 'Sant'Angiolo in Colle' by Francesco, son of the deceased 'Ceno' of Montalcino, and the purchaser, 'Ser Tuccio del quondam Francesco', a local resident of Sant'Angelo in Colle, had paid Ser Tura eight 'lire di denari sanesi piccolo'.[129] Presumably, therefore, the church did not fall in 1322. There is indeed confirmation of this in Ser Longo's endowment of the same church some 20 years later, in 1348. However, the eight *lire* paid by Ser Tuccio di Francesco was a comparatively small amount of money, if it was intended to cover the cost of complete restoration of the church. No doubt further money was required in due course to cover running repairs. It is significant in this context to recall that when Ser Longo drew up his will, he stipulated that over twice that amount of money should be given to the current rector of San Pietro, Ser Nuccio.

One possible course of events is that the church of San Pietro Vecchio, already in a fragile state by the middle of the fourteenth century, was further affected by the establishment of the new *grancia* of Santa Maria della Scala towards the end of the fourteenth century. If (as argued here) the old church of San Pietro was located between the existing northern gate of the village and the Sienese military barracks in the vicinity of *Palazzaccio*, it may even have been engulfed by the construction of new sections of wall in the vicinity of the grange, or by new building work in the vicinity of the grange. A surviving record dated 22 October 1380 does in fact make reference to the compulsory purchase of a number of properties 'presso al palazzo che a dato el comune di Siena alosspedale' (in the vicinity of the palace that the commune of Siena has given to the hospital).[130] According to this, a certain Friar Stefano di Pietro was to be allowed to buy and dispose of such property as he wished. Stefano di Pietro had in fact been recorded as the 'granciere' or master of the grange of Sant'Angelo in Colle during the previous year, and was still cited in that context in 1380 and 1381.[131]

Friar Stefano di Pietro's purchase of houses in the vicinity of the hospital's new grange may have directly affected San Pietro Vecchio, if that church complex was indeed situated in the northern part of the village. With inhabitants of nearby buildings being displaced through the acquisition or relegation of their property, the existing parish and congregation of San Pietro may even have been severely diminished. Such a course of events, combined with the overall diminution of the population of Sant'Angelo in Colle between the fourteenth and fifteenth centuries could explain not only why the church of San Pietro inside the walls was placed under the authority of the Cathedral of Montalcino in 1464, but also the subsequent disappearance or appropriation of the fabric itself.

Whatever the sequence of events, if the two panels of *Saint Peter* and *Saint Paul* had indeed originally formed part of the high altarpiece of San Pietro Vecchio, they could have been restored and/or salvaged at the end of the fourteenth century following further deterioration of the church fabric, with the intention of reinvesting them with significance elsewhere. Indeed, the fact that the frame of the *Saint Peter* panel is inscribed with his name, whereas that of *Saint Paul* is blank, could indicate that a specific attempt was made to preserve the identity of the former saint. In this context it may be significant that in 1373 Bartolo di Fredi was commissioned by the Company of Saint Peter in the church of San Francesco in Montalcino to paint the altarpiece of the Chapel of the Annunciation there.[132] Bartolo di Fredi continued working on decorations for San Francesco throughout the following decade. If a decision had been made to refresh the high altarpiece of San Pietro in Sant'Angelo in Colle at around the same time, the renowned Sienese artist producing work for the adjacent commune may have seemed the obvious person to turn to. It may even be that the authorities in Sant'Angelo in Colle turned specifically to the Compagnia di San Pietro in Montalcino, because that company carried the same *titulus* as their own church of 'San Pietro Vecchio'.

What connections, if any, may then be drawn between the two panels of *Saint Peter* and *Saint Paul* and the panel of the *'Madonna della Misericordia'*? The only firm evidence we have is that in the nineteenth century these three panels were assembled in the form of a triptych inside the parish church of San Michele Arcangelo. It seems inconceivable, however, that the panels of *Saint Peter* and *Saint Paul* were originally intended to flank the panel now known as the *'Madonna della Misericordia'*. For one thing, the three paintings differ in size.[133] Moreover, although one could argue that it was commonly the case in fourteenth-century triptychs and polyptychs that the central panel of the *Madonna and Child* was both wider and taller than those of any flanking saints, the discrepancies in artistic style between the three panels would seem to deny any early association.

A more likely sequence of events is that over time the *Madonna and Child* panel was invested with special significance, having become separated from a number of other elements that, together once constituted an altarpiece for one of the village's two churches. It may thus have been a purely practical and temporary measure in the middle of the nineteenth century to assemble the panel of the *Madonna and Child* in triptych form along with two other surviving paintings from the fourteenth century. No reason was given for the dismembering of the triptych in August 1869, when the panels of the two saints were removed to the Pinacoteca in Siena. It seems likely, however, that the decision that the central image of the *Madonna and Child* should remain in Sant'Angelo in Colle was linked with the project to restore the painting and transfer it to a new position of iconic significance on the high altar of the purpose-built Chiesa della Madonna del Rosario. In effect, the *'Madonna della Misericordia'* had become a cult image. Even now this image of the Virgin and her Child is offered particular veneration by the villagers of Sant'Angelo in Colle, during special celebrations that are organised every 25 years in her honour.

In the absence of more precise evidence, questions concerning the circumstances under which these three works of art were produced and assembled together in the parish church of San Michele Arcangelo remain, for the most part, unanswered. Nevertheless, a number of points of historical fact can be made. The most significant is that there were two churches dedicated to Saint Peter in the vicinity of Sant'Angelo in Colle in the early medieval period. One was positioned outside the walls of the village and was administered by the clergy of the parish church of San Michele Arcangelo. The clergy of San Michele were also responsible for the upkeep of furnishings of what was probably the only altar in the church outside the walls from at least the end of the fifteenth century until well into the seventeenth century. (References were made to the 'altar of Saint Peter' at the earlier date, and to altar cloths for use in the church of San Pietro in an inventory of 1674.) A second church dedicated to Saint Peter was located inside the walls of Sant'Angelo in Colle, and was still standing during the first half of the fourteenth century, albeit in a poor state of repair. This second church was administered by individual rectors, although it was also dependent in some way on Sant'Antimo, since the advice and permission of that monastery's abbot was sought in the context of raising funds for restoration work on the church in 1322. By the late seventeenth century no church with the *titulus* of San Pietro was still standing inside the walls of Sant'Angelo in Colle, although an eighteenth-century reference to 'the old church of Saint Peter' implies that there was still local knowledge that such a structure had been located inside the walls of the village at an earlier date. By contrast, the church with the *titulus* of San Pietro outside the walls to the north of the village was not only still standing in the seventeenth century, but was still being officiated by the clergy of San Michele Arcangelo, although the structure itself was in a poor state of repair. Some time around the middle of the eighteenth century, the parish clergy's responsibilities ceased in respect of San Pietro outside the walls, and no further references were made to the church in the records of the parish church. All in all, it seems likely that the church of San Pietro on the northern side of the village fell into disuse shortly after 1761 (the date at which Giovanni Antonio Pecci is said to have completed a description of the village indicating that the church of that *titulus* outside the walls of the village was still standing). In a pastoral visit of 1765, there was no reference to any such structure. By 1765, a panel identifiable as the *'Madonna della Misericordia'* was, however, set up in the small church now known as San Pietro on the southern side of the village. Surviving records from the second half of the eighteenth century make reference to the recent 'arrival' of this image. A century later, a project was put in hand to restore both the church of San Pietro and the *'Madonna della Misericordia'*, and to place the painting of the Madonna in a purpose-built church. In 1869, and possibly as early as 1862, and in any event some several decades before the completion of the new church of the Madonna, a triptych including the *'Madonna della Misericordia'* and the two panels of *Saint Peter* and *Saint Paul* was noted amongst the furnishings of the church of San Michele.

If one had set out to assemble documentary evidence in support of a hypothesis that the panels of *Saint Peter* and *Saint Paul* were originally produced for a church with the *titulus* of San Pietro inside the walls, but were subsequently adopted in the service of religious observation in a church with the same *titulus* outside the walls until some time around the middle of the eighteenth century, the facts outlined above would present a persuasive case. Without doubt, any furnishings produced for San Pietro inside the walls of Sant'Angelo in Colle must also have been severely compromised by the poor state of repair of the church complex in the early fourteenth century. Moreover, it seems clear that by the following century, and despite intervening restoration work, there was insufficient local support for the upkeep of San Pietro. By the seventeenth century the church building was no longer standing. Any moveable artefacts that had embellished the fabric must have long since been transferred elsewhere. The fact that the clergy of San Michele had been actively engaged with the affairs of the church of San Pietro 'Podere la Casella' outside the walls from an early date and were still engaged with it during the seventeenth century, may well have favoured the transfer to that church of furnishings from a pre-existing church with the same *titulus*. However, some time between 1761 and 1765, the church of San Pietro outside the walls appears itself either to have fallen into disuse or to have physically crumbled. Such an event must have resulted in any furnishings previously adopted for use during religious observations in that structure being housed elsewhere. Given the long-established relationship with San Michele, the most obvious site must have been the parish church itself. A thread of association for the panels of *Saint Peter* and *Saint Paul* can thus be traced from San Pietro Vecchio to San Pietro 'Podere la Casella' some time prior to 1676, and from San Pietro 'Podere la Casella' to San Michele Arcangelo some time between 1761 and 1765.

What, then, can be surmised about the history of the *'Madonna della Misericordia'* prior to the eighteenth century, and its association with the two panels of *Saint Peter* and *Saint Paul*? The chronological coincidence that in 1765 the *'Madonna della Misericordia'* was recorded as recently set up in the small church on the southern side of the village, and that around about the same time the church of San Pietro outside the walls on the northern side of the village was abandoned is striking. One obvious conclusion is that prior to the mid 1760s the panel of the *Madonna della Misericordia* was displayed in the church of San Pietro 'Podere la Casella', perhaps removed there some time after 1618, following the construction of the new Baroque high altar in San Michele.

There seems little doubt that by 1765 the painting of the *'Madonna della Misericordia'* was regarded as an image of some significance. This may in part have been due to its age. It may also have been due to the fact that the image had been brought to Sant'Angelo in Colle from another location. But, if, as argued here, the *'Madonna della Misericordia'* can be associated with the gold-back image noted by Ippolito Borghese as in the church of San Michele in 1618, its perceived value in the eighteenth century may have resulted from its long association with Sant'Angelo in Colle, and in particular its original position on the high altar table of the parish church.

In any event, and regardless of the precise course of events, there can be little doubt that by the second half of the eighteenth century there would have been no obvious place to display such an image other than in the small church on the southern side of the village. The installation of the Baroque altarpiece on the high altar table of San Michele and the existing ownership and *tituli* of the four lateral altars there left no opening for such an image to be displayed in any prominent position inside the parish church. The old church of San Pietro inside the walls was no longer standing. The church of San Pietro on the northern side of the village was deconsecrated, and possibly already demolished. Display on the altar of the church outside the walls on the southern side of the village must have offered the only appropriate solution.

This, then, is the sum of the village's portable decorations surviving from the time of Sant'Angelo in Colle's greatest prosperity under the protection of the Sienese Government of the Nine, and the years thereafter when the village was still closely engaged with the affairs of the *grancia* of Santa Maria della Scala: two dismembered panels that may once have adorned the high altar of a church with the *titulus* of San Pietro outside the walls of the village, and which may originally have been associated with the church of the same *titulus* inside the walls; and one image of the *Madonna and Child*, that has assumed the character of a cult image, but whose early history is unknown. Of the early fourteenth-century embellishment of the high altar of San Michele, there is no firm evidence, apart from what is revealed in the pastoral visits of 1573 and 1618. However, the fact that we can now draw so many historical threads together to form hypotheses about the original sites and circumstances of production of these decorations, including the identities of potential benefactors of just a few of the fourteenth-century panels associated with Sant'Angelo in Colle is in itself no mean feat.

In conclusion, a word about the circumstances that assist the survival of individual artefacts. Reconsideration of nineteenth-century descriptions of surviving decorations inside the parish church provides a number of insights into the embellishment of the fabric of medieval Sant'Angelo in Colle, whilst at the same time throwing light on earlier histories. According to an inventory drawn up for San Michele in 1836, the church furnishings at that period included three paintings on wood in which were depicted the figures of 'the Virgin Mary and various saints'.[134] A further entry in the same document refers to 'Tre Pitture antiche in tavola esprimente vari santi in mediocre stato'.[135] It seems clear from this that at least three of the paintings recorded in the parish church in the first half of the nineteenth century were not only old, but also in rather a bad state. That the reference in 1836 to 'the Virgin Mary and various saints' concerned the triptych consisting of the panels of *Saint Peter* and *Saint Paul* and the *'Madonna della Misericordia'* as assembled inside San Michele three decades later seems unlikely, since other evidence presented here confirms that in 1836 the *'Madonna della Misericordia'* was still displayed in the church outside the walls of the village on its southern side. Nor at first sight does it seem likely that the triptych noted in the 1836 inventory was the same as that associated with Martino di Bartolomeo, since the reference to 'various saints' implies that the existing figures of the *Archangel Michael* and *Saint John the Baptist* were not the only ones depicted in the altarpiece. As for the 'Tre Pitture antiche in tavola esprimente vari santi in mediocre stato', it is possible that such a group included the two panels of *Saint Peter* and *Saint Paul* along with a fifteenth-century panel of *Saint Bernardino* attributed to Vecchietta (also now displayed in the museum at Montalcino, and which is likewise said to have come from the parish church of San Michele in Sant'Angelo in Colle).[136] But this group of 'Tre Pitture antiche' may also have contained the two panels in pyramidal form noted in the late sixteenth-century inventory of furnishings at San Michele. If that were the case, fragments of the original high altarpiece of the parish church would have survived *in situ* until the first half of the nineteenth century. In many ways this would make sense. If the panel now known as the *'Madonna della Misericordia'* did indeed form part of a polyptych painted for the high altar of San Michele following the reconstruction of the church around the middle of the fourteenth century, other parts of the same altarpiece could have remained on the original premises even if the central panel itself was removed for display elsewhere. Indeed it was frequently the case that such dismembered parts subsequently assumed the status of a cult image. The *'Madonna della Misericordia'* is an example of this. It seems, moreover, that this was not the first, nor even the only image to achieve such status in the old frontier castle of Sant'Angelo in Colle. According to surviving records, a small chapel, which was located just outside the northern gate, and which contained an image of the Virgin, attracted considerable attention from local inhabitants until well into the eighteenth century.

This structure, which as already noted was referred to both as the 'Cappella della Madonna delle Nevi' and the chapel of the 'Madonna delle Grazie', remained standing until the early twentieth century.[137] Despite diverse vicissitudes, its internal decorations were all still visible in the eighteenth century.[138] It is not known when the chapel was founded. However, it seems likely that it was an ancient foundation. It was certainly already in existence in the sixteenth century since reference was made to it in Bishop Bossi's pastoral visit of 1576. It also seems that by that date the chapel was already in a precarious condition, since Bossi ordered Antonio Maria Forteguerri to close the chapel within six months and then destroy the fabric.[139] However, it appears that Bossi's order was not carried out immediately. Indeed, Don Brandi noted that the demolition order was baulked for several hundred years, since reference was made to the Cappella della Madonna delle Nevi in all subsequent pastoral visits right up to the suppression of the monasteries in the eighteenth century.[140] In fact, the chapel is known to have fallen out of use only in the wake of the construction of a new cemetery close to the existing northern gateway in 1786. According to a report filed by Bishop Pecci in 1788, the chapel building was at that date in a state of near ruin.[141] Around the same time it seems that the chapel's altar was demolished and the building itself turned into a mortuary chamber for the storage of funeral furnishings.[142] It continued in that guise until the early twentieth century, when the chapel was finally destroyed following the construction of the present cemetery in the vicinity of podere Ferralino.

The hypothesis is raised here that the prolonged stay of order to demolish the Cappella della Madonna delle Nevi may have been due to the fact that the chapel served as a particular focus point for local religious observations. Interestingly, and unlike pastoral visits recording other buildings inside the walls of Sant'Angelo in Colle, the structure and embellishment of the Capella della Madonna delle Nevi is described in some detail in a pastoral visit of 1768. According to this record the chapel was a 'Piccola chiesina con porta e due finestre hinc inde con ferriata, a tetto, con pitture antiche hinc inde, nel muro, altare rozzo con immagine della SS. Vergine delle Nevi e altri Santi antichi dipinti in muro con molti voti intorno' (a small church with a door and two barred windows; with ancient wall paintings, and an altar set against the wall with an image of the most sacred Virgin of the Snow and other ancient images of saints painted on the walls with many votive offerings displayed all around).[143] It seems from this that the chapel was large enough to be categorised as a small church and that the walls were extensively covered with 'old' fresco paintings. It is also clear that the embellishment of the altar consisted of an image of the *Virgin of the Snows* (probably a fresco), with a further series of frescoed images of saints on the adjacent wall.

Given the chapel's location outside the walls of Sant'Angelo in Colle, and its proximity to one of the main gates, it is hardly surprising that it was in a state of collapse by the late sixteenth century. In such a position, it must have been in the front line during any attack on the village. Yet, despite this, the embellishment of the Cappella della Madonna delle Nevi appears to have remained intact, even after the siege of Montalcino and the abandonment of the village in the middle of the sixteenth century. At no stage, either, does there seem to have been any attempt to white wash the original frescoes or to substitute them with more up-to-date decorations. Clearly, the embellishment of this particular fabric was deemed worthy of preservation even though the building itself was in a poor state of repair. But, what was so special about the decorations in the Cappella della Madonna delle Nevi? Apart from the description of the Virgin of the Snows above the altar, the eighteenth-century chronicler makes no specific reference to the individual identities of the saints frescoed on the walls of the chapel. However, the fact that a large number of votive images were recorded as displayed around the walls of the chapel would seem to imply that the inhabitants of Sant'Angelo in Colle had come to regard the chapel as under their own particular protection. Indeed, it seems that the Cappella della Madonna delle Nevi, and in particular the image of the *Virgin of the Snows* had attracted the kind of attention that was normally reserved for sites containing cult images. Such a tradition may even have helped fuel the flames of devotion generated by the panel of the *Madonna and Child* which was newly displayed in the church to the south of the walls, when the Cappella della Madonna delle Nevi itself was finally crumbling. It may also be relevant that the latter structure was also known as the chapel of the 'Madonna della Misericordia'. The title of one iconic image may thus have been transferred to another.

So what, then, can we conclude about the embellishment of the fabric of Sant'Angelo in Colle during the waning years of the Government of the Nine, and in the period under the establishment of the Government of the Twelve? Consideration of surviving fourteenth-century decorations has raised a large number of questions that are for the most part difficult to resolve. The documentary evidence is incomplete and at times contradictory. Much of the surviving artistic material is fragmentary and in a poor state of repair. However, given the condition of the old frontier castle by the mid-sixteenth century, abandoned by the Sienese and no doubt in a state of near collapse following assault by Florentine troops (if not directly on Sant'Angelo in Colle itself, most certainly in the surrounding countryside), it would be surprising if any portable or fixed artefact dating to the medieval period remained intact in the village. Portable objects in particular were subject to removal, relocation and destruction. Moreover, the villagers themselves no doubt transported their most precious artefacts away with them when seeking refuge in Montalcino before the great siege in the sixteenth century. Fixed decorations such as frescoes were compromised in other ways, not the least through being covered over by whitewashing, or suffering damage as a result of later embellishments or alterations to the structures in which they were located. Both the *Sacra Conversazione* and the image of *Saint Leonard* inside San Michele Arcangelo suffered that fate. In other cases, such as the village hospital and the church of San Pietro inside the walls, the buildings themselves no longer exist and no records survive concerning their internal decorations.

Despite this, a number of general points can be made. Surviving records in the form of pastoral visits, church inventories and last wills and testaments provide detailed information about the state of preservation and the early histories of key buildings in the southern frontier castle of Sant'Angelo in Colle. From these documents we gain insights into the administration of the different institutions. We also glean information about individual figures of authority and potential patrons. In fourteenth-century Sant'Angelo in Colle, these are identified in the main as the parish clergy, individual rectors and members of the professional class such as the village notaries. There can be little doubt, however, that powerful Sienese institutions such as the hospital of Santa Maria della Scala and the order of Augustinian Hermits also played a significant part in the everyday life and internal religious affairs of the subject commune.

Surviving wills, in particular, help to clarify relationships between the various institutions. Distinctions in the endowments made by those individual members of the local elite considered here help us reconstruct the embellishment of the fabric of two of the village's churches, as well as the chronology of their restoration and reconstruction. The detailed consideration of wills drawn up on behalf of Rosa di Piero Pecoraio, Giovanni di Paganello and Ser Longo di Ser Guccio also indicates that a particularly close relationship was established between Sant'Angelo in Colle and the Franciscan community of San Francesco in Montalcino during the period of the Government of the Nine. In addition to endowments of money for the daily needs of the friars (including the provision of decent clothing), these wills show how residents of Sant'Angelo in Colle, as well as paying attention to the upkeep and embellishment of their own local institutions, also concerned themselves with the development and decoration of religious complexes in nearby Montalcino. Ser Longo di Ser Guccio even provided money for the construction and embellishment of a chapel in the church of San Francesco there. Rosa di Piero Pecoraio for her part also considered the needs of the female branch of the Franciscan order in Montalcino. Nor was she apparently the only one to endow the *fratesse*, or female friars of that commune. Rosa's monetary contribution towards the construction of the new monastic complex of the female friars of Montalcino must clearly have boosted the affairs of that community in 1328. However, the fact that the *fratesse* already held land in the vicinity of Sant'Angelo in Colle by 1320 indicates that other local residents may already have shown favour to these female religious when drawing up their wills, and thus played their own part in stimulating building work and the embellishment of the fabric. According to the 1320 *Tavola delle possessioni*, at least one resident of Sant'Angelo in Colle, a woman identified only by the name Becca, had even joined the ranks of the female friars.

Detailed analysis of surviving decorations associated with fourteenth-century Sant'Angelo in Colle indicates that the Franciscans in Montalcino served as a source of artistic influence through the activities of artists called to embellish the Franciscan's own complex of San Francesco. It is striking how throughout this consideration of the urban fabric, art and society of fourteenth century Sant'Angelo in Colle, so many references have been made to Montalcino and in particular, to the Franciscan order there. Not only is the so-called 'Master of 1346' (a local artist and the presumed author of the *'Madonna della Misericordia'*) said to have carried out frescoes in the cloister of San Francesco in Montalcino, but Bartolo di Fredi (a leading member of the second generation of Sienese masters whose style appears to permeate the two panels of *Saint Paul* and *Saint Peter*) was in effect the artist in residence of San Francesco during the 1380s. Both these artists emerge as key players in a discussion of the embellishment of the fabric of the medieval village.

But, as the detailed analysis of the two panels of *Saint Paul* and *Saint Peter* and the fresco of the *Sacra Conversazione* has shown, Sant'Angelo in Colle under the Government of the Nine was also very obviously susceptible to the first generation of Sienese artists in the form of Ambrogio and Pietro Lorenzetti, and the work they carried out in the southern Sienese *contado*. It seems, therefore, that the embellishment of the fabric of medieval Sant'Angelo in Colle was determined not only through the imposition of outside powers and the periphery mirroring the centre, but also as a result of neighbourhood negotiations. Such two-pronged influence forms the basis of the concluding Afterword.

Notes

1 Archivio di Stato di Siena (hereafter, ASS) *Diplomatico in Caselle, casella* 892, 16 June 1348, *R. Acquisto Bandini Piccolomini*. See also Archivio Storico del Comune di Montalcino (hereafter ACM), *Archivio dell'Ospedale di Santa Maria della Croce, Convento di Ser Francesco, Campione* 10, fol. 178v and *Campione* 11, fol. 34, where Ser Longo is referred to as 'Ser Longo figlio di Ser Duccio Notaro di S.Angelo in Colle'. He was thus presumably the son of Ser Guccio d ser Francesco!

2 For an analysis of comparative wages and everyday costs, see Silvana Balbi di Caro and Gabriella Angeli Bufalini, *La Collezione Numismatica della Banca Monte dei Paschi di Siena* (Pisa, 2001), p. 131.

3 This is probably the same individual referred to as 'Mino il cherico' in June1327, see Chapter 7, footnote 17.

4 Don Antonio Brandi, *Parrocchia di S. Michele Arcangelo in S. Angelo in Colle,* typescript, 2004 (hereafter Brandi, 2004), p. 12.

5 ASS, *Diplomatico in Caselle, casella* 712, 4 June 1327, *Archivio dello Spedale*.

6 ASS, *Estimo* 24, fol. 75r.

7 Ibid., fol. 137r.

8 For an analysis of the links between local clergy and hospital officials during the early modern period, see John Henderson, 'Splendide case di cura', Spedali, medicina ed assistenza a Firenze nel Trecento', Atti del Convegno Internazionale di Studio tenuto dall'Istituto degli Innocenti e Villa I Tatti, The Harvard University Center for Italian Renaissance Studies, Florence, 27–28 aprile 1995, in Allen J. Grieco and Lucia Sandri (eds), *Medicina e Storia. Ospedali e città. L'Italia del centro-Nord, 13–16 secolo* (Florence, 1997), (hereafter 'Splendide case di cura'), pp. 15–50. See also Jean Imbert, *Les hopitaux en droit canonique* (Paris, 1947) and Francesca Carli, 'Note per una Topografia ed una Tipologia degli Ospedali extraurbani della diocesi di Siena nel medioevo', *BSSP*, 100 (1993), pp. 384–403.

9 Don Antonio Brandi, *Parrocchia di S. Michele Arcangelo in S. Angelo in Colle*, typescript, 1991 (hereafter Brandi, 1991), p. 6 and, more recently (Brandi, 2004, p. 12).

10   Archivio Vescovile di Montalcino (hereafter AVM), *Visite Pastorali*, 225, fol. 12v.

11   Ibid., – 'male ornatum absq linteis et literis necessares … potius eisit aptius canibus qa hominibus'.

12   'cubicul in quo cubile retinetur pro infirmis … e peregrines sarciatur et ano modetur, et in lecto provideatur di decenti culutra stramento obstragute et congruis linteis intra sex menses'.

13   John Henderson, *Pietà e carità nella Firenze del basso Medioevo* (Florence, c.1998), (translation of *Piety and charity in late medieval Florence*, Oxford, 1994); and 'The hospitals of late medieval and Renaissance Florence: a preliminary survey', in Lindsay Granshaw and Roy Porter (eds), *The Hospital in History* (London and New York, 1989), pp. 63–92. More recently, see Henderson, 'Splendide case di cura' and *The Renaissance hospital: healing the body and healing the soul* (Yale, c.2006), both of which also contain an overview of recent bibliography.

14   Henderson, 'splendide case di cura', p. 16.

15   In this context, see Duccio Balestracci, 'Per una storia degli ospedali di *contado* nella Toscana fra 14 e 16 secoli. Strutture, arredi, personale, assistenza' (hereafter 'Per una storia degli ospedali'), in Giuliano Pinto (ed.), *La società del bisogno: povertà e assistenza nella Toscana medievale* (Florence, 1989), pp. 37–59; and Gabriella Piccinni and Laura Vigni, 'Modelli di assistenza ospedaliera fra Medioevo ed Età Moderna. Quotidianità, amministrazione, conflitti nell'ospedale di Santa Maria della Scala di Siena', in *La Società del bisogno*, 1989, pp. 131–74. See also, Henderson, *Pietà e carità* (Florence, c.1998), and 'The hospitals of late medieval and Renaissance Florence', in Granshaw and Porter (eds), *The Hospital in History* (London and New York, 1989), pp. 63–92.

16   Henderson, 'splendide case di cura', p. 24.

17   Ilio Raffaelli, *Prima dell'economia del Brunello, Montalcino: urbanistica, demografia, cultura e società dalle origini ai nostri giorni* (Montepulciano, 2001), p. 41. For the history of Santa Maria della Croce, see Michelangelo Lorenzoni, 'L'antico Ospedale di S. Maria della Croce di Montalcino e il suo statuto del 1788', Tesi di Laurea, 1992–1993; *L'archivio Comunale di Montalcino*, Paola Giovanna Morelli, Stefano Moscadelli and Chiara Santini (eds), (2 vols, Siena, 1989–90), 2, pp. 13–31; Tullio Canali, *Libro delle Memorie dell'Origini delli Spedali di Montalcino in Toscana* (1748), transcribed by Don Antonio Brandi as *Notizie in iscorcio dello Spedale di Mont'Alcino* (typescript, 1990), (hereafter Canali, *Libro delle Memorie*). See also Adolfo Temperini, *Gli spedali di Montalcino, Montalcino* (Montalcino, 1906). It was often the case that a hospital started life in a private house belonging to an individual benefactor. In Siena, the late thirteenth-century foundation of the Ospedale di Sant'Agnese, which was established in the house of Monna Agnese di Affrettato is one such example. In Montalcino, the hospital founded by Naldo di Bindo is another. When Naldo, son of the deceased Bindo di Boncianno drew up his will in February 1347 he stipulated not only that a house belonging to him in the *contrada* of Sant'Egidio should be taken over and made into a hospital with the *titulus* Sant'Angelo, but also that the new hospital should reflect in the way it was run, the much larger institution of Santa Maria della Scala in Siena. See ASS, *Diplomatico di Montalcino*, Busta 37 bis, no. 125.

18   Canali, *Libro delle Memorie*, p. 2.

19   Lorenzoni, 'L'antico Ospedale', 1992–3, p. 5.

20   For references to Santa Lucia and the hospital of the Misericordia in Montalcino, see Canali, *Libro delle Memorie*, pp. 3–11.

21   Ibid., p. 12.

22   For a proposed reconstruction of the fifteenth-century hospital facade, see Ivo Caprioli, *Passeggiate di Primavera* (22 May 2004, Montalcino). See also ACM, *Santa Maria della Croce*, XIX (4).

23   Canali, *Libro delle Memorie*, p. 31.

24   Don Antonio Brandi, *L'Ospedale di S. Maria della Croce nel 1483. Nomina del Rettore e Inventario di Tutti i Beni mobili di Proprietà dell'ospedale*, typescript (Montalcino, 1996), (hereafter Brandi, *l'Ospedale*).

25   ACM, *Diplomatico Santa Maria della Croce*, 480.

26   Brandi, *L'Ospedale*, p. 9.

27   See Balestracci, 'Per una storia degli ospedali'; and Lucia Sandri, 'Ospedali e utenti della assistenza nella Firenze del Quattrocento', in *La società del bisogno*, 1999, pp. 61–100.

28   Sandri, 'Ospedali, e utenti', 1999, p. 85, note 45 – A Lorenzo di Niccolò, dipintore, a dì XVI di marzo per dipintura di sette lettiere negli spedali, dipinte co' l'armi di chi fece le letta per *soldi* venti l'una e per dipintura di tre lettiere sanza arme veruna, cioè dipinte tutte rosse per *soldi* tredici *denari* quattro l'una, monta in tutto *lire* nove.' San Matteo, Entrata e Uscita 1408–1411, 250, fol. 47v.

29   Alfredo Liberati, 'Nuovi Documenti Artistici dello Spedale di S. Maria della Scala in Siena', *BSSP*, 33–36 (1926–1929), pp. 147–79.

30   ACM, *Diplomatico Santa Maria della Croce*, 480, fol. 4v.

31   Brandi, *L'Ospedale*, p. 9.

32   Ibid., p. 14.

33   ACM, *Diplomatico Santa Maria della Croce*, 480, fols 4v–12, and Brandi, *L'Ospedale*, pp. 9, 14, 16, 18 and 19.

34   Alessandra Gianni, 'Iconografia della Madonna della Misericordia nell'arte Senese', in Mario Ascheri and Patrizia Turrini (eds), *La Misericordia di Siena attraverso i secoli: dalla domus Misericordiae all'arciconfraternità di Misericordia*, Arciconfraternità di Misericordia di Siena (Siena, 2004), pp. 94–101.

35   Ibid., p. 95.

36   See Gabriella Piccinni and Carla Zarrilli (eds), *Arte e assistenza a Siena. Le copertine dell'Ospedale di Santa Maria della Scala*, catalogue of the exhibition, Siena, 7 March – 31 August 2003 (Pisa, 2003).

37   See Table 3.5.

38   For a general overview of hospital architecture in the medieval period, see Dankwart Leistikow, *Dieci secoli di storia degli edifici ospedalieri in Europa. Una storia dell'architettura ospedaliere* (Ingelheim am Rhein, 1967); and M. Salvadè, 'Evoluzione dei caratteri distributive nella architettura ospedaliera', Atti del primo congresso europeo di storia ospitaliera, giugno 1960, Bologna, (Bologna, 1962), pp. 116–33.

39   Diana Norman, *Siena and the Virgin. Art and Politics in a Late Medieval City State* (New Haven and London, 1999).

40   Cesare Brandi, 'Affreschi inediti di Pietro Lorenzetti', *L'Arte*, 4 (1931), pp. 332–47. See also, Bruno Santi (ed.), *L'Amiata e le Val d'Orcia* (Milan, 1999), pp. 78–79.

See also, Soprintendenza per i beni storici artistici ed etnoantropologici per le province di Siena e Grosseto, Ufficio Catalago, schede CD – codici NAC: 9220, NAC: 9221 and 9222.

41 Santi, *L'Amiata*: pp. 44–45.

42 Ibid., p. 45.

43 Ibid., p. 73. See also, Soprintendenza per i beni storici artistici ed etnoantropologici per le province di Siena e Grosseto, Ufficio Catalago, schede.

44 Somewhat curiously, a recent guide to Montalcino that contains a section concerning Sant'Angelo in Colle appears to identify this figure as Saint Anthony, see Alessandra Dami, Raffaele Giannetti, Maddalena Sanfilippo and Giulia Zoi, *Montalcino Città delle Eccellenze*, guida ufficiale del Comune di Montalcino (Città di Castello (PG), 2009), p. 53.

45 Don Antonio Brandi (Brandi, 2004, p. 11) suggests that both frescoes were covered with whitewash shortly after Francesco Bossi's visit in 1576.

46 Brandi, 2004, p. 11.

47 See Max Seidel, 'Ikonographie und Historiographie: 'Conversatio Angelorum in Silvis', Eremiten-Bilder von Simone Martini und Pietro Lorenzetti', *Städel-Jahrbuch*, 10 (1985), pp. 77–142 (126–29).

48 In this respect, see the discussion in Chapter 4. See also Archivio di Stato di Firenze (hereafter ASF), *Diplomatico* 45, Montalcino, Sant'Agostino, 14, 17, 19, 21, 22, 23, 24, 26.

49 ASF, *Diplomatico*, 45, Montalcino, Sant'Agostino, 13. See also ASS, *Conventi*, 1089, no. 953, for a further reference to Fra Ranaldo acting in that guise in January 1304/5.

50 See ASS *Estimo di Siena*, 109, new pagination fols 23r – 26v.

51 Ibid., *Conventi*, 1089, no. 1422.

52 Norman, *Siena and the Virgin*, pp. 133–34.

53 For a recent consideration of these frescoes see Norman, *Siena and the Virgin*, pp. 139–55.

54 Ibid., p. 139.

55 Ibid.

56 Gaudenz Freuler, *Bartolo di Fredi Cini: ein Beitrag zur sienesischen Malarei des 14. Jahrhunderts* (hereafter Freuler) (Disentis, c.1994), fig. 230, p. 251.

57 Norman, pp. 145–46. See also Daniela Gallavotti Cavallero, *Lo Spedale di Santa Maria della Scala in Siena: vicenda di una committenza artistica* (Pisa, 1985), p. 73.

58 In this context see Anabel Thomas, 'Dominican Marginalia: The Late Fifteenth-Century Printing Press of San Jacopo di Ripoli in Florence', in Stephen J. Milner (ed.), *At the Margins. Minority Groups in Premodern Italy*, Medieval Cultures, vol. 39 (Minneapolis and London, 2005), pp. 192–216 (201–5 and 215, note 53).

59 In this context, see Norman, p. 141 and 230, note 50.

60 In this context, see Samuel Y. Edgerton, Jr., *Pictures and Punishment. Art and Criminal Prosecution during the Florentine Renaissance* (Ithaca, New York, 1985) and Marcia Kupper, *The Art of Healing. Painting for the Sick and the Sinner in a*

Medieval Town (Philadelphia, 2003). For another recent consideration of the location of imagery and the relationship between this and surrounding space in the early modern period, see Anabel Thomas, *Art and Piety in the Female Religious Communities of Renaissance Italy. Iconography, Space and the Religious Woman's Perspective* (New York, 2003).

61 The most recent restoration of this fresco was undertaken in 2001 under the auspices of the Soprintendenza di Siena.

62 ASS, *Diplomatico in Caselle, casella* 900, 16 December 1348, *Archivio dello Spedale.*

63 Ibid., *Diplomatico Tolomei*, Registi del Mazzo numero 11 dal 1347 al 1349: no. 181.

64 This saint is not however included in any of George Kaftal's considerations of the iconography of the saints in Italian painting.

65 This image was first discussed by the author in a series of articles published in 2010 under the title 'La Festa della Madonna', in the *Gazzettino e Storie del Brunello e di Montalcino* (Anno 3, no. 38: pp. 16–17; no. 39: pp. 16–17 and no. 40: pp. 18–19).

66 Alessandro Bagnoli, 'Una visita al museo civico e diocesano d'arte sacra', in Roberto Guerrini (ed.), *Montalcino e il suo territorio* (Sovicelle, 1998), pp. 101–53 (118–19).

67 Alessandro Bagnoli, *Museo Civico e Diocesano d'Arte Sacra di Montalcino* (Siena, 1997) (hereafter *Museo Civico*), p. 16, nos 1–2 MC and p. 52, nos 6–8MD.

68 Ibid., p. 52, no. 1DP.

69 In this respect, see Raffaelli, *Prima dell'economia*, p. 26; Don Antonio Brandi, *La parrocchia di San Michele Arcangelo in Sant'Angelo in Colle*, typescript, 1972 (hereafter, Brandi, 1972), p. 14; and Ugo Ricci, *S. Angelo in Colle nella storia e nella vita del contesto Senese e Toscano*, typescript, 1985 (hereafter, Ricci, 1985), pp. 83–84

70 Ricci, 1985, p. 83.

71 Brandi, 1972, p. 14.

72 Brandi, 1991, p. 10.

73 Ricci, 1985, pp. 36 and 83–84. See also, Ugo Ricci, *S. Angelo in Colle nella Storia. Appendice*, 1989, p. 34 and Brandi, 1972, pp. 13 and 44. See Thomas, 'La Festa della Madonna', for evidence that this church was located on the north-eastern side of Sant'Angelo in Colle. According to the *Vecchio Catalogo* of the Soprintendenza per i beni storici artistici ed etnoantropologici per le province di Siena e Grosseto (Ufficio Catalago, schede: Sant'Angelo in Colle, under Montalcino, no. 2, Chiesa di S. Michele), the panel of the *Madonna and Child* had remained from its inception in the parish church of San Michele on the second altar on the right from the current entrance door. No documentary evidence is cited in support of this, although the *scheda* in question is dated 8 October, 1909, and information contained within it is said to have been drawn from a written record compiled by 'Signor Quirino Pagni di S. Angelo'.

74 Ricci, 1985, p. 50.

75 Ugo Ricci (Ricci, 1985, p. 70) for his part cites in this context the 1775 pastoral visit made by Bishop Giuseppe Bernardino Pecci.

76 Brandi, 2004, p. 18.

77 Ibid.

78   Ibid., p. 17.

79   Bagnoli, 'Una visita', p. 119, note 33.

80   Ricci, 1985, pp. 91–92. Ricci suggests that it was only a temporary removal in
     1877, and that the painting was once again displayed in the parish church in
     1885 on the specific occasion of the feast of the Immaculate Conception, and
     in thanksgiving for delivery from a plague of cholera. Ricci maintains that the
     painting was only permanently set up on display in San Michele in 1890.

81   Brandi, 2004, p. 50.

82   According to some sources the 'Madonna della Misericordia' was transferred
     to the church of the Madonna del Rosario in 1906. Others maintain that the
     painting was set in place on the high altar in 1908.

83   Cesare Brandi, *La Regia Pinacoteca di Siena* (Rome, 1933), pp. 163–64.

84   ASS, *Manoscritti*, D 67, *Memorie Storiche Politiche, Civili, e Naturali delle Città,
     Terre, e Castella, che sono, e sono state suddite alla Città di Siena. Raccolte dal Card.
     Gio(vanni) Antonio Pecci, Patrizio Sanese* (hereafter *Pecci*), fol. 86.

85   Ibid., fol. 87. According to Ugo Ricci (*Sant'Angelo in Colle nella Storia, Appendice*,
     typescript, 1989, p. 15), Pecci drew up this account of Sant'Angelo in Colle
     between 1759 and 1761.

86   Brandi, 2004, p. 12.

87   Ibid.

88   Brandi, 1991, p. 6.

89   Brandi, 2004, p. 12. Although Don Antonio Brandi transcribed this passage
     as – 'L'altare maggiore ha una icona assai antica con l'immagine di S. Michele
     Arcangelo dipinta sul muro' – thereby in effect conceding the existence of two
     images, he in fact maintained privately that there was only one image, a fresco
     on the back wall representing the titular saint.

90   AVM, *Sant'Angelo in Colle*, Prepositura, 131, second insert, fol. 186r.

91   Brandi, 1991, p. 6. This structure remained in place until the 1960s.

92   For the re-fashioning and re-assembling of older works of art, see Cathleen
     Hoeniger, *The Renovation of Paintings in Tuscany, 1250–1500*, (Cambridge
     (England), New York and Melbourne, 1995).

93   Pinacoteca Nazionale, Siena, inv. nos 322, 303 and 409. See, also Bagnoli, *Museo
     Civico*, pp. 36 and 54, nos 14 and 15 PN.

94   Brandi, 1991, p. 5.

95   Ibid.

96   It is also relevant in this context to recall the 'beautiful large altarpiece' that is
     said to have been displayed on the altar of the hospital chapel of Santa Maria
     della Croce in the fifteenth century.

97   Brandi, *Regia Pinacoteca*, pp. 163–64.

98   See Enzo Carli, *Montalcino. Museo civico. Museo diocesano d'arte sacra* (Bologna,
     1972), inventory nos. 90 and 314. See also Pietro Torriti, *La Pinacoteca Nazionale
     di Siena* (Genoa, 1977–8), *I dipinti dal 12 al 15 secolo*, p. 127, and more recently,
     Bagnoli, *Museo Civico*, p. 52, nos 12 and 13 PN.

99 According to Francesco Brogi (*Inventario generale degli oggetti d'arte della provincia di Siena* (Siena, 1897), pp. 163–64), the two panels (which he attributed to an unknown Sienese artist) were displayed inside San Michele as early as 1862.

100 Identified by Ugo Ricci as the probable original location of the two panels.

101 AVM, *Sant'Angelo in Colle,* Prepositura, 131 (first register), fols 1r–3r.

102 Ibid., fols 4r–4v.

103 ASS, *Manoscritti D 84, Visita fatta nell'Anno 1676 alle Città, Terre, Castella, dello Stato della Città di Siena dall'Ill(ustrissi)mo Sig(no)re Bartolomeo Gherardini, Auditore Generale in Siena per la A.S. di Cosimo III de' Medici Granduca VI di Toscana* (Eighteenth-century copy), fols 72–80 (77).

104 Don Antonio Brandi, *Notizie relative a Argiano–Poggio alle mura–S.Angelo in Colle tratte dalla 'Visita fatta nell'anno 1676 dall'Ill.mo Sig.re Bartolomeo Gherardini',* undated transcription in typescript (Sant'Angelo in Colle), p. 16.

105 AVM, *Sant'Angelo in Colle,* Prepositura, 131 (in the first register), fols 136r–138v.

106 Brandi, 1991, p. 6. According to Francesco Piccolomini, the hospital of Saint Anthony Abbot owned an altar inside the church of San Michele at the time of his pastoral visit in 1573. It seems likely therefore that the first altar on the left-hand side of the church closest to the entrance was the site that had been established in the name of the hospital of Sant'Antonio Abbate. It is, indeed, possible that this site had always been reserved for religious observations in respect of the village hospital. The knights of Saint Stephen assumed responsibility for the administration of the hospital of Sant'Antonio Abbate following the death of the last member of the Brogioni family – Urania – and the subsequent demise of her husband some time during the first half of the eighteenth century. It seems likely, therefore, that religious observance in respect of the hospital of Saint Anthony Abbot continued at the same altar.

107 AVM, *Sant'Angelo in Colle,* Prepositura, 131 (fol. 1 of first register – inventory dated 1672).

108 The presumed date rests on the fact that reference was made to a parish priest of the time, Vincenzo Vincenti, and the penultimate page contains the date 1530. For a list of parish priests at Sant'Angelo in Colle during the sixteenth century, see Brandi, 2004, pp. 23–25.

109 AVM, *Sant'Angelo in Colle,* Prepositura, 131, sheet dated 1743, fol. 130r.

110 *Pecci,* p. 87.

111 AVM, *Sant'Angelo in Colle,* Prepositura, 131, in a sheet inserted after the 1492 inventory.

112 Ricci, 1985, p. 68.

113 In this context, see Brandi, 1991, p. 10, concerning a pastoral visit made to the church of San Pietro in 1616. Noting the reference to an 'immagine assai decente' above the main altar, Don Brandi presumes that its iconography must have included the figure of Saint Peter.

114 See Torriti, *La Pinacoteca Nazionale di Siena* (Genoa, 1977–8), p. 156, figure 169.

115 Holes on the left-hand side of the same panel are less deep, indicating perhaps the fixing points of a surrounding frame.

116 For Bartolo di Fredi's activities in Montalcino, see Norman, pp. 157–81

(with cross references to Gaudenz Freuler). See also Emma Lucherini, 'La pala d'altare della Cappella del Parto della chiesa di Sant'Agostino fa parte di un'opera di Bartolo di Fredi conservata a Torrita', *Gazzettino e Storie del Brunello e di Montalcino*, Anno 2, 18 (2008), pp. 38–39 and 'Il ciclo con le storie di Sant'Agostino nella cappella del coro della chiesa omonima a Montalcino', *Gazzettino e Storie del Brunello e di Montalcino*, Anno 2, 16 (2008), pp. 36–38.

117   Freuler, p. 417, note 4.

118   Ibid., p. 421, note 36.

119   Hoeniger, *The Renovation of Paintings*.

120   I am grateful to Nicola McGregor, for her comments in respect of the condition of the panels of *Saint Peter* and *Saint Paul*.

121   There is, however, clear evidence of paint loss to the ears of *Saint Peter*. Moreover, the conjunction of limbs and treatment of drapery in both panels is awkward, suggesting at the very least a misunderstanding on the part of later restorers.

122   Norman, *Siena and the Virgin*, pp. 174–81 (with cross references to Gaudenz Freuler).

123   Bagnoli, *Museo Civico*, p. 32.

124   Freuler, p. 390, fig. 343 and catalogue no. 88.

125   Ibid., p. 12, fig. 10.

126   Ibid., p. 15, fig. 13.

127   Cesare Brandi, 'Reintegrazione di Bartolo di Fredi', *BSSP*, 10, fasc. 3 (1931), pp. 206–10 (209).

128   ASS, *Manoscritti*, B10, fol. 265r.

129   According to the 1320 *Tavola delle possessioni*, the church of San Pietro owned amongst other holdings, a number of pieces of land valued around 6–8 *lire*. One of these, a piece of worked land in the area known as Prioratti valued at 7 *lire* 12 *soldi* is described as bordered on one side by land belonging to 'Ser Guccii Ser Francisci'. The same individual is recorded as owning land bordering a number of other plots belonging to the church of San Pietro. It was perhaps this individual, therefore, who acquired the piece of land recorded in the 1322 document.

130   ASS, *Ospedale* 20, fol. 109.

131   Ibid., fols 47v, 98v and 142v.

132   Norman, *Siena and the Virgin*, p. 233, note 35; p. 234, note 81; p. 235, note 100 (with cross references to Gaudenz Freuler).

133   The two saints measure 40.5 cm x 68.5 cm. The 'Madonna della Misericordia' is both wider (62.5 cm) and taller (105 cm).

134   AVM, *Sant'Angelo in Colle*, Prepositura: 131, (inside a fascicolo headed 'Stato Oilliero Lordo della Cura di S. Angelo in Colle'), fol. 5r.

135   Ibid., no. 28.

136   Bagnoli, *Museo Civico*, p. 74, no. 16PN.

137   According to a record of July 1833, the chapel, also referred to on occasion as

the 'Oratorio della Madonna' was positioned in the north-western corner of what is now an external car park, see ACM, *Archivio Preunitario (1361–1865), Ingegnere del Circondario di Montalcino, Strade e fiumi*, 1690 (hereafter *Ingegnere del Circondario*), no. 173 – Pianta Geometrica dell'andamento della strada detta delle Fonte Lontana di S. Angelo in Colle, 24 July, 1833.

138   In this context, see Brandi, 1972, p. 16, and Brandi, 2004, p. 21)

139   Ibid.

140   Ibid.

141   Ibid.

142   Brandi, 1972, p. 16. According to one surviving record, the new mortuary chapel was only erected some time after 1792, see ACM, *Ingegnere del Circondario*, no. 39, 'Parere intorno allo scampionamento di diverse strade dell sud(ett)a comunità di Montalcino', n. 111. Apparently, the reason for not having erected such a structure prior to that date was because of the existence on the proposed site of 'una stanza ad uso di piccolo Oratorio denominato il casino della Bara' (a room used as a small oratory known as the 'small house of the bier') that belonged to the Compagnia della Misericordia. According to the 1792 record, the prevailing opinion was that the small oratory should be demolished, and that its stonework should be re-used for the construction of the mortuary chapel. It was suggested that the members of the Company of the Misericordia, for their part, should be offered some other place where they could store their belongings.

143   Brandi, 2004, p. 21.

Afterword

This book, which details the ways in which medieval Siena set about garrisoning its southern *contado* (and in particular Sant'Angelo in Colle, one of its frontier castles confronting Monte Amiata and overlooking the valley of the River Orcia), has been concerned with the period between 1287 and 1355. With hindsight, we can see that this was the period when Sant'Angelo in Colle achieved its greatest significance. This was in large part because in these years Sant'Angelo in Colle was an important base in Siena's attempt to encircle and take over Montalcino, one of the remaining rebellious communes blocking the way south. That path was cleared with the final subjugation of Montalcino in 1361, and its formal incorporation in the Sienese state. Paradoxically, that victory, in which Sant'Angelo in Colle played an important part, led to Sant'Angelo's own decline.

Unlike some studies that have tended to lionise Montalcino, this book has attempted to highlight the historical significance of Sant'Angelo in Colle under the Sienese Government of the Nine. The fact that a number of key documents concerning the internal affairs of Sant'Angelo in Colle and its relationship with Siena have survived intact reflects the importance of this southern frontier castle in the eyes of the central Sienese government and its representatives, as well as illustrating the extent to which the inhabitants of Sant'Angelo in Colle established relationships with key institutions inside the city of Siena itself. Records such as the sharecropping agreements and last wills and testaments subjected to particular scrutiny here also indicate that a number of residents in Sant'Angelo in Colle were of sufficient standing to have left written records of their property and dealings. The fact that such records have survived indicates further that the stipulations laid down by these individuals, whether concerning the working of the land, the tending of livestock, or the embellishment of the fabric, were considered of sufficient importance to preserve.

Many surveys of Siena's southern *contado* appear to prioritise early modern Montalcino over Sant'Angelo in Colle, apparently ignoring the key role assumed by that southern frontier post in ensnaring its larger neighbour within the Sienese net. That said, the relationship between the two centres in the early modern period was not as clear-cut as some have assumed. Evidence presented here suggests that the historical aggression and hostility existing between Sant'Angelo in Colle and Montalcino has been exaggerated. As discussion here has shown, and despite the fact that Sant'Angelo in Colle and Montalcino were on opposite sides prior to Montalcino's final submission to, and acceptance by the Sienese in 1361, numerous links continued to be forged between the two southern communes. Indeed, during Sant'Angelo in Colle's early years as a subject Sienese commune, it seems that the Sienese government was uneasy about the continuing friendship between Sant'Angelo in Colle and Montalcino.

With this in mind, this book commenced with an investigation of local issues: territorial boundaries; land ownership; the lay-out of the urban fabric; the early fourteenth-century population of Sant'Angelo in Colle, and the extent to which this southern frontier castle was infiltrated by Sienese citizens and individuals resident in nearby communes. Apart from bringing the medieval village back to life and casting a closer eye over its early relationship with Montalcino, an underlying intention was to illustrate how such factors as professional status, the possession of property (and in particular, land) and the individual's standing in local society influenced patterns of lay piety and patronage in fourteenth-century Sant'Angelo in Colle.

As this study has shown, ownership of land could be of prime importance in establishing whether or not a particular individual could lay his or her mark on the affairs of central government, as well as on their own local environment. Endowment of land funded the administration and functioning of local and distant institutions. At the same time it imbued individual testators and their families with increased social standing and spiritual grace through the erection of chapels, the embellishment of the urban fabric, and personalised celebration of masses in their name. This in turn contributed to the testator's enduring memory and significance.

That said, the documents considered here provide a wider vista of the medieval landscape and life and work in the Val d'Orcia under the Government of the Nine. Apart from detailed information concerning ownership of land and houses and individual patrimonies, records such as the 1320 *Tavola delle possessioni* and the '1318 Boundary Document' illustrate how the land itself was intersected and marked out by oak trees, olive groves, wild pears, springs of water and internal tracks of communication. A more detailed reading of both, as well as consideration of other records such as those dealing with sharecropping and the pasturing of sheep and goats, reveals how the partitioning of land depended as much upon the personal circumstances of individual families (local residents of Sant'Angelo in Colle) as on the political machinations of the reigning authority (the Sienese government).

Given that, both the *Estimo del Contado* (and more specifically the individual entries in the 1320 *Tavola delle possessioni* for Sant'Angelo in Colle) and the *Estimo di Siena* indicate that there was a deliberate attempt to colonise Siena's southern *contado* through the purchase of land and accommodation in and around subject communes. Moreover, as this study has shown, such colonisation frequently impacted strongly on the everyday life of Siena's subject 'citizens'. Even without contracts for sharecropping and systems of letting property inside and outside the walls of Sant'Angelo in Colle, the simple clustering together by Sienese outsiders on the land, and the physical impact of property acquired by them inside the walls in close proximity to the Sienese barracks must have left the villagers in no doubt as to who were their masters. Individual bodies such as the Sienese hospital of Santa Maria della Scala and the order of Augustinian Hermits appear to have compounded that message.

Nevertheless, despite the imposition of the Sienese military, infiltration by Sienese citizens and Sienese influence in the fortification of the village and the construction of individual buildings such as the Sienese barracks, it seems that the fourteenth-century residents of Sant'Angelo in Colle maintained a strong sense of their own identity and ancient connections. In many ways this is not surprising. As discussion here has shown, the Sienese military presence in Sant'Angelo in Colle was at times patchy. It also seems that a comparatively small number of institutions and individuals were co-opted to maintain order and ensure that the residents of the southern frontier castle toed the line. While no firm evidence has emerged to show that the Augustinian Hermits contributed to such overseeing, their presence is clearly indicated in the surviving frescoes of the parish church, as well as in official tax records of the early fourteenth century. There seems little doubt, either, that officials of the hospital of Santa Maria della Scala played a significant role in the affairs of Sant'Angelo in Colle, not only during the period of the Government of the Nine, but also throughout the second half of the fourteenth century.

It also seems clear that individual Sienese residents such as Neri di Guicciardo had their fingers firmly placed on the pulse of local affairs, through their ownership of property and land. At least one of the village notaries recorded in Sant'Angelo in Colle during the first half of the fourteenth century – Giovanni di Paganello – may also have had close family links with Siena, despite being recorded as a resident of the village in the 1330s. Other officials, including the village treasurer Bindo di Accorso, although linked to Siena, were firmly rooted in the village through family connections. When it came down to the practice of daily life, it seems that age-old family connections and links established through the working of the land prevailed, even in the face of domination by the Sienese.

As the fortunes of Montalcino rose, so those of Sant'Angelo in Colle seem, by contrast, to have waned. Seven years after the drawing up of Ser Longo di Ser Guccio's will the Government of the Nine fell, and was replaced by the Government of the Twelve.[1] At about the same time, it seems as if the hospital of Santa Maria della Scala was set to leave Sant'Angelo in Colle, since in 1354 the decision was taken to let out the 'grancia' owned by them to a private citizen.[2] The fact that this was a short-term let of 12 months indicates, however, that such a move may have amounted to a temporary money-saving measure, rather than a long-term cessation of interest in Sant'Angelo in Colle. In any event, the decision by the Sienese government to abandon the barracks at Sant'Angelo during the mid 1370s seems to have had the effect of injecting new life into Santa Maria della Scala's own business in the area. For nearly three decades at the end of the fourteenth century, the affairs of the Siense hospital must have had a considerable impact on everyday life in Sant'Angelo in Colle. Not only must Santa Maria della Scala have advertised its power through the fortification and restoration of the old 'cassero' previously occupied by the Sienese military; but the affairs of the grange itself must have increased overall revenue in the neighbourhood, not least through the purchase of live stock and the sale of produce from the land.

There must have been a considerable change of impetus when the administrative headquarters of the hospital were transferred to Piana in 1400, and the grange was once more let out, this time for a period of seven years.[3] The fortified 'grancia' seems already to have deteriorated by the last quarter of the fifteenth century, since on 2 March 1485/6 permission was sought to rebuild the roof.[4] It seems that the 'palazzo overo cassaro', or palace-cum-barracks, which had once belonged to the 'Signore che anticamente era del d(e)c(t)o castello' (the lord who was once associated with the village), had been roofless for a considerable period of time – 'gia sono longissimi tempi'.[5] The petition confirmed, however, that at least some of Sant'Angelo in Colle's records (possibly including copies of its old statutes) were still in existence at the end of the fifteenth century, since reference was made to the commune's 'books', in the context of their recording the length of time that Sant'Angelo in Colle had been under the authority of Siena.

Even then, the villagers' staunch sense of independence and local pride prevailed. It seems that in March 1485/6 word was circulating that the old palace was to be sold. Evidently, the people of Sant'Angelo in Colle were anxious that this should not happen. They asked not only that the roof should be repaired, but also that neither the building itself, nor its 'piazze, confini et pertinentie' should be consigned to a third party without consultation. Here, then, is confirmation that the fortified 'grancia' of Santa Maria della Scala at Sant'Angelo in Colle (even if not the pre-existing Sienese barracks) was a complex of some size. Reference to its surrounding squares and associated structures can leave us in no doubt that the grange must originally have covered a considerable area of ground inside the medieval urban fabric. Here, also, is evidence that the hospital complex survived more or less intact, albeit without a roof, until at least the end of the fifteenth century.[6] By the middle of the following century, however, the village was deemed unfit for occupation or defence in the face of threat from Florence. When Bartolomeo Gherardini visited Sant'Angelo in Colle in 1676, the hospital complex was apparently no longer standing, and only 124 people were recorded as living inside the old centre. Of the some 100 or so *fuochi* declared in 1320, only 34 households remained. In the 300 years following the fall of the Government of the Nine, the population of the village had dwindled to less than a tenth of its earlier size. Despite this, at least one circuit of walls – traditionally symbols of inviolability – was still intact.[7]

Nevertheless, by the eighteenth century, when Cardinal Antonio Pecci drew up his survey of the cities, territories and castles belonging to Siena, the walls of Sant'Angelo in Colle were described as in large part 'razed to the ground'.[8] Pecci also reported that most of the buildings in the village were in ruins, adding that little remained above ground of the crumbled tower that, being constructed with 'grosse pietre concie' (great hewn stones), revealed the antiquity of the village. Pecci noted in addition that the sites of two gates were still evident, although one gate was completely destroyed, and the other was about to collapse.

Such a perspective implies that Sant'Angelo in Colle had reached a low point some time between the seventeenth and the eighteenth century. From that nadir, however, the village has subsequently regained some of its size and much of its prosperity. While pigs, sheep, cows and goats no longer form part of the larger picture, though they did well into the twentieth century, the local wine and oil is regarded by discerning gourmets as the best in Tuscany, if not beyond. Much of this renaissance is due to Sant'Angelo in Colle's participation in the development in the nineteenth century and subsequently of Brunello wine centred on Montalcino, politically its adversary in the medieval period, though in reality closely linked through family and other connections.

The title of a recent book, *Prima del Brunello: Montalcino Capitale Mancata*,[9] confirms the present significance of Montalcino's prime local product whilst at the same time encouraging speculation about Montalcino's earlier history. In the introduction Mario Ascheri argues that the present status or condition of any place is inevitably linked to its past. In the preface to the same book, Maurizio Buffi (the presiding mayor of Montalcino) suggests that the loss of memory or the absence of knowledge of the roots of any society inevitably results in a loss of understanding about its inherent or present identity. This much must surely be true also for the village of Sant'Angelo in Colle, ex-frontier castle under the Sienese Government of the Nine.

What Sant'Angelo in Colle was under the Government of the Nine during those seven or so decades between the end of the thirteenth and middle of the fourteenth century, how its residents responded in the light of a local Sienese military presence, and how the people, institutions and politics of other centres combined to influence the evolving urban fabric and the social welfare of the medieval village forms an intrinsic part of what we now see. Shorn of even this short period of its history, Sant'Angelo in Colle inevitably seems a lesser place. We are by nature inclined to assume that the landscape we inhabit remains unchanged, regardless of human intervention. We are as a result prone to underestimate the complexities of developments wrought over time and the significance of this in the context of our daily existence. An appreciation of the past, and an understanding of the ways in which past events affected Sant'Angelo in Colle, not only illuminates but also enriches the present: in other words, such an appreciation must be tantamount to ageing well.

Notes

1 For a recent consideration of the political and administrative changes in the wake of the fall of the Government of the Nine, see Mario Ascheri, *Lo spazio storico di Siena* (Milan, 2001), pp. 160–61.

2 This structure was presumably the comparatively modest building inside the walls of Sant'Angelo in Colle owned by the hospital prior to taking over and developing the site of the old Sienese barracks.

3 The contract, which was drawn up in 1403 between the hospital and the Sienese citizen Goro di Goro Sansedoni, stipulated a period of seven years with an annual salary of 90 florins; see Stephan R. Epstein, *Alle origini della fattoria toscana. L'ospedale della Scala di Siena e le sue terre (metà '200–metà '400)* (Florence, 1986), pp. 283–85.

4 Vincenzo Passeri, *Documenti per la Storia delle Località della Provincia di Siena* (Siena, Edizioni Cantagalli, 2002), p. 308.

5 Archivio di Stato di Siena (hereafter ASS), *Consiglio Generale*, 240, fol. 81r.

6 ASS, *Manoscritti D 84, Visita fatta nell'Anno 1676 alle Città, Terre, Castella, dello Stato della Città di Siena dall'Ill(ustrissi)mo Sig(no)re Bartolomeo Gherardini, Auditore Generale in Siena per la A.S. di Cosimo III de' Medici Granduca VI di Toscana* (Eighteenth-century copy): fols 72–80.

7 Ibid., fol. 72.

8 Biblioteca Comunale degli Intronati, Siena, *Manoscritti B.IV.8*, vol. 1, fol. 41r and ASS, *Manoscritti D 68, Memorie storiche, politiche, civili e naturali delle città, terre e castella che sono e sono state suddite della città di Siena, raccolte dal cavaliere Giovanni Antonio Pecci, patrizio sanese.*

9 Mario Ascheri and Vinicio Serino (eds), *Prima del Brunello: Montalcino Capitale Mancata* (San Quirico d'Orcia, 2007).

Bibliography

Abbreviations

BSSP – *Bullettino senese di storia e patria*

Cited manuscript sources

Florence
Archivio di Stato di Firenze
Diplomatico 45, Montalcino: S. Agostino

Montalcino
Archivio Comunale
Archivio Preunitario (1361–1865)
    Fondi diversi, Archivi di Particolari, Ser Griffo di ser Paolo
    Fondi aggregati, Convento di San Francesco
    Circondario dell' Ingegnere
Ospedale di Santa Maria della Croce
Archivio Vescovile
Visite Pastorali
Sant'Angelo in Colle, Prepositura

Pietrasanta
Archivio Storico Comunale
Campione delle Strade

Siena

Archivio di Stato

Balia

Biccherna

Consiglio Generale

Curia del Placito

Diplomatico in caselle

    Abbadia di San Salvatore

    Bichi Borghese

    Cons. Del Refugio

    Montalcino

    R. Acquisto Bandini Piccolomini

    Tolomei

Dogana

Estimo di città

Manoscritti

Ospedale Monna Agnese

Ospedale Santa Maria della Scala

Tavola delle possessioni del contado, l'Estimo

Biblioteca degli Intronati

Manoscritti

Seminario Arcivescovile, Montearioso

Pergamene del Convento di S. Francesco di Montalcino

PRINTED PRIMARY SOURCES

Montalcino

L'archivio Comunale di Montalcino, Paola Giovanna Morelli, Stefano Moscadelli and Chiara Santini (eds), 2 vols, Amministrazione Provinciale di Siena (Siena, 1989–1990).

Canali, Tullio, *Notizie Istoriche della Città di Montalcino in Toscana*, eighteenth-century copy transcribed by Don Antonio Brandi from the original manuscript in the Biblioteca Comunale, Montalcino, (typescript, 1966).

Libro di memorie dell'origine delli spedali di Montalcino in Toscana (1748), transcribed by Don Antonio Brandi as *Notizie in iscorcio dello Spedale di Mont'Alcino* (typescript, 1990).

Pecci, Giovanni Antonio, *Memorie storico-critiche della città di Siena*, facsimile reproduction, Mario Pavolini and Ennio Innocenti (eds), (Siena, Cantagalli, 1988).

Notizie storiche della città di Montalcino, with preface by Giuliano Catoni (Montalcino, ARCI, Sinalunga, Arti Grafiche Viti Riccucci S.r.l, 1989).

Siena

Archivio della Biccherna del Comune di Siena, Inventario, Ministero dell'Interno, Pubblicazioni degli archivi di stato, 37 (Rome, Siena, Tip. Ex Cooperativa, 1953).

Le Biccherne. Tavole Dipinte delle Magistrature Senesi (secoli 13–18), Ministero per i beni culturali e ambientali, Ufficio centrale per i beni archivistici, (eds), Luigi Borgia, Enzo Carli, Maria Assunta Ceppari, Ubaldo Morandi, Patrizia Sinibaldi, Carla Zarrilli (Rome, Felice le Monnier di Firenze, 1984).

Archivio dell'Ospedale di Santa Maria della Scala: Inventario, Giuliana Cantucci, Ubaldo Morandi and Sandro De'Colli (eds), (2 vols, Rome, Pubblicazioni degli archivi di Stato, 1960–62).

Il Caleffo Vecchio del Comune di Siena, Giovanni Cecchini (ed.), (vols 1–2, Florence, Leo S. Olschki, 1932 and 1934).

Il Caleffo Vecchio del Comune di Siena, Giovanni Cecchini (ed.), (vol. 3, Siena, Accademia per le Arti e per le Lettere, 1940).

Il Caleffo Vecchio del Comune di Siena, Mario Ascheri, Alessandra Forzini, Chiara Santini (eds), (vol. 4, Siena, Accademia senese degli Intronati, 1984).

Il Caleffo Vecchio del Comune di Siena, Paolo Cammarosano and Mario Ascheri (eds), (vol. 5, Siena, Accademia senese degli Intronati, 1991).

Inventario dei manoscritti della Biblioteca comunale degli Intronati di Siena, Gino Garosi (ed.), (Siena, Ciaccheri, 2002).

Gherardini, Bartolomeo, *Visita fatta nell'Anno 1676 alle Città, Terre, Castella dello stato della città di Siena dall'Ill. Monsignore B. Gherardini, Auditore Generale in Siena per la A.S. di Cosimo III de' Medici Granduca VI di Toscana*, ASS, Manoscritti D 84 [Eighteenth-century copy].

Pecci, Giovanni Antonio, *Memorie storiche politiche, civili, e naturali delle città, terre, e castella, che sono, e sono state suddite della città di Siena. Raccolte dal Cavaliere Gio(vanni) Antonio Pecci, Patrizio Sanese*, ASS, Manoscritti, D 67.

Il proemio dello statuto comunale del 'Buon Governo' (1337–39), Mario Ascheri and Rodolfo Funari (eds), BSSP, 96 (1989), pp. 350–64.

GENERAL

'Agnolo di Tura del Grasso, *Cronaca Senese*', in Alessandro Lisini and Fabio Iacometti (eds), *Cronache senesi*, Rerum Italicarum Scriptores, 15, part 6 (Bologna, Zanichelli, 1931–1939), pp. 255–564.

SECONDARY SOURCES

Ago, Renata and Angela Groppi, 'Il lavoro delle donne', in Angela Groppi (ed.), *Il lavoro delle donne* (Rome, Laterza, 1996), pp. 143–54.

Angelucci, Patrizia, 'Genesi di un borgo franco nel Senese: Paganico', in I. Deug Su and Ernesto Menestò (eds), *Università e tutela dei beni culturali: il contributo degli studi medievali e umanistici*, Atti del convegno promosso dalla facoltà di Magistero in Arezzo dell'Università di Siena, Arezzo and Siena, 21–23 gennaio 1977 (Florence, La nuova Italia, 1981), pp. 95–140.

Ascheri, Mario, 'Le "bocche" di conventi e ospedali di Siena e del suo Stato nel 1360', *BSSP*, 92 (1985), pp. 323–33.

—, 'Storia dell'ospedale e-o Storia della città', in *Spedale di Santa Maria della Scala*, Atti del Convegno Internazionale di Studi, Siena, 20–22 novembre 1986 (Siena, Pistolesi, 1988), pp. 65–71.

—, 'Siena sotto i "Nove" in un libro di W.M.Bowsky', *Nuovi studi cateriniani*, 3 (1988), pp. 126–32.

—, 'Per la storia del Territorio: un itinerario dai comuni al comune', in Carlo Avetta (ed.), *'Tintinnano'. La Rocca e il territorio di Castiglione d'Orcia* (San Quirico d'Orcia, Editoriale DonChischiotte, 1988), pp. 73–85.

—, 'Siena in the Fourteenth century: State, Territory and Culture', in Thomas W. Blomquist and Maureen F. Mazzaoui (eds), *The 'other Tuscany': essays in the history of Lucca, Pisa, and Siena during the thirteenth, fourteenth and fifteenth centuries*, (Kalamazoo (Mich.), Western Michigan University, 1994), pp. 163–97.

—, 'Un contratto per Siena: la mezzadria poderale', in Lucia Bonelli Conenna and Ettore Pacini (eds), *Vita in villa nel senese: dimore, giardini e fattoria*, (Siena, Monte dei paschi di Siena, c.2000), pp. 403–36.

—, *Lo spazio storico di Siena*, Fondazione Monte dei paschi di Siena (Milan, Arti Grafiche Amilcare Pizzi, Silvana Editoriale, 2001).

—, 'La Siena del 'Buon Governo' (1287–1355)', in Simonetta Adorni Braccesi and Mario Ascheri (eds), *Politica e cultura nelle repubbliche italiane dal medioevo all'età moderna*, Atti del convegno, Siena, 1997 (Rome, Istituto storico italiano per l'Età moderna e contemporonea 43–44, 2001), pp. 81–107.

—, Siena e la Città -Stato del Medioevo Italiano (Siena, Bettieditrice, 2003).

—, 'Montalcino nella storia; alle sorgenti del Brunello', in Mario Ascheri and Vinicio Serino (eds), *Prima del Brunello, Montalcino Capitale Mancata*, Documenti di Storia, 75, Collana a cura di Mario Ascheri, under the sponsorship of the Lions Club – Montalcino Valli d'Arbia d'Orcia, Distretto 108 La Toscana, (San Quirico d'Orcia, Editrice DonChisciotte, 2007), pp. 13–42.

—, (ed.), with Donatella Ciampoli, *Siena e il suo territorio nel Rinascimento* (Siena, Il Leccio, 1986).

—, (ed.), with Simonetta Adorni Braccesi, *Politica e cultura nelle repubbliche italiane dal medioevo all'età moderna*, Atti del convegno, Siena, 1997 (Rome, Istituto storico italiano per l'Età moderna e contemporanea 43–44, 2001).

—, (ed.), with Patrizia Turrini, *Dalla Domus Misericordiae all'Arciconfraternità di Misericordia*, Arciconfraternità di Misericordia di Siena (Siena, Protagon Editori Toscani, 2004).

—, (ed.), with Vinicio Serino, *Prima del Brunello, Montalcino Capitale Mancata*, Documenti di Storia, 75, Collana a cura di Mario Ascheri, under the sponsorship of the Lions Club – Montalcino, Valli d'Arbia e d'Orcia, Distretto 108 La Toscana (San Quirico d'Orcia, Editrice DonChisciotte, 2007).

Avetta, Carlo (ed.), *'Tintinnano'. La Rocca e il territorio di Castiglione d'Orcia* (San Quirico d'Orcia, Editoriale DonChischiotto, 1988).

Bacci, Peleo, *Dipinti inediti e sconosciuti di Pietro Lorenzetti, Bernardo Daddi ecc.in Siena e nel contado con documenti, commenti critici e 70 illustrazioni* (Siena, Accademia per le arti e per le lettere, 1939).

Bacciarelli, Vincenzo, 'Castellum de Montelatroni cum omnibus aecclesiis et capellis, muris et fossis atque munitionibus' and Michele Nucciotti, 'Insediarsi "all"estero'. L'edificazione del cassero senese di Montelaterone (1262–1266) e la prima politica amiatina del comune di Siena', in Vincenzo Bacciarelli and Paolo Pacchiani (eds), *Montelaterone: Storie, religione ed arte di un'antica cella del Montamiata* (Rome, Nuova Grafica, 2006).

—, (ed.), with Paolo Pacchiani, *Montelaterone: Storie, religione ed arte di un'antica cella del Montamiata* (Rome, Nuova Grafica, 2006).

Bagnoli, Alessandro, *Museo Civico e Diocesano d'Arte Sacra di Montalcino* (Siena, Edizioni Cantagalli, 1997).

—, 'Una visita al museo civico e diocesano d'arte sacra', in Roberto Guerrini (ed.), *Montalcino e il suo territorio* (Siena, Banca di Credito Cooperativo di Sovicille, 1998), pp. 101–53.

Bagnoli, Alessandro, Roberto Bartalini, Luciano Bellosi and Michel Laclotte (eds), *Duccio Alle origini della pittura senese* (Milan, Silvana Editoriale, 2003).

Balbi di Caro, Silvana, and Gabriella Angeli Bufalini, 'Uomini e Monete in terra di Siena', in Silvana Balbi di Caro and Gabriella Angeli Bufalini, *La Collezione Numismatica della Banca Monte dei Paschi di Siena* (Pisa, Pacini Editore S.p.A., 2001).

Balestracci, Duccio, 'Approvvigionamento e distribuzione dei prodotti alimentari a Siena nell'epoca comunale. Mulini, mercati e botteghe', *Archaeologio medievale*, 8 (1981), pp. 127–54.

—, *La zappa e la retorica. Memorie familiari di un contadino toscano del Quattrocento* (Florence, Salimbeni, 1984).

—, *I bottini acquedotti medievali Senesi* (Siena, Logge della Mercanzia, 1984).

—, 'Per una storia degli ospedali di contado nella Toscana fra 14 e 16 secolo. Strutture, arredi personale, assistenza', in Giuliano Pinto (ed.), *La società del bisogno. Povertà e assistenza nella Toscana medievale* (Florence, Salimbeni, 1989), pp. 37–59.

—, 'Firenze e Siena. Lotta per il potere nella Toscana del Duecento. Alle origini di una battaglia inutile', in *Il Chianti e la battaglia di Montaperti* (Poggibonsi, Centro di studi storici chiantigiani, 1992), pp. 7–19.

—, 'From Development to Crisis: changing urban structures in Siena between the Thirteenth and Fifteenth centuries', in Thomas W. Blomquist and Maureen F. Mazzaoui (eds), *The 'other Tuscany': essays in the history of Lucca, Pisa, and Siena during the thirteenth, fourteenth and fifteenth centuries* (Kalamazoo (Mich.), Western Michigan University, 1994), pp. 199–213.

—, (with Gabriella Piccinni), *Siena nel Trecento. Assetto urbano e strutture edilizie* (Firenze, Clusf, 1977).

—, 'L'Invenzione dell'ospedale: assistenza e assistiti nel Medioevo', in *Il Bene e il Bello. I luoghi della cura. Cinquemila anni di storia* (Milan, Electa, 2000), pp. 49–60.

—, (with Laura Vigni and Armando Costantini), *La memoria dell'acqua: I bottoni di Siena* (Siena, Protogon, 2006).

—, (ed.), *Alla ricerca di Montaperti: mito, fonti documentarie e storiografie*, Convegno, Accademia dei Rozzi, Siena 30 Novembre 2007 (Siena, Betti, 2009).

Banchi, Luciano, 'La Lira, la Tavola delle possessioni e la Preste nella Repubblica di Siena', *Archivio Storico Italiano*, ser 3, 7, part 2 (1868), pp. 53–88.

—, 'Gli ordinamenti economici dei comuni toscani nel medioevo e segnatamente del Comune di Siena, I: La Lira o l'Estimo', *Atti della R. Accademia dei Fisiocritici di Siena*, ser 3a, 2 (1879), pp. 9–80.

Banti, Ottavio, and Virgili, Enzo, 'Aspetti della vita di un comune rurale all'inizio del Trecento. Note in margine agli atti del Comune di Treggiaia (Pisa)', *Bollettino Storico Pisano*, 55 (1986), pp. 171–200.

Bargagli Petrucci, Fabio, *Le Fonti di Siena e i loro acquedotti: note storiche dalle origini fino al 1555* (Siena, Lazzeri, 1903 and Florence, Olschki, 1906) (reprint, Siena, Periccioli, c.1992).

—, *Pienza, Montalcino e la Val d'Orcia senese* (Bergamo, Istituto italiano d'arti grafiche, 1911) (reprint, San Quirico d'Orcia, DonChisciotte, 2002).

—, *Montepulciano, Chiusi e la Val di Chiana senese* (Bergamo, Istituto italiano d'arti grafiche, 1932).

Barlucchi, Andrea, *Il 'Contado' Senese all'epoca dei Nove'. Asciano e il suo territorio tra Due e Trecento* (Florence, Olschki, 1997).

Barsanti, Danilo, *Allevamento e transumanza in Toscana. Pastori, bestiami e pascoli nei secoli 15–19* (Florence, Medicea, 1987).

Bartolini, Giuseppe, Riccardo Francovich, Carlo Tronti and Marco Valenti (eds), *Sistema dei castelli e delle fortificazioni in terra di Siena* (Siena, Monte dei Paschi, 2005).

Baxandall, Michael, 'Art, Society and the Bouguer Principle', *Representations*, 12 (1985), pp. 32–43.

Belli, Maddalena, *La cucina di un ospedale del Trecento: gli spazi, gli oggetti, il cibo nel Santa Maria della Scala di Siena* (Pisa, Pacini, 2004).

Bellosi, Luciano, 'Per l'attività giovanile di Bartolo di Fredi', *Antichità Viva*, 24 (1985), pp. 21–26.

Bellucci, Gualtiero and Piero Torriti, *Il Santa Maria della Scala in Siena: l'ospedale dei mille anni, xenodochium Sancte Marie* (Genoa, SAGEP, 1991).

Bezzini, Mario, *Strada Francigena-romea, con particolare riferimento ai percorsi Siena-Roma* (Siena, Il leccio, c.1996).

Biasutti, Silvana (ed.), Don Antonio Brandi, *Il senso della memoria: ricerche sulla storia di Sant'Angelo in Colle* (Vicenza, Tecnograficarossi Sandrigo, 2010).

Blomquist, Thomas W., (ed.), with Maureen F. Mazzaoui, *The 'other Tuscany': essays in the history of Lucca, Pisa, and Siena during the thirteenth, fourteenth and fifteenth centuries* (Kalamazoo (Mich.), Western Michigan university, 1994).

Bonelli, Lucia (ed.), *Vita in villa nel senesee: dimore, giardini e fattorie* (Siena, Monte dei Paschi di Siena, *c.* 2000).

Bonucci, Bruno, *Dalla Val di Starcia si vede Montaperti'* (Siena, Edizioni di Sant'Antimo, 1998).

—, *Montalcino Pietre e storia* (San Quirico d'Orcia, Editore DonChisciotte, 1999).

Bowsky, William M., 'The Buon Governo of Siena (1287–1355): A Medieval Italian Oligarchy', *Speculum*, 37 (1962), pp. 368–81.

—, 'Medieval Citizenship: The Individual and the State in the Commune of Siena, 1287–1355', *Studies in Medieval and Renaissance History*, 4 (1967), pp. 193–243.

—, 'City and Contado: Military Relationships and Communal Bonds in Fourteenth-century Siena', in Anthony Molho and John A. Tedeschi (eds), *Renaissance studies in Honor of Hans Baron* (Florence, Sansoni, 1971), pp. 75–98.

—, *Le finanze del Comune di Siena 1287–1355* (Florence, La Nuova Italia Editrice, 1976), originally published as *The Finance of the Commune of Siena* (Oxford, Clarendon Press, 1970).

—, *A Medieval Italian Commune: Siena under the Nine, 1287–1355* (Berkeley, Los Angeles and London, University of California Press, 1981). Italian translation, *Un comune italiano nel Medioevo. Siena sotto il regime dei Nove (1287– 1355)* (Bologna, Il Mulino, 1986).

Brandi, Don Antonio, *Chiesa e Convento di S. Francesco in Montalcino* (typescript, Montalcino, 1967).

—, *Le pergamene del Seminario Vescovile di Montalcino* (typescript, Montalcino, 1970).

—, *Parrocchia di S. Michele Arcangelo in S. Angelo in Colle* (typescript, Sant'Angelo in Colle, 1972):

—, *Parrocchia di S. Michele Arcangelo in S. Angelo in Colle* (typescript, Sant'Angelo in Colle, 1991).

—, *L'Ospedale di S. Maria della Croce nel 1483. Nomina del Rettore e Inventario di Tutti i Beni mobili di Proprietà dell'ospedale* (typescript Montalcino, 1996).

—, *Parrocchia di S. Michele Arcangelo in S. Angelo in Colle* (typescript, Sant'Angelo in Colle, 2004).

—, *Notizie relative a Argiano – Poggio alle Mura – S. Angelo in Colle Tratte dalla 'Visita fatta nell'anno 1676 dall'Ill.mo Sig.re Bartolomeo Gherardini'*, undated transcription in typescript (Sant'Angelo in Colle).

Brandi, Cesare, *La Regia Pinacoteca di Siena* (Rome, Libreria dello Stato, 1933).

Brogi, Francesco, *Inventario generale degli oggetti d'arte della provincia di Siena* (Siena, Nava, 1897).

Brogiolo, Gian Pietro (ed.), *Città, castelli, campagne nei territori di frontiera, secoli 6–7,* Atti del 5 seminario sul tardoantico e l'altomedievale in Italia centrosettentrionale: Monte Barro, Galbiate (Leccio), 9–10 giugno 1994 (Mantua, SAP, *c.* 1995).

Brunetti, Lucia, 'L'Ospedale dei SS Gregorio e Niccolò in Sasso di Siena detto di Monna Agnese 1275–1446: Nascita, consolidamento e organizzazione di un'ospedale femminile per poveri, infermi e partorienti', Tesi di laurea, Università degli Studi di Siena, Facoltà di Lettere e Filosofia, Corso di laurea in storia e diritto medievale, relatore Prof.ssa Gabriella Piccinni, controrelatore Dott. Michele Pellegrini, Anno Accademico 2001–2002.

—, 'L'Ospedale di monna Agnese di Siena e la sua Filiazione Romana', *Archivio della Società romana di storia patria*, 126 (2003), pp. 37–67.

—, *Agnese e il suo ospedale, Siena, secc. 13–15* (Pisa, Pacini, 2005).

Calabresi, Ilio, 'La legislazione più antica del Comune di Montepulciano. Le quattro riforme dello statuto comunale del 1337: contenuto e valore storico', in Ilio Calabresi (ed.), *Montepulciano nel Trecento. Contributi per la storia giuridica e istituzionale. Edizione delle quattro riforme maggiori (1340 circa-1374) dello statuto del 1337*, (Siena, Consorzio universitario della Toscana meridionale, 1987), pp. 1–160.

Cammarosano, Paolo, Review of William M. Bowsky, *The Financing of the Commune of Siena: 1287–1355*, Oxford, 1970, *Studi Medievali*, ser. 3a, 12 (1971), pp. 301–22.

—, 'Le campagne senesi dalla fine del secolo 12 agli inizi del Trecento: dinamica interna e forme del dominio cittadino', in Giovanni Cherubini, Tommaso Detti, Mario Mirri, Giorgio Mori and Simonetta Soldani (eds), *Contadini e proprietari nella Toscana moderna*, Atti del Convegno di studi in onore di Giorgio Giorgetti, 1979 (2 vols, Florence, Olschki, 1979), 1, *Dal Medioevo all'età moderno*, pp. 152–222.

—, 'Aspetti delle strutture familiari nelle città dell' Italia comunale. Secoli 12–14', in Georges Duby and Jacques Le Goff (eds), *Famiglia e parentela nell' Italia medievale* (Bologna, Il Mulino, 1981), pp. 109–23.

—, *Monteriggione. Storia, architettura, paesaggio* (Milan, Electa, 1983).

—, *Italia medioevale: struttura e geografia delle fonti scritte* (Rome, La Nuova Italia Scientifica, 1991).

—, 'Il comune di Siena dalla solidarietà imperiale al guelfismo: celebrazione e propaganda', in Paolo Cammarosano (ed.), *Le forme della propaganda politica nel Due e nel Trecento*: relazioni tenute al Convegno internazionale organizzato dal Comitato di studi storici di Trieste, dall' École française de Rome e dal Dipartimento di storia dell' Università degli studi di Trieste, Trieste, 2–5 marzo 1993 (Rome, École française de Rome, 1994), pp. 455–67.

—, (with Vincenzo Passeri), *Repertorio dei toponomi della provincia di Siena, desunti dalla cartografia dell'Istituto Geografico Militare* (Siena, 1983).

—, (with Vincenzo Passeri), *I castelli del Senese. Strutture fortificate dell'area senese-grossetana* (Siena, Nuova immagine, 2006).

—, (ed.), with Riccardo Francovich, Vincenzo Passeri, Carlo Perogalli, Gabriella Piccinni and Giulio Vismara, *I Castelli del Senese, Strutture fortificate dell'area Senese-grossetana* (2 vols, Siena, Monte dei Paschi di Siena, 1976). New publication in one volume (Milan and Siena, Electa, 1985).

—, (ed.), with Vincenzo Passeri, *Città, borghi e castelli dell' area senese- grossetana: repertorio delle strutture fortificate dal medioevo alla caduta della Repubblica senese* (Siena, Amministrazione provinciale di Siena, 1984).

—, (ed.), *Le forme della propaganda politica nel Due e nel Trecento*: relazioni tenute al Convegno internazionale organizzato dal Comitato di studi storici di Trieste, dall' École française de Rome e dal Dipartimento di storia dell' Università degli studi di Trieste, Trieste, 2–5 marzo 1993 (Rome, École française de Rome, 1994).

Campana, Stefano, 'Ricognizione archeologica del territorio di Montalcino: risultati preliminari', in Alfio Cortonesi and Alba Pagani (eds), *Ilcinensia: Nuove ricerche per la storia di Montalcino e del suo territorio* (Rome – Manziana, Studi e documenti per la storia di Montalcino e della Val d'Orcia, Vecchiarelli Editore, 2004) 1, pp. 37–63.

Canali, Tullio, *Notizie Istoriche della Città di Montalcino in Toscana,* Eighteenth-century original transcribed by Don Antonio Brandi, typescript (Montalcino, 1966).

—, *Libro delle Memorie dell'Origini delli Spedali di Montalcino in Toscana* (1748), transcribed by Don Antonio Brandi as *Notizie in iscorcio dello Spedale di Mont'Alcino,* typescript (Montalcino, 1990).

Capitoni, Barbara, 'I legati al Santa Maria della Scala alla metà del Trecento. Testamenti, oblazioni e donazioni: (1344–1374),' Tesi di laurea, Facoltà di Lettere e Filosofia dell'Università di Siena, Anno Accademico 1996–1997.

Caprioli, Ivo, *Passeggiate di Primavera,* 22 May 2004, Montalcino.

Cardarelli, Romualdo, 'Studi sulla topografia medievale dell'antico territorio vetuloniese', *Studi etruschi,* 6 (1932), pp. 145–240.

Carle, Lucia, *La patria locale: l'identità dei montalcinese dal 16 al 20 secolo* (Florence, Giunta regionale Toscana; Venice, Marsilio, 1996).

Carli, Enzo, *Lippo Vanni a San Leonardo al Lago* (Florence, Edam, 1969).

—, *Montalcino. Museo civico. Museo diocesano d'arte sacra* (Bologna, Calderini, 1972).

Carli, Francesca, 'Note per una Topografia ed una Tipologia degli Ospedali extraurbani della diocesi di Siena nel medioevo', *BSSP,* 100 (1993), pp. 384–403.

Cassi, Laura, 'Distribuzione geografica dei toponimi derivati dalla vegetazione in Toscana', *Rivista Geografica Italiana,* 80, fasc. 4, dicembre (1973), pp. 389–432.

Castelfiorentino: *Storia di Castelfiorentino* (Castelfiorentino, Banca di credito cooperativo di Cambiano, 1994).

Catoni, Giuliano, 'Gli oblati della Misericordia. Poveri e benefattori a Siena nella prima metà del Trecento', in Giuliano Pinto (ed.), *La Società del bisogno. Povertà e assistenza nella Toscana medievale* (Florence, Salimbeni, 1989), pp. 1–17.

—, (and Gabriella Piccinni), 'Famiglie e redditi nella Lira Senese del 1453' in Rinaldo Comba, Gabriella Piccinni and Giuliano Pinto (eds), *Strutture familiari, epidemie, migrazioni nell'Italia medievale* (Naples, Edizioni scientifiche italiane,1984), pp. 291–304.

Cavallo, Sandra and David Gentilcore (eds), *Spaces, Objects and Identitites in Early Modern Italian Medicine* (London, Blackwell, 2008).

Cosimo Cecinato, *L'amministrazione finanziaria del Comune di Siena nel sec. 13* (Milan, Giuffrè, 1966).

Cecchini, Giovanni, 'Le grance dell'Ospedale di S. Maria della Scale in Siena', *Economia e Storia,* 6 (1959), pp. 405–22.

Ceppari Ridolfi, Maria Assunta and Patrizia Turrini, 'Il movimento associativo e devozionale dei laici nella chiesa senese (secc. 13–19)', in Achille Mirizio and Paolo Nardi (eds) *Chiese e Vita Religiosa a Siena dalle origini al grande Giubileo* (Siena, Cantagalli, 2002), pp. 247–303.

Cherubini, Giovanni (ed.), 'La proprietà fondiaria in alcune zone del territorio senese all'inizio del Trecento', *Rivista di storia dell'agricoltura,* 14 (1974), further developed in 'Proprietari, contadini e campagne senesi all'inizio del Trecento', in Giovanni Cherubini (ed.), *Signori, contadini, borghesi. Ricerche sulla società italiana del basso-medioevo* (Florence, La Nuova Italia, 1974), pp. 231–311. See also 'Proprietari, contadini e campagne senesi all' inizio del Trecento', in Giovanni Cherubini, 'Introduzione e direzione dei proprietari di beni immobili e di terre a Siena intorno al 1320 (dalla Tavola delle Possessioni)', *Ricerche storiche*, 5 (1975), pp. 357–510.

— , 'La mezzadria toscana delle origini', in Giovanni Cherubini (ed.), with Tommaso Detti, Mario Mirri, Giorgio Mori and Simonetta Soldani, *Contadini e proprietari nella Toscana moderna*, Atti del Convegno di Studi in onore di Giorgio Giorgetti (2 vols, Florence, Olschki, 1979), 1, *Dal Medioevo all'età moderna*, pp. 131–52. (Republished in Giovanni Cherubini, *Scritti toscani. L'urbanesimo medievale e la mezzadria*, (Florence, Salimbeni, 1991), pp. 189–207.)

— , 'Risorse, paesaggio ed utilizzazione agricola del territorio della Toscana sud-occidentale nei secoli 14–15', in *Civiltà ed economia agricola in Toscana nei secc. 13–15. Problemi della vita delle campagne nel tardo Medioevo*, Atti dell'ottavo Convegno Internazionale del Centro Italiano di studi di Storia e d'Arte, Pistoia, 21–24 aprile 1977 (Pistoia, Centro Italiano di studi di Storia e d'Arte, 1981), pp. 91–115.

— , 'Parroco, parrocchie e popolamento nelle campagne dell'Italia centro-settentrionale alla fine del Medioevo', in *Pieve e parrocchie in Italia nel Basso Medioevo (secc. 13–15)*, Atti del 6 convegno di storia della chiesa in Italia, Florence, 21–25 settembre 1981 (Rome, Herder, 1984), pp. 351–413.

— , 'Gli archivi per la storia locale dell'età medievale', in Giovanni Parlavecchia (ed.), *Gli strumenti della ricerca storica locale, Archivi e biblioteche*, Atti del Convegno di studio, Castelfiorentino-FI, 14 giugno 1984 (Pisa, Pacini, 1988), pp. 59–64.

— , *Scritti toscani: l' urbanesimo medievale e la mezzadria* (Florence, Salimbeni, 1991).

— , (ed.), *Signori, contadini, borghesi. Ricerche sulla societa` italiana del basso-medioevo*, (Florence, la Nuova Italia, 1974), pp. 231–311.

— , (ed.), with Tommaso Detti, Mario Mirri, Giorgio Mori and Simonetta Soldani, *Contadini e proprietari nella Toscana moderna*. Atti del Convegno di Studi in onore di Giorgio Giorgetti (2 vols, Firenze, Olschki, 1979–81).

Chianti (Il) e la battaglia di Montaperti (Poggibonsi, Clante, 1992).

Chiaudano, Mario, 'I Rothschild del Duecento. La Gran Tavola dei Bonsignori', *BSSP*, 42 (1935), pp. 103–42.

Ciampoli, Donatella, *Il Capitano del popolo a Siena nel primo Trecento. Con il rubricario dello statuto del comune di Siena del 1337* (Siena, Consorzio universitario della Toscana meridionale, 1984).

— , 'Uno statuto signorile di fine duecento: I Salimbeni e la comunità di Rocca d'Orcia novant'anni dopo la 'Carta Libertatis'', in Donatello Ciampoli and Chiara Laurenti (eds), *Gli statuti di Rocca d'Orcia – Tintinnano dai Salimbeni alla Repubblica di Siena (secoli 13–15)* (Siena, Betti Editrice, 2006), pp. 11–64.

— , (ed.), with Mario Ascheri, *Siena e il suo territorio nel Rinascimento* (Siena, Il Leccio, 1986).

— , (ed.), with Thomas Szabò, *Viabilità e legislazione di uno Stato cittadino del Duecento. Lo Statuto dei Viari di Siena*, with transcriptions by Stephan Epstein and Maria Ginatempo (Siena, Accademia Senese degli Intronati, 1992).

— , (ed.), with Chiara Laurenti, *Gli statuti di Rocca d'Orcia – Tintinnano dai Salimbeni alla Repubblica di Siena (secoli 13–15)* (Siena, Betti Editrice, 2006).

Città comunali di Toscana (Bologna, CLUEB, 2003).

Citter, Carlo, 'L'analisi di un centro-storico medievale. Sovana', *Bollettino della Società Storica Maremmana*, 66/7 (1995), pp. 7–25.

—, *L'edilizia storica di tre castelli medievali. Batignano, Istia d'Ombrone, Montepescali* (Grosseto, 1995).

—, 'L'assetto urbanistico del castello di Montepescali nel Medioevo', in Maria Serena Fommei (ed.), *Montepescali. Storia, Arte, Archeologia* (Grosseto, I Portici, 1997), pp. 33–51.

Coazzin, Silvia, 'Liberi domini totius castri.L'aristocrazia rurale 'minor' nel Senese e nella Toscana meridionale. Forme di egemonia, assetto sociale e patrimoniale di lignaggi, famiglie e gruppi consortili di castello (secc 11–14)', Tesi di dottorato di ricerca in Storia Medievale, Università di Firenze, Vigueur. Coordinatore Jean-Claude Maire Vigneur. 13 ciclo, Anno Accademico 1997/98 and 2000/01.

Cohn, Samuel K., Jr., *Death and property in Siena 1205–1800: Strategies for the afterlife* (Baltimore and London, The Johns Hopkins University Press, c.1988).

—, *The cult of remembrance and the Black Death. Six Renaissance cities in central Italy* (Baltimore and London, The Johns Hopkins University Press, 1992).

—, 'Last Wills: Family, Women and the Black Death in Central Italy', in Samuel K. Cohen, Jr., *Women in the Streets. Essays on Sex and Power in Renaissance Italy* (Baltimore and London, The Johns Hopkins University Press, 1996), pp. 39–56.

Colli, Alberto, *Montaperti. La battaglia del 1260 tra Firenze e Siena e il castello ritrovato* (Florence, Aska, 2005).

—, (ed.), *Ambrogio Lorenzetti: la vita del Trecento in Siena e nel contado senese nelle commitenze istoriate pubbliche e private: guida al Buon governo* (Siena [s.n.], 2004).

Collucci, Silvia (ed.), *Morire nel medioevo. Il caso di Siena*, Atti del convegno di studi, 14–15 novembre 2002, *BSSP*, 110 (2003).

Comba, Rinaldo, and Gabriella Piccinni and Giuliano Pinto (eds), *Strutture familiari, epidemie, migrazioni nell'Italia medievale* (Naples, Edizioni scientifiche italiane, 1984).

—, (ed.), with Irma Naso, *Demografia e società nell'Italia medievale: secoli 9–14* (Cuneo, Società per gli studi storici, archeologici ed artistici della provincia di Cuneo, 1994).

—, (ed.), with Francesco Panero and Giuliano Pinto, *Borghi nuovi e borghi franchi nel processo di costruzione dei distretti comunali nell'Italia centro-settentrionale: secoli 12–14, Cherasco (Cuneo)*, Centro internazionale di studi sugli insediamenti medievali, 2002 (Cuneo, Società per gli studi storici, archeologici ed artistici della provincia di Cuneo, 2002).

Cortonesi, Alfio, 'Demografia e popolamento nel contado di Siena: Il territorio montalcinese nei secoli 13–15', in Rinaldo Comba, Gabriella Piccinni and Giuliano Pinto (eds), *Strutture familiari epidemie migrazioni nell'Italia medievale* (Naples, Edizioni Scientifiche Italiane, 1984), pp. 153–181

—, 'Movimenti migratori a Montalcino e in Val d'Orcia nel tardo medioevo', *BSSP*, 94 (1987), pp. 9–30.

—, *Il lavoro del contadino. Uomini, tecniche, colture nella Tuscia tardomedievale* (Bologna, CLUEB, 1988).

—, 'La vita e l'olivo nelle campagne di Montalcino (secoli 13–15)', in Alfio Cortonesi (ed.), *La Val d'Orcia nel medioevo e nei primi secoli dell'età moderna*, Atti del Convegno internazionale di studi storici, Pienza, 15–18 settembre 1988 (Rome, Viella, 1990), pp. 189–212.

—, 'Agricoltura e allevamento nell'Italia bassomedievale: aspetti e problemi di una coesistenza', in Sergio Gensini (ed.), *Le Italie del tardo Medioevo* (Pisa, Pacini, 1990), pp. 391–408.

—, 'Note sull'agricoltura italiana fra 13 e 14 secolo', in *Europa en los umbrales de la crisis (1250–1350)*, Actas de la 21 Semana de Estudios Medievales de Estella, 18–22 julio 1994 (Pamplona 1995), pp. 87–128.

—, *Poggio alle Mura e la bassa Val d'Orcia nel medioevo e in età moderna*, (Poggio alle Mura, Fondazione Banfi, 1996).

—, 'Montalcino nel tardo Medioevo. Note sulla genesi di un territorio', in Roberto Guerrini (ed.), *Montalcino e il suo territorio* (Sovicille, Banca di credito cooperativo Sovicille CRAS, 1998), pp. 15–29.

—, 'Agricoltura e techniche nell'Italia medievale. I cereali, la vite e l'olivo', in Alfio Cortonesi, Gianfranco Pasquali and Gabriella Piccinni (eds), *Uomini e campagne nell'Italia medievale* (Rome and Bari, Laterza, 2002), pp. 191–260.

—, 'L'allevamento', in Giuliano Pinto, Carlo Poni and Ugo Tucci (eds), *Il Medioevo e l'Età moderna* (Florence, Polistampa, 2002), pp. 83–122.

—, 'La storia agraria dell'Italia medievale negli studi degli ultimi decenni. Materiali e riflessioni per un bilancio', in Flocel Sabaté and Joan Farré (eds), *Medievalisme: noves perspectives*, Atti del 7 Curs d'Estiu Comtat d'Urgell, Balaguer, 10–12 July 2002 (Lleida, 2003), pp. 173–94 (republished with a few alterations in *Società e storia*, 100–101 (2003), pp. 235–53.

—, 'Espansione dei coltivi e proprietà fondiaria nel tardo medioevo. L'Italia del Centro-Nord', in Simonetta Cavaciocchi (ed.), *Il mercato della terra". Secoli 13–18*, Atti della Trentacinquesima Settimana di Studi dell'Istituto Internazionale di Storia Economica 'F. Datini', Prato, 5–9 maggio 2003 (Grassina, Bagno a Ripoli, le Monnier, 2004), pp. 57–95.

—, 'Soccide e altri affidamenti di bestiame nell'Italia medievale', in Alfio Cortonesi, Massimo Montanari and Antonella Nelli (eds), *Contratti agrari e rapporti di lavoro nell'Europa medievale*, Atti del Convegno Internazionale, Montalcino, 20–22 settembre 2001, Biblioteca di Storia Agraria Medievale (Bologna, CLUEB, 2007), pp. 203–23.

—, (ed.), *La Val d'Orcia nel Medioevo e nei primi secoli dell'età moderna*. Atti del Convegno, Pienza, 15–18 settembre 1988 (Rome, Viella, 1990).

—, (ed.), *Poggio alle Mura e la bassa Val d'Orcia nel medioevo e in età moderna* (Poggio alle Mura, Fondazione Banfi, 1996).

—, (ed.), with Gianfranco Pasquali and Gabriella Piccinni, *Uomini e campagne nell'Italia medievale* (Rome and Bari, Laterza, 2002).

—, (ed.), with Federica Viola, *Le comunità rurali e i loro statuti (secoli 12–15)*, Atti dell'VIII Convegno del Comitato italiano per gli studi e le edizioni delle fonti normative, Viterbo, 30 maggio–1 giugno 2002, *Rivista storica del Lazio*, 2 vols (20–21), (2005–2006) (Rome, Gangemi, 2006).

—, (ed.), with Alba Pagani *Ilcinensia. Nuove ricerche per la storia di Montalcino e del suo territorio*, Studi e documenti per la storia di Montalcino e della Val d'Orcia, 1, (Roma–Manziana, Vecchiarelli, 2004).

—, (ed.), with Massimo Montanari, Antonella Nelli,*Contratti agrari e rapporti di lavoro nell'Europa medievale*, Atti del Convegno Internazionale, Montalcino, 20–22 settembre 2001, Biblioteca di Storia Agraria Medievale (Bologna, CLUEB, 2007).

—, (ed.), with Gabriella Piccinni, *Medioevo delle campagne: I rapporti di lavoro, politica agraria, protesta cittadina* (Rome, Viella, 2006).

Cortonesi, Gabrielle and Margherita Fontani, *Storia di un antico castello 'Suvvicille'* Pro Loco Soviville (Siena, Edizioni Cantagalli, 2006).

Coscarella, Giuseppina, Le Grancie dello Spedale di Santa Maria della Scala di Siena', in Coscarella, Giuseppina and Franca Cecilia Franchi (eds), *La Grancia di Cuna in Val d'Arbia. Un esempio di fattoria fortificata medievale* (Florence, Salimbeni, 1983), pp. 7–9.

—, 'Le Grance dello Spedale di Santa Maria della Scala nel contado senese', *BSSP*, 92 (1985), pp. 66–92.

Cronache senesi, in Alessandro Lisini and Fabio Iacometti (eds), *Rerum italicarum scriptores* 15 (Bologna, Zanichelli, 1931–39), p. 6.

Cucini, Costanza (ed.), *Radicondoli: storia e archeologia di un comune senese* (Rome, Multigrafica editrice, 1990).

Dal Pino, Franco, 'Oblati e oblate conventuali presso i mendicanti 'minori' nei secoli 13–14', in *Uomini e donne in comunità*, in *Quaderni di Storia Religiosa* (Verona, 1994), pp. 33–68.

Dami, Alessandra, with Raffaele Giannetti, Maddalena Sanfilippo and Giulia Zoi, *Montalcino Città delle Eccellenze*, guida ufficiale del Comune di Montalcino (Città di Castello (PG), Litograf Editor srl, 2009).

Del Corto, Giovan Battista, *Storia della Valdichiana* (Bologna, Forni, 1971).

Di Pietro, Gianfranco, 'Per la storia dell'architettura della dimora rurale: alcune premesse di metodo', *Archeologia Medievale*, 7, 1980, pp. 343–61.

Donati, Luigi and Letizia Ceccarelli, 'Poggio Civitella', in Alfio Cortonesi and Alba Pagani (eds), *Ilcinensia: Nuove ricerche per la storia di Montalcino e del suo territorio* (Rome–Manziana, Studi e documenti per la storia di Montalcino e della Val d'Orcia, Vecchiarelli Editore, I, 2004), pp. 15–36.

Donato, Maria Monica, 'Il Pittore del Buon Governo: Le opere 'politiche' di Ambrogio in Palazzo Pubblico', in Chiara Frugoni (ed.), *Pietro e Ambrogio Lorenzetti* (Florence, Le Lettere, 2002), pp. 201–9.

Donato, Neri di, 'Cronaca senese' in *Chroniche senesi, Rerum italicarum scriptores*, (eds) Alessandro Lisini and Fabio Iacometti (Bologna, Zanichelli, 1931–39).

Duby, Georges and Jacques Le Goff (eds), *Famiglia e parentela nell'Italia medievale* (Bologna, Il Mulino, 1981).

Duccio Alle origini della pittura senese, Alessandro Bagnoli, Roberto Bartalini, Luciano Bellosi and Michel Laclotte (eds), exhibition catalogue, Siena 4 October 2003 – 14 March 2004 (Milan, Silvana Editoriale, 2003).

Edgerton, Samuel Y. Jr., *Pictures and Punishment. Art and Criminal Prosecution during the Florentine Renaissance* (Ithaca, New York, 1985).

Elsheikh, Mahmoud Salem, 'Testi senesi dello Duecento e del primo Trecento', *Studi di Filologia Italiana*, 29 (1961), pp. 112–44.

Epstein, Stephan R., 'Dall'espansione alla gestione della crisi: L'ospedale di Santa Maria della Scala di Siena e il suo patrimonio (1260–1450)', Tesi di laurea, Facoltà di Lettere, L'Università degli Studi di Siena, Anno Accademico, 1983–1984.

—, *Alle origini della fattoria toscana. L'ospedale della Scala di Siena e le sue terre (metà '200– metà '400)* (Florence, Salimbeni, 1986).

Farinelli, Roberto and Andrea Giorgi, 'La 'Tavola delle Possessioni' come fonte per lo studio del territorio: l'esempio di Castelnuovo dell'Abate', in Alfio Cortonesi (ed.), *La Valdorcia nel Medioevo e nei primi secoli dell'Età moderna*, Atti del convegno internazionale di studi storici, Pienza 15–18 settembre, 1988 (Rome, Viella, 1990), pp. 213–56.

—, 'Radicondoli: società e territorio in una 'curia' attraverso la 'Tavola delle Possessioni'', in Costanza Cucini (ed.), *Radicondoli. Storia e Archeologia di un comune senese* (Rome, Multigrafica editrice, 1990), pp. 353–91 and 461–64.

—, 'Contributo allo Studio dei rapporti tra Siena ed il suo territorio', *Rivista di storia dell'agricoltura*, 32 (1992) n. 2, pp. 3–72.

—, *Camigliano, Argiano e Poggio alle Mura (secoli 12–14)*, presented by Alfio Cortonesi, Associazione Culturale e ricreativa Camigliano (Siena, Associazione Culturale e ricreativa Camigliano, 1995).

—, *I castelli nella Toscana delle città 'deboli'. Dinamiche del poplamento e del potere rurale nella Toscana meridionale (secoli 7–14)* (Florence, All'insegna del Giglio, 2007).

Favilli Granai, Lorenza, 'Tipografia storica del territorio di Montalcino. Insediamenti antichi nel territorio di Montalcino', Tesi di laurea, Università degli studi di Firenze, Facoltà di Magistero, relatore Giovanni Uggeri, Anno Accademico 1984–1985.

Fedeli, Paolo, *Un fratello dell'antico ospedale Santa Maria della Scala. San Bernardo Tolomei: la societa medioevale del suo tempo* (Siena, Copinfax, c.2009).

Ferri, Roberta (ed.), *La memoria dell'acqua: I bottini di Siena* (Siena, Protagon, 2006).

Fiumi, Ernestò, 'Sui rapporti economici tra città e contado nell'età comunale', *Archivio storico italiano*, 114, fasc. 1 (1956), pp. 18–61.

—, 'L'imposta diretta nei comuni medievali della Toscana', in *Studi in onore di Armando Sapori* (Milan, Istituto editoriale cisalpino, 1957), 1, pp. 329–53.

Francini, Giustino, 'Appunti sulla costituzione guelfa del comune di Siena secondo il costituto del 1274', *BSSP*, n.s. 10 (1939), pp. 11–28.

Franciosa, Luchino, *La transumanza nell'Appennino centro-meridionale* (Naples, [s.n.], 1951).

Franza, Gabriele and Nello Nanni, 'Il cassero senese di Montelaterone: Le caratteristiche architettoniche e i Cuteri del Restauro', *Amiata Storia e Territorio*, anno 13, 38/39 marzo (2002), pp. 16–18.

Freuler, Gaudenz, *Bartolo di Fredi Cini: ein Beitrag zur sienesischen Malarei des 14. Jahrhunderts* (Disentis, Desertina, c.1994)

Frugoni, Chiara, 'Il governo dei Nove a Siena e il loro credo politico nell'affresco di Ambrogio Lorenzetti', *Quaderni Medievali* 7 (1979), pp. 14–42, and 8 (1979), pp. 71–103.

—, (ed.), *Pietro e Ambrogio Lorenzetti* (Florence, Le Lettere, 2002).

Galetti, Paola, 'La donna contadina: figure femminili nei contratti agrari italiani dell'alto medioevo', in Maria Giuseppina Muzzarelli, Paolo Galetti and Bruno Andreolli (eds), *Donne e lavoro nell'Italia medievale* (Turin, Rosenberg and Sellier, 1991), pp. 41–54.

Gallavotti Cavallero, Daniela, *Lo Spedale di Santa Maria della Scala in Siena: vicenda di una committenza artistica* (Pisa, Pacini Editore, 1985).

—, (ed.), with Andrea Brogi, *Lo spedale grande di Siena: fatti urbanistica e architettonici del Santa Maria della Scala: ricerche, riflessioni, interrogativi* (Florence, La Casa Usher, 1987).

Galoppini, Laura, (ed.), *Il lardo nell'alimentazione toscana dall'antichità ai nostri giorni*, Atti della Giornata di studio, Massa, 1 settembre 2001, Deputazione di storia patria per le antiche province modenesi, *Biblioteca-Nuova Serie*, n. 168 (Massa-Modena, 2003).

Gianni, Alessandra, 'Iconografia della Madonna della Misericordia nell'arte Senese', in Mario Ascheri and Patrizia Turrini (eds), *La Misericordia di Siena attraverso i secoli: dalla domus Misericordiae all'arciconfraternità di Misericordia*, Arciconfraternità di Misericordia di Siena (Siena, Protagon Editori Toscani, 2004), pp. 94–101.

Ginatempo, Maria, 'Per la storia demografica del territorio senese nel Quattrocento: problemi di fonti e di metodo', *Archivio Storico Italiano*, 142 (1984), pp. 521–32 and 541–47.

—, *Crisi di un territorio. Il popolamento della Toscana senese alla fine del Medioevo* (Florence, Leo S. Olschki, 1988).

—, 'Il Popolamento della Valdorcia alla fine del medioevo (15–16 secolo)', in Alfio Cortonesi (ed.), *La Val d'Orcia nel Medioevo e nei primi secoli dell'età moderna*, Atti del Convegno, Pienza, 15–18 settembre 1988 (Rome, Viella, 1990), pp. 113–53.

Giorgi, Andrea, 'I 'casati' Senesi e la terra. Definizione di un gruppo di famiglie magnatizie ed evoluzione dei loro patrimoni immobiliari (fine sec. 11 – inizio sec. 14)', Tesi di dottorato di ricerca in Storia Medievale. Università degli Studi di Firenze, coordinatore prof. Giovanni Cherubini. 5 ciclo, Anno Accademico 1989–90/1992–93.

—, 'Il carteggio del Concistoro della Repubblica di Siena (spogli di lettere 1251–1374)', *BSSP*, 97 (1990), pp. 193–573.

—, (and Stefano Moscadelli), 'L'Opera di S. Maria di Siena tra 12 e 13 secolo', in Achille Mirizio and Paolo Nardi (eds), *Chiesa e vita religiosa a Siena dalle origini al grande giubileo*, Atti del convegno di studi, Siena, 25–27 ottobre 2000 (Siena, Cantagalli, 2002), pp. 77–100.

Giovannino, Fabio, *Natalità, mortalità e demografia dell'italia Medievale sulla base dei dati archeologici* (Oxford, Archaeopress, 2001).

Grieco, Allen J. and Lucia Sandri (eds), *Medicina e Storia. Ospedali e città. L'Italia del centro-Nord, 13–16 secolo* (Florence, Casa Editrice le lettere, 1997).

Grohmann, Alberto (ed.), *Le fonti censuarie e catastali tra tarda romanità e basso medioevo, Emilia Romagna, Toscana, Umbria, Marche, San Marino* (San Marino, Centro di studi storici sanmarinesi, Università degli studi della repubblica di San Marino, 1996).

Groppi, Angela, 'Lavoro e proprietà delle donne in età moderno', in Angela Groppi (ed.), *Il lavoro delle donne* (Rome, Laterza, 1996), pp. 119–63.

—, (ed.), *Il lavoro delle donne* (Rome, Laterza, 1996).

Guerrini, Roberto (ed.), *Montalcino e il suo territorio* (Sovicelle, Banca di credito cooperativo Sovicille CRAS, 1998).

Hanawalt, Barbara A., *The Late Medieval Peasant Family* (New York and London, 1985).

Henderson, John, 'The Hospitals of Late Medieval and Renaissance Florence: a preliminary survey', in Lindsay Granshaw and Roy Porter (eds), *The Hospital in History* (London and New York, Routledge, 1989), pp. 63–92.

—, *Pietà e carità nella Firenze del basso Medioevo* (Florence, Le lettere, c.1998), Italian translation of *Piety and charity in late medieval Florence* (Oxford, Clarendon press, 1994).

—, 'Splendide case di cura', Spedali, medicina ed assistenza a Firenze nel Trecento', Atti del Convegno Internazionale di Studio tenuto dall'Istituto degli Innocenti e Villa I Tatti, The Harvard University Center for Italian Renaissance Studies, Florence, 27–28 aprile 1995, in Allen J. Grieco and Lucia Sandri (eds), *Medicina e Storia. Ospedali e città. L'Italia del centro-Nord, 13–16 secolo* (Florence, Casa Editrice le lettere, 1997), pp. 15–50.

—, *The Renaissance hospital: healing the body and healing the soul* (New Haven and London, Yale University Press, c.2006).

Herlihy, David, *Medieval Households* (The President and Fellows of Harvard College, 1985), Italian translation, *La famiglia nel Medioevo* (Rome and Bari, Laterza, 1989).

—, (and Christiane Klapisch-Zuber), *Les Toscans et leurs familles. Une étude du catasto florentin de 1427* (Paris, Presse de la Fondation national des sciences politiques, 1978). English translation, *Tuscans and their families: A study of the Florentine catasto of 1427* (New Haven, Conn., Yale University Press, 1985), Italian translation: *I toscani e le loro famiglie: uno studio sul catasto fiorentino del 1427* (Bologna, Il Mulino, c.1988).

Hicks, David L., 'Sources of Wealth in Renaissance Siena: Business men and Landowners', *BSSP*, 93 (1986), pp. 9–42.

Hoeniger, Catherine, *The Renovation of Paintings in Tuscany, 1250–1500* (Cambridge, Cambridge University Press, 1995).

Imberciadori, Ildebrando, *Mezzadria classica Toscana, con documentazione inedita dal sec. 9 al sec. 14*, (Florence, Vallecchi, 1951).

—, *Amiata e Maremma tra il 9 e il 20 secolo* (Parma, La Nazione Tipografica, 1971)

—, 'Il primo statuto della Dogana dei paschi maremmani (1419)', *Note economiche*, 62 (1980–81), pp. 50–80.

Imbert, Jean, *Les hopitaux en droit canonique: du décret de Gratien à la sécularisation de l'administration de l'Hôtel-Dieu de Paris en 1505* (Paris, Librairie Philosophique J. Vrin, 1947).

Isaacs, Ann Katherine Chiancone, 'Fisco e politica a Siena nel Trecento.' *Rivista storica italiana*, 85 (1973), pp. 22–46.

—, 'Lo Spedale di Santa Maria della Scala nell'antico stato senese', in *Il Santa Maria della Scala nella storia della città*, Atti del Convegno Internazionale di Studi, 20–22 novembre 1986, comune di Siena (Siena, Pistolesi, 1988), pp. 14–29.

Klapisch-Zuber, Christiane, 'Mezzadria e insediamenti rurali alla fine del Medio Evo', in *Civiltà ed economia agricola in Toscana nei secc. 13–15: problemi della vita delle campagne nel tardo Medioevo*, ottavo Convegno internazionale, Pistoia, 21–24 aprile 1977, (Pistoia, Centro italiano di studi di storia e d'arte, 1981), pp. 149–64.

—, 'The 'Cruel Mother': Maternity, Widowhood, and Dowry in Florence in the Fourteenth and Fifteenth Centuries', in *eadem, Women, Family and Ritual in Renaissance Italy* (Chicago and London, The University of Chicago Press, 1985), pp. 117–31. First published in *Annales* 38 (1983), pp. 1097–1109.

—, 'Fonti e metodi per la storia demografica del tardo Medioevo: nascità e morte nelle famiglie fiorentine', in Daniela Romagnoli (ed.), *Storia e storie della città* (Parma, Pratiche, 1988–9) pp. 147–55.

—, 'Relazioni di parentela e vita politica a Firenze nel 14 secolo', in Christiane Klapisch-Zuber (ed.), *La Famiglia in Italia* (New Haven, Yale University Press, *c.*1991), pp. 233–54.

—, 'Le dernier enfant: fécondite et vieillissement chez les Florentins, 14e–15e siecle', in Jean-Pierre Bardet, François Lebrun and René Le Mée (eds), *Mesurer et comprendre: mélanges offerts a Jacques Dupaquier* (Paris, Presses universitaires de France, *c.*1993), pp. 277–90.

—, *La famiglia e le donne nel Rinascimento a Firenze* (Rome, Laterza, 1995).

Kupper, Marcia, *The Art of Healing. Painting for the Sick and the Sinner in a Medieval Town* (Philadelphia, Penn State University Press, 2003).

Kuehn, Thomas, *Law, Family and Women. Toward a Legal Anthropology of Renaissance Italy* (Chicago and London, The University of Chicago Press, 1991).

Lecceto e gli eremi agostiniani in terra di Siena (ed.), Corrado Fanti (Cinisello Balsamo, Silvana, 1990).

Leistikow, Dankwart, *Dieci secoli di storia degli edifici ospedalieri in Europa. Una storia dell'architettura ospedaliere* (Ingelheim am Rhein, Boehringer, 1967).

Leverotti, Franca, 'Il consumo della carne a Massa all'inizio del 15 secolo. Prime considerazioni', *Archeologia medievale*, 8 (1981), pp. 227–38.

Liberati, Alfredo, 'Nuovi Documenti Artistici dello Spedale di S. Maria della Scala in Siena', *BSSP*, 33–36 (1926–1929), pp. 147–79.

Logazzi, Luciano, 'I segni sulla terra. Sistemi di confinazione e di misurazione dei boschi nell'alto Medioevo', in Bruno Andreolli and Massimo Montanari (eds), *Il bosco nel medioevo* (Bologna, Editrice CLEB, 1988), pp. 17–34.

Lorenzoni, Michelangelo, 'L'antico Ospedale di S. Maria della Croce di Montalcino e il suo statuto del 1788', Tesi di Laurea, relatore Chiar.mo Prof. Giuliano Catoni, Università degli Studi di Siena, Facoltà di Lettere e Filosofia, Corso di Laurea in Lettere Moderne, Anno Accademico, 1992–1993.

Lucherini, Emma, 'La pala d'altare della Cappella del Parto della chiesa di Sant'Agostino fa parte di un'opera di Bartolo di Fredi conservata a Torrita', *Gazzettino e Storie del Brunello e di Montalcino*, Anno 2, 18 (2008), pp. 38–39.

—, 'Il ciclo con le storie di Sant'Agostino nella cappella del coro della chiesa omonima a Montalcino', *Gazzettino e Storie del Brunello e di Montalcino*, Anno 2, 16 (2008), pp. 36–38.

Lumia-Ostinelli, Gianna, 'Le eredità delle donne: I diritti successori femminili a Siena tra Medioevo ed età moderna', in Silvia Colucci (ed.), *Morire nel Medioevo. Il caso di Siena*, Atti del Convegno di Studi, 14–15 novembre 2002, Università degli Studi di

Siena, Dipartimento di Archeologia e Storia delle Arti, Dipartimento di Storia, con il patrocinio della Accademia dei Fisiocritici Onlus, *BSSP*, 110 (2003), pp. 318–40.

Luzzatto, Giuseppe Ignazio, 'La commenda nella vita economica dei secoli 13 e 14 con particolare riguardo a Venezia', in Giuseppe Ignazio Luzzatto (ed.), *Studi di Storia economica veneziana* (Padua, CEDAM, 1954), pp. 59–79.

Mangani, Elisabetta, 'L'orientalizzante recente nella valle dell'Ombrone', *AION*, Naples, 12 (1990), pp. 9–21.

Marcaccini, Paolo and Lidia Calzolai, *I percorsi di transumanza verso la Maremma nell'alto Medioevo* (Florence, Polistampa, 2003).

Marchionni, Roberto, *I senesi a Montaperti* (Siena, Meiattini, 1992).

Martellucci, Maura, 'I bambini di nessuno. L'infanzia abbandonata al Santa Maria della Scala di Siena (secoli 13–16)', *BSSP*, 108 (2001), pp. 9–221.

—, 'Dio li perdoni; ch'egli è stato buono rettore', *BSSP*, 110 (2003), pp. 452–88.

Martini, Giuseppe, 'Siena da Montaperti alla caduta dei Nove (1260- 1355)', *BSSP*, 68 (1961), pp. 3–56 and 75–128.

Mazzi, Maria Serena, 'Arredi e masserizie della casa rurale nelle campagne fiorentine del 15 secolo', *Archeologia Medievale*, 7, 1980, pp. 137–52.

Mirizio, Achille and Paolo Nardi (eds), *Chiesa e Vita Religiosa a Siena dalle origini al grande Giubileo* (Siena, Cantagalli, 2002).

Molho, Anthony, *Marriage Alliance in late Medieval Florence* (Cambridge, Harvard University press, 1994).

—, (ed.) with John A. Tedeschi, *Renaissance studies in Honor of Hans Baron* (Florence, Sansoni, 1970).

Moretti, Italo, 'La demografia medievale attraverso le testimonianze architettoniche e urbanistiche', in Carlo A. Corsini (ed.), *Vita, morte e miracoli di gente comune: appunti per una storia della popolazione della toscana fra 14 e 20 secolo* (Florence, La Casa Uscher, 1988), pp. 37–50.

—, (and Renato Stopani), *Romanico Senese* (Florence, Salimbeni, 1981).

Morganti, Giuseppe, 'Il Castello della Ripa d'Orcia', in Carlo Avetta (ed.), *'Tintinnano'. La Rocca e il territorio di Castiglione d'Orcia*, (San Quirico d'Orcia, Editoriale DonChischiotto, 1988).

Moscadelli, Stefano, 'Siena sotto i dodici (1355–1368): amministrazione e finanze', Tesi di laurea, Università di Siena, Facoltà di Lettere e Filosofia, 1981–1982 (Siena, 1982).

Mucciarelli, Roberta, *La terra contesa. I Piccolomini contro Santa Maria della Scala 1277–1280* (Florence, Olschki, 2001).

—, (ed.), with Gabriella Piccinni and Giuliano Pinto, *La costruzione del dominio cittadino sulle campagne: Italia centro-settentrionale, secoli 12–14* (Siena, Protagon, 2009).

Nanni, Nello, Il Cassero Senese di Montelaterone: Una Tappa contrastata nell'espansione Cittadina', *Amiata Storia e Territorio*, anno 13 marzo, 38/39 (2002), pp. 9–15.

Nardi, Lucia, 'La distrettualizzazione dello stato: I Vicariati della Repubblica di Siena 1337–1339', in Mario Ascheri and Donatella Ciampoli (eds), *Siena e il suo territorio nel Rinascimento* (Siena, Il Leccio, 1986), pp. 55–67.

—, (with Elena Brizio, Giuseppe Chironi and Cecilia Papi), 'Il territorio per la festa dell'Assunta: patti e censi di Signori e Comunità dello Stato', in Mario Ascheri e Donatella Ciampoli (eds), *Siena e il suo territorio territorio nel Rinascimento* (Siena, Il Leccio, 1986), 1, pp. 81–249.

Nardi, Paolo, 'Origine e sviluppo della Casa della Misericordia nei secoli 13 e 14', in Mario Ascheri and Patrizia Turrini (eds), *La Misericordia di Siena attraverso secoli. Dalla Domus Misericordiae all'Arciconfraternità di Misericordia* (Siena, Protagon editori toscani, 2004), pp. 65–93.

—, (ed.), *Nolens intestatus decedere. Il testamento come fonte della storia religiosa e sociale*, Atti dell'incontro di studio, Perugia, 3 maggio 1983 (Perugia, Regione dell'Umbria, Editrice umbra cooperativa, 1985).

Naso, Irma, 'La Produzione casearia europea in un trattato del tardo medioevo', in *Cultura e società nell'Italia medievale: studi per Paolo Brezzi Studi* (2 vols, Rome, Istituto storico italiano per il Medio Evo, 1988), 2, pp. 585–604.

Norman, Diana, 'Pisa, Siena and the Maremma: A Neglected Aspect of Ambrogio Lorenzetti's Paintings in the Sala dei Nove', *Renaissance Studies*, 11 (1997), pp. 310–57.

—, *Siena and the Virgin. Art and Politics in a Late Medieval City* (New Haven – London, Yale University Press, 1999).

Nucciotti, Michele, 'Il cassero senese di Montelaterone. L'Indagine Archeologica', *Amiata Storia e Territorio*, anno 13, marzo 38/39 (2002), pp. 19–23.

Orefice, Gabriella, *Castiglion Fiorentio (Arezzo)*, Atlante Storico delle Città Italiane, Toscana 4 (Rome, Bonsignori Editore, 1996).

Orlandini, Alessandro, *Gettatelli e pellegrini: gli affreschi nella sala del Pellegrinaio dell'ospedale di Santa Maria della Scala di Siena: itinerario didattico su una summa figurativa dell'assistenza ospedaliera fra Medioevo e Rinascimento* (Siena, Nuova immagine, 2002).

Os, Hendrik Willem, 'A choir book by Lippo Vanni', *Simiolus*, 2 (1967–8), pp. 117–33.

—, 'Lippo Vanni as Miniaturist', *Simiolus*, 7 (1974), pp. 67–90.

Ospedale di Santa Maria della Scala: ricerche storiche, archeologiche e storico-artistiche Ricerche e Fonti I, Collana diretta da Fabio Gabbrielli e Gabriella Piccinni, Atti della giornata di studi, Siena, 28 aprile 2005 (Siena, Protagon Editori, 2011).

Ostinelli-Lumia, Gianna, 'Le eredità delle donne: i diritti successori femminili a Siena tra Medioevo ed età moderna', in Collucci, Silvia (ed.), *Morire nel medioevo. Il caso di Siena*, Atti del convegno di studi, 14–15 novembre 2002, *BSSP*, 110 (2003), pp. 318–40.

Paccagnini, Maria Cristina, 'La Compagnia di S. Pietro in Montalcino', Tesi di laurea, Università di Firenze, Anno Accademico 1976–1977.

Paganico Porta Senese, la torre, il cassero Patrizia Angelucci, Mario De Gregorio, Federica Falchi, Ettore Pellegrini (Monteriggioni, Il Leccio, 2010).

Paone, Natalino, *La Transumanza: Immagini di una civiltà* (Isernia, Biblioteca Molisana, Isernia, Cosmo Iannone Editore, 1987).

Passeri, Vincenzo, 'La Torre di Tentennano e Castiglione', in Carlo Avetta (ed.), *'Tintinnano'. La Rocca e il territorio di Castiglione d'Orcia* (San Quirico d'Orcia, Editoriale DonChischiotte, 1988), pp. 31–43.

—, *Documenti per la Storia delle Località della Provincia di Siena* (Siena, Edizioni Cantagalli, 2002).

—, (with Paolo Cammarosano), *Repertorio dei toponomi della provincia di Siena, desunti dalla cartografia dell'Istituto Geografico Militare* (Siena, Amministrazione provinciale di Siena: Assessorato istruzione e cultura, 1983).

—, (with Laura Neri), *Gli insediamenti della Repubblica di Siena nel catasto del 1318–1320* (Siena, Università degli Studi di Siena, Dipartimento di Scienze Storiche, Giuridiche, Politiche e Sociale, 1994).

Patrone, Annamaria Nada, 'Le Pellicce nel traffico commerciale Pedemontano del tardo medioevo', in *Cultura e società nell'Italia medievale: studi per Paolo Brezzi* (2 vols, Rome, Istituto storico italiano per il Medio Evo, 1988), vol. 2, pp. 562–84.

Pavolini, Maria Luisa, 'Aspetti della politica finanziaria e comunale nel basso Medio Evo (Siena nel Due-Trecento)', *Economia e Storia* (1977), pp. 272–92.

Pellegrini, Ettore, *Il territorio senese nella cartografia antica: le carte geografiche della Toscana meridionale dalle prime rappresentazioni misurate: del Rinascimento alle elaborazioni della geodesia post illuminista* (Siena, Protagon, 2003).

—, *Viaggio iconografico nell'antico stato senese* (Ospedaletto, Pacini, 2007).

—, (ed.) *L'iconografia di Siena nelle opere a stampa: vedute generali della città dal 15 al 19 secolo*, Siena, Palazzo Pubblico, exhibition, 28 June – 12 October 1986 (Siena, Lombardi, 1986).

—, (ed.), *La caduta della Repubblica senese* (Siena, Nuova immagine, 1991).

—, (ed.), *Alla ricerca di Montaperti: mito, fonti documentarie e storiografia*, Atti del convegno, Siena, novembre 2007 (Siena, Betti, 2009).

Pellegrini, Giovanni Battista, *Toponomastica italiana* (Milan, Hoepli, 1991).

Pellegrini, Michele, 'L'Ospedale e il Comune: immagini di una relazione privilegiata', in Gabriella Piccinni and Carla Zarrilli (eds), *Arte e assistenza a Siena: le copertine dipinte dell'Ospedale di Santa Maria della Scala,* catalogue of the exhibition, Siena, Archivio di Stato (Pisa, Pacini, 2003), pp. 29–45.

—, *Chiesa e Città. Uomini, comunità e istruzioni nella società senese del 12 e 13 secolo* (Rome, Herder Editrice e libreria, 2004).

—, *La comunità ospedaliera di Santa Maria della Scala e il suo piu antico statuto: Siena 1305* (Pisa, Pacini, c.2005).

Persi, Viviana, *Il registro del notaio senese Ugolino di Giunta Parisinus Latinus 4725 (1283–1287) alle origini dell'archivio della Casa misericordia di Siena* (Siena, Accademia senese degli Intronati, 2008).

Petrucci, Armando, 'Note su il testamento come documento', in *Nolens intestatus decedere. Il testamento come fonte della storia religiosa e sociale*, Atti dell'incontro di studio, Perugia, 3 maggio 1983 (Perugia, regione dell'Umbria, Editrice umbra cooperativa, 1985), pp. 11–16.

Piccinni, Gabriella, 'I 'villani incittadinati' nella Siena del 14 secolo', *BSSP*, 82–83 (1975–1976), pp. 158–219.

—, 'In merito a recenti studi sulla mezzadria nella Toscana medievale', *BSSP*, 89 (1982), pp. 336–52.

—, *Seminare, fruttare, raccogliere: mezzadri e salariati sulle terre di Monte Oliveto Maggiore, 1374–1430* (Milan, Feltrinelli economica, 1982).

—, 'Modelli di organizzazione dello spazio urbano dei ceti dominanti del Tre e Quattrocento. Considerazioni sul caso senese', in *I ceti dirigenti nella Toscana tardo comunale*, Atti del convegno, Florence, 5–7 dicembre 1980, Comitato di Studi sulla Storia dei Ceti dirigenti in Toscana (Florence, 1984), pp. 221–36.

—, 'I mezzadri davanti al fisco. Primi appunti sulla normativa senese del '400', in *Cultura e società nell'Italia medievale. Studi per Paolo Brezzi* (Rome, Istituto storico italiano per il Medio Evo, 1988), pp. 665–82.

—, 'Ambiente, produzione, società della Valdorcia nel tardo medioevo', in Alfio Cortonesi (ed.), *La Val d'Orcia nel medioevo e nei primi secoli dell'età moderna*, Atti del Convegno internazionale di studi storici, Pienza, 15–18 settembre 1988 (Rome, Viella, 1990), pp. 33–58.

—, 'Per uno studio del lavoro delle donne nelle campagne: considerazioni dell'Italia medievale', in Simonetta Cavaciocchi (ed.), *La Donna nell'Economia secc. 13–18*, Atti della 'Ventunesima Settimana di Studi', Prato 10–15 aprile 1989, (Prato, Le Monnier, 1990), pp. 71–81.

—, 'L'ospedale di Santa Maria della Scala di Siena. Note sulle origini dell'assistenza sanitaria in Toscana (14–15 secolo)' in *Città e servizi sociali in Italia dei secoli 12–15*, Twelfth Convegno di Studi, Pistoia, 9–12 ottobre 1987, (Pistoia, Centro italiano di studi di storia e d'arte, 1990), pp. 297–324.

—, 'Le donne nella vita economica, sociale e politica dell'Italia medievale', in Angela Groppi (ed.), *Il lavoro delle donne* (Rome and Bari, Laterza, 1996), pp. 5–46.

—, 'La campagna e le città (secoli 12–15)', in Alfio Cortonesi, Gianfranco Pasquali, and Gabriella Piccinni (eds), *Uomini e campagne nell'Italia medievale* (Rome and Bari, Laterza, 2002), pp. 123–89.

—, (and Laura Vigni), 'Modelli di assistenza ospedaliera fra Medioevo ed Età Moderna. Quotidianità, amministrazione, conflitti nell'ospedale di Santa Maria della Scala di Siena', in Giuliano Pinto (ed.), *La società del bisogno. Povertà e assistenza nella Toscana medievale* (Florence, Leo S. Olschki, 1989), pp. 131–74.

—, (ed.), *Il contratto mezzadrile nella Toscana medievale*, vol. 3, Contado di Siena 1349–1518 (Appendice: la normativa, 1256–1510) (Florence, Leo S. Olschki, 1992).

—, (ed.), with Carla Zarrilli, *Arte e assistenza a Siena: le copertine dipinte dell'Ospedale di Santa Maria della Scala*, exhibition catalogue (Pisa, Pacini, 2003).

—, (ed.), *Fedeltà ghibellina, affari guelfi: saggi e riletture intorno alla storia di Siena fra Due e Trecento*, (Pisa, Pacinieditore, 2008).

Pieri, Silvio, *Toponomastica della Toscana Meridionale e dell'Arcipelago toscano* (Siena, Accademia Senese degli Intronati, 1969).

Pietro, Gianfranco di, 'Per la storia dell'architettura della dimora rurale: alcune premesse di metodo', *Archeologia Medievale*, 7 (1980), pp. 343–62.

—, (and Paolo Donati), 'Cronologia e iconografia storica dal 11 secolo alla fine del 18 secolo', in *Siena, La Fabbrica del Santa Maria della Scala*, in *Bollettino d'Arte* (Rome, Istituto poligrafico e Zecca dello Stato, 1986), pp. 5–14.

Pinto, Giuliano, 'Ordinamento colturale e proprietà fondiaria cittadina nella Toscana del tardo Medioevo' in Giovanni Cherubini, Tommaso Detti, Mario Mirri, Giorgio Mori and Simonetta Soldani (eds), *Contadini e proprietari nella Toscana moderna*,

Atti del Convegno di Studi in onore di Giorgio Giorgetti (2 vols, Florence, Leo S. Olschki, 1979), 1, *Dal Medioevo all'età moderna*, pp. 223–77.

—, 'Per una storia delle dimore mezzadrili nella Toscana medievali', *Archeologia Medievale*, 7 (1980), pp. 153–71.

—, 'I rapporti di lavoro nelle campagne senesi fra 13 e 14 secolo. Una nota sul contratto di famulato', in *Cultura e società nell'Italia medievale: studi per Paolo Brezzi* (2 vols, Rome, Istituto storico italiano per il Medio Evo, 1988), 2, pp. 683–95.

—, 'L'ospedale della Scala di Siena. Note sulle origini dell'assistenza sanitaria in Toscana (14–15 secolo) in *Città e servizi sociali nell'Italia dei Secoli 12–15*, Twelfth Convegno di Studi, Pistoia, 9–12 ottobre 1987 (Pistoia, Centro italiano di studi di storia e d'arte, 1990), pp. 297–324.

—, 'L'agricoltura delle aree mezzadrili', in Sergio Gensini (ed.), *Le Italie del tardo Medioevo* (Pisa, Pacini, 1990), pp. 433–48.

—, 'Ancora su proprietari e contadini nella Siena del primo Trecento', in Bruno Laurioux and Laurence Moulinier-Brogi (eds), *Scrivere il Medioevo: lo spazio, la santità, il cibo: un libro dedicato ad Odile Redon* (Rome, Viella, c.2001), pp. 139–50.

—, *Il lavoro, la povertà, l'assistenza* (Rome, Viella, 2008).

—, 'Dimore contadine e infrastrutture agricole', in Giuliano Pinto (ed.), *La Toscana nel tardo medioevo. Ambiente, economia rurale, società* (Florence, Sansoni, 1982), pp. 225–246.

—, (ed.), *La Toscana nel tardo medioevo. Ambiente, economia rurale, società* (Florence, Sansoni Editore, 1982)

—, (ed.), with Paolo Pirillo, *Il contratto di Mezzadria nella Toscana Medievale, I, Contado di Siena, sec. 13–1348*, (Florence, Leo S. Olschki, 1987).

—, (ed.), *La società del bisogno. Povertà e assistenza nella Toscana medievale* (Florence, Salimbeni, 1989).

Pivano, Silvio, *I contratti agrari in Italia nell'Alto Medio-evo: precaria e livello, enfiteusi, pastinato parzionaria, masseria e colonia, usufrutto vitalizio, contratto a tempo e parziaria* (Turin, bottega d'Erasmo, 1969).

Polverini Fosi, Irene, 'Proprietà cittàdina e privilegi signorili nel contado senese', *BSSP*, 87 (1980), pp. 158–66.

Raffaelli, Ilio, *Prima dell'economia del Brunello. Montalcino: urbanistica, demografia, cultura e società dalle origini ai nostri giorni* (Montepulciano, Le Balze, 2001).

Raveggi, Sergio, 'La vittoria di Montaperti', in Roberto Barsanti, Giuliano Catoni and Mario De Gregorio (eds), *Storia di Siena, I, Dalle origini alla fine della Repubblica* (Monteriggioni-Siena, Banca di credito cooperativo, 1995), pp. 79–94.

—, *L'Italia dei guelfi e dei ghibellini* (Milan, Bruno Mondadori, c.2009).

Redon, Odile, *Uomini e comunità del contado senese nel Duecento*, Amministrazione Provinciale di Siena (Siena, Accademia degli Intronati, 1982).

—, 'Il comune e le sue frontiere', in Roberto Barzanti, Giulio Catoni and Mario De Gregorio (eds), *Storia di Siena, I, Dalle origini alla fine della Repubblica* (Monteriggioni-Siena, Banca di credito cooperativo, 1995), pp. 27–40.

—, 'Le Comunità del Contado', in *Storia di Siena, I, Dalle origini alla fine della Repubblica* (Monteriggioni-Siena, Banca di credito cooperativo, 1995), pp. 55–68.

—, *Lo spazio di una città. Siena e la Toscana meridionale (secoli 13–14)* (Siena, Nuova immagine and Rome, Viella, 1999).

Repetti, Emanuele Repetti, *Dizionario geografico fisico storico della Toscana* (6 vols, Florence, Tipografia A. Tofani and G. Mazzoni, (1833–1846), ristampa anastatica, 6 vols (Reggello, FirenzeLibri, 2005).

Ricci, Ugo, *S. Angelo in Colle nella storia e nella vita del contesto Senese e Toscano* (typescript, Sant'Angelo in Colle, 1985).

—, *Sant'Angelo in Colle: Appendice* (typescript, Sant'Angelo in Colle, 1989).

Rigon, Antonio, 'I testamenti come atti di religiosità pauperistica', in *La conversione alla povertà nell'Italia dei secoli 12–14*, Atti del 27 Convegno Storico Internazionale, Todi, 14–17 ottobre 1990 (Spoleto, Centro italiano di studi sull'alto Medioevo, 1991), pp. 391–414.

Ring, Richard, 'Early Medieval Peasant Households in Central Italy', in *Journal of Family History*, 2 (1979), pp. 2–25.

Romagnoli, Ettore, *Cenni storico-artistici di Siena e suoi suburbi* (Siena, Porri, 1836). Facsimile edition, (Sala Bolognese, Forni, 1990).

Rotundo, Felicia, *L'Eremo di San Leonardo al Lago a Santa Colomba* (Rome, Kappa, 2004).

Salvadè, Mario, 'Evoluzione dei caratteri distributive nella architettura ospedaliera', Atti del primo congresso europeo di storia ospitaliera, Bologna, giugno 1960 (Bologna, 1962), pp. 116–33.

Sandri, Lucia 'Ospedali e utenti della assistenza nella Firenze del Quattrocento', in *La società del bisogno: povertà e assistenza nella Toscana medievale* (Florence, Salimbeni, 1989), pp. 61–100.

Santi, Bruno, *L'Amiata e la Val d'Orcia* (Milan, 1999).

Schupfer, Francesco, 'Precarie e livelli nei documenti e nelle leggi dell'alto Medio Evo', extract from *Rivista italiana per le scienze giuridiche*, 40, fasc. 1–3 (Turin, Bocca, 1905).

Seidel, Max, 'Ikonographie und Historiographie: 'Conversatio Angelorum in Silvis', Eremiten-Bilder von Simone Martini und Pietro Lorenzetti', *Städel-Jahrbuch*, 10 (1985), pp. 77–142.

Serino, Vinicio (ed.), *Siena e l'acqua. Storia e imagini della città e delle sue fonti* (Siena, Nuova immagine, 1997).

—, (ed.), with Andrea Brogi and Giulio Paolucci, *Civiltà delle acque: storie, miti, leggende in terre di Siena e di Maremma* ([S.I.], Chianciano Terme–Sovicille, Banca Cras stampa, 2009).

Settia, Aldo A., 'La toponomastica come fonte per la storia del popolamento rurale', in Vito Fumagalli and Gabriella Rossetti (eds), *Medioevo rurale. Sulle tracce della civiltà Contadina* (Bologna, Il Mulino, 1980), pp. 35–56.

Skinner, Quentin, 'Ambrogio Lorenzetti: The Artist as Political Philosopher', *Proceedings of the British Academy*, 72 (1986), pp. 1–56.

Siena. La Fabbrica del Santa Maria della Scala, special edition, *Bollettino d'Arte* (Siena, 1986).

Sigillo, Antonio, *Montalcino. Itinerarii turistici* (Città di Castello, tipolitografia Petruzzi, 1994).

Sordini, Beatrice, *Il porto della 'Gente Vana'. Lo scalo di Talamone fra il secolo 13 e il secolo 15* (Protagon Editori Toscani, 2000).

—, *Dentro l'antico Ospedale. Santa Maria della Scala, Uomini, cose e spazi di vita nella Siena Medievale* Fondazione Monte dei Paschi di Siena (Siena, Cooprint Industria Grafica, 2010).

Szabò, Thomas, 'La rete stradale del contado di Siena. Legislazione statutaria e amministrazione comunale del Ducento', *Mélanges de l'Ecole Française de Rome*, 87 (1975), pp. 141–86.

—, 'Il tessuto viario minore e gli statuti della Valdorcia', in Alfio Cortonesi (ed.), *La Val d'Orcia nel medioevo e nei primi secoli dell'età moderna*, Atti del Convegno internazionale di studi storici, Pienza, 15–18 settembre 1988 (Rome, Viella, 1990), pp. 155–78.

—, *Comuni e politica stradale in Toscana e in Italia nel Medioevo* (Bologna, CLUEB, 1992).

Temperini, Adolfo, *Gli spedali di Montalcino, Montalcino* (Montalcino, Tipografia 'La stella', 1906).

Thomas, Anabel, *Art and Piety in the Female Religious Communities of Renaissance Italy: Iconography, Space and the Religious Woman's Perspective* (New York, Cambridge University Press, 2003).

—, 'Dominican Marginalia: The Late Fifteenth-Century Printing Press of San Jacopo di Ripoli in Florence', in Stephen J. Milner (ed.), *At the Margins. Minority Groups in Premodern Italy*, Medieval Cultures, vol. 39 (Minneapolis and London, University of Minnesota Press, 2005), pp. 192–216.

—, 'Cosa c'è dietro il nome? Le vecchie fonti di Montalcino e Sant'Angelo in Colle: acqua, località e toponomi', *Gazzettino e Storie del Brunello e di Montalcino*, Anno 1, 7, July (2007), pp. 14–16.

—, 'Le fratesse e le mantellate terziarie della corte di Montalcino nel basso medioevo', in Mario Ascheri and Vinicio Serino (eds), *Prima del Brunello. Montalcino Capitale Mancata*, Documenti di Storia, 75, Collana a cura di Mario Ascheri under the sponsorship of the Lions Club – Montalcino Valli d'Arbia e d'Orcia, Distretto 108 La Toscana (San Quirico d'Orcia, Editrice DonChisciotte, 2007), pp. 59–90.

—, 'La Festa della Madonna della Misericordia', *Gazzettino e Storie del Brunello e di Montalcino*, Anno 3, 38 (2010), pp. 16–17; 39, pp. 16–17 and 40, pp. 18–19.

Ticciati, Laura, 'Sulle condizioni dell'agricoltura del contado cortonese nel secolo 13', *Archivio Storico Italiano*, serie 5, 10 (1892), pp. 262–79.

Torriti, Piero, *La Pinacoteca Nazionale di Siena* (Genoa, SAGEP, 1977–8). 3rd edition, Genoa, 1990).

Tortoli, Sandra, 'Il podere e i mezzadri di Niccoluccio di Cecco della Boccia, mercante cortonese a Siena, nella seconda metà del Trecento', *Ricerche storiche*, 10 (1980), pp. 239–84.

Trachtenberg, Marvin, *Dominion of the eye: urbanism, art and power in early modern Florence* (Cambridge, Cambridge University Press, 1997).

Turrini, Patrizia, 'Religiosità e spirito caritatevole a Siena agli inizi della reggenza lorense: luoghi pii laicali, contrade e arte,' part 1, *Annuario dell'Istituto Storico Diocesano Siena* (1994–95), pp. 9–128; part 2, *Annuario dell'Istituto Storico Diocesano Siena* (1996–7), pp. 144–293.

Uggeri, Giovanni, 'Questioni di metodo. La toponomastica nella ricerca topografica: il contribuito alla ricostruzione della viabilita', *Journal of Ancient Topography*, 1 (1991), pp. 21–36.

Verdiani-Bandi, Arnaldo, *I castelli della Val d'Orcia e la Repubblica di Siena* (Siena, Cantagalli, 1996) (from earlier rist. anast. Siena 1973).

Vigni, Laura and Gabriella Piccinni, 'Modelli di assistenza ospedaliera fra Medioevo ed Età Moderna. Quotidianità, amministrazione, conflitti nell'ospedale di Santa Maria della Scala di Siena', in Giuliano Pinto (ed.), *La società del bisogno. Povertà e assistenza nella Toscana medievale* (Florence, Salimbeni, 1989), pp. 131–74.

Violante, Cinzio, 'Una notizia di transumanza verso la Maremma nell'alto Medioevo', in Ilaria Zilli (ed.), *Fra spazio e tempo: studi in onore di Luigi De Rosa* (Naples, Edizioni scientifiche italiane, 1995), pp. 805–7.

Wainwright, Valerie Linda, 'Andrea Vanni and Bartolo di Fredi: Sienese Painters in their Social Context', PhD thesis, University of London, 1978.

Zdekauer, Lodovico, 'Il constituto dei Placiti del comune di Siena', *Studi Senesi*, 6, fasc. 2 (1889), pp. 152–206.

—, *Il Constituto del Comune di Siena dell'Anno 1262* (Milan, Arnoldo Forni editore, 1897). Reprint, (Arnoldo Forni, Sala Bolognese, 1983).

Index